W9-BKX-915

3 3211 00128 225 4

THE MODERN
US
WAR MACHINE

An encyclopedia of American military equipment and strategy

THE MODERN

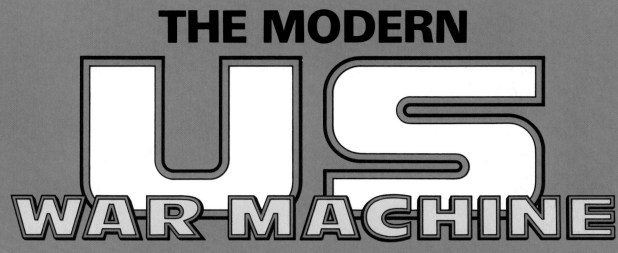

US
WAR MACHINE

An encyclopedia of American military equipment and strategy

Published by Crown Publishers, Inc
NEW YORK

OAKTON COMMUNITY COLLEGE
DES PLAINES CAMPUS
1600 EAST GOLF ROAD
DES PLAINES, IL 60016

77690

A Salamander Book

Published 1987 in the United States by
Crown Publishers, Inc.,
225 Park Avenue South,
New York, New York 10003,
United States of America.

© 1987 by Salamander Books Ltd.

ISBN 0-517-56097-6

All rights reserved. No part of this book may be reproduced, stored in a retrieval system or transmitted in any form or by any means, electronic, mechanical, photocopying, recording or otherwise, without the prior permission of Salamander Books Ltd.

All correspondence concerning the content of this volume should be addressed to Salamander Books Ltd., 52 Bedford Row, London WC1R 4LR, United Kingdom.

Credits

Editor: Ray Bonds
Contributing Editor: Walter N. Lang
Art Editor: Philip Gorton
Art Assistants: Lim & Lim
Filmset: SX Composing Ltd., The Old Mill, H&P Graphics Ltd.
Color reproduction: Rodney Howe Ltd., and Melbourne Graphics Ltd.
Jacket artwork: Wilfred R.R. Hardy, G.Av.A.
Printed in Belgium by Proost International Book Production, Turnhout.

Editor's Acknowledgments

In the process of preparing this timely volume for publication I have been fortunate in having received the help and advice of very many people and organizations. It is not possible to mention them all here, but I do thank them for their assistance. In particular, I am extremely grateful for all the efforts of and support from the Contributing Editor, Walter N. Lang; Edward A. Michalski and Bettie Sprigg of the Pentagon; and all of the Offices of Information and Audio Visual Services of the United States Department of Defense and the manufacturers of weapons and systems, who supplied almost all of the photographs which appear in this book. I also thank *Air Force Magazine* for its cooperation in allowing us to reproduce or use as reference maps which have appeared in the publication.
Ray Bonds

Contents

Foreword	8
The History of the US Armed Forces	10
The US National Security Policy	18
The US Defense Organization	30
The US Intelligence Machine	42
The US Strategic Forces	52
The United States Army	62
The United States Navy	74
The United States Marine Corps	88
The United States Air Force	100
The Soviet Threat	112
US Ground Forces Weapons	124
United States Warships	140
US Combat Aircraft	168
US Rockets and Missiles	214
Index	236

The Authors

Dr. William R. Van Cleave is Professor of International Relations and Director of the Defense and Strategic Studies Program at the University of Southern California. He is a Consultant to the Office of the Secretary of Defense; was a member of the "B Team" (Presidential Panel to Review National Intelligence on USSR, 1976-77); was Special Assistant, Strategic Policy, NSC Affairs, and SALT, Office of the Secretary of Defense (ASD/ISA, 1969-71); was a member of the US Delegation to the Strategic Arms Limitations Talks (SALT) 1969-1971. Dr. Van Cleave is also a consultant to the Central Intelligence Agency, the US Energy Research and Development Agency and to many non-Government research institutes and agencies. He has contributed to very many professional journals.

Christopher F. Foss is Military Editor of *Jane's Defence Weekly,* and author of "Jane's World Armoured Fighting Vehicles", author of two pocket books on modern AFVs and towed artillery, besides contributing to "Jane's Weapon Systems" and "Jane's Infantry Weapons". He is also former weapons correspondent to *Defence* magazine, and contributor to many professional journals.

Col. Richard S. Friedman, Military Intelligence, USA (Retd.), first entered military service during World War II in which he served as a sergeant in the US Army, assigned to the Office of Strategic Services (OSS) in the European, African and Middle Eastern Theater of Operations. He served in a variety of assignments, most recently with the US Army General Staff in Washington, as Defense and Army Attache in Budapest, Hungary, and, prior to his retirement at the end of 1984, as Deputy Assitant Director, Intelligence, on the International Military Staff of NATO Headquarters in Brussels, Belgium. Colonel Friedman was graduated from the US Army Command & General Staff College and US Army War College. Colonel Friedman is a consultant and writer on international affairs in the United States, and contributed to Salamander's "Advanced Technology Warfare".

Stephen P. Gibert is Professor of Government, Director of the National Security Studies Program, and a member of the International Research Council of the Center for Strategic and International Studies at Georgetown University, Washington, D.C. In 1980 he served on the Defense Advisory Group for President Reagan. Dr. Gibert has served as an advisor to the Asia Foundation and the Government of the Union of Burma, and has been a visiting Professor at the University of Rangoon and the US Naval War College. He is the author of "Northeast Asia in US Foreign Policy" as well as other works on international security affairs, including (as co-author) "Arms For The Third World: Soviet military Aid Diplomacy" and "Soviet Images of America". He was also Editor of *International Security Review.*

Bill Gunston is an advisor to several major aviation companies. He is a noted writer on aviation and technical affairs, being former Technical editor of *Flight International,* and Technology Editor of *Science Journal.* He is a contributor to "Jane's All The World's Air-craft" and to many authoritative international military journals. Mr. Gunston is author of many Salamander military reference books, including "Modern Fighting Helicopters", "Modern Air Combat" and "Warplanes of the Future".

John Jordan has contributed numerous technical articles on ships of the US Navy, the Soviet Navy and the NATO navies to defense journals which include *Navy International, Warship* and *Defence.* He was a consultant to the Soviet section of the 1980-81 edition of "Jane's Fighting Ships". He is co-author of Salamander's "Modern Naval Combat", "The Balance of Military Power", and author of Salamander's "Illustrated Guide to the Soviet Navy" and "Illustrated Guide to the US Navy".

Maj. Robert Thomas Jordan, USMC (Retd.) retired from the US Marine Corps on 1 April 1984 after more than 29 years of combined commissioned and enlisted service. His career was capped by his assignment as the Marine spokesman in Beirut, Lebanon, during August through November 1983. Upon his return to the US, he was in demand as a speaker throughout the United States and appeared on numerous television programs. He continued his speaking engagements after retirement and appeared on the CBS program "Crossroads" which aired 4 July, 1984. Jordan is an award-winning writer, broadcaster, photographer and artist who saw duty in Vietnam as a press escort and combat correspondent. He assisted in the planning for the returns of hostage Sgt Kenneth Kraus from Iran and POW Pfc Bobby Garwood

from North Vietnam. Formerly employed as an Associate Editor with *Leatherneck* magazine, Jordan is now Editor of *Tech-Trends International.*

Col. William V. Kennedy, Armor, USA (Retd.), has served with US Army Reserve and as an enlisted serviceman in the US Army (Regular), as well as an Intelligence Officer with the US Air Force Strategic Air Command. Formerly a faculty member of the US Army War College, Col. Kennedy is a contributor to several compendia of academic papers, including *China, the Soviet Union and the West,* and is co-author of the Salamander books, "The Intelligence War", "The Balance of Military Power", and "The Chinese War Machine".

Bruce F. Powers is a Senior Fellow at the Strategic Concepts Development Center of the National Defense University in Washington, DC. His knowledge of the capabilities of US forces was developed while serving at the RAND Corporation, the Institute for Defense Analyses, and the Center for Naval Analyses. His early career alternated between direction of studies in Washington and one-year assignments with admirals who were in command of fleets. These assignments included one at sea with the Sixth Fleet in the Mediterranean and one as Science Advisor to the Commander-in-Chief of US Naval Forces in Europe, whose headquarters were in London.

Doug Richardson is a defense journalist specializing in the fields of aviation, guided missiles and electronics. After an electronic R&D career he served as Defense Editor of the internationally respected aerospace journal *Flight International,* and as Editor of *Military Technology and Economics* and of *Defence Materiel.* He is author and co-author of numerous Salamander books, including "Advanced Technology Warfare".

Alan Ned Sabrosky (Ph.D)., University of Michigan) is Deputy for Research at the US Army War College, and former Senior Fellow in Political-Military Studies at The Center for Strategic and International Studies, Washington, D.C.; Professorial Lecturer in Government and Adjunct Professor of National Security Studies at Georgetown University; and Lecturer in Political Science at the University of Pennsylvania. A specialist in international security affairs and civil-military relations, he has taught at the US Military Academy at West Point and lectured widely at public and private defense-related institutions, including the US National War College, the Inter-American Defense College, the NATO Defense College, and the International Institute for Strategic Studies. His published work includes "Great Power games", "Military Manpower and Military Power", "Defense Manpower Policy: A Critical Reappraisal" and "Blue-Collar Soldiers".

Lt. Col. Robert C. Vasile (USA) is a recognized Army strategist and instructor with the Department of Joint and Combined Operations of the US Army Command and General Staff College. He is a subject matter expert in the field of Low Intensity Conflict and is the Army's doctrine developer for peacekeeping operations. Lt. Col. Vasile has served in Vietnam with the 5th Special Forces Group (Airborne) and the US MACV-CORPS. He holds an MA from the Monterey Institute of International Studies in International Studies — Middle East. As a foreign area specialist he also served with the United Nations Truce Supervision Organization, Palestine, and as the US Military Assistance Officer to Lebanon.

Lt. Col. Donald B. Vought, USA (Retd.) reitred from service with the US Army after 23 years of service which included three years with NATO, one year in Vietnam and one year in Iran as advisor to the Imperial Armor School. He was for seven years on the faculty of the US Army Command and General Staff College at Fort Leavenworth, Kansas, where he specialized in low-intensity warfare, intercultural communications and the study of national development as a multidisciplinary phenomenon. He is a graduate of Norwich Univeristy with M.A.s in Politcal Science (University of Louisville) and International Relations (Boston University). Lt. Col. Vought has been a frequent contributor to professional conferences and publications.

Russell F. Weigley is professor of history at Temple University, Philadelphia. He has taught also at the University of Pennsylvania, Drexel University, and Dartmouth College, and in 1973-74 he was US Army Visiting Professor of Military History Research at the US Army Military History Institute and the Army War College. He is president of the Pennsylvania Historical Association and has been president of the American Military Institute.

Foreword

by General Richard G. Stilwell, US Army (Retd.), former Commander, Eighth Army and United Nations Command, Korea; former Deputy Under Secretary of Defense for Policy.

Richard G. Stilwell General, USA (Retd.)

General Richard G. Stilwell's military career spanned 39 years and 14 campaigns in three wars. His leadership experience included command of an engineer battalion (WWII), the 15th Infantry Regiment (Korean battlefield), the United States Corps of Cadets (West Point), the Military Assistance Command, Thailand, the 1st Armored Division (Texas), the XXIV Army Corps (Vietnam), the 6th Army, and finally concurrent command of the 8th Army and the United Nations Command (Korea). Other key posts were military advisor to the first post-WWII Ambassador to Italy; Chief, Far East Division, CIA; Director, Strategy Course, Army War College; Chief of Long Range Planning at Allied Command Europe (NATO); Chief of Staff to General Westmoreland in Vietnam; member of two Presidential Commissions dealing with foreign aid programs; Deputy Chief of Staff for Plans and Operations of the US Army. General Stilwell's awards include the Department of Defense Distinguished Service Medal, The Army Distinguished Service Medal with 3 Oak Leaf Clusters, the Silver Star with Oak Leaf Cluster, the Legion of Merit with 3 Oak Leaf Clusters, the Distinguished Flying Cross, the Bronze Star with 2 Oak Leaf Clusters, the Purple Heart, numerous foreign awards and the Combat Infantryman's Badge. At his request, he was retired on 1 November 1976 in four star rank.

Subsequent to retirement, General Stilwell was a consultant to several organizations conducting defense and foreign policy oriented studies, and served as National President of the Association of Former Intelligence Officers, board member of the Committee on the Present Danger and a Co-Chairman, Coalition for Peace Through Strength.

General Stilwell returned to government service in February 1981, accepting appointment as the Deputy Under Secretary of Defense for Policy, advising on a wide range of defense and national security issues. He was responsible, inter alia, for development of the major planning document which guides overall defense programs and for the formulation of requirements and policy in the functional areas of Intelligence, security, outer space, command/control and emergency preparedness. He resigned from the position in February 1985 and currently performs consultant duties for the Secretary of Defense and the Deputy Secretary of Defense.

When *The US War Machine* was first published I lauded its substance and its timeliness. For precisely the same reasons, this completely new edition merits the attention of all who have even casual interest in world affairs. Global stability, economic growth, and increased intercourse among nations depend, in large measure, on the resolve and capability of the United States to discharge its long-standing mandate as the *de facto* leader of the free world. The past six years have been witness to favorable change in these twin determinants of effectiveness in the international competition. As to national will, the policies enunciated by President Reagan — and strongly endorsed by the American public — have answered the concerns earlier rife among allies and friends: the United States can indeed be counted upon to live up to its responsibilities. As to military sinew, the revitalization of the armed forces has been accorded top priority since the outset of the Reagan Administration. There is thus room for optimism — albeit guarded. Optimism because the trends are right. Guarded because the world environment remains highly dangerous and turbulent.

As detailed in the pages of this volume, the United States armed forces are impressive for their size, power, and versatility. Their reach is global. They possess the means for, and are geared to conduct, military operations throughout the entire spectrum of conflict from strategic nuclear exchange to high intensity conventional combat to sub-limited warfare to projection of power in support of political initiative. Backing these forces are enormous demographic resources, unsurpassed industrial capability and a pre-eminent scientific base. In the aggregate, these formidable strengths are proof positive that the United States is a military superpower. However, these strengths alone do not gauge the adequacy of the defense posture of the nation or, pertinently, of the free world. That assessment involves consideration of numerous other factors, some quantifiable and some not. Principal among these factors are the range and nature of missions assigned and the capabilities of potential adversaries.

In the years since World War II the United States military establishment has shouldered responsibilities of unprecedented magnitude and diversity. Its supreme mission — akin to that of the armed forces of any nation which acts responsibly — is to protect the American people, institutions and territory from direct and indirect attack. Beyond that, it is tasked with the contingent defense of Western Europe, Japan and numerous other nations persuant to multi-lateral and bi-lateral security arrangements to which the United States is party; all of these commitments, incidentally, involve extensive preparations for the orchestration of US and allied forces under varying coalition modes. Moreover, since the United States exercises leadership of what is, in essence, a maritime alliance its military establishment bears primary responsibility for ensuring that member states have uninterrupted use of international waters and air space and access to markets, raw materials and energy sources. Overall, those armed forces have had the generic task of preventing the threat of use of naked military force — particularly nuclear — for purpose of political or economic coercion of the nations of the free world community. Though this complex of missions has generated exceedingly heavy demands and the United States military resources have been spread correspondingly thin, the record of the last twenty years and more has been quite creditable. All major tasks have been successfully discharged. Vietnam, of course, was a conspicuous failure, albeit one due, in the main, to collapse of national will rather than inadequate military performance. In any case, past achievements are not a harbinger of the future. For one thing, the United States and her allies were spared multiple concurrent crises. For another, the United States enjoyed, for most of the period, both actual and perceived superiority in the strategic nuclear dimension, reasonably assured command of the seas and a decided edge in capability to project force to areas outside the Eurasian land mass. These favorable differentials counterbalanced weaknesses in other segments of the overall defense posture. However, expectedly, the Soviet Union has made prodigious efforts to overcome the United States' lead in these very areas and with considerable success. The nuclear advantage has been erased; the challenge on the high seas mounts; and the strategic mobility of Soviet forces steadily increases.

To be sure, the lengthening shadow cast by the Soviet military machine is not the only threat that needs to be reckoned with. But it is certainly the most ominous. The last fifteen years witnessed extraordinary increases in Soviet nuclear and conventional forces. As the build-up continues unabated all evidence points to Soviet intent to achieve dominance in every dimension of military power. Though prepared for the eventuality of armed conflict at any level and at any time, the Soviets have studied Clausewitz with consummate care. They thus aspire to advance, step by step, toward world hegemony employing every stratagem short of unambiguous war. By consequence, the principal role of the Soviet armed forces is to undergird political and economical moves to disrupt the free world alliance system, sap the vitality of the free enterprise area and isolate the United States and China. Thus, the Soviet armed forces constitute a many faceted threat.

Over two centuries, the US military has been tested, retested, and never found wanting, but its supreme challenge lies ahead. With the quantitative military balance (not only in the ground components, where Soviet advantages have been long standing, but in nuclear, naval and air dimensions as well, given the respective military trend lines) decidedly adverse and with the qualitative edge increasingly in doubt, we can assume a favorable outcome in the event of war only by the better concepts, tactics and leadership.

For the first time since the War of Independence, the United States forces are destined to be the under-dog. These predictable developments are cause for concern but they by no means portend unfavorable outcomes either in war or in military confrontation in crisis scenarios short of war. In the long history of warfare numerical advantage has rarely been the decisive factor. Nor have perceptions of relative power in crisis situations been primarily shaped by size alone. Most frequently, the major determinents of favorable issue — in campaign or in confrontation — have been superior strategy, tactical concepts, leadership, audacity and discipline. Naturally the United States and its allies cannot afford to let the quantitative gap widen appreciably more or, worse yet, accept technological inferiority. As an example, the Soviets must not be permitted to attain a politically exploitable superiority in strategic nuclear systems. Nor can the Soviets be allowed to inhibit free world projection of power or untrammelled use of the high seas. But, in the last analysis, the United States armed forces will measure up to their manifold tasks to the extent — and only to the extent — that they are able to devise the better strategy and carry out that strategy with unexcelled professionalism.

The History of the US Armed Forces

In 1985, with memory fresh of an American military success in Grenada, the President of the United States took his lady to upstate New York, to the hallowed parade fields and ivory-colored halls of West Point, to observe the "long gray line" of future regular Army officers in close-order drill. It was the same US Military Academy which had produced company commanders and field generals in every American war except the first, and where an aging General of the Army Douglas Mac-Arthur punctuated the twilight of his life with a moving speech centered on the three words at the core of an officer's life: *Duty. Honor. Country.*

By the mid-1980s, some Americans wondered if West Point, like the Air Force Academy at Colorado Springs and the Naval Academy in Annapolis, was producing managers instead of leaders; whether, indeed, career track, performance file and promotion roster had gained prevalence over duty, honor, country. Some military men feared that the typical American officer was better able to work behind a desk than lead men in battle.

As the end of the century approaches, Washington appears crowded with overweight, career-conscious officers who commute with attache case in hand and talk about systems, not about men; meanwhile Fort Bragg is sorely short of the lieutenants and captains to inspire hearts in the crucible of combat.

One recent American adventure, the Iran hostage rescue mission, shackled a tough and well-loved leader with so many layers of bureaucracy that, once the mission failed, he called it "over-managed and under-led". Too many in the professional ranks appear to want the easy solution of a "Star Wars" scenario, while too few seem ready for hard fixes in the grime and stench of the battlefield.

The pageantry at West Point evokes a bygone era. The close-order drill of the Corps of Cadets has its roots in the discipline taught by Baron von Steuben to General George Washington's Continental Army at Valley Forge in 1778, and beyond that in the necessity of eighteenth-century armies to maneuver on the battlefield as though the soldiers were automatons on parade, to maintain the line in the face of the enemy's volley firing and bayonet charge. The cadets' gray uniforms memorialize Winfield Scott's and Eleazar Wheelock Ripley's brigades of United States Regulars who charged the British at Chippewa and Lundy's Lane in Upper Canada in 1814, the first battles in which American troops were able to hold their own against approximately equal numbers of British veterans in stand-up combat throughout the battle. Scott's and Ripley's men happened to be clothed in gray because the quartermaster had run out of regulation United States Army blue.

For the United States, perpetuating ancient military memories and rituals is much more paradoxical than it is for other nations such as Britain. For Great Britain, the remote past is for the most part the nation's prominent military past; for the United States, by contrast, it is only since World War II that the nation has assuredly attained a special eminence among the military powers of the world.

It did so with abrupt suddenness. Through most of the American past, the United States was in military tutelage to Europe, almost in a colonial relationship militarily. Since 1945, military officers from all countries friendly to the United States have attended military schools in America; but until the abrupt change of World War II, Americans learned their military lessons from Europe.

Until the American War with Spain in 1898, the United States was an isolated power not participating in world military events or the world diplomacy of the military great powers. The oceans, not American ships or forts, were the source of American security. The American army was less an army of the European type than a constabulary for the patrolling of the Indian country in the West. By European standards, the American armed forces are almost armed forces without a history – which is no doubt one reason why Americans cling all the more tightly to the thin historical tradition that does exist, as in the West Point parades.

American forces in the twentieth century

Below: Despite their comparative lack of experience, the US regulars at the Battle of Chippewa (Upper Canada, July 1814) held their own against British regular infantry before inflicting a tactical defeat.

Note: This chapter substantially revised in 1986 by Salamander editorial staff.

Russell F. Weigley, Professor of History at Temple University, Philadelphia; past-president, American Military Institute.

have displayed a sensitivity about their status as newcomers. From the close of the 1775-1783 and 1812-1815 conflicts with Great Britain until World War I, the military forces of the United States did not have to test themselves against a first-rate foreign foe. General John J. Pershing, the commander of the 1917-1918 American Expeditionary Forces, was conscious of this. He knew his army was meeting first-division opponents and that he must make a good impression for the sake of his own army's morale as well as to uphold America's weight in Allied councils. Many American soldiers themselves had come to doubt, as Lieutenant Colonel James S. Pettit had put it in a prize-winning essay in the *Journal* of the United States Military Service Institution in 1906, whether the American democracy could "maintain an organization or discipline comparable to that of little Japan," let alone the Continental powers. In their final offensive of the war, the Meuse-Argonne Offensive of September 26-November 11, 1918, American troops were still suffering the disproportionately high casualties that fell to soldiers who were not battle-wise and battle-wary.

As late as World War II, the US Navy was the only great navy that had never fought in a full-scale fleet action. Because there were no Tsushimas and no Jutlands in its past, it pursued a super Jutland – a grand climatic battle against the Japanese fleet in 1941-45 – with zeal beyond the boundaries of strategic good sense. The pursuit almost produced disaster when Admiral William F. Halsey followed a Japanese decoy fleet and thus exposed the Philippine Islands invasion force at Leyte Gulf

Below: The Mexican siege of the Alamo (War of Texan Independence, 1836) has generated a crop of legends in US folklore, but is also a steady reminder of continued courage under extreme adversity.

Above: Even when fighting against their fellow countrymen, the Americans enjoyed a reputation for giving their all in battle, though this reputation was at times sadly tarnished in Vietnam.

to the main Japanese fleet in October 1944. Fortunately, the skill as well as the bravery of the crews of the smaller and older American warships was enough to discourage Japanese admirals who enjoyed material superiority.

The recency of America's emergence as a world military power has shaped the American armed forces also in matters more profound than an acute sensitivity about the thinness of the country's past military tradition. Americans still tend to regard foreign war as an extraordinary occasion. Their military history combines with the national ideology, which is derived from the liberalism of the eighteenth and nineteenth centuries, to assure them that war is an abnormal state of affairs, that it can be accounted for only in terms of an uncommon eruption of evil into the world, and that the appropriate response is to extirpate the evil by means of an all-out military assault upon it. Thus the American propensity for demanding "unconditional surrender" of their country's enemies in war. Americans have grown more sophisticated in the use of military force to serve their national interests since 1945, but popular dissatisfaction surfaced during the Korean and Vietnam wars over the application of military force in limited, measured dosages.

The discomfort of Americans over anything less than complete triumph was evident in 1983 when policy decisions – by tradition, never made by military men – required the stationing of Marines on the ground in Lebanon where they faced no sharply-defined enemy and had no victory to perceive as attainable. An unsuccessful naval air strike on December 4, 1983, against Syrian positions harassing those Marines ran afoul of the American need for visible enemies and clear solutions.

In the 1980s, Americans still expected force of arms to produce decisive solutions even if annihilation of the adversary was not possible.

Above: Another feature of US warmaking has been a high caliber of political and military leadership. During the Civil War, for example, Lincoln controlled policy and left actual operations to his generals.

Below: European operations in World War I brought forcefully home to the Americans the true nature of modern warfare; after acclimatization they acquitted themselves extremely well.

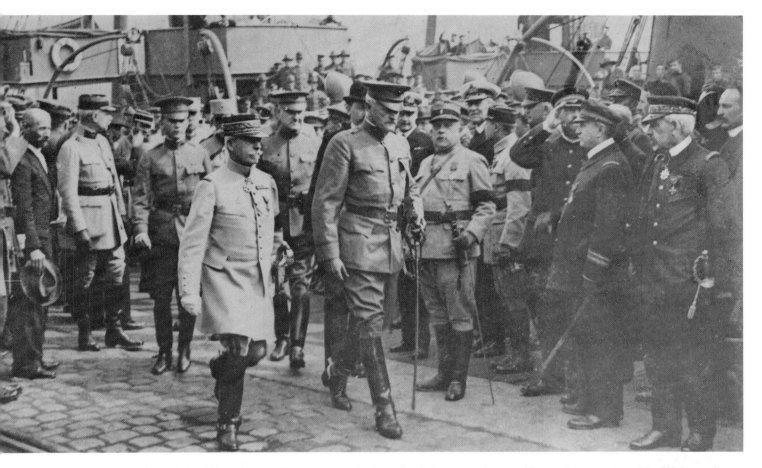

Operations in Libya and the Gulf of Sidra in February 1986 are ample proof of that. The commando raid in Iran and the air strike in Lebanon were undertaken despite, not because of, ingrained American expectations. Armed forces which had always enjoyed superb leadership still seemed to, but a nation which had fielded "citizen soldiers" in all of its wars now committed warriors with little or no link to their society, and confidence in the total solution faltered even in Grenada when elite Rangers, relaxed for a landing at Point Salines Airport, had to repack their parachutes and drop under fire when opposition proved stauncher than foreseen.

If the thirst for the total solution was foiled in Iran and Lebanon, and but briefly whetted in Grenada, by committing their developmental assets to the "Star Wars' fix of the Strategic Defense Initiative (SDI), US officers followed policymakers down a fantasy path: a high-tech defense against the transpolar ballistic missile had the classic lure of an ultimate solution, late 1980s style, so crisp and clean that it could only be American.

In the War of the American Revolution, Americans displayed the conviction nourished by their Indian wars that only total solutions would suffice. Not satisfied to expel the British from those colonies that had spontaneously risen in rebellion, the American rebels promptly in 1775 mounted expeditions to drive the British from Canada, which had not joined the rebellion. Though the conquest of Canada proved beyond the rebels' strength, the idea of again attempting it persisted throughout the war.

The American desire for total solutions made itself felt once more in the new Treaty of Paris of 1783, ending the War of the Revolution, just as it had shaped the older Treaty of Paris in 1763. Having tried and failed to conquer Canada, the new United States could hardly demand its cession. But the presumptuousness of the infant Republic was considerable nevertheless. With only the most tenuous of military claims to the vast area extending west from the Appalachian Mountains to the Mississippi River, and with the British still in

effective control of much of the area, the United States insisted that the British should not only recognize the independence of the thirteen rebellious colonies but should cede to them the whole trans-Appalachian region. The United States received the Mississippi River as its western frontier.

Lacking the Will, not the Means

It might be argued that the limitations of American military power during the Republic's early years soon curbed the tendency to seek total results from war. After all, in the War of 1812-1815 with Great Britain, the United States eventually settled for a peace reverting to the *status quo ante bellum*. Furthermore, in the War with Mexico in 1846-1848, Mexican military power and sovereignty were not exterminated; however, the US "made do" with territorial acquisitions of the former Republic of Texas plus everything west from Texas to the Pacific Ocean. But caution is necessary in ascribing even to the early and militarily weak American Republic any limited conception of the proper results of war. Though the actual peace terms of the War of 1812 were modest, they had been preceded by plenty of American talk about the annexation of Canada; it was not the will that was lacking, but the means. And in regard to Mexico in 1848, by which time American military means were more ample, President James K. Polk rushed through the Senate a peace treaty negotiated by an emissary whom he had already repudiated before the terms were arranged, in part because the President thought he must hurry lest public sentiment for the annexation of Mexico get out of hand.

Nor did the military power of the American Republic remain feeble for very long. By the 1860s, the United States mobilized against a domestic rebellion in the form of the secession of eleven of its southern states. By 1865, its great armies and navies made it the foremost military nation in the world – for a brief moment. Characteristically, with the extermination of the evils that had caused the war, the country hastily demobilized.

Above: Commander of the US forces in France during World War I, General John J. Pershing restrained himself to the military sphere and did not encroach on presidential responsibilities.

Meanwhile, for four years the American Civil War pitted hundreds of thousands against each other in an arena that was continental in extent. One of the major wars in world history and the greatest American war until World War II, it confirmed American conceptions about the nature of war and military power all the way to World War II, at the least. Once more, the United States sought a total resolution of all the issues of the war, particularly the total extermination of all of the rebellious Southern Confederacy's pretensions to sovereignty. The means of pursuing this end reflected the combination of American military experience in the Indian wars and the plenitude of United States military power by the 1860s. The means of securing the Confederacy's unconditional surrender was to be the total destruction of the Confederate armies.

When Ulysses S. Grant moved from triumphs in the western theater of war to become Commanding General of all the Armies of the United States at the beginning of 1864, he instructed each of the commanders of major army groups and field armies under him that their objective was the destruction of enemy armies. Major General William Tecumseh Sherman advancing out of the western theater toward the Atlantic coast and Major General Philip Sheridan in the Shenandoah carried this to the extreme. With Grant's advice and encouragement, Sherman and Sheridan attempted to destroy enemy armies, the Confederacy's economic ability to sustain the war, and the will of its people to persevere.

After the utter destruction of the Confederacy the United States returned with renewed vigor to fight the last of the wars against the Indians and rid the continental domain of Indian military power once and for all. As the attitudes formed from the beginning of the Indian wars helped lead the United

States to conduct the Civil War as a total war, so the experience of the Civil War diluted any humane compunctions that hitherto restrained the United States Army in dealing with the Indians. Specifically, the Army now applied the strategy of Sherman and Sheridan, aiming its blows not only at the Indians' fighting power but at their fragile economy and their ability to maintain any existence at all independent of the white man.

An American historical tradition at least as strong as the compulsion to pursue war to total victory – the fear of entanglement in Europe – kept the war with Spain in 1898 a relatively limited conflict. The Americans were content to destroy all the remnants of the Spanish Empire in the western hemisphere and the

Below: During the 20th century the USA has been able to deploy its vast industrial base to support not only its own forces but those of its allies with a veritable mass of advanced weapons and munitions.

Pacific without carrying the war to Spain itself. In World War I, the American participation came too late and was relatively too small for the American attitudes toward war to have much impact on the peace. If President Woodrow Wilson seemed generous in his peacemaking policies toward Germany, General Pershing was probably closer to the views of his countrymen in urging that the Allies should punish Germany by marching all the way to Berlin.

In World War II, the United States participated much longer and made a much larger contribution to the eventual Allied victory. The United States emerged from the war as unquestionably the greatest military power in the world. The war was a climax of American military history in that the American past fitted the United States so well to wage its part in it. Adolf Hitler's Nazi regime was an enemy so villainous that there could be almost universal agreement on the American prescription of "unconditional surrender" as the only

acceptable outcome of the conflict.

American strategists persuaded their somewhat reluctant British partners that the principal Anglo-American military effort must be a cross-Channel invasion of Europe, to confront the enemy's strength and annihilate it in the manner of Ulysses S. Grant facing Robert E. Lee. The American emphasis on the simultaneous strategy of the combined bomber offensive against Germany meanwhile echoed Sherman's and Sheridan's extension of Grant's strategy of annihilation from the enemy forces to the enemy economy.

In the Pacific, the US Navy similarly sought to annihilate the principal enemy armed force in the theater of war, in this instance the Japanese battle fleet. It drew on strategic precepts not only of the American Civil War but of the Navy's own great strategic thinker, the turn-of-the-century American prophet of sea power, Rear Admiral Alfred Thayer Mahan. From the air, the Americans wracked Japan not only with a bomber offensive com-

parable to the one waged against Germany, but eventually with the weapon representing the apotheosis of the Sherman-Sheridan manner of war.

Meanwhile, the tremendous wealth of the United States and its large population afforded it ample resources to wage a war seeking unconditional surrender through unconditional means. So well did the circumstances of World War II fit these American capacities and methods that the United States became tutor instead of pupil to most of the other military powers.

Yet the Americans have usually been loath to apply military conscription in peacetime having inherited from their British antecedents suspicion of standing professional military forces. Therefore the United States Constitution contains elaborate safeguards against military despotism, such as division of control over the federal military between the President and Congress.

So Americans have waged war zestfully when war engulfed them. But they have distrusted the professional soldiers whom they need to lead them in war because they view war as an abnormal condition. One effect has been a reciprocated distrust of American society, politics, and even democracy, on the part of the professional soldiers. Korea, to some extent, and Vietnam, to an even greater extent, served to reinforce this attitude.

The means on which Americans have historically preferred to rely to reconcile their distrust of professional soldiers and standing armies with their penchant for ferocity in war has been some form of people's army. The Continental Army of the Revolution sprang forth from these citizens' militias. The writers of the Constitution believed that state militias could fend off the potential military tyranny of a federal army. The militias gave each of the member states of the American Union enough military power, and thus a large measure of sovereignty, so they had the capacity to go to war against one another in 1861. The Confed-

eracy began life with an army already in being because it had the militia forces of the seceded states.

Today, states' sovereignty is almost wholly eroded in this area, but the National Guard and Air National Guard contingents of the separate states can usually boast officers with more experience and professionalism than the regular forces. A current problem of critical proportions is pilots deserting the regular armed forces because they can log more flying time, and sometimes fly newer equipment, in the Guard. In mid-1985, a Guard squadron in South Carolina could lay claim to having far more experienced, able officers in its F-16 fighters than could a regular squadron in the same state.

Because Americans tend to distrust a professional military – even now, when their unwillingness to have their sons drafted has given them just such a force – the military can be equally accused of bloodthirsty militarism for waging a war at all, and of pusillanimity for not waging it in the historic American mode with all available means employed! During the Vietnam crisis, the American military were thus assailed at home from right and left simultaneously, however contradictory the lines of criticism were.

A more realistic criticism is that military forces which must be kept consistently large and expensive with much of the economy at least partially dependent on their remaining large, have created a military-industrial complex whose influence on national policy is everywhere and inescapable. There is also

Left: The Korean War was a conflict that could not be won politically, but the US forces at the core of the UN armies finally stabilized an impossible stalemate and so made feasible the truce that still holds.

Below: Another great American resource has been logistical planning and co-ordination of the type that made possible the great Allied amphibious operations of World War II.

Active Duty Military Personnel, Selected Periods 1918 to 1984

Year	Army	Air Force	Navy	Marine Corps	Totals
30 June 1918	2,395,742	—	448,606	52,819	2,897,167
30 June 1939	189,839	—	125,202	19,432	334,473
31 May 1945[2]	5,983,330	2,310,436	3,359,283[1]	471,369	12,124,418
30 April 1952[3]	1,658,084	971,017	813,936[1]	242,017	3,685,054
30 June 1968[4]	1,570,343	904,850	765,457[1]	307,252	3, 547,902
31 March 1986	781,609	608,036	572,791	197,075	2,159,511
FY 1987 (programmed)	781,000	607,000	593,000	200,000	2,181,000

1 Excluding Coast Guard   3 Korean War peak
2 World War II peak   4 Vietnam Conflict peak

All information from US Department of Defense publication, "Selected Manpower Statistics" publications, except 1987 statistics, from DoD Annual Report Fiscal Year 1987.

public apprehension that having immense military power at their disposal will make Presidents excessively willing to seek a military route out of every otherwise intractable international crisis.

Distaste for a military-industrial complex aside, by the mid-1980s the US armed forces were a professional cadre (an "all-volunteer" force). Conscription of citizens was merely a memory of a previous decade. Military men – and women, who no longer served in segregated women's branches but were integral members of the force – lived their lives amidst a different language and culture than their civilian fellow citizens. Conversely, the average American under 35 had never worn a uniform and understood neither military jargon nor, often, headlines about defense issues. Having overcome crippling racial conflict and the drug problems of the 1970s and an appallingly low standard of quality in its recruits in the early 1980s (when a comic book was needed to instruct the driver of an M1 Abrams tank), the US armed forces are now attracting good people in sufficient numbers, although their retention, once trained, is low enough to constitute a glaring weakness. Current plans to upgrade from 12 to 15 carrier battle groups, for example, founder not for lack of capital ships – refurbished battleships like USS *New Jersey* are available as a stopgap – but for a dismaying paucity of trained, second-enlistment noncommissioned officers.

Despite reintroduction of draft registration in 1980, an actual draft had become a total political impossibility in the United States – but analysts look with trepidation to the early 1990s, when the number of 18-year-olds will be only three-fourths what it was in 1978. While it appears doubtful that the United States can fulfill worldwide military responsibilities for an indefinite period without a draft, the paradox remains that the current American upsurge of patriotism and support for the armed forces does not, and is not likely to, extend to support for reinstatement of national conscription.

The distaste for a "citizen's army", coupled with traditional unsettling historical conditions affecting the American war machine, ought to be pondered by all people who rely on

Left: Vietnam was a political, military and emotional disaster for the Americans, throwing the US war machine into disrepute for the ineptitude of its politico-military leadership and reliance on weight of fire (epitomized by battleship shore bombardment such as that of USS *New Jersey*, below). There were also problems with a number of tactical combat units, but the reputation of the US soldier (above) for valour was not impaired by other failings.

American military power as the principal counterweight to the might of the Soviet Union. With the Americans carrying the military leadership of the non-Communist world, a historically inexperienced hand is at the throttle and even the current improvement in US capabilities does not assure measured, patient applications of military force adjusted to complex situations. Furthermore, the American military have to contend with all the military menaces of a perilous world while also fending off constant suspicion at home.

The problems arising out of the history of the American armed forces ought to be pondered and have been emphasized here because so much depends on American military strength. American armed forces have served their country and the rest of the world's democracies far from badly. Offsetting the Soviet war machine depends on the United States to a great degree, buttressed by a large and costly American capability. The fact that Americans can still contemplate warfare in terms of complete victories bespeaks, beyond a disconcerting immoderation, to the deep reservoirs of economic strength, skilled manpower, and technological leadership they can mobilize for military purposes.

In past wars, furthermore, Americans have overcome their enemies with more than sheer material power. American fighting men have consistently displayed a considerable aptitude for battle. It was that aptitude and much more than simply the material resources of the United States that led Winston Churchill to remark on his hearing the news of Pearl Harbor and the American entry into World War II: 'I had studied the American Civil War, fought out to the last desperate inch . . . I went

to bed and slept the sleep of the saved and the thankful."

Beyond the aptitude for battle, there has also been the heartening American aptitude for military leadership, still present today in a new era when, regrettably, too many officers seem more like corporate executives than men at arms. Tradition says that the systems manager is a temporary abberation and that the tactician, the strategist, the leader can still be found in American uniform. The American officer corps performed almost immediately at a European level of professional skill as early as September 1918 with the Americans' secret, concealed movement of about a million men in a three-week period, at night and over inadequate roads and railways, from the area of their St. Mihiel offensive to the concentration area for their coming Meuse-Argonne offensive while the St. Mihiel battle was in progress. This feat was mainly the work of the young operations officer of the American First Army, Colonel George C. Marshall, Jr.

After a twenty-year interval spent in the scarcely larger than the old Indian war constabulary – plus, importantly, more study and teaching in the Army's schools – this same Marshall with apparently equal ease assumed the principal strategic and administrative leadership of the Anglo-American coalition's far-flung military forces in World War II, and carried them through to almost universal admiration. General Marshall was perhaps the best product of the American officer corps' tradition of professional excellence in the twentieth century, but he was also representative of the remarkably widespread ability of that officer corps to readjust almost overnight to command responsibilities over hundreds of

thousands of their own and Allied forces in global war. The Army's Dwight D. Eisenhower, Douglas MacArthur, Omar N. Bradley, Carl A. Spaatz, and the Navy's Ernest J. King and Chester A. Nimitz, all showed similar capacities.

Perhaps the mushroom expansion of the American armed forces has diluted the standards that in the past permitted the officers of small forces to take on large tasks so well; it is surely an understatement to say that American military leadership in the Vietnam war did not produce a George C. Marshall, although the 1980s – even in those instances where success was elusive, in Iran, in Lebanon, in Grenada – have shown strong promise by the men who were the majors and lieutenant colonels of Vietnam. Even with the preponderance of officers who look more comfortable in neckties than battle garb, the overall quality of the American professional officer corps has remained so high through so many generations that there is good reason to hope that the tradition of excellence will persist and prevail. The democracies owe much to the American professional soldiers who led in the world wars. Today, their followers may have to take men into battle using equipment named after alumni of the long, gray line – weapons named Abrams, Sheridan, Bradley – and it is on these professional heirs of a great tradition that many hopes for the future must rest.

Below: A small but important milestone in the rehabilitation of the US military's external reputation and internal pride was the 1982 invasion of Grenada, which showed the advantages of proper training and leadership at all levels.

US National Security Policy

It is not often that American presidential elections can be said to turn principally on the conduct of foreign policy and national security. It is generally agreed, however, that 1980 was such a case: foreign policy and national security issues dominated the politics of 1980, not only in the race for the presidency but in Congressional races as well. Ronald Reagan not only won a decisive victory for the presidency, but Republicans also secured a 54 to 46 majority in the US Senate.

The Republican victory in the Senate was the more remarkable of the two events. Between 1930 and 1980, the Republicans captured the Senate only in 1946 and 1952. Democrats enjoyed a Senate majority in 46 of those 50 years. Beyond this, in 1980 a number of Senate Democratic stalwarts, closely identified with President Carter's foreign policy,

such as Frank Church, the Chairman of the Senate Foreign Relations Committee, also went down to defeat. Clearly, the nation wanted new directions in national security policy.

What were the issues? Perhaps the most dramatic and emotional was the long drawn out hostage crisis; Americans felt humiliated that the Iranians had kept over 50 Americans captive so long. The incredibly bungled rescue attempt added to this sense of shame.

Perhaps the second most telling foreign policy defeat for President Carter was the failure of the the US Senate to consent to ratification of the SALT II arms control treaty. Powerful and influential citizens, such as those who made up the membership of the Committee on the Present Danger, pointed home the undeniable fact that the Soviet

Union had drawn ahead of the United States in strategic as well as conventional military power. Some Americans believed their nation was bearing an unfair share of the defense of the non-communist world. Still others were angry over the Panama Canal treaty. Unemployment in the automobile industry fueled a rising tide of resentment toward Japan. Illegal immigrants from Mexico, Central and Latin America took away jobs from Americans at the lower end of the economic spectrum.

In contrast, the 1984 presidential elections turned largely on domestic issues. President Reagan capitalized on the dramatic upswing in the economy and a resurgence of an American spirit that was dramatized by an outpouring of feeling during the summer Olympic Games in Los Angeles. Reagan's successful military action in Grenada also stood in marked contrast to the Carter failure in Iran, and provided Reagan with an additional argument to justify the substantial military buildup that had already taken place.

Reagan's first term, however, will be remembered for the introduction of the Strategic Defense Initiative, which focused attention on a possible defense against Soviet strategic ballistic missiles. SDI represents a major departure from the previous policy of Mutual Assured Destruction which holds that effective deterrence can be maintained only when both superpowers have the capacity to absorb a first strike and retaliate with massive and unacceptable destruction.

The beginning of President Reagan's second term was marked by the resumption of START (Strategic Arms Reduction Talks) negotiations with the Soviet Union. And the rise of Mikhail Gorbachev to the position of General Secretary of the CPSU marked the beginning of a generational change in the leadership of the Soviet Union.

American-Soviet Relations

The Soviet "threat" and what to do about it have preoccupied American policymakers from the enunciation of the Truman Doctrine in March 1947 until the present day. This is not surprising; since the early postwar years American leaders have been convinced that the Soviet Union is bent upon expansion, certainly in Europe, probably in the Middle East, and perhaps in Asia as well. This perception helped lead to the establishment of NATO and a more or less permanent American military presence in Western Europe. The USSR until recently was significantly weaker than the United States in strategic power and, therefore, not surprisingly, behaved with prudence and restraint during confrontations such as those in Berlin (1948 and 1961) and Cuba (1962).

The containment school of thought dominated American discussions of superpower

Above left: The tardy end to the Iranian embassy siege helped end the Carter administration, and still warns of the results of politico-military weakness.

Left: President Reagan is a staunch advocate of military strength combined with political will, and this was one of the platforms on which he was elected in 1980.

Stephen P. Gibert, Professor of Government, Director of the National Security Studies Program and a member of the International Research Council of the Center for Strategic and International Studies, Georgetown University.

Above: Under the leadership of Secretary Weinberger, the DoD has constantly emphasized the threat posed by the USSR, and the latter's growing strength.

and East-West relationships for most of the period between 1947 and 1972. However, as early as the 1948 presidential election, a new interpretation of the Cold War later referred to as "revisionism" arose on the left of the American political spectrum.

Much later, revisionism was to gain more adherents, epecially in academic circles. These university-based revisionists returned in their studies to the event of 1944-47, examined the origins of the Cold War, and found America, not Russia, wanting. According to revisionists, United States leaders such as President Truman, Secretaries Byrnes and Acheson, Senators Vandenburg and Taft, perceived aggressive designs in what were really defensive moves on Moscow's part. While it was true that the USSR wanted "friendly" nations in Eastern Europe, revisionists claimed this did not indicate a general expansionist drive. Refusing to adjust to the realities of sphere-of-influence politics, Washington adopted a moralistic pose to hide its real intentions, which were motivated by economic necessity. American policies such as the Truman Doctrine and the Marshall Plan, and the establishment of NATO were intended to facilitate economic domination of Europe to protect American export markets. Concealing this behind the rhetoric of containment, President Truman "bombarded the American people with a hate the enemy campaign", blaming it all on Soviet "aggression". This "campaign" also, according to the revisionists,

contributed to the "militarization" of American foreign policy.

Revisionists, of course, represent a distinctly minority point of view, even in the universities. For, although they labored most diligently to blame the Cold War on the West, certain facts would not go away. Among the most difficult of these was the Soviet annexation, between 1939 and 1945, of some 180,000 square miles of territory, including in Europe all of Estonia, Latvia and Lithuania and parts of Finland, Poland, and Rumania. The USSR also annexed southern Sakhalin and the Kurile Islands in the Far East and acquired a satellite in North Korea. In contrast, only China among the other major victorious powers acquired territory, laying claim to Taiwan, previously a Chinese province. First Britain and later France divested themselves of large colonial empires and the United States granted independence to the Philippines.

As the Soviet Union approached strategic nuclear parity with the United States a new school of thought emerged — the detentists. Basically, this group came to believe that the shared superpower position which arrived with parity — the total vulnerability of the United States and the Soviet Union vis-a-vis each other, and virtual invulnerability of the two countries to all other actors in the system — could become the basis for an understanding which would usher in an era of peace. At the minimum, strategic parity coupled with the doctrine and policy of assured destruction,

would provide sufficient stability so that nuclear war could be prevented and a less antagonistic superpower relationship could be established.

Athough detente concepts were articulated as early as the Kennedy-Johnson era, it was not until Nixon and Kissinger assumed power that detente became official American policy. Superpower strategic parity, it was argued, had produced a situation in which neither the United States nor the Soviet Union could expect to win a war with each other in any meaningful sense. Thus, the basis for a new and more stable relationship existed which would eliminate superpower strategic conflict so long as each possessed invulnerable second-strike forces.

At the same time, the danger of escalation of a local conflict existed, so that it had become imperative to improve Soviet-American relations. Specifically, detente would permit agreements to be made to limit the strategic arms race and allow other actions intended to "replace confrontation with negotiation". This less dangerous situation, according to President Nixon and Secretary Kissinger, had been realized in the SALT agreements of May 1972 and June 1973, ushering in a new era in American-Soviet relations.

Left: With American-Soviet relations at a low ebb after the shooting down of KAL-007 in 1983, a Soviet drilling ship watches MSC's *Narrangansett* search for wreckage.

Even in the halcyon days of detente in 1973, however, the Soviets were supplying sophisticated weapons to a large number of Third World countries. In October of that year, Egypt and Syria used advanced Russian missiles in their attack on Israel. In 1978, for the first time, the Soviet share of world arms exports exceeded that of the United States. Conventional arms transfer negotiations (CAT talks) were held between the two superpowers, but no agreement was reached. Could detente be divided with superpower competition continuing through client states, while tension in direct relations eased? The October War alert of Soviet airborne divisions and American strategic forces indicated that, indeed, detente was not divisible.

Moreover, direct relations between the United States and the USSR were also strained by the Soviet deployment of its fourth generation of ICBMs starting soon after the SALT I agreement. Highly accurate and

powerful weapons such as the SS-18 rocket were clearly destabilizing the strategic balance. The US Department of Defense warned that in the 1980s the Soviet Union would have the ability to knock out 80 to 90 percent of the US Minuteman force, while using only a fraction of the Soviet warheads. Such a disarming first strike would drastically alter the strategic balance, casting doubt on American retaliation and leaving Washington with the choice of city-busting attacks with sea-based strategic forces, or negotiation under highly unfavorable conditions.

By the late 1970s the policy of detente was clearly on the wane. President Ford forbade the use of the word "detente" within his administration. Following the Soviet invasion of Afghanistan in late 1979, the long-negotiated and controversial SALT II Treaty was withdrawn from Senate consideration. In 1980 Ronald Reagan was elected President on a platform, which included, inter alia, a com-

mitment to pursue a more forceful foreign policy and to upgrade US military forces. Although arms control negotiations continued with the Soviet government, and both superpowers pledged they would abide by the limits in the non-ratified SALT II accord, the two sides were far apart.

In essence, the Soviet Union's negotiating positions in the Strategic Arms Reduction Talks (START) are "equal reductions" from current arms levels and "equal security" with the United States. Since the USSR currently has more launchers, missiles, and throw-weight (payload), this would leave the Soviet Union numerically superior in all critical categories of strategic weapons except possibly warheads. The American position, in contrast, calls for "equal aggregates" at the end of the negotiations. To achieve equality, the USSR therefore would be required to make greater reductions. The US also rejects "equal security" if that means counting British and French nuclear weapons against US totals.

In late 1982 Soviet leader Leonid Brezhnev died and was replaced by KGB chief Yuri Andropov. The new Soviet leader immediately called for a summit meeting with President Reagan to improve the overall climate of Soviet-American relations and to further the START and intermediate nuclear forces (INF) arms reduction talks. Washington's position, however, was that the United States was no longer interested in "climate" talks. Rather, President Reagan's announced view was that the USSR must demonstrate by specific policy measures that it desired a genuine detente with the West. These concrete steps include improvement in "Soviet international behavior", especially in Afghanistan and Poland; a more "forthcoming" attitude toward arms reduction negotiations and the arresting of the Soviet military build-up; and a greater willingness on the part of Moscow to carry out in good faith the human rights provisions of the Helsinki Accords.

The downing of a Korean Airliner by the Soviets contributed to the frigid atmosphere, and relations between the two sides were further exacerbated when the Soviet Union walked out of the arms control talks in Geneva after the deployment of US Pershing II intermediate range nuclear missiles and ground-launched cruise missiles (GLCMs) in Europe. The Soviet Union, however, under Konstantin Chernenko indicated that they were prepared to resume talks with the United States once it became clear that the Reagan administration would continue in office for a second term. Reagan's announcement in March 1983 that the US would begin research on a strategic defense system has seriously complicated negotiations even though SDI as currently structured falls within the limitations of the ABM treaty.

US Security Concerns in Western Europe
It is generally agreed that, with a rough parity or a Soviet advantage in strategic forces, the conventional military balance in Europe is

Left: Reagan's determination to stand up to the Soviets has also placed a strain on American-European relations, as facts such as this graffito testify.

Right: The USA's best friend and staunchest ally in Europe has demonstrably been the British administration headed by Margaret Thatcher, an admirer of President Reagan.

becoming increasingly important. The Warsaw Pact Organization hold a quantitative advantage in forces on-line in Europe, with a 2 to 1 lead in major combat items. NATO depends on rapid reinforcement and prepositioned heavy equipment (POMCUS – Prepositioning of Material Configured to Unit Sets) to prevail in any future ground conflict. In addition, NATO counts on precision guided munitions to overcome the Pact's superiority in tanks (approximately 51,000 to 20,000 in 1985). In the future, NATO intends to deploy "high tech" systems to compensate for Warsaw Pact numerical superiorities. The US also is attempting to persuade, so far unsuccessfully, the European members of NATO to devote more resources to their conventional forces in order to raise the nuclear threshold in Europe.

At the theater nuclear level the balance of forces had to be strengthened as the Soviet Union was replacing earlier generation missiles aimed at Europe with modern, three-warhead mobile SS-20 rockets. To counterbalance this, NATO in 1979 adopted the "dual-track" decision. The first track called for the continuation of INF negotiations with the Soviet Union, and subsequently led to US proposals for the removal of all theater nuclear weapons from both the Soviet Union and Europe. This was the Reagan "zero option". The second track addressed the deployment of 464 ground-launched cruise missiles (GLCMs) and 108 new generation Pershing II missiles in Western Europe. The Soviets are particularly concerned about this deployment since their homeland could be struck by Pershing II warheads less than 10 minutes after launch.

Soviet Defense Minister Ustinov and Foreign Minister Gromyko (the latter in Bonn, in January 1983) warned that if NATO proceeded with deployment, and the United States deployed its new American-based Peacekeeper missiles, the Soviet Union would have to "answer" these additions with new Soviet deployments. President Reagan's view was that the new theater and strategic deployments were necessary to convince the Soviet Union to accept strategic and theater nuclear parity through arms control negotiations. Moreover, the current deployment of at least 414 multiple warhead Soviet SS-20 missiles (of which an estimated 243 are known to be targeted against Europe), could devastate all of Europe. In addition, it is claimed that the Soviet rocket forces have at least one "extra" missile for each SS-20 launcher. If this is so, the SS-20s might be able to deliver 2,646 warheads to their targets.

To date, the British, German and Italian governments, and also most other NATO governments, remain committed to the deployment of the 572 US theater nuclear weapons in Europe, which began in late 1983 and is expected to be completed in 1988. The Europeans remain worried, however, that the superpowers might fight a "sanctuary war" limited to Europe, with both the Soviet Union and the United States homelands spared from attack. However unrealistic this may be, American attempts to improve NATO's theater, tactical nuclear and conventional forces fuel such doubts in European capitals. European NATO doctrine since the 1950s has emphasized rapid escalation so that, in Henry Kissinger's phrase, any new war would take place "over their heads", with a central exchange of missiles directed at superpower homelands. The Europeans provide just enough conventional forces to keep the American government barely satisfied, but count on the threat of rapid escalation to strategic nuclear warfare to deter any future conflict with the Soviet Union. With this in mind, the Europeans have expressed some concern over the US Strategic Defense Initiative, some seeing it as a possible return to US isolationism or, at the very least, an alteration of US nuclear strategy that could diminish the US strategic deterrent in Europe. Others believe that the introduction of this new element could have a negative impact on START talks.

Poland Fuels NATO Rift

Another controversial issue between the US and its NATO allies concerned their respective responses to events in Poland, where in December 1981 the first legitimate workers' union in the Communist bloc was struck down by the imposition of martial law. Political responses to this action split the West as sanctions aimed at the Soviet Union or the Polish government also targeted European industry. Declaring Poland in default would cause problems for European and American banks. A wheat embargo would hurt American farmers, while limitations on other exports would injure American and especially European manufacturers.

President Reagan continued wheat exports to the USSR but banned technology exports to the Soviet Union in an effort to prevent the completion of the natural gas pipeline to Western Europe. Washington argued that Moscow could influence European political decisions by threatening to turn off the pipeline once it was in place. Further, the US government claimed that the pipeline would be the single largest generator of hard currency for the Soviet Union in the immediate future. The Europeans countered that the gas pipeline would provide only 5 percent of their energy needs and that much of the Soviet hard currency reserves go for wheat from the United States. It was all very well for Washington to maintain that the wheat export and the pipeline issues were very different and warranted separate approaches; Europeans, however, regarded this as sophistry – a weak attempt by the United States to make its European allies bear the brunt of the burden in imposing sanctions on the USSR.

The differences in interest outlined above – the relative importance of trade with the East, differing perceptions of the Soviet threat, different approaches to deterrence – threaten seriously to disrupt the Atlantic Alliance. Periodically, similar fissures have been repaired in the past. Nevertheless, Western Europe and America remain linked by economic, cultural and social ties. Europe's large population, wealth, technological resources, and industrial base make it indispensable to American security. In return, without the United States, Western Europe could not, at least in the near future, successfully resist Soviet pressures. Both Europe and the United States, therefore, will find it imperative to resolve their many differences, or at least to prevent such differences as may arise from obscuring the very real benefits of cooperation.

US Security Policy in Asia

While NATO-Europe has been and remains the principal focus of United States security concerns, Washington also maintains a sub-

stantial presence in Asia. In fact, when the Nixon administration took office in 1969, the United States had much larger military forces in Asia than in Europe. At that time it was US policy to maintain forces sufficient to fight "two-and-a-half wars". This was defined as including a possible conflict between NATO and Warsaw Pact forces, a war between the United States and the People's Republic of China, and a "half-war" contingency elsewhere.

When US troop commitments were revised downward from a "two-and-a-half" stance, it might have been supposed that force reductions would have occurred around the world. Instead, between 1969 and 1975 the United States withdrew from Asia some 702,000 military personnel; by contrast, the US force presence in Europe was not reduced. Empirically, if not in theory, the Nixon administration not only terminated the Vietnam conflict but reverted to a "European-first" military posture. Elsewhere, military aid was to take the place of American soldiers. Europe was to get US troops: Asians were to get US dollars.

Such a policy was both required and justified by the downgrading of the "Chinese threat" to non-communist Asian nations and to US national security. This was accomplished through the secret Kissinger mission to Beijing in 1971, followed by the Nixon trip in 1972, although full diplomatic relations with the PRC were not established. By the end of the Ford administration, Nixon's statement that "Asian hands must shape the Asian future" had been given concrete reality.

Despite the drawdown of American military strength in Asia, by the time President Carter took office a broad consensus had developed that Korea and Japan remained important to US global strategy. There was also general agreement that the continuing hostility between Moscow and Peking might be turned to American advantage. Stated differently, while the United States no longer intended to play a leading role in Southeast Asia, America would continue to regard Northeast Asia as a region vital to US national security. Nevertheless, Washington found it very difficult to translate this consensus into concrete policy decisions.

Korean-American Relations

Korean-American relations have been subjected to increasing stresses and strains. Although the two events may not be related, when President Nixon withdrew the Seventh Division from Korea in 1971-72, President Park declared (in December 1971) a state of emergency: martial law followed some months later (in October 1972) and in December a new constitution – referred to as the Yushin Constitution – conferred new powers on the Korean chief executive. Subsequently, four emergency decrees were issued and a number of prominent opposition leaders were arrested, including a former ROK president, Yun Po-sun. Supporters of President Park cited the new security situation in Asia and Korea in justifying more stringent political controls; critics claimed that these were only excuses to maintain a dictator whose support in the populace had waned.

These charges were echoed in the United States, where sentiment for removing the remaining US ground forces, which had surfaced periodically in the past, began building again in Washington. "Trial balloons" were floated, suggesting various "options" to the retention of American forces in South Korea, especially involving the Second Division which was positioned along the demilitarized zone (DMZ) guarding the approaches to Seoul. Whether or not there was serious sentiment in the executive branch for removing or prepositioning the Second Division, the collapse of South Vietnam in April 1975 effectively eliminated the possibility of such a move by the Ford Administration. In May, President Ford reaffirmed US treaty commitments to the Republic of Korea and in August, Secretary of Defense Schlesinger journeyed to Seoul to emphasize the President's statement by pledging that American troops would remain in Korea and that the United States would continue to assist South Korea in its armed forces improvement program. Presidential candidate Jimmy Carter in May 1976 revived the call for withdrawal from Korea of the remaining American ground forces and the tactical nuclear weapons available to them. Subsequently, the new President had been in office only about a week when his Vice President,

Walter Mondale, announced in Tokyo that US force withdrawals would begin but would be accompanied by "consultations" between Washington, Tokyo and Seoul. It was not mentioned precisely what these "consultations" would include since indeed the decision had not only been made prior to talks with the Koreans and the Japanese, but even before the new Secretary of State and National Security Advisor had had an opportunity to assess the situation. Undaunted by these rather peculiar circumstances, President Carter reaffirmed in March 1977 his intention to withdraw American ground forces, but in phases, and accompanied by "consultations" with the Republic of Korea.

President Carter's decision quite naturally raised the question as to whether adequate consideration had been given to the reasons for retaining the status quo. Possibly the most important of these was the belief that the presence of US forces in Korea is a highly significant symbol of American determination to play an important (although clearly not a dominant) role in shaping the course of change in Asia. It can be argued that the Second Division, placed as it is on the DMZ in "harm's way", indicates US will and resolve to uphold its treaty obligations and its commitments in an era when there is, regrettably, substantial reason to doubt that it intends to do so. President Carter in his press conference on 26 May 1977, replying to criticisms of his withdrawal policy, stated that the American "commitment to South Korea is undeviating and is staunch". In 1979 Carter announced that three brigades of the Second Division would remain in South Korea until 1982.

Reagan Reverses Carter Decision

When he assumed office in 1981, Ronald Reagan made it known that his administration would not implement the Carter decision to withdraw the remaining American troops from Korea. To emphasize the new policy, South Korean President Chun Doo Hwan became the first foreign leader to visit Washington after Reagan assumed the US presidency. The 11-day visit in late January and February 1981 was intended to symbolize that the new American government was committed to maintaining the defensive alliance with the Republic of Korea. Perhaps more importantly, it signaled to the rest of Asia (and to the Soviet Union) that the United States intended to remain an Asian (as distinct from just a Pacific) power; South Korea was to be the one place in continental Asia where the United States would maintain a substantial military presence, including at least some units armed with tactical nuclear weapons.

At the summit meeting, the two leaders announced that they would resume the ROK-US security consultative meetings and pledged their cooperation to further the modernization of ROK armed forces. President Reagan reaffirmed that South Korea must be a full participant in any American negotiations with North Korea (a policy which has consistently been opposed by North Korea). Furthermore, the US government stated that any unilateral American or allied steps toward North Korea which are not reciprocated by North Korea's allies with regard to South Korea would be unacceptable. This latter is an important policy stand; in practical effect, it means that Washington will not recognize and will oppose allied recognition of North Korea unless the Soviet Union and the People's Republic of China reciprocate by recognizing South Korea.

Left: US troops watch for North Korean guard movements from a United Nations Command observation post in South Korea near the Demilitarized Zone as part of the Joint Security Force.

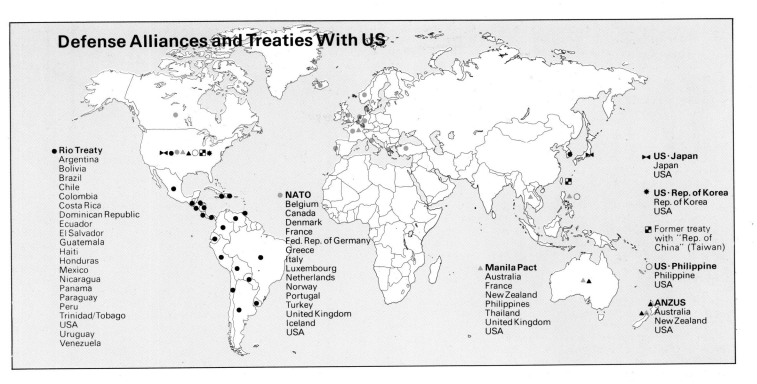

Defense Alliances and Treaties With US

● Rio Treaty
Argentina
Bolivia
Brazil
Chile
Colombia
Costa Rica
Dominican Republic
Ecuador
El Salvador
Guatemala
Haiti
Honduras
Mexico
Nicaragua
Panama
Paraguay
Peru
Trinidad/Tobago
USA
Uruguay
Venezuela

● NATO
Belgium
Canada
Denmark
France
Fed. Rep. of Germany
Greece
Italy
Luxembourg
Netherlands
Norway
Portugal
Turkey
United Kingdom
Iceland
USA

▲ Manila Pact
Australia
France
New Zealand
Philippines
Thailand
United Kingdom
USA

◄► US·Japan
Japan
USA

✳ US·Rep. of Korea
Rep. of Korea
USA

◩ Former treaty
with "Rep. of
China" (Taiwan)

○ US·Philippine
Philippine
USA

▲ ANZUS
Australia
New Zealand
USA

Cognizant of the fact that the US Second Division in Korea is the only US Army division located west of Hawaii, the current administration in Washington obviously has no plans at present to remove American military forces from Korea.

Relations with Japan

While American relations with Korea have improved since President Carter postponed further US troop withdrawals in 1979, tensions between Washington and Tokyo have steadily increased over the past decade. Two critically important issues are now sharply dividing Japan and the United States.

The first issue is trade. Between 1977 and 1980 America's trade deficit with Japan was running at about $12 billion dollars annually. By 1984 it had grown to $37 billion, its highest level ever. The American television industry disappeared to Japan some years ago and the United States became concerned that the automobile industry could also be vanquished. The Chrysler "bailout" and Detroit's dramatic recovery have dispelled these fears for the moment, but President Reagan has since lifted import quotas on Japanese automobiles, thus increasing Japanese competition once again.

Although the Japanese have placed voluntary restrictions on their exports, it is believed in the United States that the Japanese are "unfair traders". The central problem, however, lies in the fact that an unsuccessful resolution of the trade imbalance may be linked to current problems over the security relationship. There are virtually no influential defenders of Japan concerning the American-Japanese security relationship. With regard to security burden-sharing, the Japanese are much more vulnerable to the American charge of unreasonable and unfair behavior. Stated bluntly, Japan is a military protectorate of the United States, not an ally.

At the center of the controversy is Japan's unwillingness to allocate the resources necessary to contribute in a meaningful way to mutual security in Northeast Asia and the Western Pacific. In July 1982, the Tokyo government once more failed to live up to its commitments to upgrade its defenses. While

there was much discussion in Japan of the need to shoulder a greater share of the mutual security burden, the Japanese Finance Ministry set the increase in Japan's spending for 1983 at only 7.3 percent, less than the increase in 1982 over 1981 and less than that requested by the Japanese Defense Agency. While 7 percent does not seem an unreasonable increase, the total defense budget is so low that the increase amounts to only $760 million. Subsequently, in December 1982, the Finance Ministry said that the defense spending increase should be limited to 5.1 percent but this was later revised to 6.5 percent. Total spending for 1985 is projected to be about $13 billion, representing once again, less than 1 percent of Japan's gross national product (GNP). In fairness, however, Japan's gross national product is sufficiently large that its defense budget is actually the eighth largest in

the world and the third largest among non-nuclear powers.

Moreover, Japan's Asian neighbors presumably would not want Japan to procure nuclear weapons or offensive forces that could be used to intimidate countries that put up trade barriers to Japanese exports. In 1985, the Soviet Union published "Japan's Military Power", which talked about the potentially rapid expansion of the Japanese ground self-defense forces from 155,000 men to 900,000 – among other things. This is a direct and obvious reflection of the type of concern over a Japan with stronger military capability.

When Yasuhiro Nakasone succeeded Zenko Suzuki as Prime Minister of Japan, his opening statements called the United States Japan's most important trading partner and ally, and pledged his efforts to improve substantially Japanese-American trade relations.

Right: Two Japan Air Self Defense Force F-4EJ Phantoms flank a USAF F-15 during "Cope North" joint Japanese-US Air Training Exercise, scores of which have taken place since 1978.

He also cited the necessity for Japan to increase significantly its contributions to mutual security. While these kind of statements have emanated previously from Tokyo, Nakasone is considered to be by far the most pro-defense leader Japan has had in decades. His cabinet choices and his advisers also reflect an unusually strong (for Japan) defense orientation.

Nakasone is clearly and obviously very concerned about the deterioration in relations with the United States. In January 1983, the Prime Minister visited Washington for talks with President Reagan. In the course of his stay, the Japanese leader expressed his firm intention of further easing Japanese import restrictions, especially with regard to American agricultural exports. Nakasone also was quite forthright in acknowledging the need for ameliorating to the extent feasible the severe trade imbalance between the two countries. The Japanese also reminded the Americans that Japan, like the United States, currently confronts unprecedentedly large budget deficits. Nevertheless, Nakasone reiterated his previous statements in Tokyo that Japan would significantly strengthen its defense posture.

The People's Republic of China

On 19 December 1978, President Carter ended the long diplomatic hiatus between the United States and the People's Republic of China when he "derecognized" the Republic of China on Taiwan, switching diplomatic recognition from Taipei to Beijing. While the establishment of diplomatic ties with the PRC met with general approval in the United States, many in Congress were disturbed over the failure of the Carter administration to secure concessions from the PRC on the Taiwan issue.

Reflecting this, the House of Representatives in March 1979 by a 345 to 55 vote passed the Taiwan Relations Act (TRA) which pledged the United States to continue less than full diplomatic relations with Taiwan, establishing new institutions in Taipei and Washington. The Coordinating Council for North American Affairs and the American Institute in Taiwan are not dejure embassies but they continue most of the form and substance of full diplomatic relations between the United States and the Republic of China on Taiwan. Many believed that, with the election

of President Reagan the Carter decision would be reversed and diplomatic ties with Taiwan restored. Once in office, however, it became clear that the Reagan government would pursue a policy toward the two Chinas not sharply different from that of the previous government in Washington.

By late 1982, substantial obstacles still existed to close Sino-American relations. In the Shanghai Communique of 17 August 1982, President Reagan agreed to reduce US arms transfers to Taiwan contingent upon a peaceful resolution of the Two-China problem. Subsequently, the administration agreed to index US arms transfers to inflation, which led to some uncertainty as to the exact totals of future transfers. Thus the Taiwan issue remains a bone of contention. Moreover, China's military weakness has led many to believe that it was not wise for the United States to ally itself with the PRC. Beijing seemed more interested in economic modernization than in building its military forces. Signs of a possible Sino-Soviet rapprochement began to appear.

In retrospect it seems that the anti-Soviet thrust of the Reagan administration is stronger than its anti-Communist attitude.

Above: Despite continued squabbles about US support for Taiwan, the rapprochement with China continues. In June 1984 Defense Minister Zhang Aiping visited the Pentagon.

Believing in "power politics" in the classical sense and viewing the Soviet Union as the only genuine danger to the United States, Secretary Haig and his successor, Secretary Shultz, have shown a desire for close relations with the PRC to offset Soviet strength. This attitude also seems to be shared by Vice President Bush and other high officials in the Reagan government. Accordingly, American relations with Taiwan have not improved and perhaps have even deteriorated.

Several overtures – including trips by high level officials – have been made toward China in what can best be described as a developing defense relationship. The United States has said it is willing to help with defense modernization efforts in China if the purposes are

Below: A consequence of replacing New Zealand Prime Minister Robert Muldoon (here) by David Lange has been a straining of relations with the USA.

clear and the expectations realistic. President Reagan has said, "the US-People's Republic of China military relationship helps develop and maintain China as a force for peace and stability in the region and the world, while not posing a threat to other US friends and allies in the region."

Australia/New Zealand
The South Pacific, more specifically the countries of Australia and New Zealand which, with the US, make up the ANZUS Alliance, has been under considerable strain, primarily because of New Zealand's port access policies. That country's determination to bar nuclear-armed or nuclear-powered US warships from its ports, and to put the stamp of approval on that policy through parliamentary action, prompted the US in mid-1986 to announce it no longer felt bound to provide a security guarantee to New Zealand.

Australia, while pledging to continue its security ties with the US, even if the alliance does not include its neighbor, nevertheless cautioned publicly that the US should not expect its smaller allies to endorse US views on political and global issues. As Australian Ambassador F. Rawdon expressed it in June 1986, the alliance with Washington "must have that basic element of symmetry even when the size and power of the partner is so disparate".

The Philippines
The Mutual Defense Treaty of 1951 and the Military Base Agreement of 1947 are the foundations of the US security relationship with the Philippines. Staunch US supporter Ferdinand Marcos is no longer in office and was replaced in early 1986 by Corazon Aquino, who is grappling with the many problems left behind by her predecessor. US interest in continuing the *status quo* in the area is enormous, however; the proximity of its military facilities there to the international sea lanes connecting the Persian Gulf, Southeast Asia and Northeast Asia makes the *status quo* particularly important.

American Security Concerns in the Middle East
The Middle East may not be as critical to America's global posture as Western Europe or Northeast Asia, but there is no question that the Middle East is of great concern to the United States. In contrast to the sharp disagreements that exist over American policy to the USSR and the concomitant preservation of European security, and over Northeast Asian policy, there seems to be a broad consensus concerning US interests in the Middle East if there are questions as to how best to secure those interests. American policy goals are: to assist Israel in maintaining its independence and security and to settle the Arab-Israel conflict on equitable terms; to ensure access to Persian Gulf oil at "reasonable" prices, both for the United States and other oil-dependent nations, especially Western Europe and Japan; and, finally, to deny "undue" influence over the Middle East to the Soviet Union.

Policy choices with regard to the Arab-Israeli conflict must begin with the fundamental premise that the United States of necessity will have important relationships with both Israelis and Arabs for the foreseeable future. Accordingly, courses of action such as reversing alliances and "abandoning" Israel on the one hand or deliberately seeking confrontation with the Arab world through total and unquestioning support of Jerusalem on the other, are not feasible.

While there are certain aspects of the Arab-Israeli dispute which lend themselves to the formulation of alternative options, there are other aspects which have come to be imperatives in US policy. These are:

1. The existence of Israel is not negotiable. To adopt a policy position which leaves any room for doubt on this question, aside from the moral implications, would do irretrievable damage to US credibility and lead an isolated Israel to adopt a declaratory nuclear retaliation policy, with obvious dangerous consequences.

2. While the United States is committed to defend Israel's right to exist, it is not committed to particular boundaries. The United States supports UN Resolution 242 which calls for Israeli withdrawal from territories occupied in the 1967 war. That resolution envisions such withdrawal in the context of Arab recognition of Israel's right to live in peace within secure and recognized borders, not mere armistice lines.

3. The United States supports "normalization" of the conflict. This means direct negotiations of issues by the immediate participants, with external powers assisting but not dictating outcomes. It also means the acceptance of negotiations as a bargaining process in which each side makes certain concessions in order to arrive at a solution not wholly satisfactory but at least minimally acceptable to all concerned.

Above: The US contingent of the multinational 'peacekeeping' force in Lebanon had a hard time of it, confirming again that conventional forces cannot cope well with guerrilla forces on their home ground.

4. Pending resolution of the dispute, the United States must attempt to maintain a balance of military power between the two parties. It is not sufficient to maintain a military balance between Israel and the Arab opponents. While it is possible that a no-war, no-peace situation could persist a long time, the inherent instabilities make it essential to move beyond this condition to some form of settlement and US policy should be geared to this goal.

Based upon these principles, after the late Egyptian Prime Minister Anwar Sadat had made his dramatic peace visit to Israel, President Carter achieved the greatest foreign policy success of his term in office: the Camp

Below: A continued thorn in the side of Middle East problems is US support for Israel. In May 1986 Defense Minister Yitzhak Rabin and Secretary Weinberger signed an MoU for Israeli SDI work.

25

David Accords between Egypt and Israel. The Egyptian-Israeli peace treaty shattered the Arab coalition against Israel and seemingly opened the way for a genuine reconciliation between Israel and the Arab countries. Unfortunately, however, the issue of an independent Palestinian state has prevented further progress. Israel under Prime Minister Menachem Begin adopted an increasingly tougher line toward the weakened Arab front. President Reagan has been unable to persuade Israel to "freeze" new Jewish settlements on the West Bank. In contrast to previous policy, the government in Israel now shows no inclination to pursue the formula of trading territory for formal peace agreements as was done with Egypt. Rather, Israel appears to have chosen territory over peace and, by promoting Jewish settlements in the West Bank, is laying the basis for annexing the ancient lands of Judea and Samaria.

Consistent with this more aggressive policy, the Israeli government in 1982 began seeking a pretext to move into Lebanon and destroy the Palestinian Liberation Organization as a military force. The long-sought opportunity was provided by the Arab assassination of the Israeli ambassador in London. Israel's retaliation for the death of the ambassador was deliberately disproportionate in its severity, thus provoking the anticipated Arab response. This Arab attack then provided Israel with the necessary political justification to launch the desired full-scale invasion of Lebanon. In a textbook military operation, obviously well planned, Israeli forces quickly advanced to Beirut. After some weeks of negotiations, led by American envoy Philip Habib, PLO forces were evacuated from Beirut and dispersed throughout the Middle East. The Israeli triumph however, was marred by the Lebanese militia massacre of Moslem civilians in Palestinian refugee camps, ostensibly under the protection of the Israeli occupying authorities.

While it can be argued that Israel is not justified in furthering Jewish settlement in the West Bank area, and that such a policy is counterproductive, certainly Israel had the right to attack and destroy the PLO forces. Palestinians cannot expect to regard themselves as at war with Israel and not be prepared to suffer the consequences of belligerency. The military defeat and dispersal of the PLO opened up an opportunity for a genuine Arab-Israeli settlement as Israel became the dominant military power in the region. The Arabs, in contrast, were divided among themselves. Egypt and Jordan desired peace and Syria was temporarily cowed into passivity. The Soviet Union, once the strongest external supporter of the Arab states, saw its influence considerably diminished. Preoccupied with Poland and Afghanistan and concerned about the situation on its Iranian border, Moscow initially showed little inclination to become an active proponent of Israel's Arab neighbors. The situation changed dramatically, however, when Israel decided to fall back to prepared positions in Sidon and the highlands in south Lebanon. In order to fill the gap, the US, UK, France, and Italy deployed a peacekeeping force in Beirut designed to give President Gemayal's fledgling government a chance to assert itself over the diverse factions contending for power. Ultimately this mission proved unsuccessful as Syrian-supported Moslem militias took control of the Schuff mountains and terrorist groups inflicted heavy punishment on the peacekeeping forces. Facing increasing domestic pressure, President Reagan decided to disengage US forces from the region.

Under a new coalition government, Israel has begun a unilateral withdrawal from Lebanon which leaves Syria in a commanding position. In the meantime President Mubarak of Egypt has floated new ideas to press the United States back into the Middle East peace process, but President Reagan has clearly indicated that the United States will not become involved until the various Arab factions, especially the PLO, enter into direct negotiations with the Israelis.

The Persian Gulf

Although the risk of superpower confrontation has diminished on the Mediterranean side of the Middle East, the Persian Gulf area has remained volatile and dangerous. While the Camp David Accords were a success for President Carter, the Middle East also handed Carter his most telling defeat in the Iranian revolution and the American hostage crisis. Although he inherited and did not initiate a situation where Iran had become an "American surrogate" to maintain order in the Gulf, Carter accepted this state of affairs uncritically. After the Shah went into exile, the American government engaged in an embarrassing and public display of anxiety over the Shah's medical visit to the United States, breathing a sigh of relief audible all the way to Teheran when he departed. This conduct was all the more unbecoming when it is recalled that only a short time earlier the American president had lavished praise on the Shah as a great world leader.

Perhaps this episode would have been quickly forgotten, however, had it not been for the seizure of the American Embassy in Teheran. It is difficult to attribute any single factor to President Carter's defeat in the 1980 election. However, the ineffectual attempts to obtain the release of the American hostages and the completely inept rescue operation must be considered principal causes for the rout of the Democrats in 1980.

Two other events have imperiled the stability of the Gulf. The first is the Iraqi-Iranian war. The United States has attempted to remain neutral, recognizing that a decisive victory for either side could threaten other Gulf states such as Saudi Arabia and endanger the vital Persian Gulf oil supply.

More serious was the Soviet invasion of Afghanistan and Soviet attempts to destroy Afghan resistance. Irrespective of Soviet motivations, the geopolitical reality cannot be denied: control of Afghanistan will enable the USSR to dominate militarily the Persian Gulf region. Neither the so-called Carter Doctrine nor the US Central Command can alter the fundamental fact that a Soviet-dominated Afghanistan will enable Soviet air power to reign supreme over the Persian Gulf and the surrounding seas. Thus still another area of the world, if Moscow succeeds in Afghanistan, would live under the shadow of Russian military power.

Persian Gulf oil remains a vital commodity. Presently, however, there is a world oil surplus. The United States, by far the largest oil consumer in the world, can claim a major share of the credit for this more favorable situation. In 1972, the United States was consuming about 17 million barrels of oil per day and consumption was rising by 6 percent annually. This increase was halted. In 1982, a decade later, United States consumption was about 16 million barrels per day. Although the list price of Persian Gulf light crude remained at $34 a barrel in 1982 (as compared with less than $3 in 1972), its selling price in January 1985 hovered around $28 and that price was

Below: Continued US support for the legacy of the Camp David accord is attested by weapon deliveries to Egypt, and by exercises such as 'Bright Star' deployment of F-16As from Hill AFB to Egypt.

headed down further in 1986. By the year 2000, however, it is expected that the price of oil will be rising again. Also, Persian Gulf will remain the most important source of oil for non-communist and possibly communist countries as well.

As to the third US goal – preventing excessive Soviet influence in the Middle East – at the moment Soviet fortunes in the area have improved with Syria's growing influence in Lebanon. The Soviet position also would be strengthened dramatically if the USSR succeeds in turning Afghanistan into a pacified vassal state. Even if this does not happen, it is to be anticipated that Moscow will once more, at some time in the not too distant future, seek to regain an influential role in Middle Eastern affairs. Thus, preventing "undue" Soviet influence in the Middle East is a permanent task for American diplomacy.

Latin America

One of the more pleasant myths enjoyed by North Americans is that Latin America and the United States are "good neighbors", linked in a "special relationship" dictated by geography and history.

The facts are otherwise. Latin America has never been of much consequence to the United States politically, culturally or economically. One does not have to agree with the unkind remark attributed to a former high official in Washington that "Latin America is a danger pointed at the south pole" to accept the reality that only Africa has been accorded a lesser role in American national security policy. Thus it should have come as no surprise, after the failure of Secretary Haig's "shuttle diplomacy" between Buenos Aires and London, that, forced to choose, Washington backed Britain in the 1982 Falkland islands crisis. To have done otherwise would have been quite astonishing.

The reality is that the United States government has viewed its role as exercising a benevolent hegemony over hemispheric affairs, primarily concerned with making certain that Latin America followed wherever the US chose to lead in world affairs and regarded US investment in Latin America with gratitude.

Below: US pressure on Nicaragua continues, though training exercises in neighboring Honduras can provide Nicaragua and its supporters with useful propaganda against 'US imperialism'.

This felicitous state of affairs – from Washington's point of view – has been gradually undergoing change. The geopolitics of the Cold War still dictate that the areas of Soviet-American confrontation will be around the Eurasian rimland; nevertheless, the last two decades have witnessed a transition in US relations with Latin America. The old hegemonic role of the past is being replaced with, if not a relationship of equals, at least one in which Washington must demonstrate a greater regard for Latin American concerns and interests. The Latin Americans themselves have in recent years rejected their dependent status and increasingly found ways to demonstrate their unwillingness to remain subject to political domination by the United States.

Above: A DoD briefing map of the April 1986 raid by UK-based F-111s against Libya shows the long detour forced on US aircraft by refusal of overflight rights by France and Spain. This lack of co-operation infuriated the US public.

The central issue for some 20 years in US relations with Latin America has been Cuba – what to do about Fidel Castro's decision in the early 1960s to align Cuba closely with the Soviet Union. President Eisenhower first tried to "deal with" Castro and then largely ignored Cuba. President Kennedy inherited a plan to overthrow the Castro regime but failed, although he did succeed in the crisis of 1962 in disrupting Soviet plans to use Cuba as an intermediate range missile base. Presidents

Johnson and Nixon tried economic and political sanctions. President Ford and especially President Carter attempted to entice Cuba into a more satisfactory relationship through promising various economic benefits of cooperation. Whatever the reasons – ideological, idiosyncratic, economic, megalomaniacal – all efforts failed.

Washington's troubles with Havana began in 1959 when Cuba's agrarian reform policy included the nationalization of the agricultural holdings of American citizens. To this injury Cuba added insult when it opened diplomatic and trade relations with the Soviet Union and began to provide assistance to other Marxist-oriented Latin American revolutionary movements. Washington responded first with the abortive CIA-sponsored raid on the Bay of Pigs, then compelled the Soviet Union to withdraw its missiles in 1962, and in 1964 led the movement by the Organization of American States (OAS) to impose sanctions on Cuba. Cuba became increasingly dependent for its economic survival on its distant patron, the Soviet Union. For the first time in history, Moscow had established a genuine alliance in the Western Hemisphere.

The United States reassessed its Cuban policy after President Ford assumed office and made several overtures to Castro. Washington dropped its insistence that Havana break off relations with Moscow as a precondition for restoring diplomatic ties with the United States; restrictions on American-owned firms abroad doing business with Cuba were modified; the US agreed in the OAS to ease OAS sanctions against Cuba; and wide-ranging discussions between the United States and Cuba began. This rapprochement ended, however, when Castro dispatched some 36,000 Cuban troops to Angola to assist the Marxist-oriented Popular Movement for the Liberation of Angola. Cuban troops also were sent to Mozambique, ostensibly to prevent an invasion by South Africa.

Subsequently, President Carter attempted to improve relations with Castro after Cuba allegedly withdrew much of its armed forces from Angola. As Ford's initiative had foundered on Castro's Angolan intervention, so Carter's collapsed when in 1978 Cuba dispatched some 20,000 Cuban soldiers to Ethiopia to assist that Marxist regime in its struggle with Somalia. By the end of President Carter's term, even those persons in the United States most willing to have a reconciliation with Cuba had to admit that Cuba and the Soviet Union were coordinating military efforts to assist Marxist movements both in Africa and Central America. Under

such circumstances, it is not surprising that the Reagan government, upon assuming office in 1981, made it known that no further overtures would be made to Cuba unless Havana ceased to act a proxy warrior for the Soviet Union.

The Reagan administration not only toughened the US stand against Cuba but also toward the Marxist revolutionaries in Central America, especially in El Salvador and Nicaragua. Congressional opposition, however, and the (spurious) cry of "No more Vietnams" have prevented stronger US efforts in the Central American area. The timely rescue operation of US citizens on the little-known island of Grenada proved to be the exception as US troops moved in force to depose a Cuban-backed Marxist junta that had taken over the island. The administration justified its move on the grounds that US citizens were in danger and that the democratic governments on surrounding Caribbean islands had requested US assistance. The Grenada operation in retrospect had a greater significance, however, by giving credence to the Reagan position that the United States would back its foreign policy with force.

From a strategic standpoint the mission was also necessary as a Soviet-Cuban toehold in the southern Caribbean would have provided further opportunities to destabilize Central

Above: Rescued American medical students wave to US troops as they prepare to board aircraft bound for the United States. US forces quickly dealt with the 'revolutionary' opposition, finding Cuban soldiers among them.

and South America. More importantly though, it would have provided the Soviets with a base that overlooked vital US shipping lanes. There can be no doubt that the construction of an airport on Grenada that had the capacity to receive Soviet military aircraft played an important part in the decision to invade.

Canada and Mexico

Despite Washington's preoccupation with Cuba, US relations with the states on its immediate borders are of greater importance. Canada is not only America's single largest trading partner, but more importantly, provides necessary facilities for detecting and tracking ballistic missiles – facilities which will be of even greater importance if plans for

Below: While US force presence in Central America continues to cause controversy, much of the US effort is centered around medical aid. Here US Army and Honduran personnel check children during a Medical Readiness Training exercise.

Above: Fidel Castro and a communist Cuba continue as a thorn in the USA's southern flank, the Cubans supplying training and advisors to communist elements in Central America, and their country serving as a conduit for Soviet weapons.

the Strategic Defense Initiative come to fruition. Looking to the south, until recently Washington has ignored Mexico nearly as much as it has the rest of Latin America. Now, however, the United States seems to have "discovered" Mexico. A major reason for this is the porous 3,000 mile border between the two countries. Especially since the insurgencies in Central America in the 1960s and 1970s, many Latin Americans have fled their homelands, crossed Mexico and entered the United States illegally. Others have left both Central America and Mexico itself for reasons people have always left their homelands – to seek a better life elsewhere.

Whatever the reasons, the flow of illegal

Below: Understandably and perhaps inevitably, the USA and Canada continue to maintain a close military relationship. Canada is an obvious access route for Soviet aircraft and cruise missiles targeted on the USA.

migrants from Mexico to the United States is now estimated at between 500,000 and 1,500,000 people annually. Some are undocumented workers who return to Mexico; others merge into the US population permanently. While Washington has attempted to secure Mexico's cooperation in stemming this tide, Mexico sees the illegal migration out of Mexico as a US problem but a Mexican solution to problems of her own. Mexico has a population of which half or more are under 15 years of age. The population growth is about 2.7 percent annually. Some 800,000 young people enter the job market each year but only about 350,000 jobs become available.

A second reason why Mexico has become important to the United States and to the rest of the world is the dramatic rise of Mexico as a major oil producing country. Mexico has not joined OPEC and in August 1981 made a long-term commitment to sell petroleum to the United States to fill its strategic petroleum reserve. For a time it appeared that Mexico's oil exports would provide it with the necessary capital to continue its rapid pace of industrialization. This would not only enhance American-Mexican trade relations but also would help to stem the flow of Mexicans to the United States as job opportunities improved in Mexico.

President Reagan, with his southern California background and a greater realization than most US presidents of the importance of Mexico to the United States, came to office intent on improving Mexican-American relations. (Mexico is now the third most important US trading partner after Canada and Japan.) Mexico's anti-American rhetoric of the past has now been softened. Unfortunately, however, the oil glut and the concomitant reduction in oil prices have caused severe economic setbacks in Mexico to what was an overly ambitious drive for industrialization. Currently Mexico is in the throes of a genuine economic crisis; relative to the dollar, the peso has virtually collapsed. It remains to be seen whether the recent progress in Mexican-American relations will continue.

Future American National Security Policy
Many of the problems noted here are not the result of errors in resolve or judgment, although of course some are. Rather, the era of American dominance of world politics – roughly between the end of World War II in 1945 and the signing of the SALT I treaty (signifying Soviet-American strategic parity and equality) in 1972 – has come to an end.

This was inevitable; as Europe and Japan recovered from the great world conflict it was to be expected that America's economic dominance of the world would diminish. Certainly not desirable but perhaps inevitable was the rise of the Soviet Union as a military superpower. Decolonization and the growth of nationalism and anti-westernism in the Third World impeded the tidy solutions of the past. The extraordinary rise in oil prices and the related capability of a few relatively backward Middle Eastern countries to create havoc with the global economy brought about further political and economic change.

Americans must adjust to their diminished status in world affairs. They must accept the fact that they may no longer be dictating solutions but arriving at them through the arduous process of negotiations; US allies are increasingly intolerant of a one-way superhighway that is supposed to be a two-way economic street; this may be painful, but this is the situation at present and the one which lies ahead. The United States, however, will remain indefinitely the world's largest economy. And if the United States, Western Europe and Japan collectively can contain the despotic and militaristic Soviet state, then a world in which the United States is an important but no longer the dominant nation ought to be one which Americans should accept.

The US Defense Organization

Above: President Reagan, here flanked by Secretaries Schultz (left) and Weinberger, provides the US armed forces with all-important political direction.

Below: The professional headquarters of the US forces are found in the Pentagon, nerve center of military administrative and operational planning and control.

Change is in the wind for the vast US military establishment, encompassing over three million men and women – military and civilian – deployed throughout the world and spending the staggering sum, in 1986, of $289.4 billion.

While Americans tend to blame the loss of the Vietnam War on political rather than military leadership, the failure of the 1980 attempt to rescue US hostages in Iran raised serious questions about the ability of US forces to cooperate effectively with each other. Public criticism of defense organization by the then-Chairman of the Joint Chiefs of Staff, General David C. Jones, beginning in 1982, confirmed to many that something was seriously wrong. Growing dissatisfaction with the management of the vast sums being diverted from domestic programs and economic development to defense – dramatized by revelations that outrageous sums were being billed to the government, and paid, for very ordinary items such as hammers, coffee makers, toilet seats and the like, and growing US deficits – added powerful impetus to the demand for change.

The System as it is Supposed to Work

Before examining those demands and the changes proposed, let us examine the present US defense organization and how it is designed to work.

The Department of Defense is a cabinet-level organization. Reporting to it are 12 defense agencies and the three military departments (Army, Navy and Air Force). The four armed services are subordinate to their military departments – with the Marine Corps considered a second armed service in the Department of the Navy.

The worldwide US defense command organization shown in Diagram 1 is the product of the National Security Act of 1947 as amended by subsequent legislation. It presumes that a coherent national strategy is worked out in the National Security Council – composed of the President, the Vice-President, the Secretary of State and the Secretary of Defense, assisted by a staff headed by an Assistant for National Security Affairs (often called the "National Security Adviser") – and is then approved by the President to be carried out by the various departments of government, including, of course, the Department of Defense (DoD).

The Department of Defense is the very heart of the US war machine, and is the largest bureaucracy within the American political system. The current organizational structure is shown in Table 1, and can best be understood if it is broken down into its five major levels: the Office of the Secretary of Defense (DoD), the Joint Chiefs of Staff (JCS), the military departments, the defense agencies, and the combat commands (shown in Diagram 1).

The Secretary of Defense acts as the President's principal deputy – indeed as "second-in-command" – in military matters. The Office of the Secretary of Defense, including the various Deputy, Undersecretary and Assistant Secretary staffs, numbered approximately 1,200 civilians and 500 military personnel in Fiscal Year 1985. When the department was first created the Secretary of Defense was limited to three special assistants and his total staff was only 50 people. A

Col. William V. Kennedy, Armor, US Army (Ret.), formerly Intelligence Officer, US Air Force, Strategic Air Command, and author of many works on defense-related subjects.

Deputy Secretary of Defense was authorized in 1949. Current legislation allows the Secretary of Defense to have two Undersecretaries, eleven Assistant Secretaries, a General Counsel and an Inspector General. The law does not specify the functional responsibilities or duties of the Under and Assistant Secretaries, but permits the Secretary to alter them as he sees fit.

The chain of command goes from the President to the Secretary of Defense and through the Joint Chiefs of Staff, to the unified and specified comamnders in chief, each of whom is a four-star general or admiral. The areas of responsibility for these commands are delineated in a "Unified Command Plan" (UCP) controlled, in effect, by negotiation among the services.

A unified command is composed of forces from two or more services, has a broad and continuing mission, and is normally organized on a geographaical basis. A specified command also has a broad and continuing mission, but is organized on a functional basis and is normally made up of forces from a single service. The number of unified and specified commands is *not* fixed by law or regulation and may vary from time to time.

All of the forces for support of the North Atlantic Treaty Organization (NATO) and other US alliances, such as its Mutual Security Treaty with Japan are assigned to these commands. As concerns NATO, the US commander wears two "hats". As Commander-in-Chief, US European Command, he has operational control of all US forces in his area, comprising essentially Western Europe and the Mediterranean. But as Supreme Allied Commander, Europe (SACEUR), he would command all NATO forces.

Prohibition of "General Staff"

The National Security Act and its amendments prohibit the establishment of a single Armed Forces General Staff under a supreme Chief of Staff. In part, this is a reflection of concern over the manner in which the Prussian, later the German, Great General Staff operated as a "state within a state", playing a large part in bringing Germany to military and economic ruin in two World Wars. In part, though, this concern originated with the writers of the US Constitution, most of them grandsons of Englishmen who had seen a successful general, Oliver Cromwell, establish a military dictatorship that nearly put a stop to the development of democracy.

Thus, the US Joint Chiefs of Staff (JCS) and the Joint Staff that works for them do not exercise command authority over the Joint and Specified commands. They act only as advisers to the Secretary of Defense and the President. Without Presidential Secretary of Defense authority, they cannot move a ship or a squadron. Except for the Chairman, each member is the head of his respective service and retains the right to go directly to the Secretary of Defense or the President concerning any matter that cannot be resolved by agreement among the Chiefs.

The membership of the JCS consists of the Chairman, selected by the President from any of the services, the Chief of Staff of the Army, the Chief of Naval Operations, the Chief of Staff of the Air Force and the Commandant of the Marine Corps. Each of the service chiefs is selected by the President and serves a four-year term. All the Joint Chiefs are appointed by the President subject to Senate confirmation. The Chairman is appointed for a two-year term and, except in wartime, can only be reappointed once. His term is not fixed and he serves at the pleasure of the President. During his tenure on the JCS he has no service responsibilities. Because of their tenure in office, the terms of the Chiefs carry over from one administration to the next.

The Joint Chiefs are required to perform eight specific functions within the DoD, and these can be grouped into four broad categories. First they serve as the principal military advisers to the President and the Secretary of Defense, primarily through the National Security Council system. Second, they prepare seven short, medium and long range strategic and logistic plans, which provide guidance for the development of the defense budgets, military aid programs, industrial mobilization plans, research and development programs, and the contingency plans of the operational commanders. Third, they review and comment on the plans of the operational commanders. Fourth, they assist the President and Secretary of Defense in carrying out their command responsibilities – ie, the Joint Chiefs provide strategic direction over the operational commands for the Commander-in-Chief. Their duties include coordination of the contingency plans once the plans are put into effect. The plans are drawn up by the 400 officers assigned to the Joint Staff; all of these officers remain under the control of their "parent" service throughout their tours of duty with the Joint Staff.

The Joint Chiefs are assisted by the Organization of the Joint Chiefs of Staff

Below: In military decisions the president is advised by service and intelligence chiefs, and also receives the political and economic inputs of department heads.

(OJCS), which is composed of approximately 1,600 people. Of these, about 1,300 are officers; the others are enlisted personnel and civilians. The OJCS has two major components: the Joint Staff and the other groups that support the JCS but are not part of the Joint Staff.

The Joint Staff includes the Office of the Director, Joint Staff; the Manpower and Personnel Directorate (J-1): the Operations Directorate (J-3); the Logistics Directorate (J-4); the Plans and Policy Directorate (J-5); and the Command, Control and Communications Systems Directorate (C³S).

The Military Departments

In their role as chiefs of the respective services the members of the Joint Chiefs of Staff come under the administrative control of the civilian secretaries of the Departments of the Army, Navy and Air Force (the Marines being included in the Department of the Navy).

The function of the military departments is to recruit, train and equip forces which are then assigned to the Unified and Specified commands or are held in reserve in the United States for support of contingency plans. Although sounding rather prosaic, those functions in fact give each service total control over military doctrine. There is no joint US doctrine concerning matters that the services

have chosen to reserve to themselves. The OSD can and does intervene on recruiting, training and equipping to establish guidelines and procedures. Whenever there is a conflict between a departmental position and the OSD the Army, Navy and Air Force must give way.

Defense Agencies

Table 2 shows organizations or groups within DoD which have the status of defense agencies. These organizations perform functions which are common to or cut across departmental lines. There are no specified restrictions on the number or functions of these organizations. The McCormack-Curtis amendment to the 1958 Defense Reorganization Act empowers the Secretary to create such agencies whenever he determines that it would be advantageous in terms of effectiveness, economy, or efficiency to provide for the performance of a common function by a single organization. Implicit in the amendment is the Secretary of Defense's power to disestablish or disband such agencies.

Most of the agencies are under the direct management control of the Secretary of Defense; that is, their tasks are given by and they report directly to the Secretary. The Defense Communications, Defense Mapping, and Defense Nuclear Agencies are responsible

to the JCS, generally for operational matters. The status of the Defense Intelligence Agency (DIA) is somewhat ambivalent. From its creation in 1961 through 1976, it was under the control of the JCS. In fact, as noted above, the Director of DIA serves as the J-2 for the Joint Staff. However, in 1976 control over DIA was transferred to OSD, with the provision that the JCS could still assign tasks to it directly.

Half of the agencies are headed by two- or three-star generals or admirals, while the other half are headed by senior civilians. All of the agencies are staffed by a mixed civilian military complement. The civilians are generally in a permanent career status while the military personnel are assigned for a three-year tour.

The defense agencies employed 95,000 people in Fiscaly Year 1985 About 90 percent are civilians while the remaining 10 percent are military on temporary assignment. The agencies range from the mammoth Defense Logistics Agency, which employs 52,500 people, to the minuscule Defense Legal Services Agency, which has only 76 people on its payroll. Only the Defense Logistics Agency and Defense Mapping Agency have more than 5,000 people in their group. The average size is about 6,000 and five of its 12 agencies have less than 1,000 people in their employ.

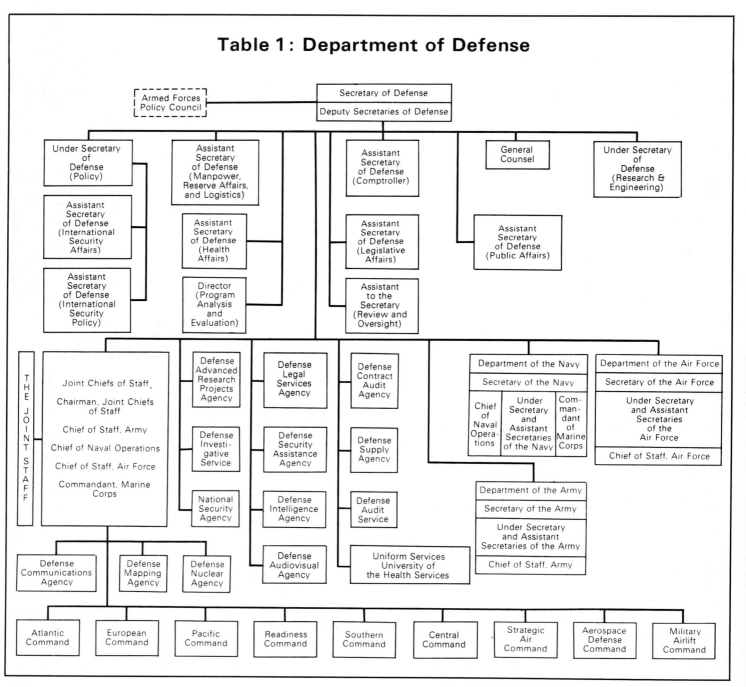

Table 1: Department of Defense

The Roles of the Agencies

The responsibilities of the agencies vary widely. The National Security Agency (NSA) is officially designated the National Security Agency/Central Security Service. It has a two-fold responsibility. NSA safeguards the communications of the armed forces and monitors the communications of other nations for the purpose of gathering intelligence. The three-star director of NSA also heads the Central Security Service. Because of the classified nature of its operation, there are no figures available on the number of NSA employees.

The purpose of the Defense Advanced Research Projects Agency (DARPA) is to maintain technological superiority for the US in the field of military hardware. DARPA undertakes and carries through to feasibility demonstration those projects which meet one of the following criteria: those with high potential payoffs but with too high a risk for the individual services to obtain budget approval; projects which may involve major technological advances or breakthroughs; and projects which could have broad utilization within the entire department. After DARPA has explored a concept and determined it to be feasible, control of the project is turned over to an appropriate military service.

The Defense Nuclear Agency (DNA) is the present name of the "Manhattan Project" group, the Armed Forces Special Weapons Project, and later the Defense Atomic Support Agency. DNA manages the nuclear weapons stockpile, develops and monitors a National Nuclear Test Readiness Program, and maintains liaison for DoD with other governmental bodies concerned with nuclear matters. Actual production of nuclear weapons is the responsibility of a separate Department of Energy.

The newest of the Defense agencies is the Strategic Defense Initiative Organization, which received its interim charter on April 24, 1984. Its well known objective is to provide support for President Reagan's initiative to eliminate the threat posed by nuclear ballistic missiles.

SDIO engages in research and development projects essential to the success of this program; it also arranges for, manages, an directs the performance of work connected with assigned research projects by the military departments, other government agencies, private business, and educational and research institutions. It presently has a staff of slightly more than 100 people.

The primary function of the Defense Communications Agency (DCA) is to provide support for the World-Wide Military Command and Control System, the National Military Command System, the Defense Communications System and the Military Satellite Communications (MILSATCOM) System.

The Defense Intelligence Agency (DIA) manages all of the defense intelligence programs and provides intelligence support to the Secretary of Defense and the JCS. DIA relies upon the resources of the armed services for intelligence collection and supervises the development of intelligence by the services to meet their own particular needs.

The design and procurement of weapons is a major responsibility of the service departments. However, since thousands of items used – ranging from typing paper to that famous hammer – are common to all of the services, attempts have been made to provide a common source with the economies obtainable from buying *en masse*. Hence, the Defense Logistics Agency which supports the military services, other DoD components, federal civil agencies, foreign governments, and others (as authorized), by buying, storing, and distributing assigned materiel commodities and items of supply, including weapon systems, and providing logistics services directly associated

Table 2: Defense Agencies

Agency	Founded	Reports to	Personnel		
			Military	Civilian	Total
National Security Agency	1952	OSD	Classified	Classified	Classified
Defense Advanced Research Projects Agency	1958	OSD	26	153	179
Defense Nuclear Agency	1942	JCS	483	633	1,116
Defense Communications Agency	1960	JCS	1,463	1,667	3,130
Defense Intelligence Agency	1961	JCS/OSD	1,805	2,607	4,412
Defense Logistics Agency	1961	OSD	965	46,757	47,722
Defense Contract Audit Agency	1965	OSD	—	3,536	3,536
Defense Audit Agency	1976	OSD	—	393	393
Defense Security Assistance Agency	1971	OSD	24	83	107
Defense Mapping Agency	1972	JCS	436	8,375	8,811
Defense Investigative Service	1972	OSD	142	2,446	2,588
Defense Audiovisual Agency	1979	OSD	128	472	600
Defense Legal Services Agency	1981	OSD	2	54	56
Uniformed Services University of the Health Services	1972	OSD	96	606	702
Total			5,570	67,782	73,352

Above: The US war machine makes wide use of computerization in all its diverse forms. Here a cartographer edits a computer map system to eliminate anomalies

Below: Central to the running of any US organization is effective communication with the media through briefings such as this by Deputy Secretary William Taft IV.

with the supply management function, contract administration services, and other support services.

The role of the Defense Contract Audit Agency (DCAA) is to perform all the required contract auditing for DoD and to provide accounting and financial advisory services regarding defense contracts to DoD components which have responsibility for procurement and contract administration. The functions of DCAA include evaluating the acceptability of costs claimed or proposed by contractors and reviewing the efficiency and economy of contractor operations. Many other agencies of the federal government also make use of DCAA services.

The Defense Security Assistance Agency (DSAA) was established to provide greater emphasis to the management control of such security assistance plans and programs as military assistance and foreign military sales.

The Defense Mapping Agency (DMA) was established to consolidate and improve the efficiency of defense mapping, charting, and geodetic operations. DMA relies almost completely on the individual services for research and development and data collection.

The primary function of the Defense Investigative Service (DIS) is to conduct personnel security investigations on DoD civilians, military personnel, and industrial and contractor personnel involved in defense business. DIS also conducts some criminal investigations and crime prevention surveys for DoD.

The Defense Legal Services Agency was established to provide legal advice and services for OSD and its field activities and the defense agencies; it provides technical support and assistance in developing the DoD legislative program; it provides a centralized legislative and congressional document reference and distribution point of the department; and it maintains the department's historical legislative files. The General Counsel serves as the Director of DLS.

Field Commands

The operating forces of the Department of Defense are presently broken down into seven unified and three specified commands. Five of the seven unified are theater or area commands: Atlantic, Pacific, European, Central and Southern. The sixth unified command, the Readiness Command, is composed of forces from the Army and Air Force based in the continental United States. The Readiness Command is in effect our ready reserve or contingency command. Its primary mission is to make its forces available to reinforce the other unified or area commands.

US Space Command became the seventh unified command in September 1985 and placed United States space forces into a single, joint military organization. The new command is charged with operating and protecting space systems and providing integrated tactical warning and assessment of space, missile, and air attacks on the continental United States.

The three specified commands are the Strategic Air Command, Aerospace Defense Command, and the Military Airlift Command, although the Aerospace Defense Command was expected to be disestablished in late 1986. Each of these commands is composed primarily of Air Force components.

Each unified command is headed by a four-star general officer. The Atlantic and Pacific Commands have always been headed by Navy admirals, while the European, Southern, Central and Readiness Commands are normally under the control of an Army officer. Space Command is headed by an Air Force general, as are the three specified commands. The commanders of the unified and specified commands are responsible to the President and the Secretary of Defense for the accomplishment of their military missions. They have full

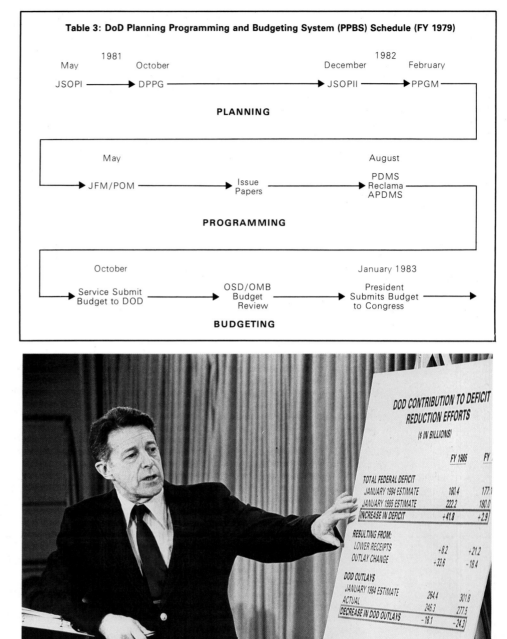

Table 3: DoD Planning Programming and Budgeting System (PPBS) Schedule (FY 1979)

	1981			1982	
May		October		December	February
JSOPI ——▶		DPPG —————————————————▶		JSOPII ——▶	PPGM ——

PLANNING

May			August
JFM/POM ——————————▶		Issue Papers ——————▶	PDMS Reclama APDMS

PROGRAMMING

October		January 1983
Service Submit Budget to DOD ——▶	OSD/OMB Budget Review ——▶	President Submits Budget to Congress ——▶

BUDGETING

Above: Key issues require the top man, and in February 1985 Secretary Weinberger briefed the media about the Department of Defense budget for Fiscal Year 1986.

operational control over the forces assigned to them – including overall aspects of personal advancement – and these forces cannot be reassigned or transferred except by the Secretary of Defense, although the JCS provides strategic guidance and direction to these commands through the various joint planning and intelligence documents, but without exercising operational control over them. The role of the Joint Commander extends only to "operational control" in time of war or other emergency.

The unified and specified commands are assisted by a joint staff and the commanders of the service forces or components assigned to them. In some of the commands, the unified commander also functions as a component commander. For example, the Commander-in-Chief of the Atlantic also serves as the Commander of the Atlantic fleet. Some of the unified commanders also are allied commanders. For example, the Commander-in-Chief of Europe is also the Supreme Allied Commander, Europe.

Logistics and administrative support of the 10 combat commands is the responsibility of the military departments. This permits the operational commander to focus on strategic and technical matters and to take advantage of pr-existing channels for logistics and administrative support.

The officers assigned to the regional Joint

Staffs are as firmly in the hands of their "parent" services as their counterparts in the Joint Staff in Washington. At least equally important, the forces assigned to those Joint headquarters remain firmly in the hands of the separate military departments in everything save "operational control" in time of emergency.

The doctrine under which each of those forces operates is developed by the parent service, not by the Joint commander. Thus, the US Army and US Air Force in Europe are operating under an "Airland Battle" doctrine that calls for giving up large tracts of West German territory in order to gain maneuver room for counterattacks. That doctrine is unacceptable to the West Germans and other NATO Allies. Indeed, Gen. Bernard W. Rogers, the US and Supreme Allied Commander in Europe has publicly disowned the doctrine as unacceptable in the special context of the European environment.

The several US military services remain to this day as firmly in control of their own budgets and policy as ever they were before World War II. Each has a complete general staff in Washington (mostly in the Pentagon), able to draw upon the academic resources of the several war colleges in formulating as many separate "national" strategies.

Organization or Disorganization?
From all of this it might be concluded that there is considerably more disorganization than organization to the US Defense establishment. The fact that the US military services operate at a high degree of efficiency throughout the world day in and day out says the opposite.

The Budget Cycle
The Director, Program Analysis and Evaluation, and his personnel serve as the Defense Secretary's analytical staff. It is their job to evaluate all of the proposals submitted to the Secretary to ensure that they are in accord with the established objectives and are cost effective. Their main function is to analyze the programs submitted by the military departments and agencies during the budgetary process.

This latter is the principal instrument by which the Secretary of Defense manages the Defense Department. Since 1961 the defense budget has been compiled under a Planning, Programming and Budgeting System (PPBS), the foundation of a Five-Year Defense Program (FYDP). At any given moment the documents associated with this system contain the approved programs with their estimated costs projected over a five-year period. Actual appropriations, however, are on a year-to-year basis so that the five-year projection is constantly subject to change. The planning portion of the annual cycle begins in May and continues to the following February. The Secretary then issues the "Defense Guidance".

In the words of Secretary of Defense Caspar W. Weinberger, "The Defense Guidance . . . is national strategy, the national objective . . . to

protect the national interest. Then the services bring in their POM's (Program Objective Memoranda) by which they tell us the amounts they will need to carry out the objectives . . . Those are then [submitted] to the Defense Resources Board (an advisory committee consisting of all senior Departmental civilian officials plus the Chairman of the Joint Chiefs of Staff).

"The Board," according to Secretary Weinberger, "holds hearings for the commanders [of the subordinate defense commands] . . . At every one of those meetings all of the Joint Chiefs are present . . . Then we have the final guidance from the President as to what the total defense budget will be,"

As finally presented to Congress the defense budget is organized into categories such as "Personnel", "Procurement", "Operations and Maintenance", etc. Within the Department, however, the budget is managed as functional components such as "Strategic [Nuclear] Forces", "General Purpose Forces", etc.

The legislative phase of the defense budget process begins in mid-January upon receipt of the President's budget and usually lasts until late September when the budget is supposed to be sent to the White House for signature.

The principal Congressional committees dealing with defense are the Budget Comitees of the House of Representatives and the Senate – which set overall spending ceilings – and the Armed Services and Appropriations committees of the two chambers. There are separate bills for authorizations and appropriations. The differences between and among them are resolved in conference by joint House-Senate committees. Under current law appropriations can be approved only from one year to the next, even though Congress may have authorized longer-term purchases for ships, aircraft and other "long lead-time" equipment. Each such purchase, therefore, is

reviewed and is in some jeopardy of cancellation during each annual budget cycle.

Command, Control, and Communications
The command, control, and communications (C³) systems of DoD are the means through which the National Command Authorities (the President and the Secretary of Defense) and, under their direction, the military commanders control and employ the military strength of the United States. These C³ systems are composed of satellites for warning, surveillance, meteorology, and communications; ground and undersea systems; ground, shipborne, and airborne command facilities, worldwide voice, telephone, teletype, and automatic data networks; and information processing systems. A secure, well designed and efficient C³ system is vital to the success of DoD in fulfilling its primary mission of employing military force in support of national policy. A poor C³ system can undo the best efforts of even an administratively sound organizational structure and a cost effective military force.

An overview of the present C³ structure is portrayed in Diagram 1. At the center are the National Command Authorities (NCA) – the President and the Secretary of Defense. The NCA exercise command and control over deployed forces through the Joint Chiefs of Staff. The JCS are supported directly by the National Military Command System (NMCS), which consists of the National Military Command Center (NMCC) in the Pentagon, the Alternate National Military Command Center (ANMCC), based near Washington, and the National Emergency Airborne Command Post (NEACP), along with their support equipment. These facilities provide the personnel and equipment which can receive, evaluate and display information as well as execute national decisions for direction and

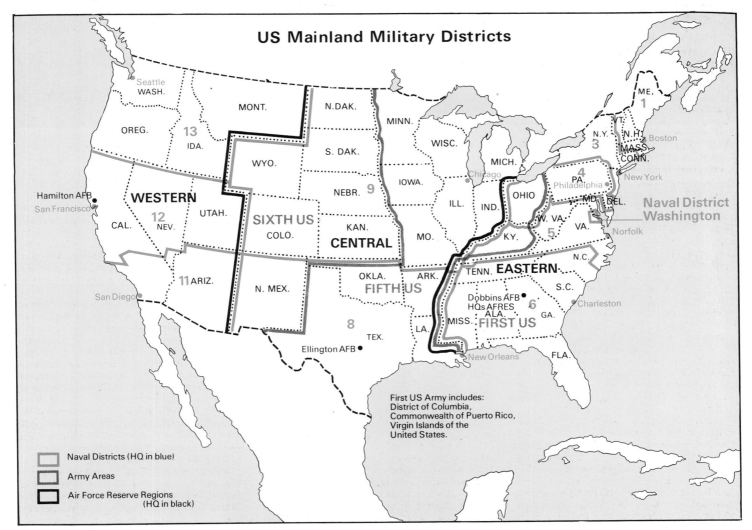

US Mainland Military Districts

First US Army includes:
District of Columbia,
Commonwealth of Puerto Rico,
Virgin Islands of the
United States.

☐ Naval Districts (HQ in blue)
☐ Army Areas
☐ Air Force Reserve Regions
(HQ in black)

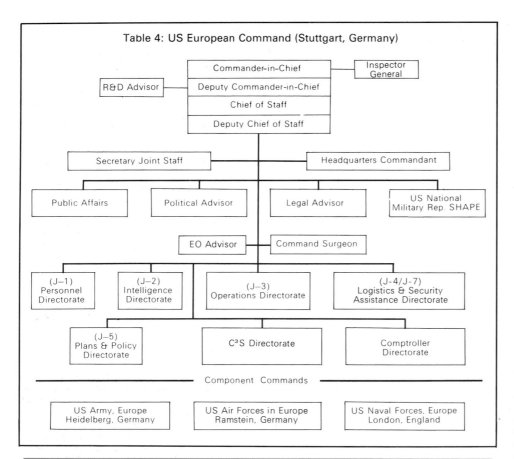

Table 4: US European Command (Stuttgart, Germany)

R&D Advisor

Commander-in-Chief — Inspector General
Deputy Commander-in-Chief
Chief of Staff
Deputy Chief of Staff

Secretary Joint Staff — Headquarters Commandant

Public Affairs — Political Advisor — Legal Advisor — US National Military Rep. SHAPE

EO Advisor — Command Surgeon

(J–1) Personnel Directorate — (J–2) Intelligence Directorate — (J–3) Operations Directorate — (J–4/J–7) Logistics & Security Assistance Directorate

(J–5) Plans & Policy Directorate — C³S Directorate — Comptroller Directorate

Component Commands

US Army, Europe Heidelberg, Germany — US Air Forces in Europe Ramstein, Germany — US Naval Forces, Europe London, England

Above: Command of the US forces is maintained under all contingencies, such a capability being provided in the nuclear scenario by the Boeing E-4B NEACP aircraft.

Below: Airborne command and communication links inevitably depend on airfields, it is essential that the availability of such bases is constantly monitored.

control of the forces. Alerting procedures and the redundancy of the facilities, coupled with the NEACP's airborne capability, provide for an important degree of survivability.

The NMCS is under the control of the JCS. The chairman of the JCS is responsible for the operation of the three elements in this system. He is assisted in this job by the Director and Deputy Director of Operations (J-3). The Director of the Defense Communications Agency is the NMCS systems engineer and technical supervisor for the entire NMCS.

The second diagrammatic ring around the NCA represents the Defense Communications System (DCS). The DCS is the "in-place" worldwide system which serves as the foundation for wartime communication needs. It provides for common-user communication requirements and extends high volume command and control capability throughout the United States, Europe and the Pacific. Included are subsystems for voice communications by the Automatic Voice Network (AUTOVON), secure voice communications by the Automatic Secure Voice Network (AUTOSEVOCOM), and secure message and data transmission by the Automatic Digital Network (AUTODIN). For the most part, these systems consist of fixed equipment and facilities and interconnect with the primary and alternate fixed or mobile command posts of the key decision makers.

Overseas, the DCS is mostly government-owned; in the US, it is leased from commercial carriers. It serves the entire Defense community with over 1,100 AUTODIN terminals and 17,000 direct AUTOVON subscriber access lines. The systems which comprise the DCS have a preempt capability so that essential command and control messages can be accorded precedence over routine traffic. The DCS system is operated and maintained by the Defense Communications Agency.

The last ring in the diagram represents the mobile and transportable facilities and tactical networks organic to the military field forces. Also included here are the post, camp, station and base fixed, internal communications systems. The communications networks of the operating forces are the means by which the highly mobile forces are maneuvered by their commanders. DoD has the capability to link the various tactical systems through the DCS to the NMCS to allow the National Command Authorities to communicate with unified and specified commanders in crisis spots and then with the on-scene commanders represented on the outer ring.

Funding and Control
The pie-shaped segments in the diagram represent the Worldwide Military Command and Control System (WWMCCS). This system includes the communication systems of the unified and specified commands, and the special systems used for control of nuclear forces. This portion of the communications network has survivability characteristics which are too expensive for incorporation in all systems but which are necessary for execution of essential functions in the event of stress, degradation, or deliberate attack. Some of the survivability characteristics are physical hardening, mobility, redundancy, antijam protection and electromagnetic pulse protection. That portion of WWMCCS designated the Minimum Essential Emergency Communications Network (MEECN) encompasses the maximum survivability and reliability features needed for essential network performance in a stressed environment. The MEECN is dedicated to providing the highest possible assurance of command and control of US strategic nuclear forces during and after any nuclear attack on the United States, which includes an attack on the communications systems.

Diagram 1: World Military Command and Control Network

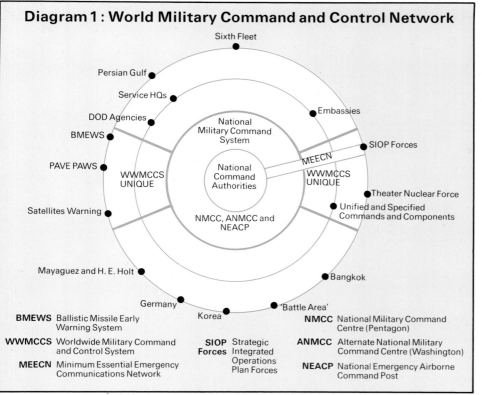

BMEWS Ballistic Missile Early Warning System		**NMCC** National Military Command Centre (Pentagon)
WWMCCS Worldwide Military Command and Control System	**SIOP Forces** Strategic Integrated Operations Plan Forces	**ANMCC** Alternate National Military Command Centre (Washington)
MEECN Minimum Essential Emergency Communications Network		**NEACP** National Emergency Airborne Command Post

The perimeter of the second ring contains examples of the intermediaries through which directives would flow on their way to and from the field forces. For example, communications with most operating or deployed forces would be channeled through the unified and specified command, while communications with a military advisory group in a particular country would be handled by the embassy.

The perimeter of the outer ring contains selected examples of different areas and types of forces. The strategic nuclear forces or SIOP (Strategic Integrated Operations Plan) forces use the MEECN while theater or tactical nuclear forces communicate through WWMCCS. Communications between the NCA and the Sixth Fleet in the Mediterranean or the US Seventh Army in Germany would use the Defense Communications System and would go via the European Command. Com-

munications among units of the Sixth Fleet and the Seventh Army would take place via the tactical communications net.

The C³ systems and procedures must be adaptable to rapidly changing situations ranging from day-to-day activities through crisis to conventional and nuclear war – including surprise attack on the United States – and programs have been structured to address this need. The interrelationship of force postures, levels of conflict and the command and control function required at each level is illustrated by Diagram 2.

Despite the survivability features mentioned above (including the possibility of evacuating the President and other high-ranking officials to alternate command facilities in underground bunkers within about 75 miles (120km) from the capital, or to airborne command posts) the C³ system is still con-

sidered to be vulnerable to surprise attack, since most of it is operated day by day in the city of Washington DC by means of commercial telephone and personal visits within and among buildings that offer only nominal protection against enemy attack. Even if, with substantial warning, the President and his important command officials could be removed to safety the communications linking those alternate command posts with worldwide US forces (by cable, microwave, satellite, etc.) would be highly vulnerable to the electromagnetic pulse released by nuclear detonations, even when those detonations occurred high in space without direct damage to structures on Earth. It is this vulnerability. which in somewhat different ways affects the Soviets as well, that pushes any modern defense organization toward the nightmare of a surprise or preemptive "first strike" with nuclear weapons in a major crisis.

Proposals for Change
To a considerable extent, it was this vulnerability that led Gen. David C. Jones, former Chairman of the JCS, to launch the current re-evaluation of US defense organization. In the past, General Jones argued, the US depended upon getting its organizational problems in order after war had begun. Now, he warned, efficient organization may be the most important factor in deciding whether a modern nation survives to continue a war beyond the first few hours.

Although it has not yet become a primary focus of debate, there is a further, historic diffusion of military control in the US system, dictated by the Constitutional provision that the "militia" – the entire able-bodied male population – be left under the control of the 50 State governors. In modern terms, the militia is divided into an "Organized Militia", now known as the National Guard, and the "Common Militia", consisting essentially of all males not serving in the National Guard. The Governors are the commanders-in-chief of the respective National Guard establishments, but these are dependent upon Federal authorities for pay, equipment, training and almost all other elements of warfare. The Governors also have authority to order all the Common Militia into military service in time of invasion or a disaster such as a nuclear

Diagram 2: The Changing Role of Communications, Command and Control (C³) in Escalation Control

Posture of forces	Levels of Activity	C³ Support Function	Required C³ Capability
Strategic Reserve Engaged Strategic Forces Engaged	Strategic Nuclear War	Reconstitution Termination Execution Info for Decision	Function under Attack Physical Survivability Jam Nuclear Effects Resistant
Selected Strategic Forces Engaged Tactical Nuclear Forces Engaged	Theater Nuclear War	Positive Control over Employment of Tactical Nuclear Weapons	Secure Communications Jam Nuclear Effects Resistant and Support for Planning
General Purpose Forces Engaged (Non-Nuclear)	Theater Conventional War	Interoperate with Allies Joint Worldwide Operations	Systems Interoperability Secure Communications Survive Conventional Attack
Isolated Engagements Limited Deployment (Show of Force)	Crisis	Rapid Effective Response Two Way Info Flow	Mobility of C³ Assets Secure Communications Jam Resistant
Normal Readiness	Day-to-Day	Training and Exercises Situation Monitoring Access to Intel and Warning* Contingency Planning	Efficient Operations Quality Service Force Connectivity Secure Communications

Negotiate/Terminate — Control of Escalation

☐ Areas Indicate Transition Between Levels. Capabilities in these Areas are Key to Smooth Orderly Transition
*Warning Systems Covered Under Strategic Defense Programs

attack.

The purpose of this deliberate diffusion of power was to prevent any one person, in particular the President or his principal military subordinates, from having full control of the means by which to achieve a military dictatorship.

In the time of war or other national emergency the President can "call" or "order" the National Guard into Federal service, but only for the length of the emergency. Under the "call" the National Guard retains its State character. This provision of law is used during only brief emergencies, such as occurred during civil rights disturbances in the 1960s. Under an "order" the National Guard is fully integrated into the Federal military forces until the end of a war or similar extreme emergency.

In addition to the National Guard (now divided into Army and Air Force components) there are Federally controlled reserve forces in each service, including both units and pools of individuals. As is obvious, there are large areas of ambiguity in this system and it is these that are largely at the heart of demand for change, focused – at least at the present time – around the refusal of certain governments to permit members of the Guard to participate in exercises overseas.

Controversy over the "600-Ship Navy"

Largely in response to the criticisms voiced by General Jones, Sen. John Tower (then Chairman of the Senate Armed Services Committee) conducted a series of hearings beginning in December 1982, and continuing until November 1983, and covering every aspect of defense organization.

While the Tower hearings were in preparation there occurred a remarkable series of public hearings conducted by the US Merit System Protecton Board at Harrisburg, Pennsylvania, 8-11 August 1983, which tended to dramatize many of the criticisms General Jones had made concerning an excessive role for the several military services and a tendency toward bitter inter-service conflicts.

In short, the Harrisburg hearings revealed that there is a major struggle underway on the part of the US Army to block funding of the full 600-ship Navy that President Ronald Reagan had announced when taking office as the centerpiece of his military buildup.

While Secretary of the Navy John F. Lehman, Jr, did not originate the "maritime strategy" which figured so prominently in the hearings he did succeed in making its principal expression – the 600-ship Navy – a major part of the Reagan Administration's defense program. In large part he was able to do that because the "maritime strategy" was also the traditional military strategy of the Republican Party.

In the Lehman version of a maritime strategy, the new and larger Navy is to carry the attack, in the event of war, directly to the shores of the Soviet Union – principally against the Soviet Northern Fleet based in the vicinity of Murmansk and the Soviet Pacific Fleet. The principal deficiency of this strategy is that it doesn't say what is to happen if the naval attacks on the Soviet shoreline were to be successful. This lack of a "thought-through" element is characteristic of a strategy developed without full Joint participation and with the interests of only one service chiefly in mind. It is comparable to the over-emphasis on strategic bombing that the US Air Force had picked up from the writings of the Italian Gen. Giulio Douhet and attempted to make the be all and end all of US strategy in the 1950s.

The Reagan Administration sought to head off a conflict over the maritime strategy by having its then National Security Adviser, William P. Clark, announce that the Administration would follow a "balanced forces"

Above: Navy Secretary John Lehmann and Rear Admiral Andrew Giordano at one of many press conferences called in response to media outcry about supply procurement.

Below: Army Secretary John Marsh Jr presents the Army Distinguished Civilian Service Award to Senator John Tower for his aid for defense programs.

strategy (that is, maintaining essentially the service budgetary balance that the Reagan Administration found when taking office) as well as pursuing the maritime strategy by which the 600-ship Navy had been launched.

The inevitable clash implicit in these opposing strategies seemed sure to be hastened in the light of a "leak" to the *Washington Post* (several months previously) of a finding by the Defense Resources Board that the Reagan defense program was already at that time underfunded by no less than $750 billion, or nearly 50 percent of the total of $1.6 trillion planned to be spent at its inception. The discrepancy was later confirmed by General Jones in testimony during the Tower hearings.

The Defense Resources Board (see Table 2) consists of the principal civilian officials of the Department of Defense plus the Chairman of the Joint Chiefs of Staff. As mentioned earlier, it meets as an advisory board to reconcile conflicting claims for resources and to arrive at a plausible funding level that the Secretary can then use in the "Defense Guidance" document by which he sets policy for the military departments and other agencies for planning future budgets. Since planning never was adjusted to accommodate the $750-billion discrepancy the Army, as became apparent from the documents made public during the Harrisburg hearings, saw itself facing what one of its senior civilian aides called an "onslaught" from the Navy threatening many of its major programs.

Lack of a National Strategy

In contrast to the neat arrangements of the organizational charts, former General Jones testified at the Tower hearings on 16 December 1982, that "We truly do not have a strategy." Re-emphasizing the *Washington Post* story, General Jones told the Senate Armed Services Committee, "You know and I know that $1.6 trillion will not pay for what we have started."

How the military services had regained control of the decision-making process within the Department of Defense was vividly illustrated by General Jones in an earlier testimony that was made part of the Tower hearings. The result of this process, General Jones testified, is that, in Vietnam, "Each service, instead of integrating its efforts with the others, considered Vietnam its own war and sought to carve out a large mission for itself. For example, each fought its own air war, agreeing only to limited measures for a coordinated effort."

Three unified commanders – Europe, Central America and the Atlantic – testified that the total control of the various armed services over the resources at their disposal severely limited integration of the forces under their command.

How things got that way was explained in a subsequent hearing by former National

Security Adviser Zbigniew Brzezinski. In the 1950s, according to Dr Brzezinski, President Dwight D. Eisenhower established a strategic planning board composed of senior inter-agency officials. That board was disestablished by President John F. Kennedy and never reconstituted. "In its absence," Dr Brzezinski testified, "a longer term vision is occasionally shaped by strong-minded individuals. . . . More often, there is simply the lack of a broader integrated strategy."

In the view of former Deputy Secretary of Defense for Policy Robert W. Komer and other authorities, the individual who exercises the greatest long-term influence on the direction of US strategic planning in the Reagan Administration is Secretary of the Navy John Lehman, Jr.

The ability of the National Security Council to develop a cohesive national strategy in the years after President Eisenhower left office resulted, in the view of Sen. Barry Goldwater, now Chairman of the Senate Armed Services Committee, in turning back the clock to "the old [service] politics of who gets what regardless of why we do or do not want it".

Former Defense Secretary Elliot Richardson, speaking of the same problem, said, "If you don't have a coherent picture in the first instance of what you are trying to do, then, of course, every subcomponent of each service can become a competitive initiating source of demand for something or other, no matter

where it fits."

Dr Brzezinski related this, also, to the failure of the Iran raid. "Interservice interests," Dr Brzezinski testified, "dictated very much the character of the force that was used. Every service wished to be represented in this enterprise and that did not enhance cohesion and integration."

One major reason that the National Security Council is unable to develop a cohesive strategy, according to the testimony of former Secretary of Defense Harold Brown, is the weakness of the military advice forthcoming from the country's highest military authority – the Joint Chiefs of Staff.

"When I dealt with the Joint Chiefs of Staff," Dr Brown said, ". . . I found [the individuals] very wise, very thoughtful on most matters, not all, but on most matters. . . . When I turn [to] what kinds of papers came out of the system, and what kind of positions came out of the system, it really is a Dr Jekyll and Mr Hyde situation because what came out then was . . . most of the time a perfectly adequate, pedestrian output, but on important issues or contentious issues, especially where service interests were involved – either a useless logrolling product, or else downright mischievous by suggesting something that obviously couldn't work. . . . On procurement [of major weapons systems] you always get logrolling. But on operations you would get a situation where the most important thing

Below: Providing rapid access to the Soviet high command in critical moments is the Washington-Moscow Direct Communications Link, known as the "hot line".

would be that nobody's ox got gored, but everybody had a piece of the action and that there was no substantial shift in the previously negotiated responsibilities."

"The services themselves," Secretary Brown states, "cannot eliminate the waste, correct the operational difficulties, or resolve the conflicts over roles and missions. Efforts by civilians in the Office of the Secretary of Defense to resolve them, through procurement decisions or new ideas about strategy and tactics, are better than nothing. But they are not nearly so appropriate as military efforts to that end, in the JCS for example, and their Joint Staff. Unfortunately, those bodies as now constituted are unable to resolve such issues."

There seems to be an emerging consensus – both within the Department of Defense and the United States Congress – on the need for reorganization. While the details have yet to be settled, changes are expected to involve more authority for the JCS and unified and specified commanders.

Defense Organization Additions
Seldom is anything deleted from the US defense organization; growth is constant. Thus, while the anomaly of the failed 1916 attempt to supplant the National Guard still burdens the US taxpayer with scores of unneeded headquarters the Defense Department is providing for its accumulating missions in space by organization of a US Space Command late in 1985.

Questionable Additions
While there scarcely can be any argument with the need for a Space Command there is considerable doubt about the wisdom of other recent appendages to the defense organizational structure.

At least in terms of size – several hundred officers and enlisted people under a full general – the US Central Command, designed to respond to crises in the Persian Gulf and Southwest Asia regions, seems a dubious proposition to many observers. Indeed, the Command was cited during the Tower hear-

ings as a form of "double-entry bookkeeping" in that it has no forces assigned but must draw forces from NATO or other assignments if required to perform any meaningful mission. In the meantime, former Joint Chiefs Chairman Maxwell D. Taylor, studies by the Congressional Budget Office and other critics have questioned whether any element of the Central Command can get to the locales intended in time to be of any use. The fact that the Central Command never has been able to find a place in the relevant region for a forward headquarters seems to validate this concern. A more reasonable, and certainly less expensive alternative would be to combine Central Command with the Readiness Command which under a previous title ("Joint US Strike Command") once had responsibility for the Central Command's assigned regions.

Even more dubious is the amalgamation of "Special Operations" units in response to a variety of real or perceived threats ranging from terrorism to Soviet subversion in Central America. The units concerned include US Army Special Forces ("Green Berets") and Rangers – organized within a US Army Special Operation Command at Fort Bragg, North Carolina – the US Navy Sea, Air and Land (SEAL) teams, Marine reconnaissance units and the 23rd Air Force at Scott Air Force Base in Illinois, a collection of varying type aircraft capable of missions ranging from insertion of agents behind enemy lines to heavy automatic weapons firepower from Vietnam-era modified transports. Altogether these units are thought to total about 30,000 active and reserve personnel, exceeding by many times over the combined military and police units assigned by all of the remaining members of NATO to this type duty. What all these people might be doing has caused considerable worry in the US Congress, particularly in light of persistent reports that US servicemen are being used to train and possibly to accompany the so-called "Contras" seeking to overthrow the government of Nicaragua, in direct violation of laws forbidding such support.

It is this tendency of military authorities in

Above: Special operations have resumed an important niche in US Army affairs, thus absorbing much high-quality manpower.

whatever time or country to skirt or circumvent the law that makes many in Congress worry that any strengthening of the military command and control system – in particular in the context of the growing passion for secrecy in the Reagan Administration – will lead to a "Prussian General Staff" and a growing intrusion of the military into American life and government.

In late 1986, the Joint Chiefs of Staff recommended to the Secretary of Defense that a new Special Operations Force Command be created, which would be headed by a three-star general or flag-rank officer. Headquartered in Washington, DC, this commander would report to the Secretary of Defense through the JCS in the same manner as a combat commander. He would also function as special operations adviser to the Chairman, JCS.

Certainly the Special Operations amalgamation is a monument to the repeated testimony by present and former high-ranking military officers and civilian officials that, no matter what the mission, each service fights for a "piece of the action". Thus it appears that legitimate missions that would have called for no more than a few thousand men – certainly far less than 10,000 – grouped under the Army's Special Operations Command, regardless of "parent" service, have been used perhaps to double the cost both in manpower and dollars.

Thus, the second Reagan Administration and indeed the rest of the 1980s seem certain to be a period of search and testing in which it will be determined whether the United States can regain control of its vast military bureaucracy, or whether as has happened to every republic in the past, the military bureaucracy will consume the economy and the freedoms it is supposed to protect.

Right: One spur to the special operations revival was the disastrous Tehran rescue mission launched from USS *Nimitz* in 1980.

U.S. Army Special Operations Forces

1. Active Components
  a. 1st Special Operations Command (1SOCOM)
                                        Ft. Bragg, N.C.
    (1) Special Forces (SF):
      (a) 1st SF Group   Ft. Lewis, Washington
          1/1 SF BN   Torii Station, Okinawa
      (b) 5th SF Group   Ft. Bragg, North Carolina
      (c) 7th SF Group   Ft. Bragg, North Carolina
          3/7 SF BN   Ft. Gulick, Panama
      (d) 10thSF Group   Ft. Devens, Massachusetts
          1/10 SF BN   Bad Tolez, Germany
    (2) Rangers (RGR):
      (a) 75th Ranger Regt. HQ   Ft. Benning, Georgia

      (1) 1st Ranger Bn   Ft. Stewart, Georgia
      (2) 2nd Ranger Bn   Ft. Lewis, Washington
      (3) 3rd Ranger Bn   Ft. Benning, Georgia
    (3) Psychological Operations (PSYOPS)
      4th PSYOPS Group   Ft. Bragg, North Carolina
      (1) 1st PSYOPS Bn   Ft. Bragg, North Carolina
      (2) 6th PSYOPS Bn   Ft. Bragg, North Carolina
      (3) 8th PSYOPS Bn   Ft. Bragg, North Carolina
      (4) 9th PSYOPS Bn   Ft. Bragg, North Carolina
    (4) Civil Affairs
      96th Civl Affairs Battalion Ft. Bragg, North Carolina
    (5) Aviation
      160th Aviation Battalion   Ft. Campbell, Kentucky

2. Reserve Components:
  a. Special Forces (SF)
    (1) 11th SF Group   Ft. Meade, Maryland
        (Army Reserve)
    (2) 12th SF Group   Arlington Heights, Illinois
        (Army Reserve)
    (3) 19th SF Group   Salt lake City, Utah
        (National Guard)
    (4) 20th SF Group   Birmingham, Alabama
        (National Guard)
  b. Aviation
    45th Aviation Battalion   Oklahoma
    (National Guard)

U.S. Air Force Special Operation Forces

1. Core Forces

Active

  a. 23rd Air Force   Scott AFB, Illinois
    (1) 1723 Combat Control Squadron   Hurburt Fld, Florida
      (a) Det 1   Rhein-Main AB, Germany
      (b) Det 2   Clark AB, Philippines
  b. 2nd Air Division   Hurburt Fld, Florida
    (1) Det 1 (UH-1N)   Howard AFB, Panama
    (2) 1st Sp Ops Sqdn (MC-130E)   Clark AB, Philippines
    (3) 7th Sp Ops Sqdn (MC-130E)   Rhein-Main AB, Germany
  c. 1st Special Operations Wing   Hurburt Fld, Florida
    (1) 8th Sp Ops Sqdn (MC-130E)   Hurburt Fld, Florida
    (2) 16th Sp Ops Sqdn (AC-130H)   Hurburt Fld, Florida
    (3) 20th Sp Ops Sqdn (HH-53H)   Hurburt Fld, Florida
    (4) Sp Ops Photo Processing & Interpretation
        Facility (SOPPIF)   Hurburt Fld, Florida
    (5) Sp Ops Weather Team (SOWT)   Hurburt Fld, Florida

Reserve

  d. 302th Sp Ops Sqdn (HH-3/CH-3)   Luke AFB, Arizona
  e. 711th Sp Ops Sqdn (AC-130A)   Duke Fld, Florida

National Guard

  f. 193rd Sp Ops Gp (EC-130/RR)   Harrisburg International
                                                                    Airport, Pennsylvania

2. Augmenting Forces
  a. 339th Air Rescue & Recovery Wing (ARRW)   Eglin AFB, Florida
    (1) 55th Air Rescue & Recovery Sqdn
        (HC-130P/N & UH-60A)   Eglin AFB, Florida

    (2) 67th Air Rescue & Recovery Sqdn   RAF Woodbridge, G. Britain
        (HC-130N/P & HH-53C)   McClellan AFB, Calif.
  b. 41st Rescue & Weather Recon Wing (RWRW)   McClellan AFB, Calif.
    (1) 41st Air Rescue & Recovery Sqdn
        (HC-130N/P & HH-53C)   McClellan AFB, Calif.
    (2) 31st Air Rescue & Recovery Sqdn (HH-3E)   Clark AB, Philippines
    (3) 33rd Air Rescue & Recovery Sqdn (HC-130P/N)   Kadena AB, Japan
    (4) 38th Air Rescue & Recovery Sqdn (HH-3E)   Osan AB, Korea

3. Collateral Assets
  a. 21st Air Force
    (1) 317th Tactical Airlift Wing (C-130)   Pope AFB, N. Carolina
    (2) 435th Tactical Airlift Wing (C-130)   Rhein-Main AB, Germany
    (3) 437th Military Airlift Wing (C-141)   Charleston AFB, S. Carolina
    (4) 438th Military Airlift Wing (C-141)   McGuire AFB, New Jersey
  b. 22nd Air Force
    (1) 62nd Military Airlift Wing (C-130 & C-141)   McChord AFB, Washington
    (2) 463rd Tactical Airlift Wing (C-130)   Dyess AFB, Texas
    (3) 314th Tactical Airlift Wing (C-130)   Little Rock AFB, Arkansas
    (4) 316th Military Airlift Group (C-130)   Yokota AF, Japan
    (5) 374th Tactical Airlift Wing (C-130)   Clark AB, Philippines
    (6) 63rd Military Airlift Wing (C-141)   Norton AFB, California

U.S. Navy Special Operation Forces

1. Active Components
  a. Special Warfare Group One   **Coronado, California**
    (1) Sea-Air-Land (SEAL) Team – 1   Coronado, California
    (2) Sea-Air-Land (Seal) Team – 3   Coronado, California
    (4) Special Boat Squadron – 1   Coronado, California
    (5) SEAL Delivery Vehicle Team – 1   Coronado, California
    (6) Naval Special Warfare Unit – 1   Subic Bay, Philippines
    (7) Light Attack Helicopter Unit – 5   Point Mugu, Hawaii
  b. Special Warfare Group Two   **Little Creek, Virginia**
    (1) Sea-Air-Land (SEAL) Team – 2   Little Creek, Virginia
    (2) Sea-Air-Land (SEAL) Team – 4   Little Creek, Virginia
    (3) Special Boat Squadron – 2   Little Creek, Virginia
    (4) SEAL Delivery Vehicle Team – 2   Little Creek, Virginia
    (5) Naval Special Warfare Unit – 2   Machihanish, G. Britain
    (6) Naval Special Warfare Unit – 4   Roosevelt Roads, Puerto Rico
    (7) Light Attack Helicopter Unit – 4

2. Reserve Components
  a. East Coast Units
    (1) Special Warfare Task Group Alpha 104   Elizabeth, New Jersey
    (2) Special Warfare Task Group Bravo 206   Little Creek, Virginia
    (3) Special Warfare Group Two Det 106   Little Creek, Virginia
    (4) Special Warfare Group Two Det 208   Miami, Florida
    (5) Special Warfare Group Two Det 305   Columbus, Ohio
    (6) Special Warfare Group Two Det 402   Bronx, NYC, New York
    (7) Special Warfare Group Two Eng Spt Det 110   Austin, Texas
  b. West Coast Units
    (1) SEAL PAC 119   Coronado, California
    (2) Special Warfare Group One Det 119   Coronado, California
    (3) Special Warfare Group Two Det 220   San Francisco, California

The US Intelligence Machine

The international military environment differs in many critical respects from that which existed at the end of World War II. Besides the massive lethal power possessed by the superpowers, there is something of a reliance on proxy nations to achieve the goals of individual states. A new form of warfare – terrorism – has grown. Moreover, the term "low intensity conflict" has entered the vocabulary to help describe the gray areas in the spectrum of conflict.

As of 1986, there were 42 conflcits of varying degrees involving 4 million people. These included wars, rebellions and civil uprisings – although few nations have declared war upon each other. This ambiguity about hostility has in turn placed a particular premium upon effective Intelligence.

How the US and Soviet governments perceive the world around them is a matter of life and death for hundreds of millions of people. An erroneous evaluation of, say, a surge in military communications traffic coupled with deployments of submarines and other naval vessels and large-scale troop exercises in Germany or along the Soviet frontiers with China and Japan conceivably could lead to a decision to "pre-empt" a perceived "enemy" offensive whether by conventional or nuclear weapons.

On the US side, the job of seeing to it that such a miscalculation does not occur rests with three major Intelligence organizations: the Central Intelligence Agency, the Defense Intelligence Agency and the Bureau of Intelligence and Research of the US State Department. Before examining these agencies and how they relate to one another it is useful to digress for a moment and ask, "What *is* Intelligence?"

Intelligence and "Covert Actions"

Unfortunately, the public understanding of this term in recent years has become obscured by the use of Intelligence organizations in both the United States and the Soviet Union to provide an "umbrella" or "cover" for paramilitary "covert" actions that have nothing to do with the gathering and careful analysis of information, the true nature of Intelligence.

It is equally unfortunate that Intelligence has come to be thought of primarily as a military or quasi-military activity. In fact, an accurate understanding of political and economic events and trends may be far more important than information about military systems and events; as Prussian Maj. Gen. Carl von Clausewitz pointed out long ago in his classic study *On War*, wars have their beginning, and their end, in the political realm, not the military – and politics, more often than not, is shaped by ecnomics.

Nor should Intelligence be seen as focussed only on perceived "enemies". Although the Intelligence organizations of the United States, Japan and the North Atlantic Treaty Organization allies are all focussed on the military threat posed by the Soviet Union and its Warsaw Pact allies they also keep a wary eye on each other. The NATO European allies become greatly worried, for example, when they suspect that the United States is dealing too directly with the Soviet Union, "over the heads" of its allies. So a careful watch is

maintained by the diplomats (including military attaches) of all of those countries to penetrate as much as possible the secret councils of the US Government, and the US does the same thing as concerns its allies.

In some ways of even more immediate importance than the military "threat" is economic Intelligence. Thus, in a recent trap set for Soviet agents, the principal *counter*-Intelligence organization of the US Government found when the trap was sprung that it had caught not Soviets, but an impressive collection of Japanese electronics specialists intent on staying abreast of or getting ahead of the US electronics industry.

Indeed, the Soviet troops and missiles might never come, but the struggle for economic survival goes on relentlessly. Only those who are keenly aware of what is happening in that vast international marketplace will meet the test of survival, or at least of attaining and maintaining a marginally acceptable level of prosperity. Only a network of highly trained

Above: Headquartered at Langley, Virginia, the CIA is one of several US Intelligence agencies, but has sole direct-reporting access to the president.

observers and analysts can provide such security.

Despite their varying titles, all of the principal US Intelligence agencies recognize the importance of considering all the various categories of Intelligence, ranging from political and military to economic and sociological, and even to the psychology of foreign peoples and their leaders.

Origins in World War II

US Intelligence came into its own only in the aftermath of World War II, and then with a serious internal flaw that has burdened and hindered its primary mission ever since. The successful Japanese attack on Pearl Harbor, Hawaii, on 7 December 1941, was a failure of

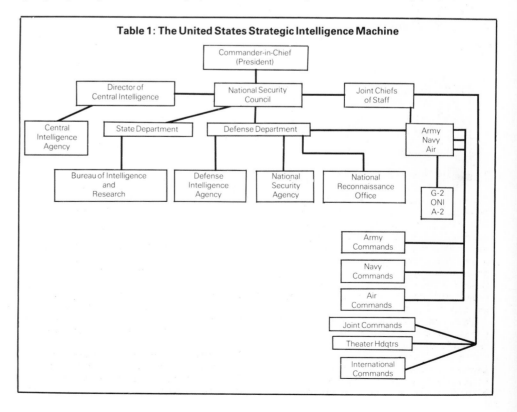

Table 1: The United States Strategic Intelligence Machine

Col. William V. Kennedy, Armor, US Army (Ret.), formerly Intelligence Officer with US Air Force, Strategic Air Command, and author of many works on defense-related subjects.

What is intelligence?

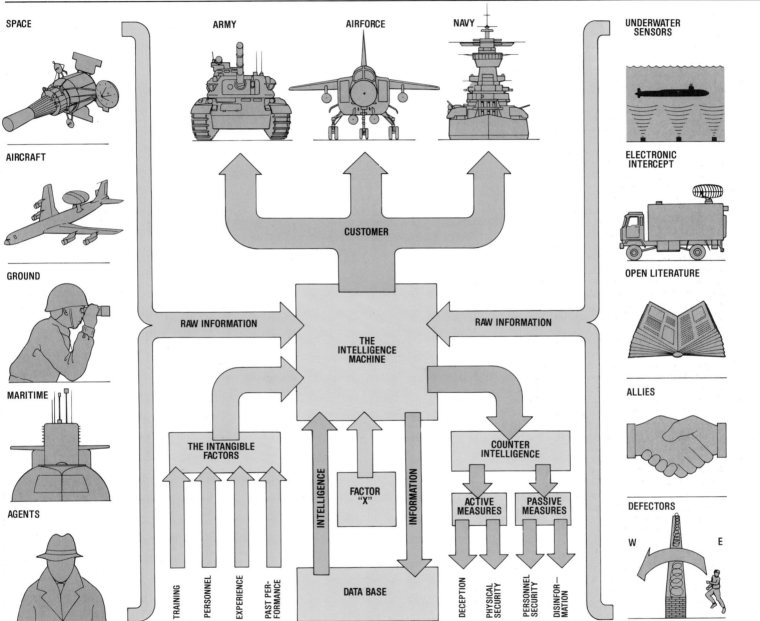

SPACE

AIRCRAFT

GROUND

MARITIME

AGENTS

ARMY · AIRFORCE · NAVY

CUSTOMER

RAW INFORMATION — RAW INFORMATION

THE INTELLIGENCE MACHINE

THE INTANGIBLE FACTORS

INTELLIGENCE · FACTOR "X" · INFORMATION

TRAINING · PERSONNEL · EXPERIENCE · PAST PERFORMANCE

DATA BASE

COUNTER INTELLIGENCE

ACTIVE MEASURES · PASSIVE MEASURES

DECEPTION · PHYSICAL SECURITY · PERSONNEL SECURITY · DISINFORMATION

UNDERWATER SENSORS

ELECTRONIC INTERCEPT

OPEN LITERATURE

ALLIES

DEFECTORS

The Intelligence Machine

The military Intelligence machine is very expensive business, which in the more important countries is active every hour of every day of the year. The fuel of these mighty machines is raw information, sucked in from many sources and then processed to create political and military intelligence.

Space is currently the Intelligence man's dream, with satellite sensors able to roam at will over every country.

Aircraft have radar and other sensors which can see far into hostile territory, and which can feed the "take" down to their bases in "real time".

Ground sensors range from radars and remote sensors to the foot soldier with binoculars. The main problem is range limitation by terrain and weather.

Maritime surveillance includes surface ships and submarines carrying a diversity of sensors to roam over the world's seas, limited only by "territorial waters".

Agents are the traditional source of the most vital information because they can penetrate the heart of the hostile system to gather cold facts and also the enemy's "feel", methods and intentions.

Underwater sensors now cover large areas of the ocean floor, particularly in the "choke points", and are designed for information not only on ship and submarine movements, but also on the ocean itself.

Electronic warfare is today one of the most important means of information-gathering. Radio, radar and microwave intercepts can provide raw data, and also build up a picture of deployments, etc.

Open literature, films and videos often provide factual information as well as insights into thought and moral processes.

Allies are frequently a valuable source of information, and also help to spread the load in this very expensive undertaking.

Defectors are invaluable prizes because, like the better agents, they can give in-depth information about their specialities.

Data base is the pool of knowledge built up by the Intelligence machine over the years, and provides the background against which new data can be analyzed effectively.

Intangible factors such as quality of personnel and training condition the basic efficiency of the Intelligence machine.

Factor X is the "lucky" ability to have the right men at the right spot and time.

"Intelligence" on a grand scale – political, economic and, ultimately, military.

More precisely defined, the Pearl Harbor disaster represented a failure of Intelligence coordination, analysis and dissemination rather than a failure of collection. Also involved was failure in another area above and beyond that of Intelligence, that of "strategic assessment'.

Japan's precarious political situation, stemming from its lack of domestic natural resources and its already over-extended military empire was known in detail in Washington. The volatile nature of the militarists who had gained control of Japan also was known from the excellent reporting of American and friendly European diplomats, journalists, and scholars. Putting those elements together should have foretold the consequences of imposing ever more severe economic and political sanctions on Japanese expansionism. Even given this failure of adequate strategic early warning, sufficient information about an impending Japanese attack on Pearl Harbor was available in time to have precluded the devastating surprise that occurred, had the US military been adequately coordinated and sufficiently alert.

The bits and pieces that go into forming a mosaic of this sort are not in themselves "Intelligence". They are identified at the early, collection stage only as "information", and initially they seldom provide anything but a very muddled and confusing "picture". It is through the process of analysis, or "evaluation", that the collected information is tested for reliability and formed into an assessment that, hopefully, will present a true and timely portrayal of what actually is occurring, or better still, of what is about to occur.

The accompanying illustrations show how that process works. Of special importance is the influence on the Intelligence process of "The Intangible Factors" shown on the left side of the chart. These constitute the huge human variable in the process by which the ultimate assessment can provide brilliant and sometimes startling insights, or by which the entire process can be short-circuited.

At the brilliant end of the scale, it was Winston Churchill's grasp of history, politics and, above all, of human motivations and predelictions that led him to conclude in 1941 that Hitler's Germany was about to attack the Soviet Union, even though Churchill's own Intelligence subordinates, looking at the same information, had reached the opposite conclusion. It was Soviet dictator Josef Stalin's emotional block, based on wishful thinking,

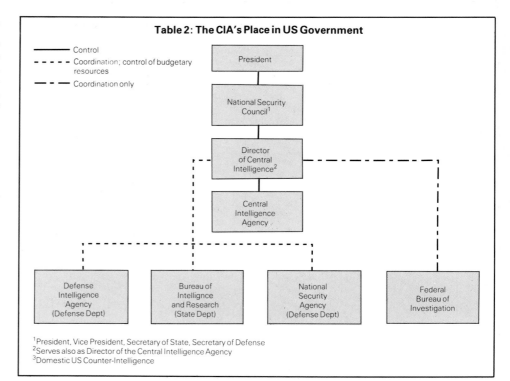

Table 2: The CIA's Place in US Government

— Control
- - - Coordination; control of budgetary resources
– · – Coordination only

President

National Security Council[1]

Director of Central Intelligence[2]

Central Intelligence Agency

Defense Intelligence Agency (Defense Dept)

Bureau of Intelligence and Research (State Dept)

National Security Agency (Defense Dept)

Federal Bureau of Investigation

[1]President, Vice President, Secretary of State, Secretary of Defense
[2]Serves also as Director of the Central Intelligence Agency
[3]Domestic US Counter-Intelligence

that prevented him from taking advantage of the warning Churchill provided.

The same sort of thing goes on at much lower levels as, for example, when a young US State Department Intelligence analyst cut short a conversation with a journalist at a recent meeting of the US Association for Asian Studies when she was told that Japanese sources had expressed serious concern over the possibility that the island of Taiwan (Formosa) might return to the control of the Chinese mainland government. Having invested a large part of her life in acquiring an advanced degree in Chinese language and, knowing that if she were seen by the People's Republic as being on the "wrong" side of the Chinese issue any meaningful dealings with the Peking government might be closed off to her, she was not about to consider information that conceivably could jeopardize her career.

Thus, too, policy-makers often fall into grave error even when the information that could have produced an entirely different assessment is only a desk or two away. The combination of US Intelligence organizations that came into being after World War II was supposed to correct the organizational flaws that led to the Pearl Harbor disaster, and to

contain safeguards against the "short-circuiting" of vital information by prejudiced or bureaucratic barriers.

The US Intelligence Machine Today

The present US Intelligence structure is founded in the National Security Act of 1947, the legal instrument by which the United States sought to correct the organizational and Intelligence deficiencies identified during World War II. At the apex of this Intelligence structure is the Central Intelligence Agency (CIA). As defined in the 1947 act and subsequent legislation, the Director of CIA was designated a "first among equals", responsible for coordinating the efforts of all of the country's Intelligence organizations and of presenting to the President the accurate, timely assessment so conspicuously absent at the time of the Pearl Harbor attack. How this arrangement relates to the overall US Intelligence "community" is shown in Table 4.

The CIA has the principal responsibility for the sort of traditional *clandestine* Intelligence-gathering dramatized and frequently over-dramatized in "James Bond" type movies and a vast "spy" literature.

The model in modern times for virtually all

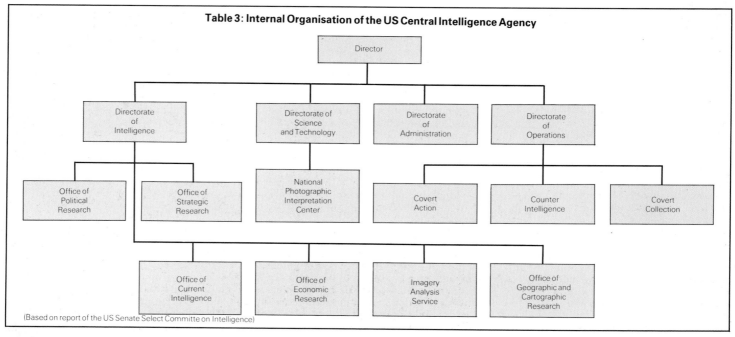

Table 3: Internal Organisation of the US Central Intelligence Agency

Director

Directorate of Intelligence

Directorate of Science and Technology

Directorate of Administration

Directorate of Operations

Office of Political Research

Office of Strategic Research

National Photographic Interpretation Center

Covert Action

Counter Intelligence

Covert Collection

Office of Current Intelligence

Office of Economic Research

Imagery Analysis Service

Office of Geographic and Cartographic Research

(Based on report of the US Senate Select Commitee on Intelligence)

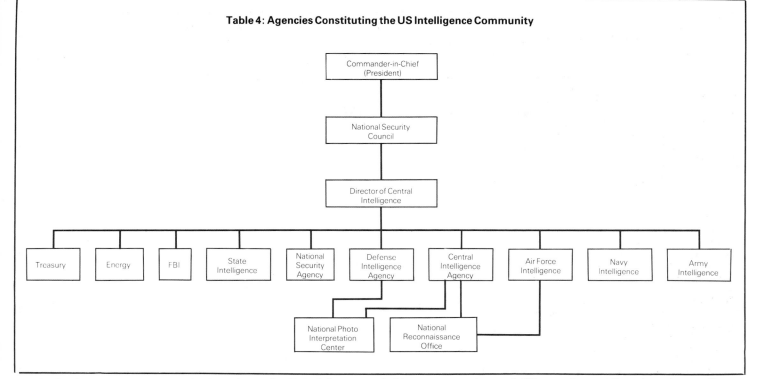

Table 4: Agencies Constituting the US Intelligence Community

```
                    Commander-in-Chief
                        (President)
                            |
                   National Security
                         Council
                            |
                  Director of Central
                      Intelligence
                            |
  ┌──────┬──────┬─────┬──────────┬──────────┬──────────┬──────────┬──────────┬──────────┬──────────┐
Treasury Energy FBI  State    National   Defense    Central   Air Force   Navy       Army
                   Intelligence Security  Intelligence Intelligence Intelligence Intelligence Intelligence
                              Agency      Agency      Agency
                                            |          |
                                    National Photo  National
                                    Interpretation  Reconnaissance
                                        Center        Office
```

such clandestine operations is the British Secret Service, often referred to as MI-6 although that is no longer its official designation. As it evolved during and since the reign of Queen Elizabeth I, the British Secret Service came to be structured along the same lines as the diplomatic service, since the embassies provided two important assets: "cover" for agents of the Secret Service in the form of legitimate diplomatic posts; and secure communications via protected diplomatic pouches and, in more recent times, coded electronic signals systems.

The clandestine service of the CIA, and of its principal opponent in "the Intelligence war" – the Soviet KGB – operate in essentially the same manner. That is, there is a CIA "chief of station" in each US embassy or consulate of any importance operating under some innocuous diplomatic title. That agent and his or her assistants seek to enlist the services of disaffected, sympathetic or simply avaricious local citizens who can furnish important information. This is transmitted via the elaborate system of microdots, invisible writing, miniaturized cameras, sophisticated electronic devices, etc., familiar to all readers of spy novels. The chief of station is then responsible for preparing reports which are transmitted via diplomatic pouch, if time permits, or by electronic means in more urgent cases.

A more open, internationally accepted form of "spying" is carried out by the uniformed military attaches accepted by all nations except those, such as Iran, which have repudiated the diplomatic system. The attaches coordinate their work with the CIA, but they come under direction of a separate agency, the Defense Intelligence Agency.

The greatest value of the true clandestine agent is his or her ability to discover intentions. That depends, of course, on how highly placed the spy may be in society and government. So far as is known, the CIA has had only two major successes in this regard. The first was Soviet Col. Oleg Penkovsky, who in the early 1960s delivered to the CIA large quantities of information concerning Soviet weapons, forces and military doctrine. With all such agents, however, there is always the danger of double-dealing. In regard to the Penkovsky case, British author Chapman Pincher, basing his judgement on sources in the British counter-Intelligence service and among Soviet defectors, suggests that the Penkovsky affair may have been an elaborate "plant" by which

the United States was led into guaranteeing the security of the Communist Castro regime in Cuba.

More recently, in 1975, Arkady N. Shevchenko, the most highly placed Soviet diplomat in the United Nations Secretariat, simply "walked into" US hands and was employed for 32 months before his open defection in 1978 as a US spy in the highest councils of the Soviet government.

Use of Open Sources
Much less exciting, but often more dependable, are the "open" sources upon which the CIA, and all such agencies, depend for by far the greater part of the information that goes into Intelligence assessments. These include the vast array of technical, trade and general readership publications produced throughout modern societies. Attendance at trade shows and academic symposia is another important source of information. A standard source for centuries has been business representatives, journalists, scholars and other travelers who have been willing to report their observations to their home governments. Unfortunately, a considerable part of this valuable source is closed to the CIA because of the unsavory reputation acquired by the "covert action" staff grafted into the CIA at its inception, deriving from a succession of undeclared wars such as that conducted by the CIA in recent years in Central America.

Results of these open and clandestine activities are reported on a "need-to-know" basis to all agencies of the US Government dealing with foreign affairs. Much of this information is also made available to US allies. This is done by means of regular Intelligence publications, some secret, some available to the public, or where the matter is urgent, by cable or personal messenger. That, however, does not guarantee that the officials concerned will act on the information. Thus Israel failed to heed repeated warnings of an Arab military build-up, in 1973, because the CIA data did not fit in with Israeli preconceptions.

In return for Intelligence transmitted to allies, the CIA receives a vast and important flow of information from the Intelligence services of those nations. Israel is unique, however, in that while receiving enormous assistance in Intelligence and other resources from the United States it attacked a US Navy electronic Intelligence-gathering ship, the USS *Liberty*, during the 1967 Middle East war,

killing and wounding American sailors, apparently because it did not want to have the United States monitoring its military communications.

While the CIA reports go directly from the source to US or Allied recipients, most are channeled through a staff of thousands of analysts, specialists in the country concerned, or in particular academic disciplines, principally economics, political science and military affairs.

The CIA is the principal US Government agency responsible for monitoring foreign broadcasts. The results of this service are available to the public through the Foreign Broadcast Information Service. That pertains, of course, only to commercial or government public radio and television broadcasts, not to coded signals.

Air and Satellite Reconnaissance
Beyond the traditional and still invaluable techniques, the CIA led the way to development of an Intelligence technique that changed the nature of modern espionage and reconnaissance. About 1960, the CIA, working closely with the US Air Force, developed satellite vehicles with extraordinarily sensi-

Below: Orbiting close to a hostile frontier, the TR-1 can "see" deep into the enemy's rear areas for the purposes of reconnaissance or tactical attack.

tive cameras and other sensing devices that enable US Intelligence analysts to survey large portions of the Earth's surface in relatively short periods of time so as to detect objects of a very small size. This photographic imagery was a further development of World War II aerial photographic reconnaissance as brought to a high state of efficiency in the U-2 and SR-71 high-altitude photo-reconnaissance aircraft.

The excellence of the satellite photography is suggested from the publication, in August 1984, of photographs showing a new class of conventional aircraft carrier under construction by the Soviet Navy at a Black Sea shipyard. So detailed are the photographs that it is possible to determine the precise stage of construction and to predict from that when the ship will be ready to take its place in the Soviet Fleet, which will be a momentous step toward enabling the Soviet Union to project its sea power far beyond its present capabilities. Many claims have been made as to the clarity of satellite photographs, popular ones being that reconnaissance satellites can clearly photograph a ball on a golf course, or reveal headlines in a newspaper.

It is similar satellite photography that has enabled the United States to identify strategic and intermediate-range missile sites all over the Soviet Union and to estimate with a high degree of accuracy the range, yield and motive power of the missiles and the state of "hardness" or vulnerability of the underground silos and other structures in which the missiles are housed.

How the Satellites Work
Although the satellites themselves, the systems that put them into orbit and the electronics that guide them are enormously complex, the basic principles of satellite surveillance are simple. By control of launch velocity, the place at which the satellite will go into orbit around the Earth can be determined with great precision. Depending upon the results desired this orbit can be a few hundred or many thousands of miles above the Earth.

By placing the satellite in a polar orbit, circling the globe generally from the North Pole to the South Pole, the cameras emplaced in the satellite can scan about 1,500 miles (2,415km) of a selected swath of the Earth's services on each orbit. Which section of the Earth is to be photographed is determined by ground controllers or pre-set programs. Thus US satellites can be designed to photograph the Soviet Union and peripheral areas in successive orbits. If spaces remain between the successive orbital sweeps, the cameras can be adjusted to cover those in succeeding days. Where it is desired to keep a certain portion of Earth under continuous surveillance a satellite can be positioned in "geosynchronous" orbit (or 23,600 nautical miles above the Earth), coordinating its velocity once in orbit

so as to match exactly that of the Earth's rotation. These systems, however, are not perfect. Given a Soviet land mass of 8.6 million square miles (22.3km^2) it is possible that clouds or other weather patterns will interrupt coverage. It is conceivable, therefore, that the Soviets could take advantage of such periods, as well as periods of darkness, to move equipment or to work on projects that it wishes to keep hidden, hiding the equipment or covering work sites in time to escape surveillance when the weather clears or daylight returns. Efforts are being made to "see through" night and bad weather by use of infrared photography and other technologically advanced sensors.

Recovery of the satellite film posed considerable difficulties in the past when it was necessary to parachute the film packages from reentry vehicles detached from the satellite and then to dispatch aircraft to snag the descending parachutes before they became lost in the ocean. Although this system still is in use for some of the older equipment, it is now possible to obtain near "real-time" photography from the satellites by translating the film into electronic signals and then transmitting these to an Earth station via a relay satellite.

In the parlance of international arms control negotiators, these surveillance systems are called "the national technical means of verification" – the means by which the United States determines what the Soviet Union has and what it might be willing to give up in trade for US concessions. This process has been considerably complicated by the fact that it is impossible to be certain from satellite or aerial photography whether cruise missiles and other dual-purpose systems are equipped with conventional or nuclear warheads.

Satellite Vulnerability
As the chart shows, the photographic satellites, such as KH-11 and Big Bird "fly" at relatively low altitudes from less than 100 miles (160km) to around 400 miles (650km). It is this relatively low orbit that makes such satellites vulnerable to anti-satellite weapons such as the ground-based rocket tested in recent years by the Soviet Union and the far more efficient US anti-satellite weapons, now under development, to be launched from an F-15 Eagle fighter aircraft.

Recent US space shuttle missions reveal a dramatic new method to counter hostile satellite surveillance – the possibility actually to capture a satellite or by having teams of astronauts examine it and perhaps remove or alter its photographic capsules without disrupting or destroying the satellite as such.

Because of satellite sensitivity to weather, enemy interference and other limitations, high-performance manned aircraft such as the U-2, TR-1 and SR-71 continue to have an important role in Intelligence-gathering. Such aircraft can be deployed much more quickly

than satellites in an emergency and their human pilots have a much higher degree of flexibility in situations calling for decisions that cannot be programmed into a satellite.

Although, as indicated earlier, the CIA played a key role in initiating worldwide photographic surveillance by aircraft and later by satellite, the means of conducting such surveillance are actually operated by the US military services. Thus, the coordinating function vested in the CIA is vital, nowhere more so than in space monitoring of radio communications.

The SIGINT Satellites
These "Signal Intelligence" (SIGINT) satellites received an unusual amount of public attention in December 1984, when, for reasons yet unknown, the US Department of Defense went to unusual lengths to focus news media attention on the supposedly "secret" aspects of the Space Shuttle "Discovery" to be launched in January, 1985. As a result it came to worldwide attention that "Discovery" would be placing in orbit a SIGINT satellite designed to monitor Soviet communications.

Many such satellites had previously been put into orbit to "eavesdrop" on Soviet civilian and military communications and on aircraft and missile control and other radars. From an analysis of such information it is possible to learn that major military exercises or more ominous military ventures are underway, the frequencies used by air defense and other radars and, by means of elaborate code-breaking ("cryptologic") procedures, to learn what Soviet officials are talking about to each other.

While the CIA continues to be responsible for coordination of information received from the SIGINT satellites with that developed by other agencies and the CIA itself, the US agency primarily concerned with SIGINT is the National Security Agency (NSA) whose headquarters are at Fort George G. Meade, Maryland, several miles from the Pentagon and the CIA headquarters located in McLean, Virginia. It is here that the huge amounts of information literally pulled from the air and space each day are analyzed, together with information received from closely integrated Army, Navy and Air Force "security agencies". Since the number of such intercepts is far beyond any manual means of tabulation most of the sorting of data is done by banks of computers programmed to "watch" for special danger signals, such as the volume and pattern of radio traffic and other electronic emissions that would likely precede an enemy attack.

Elaborate modern encoding equipment presents an enormous challenge to the code-breaker, but as the history of World War II demonstrated there is no such thing as a perfect device. Signal Intelligence, however, does not depend on the actual breaking of codes. Any electronic device betrays "secrets" about itself from the moment it is turned on, or even from the moment it is photographed, perhaps by satellite. Direction finding equipment can locate the transmitter and by relating it to other transmitters identify complete political and military chains of command and organizational structures. The frequency on which a radio or radar set transmits also is a vital element of Intelligence, in that once such a frequency is known, weapons can be keyed to that frequency, riding it directly to the source and destroying it. The sheer volume of radio and other electronic signals is important. By establishing the norm for such "traffic", it is possible to establish from an increase or decrease in volume that something unusual is

Left: Where the recovery of satellite data demands physical methods such as the return of exposed film, the re-entry capsule is air-caught by a special C-130 Hercules.

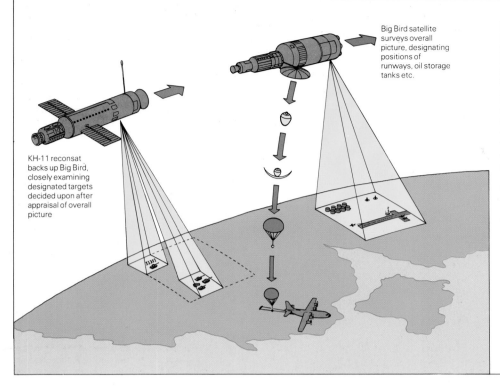

KH-11 reconsat backs up Big Bird, closely examining designated targets decided upon after appraisal of overall picture

Big Bird satellite surveys overall picture, designating positions of runways, oil storage tanks etc.

BIG BIRD

Big Bird reconsats like these shown here have replaced the area coverage satellites of the 1960s and early 1970s. With high resolution cameras, they provide broad views from which specific targets are selected for discriminatory analysis. Some pictures are returned to earth in recoverable capsules, as shown. Infra-red pictures can reveal the presence of heat-generating equipment and camouflage systems. Big Bird is backed up by the KH-11 digital reconsat which can take TV images of high clarity. both will be replaced by new reconsats launched by Shuttle. Being retrievable, they will save money through re-use.

A typical mapping operation works to a plan of target allocations, the coordinates of specific regions falling into a grid of orbital opportunities presented to the satellite on each successive pass. Many tasks require monitoring role rather than probing which, unlike the former, seeks to gather new information about some unknown or unclear activity; with so much long-term monitoring there are few sudden reconnaissance needs and most Intelligence traffic is made up of component pictures blending to present a series of indicators such as might be presented by observation of a missile being slowly prepared for a test flight. Such information is fed to other Intelligence operators so that telemetry or electronic ferrets can be activated.

occurring. Other collection means, such as satellites, aircraft or human agents can then be "targeted" on the area to determine the nature of the activity.

Often, the pace of operations is such that risks must be taken and military or governmental signals traffic conducted "in the clear". Something of that sort occurred in September 1983, when a befuddled and confused Soviet air defense system stumbled into shooting down a Korean airliner that had overflown the Soviet Pacific coast. Japanese electronic Intelligence specialists were able to pick up and record most or all of the Soviet ground-to-air and air-to-ground transmissions, providing important information about the workings and vulnerabilities of the Soviet air defense system.

The importance of SIGINT is so great that an entirely new field of electronic countermeasures (ECM) has emerged by which to "blind" and "deafen" foreign electronic reconnaissance and the weapons it serves.

The CIA and the US military services also deploy a vast array of monitoring stations to acquire the telemetry involved in testing of new Soviet weapons. This involves interception and interpretation of the signals transmitted from experimental missiles and their warheads so that US and allied analysts can determine the range, explosive power and vulnerabilities of the new weapons.

In terms of day-to-day Intelligence operations, this SIGINT work by NSA and related US and Allied agencies is the most important of all US Intelligence activities. The photographic satellites can "report" what is already there, but it is SIGINT that has the capacity to say what will be there tomorrow, or at least in the next few hours or minutes. In that predictive capacity, SIGINT is exceeded in importance only by the slim chance that a defector or a spy in a key position might be able to provide that most vital of all Intelligence – enemy *intentions*.

The Defense Intelligence Agency

Although the information produced by NSA is immediately available to CIA, the agency itself comes under the jurisdiction of the Department of Defense (DoD). Co-equal with NSA in DoD is the Intelligence agency of the US military Joint Chiefs of Staff. This is called the Defense Intelligence Agency (DIA).

DIA was established in 1961 with the aim of consolidating the disparate Intelligence activities of the Army, Navy and Air Force. In terms of specific Intelligence "products" one of the most important sub-elements of DIA is the worldwide Defense Attache system by which military officers are assigned to US embassies and consulates as internationally accepted, often fully uniformed "spies". In return, of course, the United States and all other countries – barring international outlaws such as Iran and Libya – accept the assignment of foreign military attaches in their own capitals, except where the military attaches are caught dealing in illegal, clandestine activities.

DIA also conducts Intelligence studies in the fields of broad military strategy, politics and economics in parallel with work done at CIA. This provides a viewpoint independent of CIA which, properly used and evaluated, enables policy-makers to develop a broader understanding of issues that might be ignored or even suppressed if there was only a single channel for national Intelligence assessment.

Although the DIA was intended to consolidate military Intelligence assets, in fact each of the services has maintained its own independent Intelligence staff.

The Intelligence "Chain"

The service Intelligence system begins with literally the eyes and ears of individual soldiers, sailors, marines and airmen. This is true in a very direct sense of the US Armored Cavalry troopers who patrol the borders between West Germany and its Warsaw Pact neighbors. A step removed but no less important is the naval aviator aboard a P-3C Orion long range patrol aircraft who listens to sonobuoys dropped into the ocean for the telltale "signature" of a Soviet submarine identified previously, perhaps by being trailed from its home port by a US nuclear attack submarine. Where the validated information thus gained pertains exclusively to local operations it is called "tactical" Intelligence. Where it pertains to operations involving an entire theater or even the world as a whole it is called "strategic" Intelligence (a term which is also applied to the overall assessment of a foreign nation's economy and political establishment). In many cases a particular item will have both tactical and strategic significance.

This "raw" data about the movements of

men, ships and aircraft of a potential adversary is passed up through an increasingly complex chain of military Intelligence staffs and eventually into the DIA and CIA networks where it is considered in relation to all the other millions of bits and pieces of information received every day from satellite, diplomatic and other sources.

Once sifted through the Washington evaluation process, the resulting "approved" Intelligence is sent back down through the chain of command throughout the world. In the US system a vast amount of data is transmitted in this process, providing military staffs at all levels with a very wide view of what is happening throughout the world. That can sometimes be a danger, as when Iranian revolutionaries stole and published a large number of Intelligence documents from the US Embassy in Tehran. The United States prefers to take such risks, however, to assure that even its lowranking soldiers and diplomats can have an understanding of their importance in the entire scheme of things. Experience has shown that people so informed are able to recognize and report a much greater amount of important information than people who are kept in ignorance except for a very narrow range of their own immediate responsibilities – a major weakness of the Soviet system.

The method by which this finished Intelligence is transmitted takes several forms. Strategic Intelligence of long-term significance usually is transmitted in printed form by means of various booklets and magazines produced by the several agencies. Tactical Intelligence of more immediate concern is transmitted by electronic means through the Worldwide Military Command and Communications System (which is maintained by the Joint Chiefs of Staff) with various priorities assigned ranging from "Flash" – limited to the outbreak of hostilities – to "Routine". Some of these messages will be transmitted via land lines or underseas cable, the most secure means, or by encoded radio signals. In some circumstances, especially sensitive strategic Intelligence is transmitted only via armed human courier exclusively aboard US military aircraft. Once received, it is the job of the staff Intelligence officer to see to it that the information is brought to the attention of those who "need to know" by personal visit, formal briefings or staff memoranda.

Despite the huge resources poured into the governmental systems, the best strategic Intelligence in terms of political and economic data is still that provided by the press of Western Europe, North America and, although sometimes limited by excessive partisan political and ideological content, Japan. In short, the citizen of those countries who has a reasonably good background in foreign and military affairs and who has the time to study the principal sources generally can anticipate an international crisis at least as early and often well ahead of the official Intelligence agencies. This is due to the cumbersome bureaucratic processes of all such agencies and to their often insurmountable biases, such as that already mentioned concerning the refusal of the Israelis in 1973 to accept US warnings of a surprise attack. Thus, anyone familiar with the frequent US expressions of concern over a large airfield being constructed on the island of Grenada with Cuban support would not have been surprised at US military intervention when an internal political upheaval in the island's government created a reasonable pretext. Often, and Grenada may be the most recent example, the best strategic Intelligence the US Government possesses is literally what it reads in newspaper stories by journalists of known competence.

Gaining the Long View

As indicated earlier, satellite and aerial photography can often tell us that something important has occurred, and SIGINT can often foretell that something is about to occur. Even SIGINT at its best, however, is generally limited to a very short view into the future, measured usually in a matter of days. Yet those highly technical Intelligence activities absorb the energies of tens of thousands of people and of billions of dollars each year, an estimated $4 billion per year to run the NSA alone.

The long view of Intelligence is the province of a relatively small group of people in CIA, DIA and the military staffs, but most notably in the Bureau of Intelligence and Research of the US State Department. These are the people responsible for performing the drudgery of winnowing out from a vast amount of information, including the world press, the long-range political and economic trends by which military forces are controlled or set in motion.

The important role played by the State Department's Bureau of Intelligence and Research derives from the fact, that the State Department operates the US embassies and consulates abroad. Information gathered by the staffs of those diplomatic offices is sent to Washington by pouch, routine radio or cable messages or through CRITCOM (Critical Communications Net) by which high-priority messages can be sent in code and delivered to the addressee in Washington within the hour.

As is typical throughout all modern Intelligence networks the technical quality of this communications system sometimes exceeds that of the information that is transmitted through it. When several years ago, for example, a political officer in a US embassy in Asia was asked what he thought the effect would be in the rest of Asia if the Soviets decided to move into Sinkiang (China's Northwest province) he replied, "First you must tell me, where is Sinkiang?" Having been transferred in from Bonn, West Germany, three months before it was readily apparent that not much could be expected of this source for some time to come, no matter how good the technical means of communication.

By the same token, the best sort of reporting from the embassies and the most rapid means of communications can be negated by inadequate training or experience on the part of recipients. The State Department seems to

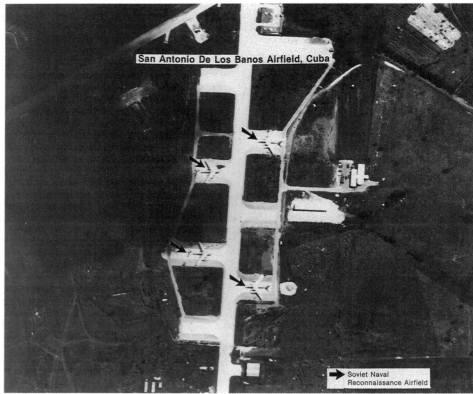

San Antonio De Los Banos Airfield, Cuba

➤ Soviet Naval Reconnaissance Airfield

have difficulties with geography at that end of the wire also. During a discussion in the Pentagon in May 1979, for example, it was suggested that to strengthen the US position in Northeast Asia the island of Attu in the Aleutians chain be fortified. A high-ranking representative of the State Department Bureau of Intelligence and Research responded, "Does that belong to us?" Attu and the entire Aleutians chain, of course, are part of Alaska. Happily the chairman of that Pentagon meeting, Ambassador Michael Armacost, is an Asian specialist who has now been advanced to the post of Undersecretary of State so, presumably, Attu is now fully identified.

There are apparently not one, but three channels of communications from the US embassies and separate consulates, one each for the State Department, the Central Intelligence Agency and the Defense Intelligence Agency, the latter via the military attaches. It is not clear whether the Ambassador, the senior State Department representative, has much control over what the attaches report. Apparently he or she has no contol over anything that the CIA does despite the danger that implies to overall US foreign relations. The embassies provide the secure rooms, of course, from which attache and CIA reporting is conducted, but whether there is much

Above: Reconnaissance by satellite or aircraft plays a vital role in determining factors such as Soviet use of airfields which could prove a threat to US interests.

rapport or coordination other than that seems open to question, given the often mutual jealousies of the three agencies, as reported by former CIA agent Frank Snepp and other authors writing of the Vietnam debacle.

In general, interviews with State department regional desk officers and other officials who are the recipients of Bureau of Intelligence and Research analyses suggest that the final judgment as concerns quality is somewhat analogous to the journalistic judgment on television newspersons – that "They are only as good as the newspapers they read."

In short, much more than half and in some special situations *all* of what the Bureau of Intelligence and Research receives from the embassies comes from "open" sources, chiefly newspapers. During the revolution of 1974 in Portugal, for example, the State Department readily acknowledged to other government

Below: Clandestine overflights of Vietnam in recent years have revealed indications (possible serial numbers and initials) of American MIAs still on the run.

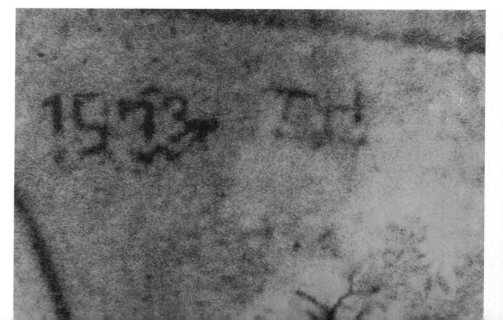

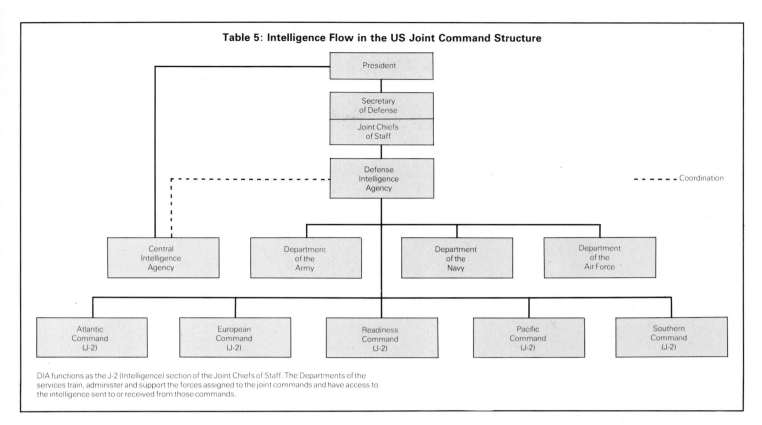

Table 5: Intelligence Flow in the US Joint Command Structure

President

Secretary of Defense

Joint Chiefs of Staff

Defense Intelligence Agency

- - - - - Coordination

Central Intelligence Agency

Department of the Army

Department of the Navy

Department of the Air Force

Atlantic Command (J-2)

European Command (J-2)

Readiness Command (J-2)

Pacific Command (J-2)

Southern Command (J-2)

DIA functions as the J-2 (Intelligence) section of the Joint Chiefs of Staff. The Departments of the services train, administer and support the forces assigned to the joint commands and have access to the intelligence sent to or received from those commands.

agencies that all it knew of the situation was what it read each day in the *New York Times*, the US diplomatic staff there having all being locked up in the embassy. That is not an uncommon development in such a situation, in that dissident groups are willing to permit journalists, even of an "enemy" government or society, to roam with a fair degree of freedom because the dissidents are contending for world public opinion. It is therefore perhaps as much a credit to US and Western journalism generally that US Senate investigators found, in the 1970s, that the small State Department Intelligence bureau together with DIA's military attaches produced the most reliable foreign political and economic Intelligence available to the US Government.

Other US Intelligence Agencies

As shown in Table 4, other agencies of the US Government make important contributions to the Intelligence process. The most important in terms of day-to-day operations is the Federal Bureau of Investigations (FBI). Although embarrassed during 1984 and 1985

Below: Totally unglamorous, HUMINT (human intelligence) is one of the most important features of tactical reconnaissance.

by the indictment of two of its high ranking agents, one for espionage and one for accepting bribes from drug dealers, the FBI has a remarkable record of efficiency as a counter-Intelligence agency. It so effectively infiltrated the US Communist Party during the period 1930 to 1950 as to render the Party impotent as an effective agency of espionage and potential subversion. Although it routinely reported that there was little or no evidence of foreign control of US anti-war groups during the Vietnam era, the very means by which it compiled that data, essentially infiltration of agents and use of informers, came under severe criticism.

As a by-product of all of these activities, the FBI has accumulated a mass of data about the Soviet Intelligence agencies, the KGB and its military counterpart, the GRU. On occasion this data has enabled the FBI to seize carefully trained Soviet agents the moment they entered US territory.

The FBI is a part of the Department of Justice and as such reports to the chief of that department, the Attorney General. The FBI has been under intermittent pressure from expansionist tendencies in the CIA, whereby the CIA has sought to intrude upon or take over entirely the FBI's domestic internal security function. So far, however, the FBI has

been able to resist these incursions, largely with the help of Congressmen concerned about an undue concentration of secret power in the CIA. At the present time, the FBI is the central authority on the conduct of Intelligence activities within the US. In fact, the CIA and military services must coordinate with the FBI on domestic operations.

Closely linked with the FBI in the department of Justice is the recently created Drug Enforcement Administration (DEA). By the nature of this work, DEA develops a large volume of Intelligence not only about the international drug traffic but also about the political and economic systems throughout areas of the world prominent in the production and shipment of narcotics, principally Latin America, the Middle East and South Asia.

The Treasury Department contributes important information gleaned from its day-to-day familiarity with international monetary transactions. Equally important is the contribution of the US Department of Commerce whose primary function at present is to analyze and devise methods of coping with the expanding imbalance in US foreign trade. Intelligence gained by the Treasury and Commerce departments through their dealings with foreign matters and businesses is of crucial importance in enabling US industry to counter its foreign competition.

Although Intelligence concerning nuclear weapons would appear to be primarily the concern of the DIA and CIA, the fact of the matter is that in the US system most of the technical experts required for study and analysis are in the Department of Energy. This derives from the fact that the Department of Energy absorbed some years ago the separate agency responsible for the production of nuclear weapons. That came about, in turn, because of the belief – mistaken as it turned out – that the nuclear energy program would so dwarf the weapons program as to make it desirable to bring them under a single administrative "roof".

How Effective is the US Intelligence Machine?

How well does this huge and expensive Intelligence machine work? It works superlatively well in maintaining a precise count of things that are countable. Thanks to the technical excellence of the US air and space surveillance system, the non-Communist world has a precise understanding of the extent of the Soviet nuclear arsenal. The number of Soviet ships, tanks, artillery pieces and other major items of military "hardware" is also known to within a rather small margin of probable error. Thanks to US SIGINT capabilities and those of its allies, primarily in Europe and Japan, the world has a reasonably good idea of the deployment of the Soviet armed forces and their command structure. US Defense Intelligence Agency analysts say that they feel they have a reliable count on Soviet aircraft shot down by Afghan guerrillas from photographs and infrared satellite pickup of wreckage on the barren Afghanistan terrain.

Some question arises, however, as to whether the Intelligence produced in Washington from all of these sources is getting to whom, where and when it is needed.

For example, one of the factors leading to the abortive US hostage rescue mission in Iran in 1979 was the failure of the military planners to take into account severe dust storms. Also, after US troops landed on the island of Grenada in the Caribbean in October 1983, it was revealed that they were operating with ordinary road maps, although the island had been publicly identified for years as a major area of US security concern stemming from Soviet and Cuban influence. These lapses may have less to do with deficiencies in the Intelligence system, however, than with the weaknesses in US defense organization and planning discussed elsewhere.

The record of the US Intelligence services in the realm of Strategic Intelligence has been spotty. The failure to assess properly the impact of Muslim fanaticism in Iran and throughout the Middle East generally is now recognized to have been the product of an overly close identification by all US agencies, the Intelligence services included, with the government of the Shah of Iran. To a somewhat lesser degree, judgments also may have been skewed by over-dependence on Israeli Intelligence services. Certainly the consequences of excessive US identification with the Israeli-supported Christian Phalangist party in Lebanon were not adequately considered by the US Government, although that does not mean necessarily that the Intelligence services failed to provide adequate warning. The resulting ignominious US withdrawal from the Lebanon, after heavy loss of life at the hands of Muslim fanatics, was a defeat for US interests throughout the Middle East.

Why the US Intelligence agencies were so closely identified with the Shah of Iran is easily understood from the fact that it was the Central Intelligence Agency that helped to bring the Shah to power in 1953, displacing a government that, compared to what eventually replaced the Shah, now seems moderation and enlightenment itself.

It would seem obvious that an Intelligence agency designed to gather information should not have been involved in the overthrow of one government and the establishment of another. Common sense tells us, after all, that people who have staked their reputations and perhaps their careers on the success of a particular leader or government are not likely to view that commitment with professional detachment. The CIA got that contradiction of roles and missions thrust upon it by an accident of history.

The OSS "Implant"

The intention of Congress in 1947 was to establish a "pure" Intelligence agency whose sole function would be to overcome the deficiencies of Intelligence management that led to Pearl Harbor. In the process of its creation, however, CIA had attached to it by Presidential initiative the remnants of the World War

Above: Soviet Intelligence scours the West for technological Intelligence, the US Secretary of Defense claiming that 5,000 Soviet defense projects have benefited.

II Office of Strategic Services (OSS), primarily a "covert" paramilitary agency that had performed well during World War II but which was in danger of going out of existence if it could not find a bureaucratic "home". In the view of its members, that "home" would preferably be found outside the military structure and discipline of the Department of Defense.

The outbreak of the Cold War in 1948 with the Soviet takeover of Czechoslovakia seemed to suggest that the paramilitary services the OSS offered might be useful in countering Soviet subversion. So, without Congressional license, the OSS was incorporated into the CIA and to this day forms one of its structural elements. Although such "covert" operations involve a relatively small proportion of the overall CIA staff they have dominated for at least the past 15 years virtually everything the public knows, or thinks it knows, about the agency, and the world's view of US Intelligence operations.

How disproportionately powerful the covert operations group within the agency itself has become is illustrated by the fact that *all* of the CIA Directors who have come up from within the agency or who had an Intelligence back-

ground before becoming Director have come from the relatively small OSS covert action staff. In short, what the history of the CIA has demonstrated is that operations requiring intense, day-to-day management will always crowd out and obscure the seemingly less immediate and certainly less spectacular, plodding work of the true Intelligence analysts unless special provision is made to segregate and foster the work of the analysts. That supposedly is what the CIA was intended to do.

In an article entitled "Why I Quit the CIA", published in *The Washington Post* on 2 January 1985, John Horton, a former high-ranking CIA official, charged that CIA Director (and OSS veteran) William J. Casey's personal involvement in directing a "covert" war in Central America has led him to demand that agency Intelligence assessments support the policies of the Reagan Administration. In the process, Horton shed considerable light on the process by which US national Intelligence assessments evolve.

The National Intelligence Estimate

"A National Intelligence Estimate," Horton

Below: Computers such as these FBI systems have done much to streamline and enhance the processing of raw data to permit faster and more accurate extrapolation of vital Intelligence.

wrote, is not simply an intelligence report or a bit of analysis, nor should it be any one man's opinion. It is the product of the deliberation of representatives of all the intelligence agencies dealing with foreign affairs. As a member of the National Intelligence Council, the national intelligence officer (responsible for a particular region or function) chairs the writing of the estimate. Being in the chair may give him more influence than one of the representatives from CIA, from State or Army or Navy or Air Force or the Marines, or from the Defense Intelligence Agency. It may not. But the result should reflect the views of all the agencies and differences in their views. It is not or should not be blandly unanimous, and it should reflect doubts as well as disagreements."

Horton states that "William Casey differs from previous directors of Central Intelligence in that he is part of the policy-making group where Central America is involved as much as he is the President's chief Intelligence officer."

In fact, Casey's role in the Reagan Administration has done no more than personify the dichotomy built into the Central Intelligence Agency in the late 1940s by involving the agency in operations that were certain to overshadow its primary function. It will be impossible for any Director of Central Intelligence to be free of the charge of bending Intelligence to suit operational objectives as long as this dichotomy remains.

The Horton article suggests another serious flaw in the American Intelligence system. Why, if there is a Defense Intelligence Agency staffed, as it is, by experienced Intelligence officers from all of the US military services, should there also be representatives of each of those services on the National Intelligence Council?

In short, the services do not trust their individual representatives in DIA to protect the *bureaucratic* interests of the several services. That, in turn, reflects the fact that each of the US military services has been left free to develop its own version of the foreign "threat" and to develop its own "national" strategy, conveniently enough advancing and protecting key service interests. The weaknesses in the Joint Chief of Staff system and the US national military planning system that permitted this aberration to occur are discussed in the chapter on "Defense Organization".

The presence, of course, of the specifically bureaucratic representatives of the services on the National Intelligence Council places a severe limitation on military members of DIA who must look to their "parent" service for assignments and promotions. The same applies to service members serving with CIA. The chances, therefore, of obtaining frank and balanced viewpoints in the National Intelligence Council are much less than Mr Horton indicates.

US Counter-Intelligence

Although it is not a function of Intelligence-gathering *per se*, the effectiveness of US Counter-Intelligence plays a major role in protecting whatever advantages the United States might have in the collection and assessment processes. The CIA has scored numerous successes in winning over or at least securing the safety of defectors, sometimes of high rank, from the Soviet Union and its satellite nations. Failures in such work tend to be hidden in the murky world that John LeCarré has so effectively described in his novels. Closer to the surface, and the light, is the work of the Federal Bureau of Investigation and the internal security system of the several US departments in controlling the activities of foreign spies within the United States.

Although there have been many notable

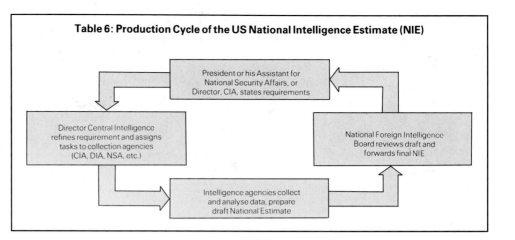

Table 6: Production Cycle of the US National Intelligence Estimate (NIE)

President or his Assistant for National Security Affairs, or Director, CIA, states requirements

Director Central Intelligence refines requirement and assigns tasks to collection agencies (CIA, DIA, NSA, etc.)

National Foreign Intelligence Board reviews draft and forwards final NIE

Intelligence agencies collect and analyse data, prepare draft National Estimate

successes, there also has been a chain of worrisome failures, one of the most damaging being the betrayal to the Soviet Union in the late 1970s of important satellite reconnaissance systems by John Boyce and Andrew Daulton Lee (two "spoiled brats" of affluent American suburban society), and William P. Kampiles, a former CIA employee. In October 1984, apparently for the first time in FBI history, one of the FBI's own agents, Richard Miller of the agency's Los Angeles office, was arrested and charged with passing secret documents to one Svetlana Ogorodnikova, an attractive supposed Soviet "defector" with whom Miller was reportedly carrying on an affair. The case entered the realms of the bizarre when Government documents released to the press reported that Miller had been stealing, among other things, candy bars, and that Miller's boss had exhorted him to repent for his sins.

More serious, however, was the John Walker spy ring which operated between 1974 and 1983. Navy officials said the ring, which included Walker, his brother and son, as well as others, gave the Soviets the keys to codes used for all secret messages to the Pacific. Others have labeled it the biggest haemorrhage in the history of US military secrets.

Human frailities being what they are, and taking into account the enormous sums of money and apparently ample supply of temptresses the Soviets are able to deploy, it should not be any great surprise that every so often they find their target. What reasonable actions can be taken to restrict such Soviet espionage without turning democratic societies into mirror images of the totalitarian regimes they are fighting is one of the most difficult tasks facing the US and other democratic governments.

Restrictions on Export of Technology

Spreading high technology capability in the Third World creates its own special problems in averting transfer of sensitive technology to hostile nations. This obviously complicates the task for Intelligencies agencies.

In January 1985, a common-sense arrangement was reached between the US Department of Defense and the US Department of Commerce to restrict Soviet access to actual or potential US military technology by requiring that licenses for export of new defense-related technology be reviewed by the Defense Department, but under a tight deadline to assure an early decision. More controversial have been Reagan Administration attempts to restrict in various ways the publication of basic research. The scientific community has argued that such restrictions almost certainly backfire in that technological progress cannot occur in a tightly controlled national environment. Still more controversial is the increased use of lie detectors to determine the "patriotism" of government employees and a massive attempt to bind government em-

ployees to a lifetime censorship obligation. Congress has intervened to limit use of both the lie detectors and the lifetime censorship agreements, but the controversy is by no means resolved.

Also likely to be controversial is a proposal by the National Security Agency that the US Government and private industry purchase some 500,000 interception-proof telephones at a cost of approximately $35,000 each to limit or prevent Soviet eavesdropping. According to David Burham of the *New York Times*, each telephone "would have a small computer that would transform the voice signals into a stream of coded digits." A computer on the receiving telephone would reconvert the signal to understandable voice. Only a few hundred such telephones are thought to be in use in the US Government at the present time. The problem arises from the fact that, according to the American Telephone and Telegraph Company, some 70 percent of US telephone conversations are transmitted by easily intercepted microwave or satellite signals.

The Soviet System has its Faults

Discussion of the defects as well as the strengths of US Intelligence is possible, of course, because that system is the servant rather than the master of a free society. Discussion of similar subjects in the Soviet Union would lead quickly to a prison cell, or worse, but that does not mean that the KGB and the GRU, the Soviet counterparts of the CIA and DIA, are any less free of defect. On the contrary, we have it on the word of no less an authority than the former Chief of the Soviet General Staff that the Korean airliner shot down by the Soviets in September 1983, over the Sea of Japan had overflown "the most important nuclear installation in the Soviet Union," Petropavlovsk on the Kamchatka Peninsula, before the elaborate Soviet Intelligence, command and control system could make up its mind what to do about it – and then it did the wrong thing.

There is still doubt that the airliner had been fully indentified by the time it was shot down, which prompts the conclusion that there was a monumental failure of Soviet Intelligence, bespeaking weaknesses that might eventually require revision of the world's estimates of Soviet vulnerabilities, particularly as concerns ability of manned bombers to penetrate Soviet airspace. Whether or not such an Intelligence failure did occur, it is plain that major faults in the command and control system manifested themselves. Without an efficient command and control system the best Intelligence in the world is useless.

From this and many other instances of Soviet difficulty in, or inability to, react efficiently in the face of fast-breaking events it can be concluded that for all its faults the US Intelligence system still has a major advantage. Upon the retention of that advantage may depend the peace of the world.

The United States Strategic Triad

The term "strategic forces" is an ambiguous one and trying to define it precisely can be a fruitless task. In any traditional strategic sense, confining the term to those intercontinental nuclear forces directed essentially toward the USSR, as is the tendency in the US, is an impoverishment of the term. This chapter deals with forces implied by the narrow sense of the term "stragetic nuclear forces" – those intercontinental offensive and defensive systems designed principally to cope with similar Soviet forces.

Following the categorization of the Defense Department's "Annual Report to the Congress", strategic nuclear forces encompass intercontinental ballistic missiles (ICBMs); submarine-launched ballistic missiles (SLBMs); long-range bombers armed with gravity bombs, short-range attack missiles, and air-launched cruise missiles; plus associated command, control, communications and intelligence (C^3I) systems. Due to the paucity of American bomber defenses, the absence of a ballistic missile defense, the general-purpose force nature of antisubmarine defense, and the very small and unorganized civil defense effort in the US, this section must of necessity focus on the strategic offensive forces.

Below: Start of the 12th Peacekeeper ICBM test flight on 21 May, 1986. The 10 unarmed Mk 21 re-entry vehicles successfully impacted the Kwajalein target area after a 30-minute flight.

The existing mix of US strategic offensive forces – the Minuteman, Titan II and Peacekeeper ICBMs, the Polaris and Poseidon SLBMs, and the FB-111, B-1B and B-52 strategic bombers – has become known as the Triad, a descriptive term that has come to connote prescriptively the complementarity or synergism of the three forces. The term and its rationale have become so entrenched that it is difficult to remember that the particular Triad forces were developed and their deployment begun before their complementarity was well appreciated. Nevertheless, the rationale for a force mix that presents an enemy with very different offensive and defensive problems and that dovetails individual strengths and weaknesses into a more capable whole is eminently persuasive.

Before moving to present and future US strategic forces and policies, it will be helpful to outline the development of American strategic nuclear forces and the changes in American thinking about those forces.

Prologue to a Strategic Force

While the United States had pioneered the development of atomic weapons, it did not in fact start to produce a stockpile until the late 1940s. "Atomic diplomacy" certainly did not exist without the atomic military means. A foreign policy of containment, formulated by 1947-48, lacked the military support and military strategy necessary to such a policy. A growing recognition within the United States

government that American military strength was seriously lacking was nurtured by the developing Cold War and Russia's acquisition of atomic weapons technology in 1949. Early in 1950, a National Security Council Report (NSC-68) summed up the situation, warned of broad-gauged Soviet military superiority and increasing threats to the West unless appropriate countermeasures were immediately taken, and recommended a crash program to build up America's nuclear and general-purpose forces. The attack on the Republic of Korea then served as the catalyst for rearmament.

In 1953, the new Eisenhower Administration inaugurated a broad economically oriented strategic program, the "New Look", which imposed severe budget constraints on the military, but at the same time selectively emphasized strategic air power, the development of a family of nuclear weapons and North American air defense.

The Korean War gave impetus to the development and production of the B-52, an eight-jet-engine heavy bomber; while it continues to be the bomber mainstay of the Triad today, this is gradually changing as more B-1Bs arrive "on the ramp". Some 15 B-1Bs became operational in late 1986 and deliveries are expected at the rate of four per month until 100 are in place in 1988. The B-52 was first flown in 1952 and was first delivered to SAC in 1955. Between 1955 and 1962, when the last B-52 was delivered, a total of more than 700 B-52s of various classifications and capabilities were produced.

The story of American strategic ballistic missiles is an interesting one, and clearly one where technology did not lead automatically to decisions on strategic forces; rather, technology encountered much resistance and was successfully turned into modern weapon systems only after the efforts of a few dedicated and determined people. One study of the American ICBM program summarizes it as "a long pattern of disbelief, neglect, and delay".

In 1947, US Air Force research long-range ballistic missiles were cancelled altogether and not resumed until after the start of the Korean War. By 1953, less than $2 million was spent on such research. During 1953-55, however, technological developments, evidence of a concerted Soviet rocket program, and – most particularly – the efforts of a few civilians changed neglect into a high priority development program.

The initial US ICBM programs, the Atlas and Titan, involved large liquid-fueled missiles. In 1955, however, a breakthrough in solid fuel technology led to the Air Force Minuteman ICBM and the Navy Polaris SLBM programs – more compact, solid-fuel missiles for deployment, respectively, in underground silos and submarines, which resulted in a missile force with much greater survivability against a surprise attack.

The shock produced in America by the full range flight test of a Soviet ICBM in August 1957, well before any US ICBM was ready, followed by the launches of the world's first man-made satellites, Sputnik in October and Sputnik II in November, caused further acceleration of the American missile programs.

Dr. William R. Van Cleave, Professor of International Relations, and Director of the Defense and Strategic Studies Program, University of Southern California.

Above: The B-52G is still a formidable weapon with the EVS nav/attack system, upgraded defenses and an underwing armament of AGM-86B cruise missiles, but is now in the twilight of its career.

Right: Half the US Navy's SSBNs now carry the Trident C-4, seen here in a December 1984 test launch off Florida. The eight Mk 4 MIRVs each have a CEP of about 500 yards (457m), but Mk 500 MaRVs may be retrofitted.

Minuteman I, with a 5,500nm range and somewhat less than 2,000 pounds throw-weight or payload, was flight tested in February 1961, and first became operational in December 1962. The first fully operational Minuteman squadron was assigned to SAC in February 1963. Minuteman II, a follow-on missile of somewhat longer range and slightly more payload, but with more accuracy, became operational in 1965.

The first SLBM nuclear-powered submarine, the USS *George Washington*, successfully launched a Polaris from underwater in July 1960, and became fully operational in 1961. Early boats were equipped with an interim 1,200nm missile (the A-1), until the 1,500nm A-2 and later the 2,500nm A-3, equipped with three warheads (not independently targetable), became standard.

Transitions to a Modern Force and New Doctrine

The Eisenhower strategic doctrine, initially based upon maintaining superiority in strategic nuclear forces, was changed to one of "sufficiency" by 1956-57. As Secretary of the Air Force Quarles expressed it, sufficiency

Above: Now almost gone from front-line service, the Titan II has 9-megaton W-53 warhead in a Mk 6 re-entry vehicle with a relatively poor CEP of 1,425 yards. This is a silo test launch from Vanbenburg.

depended, not necessarily upon being superior in forces or capabilities, but upon having the "forces required to accomplish the mission assigned".

In 1961, a new Administration and a new civilian team in the Department of Defense assumed office, persuaded that a change was in order away from Eisenhower's Sufficiency doctrine and the strategy of "Massive Retaliation". "Flexible Response", whereby the flexibility of both general-purpose and strategic nuclear forces was to be increased, was adopted as policy. At the same time, however, the "systems analysts" who came to dominate the Pentagon sought a more systematic and measurable approach to planning strategic forces, an analytical and quantifiable theory to determine as precisely as possible "How Much is Enough?" The evolution of American strategic thinking during the 1960s was the story of a contest between true Flexible Response, which tended to drive strategic force requirements upwards, and the analytical techniques and arms control corollaries of calculable force limitations, which depressed requirements.

From this contest, the term "Flexible

Response" was supplanted by the doctrine of "Assured Destruction" (AD) and the later concept of "Mutual Assured Destruction" (MAD). Originally only one of several analytical tests to aid judgment on the adequacy of forces, AD became the principal criterion, then the dominant strategic concept of the American defense community, and finally a philosophical base for theories of a mutual deterrence strategic stability, and strategic arms limitation. It became the necessary "conceptual framework for measuring the need and accuracy of our strategic forces".

Cost-effectiveness considerations along with the progressive development of American Assured Destruction thinking led to reductions in planned levels of Minuteman and Polaris early in the 1960s. ICBM levels were lowered to 1,000 Minuteman and 54 Titan II. Polaris levels were set at 41 boats with 656 missiles. By the mid-1960s the decision had been made to level off American strategic offensive forces at the levels then existing.

Evolution of American Doctrine: the 1960s, Superiority to Parity

In his famous Ann Arbor, Michigan, address in 1962, Secretary McNamara set forth the tenets of a Flexible Response Doctrine based upon counterforce and damage limiting. Military strategy, he said, "should be approached in much the same way that more

conventional military operations have been regarded in the past. That is to say, principal military objectives . . . should be the destruction of the enemy's military forces, not of its civilian population." Deterrence of nuclear war would be based upon the ability to limit damage in the event of war, which would be accomplished by US possession of the means to destroy an enemy's military capability by targeting restraint (*vis-à-vis* cities) on our own part, backed by the ability to escalate should the enemy do so.

Although biographers of McNamara generally agree that his thinking was moving away from this strategy by 1964-65, the Defense Reports of those years repeated the same theme: in addition to an Assured Destruction capability, American forces "should have the power to limit the destruction of our own cities and population to the maximum extent practicable . . . a damage-limiting strategy appears to be the most practical and effective course for us to follow." Moreover, contradicting later assertions that Pentagon studies did not support damage-limiting strategies, one Report stated directly: "In every pertinent

Right: A Minuteman II of the 44th Strategic Missile Wing in its silo at Ellsworth AFB, South Dakota. Current strength is 450, serving with nine squadrons of three SAC wings.

case we found that forces in excess of those needed simply to destroy Soviet cities would significantly reduce damage to the US and Western Europe." Assured Destruction and Damage Limiting were thus at this time the dual pillars of American strategic policy.

Change, however, came rapidly. More emphasis in public statements (and in target and force planning) came to be placed on Assured Destruction, now based upon the judgmental criterion of "unacceptable damage" measured in presumed fatalities and gross industrial destruction. Concurrently, Secretary McNamara began to disparage both damage limiting and countermilitary targeting. Flexible Response options gave way in emphasis to countercity AD.

From Assured Destruction grew the mutual deterrence concept of Mutual Assured Destruction (MAD). *Both* sides were to have an AD capability against the other, and – ideally – essentially no other strategic force capabilities. Neither should develop capabilities that would appear to call into question the other's AD capability; hence, offensive and defensive capabilities that might do so were to be avoided to the extent feasible. It was not merely that such capabilities were not achievable at prices the decision makers were willing to pay; they were to be avoided as incompatible with stability based upon MAD. MAD was as much an arms limitation concept as a strategic one. Thus, it was not so much that forces to counter the enemy's AD capability would upset mutual deterrence as that they would 'Fuel an arms race". As McNamara's Assistant Secretary of Defense expressed it, "any attempt on our part to reduce damage to our society would put pressure on the Soviets to strive for an off-setting improvement in their assured-destruction forces, and vice versa. ... This 'action-reaction' phenomenon is central to all strategic force planning as well as to any theory of an arms race." The corollary to this presumed "action-reaction" determinism was inaction-inaction. If the US were to raise from challenging a Soviet AD capability, the Soviets would be satisfied and would have no need to build up their forces further. Hence, a policy of self-restraint was adopted, and strategic force parity (later termed Sufficiency by the Nixon Administration) was substituted for the goal

of Superiority. American strategic nuclear force expenditure declined, from over $18 billion (in FY1974 dollars) at the start of the 1960s to less than one-half that by 1967-68.

Soviet strategic forces were growing during this period of time, but it seems clear that this growth was not the reason for the changes in American policy. The US intelligence community chronically underestimated the growth of that force and placed very modest AD objectives on the growth. In 1965, Secretary McNamara asserted that the "Soviets have decided that they have lost the quantitative race and they are not seeking to engage us in that contest . . . there is no indication that the

Below: Now out of service with the US Navy, the Polaris A-3 was the definitive version of this pioneering SLBM series and offered modest range and CEP with an adequate payload of three 200-kiloton multiple re-entry vehicles (MRVs).

Soviets are seeking to develop a strategic nuclear force as large as our own."

The change came, instead, from the progressive development of the concepts and beliefs noted above, a presumed disutility of strategic forces for anything save AD, and the goal of strategic stability (MAD) through arms limitations agreements that would be possible only when the Soviets were satisfied with their own AD capability.

Technological Developments
Technological progress and force modernization may be constrained by neglect, or by policy when it seems to clash with doctrinal preferences and arms control aspirations, but technology generally advances. The problem is to adapt policy and technology to one another. While these policies were evolving, technological progress was occurring in three notable areas that seemed incompatible with

those policies: ballistic missile guidance, which promised very good accuracies for ICBMs; multiple warheads, or reentry vehicles, for single missiles, each of which could be independently targeted (MIRV); and anti-ballistic missile (ABM) systems.

The MIRV (Multiple Independently Re-Targetable Vehicle) was originally a cost-effectiveness concept whereby expanded target coverage could be provided without increasing the size of the missile force. As evidence began to accumulate in the middle 1960s of a Soviet ABM program and air defense expansion, and in the later 1960s of a Soviet counterforce capability against American ICBM silos, two supplementary reasons for MIRV were added: to counter a Soviet ABM and to reduce the ABM capability of SAM (surface-to-air missile) air defenses; and to increase the capability of deterrent forces surviving any possible first strike. The quandary of MIRV and MAD was eased by deliberately avoiding effective hard target MIRVs (high yield, high accuracy), and designing them mostly to offset ABM and to increase soft target coverage.

In 1965, development of Poseidon – a new SLBM eventually to be equipped with some ten small, .04 MT warheads – was approved. The system seemed ideal for countering an ABM and targeting soft urban-industrial targets; it did not pose a threat to ICBM silos. MIRV was also adapted to an Air Force follow-on to Minuteman. Minuteman III (with about 2,200 pounds of throw-weight or payload capability) was designed to be equipped with three MIRV warheads, each of .17 MT. This system, with MIRV, was first tested in 1968, but neither it nor Poseidon would be deployed prior to the beginning of Strategic Arms Limitation Talks (SALT) in 1969. Deployment of the first Minuteman III was scheduled for summer 1970, and the first Poseidon-equipped SSBN was to be delivered in 1971. Hence, MIRV became a major SALT issue in the US. In the second session of SALT, in the spring of

Below: The re-entry of six unarmed Mk 12 RVs delivered by a pair of Minuteman III ICBMs to a point above Kwajalein atoll during a 1979 exercise graphically highlights the "footprint" of coverage achievable by such MIRVs.

1970, the US proposed an agreement banning MIRVs, which was rejected by the USSR, even though it would have also banned ABMs. The Soviet Union did not link the two systems in the US arms control sense.

ABM, even more than MIRV, was widely deemed inconsistent with MAD concepts and US SALT aspirations. American policy through the 1960s had been to continue ABM development but to forego deployment. Steady advances in the technology, however, combined with Soviet development, strained that policy. A reluctant decision to proceed with deployment was made in 1967, but the deployment was designed and rationalized to be consistent with a MAD relationship with the USSR. Initially, that meant casting the program in terms of a light area defense not heavy enough to cause Soviet concern about its AD capability.

Early in 1969, the Nixon Administration modified that plan. The new deployment plan, named Safeguard, emphasized the defense of Minuteman ICBM silos, whose future vulnerability was projected. Eventual expansion of the deployment to 12 ABM sites would be decided on an annual basis, depending upon progress in SALT and developments in Soviet counterforce capabilities. SALT agreements could still be reached to limit, or possibly ban, ABM deployment. (It might be noted that ABM defense of retaliatory forces would be logically consistent with MAD. Such a defense would not reduce an enemy's AD capability, but would only preserve one's own. In SALT, that defense might be reduced or obviated altogether if agreements reduced the projected threats to US ICBM forces. In this vein, it is noteworthy that the major Soviet initiative to stop US ABM deployment in SALT came *after* the area defense component of Safeguard was abandoned by the US in 1970, and ABM plans became restricted to defense of Minuteman. Coupled with Soviet disinterest in banning MIRV, this should have clearly revealed the Soviet strategic emphasis on counter-force rather than MAD.)

By the end of the 1960s, the focus of US strategic force attention was on SALT. The Soviet Union had roughly drawn equal with the US, at least in the central strategic forces to be the subject of SALT, and "parity" was established. United States SALT expectations

were high. While there were major studies of future US strategic force requirements and force modifications, they were SALT dominated and their recommendations were largely held in abeyance pending the outcome of SALT.

Early American expectations were not met. United States ABM deployment was limited by SALT to one ICBM site (since dismantled), but neither MIRV nor the continued growth and improvement of Soviet forces was constrained. The earlier US decisions to freeze numerical levels of the TRIAD and to improve the capabilities of the force qualitatively at only a modest, SALT-related pace, failed to induce the Soviets to freeze their own strategic force levels or to show any similar restraint. In retrospect it must be concluded that US restraint and the concept of MAD merely contributed to the opportunity for the Soviet Union first to achieve parity, then to gain superiority in major quantitative comparisons of strategic forces, and finally to convert the latter to a counter-force and war-fighting advantage.

A "New" American Strategic Doctrine
The Nixon Administrative had formalized a set of criteria that defined "Sufficiency" for American strategic forces. In addition to the Assured Destruction criterion, Crisis Stability (ie, avoiding major force vulnerabilities), equivalent destructive capability with the USSR, and defense against light attacks were to comprise Sufficiency. In concept, there began to be a move away from the previous emphasis and reliance on Assured Destruction. Presidential statements and Department of Defense Reports began to suggest new interest in more selective targeting and in escalation control, both to enhance deterrence and to hedge against its failure. In the early 1970s, after SALT had failed to dampen the Soviet build-up, a government study spearheaded by the Office of Secretary of Defense produced what might be regarded as a new doctrine of Sufficiency.

On the basis of this study, Secretary of Defense James R. Schlesinger first announced in a press conference on 10 January 1974, that there had taken place "a change in the strategies of the United States with regard to the hypothetical employment of central strategic

forces. A change in targeting strategy as it were."

Because of the enormous growth of Soviet strategic force capabilities, he said, "the range of circumstances in which an all-out strike against an opponent's cities can be contemplated has narrowed considerably and one wishes to have alternatives for the employment of strategic forces."

The FY1975 Department of Defense Report set forth what might be regarded as a new set of "sufficiency criteria", describing as the "principal features that we propose to maintain and improve our strategic posture" the following:

"... a capability sufficiently large, diversified, and survivable so that it will provide us at all times with high confidence of riding out even a massive surprise attack and of penetrating enemy defenses, and with the ability to withhold an assured destruction reserve for an extended period of time.

"... employment of the strategic forces in a controlled, selective, and restrained fashion".

AD was not to be measured arbitrarily in terms of population fatalities, but rather in terms of objectives of greater political-military relevance to a war and its aftermath (hence, linking deterrence to political postwar objectives and relationships); principally, reduction of the enemy's post-attack political-economic recovery capability and postwar political-military power.

Short of such major exchanges, however, the US goal was again to limit damage to the extent feasible, through targeting restraint and discriminate targeting, multiple options to fit the situation, and targeting of military forces, soft and hard.

American strategic forces, however, were only partly affected by this explicit change in planning. On the one hand, steps were taken to improve the targeting and ability to retarget the Minuteman force and plans were made to improve Minuteman accuracy and to install a more powerful warhead on Minuteman III (the Mark 12-A). In addition, the development of the Trident I (C-4), which would have more flexibility than the basically soft-point target Poseidon, was carried forth. On the other hand, force planning remained constrained both by existing SALT-I agreements and the then-anticipated SALT-II limitations.

At the same time, however, a new attitude toward SALT was reluctantly developing, which, along with the unprecedented and still increasing pace of Soviet strategic programs, precipitated new interest in strategic force programs. The United States had continued to exercise restraint, even in the face of a rapidly developing Soviet threat, in the hope that SALT agreements would ease strategic stability. SALT-II, however, was making no progress toward such limitations. Instead, it became increasingly clear that an acutely dangerous strategic imbalance would occur unless the US took major steps to prevent it. SALT agreements, clearly, could not themselves do that.

Funds were provided for force programs scheduled to ease the problems that the United States would otherwise face by the early to middle 1980s: new, more capable ICBM (MX), redeployed to reduce its vulnerability; Trident submarines and missiles to augment the FBM force; the B-1 bomber to replace or supplement the aging B-52; and a family of cruise missiles suitable for launch from a variety of platforms.

In 1977, however, a new Administration, more sanguine about SALT and skeptical about SNF programs, decided upon a different approach. It immediately cut nearly $3 billion from the proposed FY1978 Defense budget, and reduced, delayed or – as in the notable case

of the B-1 bomber – cancelled major strategic force programs. At the same time, it enthusiastically placed the highest priority on a SALT-II agreement.

Current and Future Doctrine and Forces

The rethinking of American strategic doctrine continued under the Carter Administration. Neither President Carter nor Secretary of Defense Harold Brown seemed closely in tune with the concepts and objectives enunciated in 1974. Both seemed personally closer to the philosophy of Mutual Assured Destruction and minimum deterrence. However, the administration commissioned a major study of strategic deterrence and US objectives should deterrence fail, of Soviet doctrine and capabilities, and of the rationale underlying existing American doctrine. Consuming nearly two years, the study reaffirmed the policy and requirements announced in 1974. Accordingly, the FY1980 Defense Report of Secretary Brown announced a "Countervailing Strategy" policy, based upon the objectives set forth in 1974.

The FY1980 Defense Report stated that "we must insist on essential equivalence with the Soviet Union", and to fulfil the aims of a "Countervailing Strategy", US forces must be capable of surviving even a well-executed surprise attack and then be able to "penetrate enemy defenses and destroy a comprehensive set of targets in the USSR with whatever

Above: Seen in the form of the first producton article, the B-1B offers much improved penetration and weapons capability compared with the B-52. But there are problems with fuel leaks.

timing, and degree of deliberation and control, proves desirable, if necessary, inflict high levels of damage on the Soviet society, particularly those elements the Soviet leadership values – regardless of the measures the Soviets might take to limit the damage, and still retain a reserve capability." The capability to attack military targets selectively and to control escalation in the event that deterrence should fail was also emphasized. During 1980, this was confirmed as official national policy with the issuance of Presidential Directive 59 (PD-59).

That major threats to American strategic forces were rapidly developing was openly acknowledged. Secretary Brown warned in the FY1980 Report that "it would be a mistake to underestimate the problems created by the military buildup of the Soviet Union", and that "it may be too late if we wait much longer" to react. Furthermore, he reported: "Our most serious concerns – which we need to act now to meet – are about the period of the early-to-mid 1980s." By that time it was acknowledged that essentially all comparisons of strategic force capabilities would favor the Soviet Union, that American ICBMs would have questionable

survivability, that the bomber force would be vulnerable to a surprise attack (only about 25 percent were kept on ground alert), and that Soviet active and passive defenses could greatly mitigate the effectiveness of surviving retaliatory forces. The Chairman of the Joint Chiefs of Staff termed this an "acutely dangerous imbalance" in his 1979 report to Congress.

It was this situation in general, and the vulnerability of land-based deterrent forces in particular, that gave rise to the term "Window of Vulnerability" during the 1980 Presidential campaign.

The Carter Administration's SNF modernization program was a mixed one, heavily influenced by the pursuit of SALT-II. Strategic force spending was held to about 8 percent of the defense budget. The program to acquire the B-1 bomber, with its improved survivability (through faster getaway and nuclear hardening) and better penetrability of Soviet air defenses, was cancelled. Emphasis was changed to air-launched cruise missiles to be carried by the aging B-52 force. Research, however, was continued on advanced technology (or "stealth") aircraft; this technology results in weapon systems with low radar cross-sections that can negate air defenses.

For the submarine force, Carter continued Ford's plans to produce a larger, more advanced SSBN, the Trident, but deferred the scheduled IOC of the first boat from 1979 to 1981. A new, longer-range SLBM, the Trident I (or C-4), would be retrofitted into some of the existing Poseidon submarines and then be carried by the first Trident boats. R&D was authorized for the advanced Trident II (D-5) SLBM, which would add new targeting flexibility to the SLBM force, but there was no commitment to production. The D-5, expected to be deployed at the end of the 1980s, will be the first SLBM capable of retaliating effectively against Soviet hardened targets.

The centerpiece of the Carter SNF program was the MX ICBM, a missile much larger (about 2½ times heavier) and more capable than the Minuteman III, to be equipped with 10 MIRVs having better hard-target capability. Since such a missile by itself, vulnerably employed, might be more of a tempting

target than an effective weapon, plans were made to base it in a multiple protective shelter (MPS) mode. In this system, each of the 200 planned MX missiles would be shuttled among 23 shelters so that any Soviet attack would need to destroy all 23 shelters simultaneously in order to destroy one missile. (In effect, this converted an unfavorable targeting ratio – 2 Soviet warheads for 10 US – to a more favorable, and hence more stable, ratio – 23 to 46 Soviet warheads, depending upon the hardening of the shelters, for 10 US). An option would also be retained to add an ABM defense to the system as necessary.

The "window of vulnerability" problem, however, was that the existing US ICBM force would be vulnerable to a fraction of available Soviet ICBM warheads by the beginning of the 1980s, while the Carter system would not be fully deployed until the end of the decade. In addition, given the Carter SNF program, Soviet strategic nuclear superiority would continue to grow at least through the 1980s. The question was: How could the United States expect to pass safely through a decade of vulnerability and inferiority?

Mr Reagan, both as candidate and as President, acknowledged the severity of these problems and emphasized the need to move rapidly to reinvigorate US SNF. Prior to his election, Mr Reagan declared that "our nuclear forces must be made survivable as rapidly as possible to close the window of vulnerability before it opens any wider".

In 1981, President Reagan launched a five-part modernization program to improve US forces in all three legs of the strategic Triad. Its fundamental purpose was to revitalize those forces and reverse the relative decline in US capabilities. The ultimate goal, of course, was to ensure a stable deterrent and create, in the administration's view, a favorable atmosphere for arms reductions. As late as mid-1986, the White House was urging the US Congress to maintain the considerable momentum that had been built behind the President's program. Its five elements consisted of:

Bombers/Cruise Missiles. The 1981 program called for modernizing existing forces with two

Above: The US Navy's prime SSBN bases are at Charleston in South Carolina, Kings Bay in Georgia and Bangor in Washington, all capable of re-arming boats with the current SLBM mainstay, the Trident C-4.

bombers – the B-1B and the Advanced Technology ("stealth") Bomber. The B-1B will initially be fielded as penetrating bombers armed with short-range attack missiles and gravity weapons, with B-52s continuing to be transferred to a standoff role. Concurrently, more than 1,500 air-launched cruise missiles have been deployed on B-52Gs and on some B-52H models. An advanced cruise missile – a stealthy, long range, highly accurate missile that will be carried on B-1B and B-52 bombers – is expected to be operational in the late 1980s. The advanced technology bomber (ATB) also employs low observable technology and is now in development. The bomber is expected to become operational in the early 1990s.

Trident Submarine/D-5 SLBM. An exceptionally quiet ballistic missile submarine, the Trident is designed to be part of the strategic Triad into the 21st Century. There are seven Tridents now in commission and the eighth began sea trials in May 1986. The ninth and all subsequent Tridents (a request for a 14th is in the Navy's FY87 budget) will carry the larger and more capable Trident II D-5 sea-launched ballistic missile. Earlier-generation C-4 SLBMs now on the first eight Tridents will ultimately be replaced with D-5s. The Trident II D-5 missile is now in full-scale development and will be deployed at the end of the 1980s in two versions, carrying either the Mk 4 reentry vehicle currently on the C-4, or the higher yield Mk 5 reentry vehicle, which is in concurrent development with the D-5.

Intercontinental Ballistic Missiles. A survivable, flexible ICBM force with hard-target capability is essential to US strategic doctrine. A presidential panel chaired by Lieutenant General Brent Scowcroft (subsequently known as the Scowcroft Commission) recommended in 1983 that 100 Peacekeeper (formerly MX) missiles be deployed as quickly as possible. The Congress agreed – at least in part – and approved 50 for deployment. Its

The Triad

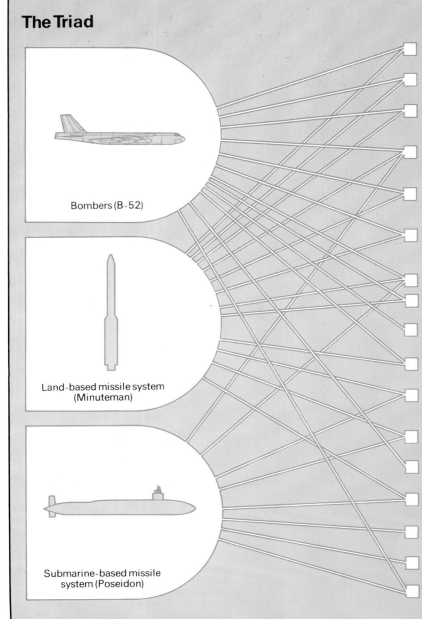

Bombers (B-52)

Land-based missile system (Minuteman)

Submarine-based missile system (Poseidon)

Capabilities of the Triad

RANGE – Up to 5500 nmi to allow full target coverage from any of several "safe" basing positions

PAYLOAD – Sufficient yield and quantities to allow conservative targeting and compensation for system errors

ACCURACY – Sufficient accuracy in conjunction with weapon yield to allow targeting of soft or hard targets with acceptable probability of destruction

PENETRATION – Capability to penetrate enemy strategic defense systems through inherent adaptability to advanced penetration techniques

FLEXIBILITY – Instantaneous capability to retarget or reallocate weapons with a choice of many engagement options and modes

COMMUNICATIONS – Constant, two-way, high-speed, reliable secure communications between command levels and weapon system

RELIABILITY – Extremely low failure rate

SECURITY – Ability to maintain constant surveillance over the physical security of the weapon

RECALL – Capability to recall, recover and reuse weapon at any point in conflict until it reaches the target area

AVAILABILITY – Capability to maintain a high state of operational alert status for the force

SURVIVABILITY – Provides characteristics such that the enemy cannot destroy the weapon system and thus nullify its deterrent capability

POST-ATTACK LIFE – Capability to operate in a post-attack mode for an extended time; i.e., many weeks to several months

ASSESSMENT – Capability to provide instantaneous assessment of weapon success or failure to accomplish its intended mission.

REACTION TIME – Capability to complete weapon mission within seconds of the time an engagement decision is made

COLLATERAL DAMAGE – Capability to limit damage to U.S. cities and population should an enemy first strike occur

ARMS CONTROL – Capability to adapt to any arms control agreement which might be desirable and negotiable

CRISIS MANAGEMENT – Capability to keep a low level of conflict or limited nuclear engagement from escalating into an all-out engagement

---

flight test program was successful and the missile was expected to achieve IOC in Minuteman silos in December 1986 at F. E. Warren Air Force Base, Wyoming.

The Scowcroft Commission also recommended development of a new, small, mobile ICBM, which has been dubbed "Midgetman" by the press. The small ICBM was ready for full-scale engineering development in late 1986; questions had arisen on whether it should have MIRV capability.

Command, Control, Communications and Intelligence. A whole series of programs is embraced in this arena, including the Pave Paws phased-array radar program (with two sites operational and an additional two slated to become operational in 1987) that will provide warning and assessment of any attacks from SLBMs, and the Ballistic Missile Early Warning System (BMEWS), designed to provide the same capability against ICBMs. Unlike Pave Paws, which is designed to warn of an attack on the continental United States, BMEWS provides early protection and warning to the North American continent, Europe and the United Kingdom. These radars are

Right: High hopes are entertained for the proposed "Midgetman", a light ICBM intended for basing in hardened vehicles designed to travel over large semi-desert regions to prevent counter-force attacks.

being upgraded first in Thule, Greenland (1987), followed by Clear, Alaska, and Fylingdales, UK.

Other C³I efforts are being directed at satellite and other communications systems – the most important of which is likely to be the MILSTAR Satellite Communications System. This system, which has been described as "revolutionary", is expected to achieve full operational capability in the 1990s. It will permit a deployed crisis reaction force ashore in some remote part of the globe to communicate securely to a senior commander embarked offshore, or the National Command Authorities. It will also be deployed on the B-1B, thus permitting the same capability anywhere in the world.

Strategic Defense Initiative
In a televised address on 23 March 1983, President Reagan announced a truly innovative aspect of SNF modernization, a commitment to research and hopefully develop over the long term effective defenses against ballistic missiles. The President announced that new technologies offered the potential for effective defenses against ballistic missiles, and he urged that US strategy be based on saving rather than avenging lives.

The Strategic Defense Initiative promptly became dubbed "Star Wars" by a largely hostile press. Although advanced applications of the SDI would undoubtedly utilize space systems, the President's speech did not pre-judge the matter but included any means of ballistic missile defense, ground-based or space-based, terminal or mid-course, near or long term. The President's hope was eventually to provide an effective national defense, but nearer term goals included the possibility of a defense of vulnerable land-based deterrent forces.

Although the Soviets have consistently emphasized the importance of a variety of defensive systems, and by 1985 had developed the basis for a rapidly deployable land-based ABM system, defensive systems had long been a missing element in US SNF plans – largely because of the conceptual influence of "Assured Destruction". Defensive systems, it could be argued, were, however, necessary to any strategic doctrine serious about escalation control and damage limiting (as was official US strategic doctrine); and, more modestly, could contribute to strategic stability by improving the survivability of deterrent forces. Defensive systems, could thus provide varying benefits, depending upon degree and effectiveness of coverage, for deterrence and for reducing damage in the event that deterrence failed.

The US SDI program is not a commitment to

Below: Vast effort is now being expended on SDI research. Typical is this Hughes/US Navy laser beam director, designed to track a target aircraft and focus the attack by High Energy Chemical Laser.

deploy ballistic missile defenses. As Secretary of Defense Caspar W. Weinberger emphasized in the 1986 Annual Report to the Congress, SDI "was established as a research program to investigate the feasibility of advanced defensive technologies to provide a better basis for deterring aggression, strengthening stability, and increasing the security of the United States and our allies. It also seeks to reduce and, if possible, eliminate the threat posed by ballistic missiles."

Were one to rely solely on the media, one might believe that, with these programs, the US was embarked on a major SNF buildup or "arms race". In fact, the programs are modest, and the real question is whether, in view of the enormous disparity of effort between the US and the USSR, they are adequate.

Since the essence of US strategic policy is deterrence, it is essential that *surviving* forces – ie, those that can endure enemy attacks – be capable of accomplishing the strategic missions set for them. The Reagan Administration has affirmed its commitment to the strategic doctrine and objectives that have evolved since the early 1970s, which the Carter Administration grouped under the terms "Countervailing Strategy" and "Essential Equivalence". This requires a diversified and complementary strategic force capable of surviving "well-executed surprise attacks", and fulfilling a range of missions, including flexible targeting and escalation control. In addition, in both perception and reality, it should equal the strategic force capabilities of the USSR.

It has been popular in Western media to portray the strategic policy and doctrine of the Reagan Administration as a sharp break from what had gone before, with a new emphasis on "nuclear war-fighting". Nothing could be further from the truth. The Reagan strategic doctrine is merely a continuation of what has existed officially for over 10 years. As Secretary of Defense Weinberger accurately emphasized, the Reagan Administration's policy of "seeking to enhance deterrence and to limit the level of destruction by having flexible and enduring forces is not new. It has been squarely in the mainstream of American strategic thinking for over two decades." Not only would such capability enhance deterrence, but if deterrence fails, "the dividends of a viable war-fighting defense are unquestionable." Under President Carter, Secretary of Defense Harold Brown had emphasized the same theme, rejecting any distinction between a "deterrence-only" strategy and one based on a "war-fighting capability". In 1980, he said, "There is no contradiction between this attention to militarily effective targeting ... and our primary and overriding policy of deterrence."

Reflecting the continued shift away from Assured Destruction, the FY1984 Department of Defense Annual Report to Congress stated: "We need to be able to use force responsibly and discriminately, in a manner appropriate to the nature of a nuclear attack." The threat to destroy cities and civilians in retaliation "is neither moral nor prudent. The Reagan Administration's policy is that under no circumstances may such weapons be used deliberately for the purpose of destroying populations."

The attempt to provide offensive forces capable of selective targeting of enemy military forces and the SDI are manifestations of that doctrine. The real question – one certain to be at the core of continuing debate – is whether US SNF capabilities and programs are sufficient to support such a doctrine.

Arms Control
In March 1985 the United States and the Soviet Union began simultaneous arms control talks addressed to three types of nuclear

War in space

The diagram shows how war in space may proceed. At the outset each side tries to blind the other by hitting early-warning and communications satellites. Air-launched ASATs (1) and co-oribtal ASATs (2) may be used for this purpose. Land-based missile launchers (3) are accompanied by missiles from submarines (4). Early-warning satellites (5) monitor these and tracking data is relayed via communications satellites (6) to ground control (7). Engagement of the missile starts as soon as possible. A submarine-launched, nuclear-pumped X-ray laser (8) and orbiting laser battle stations (9) start to destroy the attacking missiles. Surviving missiles dispense their warheads and decoys (10). A ground-based laser (11) engages the warheads through orbiting mirrors (12). Electromagnetic rail-guns (13) and satellites armed with small rocket interceptors (14) also attack surviving warheads. Remaining warheads are tracked by airborne (15) and ground-based (16) sensors. Ground-based interceptors (17) are launched to destroy warheads in various ways. Finally, as warheads approach their targets, they encounter terminal "swarmjet" defenses (18). Each side also tries to disrupt the other's space defenses using mines (19) and other ASAT weaponry (20).

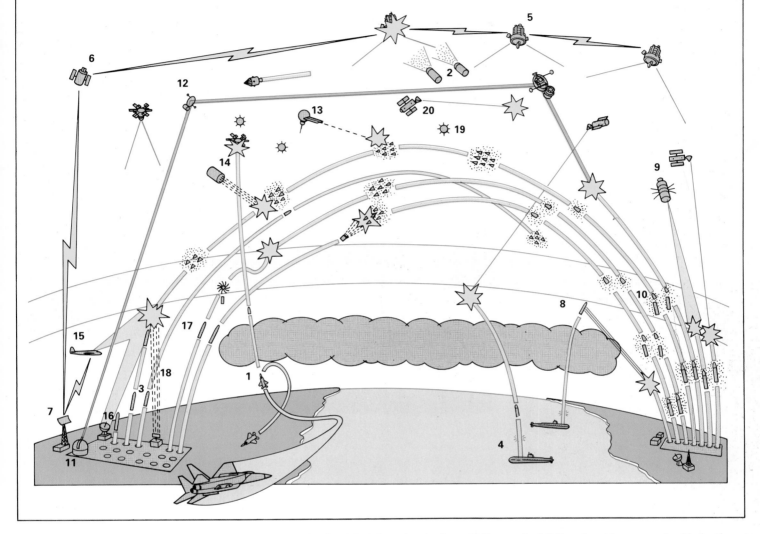

arms: theater nuclear forces, strategic offensive forces, and strategic defensive forces. This marked a resumption of the arms control negotiations that had ended more than a year previously with the walk-out of the Soviet Union (in response to the first deployment in Europe of NATO long-range theater forces, after the Soviets had deployed nearly 400 SS-20 launchers with refire missiles and more than 2,000 warheads!).

In 1981, the Reagan Administration, conscious of the failed record of arms control and the failure of Carter's SALT II agreement, approached strategic arms control cautiously. It vowed that there would no longer be agreements for the sake of agreement – rather, agreements must be militarily meaningful and promote stability. It also sought meaningful units of limitation, and actual reductions not only in weapons but in their destructive potential. Up to then, SALT had only limited "launchers" and had placed no limits whatsoever on numbers of missiles or warheads. To emphasize the new approach, the Administration renamed SALT as START, or Strategic Arms Reduction Talks. The US position from the beginning and through the spring of 1983 was based on substantial reductions in both the number of deployed strategic ballistic missiles and missile warheads. When the Soviets showed absolutely no interest in this

approach, the Administration in June 1983 modified its approach and indicated a willingness to address any number of missile limitations of interest to the Soviet Union, while retaining the goal of deep reductions. Despite this flexibility, no progress had been made by the time of the Soviet walk-out.

Soviet arms control intransigence was underscored by two major developments: continued expansion of Soviet strategic force programs across the board, and, at the same time, expanding Soviet violation of existing arms control agreements. In accordance with a Congressional mandate, President Reagan released in January 1984 an in-depth analysis of seven specific examples of Soviet arms control non-compliance. This unprecedented report was of profound significance. For the first time, an American Administration officially and openly acknowledged that the Soviet Union is in violation of the very arms control agreements that had been regarded by many as essential to security. During 1984, a two-year study by the President's General Advisory Committee on Arms Control, which cited 17 Soviet violations of existing agreements and concluded that a systematic pattern of violation existed, was released to Congress. And on 1 February 1985, the President released an up-dated report to Congress. This report reaffirmed the earlier one, on the basis

of additional evidence, and added other specific examples of violations.

It seems clear that Soviet non-compliance, when coupled with Soviet strategic force activities, reveals a fundamentally different approach to strategic arms and to arms control than that of the United States. This approach clearly calls into serious question the security benefits that might be expected from arms control. Nonetheless, and despite Soviet violations, the Reagan Administration has assigned high priority to arms control negotiations.

The Reagan administration's strategy for reducing and controlling arms is quite different from that of its predecessors. Based on the premise that the US should learn from the experience of Soviet violations of past treaties, it emphasizes four points: protecting and defending vital US interests by reducing the risk of nuclear war to the lowest possible level; treating arms reductions as a component of larger national security policy; negotiating agreements that reduce arms instead of legitimizing further increases in their numbers; adopting initiatives independently (without Soviet concurrence or agreement) that can be taken to reduce the risks that nuclear weapons will ever be used through accident, miscalculation or failure of communications.

The United States Army

With some 781,000 personnel, the regular US Army constitutes the principal land fighting element of the US armed forces. United States military involvement in Vietnam (circa 1965-73) provided combat experience for a professional generation of officers and NCOs. This experience was, however, obtained at a price. National focus on the Vietnam struggle inhibited research and development of weapons and support systems for more conventional battle in different geographical environments. Similarly, Army organizational development suffered a "decade of neglect". Subsequent to the Vietnam War, Army modernization was low on the list of priorities, thereby slowing the transition from the Southeast Asian orientation to a force capable of employment on a global scale.

Geopolitical factors pose some considerations which affect Army structure and doctrinal development. The most prominent of these is the problem of projecting military power abroad. A question which influences Army planners is how to structure forces for possible employment anywhere in the world when the various areas and different types of employment each call for a fundamentally different force.

The need to have the capability to project military power across the world's major oceans influences US defense planners in significant ways. First is the need for air and sea forces capable of moving and sustaining Army units as well as carrying out combat functions in their own elements. As a result the Army is consistently allocated about 25 percent of the military budget whereas the Navy and Air Force each draw over 30 percent.

Another factor arising from the need for power projection which influences armed service planners is interservice cooperation. The necessity for unified effort involving Army, Navy and Air Force elements has prompted development of a Joint Staff system and an accompanying philosophy of cooperation. As a result, US military services have unusually close working relationships which are routinely exercised. The US Army, as the major land fighting element which is ever-sensitive to the logistics of overseas operations, plays a leading role in the joint service arena.

It is evident that US Army planners of the 1980s face several problems which go beyond the budget and manpower constraints inherent in democracies – problems which arise from America's worldwide defense commitments. The US Army has to be prepared to operate in widely varying geographical and climatic conditions as well as at different levels of conflict intensity. It has to be ready to fight on a relatively unsophisticated battlefield as well as against numerous, highly mechanized, technologically sophisticated forces typified by those of the Warsaw Pact. Additionally, activities, other than conventional combat, which are carried out in support of national interests at the lower end of the conflict spectrum place demands upon the Army and army personnel that are fundamentally different from those of traditional armed conflict.

Against this galaxy of needs, US assessments of possible military threats in the 1980s led the Army's leadership to several conclu-

sions. One was that, given the numerical and technological realities, US forces could not win relying primarily on attrition and a tactical doctrine focused on defense. A related conclusion was that, while the Army would have to be organized and equipped to win on the conventional battlefield, it would also have to be prepared to respond to enemy-initiated use of chemical or nuclear weapons. The third conclusion was that the needs (force structure, equipment, training) of Low Intensity Conflict (LIC) were not always compatible with the needs of the forces designed for conventional combat.

These conclusions prompted two efforts which are having profound effects on the US Army today. One is a new operational doctrine, which has been labeled the Airland Battle, along with organizational changes of the field forces (Corps, Divisions and divisional units) to accommodate the new doctrine and the new weapon systems scheduled for distribution over the next decade. The second effort focuses on the lower end of the conflict spectrum, (ie, organizing, equipping and training army personnel to perform the variety of tasks associated with Low Intensity Conflict).

High- and Mid-Intensity Conflict: US Army Operational Doctrine

The principles of US Army doctrine, and therefore the shape and form of the ground forces are heavily influenced by economics, existing attitudes of the American people, and the perceived potential threat. US and NATO strategists envision the most powerful threat, although a less probable threat, as coming from the Soviet Union or the Warsaw Pact, and being principally directed against Western Europe. Therefore, US ground forces

Above: Advanced technology or not, it is ultimately the soldier who occupies the ground that determines the outcome of any war, and in this the US infantry is becoming increasingly skilled.

are structured, and doctrine is developed, to address a potential war in Europe. In an attack by the Warsaw Pact with little or no early warning, the Pact would enjoy a quantitative advantage in divisions, tanks, artillery and aircraft. To counter this numerical advantage, the United States has developed qualitatively superior equipment, and an operational doctrine that is designed to defeat an attacking numerically superior enemy. Airland Battle doctrine calls for synchronization of all weapons and logistics systems in support of the commander's concept of the battle. US tanks, infantry, artillery, attack helicopters and close air support by high performance aircraft as well as logistics systems are mutually supporting and focused on the organizational mission.

The US Army's operational doctrine, as promulgated in 1976, called for countering the enemy – ie, responding to the enemy's initiatives – an essentially defensive orientation. The current doctrine, which was officially approved in 1982, might best be summarized as follows: to secure the initiative and exercise it aggressively to defeat the opposing forces. This new and more aggressive style is having far-reaching effects on Army training and organization. It calls, for instance, for greater use of maneuver and a greater recognition of human factors as elements of battle. As much an attitudinal change as a physical one, there are four tenets derived from Airland Battle Doctrine.

Lt. Col. Donald B. Vought, US Army (Retd.), former specialist instructor, US Army Command and General Staff College, Fort Leavenworth, Kansas,
and
Lt. Col. David C. Vasile, instructor, Department of Joint and Combined Operations, US Army Command and General Staff College.

The first is *initiative* – to gain the ability to act and thereby cause the enemy to react to US forces rather than the reverse. Inevitably gaining and retaining the initiative will entail risks wherein the commander's judgment becomes the final determinant of where he can afford weakness in order to increase strength at the critical point(s).

Another tenet is *depth* – a three dimensional consideration. Battlefield depth is time, resources and distance. These elements in combination provide momentum in the attack and elasticity in the defense. US commanders are expected to use their resources to gain depth for themselves while denying depth to their opponent. To do this, they will fight the "deep battle" (ie, the battle against enemy uncommitted, or follow-on, forces). By delaying, disrupting and/or destroying the enemy's second echelon forces, the opponent is deprived of their use, thereby isolating his committed forces which are then destroyed in close-in battle.

The third tenet is *agility* – acting faster than the enemy. This involves not only the mental flexibility to analyze, decide and plan in the face of constantly changing circumstances, but to do so more rapidly than your opponent.

Equipment and information systems which allow the commander to know about critical events as they occur are needed to support agility, as are organizational procedures which permit the rapid tailoring of forces with the proper mix of personnel and equipment to capitalize on opportunities.

Synchronization is defined as an all-pervading unity of effort. Implicit in the other tenets, synchronization goes beyond the mere coordination of diverse actions; it is considered to apply in joint service and allied operations as well as at lower levels. Fundamental to synchronization is awareness of the higher commanders' intentions so that all levels and activities involved are in pursuit of the same goals.

Operationally, current doctrine calls for a tripartite view of the contemporary battlefield. While inextricably interrelated, the three concurrent battles are labeled Deep Battle, Close-In Battle, and Rear Battle. Not only are the three dependent on each other and therefore coequal, but planning must also take into account conventional, nuclear, and chemical environments. Deep Battle is the aspect which raises the most questions. Essentially, it involves disrupting, delaying or

destroying second and succeeding echelons of enemy forces to prevent them from influencing the close-in battle. The tactic is particularly important because successful application prevents the enemy from massing at the critical point and time.

The term "window of opportunity" has been applied to operation of Deep Battle techniques. The commander determines at what point in time he needs particular enemy units isolated or capabilities reduced to win the close-in battle. This then becomes the window of opportunity toward which Deep Battle efforts are directed. While conceptually simple, the demands on planning, target acquisition and attack resources are inordinate. Valuable targets in the Deep Battle are not always the same as those for the close-in battle. Bridges, defiles or bridging equipment may constitute "higher payoff" targets than maneuver units when the purpose is to prevent the enemy's second echelon from joining the close-in battle.

Deep Battle is fought at the brigade, division, and corps levels with each level operating in a different context (ie, concerned with different size enemy units and using different weaponry for their attack). The corps, however, is considered the key for Deep Battle planning

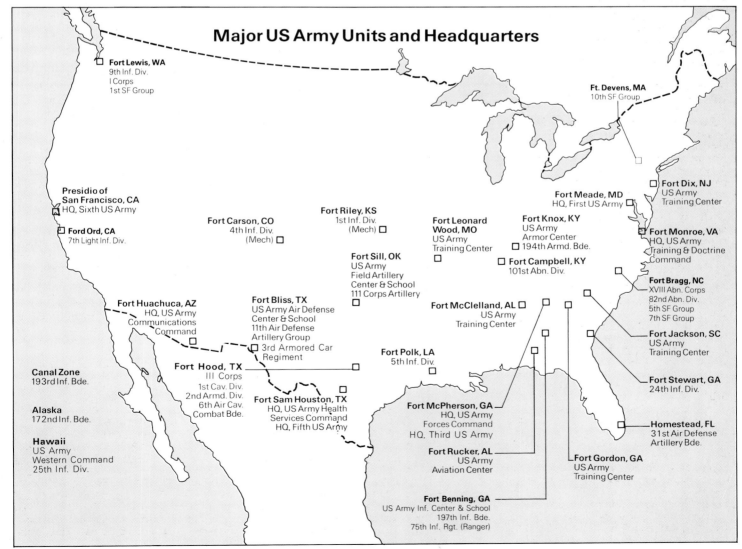

and operations. Corps is the focal point for intelligence and target acquisition information from national and allied sources as well as for joint planning with the Air Force for employment of tactical aircraft.

Offensive Operations

Fundamental to the US Army's offensive operations are five characteristics – concentration, surprise, speed, flexibility and audacity. Concentration to achieve local superiority followed by rapid dispersion to disrupt the enemy defensive efforts involves logistics as well as maneuver planning and execution. The definition of surprise has been expanded somewhat to include avoiding enemy strength and attacking his weaknesses. Speed includes any and all actions which promote the enemy's confusion as well as contributing to friendly maneuver. Flexibility in an environment where forces may cover 30 or more miles (48 or more km) a day, calls for the ability to exploit opportunities as they arise. Audacity recognizes risk but rejects tactical gamble.

Types of offensive operations describe the purpose rather than a method and have not changed from earlier listings; movement to contact – hasty attack – deliberate attack – exploitation – pursuit.

Movement to contact is intended to develop the situation while maintaining the commander's freedom of action. Organization for a movement to contact calls for a covering force

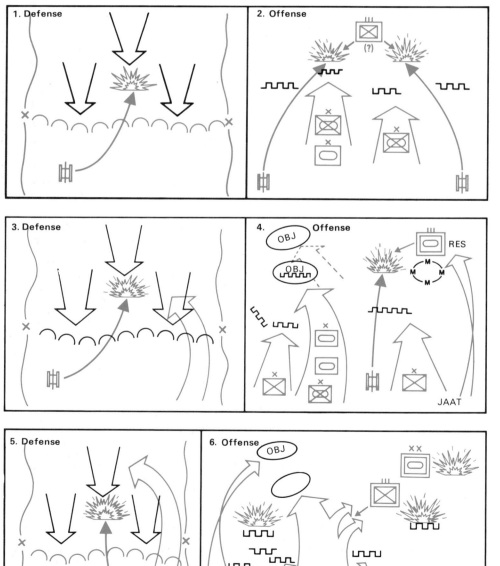

1–2: DELAY OF FORCES TO PREVENT REINFORCEMENT

The first form of depth attack is used both when in defense (1) and in attack (2). The aim is to disrupt the enemy forces in depth, particularly the second echelon, to delay (or even prevent) their arrival in the battle area. This enables the enemy forces in contact to be isolated and then defeated in detail. Deception, offensive electronic warfare, artillery fire, counter-battery fire and air interdiction will all be used in this form of deep battle. The commander must decide when he needs particular enemy units isolated in this way, and this is the window of opportunity towards which all efforts are directed.

3–4: DELAY IN ENEMY FORCES TO ALLOW MANEUVER COMPLETION

The second concept also involves attacking the enemy deep forces with fire. Its aim, however, is not so much to prevent the reinforcement of committed forces, as in (1) and (2) above, but rather to prevent them from interfering with own forces' attacks or counterattacks against the flanks or rear of enemy close-battle forces. Valuable targets in the deep battle may be different from those in the close-in battle; for example, bridges may be higher value targets than tactical units when the aim is to prevent the arrival and deployment of the second echelon.

5–6: DECISIVE DEEP ATTACK

The third form of tactical operation in this concept is both more complex and more difficult to achieve. It involves the engagement of the enemy follow-on echelon with both firepower and maneuver forces at the same time as the close-in battle continues. This is designed to stop the enemy from massing, to deprive him of momentum, and, most important of all, to destroy his force in its entirety. This will require the use of every combat and support element in close harmony. It will also require very close coordination between Army air and ground maneuver forces, artillery, electronic warfare, and Air Force battlefield interdiction.

Left: **Tactical mobility is a cornerstone of the US Army's offensive and defensive thinking, and the UH-60A Black Hawk is thus a potent asset, especially when gunships such as the AH-1 (background on the right) can be provided for support.**

of highly mobile units to find the enemy and provide time for the main body to deploy. An "advance guard" is provided to prevent light enemy resistance from delaying the main body and to facilitate movement by obstacle removal or bridge repair. The "main body" moves on multiple routes in the form of combined arms teams with their logistical support or as "pure" units which are prepared for cross attachment and rapid deployment. Ground units serving as "flank" and "rear guards" are detached from the main body to increase security during movement.

Hasty attacks are called for as a result of a meeting engagement or a successful defense. Speed in concentrating forces and surprise compensate for the lack of thorough preparation. A well-organized defense usually requires a *deliberate attack* involving the full range of weaponry and techniques.

Exploitation and *pursuit* follow successful attacks. Commanders exploit a successful attack by aggressively moving to disrupt enemy defenses after a penetration has been made. Pursuit of a withdrawing enemy calls for the commander to maintain pressure, thus

preventing the enemy from organizing a delaying action.

Defensive Operations

As with the offense, the changes in defense called for in the 1982 Operations Manual are more spirit and operational style than mechanical or definitional. The defense is considered more a matter of purpose than form with offensive combat characterizing operations. There is not a single deployment or technique prescribed for the defense. Commanders are expected to combine elements of the static and dynamic forms in light of their mission, terrain, relative strength and mobility. In this context, "static" defense implies retention of particular terrain and tends to rely on fire power to destroy the enemy. "Dynamic" defense orients more on the enemy force than on retention of terrain objectives and tends toward greater use of maneuver against attacking forces.

Deep Battle techniques have affected the role and subsequently the composition of the "covering force". In order to gain maximum effects from the enemy's early deployment, which may reveal his intentions, the covering force not only establishes contact but develops the situation. Ideally, the covering force will defeat the enemy's lead elements while Deep Battle actions delay follow-on units by aerial interdiction and other means. Covering forces may be organized around tank-heavy task

Current Division Forces		
	Active Duty Div (Bdes)	Reserve Component Div (Bdes)
AR	4 (12)	2 (6)
Mech Infantry	6 (16) +2 Reserve	1 (3)
Infantry	3 (8) +2 Reserve	5 (15)
LID	1 (2) +1 Reserve	
Air Assault	1 (3)	
Airborne	1 (3)	
Total Div (Bdes)	16 (44)	8 (24)
1 LID 1985	17 (46)	
Separate Bde (Incl 4 RO)		
AR	1	4
Mech Infantry	1	7
Infantry	0	5
CBAC	1	0
Armored Cav Rgt	3	4
Theater Force Bdes	3	4
Total Separate Bdes	9	24

forces with aviation, artillery, air defense artillery, engineer and intelligence support. The covering force is expected to employ a full range of tactical options in halting and forcing the enemy to deploy; delay alone will not

---

7–8: AREAS OF INFLUENCE AND INTEREST

The area of influence (7) is the operational area assigned to a commander within which he is capable of acquiring and fighting enemy units with assets organic to his command, plus any assigned to him in support of the particular operation. The size of the area will vary according to the prevailing conditions and the superior officer's plans. The latter also designates the front and flanking boundaries of the area. The area of interest (8) extends beyond the area of influence to include any enemy forces capable of affecting operations by the formation concerned.

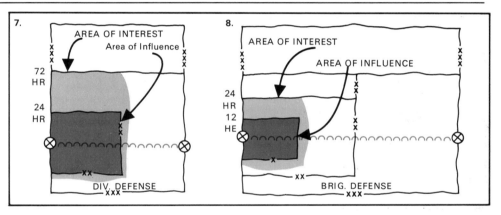

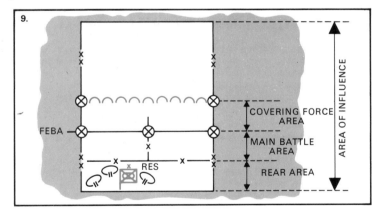

9. ORGANIZATION OF THE DEFENSE

The purpose of the defense is to provide an opportunity to gain the initiative, and commanders are expected to combine elements of static and dynamic tactical action. With this increased emphasis on offensive action and agility, reserve forces have become particularly important for counterattacks.

AIRLAND BATTLE 2000

The US Army's most recent battle methodology is a totally new concept entitled AirLand Battle 2000. The central idea is a strategic defense of NATO's central region by aggressive tactics, which would include immediate, sustained and simultaneous attacks both in depth and on the line of contact.

Based on a 20-year Soviet threat projection, assessments conclude that the US Army, heavily outnumbered in both men and equipment, would be foolish to fight a war of attrition. Rather, the

plan is for the Army to defend offensively, to strike quickly at Soviet assault echelons, while seeing subsequent echelons, in an attempt to finalize this stage of the battle before the enemy's follow-up armies join the fray. The intention is to attack the enemy throughout the depth of his formation with air, artillery and electronic means, and by use of high maneuverability. It is planned to confuse the enemy and cause him to fight in more than one direction, by deploying ground maneuver forces to the rear of his advance echelons. The Army will take advantage of the Soviet tactics which (as they exist today) mean there is an inevitable time-lag between follow-on echelons, such periods normally being lulls in the intense fighting. AirLand Battle tactics will upset the enemy's advance timetable, and force him to change his plans even to the extent of altering routes or splitting forces, so that hopefully subsequent defending forces will not have to face enemy forces too strong for them to defeat.

A scenario would have a US Army brigade attack the enemy's first echelon assault regiments while "seeing" the first echelon assault divisions. These are attacked by a US Army division, which at the same time "sees" the first echelon assault armies. These in turn are attacked by the US Army corps which must also disrupt the timetable of the second echelon divisions of the first echelon armies.

The depth attack, penetrating as much as 200 miles (321 km), would be by fully integrated air forces (hence the air-land aspect), indirect fire systems and by deep penetration ground units. The concept will entail small combat units which will operate relatively independently of each other. It also includes tactics for fighting in 360 degrees to meet the threat posed by the Warsaw Pact tactics; indeed, almost challenging them to attempt to surround the Army's agile combat forces. The concept will depend heavily on new technology, especially in communications, and in the rapid collection and assessment of intelligence data. Brigade commanders will have to know their superior commanders' intent, rather than have constant dialogue with them, thus combining the strategic and tactical levels.

Organization of the Department of the Army

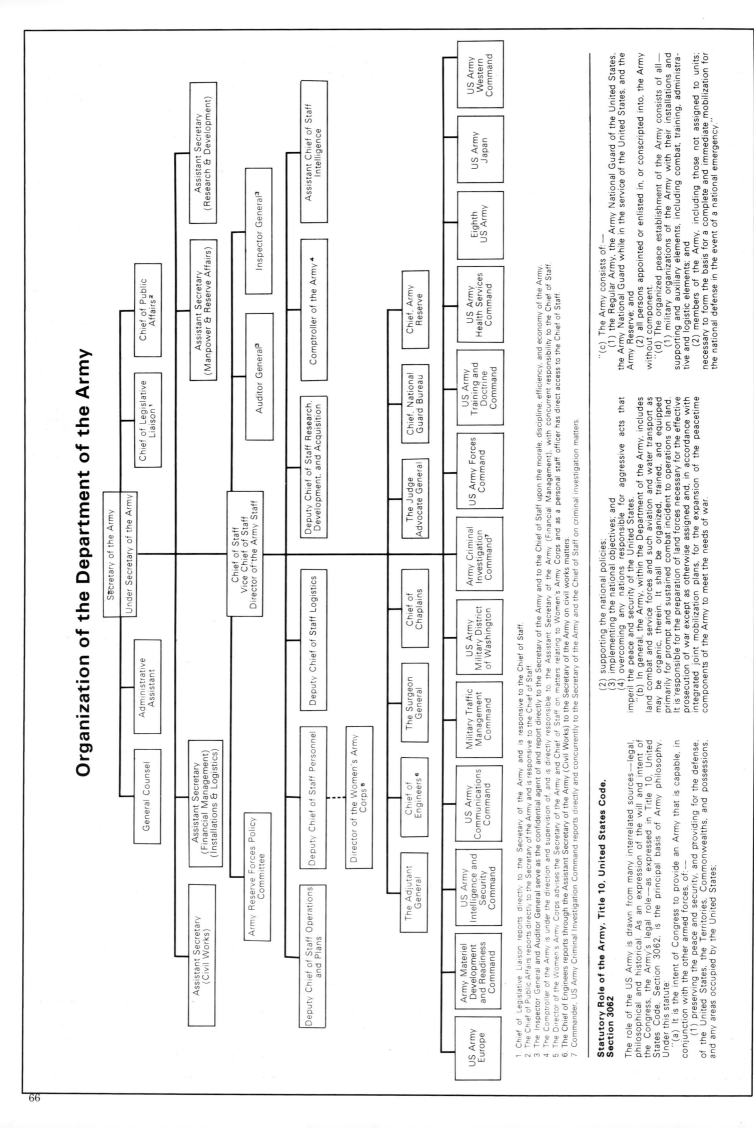

1. Chief of Legislative Liaison reports directly to the Secretary of the Army and is responsive to the Chief of Staff.
2. The Chief of Public Affairs reports directly to the Secretary of the Army and is responsive to the Chief of Staff.
3. The Inspector General and Auditor General serve as the confidential agent of and report directly to the Secretary of the Army and to the Chief of Staff upon the morale, discipline, efficiency, and economy of the Army.
4. The Comptroller of the Army is under the direction and supervision of, and is directly responsible to. the Assistant Secretary of the Army (Financial Management). with concurrent responsibility to the Chief of Staff.
5. The Director of the Women's Army Corps advises the Secretary of the Army and Chief of Staff on matters relating to Women's Army Corps and as a personal staff officer has direct access to the Chief of Staff
6. The Chief of Engineers reports through the Assistant Secretary of the Army (Civil Works) to the Secretary of the Army on civil works matters.
7. Commander, US Army Criminal Investigation Command reports directly and concurrently to the Secretary of the Army and the Chief of Staff on criminal investigation matters.

Statutory Role of the Army, Title 10, United States Code, Section 3062

The role of the US Army is drawn from many interrelated sources—legal, philosophical and historical. As an expression of the will and intent of the Congress, the Army's legal role—as expressed in Title 10, United States Code, Section 3062, is the principal basis of Army philosophy. Under this statute:

"(a) It is the intent of Congress to provide an Army that is capable, in conjunction with the other armed forces, of:—

"(1) preserving the peace and security, and providing for the defense, of the United States, the Territories, Commonwealths, and possessions, and any areas occupied by the United States;

"(2) supporting the national policies;

"(3) implementing the national objectives; and

"(4) overcoming any nations responsible for aggressive acts that imperil the peace and security of the United States.

"(b) In general, the Army, within the Department of the Army, includes land combat and service forces and such aviation and water transport as may be organic, therein. It shall be organized, trained, and equipped primarily for prompt and sustained combat incident to operations on land. It is responsible for the preparation of land forces necessary for the effective prosecution of war except as otherwise assigned and, in accordance with integrated joint mobilization plans, for the expansion of the peacetime components of the Army to meet the needs of war.

"(c) The Army consists of:—

"(1) the Regular Army, the Army National Guard of the United States, the Army National Guard while in the service of the United States, and the Army Reserve; and

"(2) all persons appointed or enlisted in, or conscripted into, the Army without component.

"(d) The organized peace establishment of the Army consists of all—

"(1) military organizations of the Army with their installations and supporting and auxiliary elements, including combat, training, administrative and logistic elements; and

"(2) members of the Army, including those not assigned to units, necessary to form the basis for a complete and immediate mobilization for the national defense in the event of a national emergency."

usually suffice. Withdrawal will normally not be uniform but take place only when forced by enemy pressure. Elements of the covering force which can do so remain forward of the main battle area, hindering enemy operations, adding to the commander's surveillance capabilities, and when possible, attacking enemy forces from the flank or rear.

With the increased emphasis on offensive actions and battlefield agility, reserve forces become particularly important to the commander. Formally designated reserves usually only apply at brigade and higher levels. Here, however, reserves may constitute a third of the force. Since the purpose of defense is to provide an opportunity to gain the initiative, reserves (whether fire power or maneuver units) will be employed in decisive actions rather than simply restoring the defensive position.

The heightened emphasis on rear battle is a function of the increased demands on command and control systems as well as the high volume of fuel and ammunition consumption which the battlefield of the future will entail. Combat support and combat service support (logistics) units will be dispersed to avoid presenting lucrative targets but must be mutually supporting for possible rear area combat operations. The commander's allocation of resources and placement takes into account the probabilities of enemy air mobile, nuclear, chemical and conventional air attack along with sabotage and unconventional warfare.

The Corps

Organizational implications of the Airland Battle doctrine are extensive. All levels of operational forces must be modified to support the new doctrine and to accommodate the rapidly changing technology. While never intended to be organizationally rigid, the type of corps which has been designed for the European Theater is shown below.

The heavy corps design envisions operating with from two divisions to five divisions. A typical corps will have a minimum strength of some 60,000 personnel, less assigned divisions, and be capable of expansion as needed. Design considerations include provisions for coordination with allied forces and the increased operational participation with US Tactical Air Forces.

The Division

A total of 18 divisions make up the active army ground combat force. Within these divisions are found combat support elements consisting of artillery, air defense artillery, military Intelligence, signal, chemical and engineers. Combat service support elements consisting of quartermaster, transportation, military police, medical services, and those others responsible for the care and maintenance of the Army are also organic to the division.

The division is the largest force that is trained and fought as a combined arms team. It is a balanced, self-sustaining force that normally conducts operations as part of a larger force, but is capable of conducting independent operations, especially when supplemented by additional combat support and combat service support elements. Normally, the division fights as part of a corps, with two to five divisions making up the corps force. The division is designed to fight conventional operations, or a mixture of conventional and chemical-nuclear operations, in any part of the world.

While the division is the basic combined arms formation, it is the battalion (rather than the regiment, as is the case with the Soviet Ground Forces) that is the basic maneuver unit. The battalion fights as part of a brigade, with normally three to five battalions comprising a brigade. Each division has three brigade headquarters to which battalions are assigned as the command sees fit.

Heavy maneuver battalions – armor and mechanized infantry – fight best in open country using terrain to maximum advantage. The light maneuver forces – rifle infantry, air assault infantry, airborne infantry, and ranger infantry – are ideally suited to more restricted terrain where close-in fighting becomes the norm. The maneuver elements of the division are grouped together under brigade control in accordance with the terrain, the enemy they face, and the mission they must accomplish.

Tank and mechanized infantry battalions rarely fight as pure organic units, but are cross-attached or task-organized by the brigade commanders to perform specific mission tasks to utilize more fully their capabilities

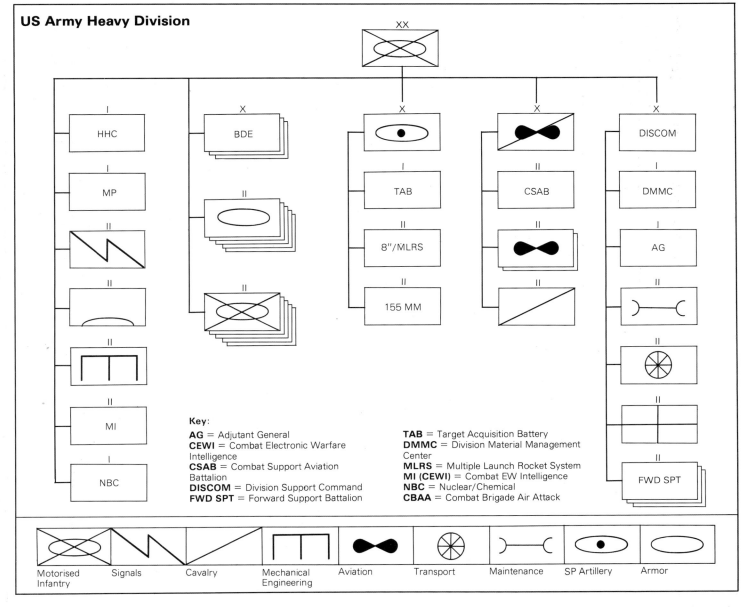

US Army Heavy Division

Key:
AG = Adjutant General
CEWI = Combat Electronic Warfare Intelligence
CSAB = Combat Support Aviation Battalion
DISCOM = Division Support Command
FWD SPT = Forward Support Battalion

TAB = Target Acquisition Battery
DMMC = Division Material Management Center
MLRS = Multiple Launch Rocket System
MI (CEWI) = Combat EW Intelligence
NBC = Nuclear/Chemical
CBAA = Combat Brigade Air Attack

Motorised Infantry | Signals | Cavalry | Mechanical Engineering | Aviation | Transport | Maintenance | SP Artillery | Armor

and offset each other's vulnerabilities. After the division commander has visualized how he wishes to fight the battle, he allocates maneuver units to the brigade commanders, who in turn cross-attach these forces to optimize the weapon systems of each unit. The resultant battalion task forces are a combination of tank and mechanized infantry companies under the command of a battalion commander. A tank-heavy force would normally be structured to operate in open, rolling terrain, while the mechanized-infantry-heavy task force is better suited to operate in more restricted terrain and built-up areas. An even mix of tank and mechanized infantry results in a balanced task force that provides great flexibility to the commander. A balanced force would normally be structured when information about the enemy is vague or when the terrain is mixed and variable.

Tank Battalion

The tank battalion has 543 officers and enlisted personnel organized into four companies and an HQ company. Each tank company has three platoons of four tanks each. Maintenance and support functions are consolidated in the battalion HQ company, as are an Armored Cavalry Platoon and a six-tube mortar platoon. Currently, tank battalions may have M60A1, M60A3 or the M1 Abrams tank. The M60A1 has a 105mm gun which is highly effective at 2,190 yards (2,000m) and a cruising range of 310 miles (500km) at a steady 20mph (32kmh). The M60A3 has a similar chassis but its main gun is stabilized for firing on the move. It also has a laser range finder and solid state computer and thermal shroud, which have enhanced the tank's first-round hit capabilities. The M1 Abrams tank is the newest system and will replace the several models of M60 over the next few years and into the early 1990s. Through FY1985, 4,168 M1s have been delivered to the Army, with production now increased to 70 tanks per month. The total projected US Army requirement is for 7,467.

The new tank battalion is designed to employ 58 of the M1 tanks. With its improved day and night fire control capability, compartmentalized fuel and ammunition storage and stabilized gun, the Abrams is the primary ground combat weapons system of the US Army for the 1980s. The M1 has been judged capable of operating during a 24-hour combat day without the need to refuel. The 60-ton Abrams has a top speed of 45mph (73kmh) and cruising range of 275 miles (440km). While it will eventually be equipped with a 120mm smoothbore gun of German design, the initial Abrams will have the British-designed M68E1 105mm gun, which is standard main armament on US and most other NATO tanks.

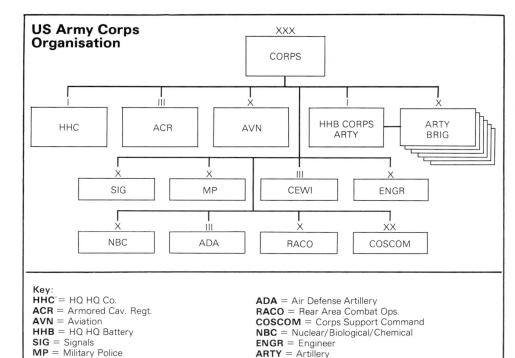

US Army Corps Organisation

Key:
HHC = HQ HQ Co.
ACR = Armored Cav. Regt.
AVN = Aviation
HHB = HQ HQ Battery
SIG = Signals
MP = Military Police
CEWI = Combat EW Intelligence

ADA = Air Defense Artillery
RACO = Rear Area Combat Ops.
COSCOM = Corps Support Command
NBC = Nuclear/Biological/Chemical
ENGR = Engineer
ARTY = Artillery

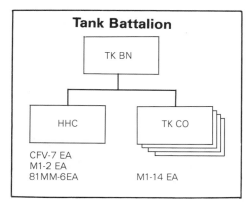

Tank Battalion

TK BN

HHC — TK CO

CFV-7 EA
M1-2 EA
81MM-6EA

M1-14 EA

Mechanized Infantry Battalion

The mechanized infantry battalion has 844 officers and enlisted personnel organized into four mechanized rifle companies, an anti-armor company and an HQ company. The four-rifle company configuration allows for cross-attachment with the similarly structured tank battalions. Each rifle company has three platoons of three 9-man squads each. Maintenance and support functions are consolidated in the battalion HQ company, along with a scout platoon and a mortar platoon. The anti-armor company has three platoons of two sections each, and contains a total of 12 Improved TOW Vehicles. (The TOW has a 3,280 yards/3,000m range.) Each rifle company has 9 Dragon (1,093 yards/1,000m range) man-portable anti-armor guided missiles.

The improved Bradley Fighting Vehicle (BFV) is designed to provide the infantry with cross-country mobility and speed that complement that of the Abrams tank. The 25-ton BFV has a top speed of 42mph (67km/h) and a cruising range of 300 miles (480km). It carries a 25mm automatic cannon and a 7.62mm co-axial machine gun in a two-man turret equipped with day and night thermal sights. There are 54 BFVs in each mechanized infantry battalion.

The mechanized infantry usually operates as part of a combined arms force. The infantrymen remain mounted in their carriers until they are required to assault or forced to

Above: Criticism has been levelled at the M2 Bradley for its supposed vulnerability on the armored battlefield, but the type is a potent companion for the M1 and M60 MBTs.

US Armored and Mechanized Infantry Divisions in Europe

		Armored Div.	Mechanized Inf. Div.
Tank Battalions		6	5
Mechanized Infantry Battalions		5	6
Major Weapons Systems			
M60A1			
M60A3	Tanks	324	316
M1			
*M113	APC	418	463
M113 TOW	Anti-	152	170
Dragon	armor Systems	244	284
M109A1	Arty.	72	72
M110		12	12
Chaparral	Air Defense	24	24
Vulcan	Gun/	24	24
Stinger	Missiles	72 teams	72 teams

*The BFV is replacing the M113

dismount by the enemy. The carriers displace to protected positions to provide supporting fire. The new infantry fighting vehicle will greatly enhance the infantryman's ability to fight while mounted and protected.

Combat Aviation Brigade (CAB)
This organization of approximately 1,200 officers and enlisted personnel is designed to consolidate the aviation assets of the division as well as to provide an additional control headquarters. In addition to its headquarters troop, the CAB has two attack helicopter battalions, a General Support AVN Company, a Combat Aviation Company, and a Reconnaissance Squadron. Recent organizational changes include the establishment of a Long-range Surveillance Detachment of some 50 personnel in the Reconnaissance Squadron to supplement the Division's Intelligence gathering capabilities. A further change has transferred the aircraft maintenance company from the CAB to the Division Support Command in order to allow the CAB commander to concentrate on the employment of the Division air assets.

The principal weapons of the Apache Attack Helicopter Battalions are their 21 Attack Helicopters (AH-64) and 13 Observation Helicopters (OH-58C). The AH-64 is capable of speeds of 197 knots (227mph/363kmh). It can cruise at 145 knots (167mph/268kmh) carrying 8 Hellfire missiles, Hydra 70 rockets and 320 rounds of 30mm ammunition and enough fuel for nearly 2 hours of flight. This day/night/ adverse weather capable aircraft is considered highly combat survivable and with auxiliary fuel tanks has a range of 800 nautical miles (1,480km). The first Apache unit was fielded in early 1986, and the FY87 budget provided for the procurement of 144 units at a rate of 12 per month. The current program calls for a total buy of 625 Apaches.

The OH-58C is capable of speeds up to 120 knots (138mph/222kmh) and with its radar warning and heat suppression systems pro-

Right: Using its stabilized main gun and advanced fire-control system, the M1 MBT can fire on the move with excellent probability of scoring a first-round hit while itself remaining a difficult target.

Below: Allocated at the scale of 27 launchers per corps, the MLRS offers the capability for massive destruction in the rear areas of formations attacking US units – if resupply of rockets can be assured.

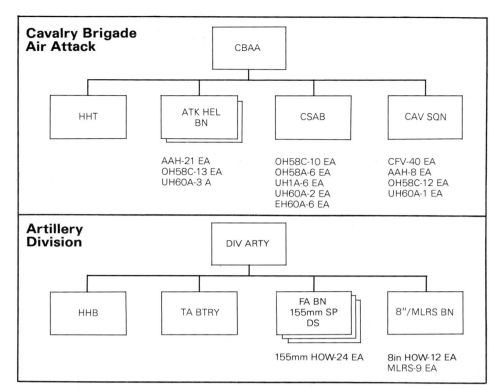

Cavalry Brigade Air Attack

- CBAA
  - HHT
  - ATK HEL BN
    - AAH-21 EA
    - OH58C-13 EA
    - UH60A-3 A
  - CSAB
    - OH58C-10 EA
    - OH58A-6 EA
    - UH1A-6 EA
    - UH60A-2 EA
    - EH60A-6 EA
  - CAV SQN
    - CFV-40 EA
    - AAH-8 EA
    - OH58C-12 EA
    - UH60A-1 EA

Artillery Division

- DIV ARTY
  - HHB
  - TA BTRY
  - FA BN 155mm SP DS
    - 155mm HOW-24 EA
  - 8"/MLRS BN
    - 8in HOW-12 EA
    - MLRS-9 EA

vides a survivable observation capability which can operate at night.

Division Artillery

With slightly over 2,500 personnel, the Division Artillery organization follows traditional principles of direct support for the maneuver elements. Each 155mm self-propelled howitzer battalion routinely supports one of the division's brigades. These battalions are fully mobile and can split their component batteries into two sections capable of independent operation. The Multiple Launch Rocket Systems (MLRS) battery provides the division with an organic rocket capability as well as longer range weapons to fight the Deep Battle envisioned in the Airland Battle doctrine. Recently, changes have been made in the Division Artillery organization to reduce the division's logistical requirements. Here-to-fore, the division had a General Support Battalion which had 203mm (8in) howitzers along with an MLRS battery. Moving the 8in howitzers to corps control has both enhanced the corps commander's ability to influence the battle and eliminated the division's logistics needs associated with that weapons system. Growth potential exists in the MLRS to add a terminal guided warhead – to defeat armor – and a binary chemical warhead.

The division's Air Defense Artillery Battalion (ADA) has undergone a similar reorganization. In the early 1980s, divisional ADA battalions were structured to include Chaparral missiles for the defense of the division rear area. Currently, the Chaparral systems are being transferred to the corps in consonance with the philosophy of focusing the division's attention forward. Divisional ADA resources are now concentrated on defending the brigade areas while the division rear will rely more heavily on the corps ADA brigade for defense against enemy air strikes.

Division Support Command (DISCOM)

With nearly 3,000 personnel, the Division Support Command (DISCOM) consolidates logistics functions under a single commander. The DISCOM is organized to provide a mix of support services to the brigades (three forward support battalions – FSBs) and those elements in the division rear (the main support battalion). Through habitual assignment of FSBs to their supported brigades, the working relations between supported and supporting units are routinized thus facilitating logistics at the crucial point of delivery to the user.

Reserve Forces

Any prolonged armed conflict undertaken by the US Army would involve employment of Reserve Components (RC). United States RC forces are the contemporary form of a long tradition of citizen soldiers which pre-dates the nation's founding. Current planning calls for half of the Army's wartime strength to come from the Reserve Components, both National Guard and Army Reserve.

The Army National Guard, numbering 450,500 in FY86 is organized into 10 divisions, 14 separate brigades, 4 armored cavalry regiments as well as 4 brigades and 7 battalions which are designed to "roundout" or fill regular army formations. When not activated (ie, called into military service by the federal government), the National Guard's personnel constitute a military force at the disposal of the states and territories. They function as needed in time of emergency to protect life and property and preserve public safety in their own home state.

The Army Reserve had a FY86 programmed end strength of 310,700 organized in units and as individuals to augment and fill various units and installations should the need arise. Reserve personnel constitute a major source of combat support and combat service support as

---

US Maneuver Forces mix and Locations

Armored Divisions
Ansbach, Germany
1st Armored Division
6 Armored   5 Mechanized

Fort Hood, Texas
2nd Armored Division
5 Armored   5 Mechanized
(3d Brigade in Germany)
(2 Armored   1 Mechanized)*

Frankfurt, Germany
3d Armored Division
6 Armored   5 Mechanized

Fort Hood, Texas
1st Cavalry Division
4 Armored   4 Mechanized
(2 Armored   1 Mechanized)*

Mechanized Divisions
Wurzburg, Germany
3d Infantry Division
6 Mechanized   4 Armored

Fort Carson, Colorado
4th Infantry Division
5 Mechanized   5 armored
(3d Brigade in Europe)
(1 Mechanized)

Fort Polk, Louisiana
5th Infantry Division
2 Armored   1 Mechanized (3 Infantry)*

Bad Kreuznach, Germany
8th Infantry Division
6 Mechanized   5 Armored

Fort Riley, Kansas
1st Infantry Division
5 Mechanized   5 Armored
(3d Brigade in Europe)
(1 Mechanized)*

Infantry Divisions
Korea
2nd Infantry Division
5 Infantry   2 Mechanized   1 Armored
(Still has HJ Battalion)

Fort Ord, California
7th Light Infantry Division
6 Infantry   (3 Infantry)*

Fort Stewart, Georgia
24th Mechanized Division
6 Infantry   (1 Armored   3 Mechanized)*

Fort Stewart, Georgia
24th Infantry Division
6 Infantry   (1 Armored   3 Mechanized)*

Hawaii
25th Infantry Division
6 Infantry

*Reserve Component Roundout Battalions.

Air Assault Divisions
Fort Campbell, Kentucky
101st AASLT Division
9 Infantry (Ambl)   1 Tank Dest   1 Attack Hel

Airborne Divisions
Fort Bragg, North Carolina
82nd Airborne Division
9 Infantry (Abn)   1 Armored (Lt)

6th ACCB
Fort Hood, Texas
2 Attack Battalions   1 Air Cavalry Battalion

172d Infantry Brigade (Sep)
Fort Richardson, Alaska
3 Infantry

197th Infantry Brigade
Fort Benning, Georgia
1 Infantry   1 Mechanized   1 Armored (1 Mech)*

194th Armored Brigade
Fort Knox, Kentucky
2 Armored   1 Mechanized

Berlin Brigade
3 Infantry   1 Armored Company

193d Infantry Brigade
Panama
2 Infantry   1 Mechanized

2d Armored Cavalry Regiment
Nürnburg, Germany
3 Cavalry Squadron

3d Armored Cavalry Regiment
Fort Bliss, Texas
3 Cavalry Squadron

11th Armored Cavalry Regiment
Fulda, Germany
3 Cavalry Squadron

Ranger Battalions
Fort Benning, Georgia
3 Bn. 75th Infantry

Fort Lewis, Washington
2d Battalion (Ranger)   75th Infantry

Airborne Task Force (TF)
Italy
1 Airborne (+)

Totals (Active/Roundout)

Infantry 38/9		Armored 48/6	
Airborne 10		Armored Cavalry 21	
Air Mobile 9		Air Cavalry 6	
Mechanized 47/8		Attack 3	
Ranger 3		Tank Des 1	

---

well as training organizations needed by the Army in the event of national emergency. Unlike the National Guard, the Reserve forces do not have responsibilities to the states in which they live. Some 20 percent of Army Reserve would be deployed within 30 days after mobilization and another 60 percent are scheduled to deploy between 30 and 60 days after mobilization.

Planned early deployment of RC forces raises questions concerning the training and equipping of reserves, both Army National Guard and Army Reserves. Efforts to get maximum training in the time available are ongoing and have been generally successful in the early 1980s. A similar problem concerning equipment shortages and the use of obsolete equipment is less amenable to solution. Recent moves to procure the same equipment for the reserve components as is being used by the regular army have begun to take effect, but there are still questions of equipment interoperability and the sustainability of reserve units.

Deployment Considerations

While the organization, equipment and training of most ground forces are based on

fighting in the European environment, with emphasis on armored and mechanized forces, recent Soviet demonstrations of the capability and willingness to project military power directly or through proxy forces, has caused some re-evaluation of deployment considerations for US forces. The introduction during the 1980s of increasingly heavier tanks and infantry fighting vehicles and a host of mechanized supporting systems will significantly enhance the fire power and mobility of deployed forces in Europe. These same changes will significantly increase the strategic airlift and sealift required to move reinforcing units across the Atlantic.

In case of conflict between NATO and the Warsaw Pact, several factors combine to help alleviate the deployment problem. The existence of a forward base and depot structure in place in Europe, and the attendant ability to preposition both unit sets of equipment and required sustaining supplies allows rapid airlift of personnel with minimum accompanying equipment. The Army prepositioning program – called POMCUS, for Prepositioned Material Configured to Unit Sets – calls for six division sets of equipment. The equipment fill for the last set began in 1986. Recent agree-

Major US Army Units and Headquarters in Germany

NETHERLANDS

Hamburg

• Bremen

□ **Garlstedt**
2nd Armd. Div. (FWD)

• Hannover

Berlin

Berlin Bde

WEST GERMANY
(Federal Republic
and West Berlin)

• Dortmund

• Cologne

• Bonn

EAST GERMANY

□ **Frankfurt**
V Corps
3rd Armored
Division

Bad Kreuznach □
8th Infantry
Division

□ **Würzburg**
3rd Infantry
Division

□ **Heidelberg**
HQ, US Army
Europe and
Seventh Army

□ **Ansbach**
1st Armored
Division

Moerhingen □
VII Corps

FRANCE

□
Goppinggen
1st Inf. Div. (FWD)

Munich

SWITZERLAND

Major US Army Units and Headquarters in Korea

CHINA

NORTH
KOREA

SEA OF
JAPAN

• Pyongyang

Camp Casey
□ 2nd Infantry Div.
Yóungsán □□
HQ, Eighth   Soul (Seoul)
US Army

SOUTH
KOREA
28,486

• Pusan

Additionally, there are
2,364 US Army personnel
serving in Japan

---

ments between the United States and its European NATO allies will provide at least initial support by host nation support units, again reducing initial requirements to deploy logistical support forces with combat units. The commitment of European civilian cargo ships and aircraft to the deployment effort will further ease the burden on US resources. Finally, the advantage enjoyed by NATO forces in terms of familiarity with the terrain, established command and control systems, and exercise experience (including annual deployment exercises) combine to offer a high degree of assurance that timely reinforcement of Europe is feasible.

A similar set of circumstances, combined with a reduced requirement for armor and mechanized forces applies to deployment considerations for an outbreak of hostilities in Korea, although the distances involved are far greater.

No such advantages are currently found, however, when possible contingency requirements for Southwest Asia or other potential areas of conflict are considered. The requirements to maintain the capability to deploy forces rapidly to areas of the world where no US troops are forward deployed in peacetime,

where no alliances currently exist and where equipment and supplies cannot be stockpiled in advance presents the Army with severe challenges. Since such forces must not only be relatively lightly equipped for ease and rapidity of movement, yet possess sufficient fire power to combat a mechanized enemy, the Army is constantly testing new organizational concepts and high-technology weapon systems to provide the required levels of both fire power and deployability. Other specially trained and equipped units (air assault, airborne and ranger) provide a current rapidly deployable force for worldwide contingencies.

The wide range of possible contingencies is reflected in the combat forces identified for employment with the basic Rapid Deployment Force (RDF), which include the 24th Mechanized Division, the 82nd Airborne Division, the 101st Air Assault Division, the 6th Cavalry Brigade (Air Combat), plus Rangers, Special Forces and support forces. This does not mean that all of these units would be committed to all RDF contingencies, merely that a wide mix of heavy and light forces is available for tailoring packages of Army, Air Force, Navy and Marine elements to meet specific circumstances.

The Invasion of Grenada, 1983

The US military intervention in Grenada in October 1983, provides an example of a contingency wherein armed forces are employed but where the level of violence is significantly less than that found in a contemporary mid-intensity war. The entire operation from landing until the cessation of hostilities took only nine days and significant resistance was ended by the fifth day.

Briefly, the operation began in the early morning hours of 25 October, with a Marine rifle battalion making a heliborne landing on the island's north coast to seize the airfield at Pearls while Army Rangers conducted an air assault on the airfield at Point Salines in the south. The Marines encountered little resistance. In the south, the Rangers met stiffer resistance from the Cubans and elements of the Grenadan People's Revolutionary Army (PRA) but were still able to secure the Point Salines airfield as well as rescue the American students at the True Blue campus adjacent to the airfield by mid-morning. That afternoon the Army units at Point Salines defeated a force of some 100 PRA supported by three Soviet-manufactured armored cars in the only organized counterattack of the campaign.

On 26 October, the American students found at the True Blue campus began to be evacuated from Grenada on the aircraft bringing in elements of the Army's 82nd Airborne Division to replace the Rangers. Later in the day Rangers rescued the American students at the Grand Anse campus near St Georges in a classic air assault operation which took only 26 minutes to secure the campus area. By. nightfall on the 26th some 600 prisoners and detainees had been gathered as the Army and Marines, along with elements of the Caribbean Peacekeeping Force, moved to eliminate armed resistance.

In general terms, Grenada was a military success, having been carried out expeditiously and with light casualties. Perhaps more significantly, there had been little loss of life or destruction of property among the Grenadan population. The latter situation is attributable to the strict rules of engagement under which US forces operated.

Criticism of the Grenadan operation focuses

Above: Long-range operations are a primary task for the men of the 82nd Airborne Division.

Below: The Army has emphasized high mobility in equipping its forces for low intensity conflict.

more on the problems experienced in coordinating the actions of the services and the seemingly excessive number of combat forces involved than on unit operations or equipment failure. Joint operations, as well as joint planning, are highly complex matters and demand constant exercise to be effective. Given the situation on the ground on 25 October, the decision to bring in more combat units from the 82nd Airborne Division than had been planned (six rather than two battalions) is understandable. The Cubans and People's Revolutionary Army conducted little organized resistance, but because they remained armed and dispersed as individuals and small groups the extent of opposition could not be determined. The fact that the American medical students were not all at the True Blue campus added to the problem. Under the circumstances a prudent commander would opt for more combat power even if – as it turned out – it was not all needed.

Low Intensity Conflict (LIC)

The US Army has focused on Europe as the area of highest military risk since the dissolution of the World War II coalition against Nazi Germany. The threat posed by the massive forces of the Warsaw Pact has been countered by a build-up of NATO forces and more recently by US force modernization efforts. In the late 1970s, however, the US perception of the threat to peace was revised in light of the demonstrated Soviet willingness and capacity to project forces beyond its own border regions. Through the use of surrogates and an ever increasing capability to project its own forces, the Soviet Union has indicated that the stalemate in Europe does not apply on a global scale. While conflicts in the more remote areas of today's world may not have the same significance for the US as a clash in Europe, US interests are frequently involved and these small Low Intensity Conflicts cannot be ignored. Just as US threat perception has broadened to include the possible need for armed forces to be employed in areas traditionally considered to be of little concern, the US Army has accepted the need to have forces ready and able to respond to situations short of war (ie, rescues, insurgencies, and actions against terrorists). The Army and Air Force activated the Center for Low Intensity Conflict at Langley Air Force Base, Va., in early 1986. It represents, in the words of their joint announcement of the center, "an effort between the services to improve the Army and Air Force posture for engaging in low intensity conflict, to elevate awareness of the role of military power in low intensity conflict, and to provide an infrastructure for the eventual transition to a joint, and perhaps interagency, activity."

Light Infantry Division (LID)

A number of programs have been undertaken since 1980 when the Army began to address the need to respond to low intensity conflicts ranging from terrorism through insurgent war. One initiative, which is designed to respond to the strategic realities of today's world, is the establishment of the Light Infantry Division.

The light division concept does not subsume the requirement for continuing modernization of heavy forces. It does, however, meet the requirements for a quick reaction to a land conflict by a force which can be rapidly deployed for contingency situations or for deployment in a conventional war scenario. Such a unit can be employed to contain a low level conflict or, as a show-of-force element, possibly preclude the outbreak of armed hostilities.

The force structure design is still under refinement, but the basic concept is being applied to the 7th Infantry Division. The

conversion process is now complete and a light division of slightly more than 10,000 soldiers will soon be ready for a broad range of missions. It was certified during FY86 by exercises up through division level. The Army's 10th Mountain Division (Light Infantry), Fort Drum, NY, was activated in December 1984. The 6th Light Infantry Division, was added to the force structure in 1986 and is based in Alaska. These new light infantry divisions, like the prototype 7th, are to be organized and equipped as rapidly deployable foot-mobile fighters. The basic organization of the light infantry division includes three infantry brigades, a division artillery, a combat aviation brigade, division troops and division support command.

Although the force structure allows the division to be transported in less than 500 C-141 sorties, its organic fire power is marginal to meet an opposing conventional force supported by armor. Moreover, the division must rely on support units as augmentation to give the division sustained combat power for prolonged periods. The force planners envision a contingency scenario which pits the division against lightly armed conventional forces or guerrillas in strength. In a mid-intensity scenario the division unaugmented lacks the mobility and punch required for the sophisticated modern battlefield. Structured as it is, the light division's employment must emphasize the tactical use of terrain.

The US Army's current light infantry structuring process should be concluded by 1989; the efforts are intended to provide a fighting force to respond to those military needs which fall between the heavy formations designed for employment in Europe or Northeast Asia and the Special Operations Forces designed for unconventional missions.

Special Operations Forces (SOF)

Activated in October 1983, the US Army's 1st Special Operations Command (SOCOM) brings the various special operations forces under single control. With headquarters at Ft Bragg, NC, and commanded by a major general, 1st SOCOM is strong evidence that the US leadership is formally preparing to counter the threat posed by "small dirty wars" (ie, terrorism and insurgency). The resolve which lies behind this light force preparation is welcome to those allies who have perceived

the US as a superpower militarily paralyzed from the effects of the long Vietnam war.

SOF have existed in US force structure under various labels and in various configurations since World War II. As with any "special" type of unit in an Army, there have been questions of utility and cost effectiveness which caused SOF's fortunes to wax and wane over the years. In the aftermath of Vietnam, SOF experienced a decade of neglect more pronounced than that of the army as a whole. American recognition of the reality of low intensity conflict and the long term need to have military options to employ in LIC led to renewed interest in SOF in the 1980s.

The SOF includes five components within the Army – Special Forces, Rangers, civil affairs and psychological operations units and Special Operations Aviation. These highly trained and uniquely equipped forces are designed to accomplish strategic and tactical missions as prescribed by the National Command Authority (NCA) through the Joint Chiefs of Staff.

Organized around the 12-man "A" detachment, Special Forces units have four primary missions. These missions are conducted across the entire spectrum of conflict and include foreign internal defense, unconventional warfare, strategic reconnaissance and strike operations.

Because of their language capability and geographic area orientation, Special Forces are frequently deployed on foreign internal defense missions to assist friendly countries in the improvement of their security posture. This is, and will remain, a constant peacetime mission.

There are four Special Forces Groups under the command of 1st SOCOM. One of these groups, the 1st SF Group was activated in 1984 and is located at Ft Lewis. One of its three battalions will be forward deployed to Okinawa. The 5th Group is located at Ft Bragg along with the 7th Group. The 7th Group has one battalion forward deployed in Panama. The battalion in Panama has been responsible for the majority of the training provided to the armies of the Central American Republics in recent years.

The 10th Special Forces Group is located at Ft Devens, Mass., with one battalion forward deployed to West Germany. This battalion is under the control of the US European Com-

mand.

The US Army's Ranger units have a mission to conduct strike operations. Organized as three battalions with a newly formed regimental headquarters, Rangers proved their utility in Grenada. Some controversy continues as to whether Rangers are SOF and as such under the supervision of 1st SOCOM, or should be categorized as light infantry forces. The distinction is training. Rangers are airborne-qualified and experts in small unit commando type tactics. They train vigorously in peacetime and give credence to the maxim, "Those units perform well in war the operations for which they have trained in peace".

One Ranger battalion, 1st Battalion 75 Infantry is located at Savannah, Ga, while the 2nd Battalion is located at Ft Lewis, Wa. The 3rd Battalion along with the newly formed regimental headquarters is located at Ft Benning, Ga, which is home to the Ranger School.

The 4th Psychological Operations Group is the only unit of its kind in the active component and one whose function multiplies combat power out of proportion to its numerical strength. The 4th Group is stationed at Ft. Bragg, NC, and consists of four battalions. Psychological Operations (PSYOP) has been traditionally relegated to a distinctly secondary role by US defense officials. Even today the majority of PSYOP units are found in the Reserve Components. A recent training program designed to make US soldiers aware of Soviet PSYOP capabilities and techniques suggests another look at PSYOP units is under way.

Like PSYOP, the Civil Affairs (CA) battalion in the active component has received little emphasis. The US Army has one battalion, the 96th Civil Affairs Battalion at Ft Bragg, NC, which consists of four companies. The utility of Civil Affairs personnel in the developmental aspects of Internal Defense and Development doctrine may prompt a new look at the army's CA resources.

Special Operations Aviation units include Army rotary wing units and Air Force fixed wing aircraft. These air assets train with, and are dedicated to, the support of SOF missions.

Below: Hand-to-hand combat training is increasingly important for the Army's Special Operations Forces.

The United States Navy

The far-flung successes of the US Navy as World War II ended made it dominant in many parts of the world. This dominance continued after demobilization and into the 1960s, when a Soviet fleet first posed significant challenges to it. Today's US Navy has 553 ships and 581,000 men and women on active duty. It deploys versatile, capable fleets overseas and operates additional effective forces closer to the United States. It remains the most capable navy in the world; and capable navies exert control over the oceans.

Forces that have Shaped the Navy
The most important force shaping the US Navy is a set of broad national objectives. These are discussed first, followed by descriptions of the Navy's most likely conflicts and its peacetime posture. The likely conflicts point out the characteristics of opponents most needing US Navy attention. Improvements in technology create opportunities to shape a navy; limited budgets impose constraints. These, too, are discussed.

US Objectives for its Navy
The United States, together with allied and friendly countries, hold sway in much of the World Ocean, a loosely-defined geographic area tied together by economic interdependence using the seas. The seas and airspace surrounding the United States serve as a convenient means for access to other members of the World Ocean as well as the final bastions for defense of the US homeland. Therefore, their control is vital to the security of the nation.

US peacetime objectives include ensuring free use of the seas by friendly merchant shipping, and influencing events far from US shores. As foreign trade by the United States grew during the past century, its Navy grew to insure the uninterrupted flow of that trade. One reason US Navy ships are deployed far from US shores is to maintain that flow by deterring potential threats to it. These deployed forces also affect events on land by their ability to project naval power ashore. Earlier in this century, intervention ashore meant several miles – the range of a naval gun or an independent landing party. More recently, carrier-based aircraft and helicopter-borne Marines extended intervention ranges to tens and even hundreds of miles. Cruise missiles now proliferating aboard ships extend the range still farther.

Because the seas are an international highway, naval forces can move freely in peacetime. This flexibility becomes very important in crises, when naval forces can help signal their governments' intent by the stations they assume. Some of this stationing can be threatening, but if done outside territorial waters, the ability to stop short of combat and withdraw is retained. If, on the other hand, land forces are to influence crises, they must generally be so placed that the act of placement is itself hostile. Naval forces are therefore often preferred for crisis management. US naval forces bring a wide range of potential capabilities to a crisis – from a few interceptor sorties that can cover the ground forces of a small ally to large air strikes or amphibious assaults. This versatility gives added flexibility to the US Government in a crisis (as it did during the simultaneous 1958 demands of the Lebanon landing and the Taiwan Strait crisis). If the crisis turns to combat, this versatility permits US participation without the full-scale commitment implied by the introduction of sizable ground forces. If a full-scale commitment is decided upon, naval forces are often – because of their position and the range of their capabilities – the first committed. (The first American strikes against North Vietnam, for instance, were conducted by US Navy forces in 1964. The demand for air sorties to support friendly troops in South Vietnam rose quickly in 1965. Even though it may be less expensive to fly air sorties from land bases, such bases take months to build. While construction was going on in 1965, an extra carrier flew the sorties needed.)

When a crisis does turn into a conflict, one US objective is to control its intensity. Because the United States has major interests overseas, including the well-being of many allies there, local conflicts that spill over can be very damaging. Employing needed US Navy capabilities far from US shores enhances the likelihood of keeping conflict confined, and also away from North America or other areas of vital concern.

In addition to operating at long distances, the US Navy is expected to respond promptly and to continue to fight for months or even years. The requirement to go into action quickly means that naval forces must be nearby and ready. This is achieved by keeping them manned and equipped and exercising them regularly. The exercises stress likely

Below: The massive 16in (406mm) main guns of the USS *Iowa* and her three sisters offer unrivalled shore-bombardment capability in hulls virtually invulnerable to all but nuclear weapons.

Bruce F. Powers, Senior Fellow, Strategic Concepts Development Center, National Defense University, Washington, DC.

combat employment and tend to be more sophisticated the closer the forces are to the scene of their likely employment. In particular, the forces regularly stationed in the Mediterranean Sea, the Indian Ocean, and the western Pacific Ocean conduct multi-ship exercises that stress several types of naval warfare within the space of a few days. They also exercise with both other US and allied forces.

The requirement to fight on also influences the design of the US Navy. Staying power is built into individual ships; it is also achieved by providing both relief warships and ships that can replenish warships engaged in combat with ammunition, fuel, spare parts, and food. The replenishment ships permit warships to keep fighting, and to do so several thousand miles from the United States rather than returning home for replenishment. A network of overseas bases increases the flexibility and decreases the distance over which these replenishment ships must sail. Typically, warships retire a hundred miles (160km) or more from the combat area to replenish and then return to it. When warships need repairs or crew rest, the relief warships fill their place. Relief warships operate near the coasts of the United States in peacetime.

Specific Missions

To achieve the objectives described above, US Navy officers focus on missions. The most important is establishing and maintaining control of sea and air space. Other missions are to project air, missile, or amphibious forces ashore and to operate in peacetime in ways that reassure allies and warn potential foes.

Establishing sea control is generally viewed as a prerequisite to projecting naval forces ashore. For example, moving a division or more of troops to assault a distant shore requires many transport vessels. Such ships are lightly armed; their path must be kept safe from opposing forces. Once an amphibious or carrier force has reached its operating area, control of the sea and air space there is also necessary; if control of the operating area is subject to interruption, projection of air or landing forces ashore cannot be achieved reliably.

The relative emphasis placed on each Navy mission has been shifting since World War II. Such broad objectives as ensuring free use of the seas and influencing distant events ashore have remained fixed. But specific Navy missions, such as projecting forces ashore, have shifted in relative importance as technology and the capabilities of potential opponents have evolved.

During the Korean War, for instance, ships of the US Navy (numbers grew to over a thousand) and of some other UN-member navies operated several thousand miles from home waters. Unchallenged at sea, this force devoted itself entirely to air attack of targets ashore, shore bombardment with naval guns,

Right: The new VLS in Ticonderoga class CGs provides great tactical flexibility and improved missile capacity. This is USS *Bunker Hill* in the process of firing a trial salvo of three Standard SAMs from her forward 61-cell VLS complex.

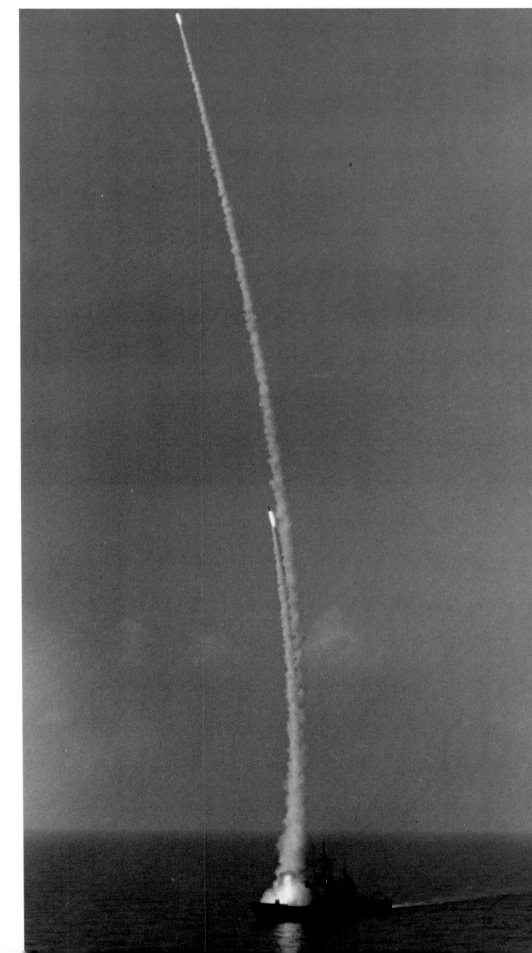

and amphibious landings.

About that time, as part of a general implementation of the nuclear deterrence concept, US Navy aircraft aboard carriers were assigned the mission of delivering nuclear weapons on targets in the Soviet Union. This mission influenced the design of carriers and their aircraft. Aircraft were made larger to carry the large nuclear devices of the time and to strike targets at ranges of a thousand or more miles. The carriers themselves were built larger to accommodate the larger aircraft. Except for amphibious transports, the Navy operated most of its other large surface ships with the carriers.

Beginning in 1960, the carriers gradually transferred the mission of long-range delivery of nuclear weapons to submarines – nuclear-powered submarines firing ballistic missiles with nuclear warheads. The early Polaris and now Poseidon and Trident missiles can be launched from beneath the ocean's surface against targets in the Soviet Union or elsewhere.

As the carriers turned over the mission of delivery of nuclear weapons to submarines, their mission was again focused on attacking closer targets. This shift of attention was accelerated in 1964-72 by the requirements for air support during the Vietnam War. Here, as in Korea, the absence of a naval threat permitted the carriers to mount sorties with maximum non-nuclear bombloads from close to shore and free their escorts occasionally to bombard it.

Potential challenges at sea have compelled shifts in emphasis among Navy missions. The Soviet Navy began its first regular deployments outside home waters, to the Mediterranean Sea, in 1964. In 1967, such deployments became continuous. During that year, an Egyptian vessel launched a cruise missile at

the Israeli destroyer *Eilath* and sank it. Similar missiles were carried by some of the Soviet ships that had recently arrived in the Mediterranean. There – and, later, elsewhere as US Navy operations in Vietnam decreased – the Navy developed and exercised procedures for dealing with opposing surface forces armed with cruise missiles.

In short-term crises that call for the application of naval power ashore at places where the Soviet Navy concentrates forces, virtually all US Navy resources in the vicinity will have to be directed to dealing with the concentrated Soviet forces before USN attention can return to events ashore. In places where the Soviet Navy is absent or weak – such as in some Third World settings – the threat of the US Navy's unfettered activities is reduced, and so some USN attention can be concentrated on events ashore from the outset.

Submarines, particularly in the Atlantic Ocean, have long been a major concern to the US Navy. German submarines nearly stopped the Atlantic flow of supplies to Europe in 1917 and again in 1942. After 1945, the Soviet Union expanded its large submarine force. To deal with the resultant threat to their freedom of action, US aircraft carriers are therefore allotted antisubmarine helicopters and fixed-wing antisubmarine aircraft. In addition to those fitted with ballistic missiles, nuclear-powered attack submarines have entered the US Navy in large numbers, adding significantly to its antisubmarine strength. However, the ongoing modernization of the Soviet Navy's attack submarine force has kept US Navy attention on Soviet submarines.

Although the first nuclear weapons for delivery by carrier-based aircraft were designed for use against the Soviet homeland, later nuclear weapons were developed for both offensive and defensive war at sea. Such weapons are no longer limited to aircraft carriers; they include depth charges and surface-to-air missiles.

Likely Wartime Employment
The Secretary of Defense has directed the Navy to be ready to assist allies if NATO is attacked by Warsaw Pact Forces, to be similarly ready to aid Japan and South Korea, to

conduct operations near the Persian Gulf, to handle similarly-scaled contingencies elsewhere, and to manage crises. US forces are tasked to be able to deal with the NATO war and with combat elsewhere as well. For the Navy the current planning assumption could mean simultaneous fighting in three oceans – Atlantic/Mediterranean, Indian, and Pacific.

A NATO war would place great stress on all US forces, including those of the Navy. In such a war, they might be called upon to provide NATO ground forces with air support from carriers or to assist by landing Marines. To do either would require control of sea and air space in the vicinity. If the war went on for weeks or months, extensive sea control operations would be required of NATO navies so that NATO armies and air forces engaged in Europe could be supplied by merchant shipping from North America. Any of these missions, moreover, might involve use of tactical nuclear weapons.

With or without nuclear weapons, the US Navy might be expected to participate extensively in such sea control while providing NATO land forces – especially in the exposed flanks of northern or southern Europe – with more direct support. In such a conflict, the US fleet would have to help fend off Soviet attacks at sea and cope with Warsaw pact air defenses ashore. NATO, with the combined capabilities of its navies including the US Navy, would find its hands full in dealing with these threats. If the US Navy were called upon to fight a lesser war elsewhere at the same time, NATO would be especially taxed.

Crises in the Middle East, Persian Gulf, or Korea might require US forces, and the US Navy would probably play a large role in these contingencies. Because of its access to each area from the sea, the Navy's capabilities and flexibility make it a tool the US Government is apt to use in these more geographically constrained wars. It was once thought that combat in these more remote areas would be less intense than NATO combat or that opponents would be weaker than the Soviet Union. But the diffusion of advanced weaponry to these areas over the past 10 to 15 years calls for the best the US Navy has; aircraft such as the highly sophisticated F-14 interceptor designed

Below: Now in reserve, USS *Thomas Jefferson* was built as an Ethan Allen class SSBN but converted to an SSN when her obsolete Polaris SLBMs were phased out. Two sisters serve as special-mission submarines for clandestine insertion/extraction missions.

Above: The F-14A has a comparatively poor powerplant, and the type is to be revised as the F-14D with the more powerful and reliable F110 as well as upgraded avionics. These are Tomcats (background) of USS *Saratoga* during the Libyan crisis of 1986.

Below: CVs can operate only in conjunction with powerful cruisers such as these, and the provision of nuclear-powered escorts for CVNs generates unexcelled operational flexibility.

for use against the Soviet foe may face Soviet aircraft flown by non-Soviet pilots. Soviet entry into such contingencies would further complicate and enlarge the Navy's tasks.

Conflicts of yet smaller scope are rising in relative likelihood of occurrence. Within the Third World, rapid political changes – caused by burgeoning populations, religious upheavals, resource discoveries, and the like – and growing military power made available by purchases of advanced-technology weaponry by newly-rich nations all combine to form a dangerous mixture. The resulting explosions,

when viewed against the background of increasing economic interdependence in the world, can be more disruptive than a decade or two ago. Containment and neutralization of them will sometimes fall to the United States. If called upon to deal with such explosions, the Navy will have to be flexible, deft, and controlled to avoid making the mixture even more explosive.

Peacetime Deployment Posture

The peacetime deployment posture of the US Navy reflects two compromises. One is between those areas of the world deemed most important in the political-economic sense and where the Navy is most likely to be employed in wartime and crises. The other compromise is between placing ready forces close to those areas and holding some back for a surge.

In peacetime the US navy deploys forward one-seventh to one-third of its warships – depending on class. A total of 13 carriers make up the current active pool of deploying carriers. Current practice has a third of the active aircraft carriers thousands of miles from the United States. On a typical day at least one US carrier is deployed to the Mediterranean Sea, at least one other to the western Pacific Ocean, and another operates in the Indian Ocean. A fourth is usually either in the Mediterranean Sea or western Pacific. (Carriers deploy overseas for approximately six months at a time.) These four carriers are backed up by nine other active carriers assigned to bases in the continental United States. Because of the great distances from home and a policy of "relief on station", one of the nine is often enroute to or from one of the forward stations. The carriers based in the United States are in various states of operational training and repair, including one or two in overhaul. (In addition, during the 1980s, the four carriers commissioned in the 1950s are undergoing extraordinarily extensive 28-month overhauls, one at a time. These overhauls will extend the carriers' lives by 15 years.)

A carrier, its embarked aircraft, their pilots, the escorting ships, and their crews customarily train together for a deployment. This period of preparation builds working relationships and mutual confidence. Training includes advanced exercises in, for example, the North Atlantic during preparation for deployment to the Mediterranean. When a group of ships that includes an aircraft carrier deploys, it generally operates together as a battle group. Amphibious ships are similarly grouped; because the Marines make up a single fighting unit once they have landed and their effectiveness ashore depends partly on how well their landing is coordinated, there are obvious advantages to grouping their transports.

Forward deployed ships move regularly for exercises and port visits. The forces deployed forward are ready for combat, some of those to the rear are ready to augment those forward, and all have the ability common to all naval forces – freedom to move in crises. In cases of potential conflict, the carriers in that part of the world, together wih escorts and other ships such as transports, are usually moved closer to the trouble spot. An additional carrier with supporting ships is sometimes dispatched from the United States. At least one such carrier on each coast can be dispatched immediately, arriving in the Mediterranean in 4 to 5 days, in the western Pacific in 8 to 10, or in the Arabian Sea in 12 to 25 – depending on the risks in using the Suez Canal. Another carrier on each coast can be dispatched 3 to 5 days later.

If a war lasted six months and theaters elsewhere could spare a temporary loan of forces, as many as 12 carriers could be sent to the combat theater. A war lasting years might require construction of additional carriers.

US/USSR Maritime Bases and Facilities

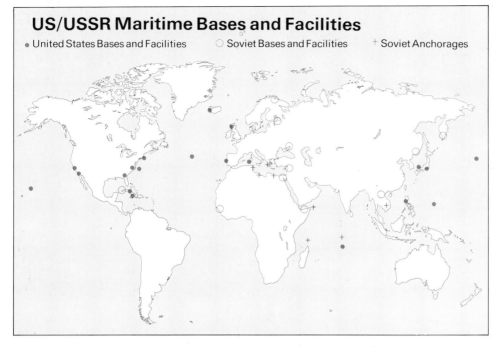

• United States Bases and Facilities   ○ Soviet Bases and Facilities   + Soviet Anchorages

Table 1: Evolving Composition of the US Navy

	FY 1980	FY 1986	FY 1987
Aircraft carriers	13	13	14
Battleships	0	3	3
Cruisers/destroyers	107	101	104
Frigates	71	113	115
Nuclear-powered attack submarines	74	97	99
Diesel-powered attack submarines	5	4	4
Ballistic missile submarines	40	38	39
Strategic support ships	8	6	6
Amphibious ships	66	62	62
Patrol combatants	3	6	6
Mine warfare ships	3	3	4
Underway Replenishment ships	48	54	57
Support forces ships	41	54	53
Total	**479**	**554**	**567**

Naval Bases

Naval bases in the United States provide the full range of services needed, including overhaul, refueling, aircraft rework, ordnance storage, sensor calibration, and recreation. US Navy bases overseas tend to provide a narrower range of services. Overhauls typically are not done overseas, nor are repairs that can be deferred until the end of a deployment. Overseas bases exist to provide the services a deployed fleet must have to stay ready. In wartime, large-scale operations using Marines are often conducted to seize such bases overseas.

One way to ease the burden of a peacetime policy that puts so much of the fleet's warships forward is to station some of them overseas indefinitely, saving transit time. But, because virtually all overhauls are done in the United States, indefinite overseas stationing has not been adopted. Instead, a compromise has been arranged for some submarine and destroyer tenders, the command ships that serve as flagships overseas, and some combatant ships. It is known as "homeporting", and assigns some ships overseas for the full 4 to 7 years between

overhauls. In the mid-1970s, a squadron of destroyers was "homeported" in Greece for three years. An aircraft carrier, a cruiser, a conventionally powered submarine, and a squadron of destroyers are based that way in Japan, and a cruiser is "homeported" in the Philippines.

Past Technological Improvements

The US Navy converted its ships from sail to steam in the second half of the nineteenth century. Steam required coaling stations along the routes. Because steam made large-scale operations more reliable, fleets could

Below: A catapult officer of USS *Coral Sea* gives the order to launch an E-2 Hawkeye, the US Navy's highly effective airborne early warning/command system and combat aircraft force multiplier.

Above: The US Navy is recommissioning four battleships like USS *New Jersey*, and using them at the core of multi-role Surface Action Groups.

sustain coverage of larger areas. Since conversion from coal to oil, which is more easily transferred at sea than coal, direct and frequent dependence on bases for refueling has decreased. (The bases now serve more as storage points for such consumables as ammunition, jet fuel, and oil for ships, and as transit points for the spare parts on which the fleet increasingly depends.) Thirteen of the Navy's surface ships, being propelled by nuclear power plants, are virtually free of the usual refueling requirements; however, the four large aircraft carriers, *Enterprise, Nimitz, Eisenhower*, and *Vinson*, need occasional replenishment of their aviation fuel. (A conventionally propelled carrier must, every few days, take on ship fuel as well as aviation fuel.) All US Navy submarines constructed since 1956 have nuclear propulsion, making them less vulnerable to radar and visual detection than the diesel-electric submarines that regularly have to break the surface of the water.

The outcome of sea battles has always depended, in large part, on the ranges at which ships could detect each other, on fire control systems, on weapon ranges, and on the ability of ships to absorb hits. The introduction of ironclad ships over a hundred years ago was followed by the development of armor-piercing ammunition for naval guns. The range of these guns was slowly extended to the range of the visual horizon, about 20 miles (32km), and then slightly beyond. Accuracy also improved with the introduction of rangefinders, computers, and radars. Aircraft first operated from ships to extend the range at which targets could be detected and identified – beyond ship horizons – so that naval gunfire could be concentrated against them. Later, the aircraft began to carry bombs and torpedoes. World War II proved surface ships to be vulnerable to attacks by aircraft; the carrier became the preeminent ship of the line. As with naval guns earlier, the range of aircraft operating from ships was increased, and their speed was

improved by the introduction of jet engines in the late 1940s. This was followed by increases in the speed and altitude of aircaft designed to fight other aircraft and in the range and bombload of aircraft designed for strike roles.

Detection of targets had been largely visual, but World War II brought radar and sonar to ships, and radar to aircraft. Shipborne radar permitted detection of air targets far beyond the range of naval guns; guided antiair missiles began to replace guns in the mid-1950s to take advantage of the larger detection range made possible by the radars and the greater accuracy of the missiles. In the late 1970s, Harpoon surface-to-surface missiles began to supplant still more naval guns; the introduction of Tomahawk surface-to-surface missiles in the early 1980s continued that trend. For several reasons – among them to return 16-inch guns to the fleet, to increase the size of the Navy relatively inexpensively, and to insure that large numbers of cruise-missile hits can be taken by some ships – four World War II battleships are being reactivated during the 1980s. The last of these ships – the *Wisconsin* – is expected to be recommissioned in 1989. These 58,000-ton battleships are being modernized with Harpoon and Tomahawk, but nonetheless will often operate under the cover of aircraft from carriers.

High-powered shipborne sonars, such as the SQS-26, which arrived in the 1960s, extended the range at which submerged submarines could be detected. Airborne radar used at first for antisubmarine work and detection of surface ships was later extended to antiair warfare. Radar allowed interceptors to detect other aircraft beyond visual range; air-to-air missiles of greater range than air-to-air guns soon followed. The heat-seeking (passive infra-red homing) Sidewinder of 2 to 3 miles (3 to 5km) range came first. Its early models had to attack from the rear of the target. The Sparrow missile followed, permitting attack at 10 to 15 miles and from any heading because of its radar guidance. Only one Sparrow at a time could be controlled by the F-4 interceptor that had fired it. This limitation was overcome in the mid-1970s by introduction of the F-14 interceptor with 104nm (191km) range Phoenix missiles.

Force Coordination

The arrival of long-range weapons and sensors in quantity in the US fleet has made coordination of forces especially important. When several ships and aircraft operate together in a battle group, as is customary, the capabilities of their sensors and weapons overlap, often beyond the range at which any one of the ships or aircraft could, alone, destroy the target. Coordination of the sensors or weapons on several ships, aircraft, or at points ashore is needed to take advantage of the overlap.

Coordination occurs by visual signals, as well as by radio, which was added in the past 75 years, and by high-speed computers, which arrived in the past 25. All US Navy aircraft carriers, all cruisers, and several other surface ships have the Navy Tactical Data System (NTDS), providing computer-assisted target tracking and quick radio exchange of tracking data among ships. The 1980s are bringing the more sophisticated AEGIS control system (described later) into the fleet.

The carrier-based E-2C Hawkeye surveillance aircraft, whose capabilities include a look-down radar for detecting and tracking low-flying targets that ships may not be able to detect, has an Air Tactical Data System comparable to the NTDS. It permits linking with the ships' NTDS, so that tracking data can be shared among all units. (Ships also have the potential to draw on the tracking data produced by the larger, land-based E-3 AWACS aircraft.) The most recent version of the land-based P-3 submarine aircraft has the computer and communications capability to participate in this linking; carrier-based interceptors do, too. Though ships without NTDS have significant radio capacity and other means of control, the margin provided by NTDS often causes an NTDS ship to be chosen by a battle group commander as his flagship.

Recent Combat Experience

The coordination capability of the US Navy has been displayed many times, most recently in 1986 in the Gulf of Sidra incident, but never more impressively than in the Gulf of Tonkin in 1972. Five aircraft carriers with attendant escorts, air control ships and replenishment ships operated together in the Gulf of Tonkin. At times, this force operated more than a hundred aircraft simultaneously in combat, tracking both them and potentially hostile aircraft, providing aerial refueling aircraft as needed, recovering downed pilots whose planes had been hit over North Vietnam, tracking surface targets, keeping watch for submarines, and refueling and rearming ships while in motion.

Table 2: Fleets of the US Navy

Fleet	Operating Area	Home Port of Flagship
Second	Atlantic Ocean	Norfolk, Virginia
Third	Eastern Pacific Ocean	Pearl Harbor, Hawaii (headquarters ashore)
Sixth	Mediterranean Sea	Gaeta, Italy
Seventh	Western Pacific Ocean and Indian Ocean	Yokosuka, Japan

Increases in Ship Size

Because ships now carry radars, sonars, missile systems, and coordinating computers, the ships are larger than ever before. The equipment itself, its large demand for power, the additional men that must operate it, and greater comfort for those crews all have contributed to this growth. So have greater magazine and fuel capacities, to lengthen the time between replenishments. Most classes of US Navy ships have at least doubled in size since World War II. The newest aircraft carriers displace nearly 92,000 tons when fully loaded. However, despite added manning for sophisticated weapon systems, the ratio of manpower to ship tonnage is down sharply from World War II. Rising relative manpower costs have induced it; automation and streamlined damage-control measures have permitted it.

Constraints on the US Navy

The US Navy, along with the other services, faces obstacles in achieving the objectives the United States has for it and in taking advantage of the technological opportunities it creates and that are presented to it. One obstacle is limited funds. Although almost $99,015 million was spent in Fiscal Year 1985 on the US Navy and Marine Corps (whose aviation and amphibious budgets are closely coordinated), many programs compete for these funds. A proposed budget is sent to the Secretary of Defense, and competes for the funds available to the Defense Department. Similar competition occurs as the budget moves through Congress for final approval. The net result is that most programs do not get all the funds their Navy sponsors seek. The reductions take on meaning when another obstacle, the capabilities of potential opponents, is considered.

The principal potential opponent of the US Navy is the Soviet Navy. It has more ships than the US Navy, though less tonnage. The sophistication and breadth of its operations have increased substantially in the past 20 years. The posture of the Soviet Navy had been principally defensive, emphasizing protection of the Soviet homeland by denying portions of the nearby seas to Western navies. Such denial capabilities have taken greater focus in the apparent Soviet intent to preserve their ballistic-missile submarines in bastions north and east of the USSR. Moreover, deployments by the Soviet Navy far from the Soviet Union have become common and threaten localized denial or at least neutralization of Western navies near trouble spots.

During crises, US and Soviet ships tend to intermingle. At such close quarters, the potency of Soviet shipboard missiles, when combined with proximity to Soviet bases for missile-equipped aircraft, as in the Mediterranean or South China Sea, makes a massed attack particularly threatening. Conversely, if US forces were to take the initiative in such circumstances, they would pose a serious threat to the Soviet Navy. The advantage to the force that strikes first inhibits the action both governments take with their fleets.

Some obstacles to orderly development of a navy cannot be foreseen. In the case of the US Navy, the Vietnam War was such an interruption. Its emphasis on projection of force ashore demanded high expenditures of operating funds for carriers and their aircraft, for ships with naval guns, and for the unexpectedly large amounts of ammunition used. At the same time, the Navy's share of the Defense budget shrank because the combat loss rates of Army and Air Force equipment ashore had not been foreseen. The net result for Navy forces designed for sea control was accelerated obsolescence and relative inattention to replacement forces.

US Navy Composition and Organization Today

Table 1 shows the composition of the US Navy over the past 7 years. The numbers of nuclear-powered attack submarines, frigates and cargo ships have grown significantly. Groups

Above: The superb S-3A packs massive anti-submarine detection and attack capability into a small airframe.

Left: All carriers are limited by supplies of ordnance and aviation spirit, while conventionally-powered units such as USS *Saratoga* additionally require main engine fuel. Hence the importance of fleet oilers such as the Mispillion class *Navasota* and her 150,000 barrels of fuel.

of US Navy surface ships tend to be built around a carrier, battleship, amphibious ships or replenishment ships. In wartime, each such group will need accompanying surface combatants. Twenty to thirty of them will provide defense as the lightly armed amphibious ships transit to the landing area, and shore bombardment once there. A like number would escort the 8 to 10 groups of underway replenishment ships that would be needed to keep fighting ships on station. Yet others would be needed for convoy duty.

Besides the 553 ships in the Navy, there are 5,700 aircraft, with roughly one-quarter of them operated by the Marine Corps. Approximately 1,000 are aboard large aircraft carriers. Another few hundred, mostly helicopters, are aboard smaller ships, including amphibious assault ships. Land-based aircraft include 24 squadrons of 9 P-3s each.

Some attack submarines would be assigned to antisubmarine work in wartime, including 1 to 3 submarines to each of the battle groups built around a carrier. These groups also would each include more than 5 surface combatants and be supported by their own carrier-based aircraft and by P-3s.

Each ship and aircraft in the US Navy is assigned to one of four fleets for operational control. Table 2 shows the four fleets and their

customary operating areas. The fleet to which any one ship or aircraft is assigned changes with time. Deployments overseas mean assignment to the Sixth or Seventh Fleet for several months. The approximate peacetime composition of those fleets is shown in Table 3. After a deployment is concluded, the ship or aircraft squadron returns to the Second or Third Fleet, respectively. Then, the ship or squadron begins a new training cycle.

The overall management of this rotation is conducted by Navy commanders-in-chief – one for each theater. The organization of operational control is shown in Table 3, where the locations of the headquarters of the commanders-in-chief are also shown. The US Navy organization for management of force rotation is not symmetrical. In the Pacific Fleet, forces in the Third Fleet preparing for deployment are still controlled by the same commander-in-chief when assigned to the Seventh Fleet. When forces are moved to Sixth Fleet from Second Fleet, their operations are controlled by separate commanders-in-chief. This asymmetry stems from the unified command structure of worldwide US forces. That structure (not shown in Table 3 but included in the chapter on organization) keys on four distant theaters: the Pacific, Atlantic, European, and "Central" – the last a unified command encompassing Southwest Asia and the Persian Gulf.

US Navy and Marine Corps forces are integrated within fleets as shown in Table 4. (It was Task Force 62 that spent 1½ years at Beirut airport until early 1984.) One level up, the forces of the US Army, the integrated US Navy/Marines, and the US Air Force report to their theater commanders-in-chief through commanders-in-chief such as those of the Navy shown in Table 3. (The MidEast Force is a 20-year-old 3 to 5 ship entity that has

Above: The plot develops on the vital Naval Tactical Data System board of a Spruance class DDG, providing the command crew with an accurate and real-time tactical picture of the current situation.

operated largely within the Persian Gulf.) Since late 1979, about 20 ships under Seventh Fleet control have operated in the nearby Arabian Sea. The addition of Arabian Sea commitments along with increased exercise activity off central America since 1982 has, despite growth in the size of the fleet, increased peacetime stress on it.

The commanders-in-chief of the Pacific and Atlantic Fleets each have several subordinate commanders charged with administrative control of various types of forces. Each of these subordinate commanders tends to be concerned with one type of ship only – such as a submarine – and is responsible for development of tactics and doctrine, providing manpower, spare parts, appropriate safety standards, etc., for the ships. The ships and aircraft assigned to the Sixth Fleet are under the administrative contol of the commander-in-chief, Atlantic Fleet.

The navy commanders-in-chief are autonomous in some respects. Operating doctrine and procedures for their forces can vary but, because the forces and personnel under their control rotate, these variations are not significant.

The ultimate unifying influence in the US Navy is provided by the Chief of Naval Operations (CNO). Despite his title, the CNO commands no forces. He does, however, select the forces that will make up the Navy. He does so by considering the operational problems faced by fleet commanders, the postulated threat, guidance on US strategy from the Secretary of Defense, emerging technologies, available manpower, and budget constraints. Much of the CNO's impact comes 5 to 35 years after his decisions have been made. But, during his four-year term of office, the CNO is also responsible for more immediate concerns – the provision of manpower and other resources to the fleet commanders-in-chief and for overall Navy policies.

The US Navy has 581,000 men and women on active duty; all are volunteers. Since graduation from secondary school increases the chances of successful completion of enlistment and of the Navy's many schools that

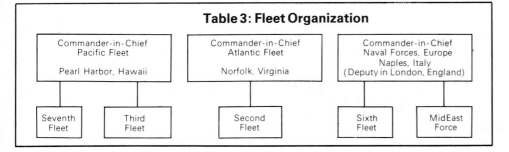

Table 3: Fleet Organization

Commander-in-Chief Pacific Fleet Pearl Harbor, Hawaii		Commander-in-Chief Atlantic Fleet Norfolk, Virginia	Commander-in-Chief Naval Forces, Europe Naples, Italy (Deputy in London, England)	
Seventh Fleet	Third Fleet	Second Fleet	Sixth Fleet	MidEast Force

Above: The US Coast Guard is a separate military service in its own right, but in war can be placed under the operational control of the US Navy, which would find boats such as the cutter *Munro* useful for escort and anti-submarine warfare.

Right: With its major assets formed into battle groups each centered on a CV, the US Navy fully appreciates the value of up-to-date tactical information such as that of the Command Support System with input from space, air, surface and submarine sources.

prepare recruits to operate and maintain increasingly sophisticated equipment this key indicator is looked at carefully. Currently, some 89 percent of Navy recruits have completed secondary school.

The Naval Reserve stabilized at 220,610 men and women at the end of December 1985; 131,344 of them drill regularly and are the Navy's primary source of immediate mobilization manpower. Some serve in complete operational entities such as ships, squadrons, and construction battalions. At present, there are 14 ships that can be mobilized immediately: a destroyer, eleven frigates, and two tank landing ships. Reserve aircraft operate around the world. Two of six reserve light attack squadrons received the modern F/A-18 "Hornet" aircraft in 1986. Reservists provide a pool of skills that add to the active Navy's flexibility. For example, nearly 400 volunteer reservists relieved regular crew members aboard the battleship *New Jersey* during Christmastime in 1983 while the ship was on station off Lebanon.

A discussion of total available naval resources would be incomplete without consideration of the US Coast Guard. In peacetime, it is part of the Department of Transportation; in wartime, part of the Department of Defense.

The Coast Guard's ships include approximately 250 cutters (the Coast Guard calls icebreakers, patrol boats and other ships "cutters" – as long as they are 65 feet in length) and more than 2,000 smaller "boats". The Coast Guard also has 198 aircraft and 38,000 men and women on active duty. Its peacetime

activities are centered on search and rescue, aids to navigation, and law enforcement among civil traffic near US coasts, but its wartime missions include port security, antisubmarine warfare, convoy escort, and mine countermeasures. Preparation for filling out Navy capabilities in wartime thus competes with peacetime activities. The rise in demand for peacetime service, particularly the rapidly rising demand for law and treaty enforcement, is placing significant stress on the Coast Guard's training for wartime. Nevertheless, the Coast Guard remains ready to contribute: for example, a cutter, a C-130 aircraft, and two search and rescue platforms participated at Grenada on invasion day in October, 1983. Later, four cutters, three patrol craft, and a buoy tender helped consolidate the invasion's results.

Capabilities of US Navy Active Forces
The US Navy is structured to assert control over the oceans and, when necessary, over adjacent territory; the Soviet Navy, on the other hand, is structured to deny that control.

In antisubmarine warfare, the US Navy enjoys significant technological advantages that are buttressed by geographical advantages. US submarine sensors permit detections that allow attacks to be made at long range. Off-ship sensors and information-processing capabilities permit tracking of submarines, thus increasing the likelihood that attacks will be successful. Widespread and well-placed US air bases for operation of P-3 antisubmarine aircraft give them an advantage. Because the large Soviet submarine force must move out of home waters in wartime if it is to help deny contested areas to Western naval forces, and since the exit from those waters to the North Atlantic in particular, is narrow, US defenses can be concen-

trated. Attack submarines could be stationed in barriers to take advantage of this.

Despite these US advantages, the size of the Soviet force and the slow pace of any anti-submarine campaign is apt to present vexing problems. If the Soviets deploy their submarine significantly before combat, high initial US losses are possible.

The Soviets learned well the lesson taught by Japanese "kamikaze" attacks on American and British surface ships toward the end of World War II. Cruise missiles (low-flying homing weapons) have been fitted on some Soviet submarines and are now widely deployed on Soviet cruisers and destroyers. These pilotless missiles are directed against surface ships; they can be redirected in flight. They have proved their potency, as in the *Eilath* sinking and, when fired by aircraft, in the 1982 sinkings of the British Royal Navy's HMS *Sheffield* and the *Atlantic Conveyor* near the Falkland Islands.

The intermingling of forces that sometimes occurs in crises tends to offer great advantage to the side that shoots first if it is willing to incur the risks of a war. The potential harm to US surface ships from Soviet cruise missiles fired from intermingled positions is made more severe by the added possibility of prompt follow-up attacks with torpedoes fired by submarines. This combination, if effectively delivered, could disable many US ships. Still more could be lost to air-launched cruise missiles. If attacks by Soviet land-based "Backfire" bombers equipped with antiship missiles were coupled with surface-fired missile and submarine torpedo attacks, defenders would have their hands full.

With reasonable prospects for eventual, if not immediate, establishment of sea control, US capabilities to project naval power ashore can be addressed. It is here that most of the

Above: Now equipping US Navy and Marine Corps squadrons, the F/A-18 provides an unrivalled air combat and attack capability of excellent range.

combat experience gained in Vietnam resides. Each US aircraft carrier is a potent force. Its 24 A-7s or F/A-18s, 10 A-6s, 24 F-14s or F-18s, and 25 to 30 other aircraft can mount a devastating strike of about 40 aircraft at several hours' notice. In a strike of this kind, half the aircraft may carry bombs or air-to-surface missiles. The loads possible on today's carrier-based aircraft mean that such a strike could deliver 75 tons of bombs on targets as far as 300 to 400 miles (480 to 640km) from the carrier. When, instead of major strikes, more routine production of sorties is required, as often happened in Vietnam, a large carrier is capable of 110 to 120 sorties a day when operating aircraft for 12 hours and then resting for 12. This performance is possible at night as well as in daylight, and is readily sustained for a month or more.

Such output can be interrupted, however. The example of the North Vietnamese Air Force shows how. This force of no more than 100 fighter aircraft prevented carriers in the Gulf of Tonkin and larger numbers of US Air Force bases ashore from achieving maximum output. The usual way to measure fighter performance is the exchange ratio: in the case of the Vietnam War, the number of MiGs lost versus US fighters lost. The MiGs initially held their own at that, but were later over-whelmed. However, detections of MiGs near US strike groups over North Vietnam sometimes caused heavily-laden attack aircraft to jettison their bombloads before reaching the target so as to decrease their vulnerability to the MiGs. This, too, is a useful measure of the effect of the North Vietnamese Air Force. The

most subtle measure captures the most pervasive effect the MiGs had. Ten to fifteen percent of the sorties flown from carriers in the Gulf of Tonkin were launched with air-to-air missiles instead of air-to-ground bombs in case MiGs should appear; they almost never did. Thousands of sorties that might have carried bombs did not. Similarly, the threat from North Vietnamese surface-to-air missiles diverted thousands of other USN, USMC, and USAF sorties to suppression by jamming or direct attack on the SAM firing sites.

Despite the possibilities for interruption of carrier strikes or diversion of some of their aircraft to other missions, a US carrier near a friendly country's shoreline poses a considerable problem for a potential aggressor. Similarly, the amphibious assault capabilities of US Marines embarked in Navy ships permit rapid landing of an effective force. Amphibious transports can move at 20 knots (37km/h) and thereby create uncertainty regarding the

choice of a landing site. The large replenishment force of the US Navy can keep up with the amphibious force. It can also replenish the faster carrier battle groups while they are underway, day or night.

Despite many strengths, the US Navy is notably weak in some areas. The problems of dealing with massed missile attacks have already been mentioned. Groups of ships without carriers are limited in their ability to detect, identify, and track ships beyond visual range. As a result, effective use of the surface-to-surface Harpoon and Tomahawk missiles that are being installed in large numbers of surface combatants will be limited to visual or radar ranges unless sensors on aircraft or elsewhere can help. The threat of large-scale use of mines by the Soviet Navy is not matched by large-scale countermeasure forces or exercises in the US Navy – the present active inventory includes only three mine warfare ships. This is in the process of being redressed.

Above: USS *Vincennes* is a Ticonderoga class escort cruiser, a type optimized in sensors and weapons for the defense of carrier battle groups against saturation attack by aircraft and anti-ship missiles.

The Navy's current plans called for 14 "Avenger" (MCM-1) Class ships and 17 "Cardinal" (MSH-1) Class Minesweeper Hunters. Eleven MCMs were funded through 1986; the lead ship of the MSH-1 Class was funded in FY84, and four more were appropriated in 1985. The substantial ability of the US Navy to manage massed forces at sea has depended on high-frequency (HF) radio communications. These transmissions, readily detectable at ranges beyond the horizon and susceptible to interference by jamming, are another weakness of the US fleet. The fleet's vulnerability to nuclear attack will be addressed later.

Tomorrow's US Navy
The composition of any navy changes slowly because ships normally have useful lifetimes of 20 to 40 years. (Aircraft last about half as long.) In 1963, the US Navy was composed of 916 ships, many of which were built towards the end of World War II and many were retired by the mid-1970s; many others were constructed during the 1950s, as Korea and the Cold War pushed up the size of the Navy. In 1963, the US Navy had 24 aircraft carriers; nine were smaller ones configured for antisubmarine work. The conversion to a nuclear-powered submarine force had just gotten underway; the Navy has five diesel-powered submarines still in commission, but all are more than 25 years old.

Continued growth in the number of US Navy ships is planned for the coming decade. The navy goal is 600 ships by the end of 1989. Some 19 new ships were delivered in 1985. In mid-1986, there were 84 naval ships either under construction, conversion or reactivation at 17 different shipyards throughout the United States.

Table 4: Peacetime Composition of Deployed Fleets

Sixth Fleet
Task Force 60
  1 to 2 carriers
  10 to 14 surface combatants

Task Force 61
  5 amphibious ships

Task Force 62
  1 reinforced USMC battalion

Task Force 63
  6 to 7 underway replenishment ships
  4 auxiliaries

Task Force 66
  6 attack submarines

Task Force 67
  1½ maritime patrol squadrons
  1 reconnaissance squadron

Task Force 68
  Special Operations

Task Force 69
  4 to 5 attack submarines

Seventh Fleet
Task Force 71
  Flagship, 7th Fleet

Task Force 72
  3½ maritime patrol squadrons
  1 reconnaissance squadron

Task Force 73
  7 to 9 underway replenishment ships
  6 to 7 auxiliaries

Task Force 74
  6 attack submarines

Task Force 75
  20 surface combatants

Task Force 76
  8 amphibious ships

Task Force 77
  1 to 2 carriers
  12 to 19 surface combatants

Task Force 79
  2 reinforced USMC battalions

Task Force 70
  (Indian Ocean force of about 20 ships
  seconded from the other Task Forces
  in this table)

New Ships and Aircraft

Seven Ohio Trident ballistic-missile submarines have been commissioned, five are being built, and two more are on order. These large (18,700-ton) submarines carry 24 ballistic missiles each. The C-4 missiles have a 4,350 mile (7,000km) range, permitting operation of the submarines over a much wider area than the Polaris submarines with Poseidon missiles they replace. The ninth Trident submarine will be the first fitted with the longer-range and more accurate D-5 missile in 1989. The increase in operating area, the increased number of missiles per submarine, the quieter operation, improving accuracy, and the expected reduction in frequency of overhauls should all make the Trident a potent ballistic missile deterrent force.

Before proceeding with a description of other weapon systems that will soon be entering the US fleet, it is worth noting that eventual performance in the fleet seldom matches predeployment claims. Those claims are generally made with implicit assumptions of near-perfect maintenance, a cooperative atmosphere or ocean, and perfect information available to commanders. Though such assumptions are unjustified, they color nearly all descriptions of future weapon systems.

Two types of Light Airborne Multipurpose System (LAMPS) helicopters are employed on Navy surface ships to extend their antisubmarine warfare capability. The first system (LAMPS Mark I) is the SH-2F and is the primary ASW sensor for more than 80 surface combatants. It is expected to remain so through the year 2000, and, therefore, its capability is continuously upgraded. Specific upgrades include T-700 engines, onboard sonobuoy processing capability, 99 channel sonobuoy capability and secure tactical navigation data link.

The SH-60B "Seahawk" is the air subsystem of the LAMPS Mark III system scheduled for FFG-7, DD-963, and CG-47 class ships. The total system includes the "Seahawk", the ship's electronics, a helicopter landing system and helicopter support facilities. This computer-integrated, ship/helicopter combat system is designed to increase the flexibility, combat range and effectiveness of surface combatants. LAMPS Mark III was first deployed on four frigates in 1985 and has demonstrated high performance capability; the Navy hopes to acquire 47 Seahawks over the next five years.

It has been 25 years since nuclear-powered attack submarines began joining the US fleet in quantity. These boats were of 3,400 to 4,000 tons submerged displacement. Their replacements, the SSN-688 class of 6,900 tons submerged displacement, have already joined the fleet in numbers and will continue to do so through the 1980s. The 688-class boats are much quieter than their predecessors, and are fitted with the long-range BQQ-5 hull-mounted sonar. By 1990, 52 of them are expected to be in the US fleet. A replacement, SSN-21 (the "Seawolf" class), is on the drawing boards. A fully funded lead ship of this class has been requested for FY1989.

Anti-air warfare capabilities in the US Navy should also be upgraded by the arrival of new systems. Prominent among these is the Aegis combat system, which was introduced with the commissioning of the cruiser *Ticonderoga* in 1983. Aegis depends on the SPY-1 phased array radar permitting automatic detection and tracking, and on the medium-range Standard surface-to-air missile. Eventually, at least one Aegis cruiser will operate with each carrier battle group. Anti-air capabilities are also being upgraded by installation of two Phalanx close-in defense systems, designed to shoot down missiles that pass through the ship's outer defenses.

The US Navy's amphibious force has been

Table 5: Department of the Navy Shipbuilding and Conversion, Navy (SCN) Five Year Plan						
	FY 1983	FY 1984	FY 1985	FY 1986	FY 1987	FY 1983–FY 1987
New construction						
Aircraft carrier (CVN-72/73)	2	—	—	—	—	2
Trident submarine (SSBN)	2	1	1	1	1	6
Attack submarine (SSN-688)	2	3	4	4	4	17
AEGIS cruiser (CG-47)	3	3	3	4	4	17
Destroyer (DDG-51)	—	—	1	—	3	4
Destroyer (DD-963)	—	—	—	2	1	3
Frigate (FFG-7)	2	2	2	3	3	12
Ocean surveillance ship (AGOS)	—	1	—	2	3	6
Mine countermeasures ship (MCM)	4	4	5	—	—	13
Coastal minehunter (MSH-1)	—	1	—	5	5	11
Dock landing ship (LSD-41)	1	1	2	2	2	8
Amphibious warfare ship (LHD-1)	—	1	—	—	1	2
Fast combat support ship (AOE)	—	—	1	1	2	4
Fleet oiler (TAO)	1	3	4	4	6	18
Salvage ship (ARS)	1	1	—	—	—	2
Cable laying ship (T-ARC)	—	—	—	1	—	1
Nuclear cruiser (CGN-42)	—	—	—	—	1	1
Ammunition ship (AE)	—	—	1	2	1	4
Destroyer tender (AD)	—	—	—	1	1	2
Conversion/acquisition						
Battleship activation (BB)	1	1	1	—	—	3
FBM supply ship (TAK) (C)	—	—	1	—	—	1
CV-SLEP	1	—	1	—	1	3
Fast logistics ship (TAKRX) (C)	4	—	—	—	—	4
Survey ship (TAGS) (C)	—	—	2	—	—	2
Hospital ship (TAHX) (C)	1	1	—	—	—	2
Range ship (TAGM) (C)	—	—	—	1	—	1
Total number of ships	**25**	**23**	**29**	**33**	**39**	**149**

A total of six Trident submarines are budgeted for the five-year period. A total of 17 each SSN-688s and CG-47s are budgeted through 1987, with a fairly level stream of construction planned for both during the five-year period. Likewise, a total of 12 FFG-7s are budgeted through 1987 with either two or three scheduled in each of the five years. In the case of Mine Countermeasure Ships (MCMs), however, all of the new construction of 13 ships are budgeted for the first three years of the five-year period. Eighteen fleet oilers (TAOs) are budgeted for FY 1983 through FY 1987.

Source: US Secretary of Navy testimony before Defense Subcommittee Senate Appropriations Committee (RADM Miller statement) March 1982.

upgraded by delivery of five amphibious assault ships (Tarawa class LHAs) with flight decks large enough for potential operation of tactical aircraft. They offer large flight decks for helicopter lift of troops and cargo to the beach, well decks for ship-to-shore landing craft carrying tanks and other heavy equipment, and enough internal capacity to carry a reinforced battalion of troops and equipment. Until now, USMC battalions deployed at sea were generally spread among four or five ships.

Marine Corps forces are being made more rapidly deployable by the creation of three squadrons of Maritime Prepositioned Ships (MPS). The four or five ships in each MPS squadron will carry the equipment for a Marine air/ground force of approximately 15,000 men. The men will be airlifted to the objective area to link up with the equipment. As the link-up will have to occur in a relatively benign setting, it does not represent the same forcible entry capabilities as do Marines in amphibious assault ships. But a benign setting could mean a sizable, well-equipped Marine force would be operating ashore quicker.

The first MPS squadron was loaded in late 1984 and operates in eastern and northern Atlantic waters. The second, which was completed and loaded in 1985, will replace five prepositioned ships in the Indian Ocean and operate in that area. The third was completed in 1986 and will operate in the western Pacific.

Defense against antiship cruise missiles is being buttressed by widespread deployment of NATO Seasparrow missiles on US surface ships, including both combatants and replenishment ships. This system employs the 20-year-old Sparrow air-to-air missile in a surface-to-air mode with a range exceeding five miles (8km). Seasparrow and Phalanx are aboard the battleships and 1950s carriers as they emerge from 1980s refits. Several other NATO countries and Japan are also deploying Seasparrow on their ships.

The longer range Tomahawk is augmenting the 60-nautical mile (110km) Harpoons that are now on many ships. With LAMPS aboard the firing ship, identification of targets at ranges beyond the horizon is possible. LAMPS III extends that range further, as do satellite systems that detect and identify surface targets.

In fact, systems – including those that use satellites – that stress management and processing of information rather than direct destruction of targets are claiming an increasing share of US Navy resources; this will continue into the 21st century. Another current example is a set of communications satellites that use ultrahigh-frequency (UHF) radio signals. UHF radio cannot be detected beyond the 20-mile (32km) line-of-sight horizon of the transmitting ship. Since the satellite is above the ship, it can receive the signal and relay it to distant points without betraying the position of the transmitting ship.

The sophisticated swing-wing F-14s began replacing F-4 interceptors in the mid-1970s, and that modernization is now essentially complete. The F-14s are expensive, and a less costly complement to them was therefore sought for carrier service. The F/A-18 began appearing in the Navy and Marine Corps in 1982. Initially conceived as a relatively simple aircraft, the addition of many features has driven the cost for a massive planned purchase of almost 1,400 aircraft above $40,000 million. Despite a cost approaching that of an F-14, the F/A-18 offers an advantage by using the same airframe for an attack airplane, the A-18, which will replace the A-7s. The first carrier deployment overseas with F/A-18s began in 1985.

The effectiveness of all carrier-based interceptors has been increased by deployment of an improved version of the Sidewinder air-to-air missile. More than 1,000 copies of the upgraded version of the Sidewinder (the AIM-9M) will be acquired in both FY1986 and FY1987. Because of greatly increased sensitivity to the heat emitted by opposing aircraft, the new Sidewinder is not limited to attacks from the rear of its target, but can be used from any bearing. Its potency was proven when fired by British Harriers in the 1982 Falklands campaign.

Unanswered Questions

Some characteristics of the future US Navy cannot be seen clearly. The major questions include:
1. Which should be stressed more in structuring the Navy, global conflict with the Soviets or regional conflicts not necessarily involving them?
2. What is the role and future distribution of aircraft at sea?
3. How vulnerable are surface ships?
4. Can distant targets be located and identified accurately enough to use Navy surface-to-surface missiles at their maximum ranges?
5. How many surface ships should have nuclear propulsion?
6. How should attacks that employ nuclear weapons be countered?

Each question will be addressed in turn.

Should the Navy be structured for wars against concentrated Soviet naval forces and homeland territory or for less-concentrated Soviet forces and intervention in the Third World? How large and sophisticated should it be? These questions underlie much of the current debate over the future US Navy. The concentrated Soviet alternative is demanding and therefore will be costly. The choice will affect the entire Navy; its effect can be seen clearly in carrier and amphibious forces.

If the US Navy and Marine Corps are to be used against concentrated Soviet forces, enough carriers must be built to make sure that – after losses – enough will be operating near Eurasia's coasts when their air sorties are needed. (They are expected to be necessary in the Mediterranean, Far East, and Arabian Sea, may be necessary in northern Europe, and could even be required in central Europe.) Similarly, if USMC ground forces were employed in central Europe or against Soviet concentrations elsewhere, they might require more tanks and other heavy equipment than they now have. If such ground forces were to move to Eurasia in amphibious ships, those ships would need more capacity.

If, on the other hand, naval challenges to Soviet forces close to USSR borders could be sidestepped and if NATO land armies could hold the line without help from amphibious troops, then the carriers and Marines could concentrate on preparations for Third World operations. This would mean fewer sub-

marines and might mean fewer carriers would be needed in the US inventory, and that their aircraft might not face opponents as concentrated as those in Europe. For the Marines, it would probably mean lighter forces designed to intervene quickly and withdraw quickly.

Whether the Navy is oriented toward the Soviet periphery or toward the Third World, the future of sea-based aircraft will be the subject of continuing debate. There is general agreement that aircraft based on ships will be a continuing feature of the US Navy, but how many aircraft, their design, and that of the ships that will operate them is not entirely clear. If the Soviets can attack several carriers successfully, a significant portion of the US Navy's offensive punch would be blunted.

A possible answer lies in aircraft that can take off and land vertically or over a runway a few hundred feet in length. Vertical or short takeoff and landing (V/STOL) technology may produce aircraft that can perform in flight as effectively as conventional aircraft. If V/STOL aircraft that capable can be developed, then smaller, more numerous ships could operate the aircraft. What size ships would be appropriate to operate them? How many? How many aircraft per ship? How reliable must aircraft be that are dispatched to smaller ships if they are to continue operating from them – rather than filling their limited deck space with aircraft awaiting parts? If many ships with aircraft operate far apart, will they need additional communications? Which is more easily defeated – a force of many smaller ships or a force of a few large ships? These questions were thoroughly debated in the United States in the late 1970s. The results: keep the question of aircraft type open by continuing development of V/STOLs, but build additional large aircraft carriers.

How vulnerable are surface ships in an era of widespread cruise missiles? Proponents of submarines and of land-based aircraft say the era of navies built around surface ships is passing, and cite British ship losses in the Falklands as examples. Surface ships, however, cannot be matched for a combination of easy communications and lengthy on-station times running to weeks or months. Because of this, efforts to fashion effective defenses against antiship cruise missiles continue. These include direct defenses, such as Aegis,

Above: Showing its towed MAD "bird" in the retracted position, an SH-60B Seahawk LAMPS III helicopter cruises with the Oliver Hazard Perry class frigate USS *Crommelin*, which can carry two such helicopters.

Phalanx, and F-14s, and indirect ones, such as electronic deception and shifting radio communications to UHF.

Another element of the decentralization of US Navy offensive power is the widespread deployment of Harpoon and now the 300-mile (480km) antiship Tomahawk aboard surface combatants. These deployments are occurring as USAF antiship capabilities (eg, Harpoon-equipped B-52s) are being integrated. Taking advantage of these ranges requires a capability to detect, identify, hit with an effective warhead, and assess the damage to targets well beyond the horizon. This means integrating and passing information among ships and aircraft in such a timely and reliable fashion that doing it presents major problems to the US Navy – a navy that already has made important advances in the management of information.

How many surface ships should be propelled by nuclear power? The tactical advantages of the carefully-designed US power plants can be substantial – greater propulsion reliability and speed, and reduced replenishment frequencies. For an aircraft carrier, though, the investment in such propulsion costs up to twice as much as conventional propulsion. Over the carrier's lifetime, however, the costs of its aircraft are dominant and they do not depend on the means of ship propulsion. The tactical advantages have to be balanced against the cost differences. Building programs in the remainder of the century can produce somewhat different numbers of ships, depending on which propulsion plants are selected for them. (All carriers constructed since 1964 have been nuclear powered.)

Attacks conducted with nuclear weapons present acute problems in defending a fleet. Soviet naval writers tend not to distinguish between use of nuclear and conventional weapons. Soviet writers also stress "decisive strikes" (although some recent writings claim that naval conflict will not necessarily be brief). If strikes with nuclear weapons are to be

Above: The addition of Harpoon anti-ship missile capability has further enhanced the formidable armament load carried by the US Navy's premier maritime patrol aircraft.

Left: First US Navy ship to be fitted (October 1982) with the quadruple Armored Box Launcher for Tomahawk missiles was the destroyer USS *Merrill*.

the means to achieve these goals, defeating them will be many times more difficult than defeating conventional strikes. Because nuclear weapons are more powerful and therefore need not be as accurate, stopping more of them is necessary to protect a fleet. Depending on the size of the warheads on the attacking weapons, it may be necessary to stop *all* of them – a much more demanding task than stopping most. If systems such as Aegis and Phalanx cannot achieve it, then dispersal of defending ships may be necessary to prevent more than one from being disabled by a nuclear detonation. As the separation distance between ships increases, the communication that permits coordination of ships and aircraft becomes more difficult to maintain and the degree of synergism diminishes. If attacks with nuclear weapons are that disruptive to a fleet, then their use (or even the threat of it) offers more advantage to the side whose mission is sea denial than to the side trying to control the seas.

The Continuing Debate

The world's naval officers and other students of naval warfare have not yet reached agreement on which factors are most important in winning war at sea. It is possible to get general agreement on which factors – the ranges of weapons, quality of fighting personnel, staying power of ships, ability to mass and coordinate forces – are important. But, it is much more difficult to rank them in order of importance. It is presently impossible to relate changes in one factor to changes in another in any systematic way. Because of that, debate over how to build and operate more effective navies and how to predict which of them will prevail in combat continues. Such debate is ordinarily illuminated by combat experience, but there has been no conflict between major navies for more than 40 years. Navies are already quite different from what they were then; they will continue to change. The debate will go on.

The United States Marine Corps

For over two hundred years the Marines have participated in every major war fought by the United States, as well as in innumerable police actions and armed interventions in virtually every part of the world. The list of battle honors earned by the Marine Corps since 1775 bears testimony to its impressive record. Certainly, the performances of the Marine Corps at places such as Belleau Wood, Guadalcanal, Iwo Jima, the Chosin Reservoir, and Khe Sanh have earned it a prominent place in the lexicon of military history.

As with any military establishment, the elite US Marine Corps has its own set of traditions, reflecting an institutional interpretation of the Corps' past performance. In part, of course, such traditions are self-serving, highlighting only that which is worthy of emulation and ignoring or discarding anything that is not. Yet traditions cannot be dismissed lightly, especially in the case of a military institution. For such traditions not only influence the way in which the Corps sees itself, but how others view the Corps. They also shape the missions assigned to the Corps, and the way in which it organizes itself for battle.

Over the years, the Marine Corps has traditionally viewed itself as an elite force of infantry, highly disciplined and reliable (its motto is *Semper Fidelis*, or "Always Faithful"), which constituted the "cutting edge" of American diplomacy and power. The dictum that "every Marine was first and foremost a rifleman", while often only nominally accurate, perfected this perception. Even today, the fact that Marine ground combat formations are relatively large units with a high proportion of infantry is evidence of its continued significance.

Further, the fact that Marines were stationed aboard major naval vessels, and traditionally operated in conjunction with the fleet, made them the logical choice for expeditionary forces abroad (sometimes in conjunction with members of the Army and Navy as well). This was particularly true in the years before strategic airlift capabilities became part of the American arsenal. Even then, Marines were used as the initial ground combat forces in a variety of recent interventions (such as Lebanon, 1958; the Dominican Republic and South Vietnam, 1965; and Grenada, 1983), and as a "fire brigade" to relieve pressure on beleaguered American forces (Korea, 1950), and to evacuate American citizens in the face of enemy attack (Phnom Penh and Saigon, 1975), and join in a multinational peacekeeping force to help re-establish order in war-torn localities (Beirut, 1982-84). For the Marine Corps, in other words, being "first to fight" has had more than lyrical significance.

More recently, however, a new set of institutional traditions has been superimposed on those that originally existed. Since World War I, the Marine Corps has come to see itself as an elite assault force, in addition to whatever other qualifications it may have. The skill and ferocity of the Fourth Marine Brigade at Belleau Wood earned them the accolade of Georges Clemenceau for "saving Paris", and the name of *Teufelhunde* ("devil dogs") from the Germans whom they defeated. In that battle, and others like it, Marines fought as line infantry. A unique mission was missing, a mission that began to take shape in the years between the two world wars. First, during those interwar years, the Marines began experimenting with amphibious operations during counterguerrilla operations in several Central American republics. Second, it gained experience at the onset of World War I with amphibious operations while dealing with problems in the Pacific Basin. These traditions merged to produce an amphibious assault force whose maintenance has since been the principal *raison d'etre* for the US Marine Corps. Finally, the evolution of Marine aviation units provided the Corps with its own "air force", a bone of contention within the American armed services for years. After the reorganization of the US defense establishment in 1947, this capability allowed the Marine Corps to lay claim to being a unique, combined-arms, ground-air team with a special competence in amphibious warfare – a team which may be "task-organized" as required for the assigned mission. This was the basic configuration of the Corps when it fought in the Korean and Vietnam wars, and which it retains today.

The Modern Marine Corps

The position of the US Marine Corps in the American defense establishment today reflects a legislative legitimization of the status of the Corps at the end of World War II. That position was delineated by the National Security Act of 1947, as amended in 1952 and afterwards. It entailed a specification of: (1) the relationship of the Marine Corps to the other services in general, and to the Navy in particular; (2) the missions to be performed by the Corps; and (3) the basic force structure of the Corps.

The anomalous position of the Marine Corps within the US defense establishment is highlighted by its relationship to the other services. It is the only branch of the armed services not to be in a separate department. Instead, it has co-equal status with the department of the Navy, the Commandant Marine Corps (CMC) and the Chief of Naval Operations

The Commandant of the Marine Corps (CMC), like the other three service chiefs, acts as a military adviser to the President in his capacity as Commander in Chief of the armed forces. Until 1978 however, this "four services in three departments" organization precluded the Commandant from having a regular seat on the Joint Chiefs of Staff (JCS), although he was permitted to participate in discussions with the other chiefs on a co-equal basis on matters pertaining directly to the Marine Corps. From 1978 onwards, Congress has authorized the Commandant to sit on the JCS as a permanent and equal member.

The missions assigned to the Marine Corps fall into three broad categories. The principal mission of the Corps is to maintain an amphibious capability to be used in conjunction with fleet operations, including the seizure and defense of advanced naval bases and the conduct of land operations essential to the successful execution of a maritime campaign. In addition, the Corps is required to provide security detachments for naval bases and facilities, as well as for the Navy's principal warships. Finally, the Corps carries out additional duties at the discretion of the President.

The third feature of the Marine Corps position within the Department of Defense is also unique: the Corps is the only service to have its basic force structure defined by statutory law.

Right: US Marine Corps amphibious assault is truly a combined-arms operation, with the ground forces delivered from the sea in LVTP7 "Amtraks" and supported from the air by AH-1 SeaCobra helicopter gunships.

Below: Increased US interest in Central America is reflected by this landing exercise in Honduras as craft from the LPD USS *Ponce* maneuver against a backdrop of coast and an LST, the USS *Harlan County*.

Alan Ned Sabrosky, Deputy for Research, US Army War College
Revised and updated by
Robert T. Jordan, Editor Tech-Trends International magazine; formerly Associate Editor, *Leatherneck* magazine.

According to the amended National Security Act of 1947, the Marine Corps will maintain a regular Fleet Marine Force of no less than three divisions, three aircraft wings, and three Force Service Support Groups (FSSG). Active-duty Marine Corps force levels cannot exceed 400,000 personnel, although no minimum force levels are specified. Provision is also made for reserve components to permit the expansion of the regular Marine Corps whenever mobilization occurs.

Current Strength and Organization

The active-duty strength of the Marine Corps at the start of FY86 was 198,300 personnel, including 9,300 women. Since the late 1970s, the Marine Corps has focused on building a "quality" force. Current enlistments reflect over 97 percent high school graduates. High retention rates have permitted the Corps to be very selective in choosing initial enlistees and to discharge marginal performers from its ranks. Better pay and benefits have made it somewhat easier for all the American armed services to obtain and retain better personnel, and the Marine Corps is no exception. The uniformed active-duty force is complemented by a civilian workforce of approximately 22,000 personnel. The selected Marine Corps Reserve consisted of 40,744 reservists as of December 1985. The Marine Corps intends to have all of its reserve units up to full wartime strength by FY1990.

For nominal operational purposes, regular and reserve Marine Corps personnel are organized in four divisions (three regular and one reserve), four aircraft wings (three regular and one reserve), and four Force Service Support Groups (FSSG) (three regular and one reserve). These combat service support organizations augment division units with specialized support when required by the unit's mission. Marine divisional and aircraft wing organizations are larger than their counterparts in the other military services, reflecting the Marine emphasis on multi-purpose assault forces.

This is particularly apparent in the case of the Marine divisional structure. Even more than its advocacy of the combined-arms ground-air team organization concept, the Marine Corps retains its basic faith in the central role of infantry in combat. Thus, the 17,000-man Marine Division (counting attached Navy personnel but excluding supporting personnel who would normally deploy with

divisional units) constitutes the ground combat element of the Marine Air Ground Task Force (MAGTF).

The basic structure of the Marine Division, as it is presented in Chart 1, is essentially the old "triangular" model of World War II vintage, albeit that some changes have recently occurred or are programmed for the next five years. The Division is organized around three infantry regiments, each of which has three infantry battalions and a headquarters element.

In addition to the infantry regiments, each Marine Division has an artillery regiment with three direct support artillery battalions (equipped with 155mm towed howitzers); batteries of self-propelled artillery (155in and 8in howitzers) are also available, and currently assigned to the artillery regiments of

two divisions. Other divisional units include a tank battalion, an armored amphibian battalion, a reconnaissance battalion, a combat engineer battalion, and a headquarters battalion; and each division will soon add a new element – Light Armored Vehicle Battalion (LAVB) equipped with a new family of armored vehicles currently being developed for the Marine Corps.

For their part, the Marine aircraft wings are both large and multipurpose. They are larger than both their Air Force and Navy counterparts, and considerably more diverse in composition than an Air Force wing, which conventionally contains aircraft of only one type. The standard Marine aircraft wing will have from 18 to 21 squadrons with a total of 286 to 315 aircraft. These run the gamut from fighter-attack squadrons (with F-4s and F/A-18s),

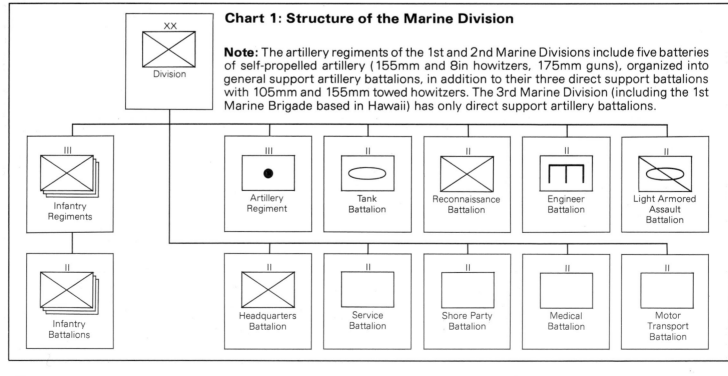

Chart 1: Structure of the Marine Division

Note: The artillery regiments of the 1st and 2nd Marine Divisions include five batteries of self-propelled artillery (155mm and 8in howitzers, 175mm guns), organized into general support artillery battalions, in addition to their three direct support battalions with 105mm and 155mm towed howitzers. The 3rd Marine Division (including the 1st Marine Brigade based in Hawaii) has only direct support artillery battalions.

Division

Infantry Regiments

Infantry Battalions

Artillery Regiment

Tank Battalion

Reconnaissance Battalion

Engineer Battalion

Light Armored Assault Battalion

Headquarters Battalion

Service Battalion

Shore Party Battalion

Medical Battalion

Motor Transport Battalion

Left: The F/A-18A has added a new dual-role fighter/attack dimension to USMC aviation strength. These are Hornets of VMFA-314, part of the 3rd Marine Aircraft Wing's Marine Aircraft Group 11.

Above: Another potent new McDonnell Douglas warplane bolstering USMC air capability is the AV-8B Harrier II, seen here with AGM-65E Laser Maverick Hughes Angle-Rate Bombing system.

light and medium attack squadrons (with A-4s, A-6s and the AV-8A/B Harriers), to tanker/transport squadrons (with KC-130s), to transport and attack helicopter squadrons (with AH-1s, CH-53s, CH-46s, and UH-1s), plus a trio of electronic warfare, observation, and reconnaissance squadrons. These squadrons are organized into three fighter/attack groups, six helicopter groups, and separate special-purpose squadrons, in addition to a wing headquarters squadron, support group, and air control group.

Task Organization and Deployment

For both administrative and operational purposes at the most general level, the Corps has traditionally paired a Marine division and a Marine aircraft wing (plus logistical support units), and divides the three active (or "regu-

lar") division-wing teams between its two principal Fleet Marine Forces (FMF). Currently, two division-wing teams are assigned to the Fleet Marine Force Pacific (FMFPAC), with responsibility for Marine Corps operations in the Pacific Ocean and Indian Ocean regions.

One of these division-wing teams, composed of the Third Marine Division (reinforced) and the First Marine Aircraft Wing, is based in the Western Pacific and Hawaii. Two-thirds of this division-wing team, comprising under normal circumstances approximately 23,000 Marines, are conventionally deployed in the Western Pacific, principally in Okinawa. The remaining one-third of this division-wing team, organized into the First Marine Brigade (reinforced), is based in Hawaii. The other division-wing team with the Fleet Marine

Force-Pacific is based on the West Coast of the United States. This team, which is structured around the First Marine Division (reinforced) at Camp Pendleton, California, and the Third Marine Aircraft Wing at El Toro, California, is principally oriented toward operations in the Pacific Basin. However, it also provides back-up forces for operations elsewhere, as in the Cuban missile crisis of 1962 and the US intervention in the Dominican Republic in 1965. The remaining division-wing is assigned to the Fleet Marine Force Atlantic (FMFLANT), which has responsibility for operations in the Atlantic Ocean, Caribbean Sea, and Mediterranean Sea regions. This team consists of the Second Marine Division, headquartered at Camp Lejeune, North Carolina, and the second Marine Aircraft Wing, headquartered at Cherry Point, North Carolina.

All major formations based within the US proper provide both individual replacements and, on a unit deployment basis, maneuver units (infantry battalions and aviation squadrons) on a rotational basis for Marine formations headquartered in the Western Pacific for

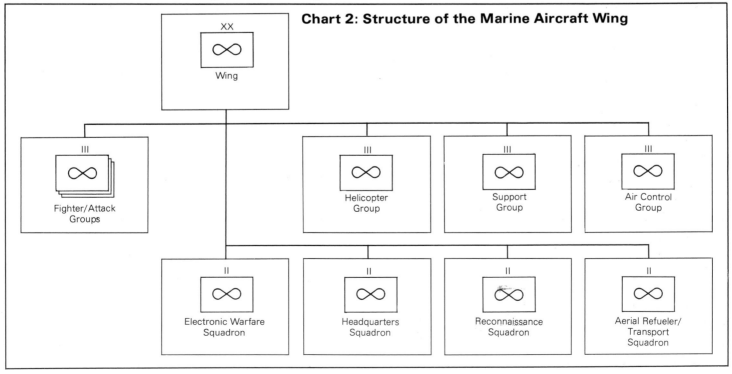

Chart 2: Structure of the Marine Aircraft Wing

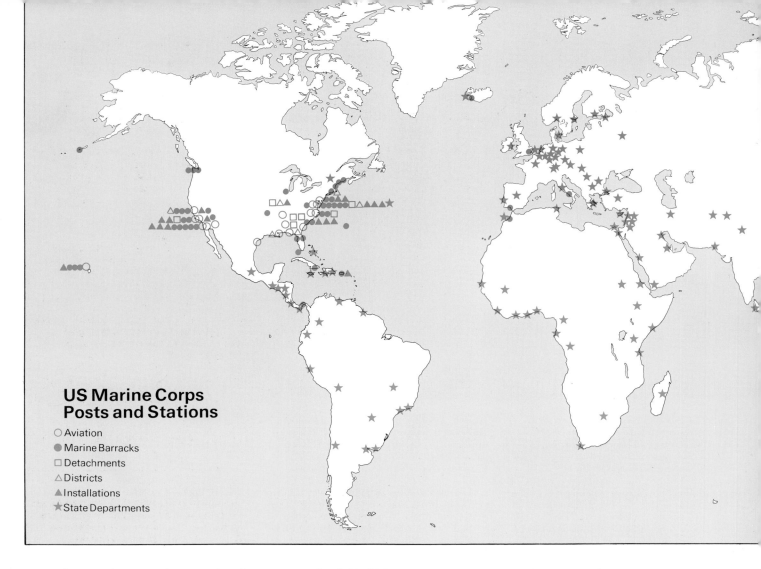

US Marine Corps Posts and Stations

○ Aviation
● Marine Barracks
□ Detachments
△ Districts
▲ Installations
★ State Departments

six-month tours of overseas duty. Reinforced infantry battalions (called "battalion landing teams", or BLTs) also form the core of Marine formations regularly assigned to the 6th Fleet in the Mediterranean and the 7th Fleet (in the Western Pacific), and are occasionally deployed elsewhere as contingencies arise, to provide American commanders with a force capable of being put ashore and committed to action at short notice. Smaller detachments of regular Marines are assigned at 32 Marine Barracks as security forces for certain US naval facilities, to ships, and to United States Embassies and Consulates in more than 100 countries.

Finally, the reserve division-wing team, made up of the Fourth Marine Division, Fourth Marine Aircraft Wing and Fourth Service Support Group is intended to augment and reinforce the regular division-wing teams or provide a fourth division-wing team in time of crisis and mobilization. Its units are located throughout the United States. Training is conducted one weekend each month and two weeks each year. Mobilization drills are conducted to ensure that readiness is maintained.

The extent of Marine assignments, both within the US and elsewhere, is apparent from the portrayal of US Marine Corps Posts and Stations in the map; the current deployment status of Marine maneuver formation (infantry battalions, helicopter squadrons and fixed-wing aviation squadrons), with their parent headquarters, is presented in Table 1.

The size of both the Marine division and the Marine aircraft wing, the built-in reliance of the division on reinforcing elements from the FMF, and the diversity and multipurpose flexibility of the aircraft wing reflect a basic element in Marine Corps organization, planning, and doctrine. This is known as the "Marine Air-Ground Task Force" (MAGTF) concept, and assumes that the relative com-

position of each MAGTF (and especially both the size and the mix of its ground and aviation combat components) would vary according to the mission it was expected to perform. The basic "building blocks" in this approach are the infantry battalion, composite aircraft squadron, and service/support group which may be combined into a Marine Amphibious Unit (MAU), smallest of the air-ground task forces at 1,800 to 4,000 Marines and sailors. Larger air-ground task forces (8,000 to 18,000 Marines and sailors) form the Marine Amphibious Brigade, or MAB, consisting of a Regimental Landing Team of two to five infantry battalions, a Marine Aircraft Group, and a Brigade Service Support Group. The Marine Amphibious Force, or MAF, may be composed of less than one or more than several division-wing teams. At 50,000 plus Marines and sailors, it is the largest and most powerful of these forces.

A number of programmes or plans are in various stages of development, all of them intended to enhance the ability of the Marine Corps to deploy combined-arms task forces more rapidly, more efficiently, and more extensively than in the past. One involves the prepositioning of equipment in certain key areas to reduce the transportation requirements for the insertion and employment of at least the initial Marine contingents. For example, it is planned to preposition in Norway equipment and supplies adequate for a 13,000-man Marine Amphibious Brigade-sized Marine Air-Ground Task Force. Under the Maritime Prepositioning of Ships (MPS) concept, Marines of the MPS brigades would be airlifted to a contingency area to link up with pre-loaded sea-delivered supplies and equipment. In this "marriage-area", the MPS Marines would organize for possible reinforcement or combat duties. The first MPS squadron, fully loaded deployed on July 30, 1984,

with an area of operations in the eastern Atlantic. The second squadron deployed in phases, and replaced the Marine Corps portion of the Near-Term Prepositioning Force in Diego Garcia in December 1985. The third MPS squadron deployed to Guam and Tinian in the Pacific in 1986.

The Marine Corps' ability to task organize is not without restrictions. The combat support elements and command and control assets available constrain the total number of MAUs and MABs which may be formed from the Marine Corps' total assets. In theory, 27 infantry battalions are available to be formed into MAUs. Current levels of amphibious shipping are insufficient to deploy 27 MAUs, however.

Doctrine and Weapons
Perhaps the single dominant characteristic of Marine tactical doctrine is the emphasis on the principle of the offensive. This applies not only to combined-arms amphibious operations, with their projected mix of seaborne and helicopter-borne assault groups attacking with naval gunfire and tactical air support, but to all other operations as well.

In theory, the tactical repertoire of the Marine Corps is as varied as that of any other modern military organization. Certainly, it includes major emphasis on the closely coordinated employment of close air support and (where available and feasible) naval gunfire support as well. Yet, in practice, it often seems that the institutional precedence given to the ability to provide assault forces, coupled with the relatively limited tactical flexibility permitted to amphibious assault forces in the initial stage of an operation, has continued to predominate. And in point of fact, it ought not to be surprising that an institution such as the Marine Corps, which has built its *persona* around the image of an assault force, should

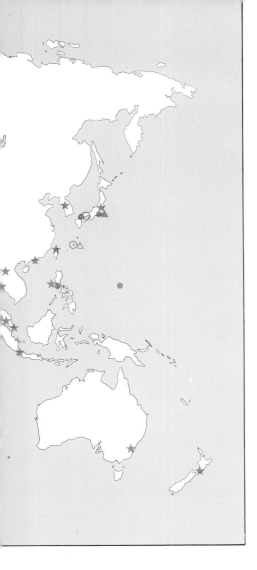

Marine Air/Ground Units

Marine Amphibious Unit
The Marine amphibious unit is the smallest air-ground task force (1,800-4,000 Marines and sailors) and is normally built around a reinforced infantry battalion and a composite aircraft squadron. It is commanded by a colonel and employed to fulfill routine forward afloat deployment requirements. The Marine amphibious unit provides an immediate reaction capability to crisis situations and is capable of relatively limited combat operations. Because of its limited, sea-based sustainability, the Marine amphibious unit will not routinely conduct amphibious assaults and may be considered the forward element of a larger Marine air-ground task force. Marine amphibious units are now continuously deployed in the Mediterranean, Western Pacific and periodically in the Atlantic and Indian oceans and the Caribbean Sea.

Marine Amphibious Brigade
A Marine amphibious brigade is the second basic type of Marine air-ground task force with 8,000-18,000 Marines and sailors and is a task organization normally built around a reinforced infantry regiment and a composite Marine aircraft group. It is commanded by a brigadier general and capable of amphibious assaults and subsequent operations ashore. During potential crisis situations, a Marine amphibious brigade may be forward deployed afloat for an extended period to provide rapid response. With 30 days of self-sustainability, the Marine amphibious brigade may be supported from its sea base, facilities ashore or a combination of both.

Marine Amphibious Force
A Marine amphibious force is the largest (50,000 plus Marines and sailors) and most powerful of the Marine air-ground task forces and normally is built around a division/wing team. However, it may range in size from less than one to several divisions and aircraft wings, together with an appropriate combat service support organization. The Marine amphibious force is commanded by either a major general or lieutenant general, depending on its size and mission. It is capable of conducting a wide range of amphibious assault operations and, with its 60 days of support, sustained operations ashore. The Marine amphibious force can be tailored for a wide variety of combat missions in any geographic environment.

Bottom left: The 5.56-mm FN Minimi light machine-gun has been adopted for the US forces as the M249 Squad Automtic Weapon, and offers a useful combination of light weight, reliability and two feed options.

Below: An M60 machine-gun post on Grenada during 1982. This undertaking showed the utility of USMC weapons and tactics, but also revealed inter-service problems and high-level tactical interference.

prefer to operate in such a manner whenever possible.

The Marine Corps has taken a number of steps to increase its firepower and its mobility in the 1980s. Improved M16 rifles have been issued as the basic infantry weapon. The traditional 13-man rifle squad is returning over the period FY86 to 88, after two years spent in moving toward 11-man squads revealed numerous problems. These squads are equipped with the new 5.56 M249 FN Belgian-made Squad Automatic Weapons (SAWs), providing them with a capability they have not had since the Browning Automatic Rifle (BAR) was phased out, in addition to the 7.62mm M60E3 machine guns and the new 60mm mortars within the weapons platoon.

The battalion weapons company now has a new heavy machine gun platoon with eight firing teams, each of which mans a vehicle with a .50 caliber heavy machine gun and the

Mk 19 40mm "machine gun" – a *de facto* automatic grenade launcher. The battalion weapons company's mortar platoon will also receive an improved version of the 81mm mortar expected to be delivered in 1989, with more range and greater lethality than the current weapon. Literally every weapon in the Marine ground arsenal will have been replaced or improved by the 1990s.

Changes are also under way in the artillery, aviation, and armor capabilities of the Corps. To enhance counterbattery capability, the Marines will acquire three target acquisition batteries over the next five years. The towed 105mm and 155mm howitzers previously in the Marine Corps divisional artillery regiments are being replaced by the M198, 155mm howitzer. Some 433 howitzers were delivered through FY85, with an additional 144 programmed throughout FY86/87. Oddly enough, however, this is also a towed weapon – something of an anomaly, given the prevailing trend in most armed forces toward self-propelled artillery. However, to retain the mobility and flexibility inherent in MAGTFs, the helicopter-transportable M198 is the ideal direct support artillery replacement.

Some 105mm howitzers, however, will be retained in a "contingency reserve" during the transition, perhaps because the new 155mm howitzers are heavier than the older 105mm weapons, and thus less mobile.

Modernization of Marine aviation is likewise proceeding, with an eye to enhancing both close air support (CAS) and tactical airlift capabilities. Three squadrons of CH-53Es, with a 16-ton lift capacity (adequate for lifting 93 percent of a Marine Division's assault echelon equipment) are now operational. Acquisition proceeds with the F/A-18 dual-purpose air-superiority/ground attack aircraft, equipped with both Sparrow III and Sidewinder missiles in addition to its ordnance. Further, the Falklands War of 1982 reaffirmed the Marine Corps' faith in the value of the Harrier V/STOL aircraft; beginning in 1985, it began taking delivery of the improved AV-8B version. Three tactical squadrons of AV-8Bs

are now operational, with an additional squadron expected to receive the aircraft in FY87.

Armor continues to receive attention. The M60A1 tanks, the mainstay of Marine Corps armor for years, will be replaced by the M1A1 120mm tank, which is expected to enter the inventory in FY90. Of greatest importance, however, is the programmed acquisition of the Light Armored Vehicle (LAV), principally, but not exclusively for the Light Armored

Above: the LVTP7 is cumbersome and slow, but it is undergoing improvement to LVTP7A1 standard with a revised powerplant and a number of important tactical features.

Below left: Some 715 M60A1s tanks are to be replaced by M60A3 MBTs, though the USMC might be better served by a larger number of lighter AFVs with comparable firepower but greater mobility.

Vehicle Battalions (LAVB) being added to each Marine division. Each LAVB will consist of 1,038 men with 145 LAVs. A total of 744 LAVs are to be acquired by the Corps, in six variants: LAV-25, antitank, command, mortar, logistics and recovery. Two other variants, the assault gun and the air defense LAVs are also being developed. When available in strength, the LAV will add considerably to the Marine Corps' combat power in fluid combat environments.

If having better air and armor capabilities adds to the ability of the Corps to wage modern war, the ability to counter an opponent's aircraft and armor is at least as important. Control of the air has always been an important element in planning amphibious operations. It is equally essential for amphibious forces ashore to have an independent capability to defend themselves against attacking aircraft. The relative dearth of armored fighting vehicles available to the MAU and its larger multiples argues for enhancing their anti-armor capabilities as well. Both anti-aircraft and anti-armor capabilities become of even greater importance to the Corps if one contemplates employing Marine units in either European or Middle Eastern theaters of operation. Even the projected augmentation of Marine aviation and armored forces will not appreciably alter this consideration.

Two surface-to-air weapons systems are employed by the Marine Corps for anti-aircraft defense. First, each of the Fleet Marine Forces has a Light Anti-Aircraft Missile (LAAM) Battalion equipped with Hawk surface-to-air missiles. The system provides medium range and altitude defense

Above: A KC-130F refuels a pair of CH-53E Super Stallions each carrying a LAV-25 combat vehicle in a scene that fully epitomizes the USMC's commitment to tactical mobility with powerful weapons.

Right: The LAV series has been ordered for the USMC, and also proposed in several other variants such as this model with a rotary-barrel cannon in a turret topped by small SAM launchers.

against hostile aircraft. Second, for close-in air defense, the Marine Air Control Group (MACG) of each Marine Aircraft Wing (MAW) has a Forward Area Air Defense (FAAD) Battery, which contains five firing platoons (75 FAAD teams with two gunners per team). The teams are equipped with the Stinger missile which is a shoulder-fired surface-to-air missile system. Normally, five Stinger teams support a MAU with a platoon (15 teams) supporting a MAB. A full battery would support a MAF-sized deployment. Each LAAM battalion also has four FAAD teams designed to augment the HAWK system coverage.

The HAWK system has been upgraded through a Product Improvement Program designed to keep the system current with the latest threat projections. This included increasing the missile's capability to operate in ECM environments. LAAM and FAAD units have been expanded and additional batteries are being added to the LAAM battalion to increase potential firepower. Missile inventories are being increased through increased procurement, thus enhancing the capacity of the expanded air defense units to sustain combat operations.

Although once limited to the 106mm recoilless rifle and the 3.5in rocket launcher, Marine Corps anti-armor capabilities have grown considerably in recent years with the addition of new weapons and improved ammunition. A replacement (the AT4) has been selected for the M72A2 Light Assault Weapon (LAW), and the Shoulder-Launched Multipurpose Assault Weapon (SMAW), now capable of defeating light armor, will soon be capable of defeating armor up to and including

that on the Soviet T-72 tank.

In addition, 40mm and .50 caliber improved munitions now provide the capability to defeat light armored vehicles. TOW-2s, with greater range and penetration, coupled with the planned improvements to the Dragon – with initial operating capability in 1990 – complete the array of anti-armor weapons.

Moreover, the new High Mobility Multi-Purpose Wheeled Vehicle (HMMWV), although not primarily designed for the anti-armor role, will have the capability to carry anti-tank missiles and Mk 19 40mm machine guns.

Last, but certainly not least for an institution such as the Marine Corps, is the question of amphibious capability, which weighs heavily in Marine Corps planning and pro-

curement. The mainstay of the amphibious assault force is the classic "Amtrac", the LVTP-7A1 and its variants, a total of 47 of all types (including 43 LVTP-7s) being in each LVT (Landing Vehicle Tracked) unit. The AAV-7A1 (Assault Amphibious Vehicle) was first fielded in 1983 and is an improved version of the LVT 7 family of vehicles. The Marine Corps has procured 327 of these AAV-7A1s in order to meet the prepositioning requirements of three Marine Amphibious Brigades.

A new type of assault craft, the Landing Craft Air Cushion (LCAC), with a 60 ton payload and a speed of 40 knots (with payload) to 50 knots (plus across-the-beach and inland capability), became operational in 1986 when Amphibious Craft Unit-5 was activated with six LCACs. While there have been some design suitability problems with the LCAC, particularly in the area of reliability and maintainability, funds for an additional 12 were contained in the FY86 budget, bringing the total number of funded units to 33. In addition to the amphibious ships (eg LHAs) currently available, the Navy is proceeding with the development and deployment of Dock Landing Ship (LSD-41) class, of which ten are to be built; the LHD-1 (General Purpose Assault Ship) of 40,500 tons displacement, is scheduled to replace the existing LPHs; and the reactivation of four Iowa-class battleships (three have been recommissioned) – all of which points in favor of greater amphibious assault capability for the Marine Corps.

Today's Marine Corps: A Net Assessment

On balance, it is clear that the Marine Corps, as it is presently configured, has a number of distinct assets. *First*, it is clearly a highly cost-effective force, providing a considerable degree of combat power at relatively low cost. In FY1982, for example, only 4 percent of the entire defense budget was allocated to the Marine Corps. For that expenditure, the Corps provided 9 percent of the military personnel, 12 percent of the general-purpose forces, 12 percent of the tactical air forces, and 15 percent of the ground combat forces in the entire US defense establishment.

Second, within its basic ground combat formations, the Marine Corps maintains a very high "tooth-to-tail" (combat:support) ratio of 60:40. This is the highest in the American defense establishment, and comes the closest of any American formation to the combat:support ratio of the very "toothy" Soviet formations.

Third, the combined-arms ground-air team concept which is at the foundation of Marine Corps operational doctrine provides a framework for the integrated use of all combat arms to a degree greater than that which exists elsewhere in the US defense establishment. In this highly flexible and well-coordinated framework, the Marines employ a very high ratio of tactical air:infantry capabilities as a surrogate for the armor and artillery which the Corps lacks (at least by Army standards). This enhances the combat power of Marine formations beyond what might be expected from an inspection of the tables of organization and equipment of the ground combat elements.

Fourth, while there is some debate about the

Above: the USN plans to acquire 11 Wasp class ships able to operate STOVL combat aircraft, helicopters, LCACs and landing craft in support of a USMC battalion landing team of 1,875+ men.

Below: Designed to operate helicopters but not landing craft, the Iwo Jima class LPHs (exemplified by the USS *Inchon*) are based on the design of World War II "jeep" carriers, and each carry 2,000+ marines.

Above: One of five new-build Maritime Prepositioning Ships, the *PFC Dewayne T. Willism* carries 22,700 tons of equipment and supplies, sufficient for one-quarter of a Marine Amphibious brigade for 30 days.

utility of a *large* amphibious capability, there is little doubt about the need to have *some* capability of this kind, as that is currently conceived in US doctrine. Here, the Corps' forte stands out. It has the greatest experience with amphibious operations, and possesses the greatest number of personnel trained to manage such operations, of any force in the world. Airborne formations certainly can deploy more rapidly than seaborne Marines. But in some instances (eg Lebanon, 1958; Dominican Republic, 1965; and the Mayaguez incident, 1975) an amphibious force on station in a trouble spot may still be preferable to a more mobile force which would have to be deployed overseas. Such airborne units are limited by available strategic airlift and don't possess the 30 day subsistence which the Marines have within their amphibious task force assets. Certainly, the amphibious assault ships (LHAs), which can carry 1,703 Marines with their artillery and armor, plus helicopters, are clear assets in this regard.

The Corps also has its share of liabilities. *First* is the fact that it is still a very "light" organization, despite current and projected changes in its mobility and firepower. "Lightness" is, of course, a relative term. Against most Asian, African, or Latin American units, a Marine battalion (reinforced) would be considered a very "heavy" unit. Yet, unless operations in the future can be limited to the Third World, the ability of the Corps to operate

effectively against much heavier Soviet formations must be considered questionable.

Second, it is very clear that the close-air support (CAS) on which the Corps has placed great reliance in the past may be challenged. The families of Soviet-designed surface-to-air missiles and radar-directed multiple automatic AA cannon have, as the 1973 Arab-Israeli war demonstrated, made reliance on close-air support questionable.

Navy-Marine planners are adamant, however, that CAS is a *must* in any future conflict. Their position is that no amphibious operation should be undertaken unless air superiority can be maintained.

Third, the Corps' ability to conduct amphibious operations with the support necessary for good prospects of success is decreasing, although not because of deficiencies on its own part. The current fleet of amphibious warfare ships is relatively new, with newer ships coming on line. There are now fewer ships, less lift and less naval gunfire (NGF) support than at the beginning of the Vietnam War. The simple fact that the United States now has the ability to provide adequate amphibious lift for only the assault echelon of one Marine Amphibious Force – barely one-half of what US planners have considered essential – cannot be considered desirable. Moreover, although the recommissioning of three battleships is considered a step in the right direction insofar as a NGF is concerned, the sharp decline in on-line capability has reached the point where the ability of a Marine assault force to make a forcible entry against a determined defense in the absence of clear tactical air superiority is doubtful. Unless these deficiencies are remedied, the ability of the Marine Corps to maintain a viable amphibious

assault capability against established opposition will become increasingly open to question.

Basic questions about the Marine Corps
After World War II and the Korean War, the need for a Marine Corps was called into question, and the post-Vietnam experience followed the pattern. Yet it was, and is, clearly in the national interest of the US to have at its disposal an elite combat force, even – and, perhaps, especially – in an era of technologically sophisticated weaponry.

It can certainly be argued that there remains a need to retain an amphibious assault capability in the modern world. But it is a very different matter to argue that there is a need for a major, multi-division amphibious capability, and that the Marine Corps should be able to participate in operations in Europe, if the need arises.

Memories of World War II notwithstanding, it is all too likely that any adversary large enough to merit, for example, a MAF-level amphibious assault would also have the capability to concentrate massive firepower on a most inviting target – such as an amphibious force, lying (even at some distance) off a shoreline, preparing to send in the landing force via helicopter and assault landing craft or armored amphibians.

The Marine Corps' over-the-horizon (OTH) strategy of assaulting a hostile beach from 25 to 50 nautical miles (45 to 90km) offshore still requires a fleet of LCAC and development of the Osprey tilt-wing aircraft to be viable. Optimistic estimates place full implementation of OTH well into the 1990s.

Despite the Corps' acquisition of the new LAVs, any commitment to a war in Europe must be limited. Engagement of heavy mechanized forces must be relegated to US Army and NATO units appropriately equipped to deal with such a threat.

The characterization of the Marine peacekeeping force in Beirut, Lebanon, as "sitting ducks" raised questions as to the suitability of Marines for such static duty. Throughout their history Marines have been called upon to endure Spartan conditions that would defeat the spirits of those less disciplined. The tragedy in Beirut caused by the terrorist attack of 23 October 1983 forced the Corps to review its training priorities. Since that event greater emphasis has been placed on counteracting terrorism and the conduct of "low-intensity" warfare.

One thing must be admitted fairly. The Marine Corps, despite extensive rationale to the contrary, has evolved to the point where its size and force structure bear only a tangential relationship to the purpose, scope, and realistic missions of an elite *force d'interventions*. Nor would augmenting the mechanized warfare capability of the Corps ease the problem.

The Future of the Marine Corps
What, then, should the Marine Corps do? It is clear that there is no rational basis for the Corps to become a second Army, replete with mechanized formations; nor to compete with the other services for the possession of a major tactical air capability; nor even to remain a "light" force in a world of "heavy" conflicts. On the other hand, it is equally clear that what really gave the Marine Corps its presumptions of uniqueness and elite status in the past reflected its institutional values more than its operational characteristics. What made the Marine Corps different was not the missions it was intended to perform. It was the overall caliber of the forces available for *whatever* missions they were called upon to carry out. And is it there that the Corps should base its future position.

In the final analysis, it is the US Marine Corps' *esprit de corps*, the indefatigable spirit of its members, which makes it the unique and elite organization it has become. The Corps' strength lies in its ability to field task-organized units, large or small, suitable to whatever mission assigned. But to remain the *Corps*, its spirit must remain intact.

Following the Vietnam conflict, it became fashionable for military strategists to attack the viability of amphibious warfare in the modern world of high technology and nuclear threat. It was also fashionable to attack the Marine Corps as being "too light to fight"; suggesting that the Corps should "heavy-up" with more mechanized armor. Events in Southwest Asia served to question the validity of these theorists, however.

The Carter Administration found that, despite an impressive array of armed might, there was insufficient tactical lift, either by sea or air, to respond to global hot spots. The Soviet invasion of Afghanistan and the collapse of the Shah of Iran's government punctuated the need for a force capable of quick intervention in the future when similar events of national concern occur. The result was the formation of the Rapid Deployment Force (now US Central Command). The Near Term Prepositioning Ships program was implemented to provide the heavy lift capability needed to support the multi-service forces which might be committed in Southwest Asia. A massive support facility was prepared at Diego Garcia, a small island in the Indian Ocean.

Critics of the RDF charged that its impressive array of disparate forces from all the Armed Services was only a "paper force" put together to assuage inter-service rivalry without thought to the practicalities involved in detaching them from their operational commands when required for RDF duty. Some of these critics suggested that the Navy-

Above: The commitment of the USMC to peacekeeping duties in Beirut during 1983 was long on rhetoric but decidedly short on practicality, as proved by the October bomb blast that killed more than 200 men.

Below: Marines clear a Beirut beach in preparation for the establishment of a garrison area. Little in standard USMC training and expertise had prepared the men for the realities of this strife-torn city.

Left: Initial planning demands 552 MV-22 Osprey multi-role VTOL transports for the USMC. In the planned assault role the MV-22 will carry two batches of 24 troops over 127 miles (204km) without refueling.

by a force of 16,500 Marines within 90 minutes from the first sortie. The potential adversary will be faced with defending 800 to 900 miles (roughly 1,300 to 1,450km) of shoreline which will be vulnerable to attack anytime during the 24 hours after the MAGTF arrives offshore.

The Marine Corps has long prided itself on its readiness and flexibility. It is continuously evaluating and responding to the dynamics of changing threat and technological environments, within the constraints of political priority in authorizing and funding such initiatives. The Corps now seems to be preparing to fight low-intensity conflicts. It sees a trend of larger nations employing surrogates to achieve the sponsoring nation's goals through terrorism and low-intensity conflict.

The Corps will continue to improve its weapons and equipment inventory. The 9mm pistol, the M60E3 machine gun, the Mk-19 40mm machine gun and an improved 81mm mortar are slated to enter the Corps' arsenal. The Light Anti-armor Weapon (LAW) will also be replaced. The M23 Mortar Ballistics computer and a battery computer system will be acquired, as well as an M60 Mineplow and an Assault Vehicle Launched Bridge. The tilt-winged Osprey replacement for the CH-46 helicopter is expected to be available during the early 1990s.

Assets, such as the Position Location Reporting System (PLRS), will enhance command and control in the future. Decoys for the AN/TPS-32 and AN/TPS-59 radars will help confuse enemy ECM. The Tactical Air Operations Module (TAOM) and the Marine Integrated Fire and Air Support System (MIFASS) will become available to assist the task force commander as well.

The Navy and Marine Corps have validated an operational requirement for future use of Remote Controlled Vehicles (RCV). During 1984 the Marine Corps activated an RCV unit within the Second Marine Division to develop concepts of employment for the RCV. A small number of Israeli Mastiff III RCVs were procured for this purpose. The Navy and Marine Corps is anxious to make the RCV operational as quickly as possible, therefore they are looking to buy "off-the-shelf" technology. Still, the RCV selected for final use will no doubt be a hybrid of production models currently available. Although concepts of deployment for the RCV are still being evolved, it is apparent that long range aerial reconnaissance will be a prime use for the unmanned aircraft. Spotting for Naval gunfire and augmentation of command and control systems, especially in the OTH concepts of future amphibious assaults, are other uses being considered.

The Marine Corps has little desire to evolve into another land army. It will continue, as it began, to provide security to Naval ships and facilities as well as security personnel for US embassies and consulates. The self-sufficient Navy-Marine amphibious task force provides the nation with a viable option of "showing the flag" almost anywhere on the globe without a declaration of war.

The ancient Chinese general, Sun Tzu, counseled that elite forces lead the attack in battle, followed by an army of common soldiers who would consolidate and set up a defense in depth. For the United States, the Marine Corps is that elite force which provides the "cutting edge" of America's armed forces. The Corps seems comfortable in that role and thus would be wise to resist the tinkering of "think-tank" theorists in the future, just as it has displayed such wisdom in the past.

Marine amphibious task force was a ready-made RDF devoid of the problems associated with the joint-service version. Such speculation has not found a very receptive audience, however. What, then, is the future of the US Marine Corps? The unprecedented funding for weapons improvement and replacement during an austere budgeting period bodes well for the Marines. By the 1990s virtually every ground weapons system and a large percent-

Below: Tactical reconnaissance is a primary battlefield requirement best met under modern conditions by RPVs such as the Israeli-developed Mastiff, which is being procured jointly by USN/USMC.

Above: The US Navy is to receive some 90 LCAC-1 air-cushion assault craft, each able to carry 60 tons of freight over a range of 230 miles (370km). The type's combat survivability has yet to be proved.

age of air weapons systems will have been improved or replaced. A new generation of amphibious ships, complemented by MPS, will provide the Corps with the capability to project the assault echelons of a MAF and a MAB (about 50,000 Marines) across a hostile beach within 7-10 days after the President so directs.

The LCAC and the Osprey tilt-winged aircraft will permit the Marines to launch an attack from 25 nautical miles (45km) offshore

The United States Air Force

In the five years between 1945 and 1950 the United States Air Force made the difficult transition from the era of leather flying jackets and air-cooled radial engines to that of near-transonic combat in swept-wing jet fighters. In the mid-1980s the service stands poised on the edge of an even more dramatic breakthrough – the era of the "electronic airplane", the first generation of warplanes whose design is optimized for electronics-based combat.

Back in the 1940s, the Soviet Union was able to match the USAF's breathless pace, tackling a similar transition which allowed it to field its own MiG-15 jet fighter in time to match the F-86 Sabre in the skies above Korea. In the three decades which followed, the USAF became the air arm against which others were measured, playing a key role in launching many of the technologies which feature in present-day aircraft. France and Britain were able to identify areas which the US was overlooking, and so were able to field unique designs such as the Mirage III and Harrier, but only the Soviet Union had the resources to match the USA in the ever-escalating race to faster and higher-climbing designs. With types such as the F-4 Phantom II, F-8 Crusader, F-111 fighter-bomber, solid-propellant Minuteman ICBM, and B-52 bomber, the USAF set a technological mark which the Soviet Union found hard to beat, while the emergence of the F-14/-15/-16/-18 generation of fighters kept the US in the dominant technological lead throughout the 1970s and early 1980s.

No other air force could equal its range of capability – more than 200 long-range heavy bombers capable of attacking targets with free-falling bombs or the latest cruise missiles, agile "dogfighters" armed with look-down/shoot-down weaponry and vectored to their targets by advanced early-warning aircraft equipped with "look-down" surveillance radar, dedicated close-support formations equipped with the heavily-armored A-10, ample reserves of older but still highly-capable types such as the F-4 Phantom and A-7 Corsair II, plus a fleet of intercontinental-range jet transports and tankers capable of projecting US military power across the globe.

Only now is the Soviet Air Force beginning to field similarly advanced fighters, but the USAF is breaking the ground for an even more advanced generation of aircraft and missiles. Weapons on the drawing board or even in flight test include concepts which would have seemed little better than science fiction a few decades ago – "stealth" bombers invisible to radar, advanced fighters able to out-maneuver and outfight any conventional aircraft, transport aircraft able to fly heavy cargoes over intercontinental ranges then land at low-grade front-line air bases, hypersonic vehicles capable of overflying any point on earth and returning to base in less than two hours.

Having only just managed to deploy aircraft able to match current US designs, Soviet defense planners must be dismayed at the prospect of returning to the drawing board to create another new generation of aircraft and equipment. Given the long-standing Soviet determination to gain equality or superiority to the West in defensive strength, the necessary new designs no doubt will be created, probably before the end of the decade, but equaling the coming generation of US "super-planes" will be a difficult task – even allowing for the current massive Soviet investment in R&D in key areas such as microelectronics, propulsion and optics.

The History of the USAF

The air arm of the United States did not achieve its status as an independent service until 1947, having been a branch of the US Army until then. It started life in 1907 as the Aeronautical Division of the US Signal Corps, later being renamed the Aviation Section of the US Signal Corps. In 1918 it became the Army Air Service, but was elevated to the status of the Army Air Corps in 1926. The latter title was retained until 1941, when a further "promotion" introduced the title Army Air Forces. Final independence came on 18 September 1947, and the service has been known as the United States Air Force since that date.

Current Organization

Main components of the USAF are Strategic Air Command (SAC), Tactical Air Command (TAC), Space Command (SPACECOM), Military Airlift Command (MAC), Air Training Command (ATC), United States Air Forces in Europe (USAFE), Pacific Air Forces (PACAF), and Alaskan Air Command (AAC). These are supported by five further Commands – Air

Strategic Air Command units

Headquarters: Offutt AFB, Nebraska

Eighth Air Force (Headquarters: Barksdale AFB, La.)
2nd, 7th, 19th, 68th, 97th, 379th, 410th, and 416th Bomb Wings (B-52/KC-135/KC-10)
380th and 509th Bomb Wings (FB-111/KC-135)
305th and 340th Air Refueling Groups (KC-135)
384th Air Refueling Wing (KC-135)
351st Strategic Missile Wing (Minuteman)
380th and 381st Strategic Missile Wing (Titan II)
11th Strategic Group
306th Strategic Wing
4684th Air Base Group
6th and 20th Missile Warning Squadron
12th Missile Warning Group

Fifteenth Air Force (Headquarters: March AFB, Calif.)
5th, 22nd, 28th, 43rd, 92nd, 93rd, 96th, 319th, and 320th Bomb Wings (B-52/KC-135)
307th Air Refueling Group (KC-135)
100th Air Refueling Wing (KC-135)
44th, 90th, 91st, 321st, and 341st, Strategic Missile Wings (Minuteman)
390th Strategic Missile Wing (Titan II)
6th, 43rd and 376th Strategic Wing
9th Strategic Reconnaissance Wing (SR-71/U-2)
55th Strategic Reconnaissance Wing (RC-135/KC-135)
7th and 13th Missile Warning Squadrons
16th Surveillance Sqn.
46th Aerospace Defense Wing

Doug Richardson, formerly Editor of *Defence Materiel*, and Defence Editor, *Flight International*.
and
Bill Gunston, Assistant Compiler of *Jane's All the World's Aircraft*; author of many technical books and papers on military affairs.

Above: Based at RAF Lakenheath, the F-111F has acquired political notoriety for its role against Libya in 1986, but remains a potent long-range interdictor.

Left: The B-1B has great offensive power combined with high survivability, but is phenomenally expensive and is to be built only in small (perhaps too small) numbers.

SAC inventory	
Bombers	
Rockwell B-1B	100*
Boeing B-52D Stratofortress	75
Boeing B-52G Stratofortress	151
Boeing B-52H Stratofortress	90
General Dynamics FB-111	63
ICBMs	
Boeing Minuteman II	400
Boeing Minuteman III	600
Martin Marietta Titan II	52
Reconnaissance aircraft	
Boeing RC-135	16
Lockheed SR-71 Blackbird	9
Lockheed U-2R	8
Lockheed TR-1	18
Airborne Command Posts	
Boeing E-4B	6
Boeing EC-135	21
Tankers	
Boeing KC-135 Stratotanker	646
McDonnell Douglas KC-10A Extender	60*
planned	

Force Communications Command (AFCC), Air Force Logistics Command (AFLC), Air Force Systems Command (AFSC), Electronic Security Command (ESC), and Air University (AU). Further support is given by 16 Separate Operating Agencies (SOAs) covering fields from commissary and safety to legal and counter-intelligence services, plus a number of Direct Reporting Units (DRUs) such as the United States Air Force Academy, Air Force Technical Applications Center and the USAF Historical Research Center.

Like that of most air arms, the USAF front-line strength can vary from year to year. During the early 1980s the number showed a slight annual increase. In Fiscal Year 1985, a total of 7,287 aircraft were in active service. A further 468 were available from the Air Force Reserve, and 1,688 from the Air National Guard. Most fighter or attack squadrons have either 18 or 24 aircraft. Bomber squadrons can have anything from 13 to 19 aircraft, 12 in the case of FB-111 units. Typical transport squadrons have 16 C-130 Hercules, 17 or 18 C-5A Galaxies or 18 C-141 StarLifters. Units operating specialized aircraft tend to vary in strength. An E-3A Sentry squadron, for example, could have between 2 and 16 aircraft.

The USAF has 91 bases in the USA, plus 47 principal bases in overseas nations. The Air National Guard and Air Force Reserve operate from a total of 87 bases in the USA.

Operational readiness declined badly in the late 1970s, with factors such as shortage of spares and poor training magnifying the stresses resulting from the transition to an all-volunteer force. Despite a massive increase

in defense spending during the early 1980s by the Reagan Administration, bigger holdings of spares, improved training, and the introduction of more reliable and easier-to-maintain equipment such as the F-16, some combat-readiness rates have continued to decline – at least in theory.

In practice the service is in better shape. Many of the highly publicized low ratings reflect recently introduced higher assessment standards, and the transition to new equipment.

Just over 80 percent of the USAF FY85 strength of 601,500 is made up of enlisted personnel. Officers account for the remaining 18 percent. More than 88,000 black personnel serve with the USAF, making up some 17 percent of the enlisted strength, and five percent of the officers. Women play an ever-growing role in USAF strength, making up about 12 percent of the total numbers.

Service personnel are well educated. More than 1,300 officers have Doctoral or professional degrees, while virtually all officers have a Bachelor's or Master's degree. The latter qualifications are also held by almost 3 percent of enlisted personnel, while more than 40 percent have some level of college education. Ninety-nine percent of all enlisted personnel have a minimum of a High School education.

Strategic Air Command
Strategic Air Command is responsible for the ground and airborne portions of the "triad" of US strategic forces, and its most visible component is the fleet of veteran Boeing B-52 Stratofortress bombers. Although newer B-1B

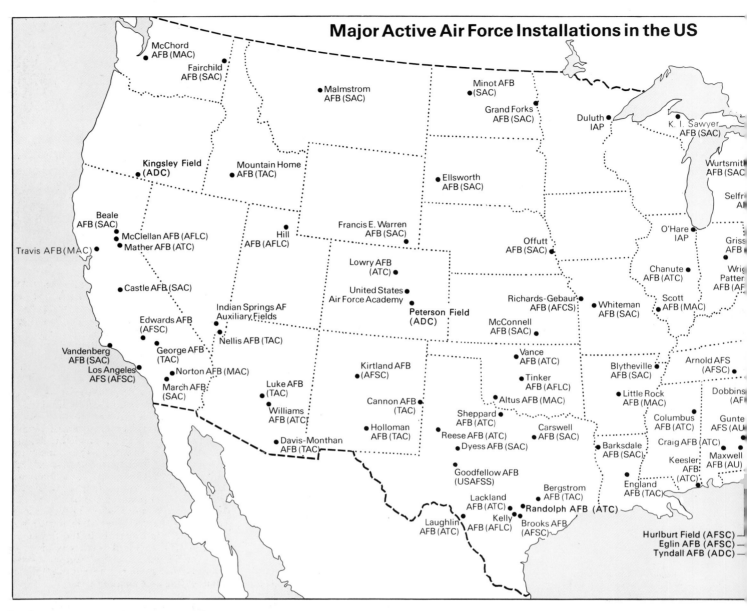

Major Active Air Force Installations in the US

McChord AFB (MAC)
Fairchild AFB (SAC)
Malmstrom AFB (SAC)
Minot AFB (SAC)
Grand Forks AFB (SAC)
Duluth IAP
K. I. Sawyer AFB (SAC)
Wurtsmith AFB (SAC)
Selfri AI
Kingsley Field (ADC)
Mountain Home AFB (TAC)
Ellsworth AFB (SAC)
O'Hare IAP
Griss AFB
Beale AFB (SAC)
McClellan AFB (AFLC)
Mather AFB (ATC)
Hill AFB (AFLC)
Francis E. Warren AFB (SAC)
Offutt AFB (SAC)
Chanute AFB (ATC)
Wri Patter AFB (AF
Travis AFB (MAC)
Lowry AFB (ATC)
Richards-Gebaur AFB (AFCS)
Whiteman AFB (SAC)
Scott AFB (MAC)
Castle AFB (SAC)
United States Air Force Academy
Peterson Field (ADC)
Indian Springs AF Auxiliary Fields
McConnell AFB (SAC)
Edwards AFB (AFSC)
Nellis AFB (TAC)
Kirtland AFB (AFSC)
Vance AFB (ATC)
Blytheville AFB (SAC)
Arnold AFS (AFSC)
Vandenberg AFB (SAC)
George AFB (TAC)
Tinker AFB (AFLC)
Little Rock AFB (MAC)
Dobbins (AF
Los Angeles AFS (AFSC)
Norton AFB (MAC)
Luke AFB (TAC)
Cannon AFB (TAC)
Altus AFB (MAC)
Columbus AFB (ATC)
Gunte AFS (AU
March AFB (SAC)
Williams AFB (ATC)
Holloman AFB (TAC)
Sheppard AFB (ATC)
Reese AFB (ATC)
Carswell AFB (SAC)
Craig AFB (ATC)
Maxwell AFB (AU)
Davis-Monthan AFB (TAC)
Dyess AFB (SAC)
Barksdale AFB (SAC)
Keesler AFB: (ATC)
Goodfellow AFB (USAFSS)
Bergstrom AFB (TAC)
England AFB (TAC)
Lackland AFB (ATC)
Randolph AFB (ATC)
Laughlin AFB (ATC)
Kelly AFB (AFLC)
Brooks AFB (AFSC)
Hurlburt Field (AFSC) —
Eglin AFB (AFSC) —
Tyndall AFB (ADC) —

bombers are coming online, this elderly giant is still the mainstay of SAC's fixed wing element, carrying nuclear missiles or free-falling nuclear bombs. In addition to the nuclear role, USAF's manned bombers can also be used to deliver conventional payloads. They can greatly boost the firepower available to tactical commanders, and fulfill naval missions such as maritime-reconnaissance, minelaying and anti-ship strikes.

When Boeing engineers designed the B-52 in the early 1950s, they could have had no idea that the aircraft would serve into the 1980s. Designed during the "cold war" at a time when the USAF urgently needed an intercontinental jet bomber and non-stop transatlantic jet airliners were still a thing of the future, the B-52 pushed the technology of its time to the limits.

Structural longevity was low on the list of priorities as the Seattle designers shaved excess weight from their eight-engined design. The original projected airframe life was only 5,000 hours, a figure which even the youngest passed more than a decade ago, but a massive structural rebuild program has prolonged service life and coped with the stresses involved in low-level flight. By 1962 Boeing had built a total of 744 B-52s, in eight major types, with a third of this fleet surviving into the mid-1980s, leaving only the -52G and -52H variants.

Most of SAC's manned bomber strength is supplied by 167 B-52G and 96 B-52H and these have an average age of more than 23 years. Both have wings which incorporate integral fuel tanks, while the -52H is powered by Pratt

& Whitney TF33 turbofan engines. The structure of the B-52H is better suited to low-altitude flight, while the tail-mounted armament consists of a single 20mm Vulcan gun rather than the quadruple 0.5in machine gun fitted to earlier models.

Maintaining this aging fleet of veterans requires a considerable engineering effort. Modification programs currently under way or planned are intended to prolong the aircraft's service life and expand its mission profile.

In order to improve avionics performance and to eliminate the problems associated with the maintenance of elderly vacuum-tube (thermionic valve) avionics, these aircraft are being re-equipped with modern solid-state electronics hardened to resist the effects of electro-magnetic pulses from nuclear explosions. The new avionics include a modernized radar, and new inertial navigation and bombing systems.

ECM systems are regularly upgraded, and the latest projects include Pave Mint (updating the ALQ-117 ECM set of the B-52G to counter new surface and airborne fire-control and missile radars), and the installation of the ALQ-172 in the B-52H to cope with current and projected airborne interceptors.

Other B-52 modernization programs will replace outdated radar equipment with modern solid-state components, install a new environment-control system, and improve communications by installing VLF/LF receiver terminals, and upgrading the SATCOM terminals. The electro-optical viewing system on the B-52G is to be updated, a digital unit will replace the existing FLIR signal proces-

sor, while the 69 aircraft not scheduled to receive ALCM will be fitted with a new integrated stores management system.

The ability of the B-52 to penetrate the latest Soviet defenses must be limited, despite the addition of the new electronic countermeasures described above. The CIA has estimated that the aircraft will remain effective until 1990.

Successful manned bomber operations in the face of the Soviet air defenses require a mix of penetrators and stand-off missile carriers. Cruise missiles will be fitted to 99 B-52G and 96 B-52H, externally in the case of the -52G, externally and internally in the case of the H model, which will be fitted with the Common Strategic Rotary Launcher for the internal carriage of ALCM, SRAM, and other weapons.

The first squadron of ALCM-armed B-52Gs became operational at Griffiss AFB, NY, late in 1982. By the end of FY84, 90 B-52G aircraft were equipped to carry ALCM, and work on converting the B-52H force started in 1985. By the end of this decade, the new Rockwell B-1B will be the primary penetrating bomber. Most B-52s will either be serving as cruise missile carriers or assigned to general-purpose missions including maritime support.

Using the current AGM-86B missile, the B-52 force will be able to reach 85 percent of all strategic targets from launch positions outside of Soviet airspace, and beyond the range of many defensive systems. Operational launch points are likely to be some 220 miles (350km) or more from the Soviet coast. In order to reach the remaining targets, bombers equipped with ALCM-B will need to penetrate into Soviet

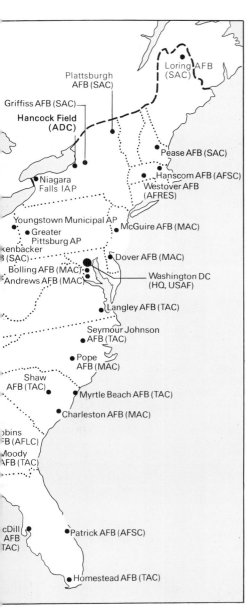

Above: The best defensive equipment US technology can devise is packed into these SAC B-52s, but massive Soviet defenses could prevent these big aircraft from even getting to their targets.

airspace, risking engagement by interceptors or SAMs.

Plans to develop a longer-ranged missile able to reach all targets from offshore launch areas, and with enough range in hand to allow USAF planners more flexibility in routing ALCM rounds along indirect flight paths were originally centered on the ALCM-C. This weapon was scheduled to enter production in the mid-1980s.

Unfortunately for SAC planners, Soviet designers did not remain inactive in the face of the threat posed by cruise missiles. Their response included weapons such as a new version of the vertically-launched Mach 6 SA-10 SAM, plus MiG-31 "Foxhound" and Sukhoi Su-27 "Flanker" interceptors armed with AA-9 shoot-down missiles. The effectiveness of these anti-cruise defenses is not fully known, but the speed with which they were devised and fielded seems to have caught the US DoD by surprise. Plans for the ALCM-C were scrapped in favor of a $1 billion project to develop an Advanced Cruise Missile utilizing the latest developments in missile guidance, propulsion and "stealth" anti-radar techniques. This project is being handled by General Dynamics, and the weapons will enter service in the late 1980s.

In the longer term, the Soviet Union is thought to be considering an anti-cruise missile defense able to engage stand-off bombers before ALCMs or ACMs have been released. This could take the form of an interceptor armed with an air-to-air missile of very long range – perhaps an air-breathing weapon in the class of the now-abandoned Martin

Marietta ASALM and targeted by the new Ilyushin "Mainstay" early-warning aircraft.

Development of the B-1

Full-scale development of the Rockwell International B-1 started in 1970. The first prototype flew on 23 December 1974, but plans to deploy a force of more than 200 were torpedoed in June 1977 by President Carter, whose Administration considered a combination of stand-off bombers armed with cruise missiles a more viable weapon.

Resurrection of the B-1 came four years later under President Reagan, when the US House and Senate Committees for Defense Appropriations ordered the USAF to develop a new bomber. GD made another attempt to propose a stretched derivative of the FB-111, but the growing support in the USA for better defense demanded that a long-range design be fielded. The result was a decision to develop and deploy two patterns of new bomber – an upgraded B-1 and an all-new design based on "stealth" technology.

Even after the cancellation of the B-1 in 1977, the prototypes continued to fly, completing their flight-test program, then being mothballed. Convinced that America would one day need the B-1, Rockwell doggedly pressed on with further studies, refining the design. When the USAF was ready for the B-1, the company could offer not the aircraft cancelled four years before but the new B-1B. Although slower than the -1A, (the result of adopting simpler fixed-geometry air intakes), the revised design has a much lower radar cross section and can carry a heavier payload. The B-1B is designed to be able to penetrate Soviet defenses, but the USAF is hedging its bets by equipping the aircraft with ALCMs. Fourteen rounds would be carried under the wings, plus a further eight on a rotary launcher in the weapons bay.

When designing the B-1A, the Rockwell team had carefully shaped the airframe to minimize the radar cross-section. By avoiding the massive slab sides and other radar-reflecting features of the B-52 configuration, they trimmed the apparent size of the new bomber as seen on radar to a tenth of that of the Boeing aircraft. The further refinements incorporated in the B-1B reduced the radar "size" of the B-1B to one hundredth that of the B-52.

On 23 March 1983, the second B-1A prototype was restored to flying status, visible evidence that the aging B-52 might at last be replaced. Tasks assigned to this aircraft included trials of the B-1B fixed-geometry engine inlets, flight control system, and composite bomb bay doors. This aircraft was followed by the fourth prototype reworked as a testbed for B-1B offensive and defensive avionics.

The first B-1B production aircraft was rolled out on 4 September 1984, and flew on 18

October. Delivery of the first operational B-1B was made on 29 June 1985, with the first squadron operational in late 1986. Rockwell hopes to hit a production rate of four aircraft per month by early 1987, completing deliveries of the planned fleet of 100 in June of the following year. At a program unit cost of $283 million, the B-1B is expensive, and there are no present plans for a follow-on order. Despite the B-1B's high performance and low radar cross-section, it seems safe to predict that its life in the penetrator role will be short, given predictable improvements to the Soviet air defenses. The Rockwell bomber is likely to serve for 25 years, but from the mid-1990s onwards will probably be confined to the stand-off role as a missile carrier.

The Advanced Technology Bomber

The Joint Bomber Study Group set up in the early 1980s to recommend a suitable design for SAC's future bomber realized this, and recommended that recently developed and highly classified "stealth" technology be applied to the design of a follow-on Advanced Technology Bomber for service starting in the early 1990s. This would replace the B-1B in the penetration role, leaving the Rockwell plane to fill the stand-off mission.

Northrop was awarded a contract to perform initial research and development on "advanced bomber concepts", but details of the program are highly classified, with the development work being carried out in closely-guarded facilities to which access is strictly controlled. No official information has "leaked" so far, but some clues may be gleaned from known areas of Northrop expertise.

It may be significant that the company's prior bomber experience is confined to the unsuccessful YB-49 Flying Wing of the late 1940s. Many experts predict that the ATB will be of flying-wing configuration, an idea which may be supported by (or might even have originated from) the fact that shortly after award of the USAF advanced bomber concepts contract, Northrop vice-president for advanced projects Lee Begin wrote a paper on the YB-49. Northrop also has significant experience in carbon-fiber technology and is a major supplier of ECM systems.

Production of the ATB is expected to follow close behind that of the B-1B. First aircraft from a planned run of up to 150 could enter service in the early 1990s, replacing the B-1B

Left: The 388th ECS Operates 24 EF-111As out of Mountain Home AFB for the electronic support of TAC units with the automated ALQ-99E high-power jammer.

in the penetration role, allowing the latter to replace the B-52 as a stand-off missile carrier. According to the US DoD, the new bomber should maintain SAC's ability to penetrate Soviet air defenses into the 21st century.

Airborne Refueling

Like most USAF aircraft, the B-52 is equipped for airborne refueling and supported by a fleet of KC-135 tankers. Up to half of these veterans are being re-engined and fitted with improved refueling equipment and avionics. These will be supplemented by up to 60 KC-10A wide-bodied cargo-tanker aircraft.

The latter will have a dramatic effect on the ability of the United States to reinforce its Allies during a crisis. A fleet of 17 KC-10A could refuel a F-4 squadron flying from the USA to Europe, and carry the associated personnel and ground equipment. To achieve the same result using the KC-135 would involve 40 tankers and a similar number used simply as transports.

Modernizing USAF's Missile Force

Faced with the threat interest posed by high-accuracy Soviet ICBMs, the US has upgraded its missile force to improve survivability, among other objectives. That force consists of 450 Minuteman IIs and 550 Minuteman IIIs,

although 50 will be displaced by the new four-stage Peacekeeper missile beginning in late 1986. Silos are being modified by the addition of an improved suspension for the missile, anti-shock mountings for the checkout equipment, additional concrete on the silo lids and the installation of bins on the silo doors to catch debris thrown up by nearby nuclear explosions.

The liquid-propellant Titan II missile is now being phased out of the SAC inventory, and should be gone by 1987. A number of accidents with this large liquid-propellant weapon raised questions of long-term safety and reliability, while the higher accuracy of the new Peacekeeper ICBM will reduce the military usefulness of Titan's heavy 9MT warhead.

Despite the attention of four Presidents and six Secretaries of Defense in 12 years, the problem of finding a suitable basing mode for the Peacekeeper (formerly MX) seemed well-nigh insuperable. President Reagan's solution was to set up the Commission on Strategic Forces (the Scowcroft Commission) which recommended that 100 Peacekeeper rounds be deployed in ex-Minuteman silos at Warren AFB in Wyoming (as a short-term measure), and the development of a new lightweight single-warhead Small ICBM which could be deployed in large numbers to increase greatly

the number of targets which Soviet ICBMs would have to destroy in order to carry out a successful "first strike". Promptly dubbed "Midgetman" by the media, the new missile will be suitable for mobile basing, probably on custom-designed blast-resistant wheeled vehicles. Early studies suggest that the Small ICBM may be around 13m long and 106cm in diameter, and weigh around 13,500kg. Such a design may be only marginally larger than the Martin Marietta MGM-31 Pershing II, but more than twice the weight.

Command and control facilities for the US strategic forces are partly maintained by a fleet of airborne command posts. The earlier examples are based on the KC-135, but the newer E-4 uses the airframe of the Boeing 747 wide-bodied airliner. Latest version is the E-4B, with improved command, control and communications equipment better equipped to survive the effects of electro-magnetic pulse radiation, and a maximum mission duration of 72 hours with airborne refueling, the limitation being due to the capacity of the engine oil tanks and the endurance of the crew.

Space Command

The day when the initials USAF will stand for United States Aerospace Force were brought closer in September 1982 with the formation of Space Command. The USAF's newest command has some 6,000 military personnel. Its commander also heads the US/Canadian North American Aerospace Defense Command (NORAD) as well as the US Space Command.

The new Space Technology Center at Kirtland AFB in New Mexico is responsible for basic space-related technology, reporting to the Space Division of Air Force Systems Command, which in turn tackles development, launch and checkout of military spacecraft. Once settled in orbit and commissioned, spacecraft are managed by Space Command. Orbiting systems for which the latter is responsible include the Satellite Early Warning System, Defense Meteorological Satellite Program, Global Positioning System (GPS) satellite system. The new Milstar comsats will be added to this list when operational.

Space Command is also responsible for the global network of missile-warning and space-surveillance sensors. Managed by the 1st Space Wing at Peterson AFB, Colorado, these pass data to the Space Defense Operations

Right: Air-superiority partner to the F-16, the F-15C currently carries potent but obsolescent AAMs as illustrated by these Netherlands-based Eagles of the 32nd TFS.

Center. Part of the USAF's Cheyenne Mountain Complex, this center is responsible for US satellite surveillance, satellite protection and ASAT programs, handling both military and civilian spacecraft.

Control of operational spacecraft and DoD Space Shuttle missions will be assigned to the Consolidated Space Operations Center currently under construction at Falcon AFS. Its capabilities will duplicate those currently at the Satellite Test Center located at Sunnyvale AFS in California, and those at the Johnson Space Center at Houston in Texas. Another facility under construction is the Test, Development and Training Center at Peterson AFB, Colorado.

Tactical Air Command

Tactical Air Command is the arm of the USAF which would provide quick-reaction air reinforcements for use overseas. It has just completed several major re-equipment programs, having deployed the F-15 Eagle and F-16 Fighting Falcon in large numbers, along with the A-10 Thunderbolt II close air aupport aircraft. The ability of the force to survive the Soviet defenses of the late-1980s and beyond has been enhanced by the massive ECM capabilities of the EF-111A Raven, the first squadron of which is already operational in the UK.

Both the F-15 and F-16 are being upgraded by improvement programs. Current F-16 production variant is the F-16C/D. Based on the earlier -16A/B, this is fitted to carry advanced systems such as the AIM-120 AMRAAM missile, Westinghouse APG-68 radar and Advanced Self-Protection jammer (ASPJ), plus the Martin Marietta LANTIRN (Low-Altitude Navigation and Targeting In Night) nav/attack pods, and Hughes AIM-120A AMRAAM missile.

Short-term improvements to the F-15 include the improved Hughes APG-70 radar, better EW systems, a new central computer, a reprogrammable armament-control system, and the AIM-120A missile. For the longer-term, the USAF will switch procurement to the two-seat F-15E dual-role fighter. Developed using experience gained from the experimental Strike Eagle program, the F-15E is an all-weather design able to fly air-to-air or deep interdiction missions. In the latter case, the aircraft will be able to carry up to 24,500lb (11,110kg) of ordnance, delivering this accurately on target with the assistance of LANTIRN.

Unfortunately for both programs, the new AMRAAM missile seems to be in trouble. For more than quarter of a century the USAF has relied on the short-range AIM-9 Sidewinder heat-seeking missile and the medium-range AIM-7 Sparrow. Both have steadily evolved, succeeding models having been fielded to counter the changing threat. (The small Falcon missile proved far less successful, and was withdrawn from production following the USAF decision to remove it from the F-4 Phantom. It now serves only on a handful of surviving F-106 fighters.)

Intermediate in size and weight between Sidewinder and Sparrow, the revolutionary AIM-120A AMRAAM fire-and-forget missile is being developed by Hughes Aircraft. Compared with existing missiles, AMRAAM offers a generally improved performance envelope (including a higher velocity and maneuver-

Left: F-16As of PACAF's 8th TFW contribute to the 'Team Spirit '85' Western Pacific solidarity and deployment exercise from Kunsan AB in south Korea.

ability) plus beyond-visual-range capability. The USN might be able to manage without AMRAAM – the weapon is specified only as a future option on the new F-14D version of Tomcat – but the Air Force urgently needs it. Until AMRAAM enters service in FY87, the F-16 Fighting Falcon lacks all-weather capability.

AMRAAM is already having cost and time-scale problems, and the USAF has even considered scrapping the program. A year before the planned IOC, the project was running six months behind schedule, while the unit cost had risen from $75,000 per missile to around $200,000.

The F-15 and F-16 were originally designed to use the P&W F100 turbofan powerplant, but in the summer of 1982 the Air Force announced that it intended to split its future fighter engine purchases between Pratt & Whitney and General Electric. This marked the beginning of a fierce competition between P&W's improved version of the F100 (with a longer-lifted core, plus a digital electronic engine-control system) and GE F110 turbofan – a more recent powerplant based on the F101 engine of the B-1 bomber and using a scaled-up fan, modified afterburner and nozzle from the GE F404 engine of the F/A-18 Hornet. Originally known as the F101 DFE, this develops 27,000lb (12,245kg) of thrust in full afterburner.

In February 1984, the US DoD announced that it was awarding 75 percent of its next year's worth of F-16 engine contracts to GE – a total of 120 engines. The P&W and GE engines both met the service's requirements, but the F110 offered improved operating characteristics and overall support costs. With the USAF now committed to competitive engine purchases, the two companies will now be free to bid for future F-15 and F-16 engine work. Individual units will not deploy both engine types – the split between F100 and F110-powered aircraft will probably be made at Wing level.

Another area of TAC improvement is that of communications. USAF efforts to develop a secure, jam-resistant radio system for the US services received a setback when the US Congress ordered that development of the planned Seek Talk system be ended. Short-term solution is the modification of existing tactical UHF sets with the Have Quick system.

Several longer-term alternatives have been explored, the preferred solution being an enhanced version of the Joint Tactical Information Distribution System (JTIDS). The basic version of this secure, jam-resistant digital data and voice communication system is already in service aboard the Boeing E-3A Sentry airborne early-warning aircraft and at selected ground sites in the USA and Western Europe; it will be deployed throughout the 1980s and into the 1990s.

New Fighter Designs

Most mysterious US fighter is the Lockheed F-19 – the "stealth fighter". Originally known as the XST (Experimental Stealth Tactical), this first flew in 1977, and probably took part in a competitive fly-off against designs. The first production batch was ordered in 1981, and the first squadron probably formed in 1983/4 at the Groom Lake facility at Nellis AFB, California.

Such is the size of Nellis that the F-19 and its rival or rivals could be test-flown in utter secrecy and away from the prying eyes of aircraft "spotters" of the official and unofficial sort – much in the same way that the A-11/YF-12 was tested in secrecy two decades before. Few outside eyes have glimpsed the new fighter, whose basic configuration – a large and rounded fuselage blended with a relatively small wing – has been likened to that of the Space Shuttle or even of the NASA lifting bodies tested in the late 1960s.

The eventual replacement for the F-15 will be the proposed Advanced Tactical Figher (ATF), a next-generation tactical fighter for air-to-air and air-to-ground missions. Concept-definition studies of the new fighter and an associated advanced technology engine started in September 1983, when the USAF awarded study contracts – each worth around $900,000 – to Boeing, General Dynamics, Grumman, Lockheed, McDonnell Douglas, Northrop and Rockwell. Proposed designs were offered to the Service in 1984, and selection of three for further 42-month study contracts was in hand in early 1985.

Although some of the companies have shown photographs of models of advanced fighter designs, these do not represent current ATF thinking. Aircraft such as the F-15 were a natural evolution of earlier designs, but in ATF the USAF hopes to make a revolutionary leap forward in aircraft capability, creating a fighter able to outfly all designs currently in production.

ATF will be able to operate in darkness and adverse weather conditions while coping with

the threat anticipated for the mid-1990s and beyond. The USAF intends to take advantage of the latest developments in aerodynamics, propulsion, avionics, materials, and manufacturing techniques, and much of the required technology will be drawn from current programs such as the AFTI/F-16, Grumman X-29 forward-swept wing demonstrator, and the "F-19" stealth fighter. Likely features of the new fighter will be vectored-thrust, for STOL performance or even in-flight agility, "stealth" technology, an integrated fire/flight control system with high-technology cockpit displays, large-scale use of built-in test and support equipment, and use of composites and advanced metallic materials.

Funding problems have already resulted in delays, and ATF will not now meet the originally planned operational date of FY93. Under current plans, full-scale engineering development is likely to begin in 1989, with the first prototype flying in 1991.

The delay might even prove useful, since the USAF will not roll out its new fighter until after rival designs such as the European Fighter Aircraft, Saab-Scania Gripen, IAI Lavi and next-generation MiGs and Sukhois have been fixed. Given adequate funding and political backing, coupled with late 1980s technology, ATF should out-class these fighters as effortlessly as the Bf-109, Spitfire and P-51 Mustang outflew open-cockpit biplanes. No other aircraft project will prove harder to beat when the Soviet design bureaux turn their hand to designing fighters for service in the mid to late 1990s. ATF could even see the final technological eclipse of Western Europe's military aircraft industry, whose EFA/ACA/ACX designs all lack the level of sophistication and performance currently planned for the US fighter.

With the disbanding of Aerospace Defense Command, TAC is now responsible for the defense of US airspace. SAC still provides long-range warning facilities to guard against missile attack, but TAC mans the small force of air-defense radars, control centers and interceptors which now guards CONUS.

The Soviet Union has not in the past possessed a bomber force capable of flying deep-penetration strategic missions into US airspace with any chance of survival. The turboprop-powered Tu-95 "Bear" (recently returned to production as a cruise missile carrier) was always vulnerable to intercepton, and by the time that the Mya-4 "Bison" was available in its definitive D-15 two-spool engined form, it too would have been an easy target for the F-102, let alone the later F-106.

The first bomber to stand a chance of penetrating deep into US airspace was the Tupolev Tu-26 "Backfire", some 130 of which serve with Long Range Aviation units. Although lacking the range for two-way missions, "Backfire" could attack US targets, then land at airfields in Latin America.

The situation will change from 1987 onwards when the Tupolev "Blackjack" variable-geometry bomber enters service. Larger and faster than the B-1, it will be the first effective intercontinental bomber fielded by Soviet Long Range Aviation. The massive airframe of "Blackjack" has sufficient internal volume for a large fuel load. Powered by four large turbofans – probably a new-technology turbofan in the thrust class of the Tu-144 supersonic airliner's Kuznetsov NK-144s – the aircraft is likely to have a range sufficient to allow wartime missions to be flown against the continental USA.

How effective it would be at avoiding the depleted US defenses is hard to assess, since this would depend on the performance of the aircraft's ECM systems. With the deployment of the AS-15 cruise missile, "Blackjack" will be able to avoid most defensive systems, launching its weapons from stand-off range.

The current USAF interceptor force consists of three TAC squadrons of F-15 Eagles, plus a rapidly declining number of TAC F-106 Delta Darts. The Air National Guard provides a further four F-106 units, one wing and three groups equipped with F-4C/D Phantoms. (The obsolescent F-101 Voodoo has now been withdrawn from ANG service.) 552nd Airborne Warning and Control Wing operates the E-3A Sentry, with squadrons deployed at three bases in the USA and at Keflavik in Iceland, and Kadena in Japan. No SAMs are deployed as part of the continental US air defenses.

A small high-technology air-launched anti-satellite (ASAT) weapon capable of destroying enemy satellites at low orbital altitudes is under development and flight testing. This consists of a modified SRAM first stage, a solid-propellant second stage rated at 6,000lb (2,722kg) thrust, and a miniature vehicle (MV) with Hughes infrared terminal seeker and conventional warhead mounted forward of a second stage.

ASAT was intended to be carried by designated air defense F-15s based at Langley Air Force Base, Va. It will be more flexible than a ground-launched ASAT system, since the carrier aircraft may be flown to a suitable geographic location for a fast-reaction interception mission before beginning its zoom climb to the point of weapon release. Ground-based systems must wait for the Earth's rotation to bring them within range of the orbiting target.

The two-stage weapon will ignite its rocket motors, climb to interception height under the control of a laser-based inertial guidance system, then carry out the final homing by passive IR seeker.

Firing trials from an F-15 began in 1983, and the first live launch against a target in space occurred successfully on 13 September 1985. A total of $322 million is sought for continuation of the ASAT program in Fiscal Year 1987, but further testing is barred until the President certifies to Congress that the Soviets conducted a similar test after 3 October 1985.

In the mid-1970s, TAC could rely on a large pool of combat-experienced aircrew from the Vietnam War, but had the good sense to ensure that this experience was not lost as these men moved to desk jobs or retired from the service. The massive Red Flag exercises held at Nellis AFB, Nevada, are unique in the West, if not in the world. Flying against typical European targets defended by F-5E "MiG simulators" and simulated Soviet ground radars, SAMs and anti-aircraft artillery, crews can develop the skills normally won in the crucial first combat sorties which inflict such massive losses on inexperienced aircrew.

Less well known are the Chequered Flag exercises under which TAC squadrons prepare for unit operations from overseas bases, Green Flag which focuses on coordinating and increasing the electronic capabilities of the

tactical air forces and other "Flag" programs intended to improve the performance of ground crews and facilities.

US Air Forces in Europe

More than 30 USAF squadrons serve in the 3rd, 16th and 17th Air Forces which make up the United States Air Forces in Europe (USAFE). Like TAC, these are being re-equipped to meet the threat posed by next-generation Soviet equipment. The F-15C and D replace the earlier F-15A/B standard, while the F-16 has almost completely replaced the veteran F-4. The sparsely-equipped A-10 is more suited to US conditions than to the often bad weather in Western Europe, but both this aircraft and the F-16 are due to be equipped with the LANTIRN FLIR system and associated wide-angle holographic HUD.

The "heavy punch" of USAFE is still the seven squadrons of F-111E and F-111F strike aircraft based in the UK. Earlier F-111A models of this variable-geometry fighter-bomber have been rebuilt to create the EF-111 Raven ECM aircraft. While the latter would jam hostile radar, USAFE's F-4G Wild Weasel aircraft would use APG-38 homing systems to locate and attack radar installations by means of Shrike, Standard ARM, Harm or Maverick missiles, plus unguided ordnance such as the Rockeye cluster munition.

The USAF is slowly being weaned away from its traditional belief that fixed bases could operate near-normally in any future European war. The fleets of MiG-23 "Flogger" and Su-24 'Fencer" strike aircraft deployed by the Warsaw Pact could create havoc on the USAFE's runways and support facilities. Much attention has been paid to the threat posed by anti-runway weapons. While these have only a short-lived effect, the loss of the avionics test and repair facilities would drastically reduce the prolonged combat-effectiveness of an F-15 or F-16 unit.

In addition to improving its runway-repair facilities, USAFE has installed blast and NBC-resistant avionics maintenance shops at Lakenheath and Upper Heyford in the UK, and at Bitburg in West Germany. Similar upgrades are planned for Hahn, Ramstein, Spangdahlem and Zweibrucken air bases in West Germany, Aviano in Italy, Soesterberg in the Netherlands, and Incirlik in Turkey.

Strategic Air Command's SR-71 Blackbird and RC-135 reconnaissance aircraft are frequent "guests" of USAFE, operating from RAF Mildenhall in the UK. Additional reconnaissance capability is now available in Europe thanks to the deployment of the TR-1. This will not attempt to overfly hostile territory but will fly along the border, using sideways-looking radar to gather information. The Precision Location Strike System planned for this aircraft will be able to locate radar systems and direct anti-radar attacks.

New technology offers improved methods of detecting and attacking massed armored formations. In order to provide a reliable means of locating and tracking moving targets at extended range, gathering the data needed by units tasked with attacking targets deep behind enemy lines, the earlier US Army Battlefield Data System (BDS), and USAF Pave Mover programs were merged in 1984, creating the USAF/US Army Joint Surveillance and Target Attack Radar System (JSTARS) airborne radar program – an ambitious project to combine the air-to-surface moving-target surveillance needs of the two services. In US Army service, the new radar will probably be carried by the Grumman OV-10D Mohawk. USAF thinking originally

Left: 'Border Star '85' matches the elderly but still useful F-4 Phantom tactical fighter with its successor, the multi-role and electronically advanced F-15 Eagle.

<table>
<tr><td colspan="2">United States Air Forces in Europe (USAFE) Major Units</td></tr>
<tr><td colspan="2">Headquarters: Ramstein AB, W. Germany</td></tr>
<tr><td colspan="2">3rd Air Force (Headquarters: RAF Mildenhall, UK)
16th Air Force (Headquarters: Torrejon, Spain)
17th Air Force (Headquarters: Sembach, W. Germany)</td></tr>
<tr><td colspan="2">Main Units</td></tr>
<tr><td colspan="2">Greece
7206th and 7276th Air Base Group (support & communications)</td></tr>
<tr><td colspan="2">Italy
40th Tactical Group (various USAFE aircraft on rotation)
7275th Air Base Group (support & communications)</td></tr>
<tr><td colspan="2">Netherlands
32nd Tactical Fighter Squadron (F-15)</td></tr>
<tr><td colspan="2">Spain
401st Tactical Fighter Wing (F-4)</td></tr>
<tr><td>406th Tactical Fighter Training Wing (KC-135/range support & weapons training)</td></tr>
<tr><td>United Kingdom
20th and 48th Tactical Fighter Wing (F-111)
81st Tactical Fighter Wing (A-10)
10th Tactical Reconnaissance wing (RF-4/F-5)
513th Tactical Airlift Wing (C-130/KC-135)
7020th Air Base Group (KC-135)
7273rd Air Base Group (GLCM cruise missiles)
7274th Air Base Group (support & communications)</td></tr>
<tr><td>W. Germany
36th Tactical Fighter Wing (F-15)
50th Tactical Fighter Wing (F-16)
52nd and 86th Tactical Fighter Wings (F-4)
26th Tactical Reconnaissance Wing (RF-4)
435th Tactical Airlift Wing (C-9/C-130)
600th Tactical Control Wing (command, control & communications)
601st Tactical Control Wing (OV-10/CH-53)
7100th Air Base Group (command, control & communications)
7350th Air Base Group (support & communications)</td></tr>
</table>

favored the Boeing C-18 (militarized 707) but the US Department of Defense is reported now to favor use of the Lockheed TR-1.

Intelligence and fire-control information from multiple sources needs to be processed by automatic systems, and distributed to tactical commanders for targeting decisions. Data from all sources will be integrated by the Joint Tactical Fusion system, an automatic means of processing, analyzing and distributing Intelligence reports from multiple sources. This will allow battlefield commanders to assess the status and disposition of enemy forces and selected targets. A more advanced fusion system able to handle real-time Intelligence data is already in development.

Once located and identified, targets will be attacked by aircraft and missiles able to deliver ordnance such as terminally-guided sub-munitions. One of the attack systems now under development is the JTACMS (Joint TACtical Missile System). This joint US Army/Air Force program is a direct follow-on to the earlier Corps Support Weapon System (Army) and Conventional Stand-off Weapon (Air Force) projects. Studies are currently in hand, and contracts for full-scale engineering development are due to be awarded in 1986.

JTACMS will be a dual-role ground and air-launched missile able to deliver a wide range of sub-munitions, including "smart" types. The specification calls for an ambitious range

Above: Designed to operate in trios for the triangulation of hostile radars in the European theatre, the TR-1 has suffered from delays with its sensor system.

of goals – the new weapon must be able to suppress battlefield defense systems, interdict supply lines and engage naval targets. Although it will not be carried by USAFE aircraft, it will provide a major increase in firepower for West-European-based US forces. The USAF plans to use JTACMS as a conventional-warhead stand-off weapon for the B-52, while the US Army intends to deploy it as a replacement for the Vought Lance.

The missile used to carry the sub-munitions will be based on the airframe of the T-22 Improved Lance, a modified T-16 round based on the Martin Marietta Patriot, or a new T-19 missile based on the AGM-69 SRAM. The T-22 and modified T-16 were test-flown during the earlier Assault Breaker program.

Most controversial new USAFE program is the deployment of new nuclear missiles to counter the Soviet SS-20 force. During the years of the Carter Administration, the European NATO allies began to question the degree to which the US Government was committed to the defense of Western Europe. The badly-handled "neutron bomb" debate did little to reassure them, but under the leadership of West Germany's Helmut Schmidt the

Alliance took the decision to modernize its tactical nuclear firepower by deploying Pershing II ballistic missiles in West Germany to replace existing Pershing I rounds, and to deploy cruise missiles in the UK, Belgium, Italy and the Netherlands. All would be deployed and manned by USAF personnel.

These deployment plans triggered off significant political protests in the countries involved. Much of this has been highly vocal, attracting much public and media attention, with the campaigners often singularly silent on the subject of Soviet deployments of nuclear or nuclear-capable systems such as the SS-20 and -22 missiles and Tu-22(M) "Backfire" bomber. Despite the activities of "peace protesters", missiles were deployed in the UK, West Germany, Italy and Belgium. The Netherland has ageed to accept deployment of the ground-launched cruise missile at Woensdrecht, part of the overall plan to deploy 464 GLCMs in five NATO countries.

Alaskan Air Command
The main "teeth" units of Alaskan Air Command (AAC) are the F-15-equipped 43rd Tactical Fighter Squadron and 21st Tactical Fighter Wing, plus the A-10 Thunderbolts of the 18th Tactical Fighter Squadron. Other aircraft include the O-2 aircraft of the 25th Tactical Air Support Squadron, T-33 trainers of the 5021st Tactical Operations Squadron, and 21st Fighter Wing's C-12 transports.

A total of 13 long-range radar sites are scattered throughout Alaska's 586,000 square miles. These 25-year-old installations are currently being modernized in a program which has already seen the creation of a Joint Surveillance System Region Operations Control Center. Located at Elmendorf AFB, this is linked to the radar sites and to remotely located surface-to-air communications facilities via satellite communications.

This policy of centralization has allowed military personnel to be withdrawn from the radar sites, which are now maintained by civilian contractors. Under the Seek Igloo program, Alaskan Air Command's radar facilities are also being upgraded by the installation of Minimally Attended Radars (MARs). The last five Seek Igloo radars were accepted at Tatalina, Cold Bay, Cape Lisburne, Cape Romanzof, and King Salmon in 1985.

AAC is clearly highly dependent on SATCOM links, but is not placing all its faith in a single link. Trials of meteor-burst communications links have already been carried out. These maintain long-distance communication by reflecting radio signals from the ionized trails left by meteors burning up in the Earth's upper atmosphere. Visually-spectacular meteors may be a rarity, but smaller meteors fall at such a rate as to make meteor-burst systems a viable back-up to normal data links. (Meteor Burst communications can also be used to direct fighter intercepts.) Unlike comsats, meteors are natural phenomena, and do not offer a target for hostile ASAT weapons.

Pacific Air Forces
Pacific Air Forces (PACAF) has the massive task of providing defence for US national interests over an area covering more than half of the Earth's total surface area. This stretches from the east coast of Africa to the Western coastline of the USA, and from the Arctic to the Antarctic. Despite this, it is severely outnumbered by the Soviet Air Force units based in the eastern USSR, having just 325 modern fighters and ground attack aircraft.

Its largest single element is the 5th Air Force based in Japan and South Korea. This includes the 18th Tactical Fighter Wing at Kadena in Japan (F-15C/D Eagle, RF-4C, plus E-3A Sentry), the 8th Tactical Fighter Wing at Kunsan in South Korea (F-16 Fighting

Falcons), the 25th Tactical Fighter Squadron at Suwon in South Korea, plus the 51st Tactical Fighter Wing and 5th Tactical Air Control Group at Osan which operate A-10, F-4E and OV-10A Bronco aircraft, respectively.

Above: USAFE's primary air assets against WarPac armor are the A-10As of the 81st TFW based at RAF Bentwaters and Woodbridge. These machines sport Mavericks and ALQ-119(V) jammer pods.

The Thirteenth Air Force in the Philippines is lower down the priority scale, since its main fighter types are the F-4E/G and F-5E. It does, however, boast a lineup of interesting special-purpose types such as the F-4G Wild Weasel, and the MH-130 Hercules. A new F-16 wing (the 432D Tactical Fighter Wing) was deployed at Misawa in Japan in 1985. The new Stinger man-portable SAM is to be deployed by the security police at PACAF bases.

Military Airlift Command

NATO plans for the emergency or wartime reinforcement of its allies in Western Europe or elsewhere rely on a combination of sealift, airlift, and the use of prepositioned stocks of military equipment and other supplies. Surface ships may be slow, but are flexible and can carry heavy loads. Only airlift can move cargoes and personnel quickly to where they are most needed.

Current USAF airlift capacity is provided by the transport aircraft of Military Airlift Command, the Air Force Reserve, and the Air National Guard. Even by airline standards, MAC is a formidable organization, operating a fleet which includes 77 wide-bodied aircraft, 281 smaller four-engined jet transports, and more than 250 four-turboprop freighters. The entire fleet, including the smaller helicopters and transports, numbers more than 1,000 aircraft. Operating out of 13 air bases in the USA, plus several overseas fields, MAC handles most of the DoD's airlift requirements. A typical year's operations can involve more than 2 million passengers and up to half a million tons of cargo, but MAC must always be ready to provide extra lift on demand. During October 1983, for example, 15,000 tons of cargo and 36,000 passengers were carried in support of the invasion of Grenada.

Usage of modern aircraft is not confined to the regular Air Force – AD reserve units fly the C-5A and C-141B, while they and the ANG are also equipped with the C-130. These forces are supplemented by the Civil Reserve Air Fleet (CRAF).

The combined efforts of these air fleets is able to transport 32.4 million ton/miles of cargo per day over inter-theater distances. Impressive although this total may seem at first sight, it is just under half of the 66 million ton/miles which a mobility study ordered by Congress in the early 1980s identified as the minimum goal for inter-theater airlift capacity. Even the latter figure does not fully represent the total air-cargo requirements demanded by the scenarios covered in the study, but is a compromise figure dictated by the high cost of airlift operations.

Long-range mainstay of the Command is the C-5 Galaxy fleet. Production of the C-5A ended in 1973, but the fleet is being rebuilt to extend service life. The existing five main wing boxes are being replaced by new components made from a stronger and more corrosion-resistant aluminum alloy. This program should be completed in 1987. The modified aircraft should have a 30,000hr service life, allowing them to serve into the 21st century.

As part of its submission to meet the USAF's 1980 requirement for a CX long-range heavy lift transport, Lockheed proposed an improved version of the Galaxy, pointing out that this could be available much sooner than an all-new design. The Galaxy did not meet all the CX requirements, but its potential availability on a relatively short timescale resulted in the CX plan being put on backburner in favor of returning the C-5 to production as described above, and continuing low-rate production of the KC-10A Extender cargo/

Left: The RF-4C remains one of the world's comparatively few dedicated tactical reconnaissance platforms, seen here as aircraft of the 15th TRS at Kadena AB.

tanker. These two projects allowed the service to improve quickly its inter-theater airlift capability, with the CX (now known as the C-17, described later) following on a later timescale. The new C-5B incorporates the new wing, improved TF39-GE-1C turbofans, modern avionics, and all the other modifications devised for the C-5A. Delivery of 50 examples began in 1986.

In another massive rebuilding program, Lockheed stretched 271 C-141A StarLifters to create the present C-141B fleet. These incorporate a refueling receptacle located in a fairing mounted on top of the forward fuselage, making the aircraft less dependent on landing rights during wartime resupply missions. Despite this rebuilding, these aircraft will require further reworking if their lives are to be extended past the end of the century – some could be retired a decade from now. Given large-scale modification, most of these hard-working strategic freighters could be good for further decades of service, being eventually retired around 30 years from now.

This fleet of long-range jets is supplemented by several smaller jet transports. MAC operates a small number of Boeing 707s under the designations C-18A and C-137. The eight C-18As are ex-American Airlines 707-323C airliners, while the five C-137s are custom-built VIP aircraft – Presidential transport "Air Force One" is one of two C-137C, while the other three are C-137B (707-120 airliners retrofitted with JT3D turbofans).

Another commercial airliner in USAF service is the McDonnell Douglas DC-9 Series 30. Some two dozen are in service – as aeromedical transports (C-9A) or for US Government use (C-9C).

Main tactical transport is the seemingly irreplaceable C-130 Hercules. Some C-130s are already more than 28 years old and require structural rebuilding, including rehabilitation of the wing center section and the fitting of new outer wing boxes.

Despite modernization schemes, old age is catching up with the MAC fleet, leaving USAF personnel to struggle with fatigued airframes and obsolescent avionics. Some aircraft seem likely to go to the breakers within a decade or so. The 1990s may well see the retirement of the more ancient examples – more than 150

Above: The C-5 Galaxy was built and rebuilt in a costly program, but provides MAC with truly global airlift capability even with massive loads.

older Hercules and some 55 StarLifters.

The USAF's long-term airlift plans are based on replacing the smaller aircraft with the new C-17. Originally known as the CX, this was the subject of a 1980 request for proposals. Boeing, Lockheed and McDonnell Douglas all offered new designs, with McDonnell Douglas being declared the winner in August 1981.

Full-scale engineering development of the C-17 is now under way. The new transport will be able to carry a 68 ton payload over a range of up to 2,940nm (5,450km). Despite its intercontinental range, the aircraft will have STOL performance, allowing it to fly heavy payloads into and out of smaller airfields of the type used by the C-130. The latter will still be needed for high sortie-rate tactical missions with smaller payloads, but the C-17 will provide a useful heavy-lift tactical capability when large loads of munitions, fuel or other supplies must be carried over relatively short range.

Technology for the C-17 was proven by the flight testing of the YC-15 tactical transport. The newer aircraft bears a distinct family resemblance to the earlier experimental design, but has a greater all-up weight and range. It retains the same high-wing configuration with pod-mounted engines, plus T-tail, but two wingtip-mounted winglet surfaces provide a distinctive recognition feature. They reduce drag, and thus lower the fuel consumption. In the case of the C-17, their installation will cut the fuel burn by around four percent. The wing will use a modern advanced aerofoil whose relatively greater thickness allows the integral tanks to carry more fuel than if a conventional aerofoil had been used. The four Pratt & Whitney F117-PW-110 turbofans and their associated fuel system will be controlled by a computerized flight-management system, allowing the aircraft to match the payload capability of the larger C-5 when operating at the longest ranges.

Smaller aircraft in MAC service include

small jet and piston-engined transports. MAC has 11 C-140B Jetstars, but these elderly and fuel-hungry aircraft are due to be replaced by 11 C-20A (Grumman Gulfstream III) executive transports. The USAF has also arranged to lease 80 Learjet 35A business jets which will be issued to MAC's Operational Support Aircraft fleet for duties such as pilot training and the transportation of high-priority personnel and cargo.

MAC also operates the recently acquired Short C-23 Sherpa EDSA (European Distribution System Aircraft) used to ferry aircraft spares and engines between USAFE bases, and several leased C-12A (Beechcraft Super King Air 200) light piston-engined twins.

In an emergency MAC's own fleet can be supplemented by more than 300 airliners and cargo aircraft owned by the 28 US airlines who participate in the Civil Reserve Air Fleet (CRAF) program. Under a recently devised scheme, the USAF is paying for the cost of setting up a modification line able to fit a cargo door and strengthened floor to the Boeing 747. First aircraft to be modified belonged to Pan American, with up to 19 due to be reworked in this way in order to improve their military usefulness. After modification, they are returned to normal airline passenger service, with the USAF paying the additional operating costs.

In addition to operating as a passenger/cargo service, MAC also supports USAF Special Operations Forces (SOF), having integrated its Aerospace Rescue and Recovery Service (ARRS) with the SOF back in 1983. Located at Scott AFB, Illinois, ARRS is probably the most exotic MAC unit. Its most publicized activity is combat search and rescue using specially equipped HC-130 Hercules plus Sikorsky HH-3 and HH-53 rescue helicopters. Most complex of the latter is probably the HH-53H Pave Low III, which carries a comprehensive avionics suite for all-weather rescue missions, including a terrain-following radar, stabilized FLIR plus Doppler and inertial navigation units.

These rotary-wing types are due to be joined in 1988 by the new HH-60D Night Hawk version of the Blackhawk helicopter. This is currently in engineering development to meet the USAF's HX requirement for a rescue helicopter able to operate at low level in darkness or bad weather. The HH-60D will carry terrain-following/avoidance radar, FLIR, a refueling receptacle plus auxiliary internal and external fuel tanks. The broadly similar -60E will have simpler avionics, and not be suitable for adverse-weather operations.

If the SOF ever sees action, it will ride into battle aboard the specialized transports of the 2nd Air Division of MAC's 23rd Air Force. Fixed wing-types include the AC-130 Hercules gunships (used to good effect in support of US Army ground units during the Grenada operation) and the MC-130E and -130H Combat Talon low-level deep-penetration transports. These are supplemented by helicopters such as the HH-53 and UH-1N, with the HH-60D Night Hawk due to follow.

ARRS also flies various models of C-130 and C-135 for weather reconnaissance, air sampling (a means of detecting clandestine nuclear testing), and to support Space Shuttle and Strategic Air Command operations.

Air Training Command
First-class equipment is almost useless without first-class personnel to fly and maintain it. Such is the USAF's commitment to quality that approximately a fifth of all USAF sorties are flown by Air Training Command. Its fleet of training aircraft currently consists of five main types – the T-37, T-38, T-41A, T-43A and UV-18B. These operate from 13 bases, but the Command also boasts six technical training centers, and a network of field training units at 96 locations worldwide. Air Force Reserve Officer Training Corps units are located at more than 150 US universities and colleges.

The Cessna T-37 is aging, and was expected to be replaced from late 1987 onwards by the new Fairchild T-46A New Generation Trainer. However, the future of this program was open to question in early 1986, due to budgetary constraints and reported "contractor cost and schedule difficulties".

In an average year, the USAF recruits about 66,000 new personnel. Basic military training is carried out at Lackland AFB, Texas, while the various technical training centers conduct more than 3,000 courses. ATC handles initial flying training, plus basic military and technical training, but can also handle undergraduate, postgraduate and professional training tasks. ATC is also responsible for training Air Force Reserve and Air National Guard personnel. Recent years have seen the US forces much criticized for poor discipline and personal motivation. Improvements may result from the "Back to Basics" program started in 1983 to re-emphasize traditional military values such as patriotism, physical training, manners and customs, and physical appearance.

Basic flying is handled by 14th, 47th, 64th, 71st, 80th and 82nd Flying Training Wings. All are located in the Central or Southern USA where the favorable climate creates training conditions greatly superior to those found in most European nations. As a result, some friendly foreign air arms send pilots and navigators to the USA for ATC training, such candidates making up about a tenth of the total. In FY83, to take an example, ATC trained 5,600 overseas airmen from more than 70 nations. At Sheppard AFB, in Texas, home of the 80th Flying Training Wing, the US and its NATO allies have set up a Euro-NATO Joint Jet Pilot program under which USAF and NATO pilots will train together.

Reserves
The United States is the only nation able to afford large-scale reserve air arms and to equip these with modern aircraft. Like the units of the regular Air Force, reserve squadrons have in many cases been upgraded with better equipment such as the F-16 and A-10.

Air Force Reserve (AFRES) is organized into three air forces – 4th, 10th and 14th. The 4th and 14th are transport formations, whose principal equipment includes five squadrons of C-5A, two squadrons of KC-10A, 13 squadrons of C-141B, three squadrons of KC-135, and 15 squadrons of C-130 Hercules. Only the 10th Air Force flies fighters and attack aircraft, this formation providing around seven percent of USAF tactical fighter strength. Main "teeth" flying units of this AF – which is based at Bergstrom AFB, Texas – are a single F-16 squadron, five F-4D squadrons, and five A-10 squadrons.

The Air National Guard provides an even larger reserve, fielding 73 percent of the USAF's interceptor force, more than half the tactical reconnaissance elements, a third of the tactical support, quarter of the tactical fighters, a third of the tactical airlift and some

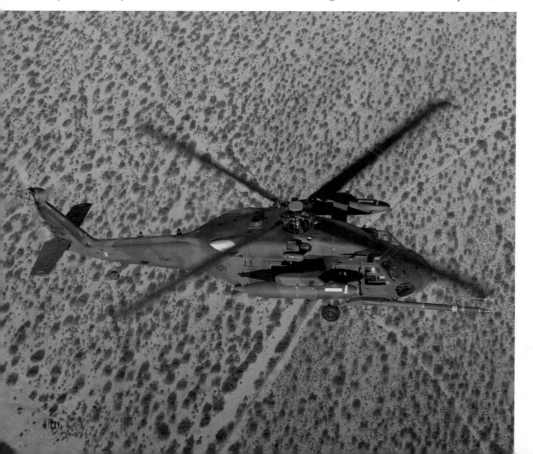

Military Airlift Command fleet (major aircraft)	
Lockheed C-5 Galaxy	77
Lockheed C-141 Starlifter	270
Lockheed C-130 Hercules	259
McDonnell Douglas C-9 (militarized DC-9)	23
Boeing C-137 (militarized 707)	5
Sikorsky CH-3/HH-3)	46
Sikorsky CH-53/HH-53	21

USAF strength	
Strategic Bombers	363
ICBMs	1,052
Fighter/attack aircraft	3,026
Reconnaissance & electronic warfare	392
Flight-refueling tankers	544
Transports	828
Helicopters	238
Utility, observation, SAR	250
Trainers	1,664
Personnel (military)	599,000
Personnel (civilian)	243,000

Left: The Black Hawk was planned for transport, but has matured into armed military/naval types, an ECM model and this HH-60A Night Hawk rescue variant.

Right: The USAF fields aircraft for every role, small and large, as exemplified by an A-37B light attack aircraft dwarfed by the monstrously costly E-3 AWACS aircraft.

17 percent of the flight refueling capability. Like AFRES, it fields a mixture of the old and new, having received its first F-15 squadron in 1985, with another unit scheduled for the Georgia ANG in FY86. Other "new recruits" are the F-16 (three squadrons will have converted to it by the end of 1986) and new-production A-7s. Other main combat types are the F-4C/D, RF-4C, F-106, A-7D, A-10, DA-37, C-130 and KC-135.

Specialized Commands
Other commands provide the back-up support without which the USAF would soon grind to a halt. Air Force Logistics Command, based at Wright-Patterson AFB, Ohio, is tasked with supplying the fuel, munitions and other ordnance, spare parts and maintenance needed by the other commands. It runs many facilities including the Logistics Support Center Europe at RAF Kemble in the UK, and the world-famous "aircraft graveyard" – the Military Aircraft Storage and Disposition Center at Davis-Monthan AFB, Ohio.

Air Force Systems Command designs, tests and purchases weapons and equipment for the operational commands, and has significant expertise in "hi-tech" areas such as avionics, armament, and guided missiles. Recent tasks have included managing the B-1 and Peace-keeper programs, evaluating the rival F-15E and F-16XL fighter prototypes, developing the JTIDS (Joint Tactical Information Distribution System) jam-resistant communications system, testing the LANTIRN (Low-Altitude Navigation and Targeting Infra-red for Night) pods, and developing technology in support of President Reagan's Strategic Defense Initiative.

Air Force Communications Command, as its name suggests, is tasked with the USAF's communications requirements, providing facilities which include strategic and tactical communications (including military comsats and links with rapid-deployment and other special-purpose forces), air traffic control, and instrument landing systems, plus the regular administrative communications and computing facilities required by the Air Force.

Electronic Security Command plays a more subtle electronic warfare role, helping with the development of EW systems, the evolution of EW tactics, and the elimination of electronic "leaks" of classified information. The command is responsible for analyzing the results of exercises such as Red Flag and of any air combat involving the USAF, and for testing EW systems and equipment. It also procures and controls the deployment of encryption equipment, and is involved in electronic intelligence gathering operations.

Air University, also a major command, provides professional military education and degree-granting and professional continuing education for officers, non-commissioned officers and civilians. Most of AU's professional military education schools are located at Maxwell Air Force Base, Ala. These include the Air War College for senior officers, Air Command and Staff College for mid-career officers, and Squadron Officer school for company-grade officers. The Air Force Senior Noncommissioned Officer Academy is located at nearby Gunter Air Force Station.

Other major AU organizations include the Leadership and Management Development Center; the Center for Aerospace Doctrine, Research, and Education; the Educational Development Center; the Air University Library; and Headquarters Civil Air Patrol. (These are all located at Maxwell Air Force Base.) In addition, AU operates the Extension Course Institute and the Air Force Logistics Management Center (at Gunter Air Force Station), and the Air Force Institute of Technology, Wright-Patterson Air Force Base, Ohio.

Above: Constant technical development is a high priority in the USAF, and this F-16B of the AFFTC has a tail-mounted camera to record AIM-120 AMRAAM firing trials. Also carried is an ALQ-119 jammer pod.

The Soviet Threat

The present US/Soviet military balance has evolved from actions and reactions occurring over a long time and involving many different political and military factors, worldwide. At the end of World War II in 1945, the United States demobilized its forces and much of its equipment, and reduced military research to a standby basis. At the same time, the Soviet Union initiated an urgent nuclear weapons, rocket and missile development, and began a long-term submarine and naval cruiser construction program while reducing its forces by a relatively smaller percentage.

Between 1950 and 1954, the US increased military spending, principally in response to demands of the Korean War; it was not a long-term program. During the thirty years since the end of the Korean War, Americans participated in the post-World War II recovery of Western Europe and Japan, assisted with the development of more than ten new, successful industrialized nations, and have continued friendly relations with all of them. Washington also forged alliances with West Germany, Italy and Japan, and established a more relaxed relationship with the People's Republic of China. During the same time, Moscow lost its former military alliance with China and has gained only Cuba, Vietnam and South Yemen to add to its reluctant East European allies.

In examining the Soviet-US military balance today, we can see the favorable political and economic factors on the US side offset in a very dramatic way by the growth of Soviet military power. The two superpowers have divergent military philosophies, doctrine and strategies, as well as differences in political and economic outlook; all affect the *how* and *why* of the numbers in any comparison.

Americans have always emphasized new technology and high quality in armaments programs. The Soviets insist, as did their Russian forebears, that "more of everything is better". The Soviets have been able to transcend great qualitative differences in the past because their philosophy recognizes technical inferiority, but seeks ways in which to circumvent its disadvantages. This approach was stressed by the great Russian military leader, Suvorov, and is the origin of the Russian and Soviet strategy – *to compensate for technical weakness by exploiting numbers.*

Soviet strategy, however, does not depend upon numbers alone. For example, it is acknowledged that Western tanks enjoy many superiorities over Soviet tanks, with superior ranges and faster rates of engagement. The Soviet response has been to field larger numbers of tanks and seek to engage and close with the enemy very quickly, thus eliminating the advantage of range. Employment of mass fire can eliminate the advantage of higher rates of engagement. As future Soviet tanks improve in quality, the advantage of numbers will persist.

The Soviet Union and its allies continue to deploy improved weapons systems designed for the entire spectrum of strategic, theater-nuclear, and conventional conflict. Despite their traditional inclination toward total secrecy, Soviet leaders have publicized certain of their advances. In the autumn of 1984, the Soviet Defense Ministry announced that the USSR was beginning to deploy a new genera-

Below: A DoD artist's impression of the new SS-25 provides a neat insight into the Soviet Union's new land-mobile and thus highly survivable fifth-generation ICBM.

tion of nuclear-armed, air-launched and sea-launched cruise missiles. He also revealed that nuclear-armed, short-range ballistic missiles had been forward-deployed from the USSR to operational sites in Eastern Europe and that additional ballistic missile submarines were on patrol in the Atlantic and Pacific Oceans. Former General Secretary Chernenko said, in speaking before the Politburo, that further actions would be taken to strengthen the Soviet Union's military capability. The successes achieved by the Soviets in both quantity and quality of systems are founded upon a combination of an aggressive research and development program together with a systematic effort to target and obtain advanced Western technologies.

Nuclear Forces

It is important to recognize that nuclear weapons, although not employed since the end of World War II, cast a shadow over any military balance. For example, in 1950 the Soviet leader, Josef Stalin, imposed a ground blockade on West Berlin. Even then, the Soviets enjoyed a vast superiority in conventional forces and had become a nuclear power. Nevertheless, when the United States and the United Kingdom responded to the blockade by mounting a massive airlift, the Soviets were unwilling to risk a war by stopping the flights. The American superiority in air force capability and nuclear weapons had not deterred the Soviets from precipitating the crisis, nor were these capabilities decisive in the final outcome; but the nuclear "umbrella" was effective in establishing the parameters of the confrontation.

Even as the Soviets modernize their fourth generation of ICBMs and deploy them with greater accuracy and survivability, deployment of a fifth generation (the SS-25) has begun. The strategic capabilities of the Soviet Navy have increased with the introduction of each new massive Typhoon class SSBN. With the new Delta IV SSBN, recently launched as the platform for the SS-NX-23 long-range MIRVed SLBM, its capabilities are further increased.

The Soviet Union now has three manned strategic bombers in production and development – the "Backfire", the "Bear-H", and the "Blackjack". With the reopening of the production lines to deliver the upgraded "Bear" turboprop bomber, 40 of which now carry the 3,000km-range, nuclear armed AS-15 air-launched cruise missile, the range and lethality of its long-range bomber force have been improved.

Although Soviet leaders have consistently repeated their commitment to "no first-use of nuclear weapons" they are convinced that a conventional war in Europe might escalate to the nuclear level and, accordingly, they have developed extensive plans to launch a massive first strike against prime NATO targets should their conventional operations be delayed, or to stop a NATO nuclear strike by launching a preemptive attack. Their current strategic and theater forces, or those under development, provide them with the means of

*The views of Col. Friedman do not purport to reflect the positions of the Dept. of the Army, or the Dept. of Defense.

Col. Richard S. Friedman, US Army (Ret.)*, formerly with Military Intelligence, US Army, and an officer with US Army General Staff; formerly Defense and Army Attache in Budapest, Hungary; and member of International Military Staff, NATO HQ.

executing their plans. Passive assets, such as civil defense forces, countermeasure troops with equipment designed to confuse and divert incoming aircraft, hardened facilities, command vehicles, and evacuation plans to protect key officials, essential workers and much of the general populace, encourage them to believe their own risks can be kept within acceptable limits.

Intercontinental Ballistic Missiles

In addition to those at test sites, the operational Soviet ICBM force consists of approximately 1,400 silo launchers of which nearly 818 have been rebuilt since 1972. All of the 818 silos have been hardened to withstand attacks by the ICBMs currently deployed by the US. These silos contain the most modern ICBMs currently deployed anywhere in the world: the SS-17 Mod 3 (150 silos); the SS-18 Mod 4 (308); and the SS-19 Mod 3 (360). Each SS-18 and SS-19 can carry more and larger MIRVs than the Minuteman III. The SS-18 Mod 4 carries at least ten MIRVs, and the SS-19 Mod 3 carries six; the Minuteman III carries only three. The SS-18 Mod 4 was specifically designed to attack and destroy ICBM silos and other hardened targets located in the United States. The SS-18 Mod 4 force now deployed is capable of destroying between 65 and 80 percent of the US ICBM silos using two nuclear warheads against each. The SS-19 Mod 3 ICBM could be assigned similar missions and could also be employed against targets in Eurasia. The SS-17 Mod 3 has similar targeting flexibility although it is somewhat less capable than the SS-19. The rest of the 508 Soviet ICBM silos are equipped with the SS-11 (28), SS-11 Mod 2/3s (420), and SS-13 Mod 2s (60). These ICBMs which were deployed in 1966 and 1973, are contained in less survivable silos and are significantly less capable; however, their destructive power is adequate against softer targets in the US and Eurasia.

Within the last year, SS-11 silos have been dismantled in compensation for SS-25 deployments. By the mid-1990s, all SS-11s will have been dismantled.

The deployment programs for all of the currently operational ICBM systems are complete, their reliability is regularly tested by live firings from operational sites and the command, control and communications system that supports the Soviet ICBM force is very modern and highly survivable. The currently operational ICBMs which the Soviets do not replace with either new or modified systems will most likely be modernized to extend their useful life. In the past such modernization has enabled the Soviets to sustain a higher level of confidence in system reliabilities for a longer period. The conclusion of the current deployment programs will also probably mean the end of any significant investment in new liquid propelled ICBMs. The Soviets already have two new solid-propellant ICBMs – the SS-25 and the SS-X-24.

The medium-size SS-X-24 is well along in its flight test program. Its deployment in the rail mobile mode could begin as early as late 1986; silo-based deployment will follow. The SS-25, similar to the Minuteman, will carry a single reentry vehicle.

Several bases for the SS-25 are almost

operational, with sliding roofed garages and support buildings for required mobile support equipment. Some 70 launchers are deployed. Recent activities at the Soviet ICBM test ranges indicate that two additional ICBMs are currently under development. It is possible that a MIRVed version of the SS-25 will be developed in the late 1980s.

Below: Long-range strategic penetration missions are the *forte* of the Tupolev "Blackjack" variable-geometry bomber, whose considerable radius is enhanced by use of the AS-15 cruise missile.

Above: The Typhoon class SSBNs are the world's largest underwater craft, truly prodigious boats each carrying 20 SS-N-20 submarine-launched ballistic missiles.

Submarine-Launched Ballistic Missiles

In January 1985, the Soviet SLBM force was estimated at 62 modern SSBMs carrying 944 nuclear-tipped missiles. This figure does not include the 13 older submarines equipped with 39 missiles currently assigned to theater missions. Twenty SSBNs are fitted with 336 MIRVed SLBMs. These 20 platforms have been built and deployed during the past nine

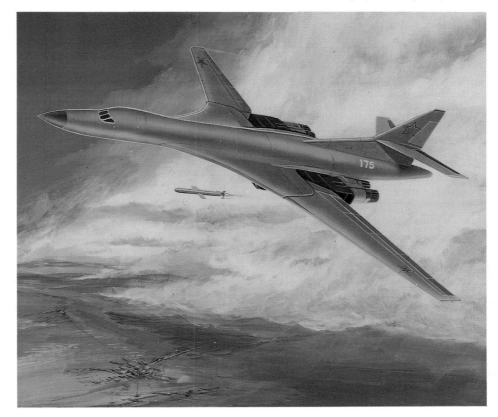

years. Two-thirds of the ballistic missile submarines are fitted with long-range SLBMs which enables the submarines to patrol in waters close to the Soviet Union where they enjoy some protection from NATO ASW operations. The long-range of the missiles allows the Soviet force to fire from home ports and still reach targets located in the United States.

Four units of Typhoon have already been completed, each with 20 SS-N-20 solid-propellant MIRVed SLBMs having a range of 5,160 miles (8,300km). Typhoon is the world's largest submarine and at 25,000 tons displacement is a third larger than the US Ohio class. By the early 1990s, the Soviets could have as many as eight of these vessels in their operational force.

Under the SALT I Interim Agreement the Soviets, since 1978, have removed 14 Yankee I units from service as ballistic missile submarines in order to remain within the 62 modern SSBN/950 SLBM limits. These units had to be removed as newer submarines were produced. Not all the Yankees have been scrapped; some have been reconfigured as attack or cruise missile submarines.

The Soviets have launched three units of a new class of SSBN, the Delta IV, which will be fitted with the SS-NX-23 SLBM, now being flight tested. This is a large, liquid-propelled SLBM with a greater throwweight, more warheads, and more accuracy than the SS-N-18, which is carried on the Delta III SSBN. The SS-NX-23 is likely to be deployed on Delta IIIs as a replacement for the SS-N-18. Flight testing of a modified version of the SS-N-20 is likely to commence soon. Based on past Soviet practice, testing of a modified, more accurate version of the SS-NX-23 may begin before the end of the 1980s.

Strategic Aviation
The Soviets have restructured their strategic bombers and strike aircraft to form five air armies subordinate to the Supreme High Command (VGK) and they are: Smolensk Air Army; Legnica Air Army; Venitza Air Army; Irkutsk Air Army; and Moscow Air Army. These armies were established to cover three specific theaters of military operations (Europe, Asia, and the United States) and yet retain the flexibility to reallocate aircraft as necessary in wartime.

Strategic aviation assets include some 180

Above: Further evidence of the Soviets' commitment to survivable nuclear capacity is provided by the highly mobile but also impressively accurate SS-20 intermediate-range missile for the theater role.

"Bear" and "Bison" bombers and about 270 "Backfire" bombers (including 125 "Backfires" assigned to Soviet Naval Aviation). The Soviets also have 397 medium-range "Blinders" and "Badger" bombers; 450 shorter range "Fencer" strike aircraft; and 530 tanker, reconnaissance, and electronic warfare aircraft.

The first new production of a strike version of the "Bear" airframe in more than 15 years has commenced. Older "Bear" aircraft, configured to carry the newer, supersonic AS-4 missile (replacing the subsonic AS-3) have been produced as "Bear-G" and several are now in service.

"Backfire" is the most modern operational Soviet bomber. It is being produced at a rate of approximately 30 per year and this rate is expected to continue through the end of the 1980s. The original design has been modified several times and further modifications are likely to be made to upgrade aircraft performance. It is a long-range aircraft capable of performing nuclear strike, conventional attack, antiship strike and reconnaissance missions. "Backfire" can be equipped for in-flight refueling, increasing its range and radius, and it could be used against the contiguous United States on high-altitude subsonic missions. Its low-altitude performance characteristics also make it a very effective weapon for support of military operations in Europe and Asia.

Some "Fencer" strike aircraft are also assigned to the air armies. "Fencer" is a supersonic, variable-geometry-wing, all-weather fighter-bomber which first became operational in 1974. Four variants have been developed. This aircraft is still in production and the number assigned to the air armies is expected to increase during the next few years.

"Blackjack", the new Soviet long-range bomber, is now in flight-testing. Larger than the B-1B, it has the same combat radius, but will be faster. "Blackjack" will be able to carry cruise missiles, bombs or both and is expected to be operational by 1988, replacing the "Bear-A" and later the "Bear-G" bombers.

A new aerial-refueling tanker based on the Il-76 "Candid" is expected to be deployed in the near future; it will improve the ability of the Soviets to conduct longer range operations.

Long-Range Cruise Missiles
The AS-15, a small, air-launched, subsonic, low-altitude cruise missile similar to the Tomahawk, reached initial operational capability with the "Bear-H" and has a range of around 1,865 miles (3,000km)

It is expected to be carried on the "Blackjack" when it becomes operational. Such a combination will increase Soviet strategic intercontinental air power capabilities in the late 1980s. The Soviets have sea-launched and ground-launched versions of the AS-15 under development.

The sea-based variant, the SS-NX-21, is small enough to be fired from standard Soviet torpedo tubes. Anticipated launch platforms for the SS-NX-21 include: existing Victor class nuclear-powered attack submarines (SSNs), a reconfigured Yankee class SSN and the new Akula, Mike, and Sierra class SSNs. The SS-NX-21 is expected to become operational this year and could be deployed on submarines near the US and allied coasts.

The ground-based SSC-X-4, a variant of the small cruise missile, probably became operational in 1986. The system is mobile and will likely follow operational procedures similar to those of the SS-20 LRINF missile.

A new larger cruise missile is also being developed as a sea-based system. Designated the SS-NX-24, it will be flight-tested from a specially converted Yankee class nuclear-powered cruise missile attack submarine (SSGN). The sea-based missile could be operational in 1987. These cruise missiles will all be fitted with nuclear warheads when they are first deployed and will be capable of attacking hardened targets. They could, with further developments, eventually become accurate enough to permit use of conventional warheads. Under conventional employment, these missiles would pose a significant non-nuclear threat to US and Eurasian airfields, and nuclear weapons sites in a non-nuclear conflict.

Non-Strategic Nuclear Forces
In 1977, the Soviets launched a concerted effort to modernize and expand their intermediate-range nuclear force with initial deployment of the SS-20. Each carries three MIRVs, thus more than doubling the number of LRINF warheads that existed in 1977. The SS-20 also has significant improvements in accuracy, range and reaction time over the missiles they replaced.

Two-thirds of the 441 SS-20s deployed are opposite NATO Europe. Some shifting of the SS-20s has been observed recently as the Soviets prepare for deployment of the SS-25 ICBM. It is not expected that any overall reduction of the SS-20 force will result from this activity. The mobility of the SS-20 system which enables on- and off-road operations enhances its survivability because detecting and targeting the missiles is difficult when they are field-deployed. The SS-20 launcher can be reloaded and refired from stocked reloads.

In addition to its SS-20 force the Soviets still maintain some 112 SS-4 LRINF missiles in the western USSR opposite NATO Europe. The Soviets also still maintain and operate 13 Golf II class ballistic missile submarines, each equipped with three SS-N-5 SLBMs. Six Golf II units are based in the Baltic where they pose a threat to most of Europe, while the remaining seven patrol the Sea of Japan. There is also a modified version of the SS-20 under flight-testing. This missile is expected to have even greater accuracy and improvements than the current SS-20.

Above: Another launch platform for the AS-15 nuclear-tipped cruise missile is the new-production Tupolev "Bear-H" turboprop-powered bomber, whose powerplant belies excellent performance.

Non-Strategic US Forces
Late in 1983, the US began the initial deployment of Pershing IIs and ground-launched cruise missiles (GLCMs) in Europe in response to the Soviet LRINF deployments. The deployment will continue until 1988, when 108 Pershing IIs and 464 GLCMs will be in place (unless a US/Soviet agreement is executed which eliminates or limits the number of LRINF missiles on both sides). The Soviet

Below: The Delta IV class SSBN is perhaps less impressive than the monstrous Typhoon class boat, but carries 16 extremely capable SS-N-23 SLBMs.

Union will maintain its significant numerical superiority in shorter range non-strategic nuclear missiles even as the US Pershing IIs replace the Pershing Is and the Soviets replace their Scuds with SS-23s. Pershing II will, however, improve the qualitative US factor. The USSR still has a numerical advantage in shorter range intermediate-range nuclear force aircraft and is reducing NATO's qualitative advantage at the same time. The balance in short-range nuclear forces (consisting of tube artillery and missiles) which was a historic advantage for NATO has shifted considerably toward the Soviets in recent years.

Short-Range Nuclear Forces
The Soviet Armies and Fronts have missile brigades equipped with 12-18 SS-1C Scud SRBMs. Over 500 Scud launchers are opposite NATO Europe and over 100 are deployed near the Soviet-Chinese border and in the Far East.

About 75 are opposite southwest Asia and eastern Turkey, and one brigade is in strategic reserve. The Scud is expected to be replaced by SS-23 with its longer range and greater accuracy; the Western Military Districts are expected to receive it first, followed by deployment to the Group of Soviet Forces, Germany. Each Front commander may also have a brigade of 12-18 Scaleboard missiles available. These are more accurate than SS-12 which they replace. Over 70 launchers are opposite NATO Europe and 40 are near the Sino-Soviet border; there is one battalion opposite southwest Asia/eastern Turkey; and one brigade in strategic reserve.

During 1984, the Soviets forward deployed Scaleboard to Eastern Europe for the first time. These Front-level missiles, normally deployed with Soviet combined arms formations, are now in a position to strike deep into NATO without having first to be moved forward. Improvements in guidance systems and control, warhead capabilities, and accuracies of the SRBMs are expected. These systems can deliver nuclear, chemical or conventional warheads closer to the forward edge of the battle area and at greater depths within the theater of military operations.

Tactical Missiles and Nuclear Artillery
Soviet Division Commanders have FROG rockets at their disposal. They are included in a FROG battalion with four launchers and the new, more accurate, longer range SS-21 which is replacing FROG in some divisions opposite NATO. In early 1985 there were some 375 FROG and SS-21 launchers in these forces. There are now 500 FROG launchers near the Sino-Soviet border; about 100 opposite southwest Asia and eastern Turkey; and about 75 in the Strategic Reserve.

The Division Commanders have some 800 nuclear-capable artillery tubes. Three new self-propelled, nuclear-capable artillery pieces are being added to the inventory: a 152mm gun, a 203mm self-propelled gun, and a 240mm self-propelled mortar.

Ground Forces Organization
The leadership of the Soviet Union has continued the Russian tradition of maintaining the large ground forces one would expect of a continental power which comprises approximately one-sixth of the Earth's land surface.

The Soviet ground forces are the largest of the five branches of the armed forces, with a peacetime strength of about 1.9 million. In peacetime, the ground forces are subordinate to 16 Military Districts. Forces in Eastern Europe are organized into four Soviet Groups of Forces (GOFs) – one each in the German Democratic Republic, Poland, Czechoslovakia and Hungary. The seven airborne divisions are directly subordinate to Airborne Forces Headquarters in Moscow and the forces in Mongolia and Afghanistan are each organized into an army subordinate to the adjacent military district. The combat power is in 213 maneuver divisions, including 12 mobilization divisions. Two divisions are being expanded to new corps-type structures.

The size and structure of the military districts and Groups varies widely. A typical military district or GOF would include several combined arms or tank Armies, an artillery division, an air defense division, several surface-to-air (SAM) brigades and an aviation component called the Air Forces of the Military District or GOF, plus other units. In wartime the major GOFs and military districts would form Fronts and a number of Fronts would conduct operations to secure strategic objectives within a designated theater of military operations (TVD). Neither the Army nor the Front has a fixed organization; each is tailored for operations in its designated area. Western forces do not have a counterpart to the Front, the closest parallel being an Army Group plus organic tactical aviation.

The basic maneuver forces of the Soviet ground forces are the tank, motorized rifle and airborne divisions. The tank and motorized rifle divisions are very mobile armored forces and both have a full complement of support elements. The tank division with 11,000 men, has 3 tank regiments and 1 motorized rifle regiment, while the motorized rifle division with 13,000 men, has 3 motorized rifle regiments and 1 tank regiment. The airborne divisions are not as mobile on the ground as the tank and motorized rifle divisions in Soviet forces, but are significantly more mobile than a US airborne division. The three parachute regiments and their combat support and service units are well-equipped with the airborne amphibious combat vehicle, the BMD.

As mentioned, two divisions have been converted into corps-like structures. These are almost twice as large as a normal tank division with more than 450 tanks, 600 infantry fighting vehicles and armored personnel carriers plus 300 artillery pieces/multiple rocket launchers. Additional units of this type are expected to be formed since they are ideal to act as high-speed Operational Maneuver Groups (OMG), which can conduct high-speed operations deep in enemy rear areas.

At divisional level, helicopter detachments are being expanded to squadrons and in some of the squadrons the number of "Hind" attack helicopters has been increased. At Army level,

Above: Known by the Soviet production designation 2S3 and by the US reporting designation M-1973, this is a modern and capable 152mm SP gun/howitzer.

about 20 attack helicopter regiments have been formed, with up to 60 "Hip" and "Hind" attack helicopters in each. Over half of these are deployed opposite NATO forces. Most of the attack helicopters are the heavily armed Mi-24 "Hind-D/E" and Mi-8 "Hip-E". These aircraft are armed with anti-tank guided missiles and 57mm unguided rockets, effective both against lightly armored targets and

Below: There is still little information about the Mil Mi-28 "Havoc", an advanced battlefield helicopter comparable to but smaller than the current Mi-24 "Hind".

Above: The "Scud" series of SSMs provides Soviet ground formations with battlefield support, having alternative HE, chemical or nuclear warheads.

personnel. Chemical or conventional bombs can also be carried on these helicopters.

The continuing Soviet emphasis on heavy-lift helicopter transport capability is seen in the recent appearance of the Mi-26 "Halo", the world's largest production helicopter. It is capable of carrying internally two airborne infantry combat vehicles or about 85 combat-equipped soldiers. Soviet helicopters are now being equipped with infrared (IR) jammers and suppressors, IR decoy dispensers and additional armor – modifications probably made as the result of lessons learned in Afghanistan. The new Mi-28 "Havoc" (which resembles the US Army Apache) is expected to be deployed soon. The newer "Hokum" helicopter will give the Soviets a significant rotary-wing air superiority capability, and has no current Western counterpart.

The Soviets are also making changes in their logistic structure. In the past, transport, supply and servicing operations were fragmented. Today, at division level, there is a materiel support battalion which includes motor transport, supply and maintenance elements. The transport vehicle inventory is about 30 percent larger than those of division

motor transport battalions. Materiel support brigades are being formed at Army and Front levels as well.

At present, the Soviets have 199 *active* tank, motorized rifle and airborne divisions. Ninety-eight of these active divisions are opposite NATO, including 30 in Eastern Europe. Fifty-three are along the border with China and in the Soviet Far East opposite China and Japan. Ten divisions (including 4 in Afghanistan) are opposite southwest Asia. Twenty divisions in the Caucasus are available for operations in eastern Turkey and southwest Asia. An additional 18 divisions are located in the Strategic Reserve military districts.

About 40 percent of the Soviet divisions (including all of those deployed outside the USSR and 6 of the 7 airborne divisions) are manned at what the Soviets consider *ready* levels – ie, they could be ready for combat in a short period of time. The remainder are cadre divisions and need about 60 days to mobilize and prepare for further training and deployment. The 14 mobilization divisions (or in-active divisions) are unmanned sets of equipment from which divisions will be formed in wartime. The ground forces include over

52,600 main battle tanks, about one-third of which are the later models (T-64/72/80 series) and more than half of these are opposite NATO Europe.

Soviet forces have approximately 59,000 armored personnel carriers and infantry fighting vehicles with which to mesh their infantry tank forces. Most of these vehicles are the BTR-60 wheeled APCs and the BMP tracked IFVs. A motorized rifle regiment in a tank division and that in the motorized rifle division are equipped with BMP. The other motorized rifle regiments of the motorized rifle divisions are equipped with BTR-60s.

The BTR-80, a follow-on to the BTR-70 and the BTR-60, has been fielded in limited numbers. It has an improved engine and drive-train with better off-the-road performance. The improved BMP-2 is replacing or augmenting the BMP. The BMP-2 has a 30mm rapid-fire gun and carries the AT-5 ATGM. The Soviets have also fielded the BMP with their airborne and air assault units and a number of light ground-pressure vehicles such as GTT/MT-LB series for employment where trafficability is poor.

The Soviets have always placed great emphasis on fire support and currently have more than 39,000 artillery pieces and multiple rocket launchers (MRLs) larger than 100mm caliber in their active inventory. Over 14 percent of the inventory are self-propelled weapons and 70 percent of these are opposite the NATO Central Region.

Air Defense Weapons

More than 4,600 SAM launchers and 12,000 AAA pieces are deployed by the Soviets at regimental through Front level – the most comprehensive troop tactical air defense system in the world! In addition to these, as many as 25,000 shoulder-fired SAM launchers are at battalion and company level and with non-divisional units.

The standard air defense for tank or motorized rifle regiments is a battery of SA-9-13 SAMs and ZSU-23-4 self-propelled AAA pieces. The SA-9 system, mounted on a wheeled transporter-erector-launcher (TEL), is being selectively replaced and augmented by the SA-13 on a tracked TEL. A follow-on to the ZSU-23-4 quad gun is expected to appear soon. A new division-level SAM, the SA-11 is beginning to be deployed. It has an onboard radar, increasing mobility and target-handling capability. The standard weapon at Army and Front level is the SA-4 which should soon be replaced by the SA-X-12.

Chemical Warfare

The Soviets are better prepared for operations in a chemical environment than any other armed force in the world. Soviet soldiers receive extensive chemical defense training and most combat vehicles are equipped with a chemical protection and chemical detection alarm system. Chemical defense troops with specialized detection and decontamination equipment are found throughout the ground forces. The Soviets have more than 80,000 active duty officers and enlisted specialists trained in chemical warfare (and more than double that number in the reserves). They have about 30,000 special vehicles for chemical reconnaissance and decontamination. Military chemical warfare schools at 200 locations teach and train Soviet troops how to protect and decontaminate themselves in combat.

Special Purpose Forces

The USSR has a special complement of forces known as Spetsnaz (Special Purpose Forces) which are controlled by the Main Intelligence Directorate (GRU) of the Soviet General Staff. These forces are trained to conduct a variety of sensitive missions abroad, including covert action. Large numbers of Spetsnaz troops have been assigned to Afghanistan, where they have become known for their ruthless aggressiveness. In peacetime, GRU-coordinated reconnaissance programs are designed to meet projected intelligence requirements for wartime. During hostilities, Spetsnaz forces would operate far behind enemy lines to conduct reconnaissance, sabotage, assassination and strike missions on special military and political targets.

Spetsnaz forces are organized into brigades; however, in wartime they would infiltrate and fight as small teams. Each brigade could field approximately 100 Spetsnaz teams. A typical team would be commanded by an officer with a

Right: The SA-9 "Gaskin" provides Soviet motor rifle and tank regiments with modest low-level air-defense capability. The system is based on the BRDM-2 chassis.

Above: Known in Soviet service as the T-74 but by the US services as the T-80, this powerful MBT has good protection and a laser rangefinder for its 125mm main gun.

warrant officer or sergeant as deputy. Other members of the teams are trained as communicators, weapons and demolitions specialists.

Air Forces

The Soviet Air Forces (SAF) have three major combat components: Strategic Air Armies (discussed under nuclear forces); Air Forces of the Military Districts and Groups of Forces; and Soviet Military Transport Aviation (VTA). There are 17 air forces in the Groups of Forces, peripheral military districts of the USSR, Mongolia, and Afghanistan. These air forces are operationally subordinate to the MD, Group or army commander and consists of combat fighters, reconnaissance craft, fighter-bombers and helicopters. (Helicopters are known as Army Aviation.) Fighter and fighter-bomber regiments can be organized into divisions or remain independent and report directly to the MDs and Groups of Forces. The reconnaissance regiments and squadrons are independent units. Helicopter units either report to the MDs and Groups of Forces or to their assigned maneuver elements.

The five Strategic Air Armies include one designed for intercontinental and maritime strike missions and four designed for support

Above: Inter-theater and global movements are greatly aided by the Soviet Union's growing fleet of new Antonov An-124 "Condor" strategic transport aircraft.

of various theater missions. Two of the latter air armies are comprised entirely of former Tactical Air Army assets. Regiments within the air armies are usually organized to divisions although some independent regiments exist. The Soviet Military Transport Aviation, the third operational element of SAF, has the

Below: Now being developed in mobile form, the SA-10 SAM was first deployed for the defense of fixed installations, suggesting a capability against missiles.

primary responsibility to provide airlift services for the Soviet Airborne Forces (VDV) and air assault units. It also provides air logistics support for other deployed Soviet and allied forces.

Soviet Air Forces have as their combat and combat support assets more than 700 bombers, almost 6,300 fighter and fighter-bombers and about 600 VTA transports. Significant assets of Aeroflot, the Soviet Civil Transport, are also available as a reserve for VTA transport.

The VTA has some 600 medium and long-range cargo transports. Il-76 "Candid" long-range jet transports have been gradually replacing An-12 "Cub" medium-range turbo-prop transports at a rate of around 30 per year. There are now 290 "Candids" and 230 "Cubs"

in the active inventory. "Candid" has significant advantages over "Cub"; in particular, it can carry twice the maximum payload over three times the distance. VTA also has about 55 An-22 "Cock" long-range turboprop transports, the only Soviet transport able to carry out-sized cargo such as main battle tanks or large missiles. However, production of the new heavy-lift An-400 "Condor" transport, bigger even than the US C-5A Galaxy, will dramatically upgrade VTA heavy-lift capabilities. It is estimated that initial deployment of "Condor" will occur in 1987 or 1988.

The Air Forces of the MDs and GOFs have about 5,440 fighter-interceptors, fighter-bombers, and reconnaissance and electronic countermeasures (ECM) aircraft which are deployed in nearly 140 regiments and squadrons. About 750 of these aircraft are assigned to Strategic Air Armies, and some 110 are in Afghanistan. The MiG "Flogger" is the most numerous fighter-interceptor, with about 1,700 aircraft. Almost 600 MiG-21 "Fishbeds" are still operational, although they are being replaced by the MiG-29 "Fulcrum", and additional regiments of the Su-15 "Flagon" continue to remain in the force. Deployment of the MiG-29 "Fulcrum" air superiority fighter proceeded into early 1986 at a steady, though limited, rate. By the end of January 1986, Soviet forces in East Germany and the far eastern USSR had begun to receive it. The new Su-27 "Flanker" also entered operational service by early 1986, with initial aircraft arriving in air defense regiments.

The "Fulcrum" and "Flanker" both have true look-down/shoot-down radar, and carry beyond-visual range AA-10 and the short-range AA-11 air-to-air missiles. Together with the "Foxhound" interceptor, these aircraft mark the transition to a new generation of far more capable Soviet aircraft.

The variable-geometry wing Su-17/-20/-22 "Fitter" series is the most common (almost

Left: The carriers of the Kiev class mark a departure for the Soviets. Though lacking CTOL aircraft capability, they are well armed with V/STOL aircraft and missiles.

800) ground attack aircraft in SAF regiments of the MDs and GOFs. The best interdiction aircraft in the Soviet inventory is the Su-24 "Fencer". Other regiments are comprised of MiG-23/-27 "Floggers", the new Su-25 "Frogfoot", and older MiG-21 "Fishbed" and Su-7 "Fitter-As".

Reconnaissance assets are composed of "Fishbeds", Su-17 "Fitters", MiG-25 "Foxbats", and Yak-28 "Brewers". Newer aircraft are beginning to replace the "Brewer", significantly increasing Soviet reconnaissance range capabilities.

NATO/Warsaw Pact Air Forces

According to official NATO estimates, the overall global total of Warsaw Pact aircraft reaches almost 13,000 aircraft of all types, of which more than 10,000 face NATO in Europe. NATO officials calculate 7,500 of these aircraft are of types which are technically capable of delivering nuclear weapons. The NATO air assets, in place in Europe (excluding those of France and Spain), include 1,960 fighter/bomber ground attack aircraft, 795 interceptors and 235 reconnaissance aircraft. NATO is understandably concerned because the introduction of new Soviet aircraft in significant numbers, replacing older, less capable ones has considerably increased the Warsaw Pact's offensive capability. Compared with previous estimates, the latest Soviet aircraft are capable of carrying up to twice the payload, with three times the range and higher speeds, as well as being operational at lower altitudes – thus rendering them less vulnerable to NATO air defenses. Their increased combat radius would allow for Warsaw Pact operations from more distant bases in case of

Above: The Soviets' northern and eastern shores host a number of SSBN bases such as that depicted with Typhoon (lower left) and Delta IV class (entering tunnel) boats.

Warsaw Pact hostilities against NATO. This would mean that NATO fighter-bombers would have to penetrate much deeper into heavy defended enemy airspace to counter-attack Warsaw Pact bases. (Soviet Air Defenses will be discussed later. The tactical air defenses have been addressed as applicable to each section in this chapter.)

Soviet Naval Forces

The Soviet Navy's power, mobility and capability for worldwide deployment can support Soviet interest abroad to a greater extent than the other branches of Soviet armed forces. Since the Soviet Navy evolved from special and particular national political requirements and geographic considerations, it differs greatly from the US Navy. Generally, the missions of the Soviet Navy are summarized as follows:

To protect Soviet strategic strike capabilities.

To carry out strategic submarine-launched ballistic and cruise missile strikes.

To counter the threat from Western sea-based strategic forces.

To achieve sea control in the approaches to the Soviet and other Warsaw Pact nations.

To conduct sea-denial operations in selected ocean areas so as to preclude Western freedom of action in these areas.

To support Warsaw Pact ground operations by protecting the sea flanks, seizing vital straits and islands, and conducting amphibious assaults.

To protect vital sea lines of communication (SLOCs) as well as interdicting Western SLOCs.

The Soviets rely on in-depth defenses in the

sea approaches to the USSR to provide immediate protection to the homeland as well as to secure access from bases to the operating areas. Most Soviet general purpose surface, submarine and naval air forces would probably be assigned initial wartime tasks within this perimeter.

Submarine Forces

Several new and improved classes of general purpose submarines are under construction, with movement toward new designs such as the "Akula" and "Sierra". This process decreased output of general purpose submarines in 1985, with only one new nuclear-powered attack submarine – a Victor III Class – launched.

The construction of "Kilo"-class diesel-powered attack submarines continued. Series production of the "Akula", "Sierra", and possibly other classes was expected to begin in earnest with additional launches in 1986.

Surface Forces

The Soviet Navy now has about 675 surface combatants. This total includes 280 principal surface combatants and 3 Kiev Class aircraft carriers. It also includes 185 patrol combatants, 77 amphibious ships, and some 130 mine warfare ships.

Currently, the largest operational ship in the Soviet Navy is the Kiev class aircraft carrier. It is armed with a variety of new weapons including a battery of 340 miles (550km) range SS-N-12 antiship missiles, over 100 long and short-range SAMs, air defense gun batteries, besides sophisticated tactical sensors, electronic warfare systems and

Below: The Kilo class diesel-electric submarine is in major production as replacement for the Foxtrot class in continental shelf and covert operations.

Left: Another powerful new type in Soviet service is the Kirov class cruiser, which packs a highly impressive missile armament into a nuclear-powered hull.

advanced communications. The flight deck can accommodate both "Hormone" and "Helix" ASW and missile guidance helicopters, as well as the Yak-36 "Forger" VTOL attack, reconnaissance and interceptor aircraft.

In 1980, when the Soviets introduced their first nuclear-powered surface warship – *Kirov*, a large guided-missile cruiser (and one of the most extensively armed vessels in the world), and the *Udaloy* and *Sovremenny* guided-missile destroyers, it became clear that their naval development had entered a new era. In 1982, they produced the *Slava* a gas-turbine-powered guided-missile cruiser with 16 SS-N-12 cruise missiles, 64 SA-N-6 air defense missiles and 40 SA-N-4 point defense missiles as well as 130mm twin-barrel dual purpose guns and a variant of "Hormone" helicopters. In 1984, *Frunze*, the second Kirov class, became operational and a third ship of this class is under construction

The most noteworthy new platform under construction is an entirely new class of aircraft carrier. Launched in December 1985 and now undergoing a fitting-out period, it is approximately 1000ft (300m) long and will displace 65,000 tons. The new carrier is an evolutionary step in the Soviet Navy's carrier program. It has a larger angled flight deck than the Kiev Class carriers, has deck-edge aircraft elevators fore and aft of the starboard superstructure, and a broad upturned bow similar to a ski jump ramp used for short-take-off-and-vertical-landing aircraft. The aircraft for the carrier's air wing are still under development; the carrier is expected to begin sea trials in 1989.

While an increasing emphasis on sea-based aircraft development is expected, Soviet Naval Aviation is expected to remain primarily land-based. With more than 1,600 aircraft, Soviet Naval Aviation today is larger than most of the national air forces in the world! Its inventory includes "Badger", "Backfire" and a "Bear-F" turboprop variant designed for ASW missions.

Amphibious Forces
Since 1968, Soviet amphibious warfare capability has improved steadily and their Naval Infantry now has some 16,000 troops allocated among the four fleets: Northern, Pacific Ocean, Baltic and Black Sea. Each Western fleet has a naval infantry brigade of some 3,000 men while the Pacific Ocean Fleet contains a single 7,000-man division. Amphibious lift for Naval Infantry is provided by a number of specialized ships, the largest of which are the two Ivan Rogov class amphibious assault transport docks (LPDs). *Ivan Rogov* can carry four "Helix" helicopters and has bow doors and a wet well-deck at the stern that can accommodate two Lebed air cushion vehicles (ACVs). This ship can carry over 500 Naval Infantry plus equipment. Additional lift is provided by Alligator and Ropucha class amphibious vehicle landing ships (LSTs) and smaller Polnocny class medium amphibious assault landing ships (LSMs).

The Soviet Navy is also the world's largest operator of military air cushion vehicles. These craft can move troops and equipment more rapidly and effectively than conventional landing craft for short distances. Air cushion vehicles like the *Gus, Lebed, Aist, Tsaplya*, and *Utenok* are deployed and would be expected to play a major role in Soviet amphibious operations.

Naval Special Purpose Forces
Like the Ground Forces, the Soviet Navy has a small body of specially trained troops in each fleet area. These naval Spetsnaz forces are assigned, in brigade formation, to each of the Soviet fleets for covert missions, including underwater demolitions.

Soviet Merchant Fleet
The Soviet concept of seapower contemplates use of all maritime resources and this includes the merchant marine and large fishing and research fleets, although they are not categorized as military forces. The operations of the merchant marine are closely coordinated with naval requirements from Moscow level down to the smallest port facility. A significant portion of logistic support required by the Soviet Navy in peacetime, particularly in distant areas, is provided by the merchant fleet. This flexibility allows the Soviet merchant ships to obtain supplies for naval use in ports where warship visits might be denied. In a crisis, the highly organized, centrally controlled merchant fleet can provide military support quickly and effectively.

Deployment of Naval Forces
The Soviet Navy is organized into four fleets – the Northern, Baltic, Black Sea, and Pacific Ocean Fleets – and the Caspian Sea Flotilla. The navy also maintains deployed forces in the Mediterranean Sea, the Indian Ocean, and off the coast of West Africa. The Soviets also continue to develop a naval and airbase at Cam Ranh Bay, Vietnam, where they now station submarines with supporting surface combatants and a composite air group.

In addition, combatant task groups often deploy to the Caribbean Sea, with stopovers at Cuban bases and ports. The Soviet navy – since the mid-1970s – has evolved toward a balanced ocean-going fleet (a true "blue water navy") capable of fighting at great distances from the USSR at nuclear and conventional levels.

Strategic Defense and Space Programs
The Soviet concept of a layered defense envisions not only the tactical air-defenses discussed earlier, but also their strategic defenses and includes space programs. Strategic defenses are vital to the Soviets' overall strategy for nuclear war. Because individual systems may have shortcomings and the possibility that any one layer of defense cannot stop all attacking weapons, the Soviet system contemplates multiple types of defensive capabilities.

The Soviets have the world's most extensive early warning system for both ballistic missile and air defense. Their operational ballistic missile early warning system includes a launch-detection satellite network, over-the-horizon radar, and a series of large phased-array radars located primarily on the periphery of the USSR. The current launch-detection satellite network can provide about 30 minutes' warning of any US ICBM launch, as can the two over-the-horizon radars, but they are less precise than the satellite net. Together, these two systems provide more reliable warning than either working alone.

The ballistic missile defense capabilities are continuing to be upgraded. The Moscow missile defenses are being enlarged and equipped with a new generation of radars, and interceptor missiles. The new SA-X-12 SAM (incorpor-

Above: The Soviets have recently introduced a number of advanced tactical aircraft, including the Sukhoi Su-27 with look-down/shoot-down capability.

ating ballistic missile capabilities) is nearly operational and other system research, such as that on directed-energy systems, continues. The only operational ABM system in the world today is that around Moscow. The original single-layer system with 64 reloadable, above-ground launchers is being upgraded to the 100 accountable under the US/Soviet ABM Treaty and could be operational by 1987.

Air Defenses
The Soviets have made significant shifts in the subordination of their air and air defense assets. The reorganization has provided them with a very efficient organization that merges strategic and tactical and air defense assets in most land border areas of the USSR. The air defense (APVO) interceptors became part of a new structure, the Air Forces of the Military District, which also includes most of the assets of the former tactical air armies.

The strategic and tactical air defense forces are impressively large with more than 9,000 strategic SAM launchers, and 4,600 launch vehicles for tactical SAMs, as well as some 10,000 air defense radars. More than 1,200 interceptors are dedicated to strategic defense while an additional 2,800 Soviet Air Force interceptors could also be used.

Deployment of the supersonic MiG-31 "Foxhound" interceptor with the Soviet's first true look-down/shoot-down and multiple target engagement capability continued in 1984. More than 100 "Foxhound" aircraft, comparable in size to the F-14 Tomcat, are deployed from Archangel to the Far East MD. Two new fighter interceptors – the Su-27 "Flanker" and the MiG-29 "Fulcrum" – with look-down/shoot-down capabilities have also been deployed. More than 100 "Fulcrums" are in operational units; the "Flanker" has only recently begun to deploy. Both are probably intended to operate with the new "Mainstay" AWACS aircraft.

The strategic SAMs form barrier, area and terminal defenses and a mixed and integrated system of aircraft, SAMs, and AAA artillery provide the USSR with the most comprehensive air defense system in the world.

Laser/Particle Beam Weapons
More than 10,000 scientists and engineers and more than a half dozen major research and development facilities and test ranges are involved in the Soviet laser program. The research is being conducted on three types of gas lasers considered promising for weapons applications: the gas dynamic laser, the electric discharge laser, and the chemical laser. The Soviets also are aware of the military potential of visible and very short wave-length lasers. They are investigating excimer, free-electron, and x-ray lasers.

In the area of particle beams, the Soviets

have been involved in research since the late 1960s. Official estimates are that they may be able to test a prototype particle beam weapon in the 1990s that would be capable of disrupting the electronics of satellites. A weapon designed to destroy satellites could follow later.

Space Programs

The Soviet concept of warfare embraces the philosophy of combined arms in which all types of forces are integrated into military operations. Space assets play a major role in this concept and the Soviet drive to use space for military purposes is an integral part of Soviet military planning.

Space Programs

They have made progress in their space plane and space shuttle programs, and the first flight of a Soviet shuttle is expected in late 1986 or 1987. Furthermore, they now operate several space-based reconnaissance and surveillance systems, two of which have no US counterparts. The latter are the nuclear-powered Radar Ocean Reconnaissance Satellite (RORSAT) and the Electronic Intelligence Reconnaissance Satellite (EORSAT), both of which are used to locate and target naval forces.

They have also pressed ahead with the development and deployment of the GLONASS,

Below: Though the Soviets condemn the US SDI programme, they too are involved in advanced defense technology work with development models such as this laser capable of interfering with satellites.

a global navigation satellite system. Fully developed, this system will provide three-dimensional (latitude, longitude, and altitude) positioning information.

In the area of launch systems, the Soviets have continued launch pad compatibility testing for its heavy-lift vehicle (a Saturn V class booster) and flight testing of its Titan III class medium lift vehicle. The former will apparently be used to launch the Soviet shuttle orbiter and be able to carry payloads of about 100,000 kilograms, enabling the assembly of large modular space stations in orbit. The latter may be used to launch the Soviet space plane, which is a different program from the space shuttle. It could be used for real-time reconnaissance missions, satellite repair and maintenance, crew transport, space station defense, and satellite inspection or destruction.

When these new launch systems become operational, the Soviets will have 10 different types of expendable launch vehicles and two reusable manned space vehicles.

Conclusion

Soviet military power has been acquired in a steady, consistent and generally efficient manner over a long time. Because it relies upon what others are dissuaded from doing, Soviet military power is relatively fragile. If the US or its allies elected to devote anything approximating the percentage of their resources to military power that the Soviet Union does, clearly their relative power would exceed that of the Soviet's in only a few years. Past US and allied efforts have never defined their maximum potential.

The US and its allies must maintain a military capability which convinces the Soviet leadership that the costs of aggression far outweigh any possible gains. The goals of arms reductions and world peace could be achieved under these conditions.

The strategy adopted by the US and its allies of nuclear and conventional deterrence is viable to the degree that they can raise and maintain forces that are properly manned, trained and equipped. For forty years, this strategy has been effective in preventing a major conflict in Europe. With the increasing global challenge, the US and its allies must develop an accurate and comprehensive understanding of the Soviet challenge and undertake the steps necessary to maintain an effective deterrent to the *threat* of force as well as its employment. At the same time, national leaders must continue to seek realistic, equitable and genuine arms reductions which can contribute to global stability and the peace and security of all nations. This is not simple, cheap or without frustration, but the alternatives are predictably far worse.

To conclude this chapter, the discussion of deterrence is set forth succinctly as it was defined in the report of the Scowcroft Commission: *"Deterrence is not an abstract notion amenable to simple quantification. Still less is it a mirror-image of what would deter ourselves. Deterrence is the set of beliefs in the minds of the Soviet leaders, given their own values and attitudes, about our capabilities and our will. It requires us to determine as best we can, what would better deter them from considering aggression, even in a crisis – not to determine what would deter us."*

US Ground Forces Weapons

M48

Type: Medium tank.
Crew: 4.
Armament: One 105mm M68; one 0·3in M1919A4E1 machine gun co-axial with the main armament (some have a 7·62mm M73 MG); one 0·5in machine gun in commander's cupola.
Armor: 12·7mm-120mm (0·50-4·8in).
Dimensions: Length (including main armament) 28·3ft (8·686m); length (hull) 22ft 7in (6·882m); width 11ft 11in (3·631m); height (including cupola) 10ft 3in (3·124m).
Weight: Combat 108,000lb (48,989kg).
Ground pressure: 11·80lb/in² (0·83kg/cm²).
Engine: Continental AVDS-1790-2A 12-cylinder air-cooled diesel developing 750hp at 2,400rpm.
Performance: Road speed 30mph (48km/h); range 288 miles (463km); vertical obstacle 3ft (0·915m); trench 8ft 6in (2·59m); gradient 60 per cent.
History: Entered service with the US Army in 1953.

The hull of the M48 is of cast armor construction, as is the turret. The driver is seated at the front of the hull with the other three crew members located in the turret, with the commander and gunner on the right and the loader on the left. The engine and transmission are at the rear of the hull, and are separated from the fighting compartment by a fireproof bulkhead. The suspension is of the torsion-bar type and consists of six road wheels, with the drive sprocket at the rear and the idler at the front. Depending on the model there are between three and five track-return rollers, and some models have a small track tensioning wheel between the sixth road wheel and the drive sprocket. The main armament consists of a 105mm gun with an elevation of +19° and a depression of −9°, traverse being 360°. A 0·3in M1919A4E1 machine-gun is mounted co-axially with the main armament. The cupola can be traversed through 360°, and the machine-gun can be elevated from −10° to +60°.

The M48 can be fitted with a dozer blade, if required, at the front of the hull. All M48s have infra-red driving lights and some an infra-red/white searchlight mounted over the main armament. The type can ford to a depth of 4ft (1·219m) without preparation or 8ft (2·438m) with the aid of a kit.

The first model to enter service was the M48, and this had a simple cupola for the commander, with the machine-gun mounted externally. The second model was the M48C, which was for training use only as it had a mild steel hull. The M48A1 was followed by the M48A2, which had many improvements including a fuel-injection system for the engine and larger capacity fuel tanks. The M48A2C was a slightly modified M48A2. The M48A3 was a significant improvement as this had a diesel engine, which increased the vehicle's operational range considerably, and a number of other modifications including a different fire-control system. Latest model is the M48A5, essentially an M48A1 or M48A2 with modifications including an M68 main 105mm gun, new tracks, a 7·62mm M60D co-axial machine-gun and a similar weapon on the loader's hatch, plus many other detail modifications. One interesting modification is the fitting of an Israeli-developed low-profile cupola.

Earlier M48A1, M48A2C and M48A3 in the US inventory (some 1,809

M60

Type: Main battle tank.
Crew: 4.
Armament: One 105mm gun; one 7·62mm machine gun co-axial with main armament; one 0·5in anti-aircraft machine gun in commander's cupola.
Armor: 12·7mm-120mm (0·5-4·80in).
Dimensions: Length (gun forward) 30ft 11in (9·436m); length (hull) 22ft 9½in (6·946m); width 11ft 11in (3·631m); height 10ft 8in (3·257m).
Weight: Combat 114,600lb (51,982kg).
Ground pressure: 11·24lb/in² (0·79kg/cm²).
Engine: Continental AVDS-1790-2A 12-cylinder diesel developing 750bhp at 2,400rpm.
Performance: Road speed 30mph (48km/h); range 280 miles (450km); vertical obstacle 3ft (0·914m); trench 8ft 6in (2·59m); gradient 60 per cent.
History: The M60 entered service with the US Army in 1960

In the 1950s the standard tank of the United States Army was the M48. In 1957 an M48 series tank was fitted with a new engine for trials purposes and this was followed by another three prototypes in 1958. Late in 1958 it was decided to arm the new tank with the British 105mm L7 series gun, to be built in the United States under the designation M68. In 1959 the first production order for the new tank, now called the M60, was placed with Chrysler, and the type entered production at Detroit Tank Arsenal in late 1959, with the first production tanks being completed the following year.

From late in 1962, the M60 was replaced in production by the M60A1, which had a number of improvements, the most important being the redesigned turret. The M60A1 had a turret and hull of all-cast construction. The driver is seated at the front of the hull with the other three crew members in the turret, commander and gunner on the right and the loader on the left. The engine and transmission are at the rear, the latter having one reverse and two forward ranges. The M60 has torsion-bar suspension and six road wheels, with the idler at the front and the drive sprocket at the rear; there are four track-return rollers. The 105mm gun has an elevation of +20° and a depression of –10°, and traverse is 360°. Both elevation and traverse are powered. A 7·62mm M73 machine-gun is mounted co-axially with the main armament and there is a 0·5in M85 machine-gun in the commander's cupola. The latter can be aimed and fired from within the turret, and has an elevation of +60° and a depression of –15°. Some

60 rounds of 105mm, 900 rounds of 0·5in and 5,950 rounds of 7·62mm ammunition are carried. Infra-red driving lights are fitted as standard and an infra-red/white light is mounted over the main armament. All M60s have an NBC system. The tank can also be fitted with a dozer blade on the front of the hull. The M60 can ford to a depth of 4ft (1·219m) without preparation or 8ft (2·438m) with the aid of a kit. For deep fording operations a schnorkel can be fitted, allowing the M60 to ford to a depth of 13ft 6in (4·14m).

Right: The M60A3 is armed with the 105mm M68 rifled gun and still provides the backbone of US Army armored formations.

Christopher F. Foss, Military Editor of *Jane's Defence Weekly,* author of *Jane's World Armoured Fighting Vehicles;* Editor of *Jane's Armour and Artillery* and *Jane's Military Vehicles and Ground Support Equipment.*

tanks) have been updated to M48A5 standard and serve with Army National Guard and reserve units. Some M48A1 and M48A2 chassis were to have been used for the Sergeant York DIVADS, but this is now defunct.

Three flamethrower tanks were developed: the M67 (using the M48A1 chassis), the M67A1 (using the M48A2 chassis) and the M67A2 (using the M48A3 chassis). Also in service is an M48 Armored Vehicle-Launched Bridge. This has a scissors bridge which can be laid over gaps up to 60ft (18·288m) in width.

Below: The M48 series is decidedly elderly, but retains a certain combat value when upgraded with the 105mm M68 gun.

Below: The chassis has a number of other roles, including the core of an armored vehicle-launched bridge.

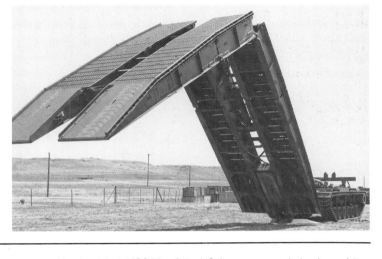

The M60A2 was a special model armed with a 152mm gun/launcher but has now been phased out of service. Current production model is the M60A3 with numerous improvements including stabilization of main armament, top loading air cleaner fitted, passive searchlight over main armament, new tracks with removable pads, tube over bar suspension, RISE engine, thermal sleeve for main armament, laser rangefinder, passive night vision devices, new MAG 7·62mm MG, smoke dischargers each side of turret, muzzle reference system, engine smoke dischargers and improved personnel heater. Most M60A1s of the US Army are now being brought up to this new standard, with the aim of an M60A3 fleet totalling 7,352 (1,691 from new production and 5,661 from conversion of M60A1s in Army depots). Of these, 3,786 will be the M60A3 TTS version, which has all the improvements listed above, plus a tank thermal sight. By 1981 total production of the M60 series of MBTs had amounted to over 10,600 vehicles with the final vehicles being completed in 1985. Specialized versions of the M60 series include the M60 armored vehicle launched bridge and the M728 Combat Engineer Vehicle which is fitted with a bulldozer blade, 152mm demolition gun and an A-frame for lifting obstacles which is pivoted at the front of the hull. The basic vehicle can also be fitted with roller type mineclearing equipment or a dozer blade.

Below: The M60 is automotively sound, well armored and provided with adequate offensive armament, but suffers from the inherent tactical limitations imposed by its considerable height, especially when the 0·5-inch AA machine-gun is fitted in the commander's cupola.

M1 Abrams

Type: Main battle tank.
Crew: 4.
Armament: One 105mm M68 gun; one 7·62mm machine gun co-axial with main armament; one 0·5in machine gun on commander's cupola; one M240 7·62mm machine gun on loader's hatch (see text).
Armor: Classified.
Dimensions: Length (gun forward) 32ft 0½in (9·766m); length (hull) 25ft 11¾in (7·918m); width 11ft 11¾in (3·655m); height 7ft 9½in (2·375m).
Weight: 120,000lb (54,432kg).
Engine: Avco Lycoming AGT-T 1500 HP-C turbine developing 1,500hp.
Performance: Road speed 45mph (72·4km/h); range 275 miles (443km); vertical obstacle .4ft 1in (1·244m); trench 9ft (2·743m); gradient 60 per cent.
History: First production vehicle completed in 1980.

By 1986 over 3,000 M1s had been built and the tank is now entering service at an increasingly rapid rate. The first units to field the M1 were the three armored battalions of 3rd Infantry Division (Mechanized) who proudly gave the tank its European debut in 'Exercise Reforger' in August 1982. The US Army has a requirement for some 7,058 M1s by the end of Fiscal year 1989. From 1987 it is expected that the 105mm M68 rifled tank gun will be replaced by the 120mm Rheinmetall smooth bore gun which is being produced under the designation XM256; this will fire both West German and American ammunition, although there have been more problems in adapting the turret to take the West German gun than had been anticipated.

The M1 has a hull and turret of the new British Chobham armor, which is claimed to make the tank immune to attack from all shaped-charge warheads and to give dramatically increased protection against other anti-tank rounds, including kinetic energy (i.e., APDS and APFSDS). It has a crew of four; the driver at the front, the commander and gunner on the right of the turret, and the loader on the left. The main armament consists of a standard 105mm gun developed in Britain and produced under license in the United States and a 7·62mm machine-gun is mounted co-axially with the main armament. A 0·5in machine-gun is mounted at the commander's station and a 7·62mm machine-gun at the loader's station. Ammunition supply consists of 55 rounds of 105mm, 1,000 rounds of 12·7mm and 11,400 rounds of 7·62mm. Mounted each side of the turret is a bank of six British-designed smoke dischargers. The main armament can be aimed and fired on the move. The gunner first selects the target, and then uses the

Below: An M1 Abrams MBT under way in typical tank country during Exercise "Reforger '82" in West Germany.

M551 Sheridan

Type: Light tank.
Crew: 4.
Armament: One 152mm gun/missile launcher; one 7·62mm machine-gun co-axial with main armament; one 0·5in anti-aircraft machine-gun; four smoke dischargers on each side of turret.
Armor: Classified.
Dimensions: Length 20ft 8in (6·299m); width 9ft 3in (2·819m); height (overall) 9ft 8in (2·946m).
Weight: Combat 34,898lbs (15,830kg).
Ground pressure: 6·96lb/in^2 (0·49kg/cm^2).
Engine: Detroit Diesel 6V53T six-cylinder diesel developing 300bhp at 2,800rpm.
Performance: Road speed 45mph (70km/h); water speed 3·6mph (5·8km/h); range 373 miles (600km); vertical obstacle 2ft 9in (0·838m); trench 8ft 4in (2·54m); gradient 60 per cent.
History: Entered service with United States Army in 1966 and still in service.

In August 1959 the United States Army established a requirement for a "new armored vehicle with increased capabilities over any other weapon in its own inventory and that of any adversary". The following year the Allison Division of General Motors was awarded a contract to design a vehicle called the Armored Reconnaissance Airborne Assault Vehicle (ARAAV) to meet the requirement. The first prototype, designated XM551, was completed in 1962, and this was followed by a further 11 prototypes. Late in 1965 a production contract was awarded to Allison, and the first production vehicles were completed in 1966, these being known as the M551 or Sheridan. Production was completed in 1970 after 1,700 vehicles had been built.

The hull of the Sheridan is of all-aluminum construction whilst the turret is of welded steel. The driver is seated at the front of the hull and the other three crew members are in the turret, with the loader on the left and the gunner and commander on the right. The engine and transmission are at the rear of the hull. The suspension is of the torsion-bar type and consists of five road wheels, with the drive sprocket at the rear and the idler at the front. There are no track-return rollers. The most interesting feature of the Sheridan is its armament system. This consists of a 152mm gun/launcher which has an elevation of +19° and a depression of −8°, traverse being 360°. A 7·62mm machine-gun is mounted co-axially with the main armament, and there is a 0·5in Browning machine-gun on the commander's cupola. The latter cannot be aimed and fired from within the turret, and as a result of combat experience in Vietnam many vehicles have now been fitted with a shield for this weapon. The 152mm gun/launcher, later fitted to the M60A2 and MBT-70 tanks, can fire either a Shillelagh missile or a variety of conventional ammunition including HEAT-T-MP, WP and canister, all of

laser rangefinder to get its range and then depresses the firing switch. The computer makes the calculations and adjustments required to ensure a hit.

The fuel tanks are separated from the crew compartment by armored bulkheads and sliding doors are provided for the ammunition stowage areas. Blow-out panels in both ensure that an explosion is channeled outward. The suspension is of torsion-bar type with rotary shock absorbers. The tank can travel across country at a speed of 30mph (48km/h) and accelerate from 0 to 20mph (0 to 32km/h) in seven seconds, and this will make the M1 a difficult tank to engage on the battlefield. The M1 is powered by a turbine developed by Avco Lycoming, running on a variety of fuels including petrol, diesel and jet fuel. All the driver has to do is adjust a dial in his compartment. According to the manufacturers, the engine will not require an overhaul until the tank has traveled between 12,000 to 18,000 miles (19,312 to 28,968km), a great advance over existing tank engines. This engine is coupled to an Allison X-1100 transmission with four forward and two reverse gears. Great emphasis has been placed on reliability and maintenance, and it is claimed that the complete engine can be removed for replacement in under 30 minutes.

The M1 is provided with an NBC system and a full range of night-vision equipment for the commander, gunner and driver.

Above: Given the size of the M1's muzzle flash, a high single-shot hit probability is vital for night operations.

Below: In definitive form the M1 is to sport a 120mm smooth-bore gun produced in the USA under Rheinmetall licence.

Below: The gunnery problems of modern MBTs require advanced solutions, as indicated by the gunner's position in an M1.

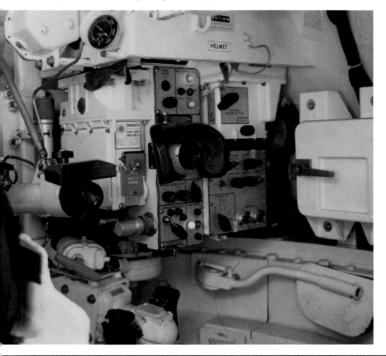

---

them having a combustible cartridge case. The Shillelagh missile was developed by the United States Army Missile Command and the Philco-Ford Corporation, and has a maximum range of about 3,281 yards (3,000m). The missile is controlled by the gunner, who simply has to keep the cross-hairs of his sight on the target to ensure a hit; however, severe problems exist in "capturing" the missile, making it of little value at ranges under 1,300 yards (1,200m). The missile itself weighs 59lbs (26·7kg) and has a single-stage solid-propellant motor which has a burn time of 1·18 seconds. Once the missile leaves the gun/missile-launcher, four fins at the rear of the missile unfold and it is guided to the target by a two-way infra-red command link which eliminates the need for the gunner to estimate the lead and range of the target. A Sheridan normally carries ten missiles and 20 rounds of

ammunition, but this mix can be adjusted as required. In addition, 1,000 rounds of 0·5in and 3,080 rounds of 7·62mm ammunition are carried. The Sheridan is provided with a flotation screen, and when erected this enables the vehicle to propel itself across rivers and streams by its tracks. Night-vision equipment is provided as is an NBC system.

The M551 has not been a success. Its development was long and expensive, and a further in-service product-improvement program has failed to bring it up to an acceptable standard. As a result, it has long since been replaced by the M60 in reconnaissance units of the US Army in Europe. It remains in active use only at the National Training Center, Fort Irwin, where it is used to stimulate Soviet Army vehicles, but some redundant chassis may be used as interim self-propelled anti-tank guns for 9th Infantry Division.

Below left: The most notable feature of the M551 is main armament able to fire Shillelagh missiles or HEAT rounds.

Below: Sheridan light tanks on the move, showing the type's low silhouette and large-caliber main armament.

Below: The M551 was designed to be highly air-portable, and can be carried by all US tactical and strategic transports.

M2/M3

Type: (M2) Infantry fighting vehicle; (M3) Cavalry fighting vehicle.
Crew: 3 plus 6.
Armament: One 25mm Hughes "chain-gun"; one 7·62mm machine-gun co-axial with main armament; twin launcher for Hughes TOW ATGW.
Armor: Classified.
Dimensions: Length 21ft 2in (6·45m); width 10ft 6in (3·20m); height 9ft 9in (2·97m).
Weight: 50,000lb (22,680kg).
Ground pressure: 7·7lb/in² (0·54kg/cm²).
Engine: Cummins (VTA-903T water-cooled 4-cycle diesel developing 506bhp.
Performance: Road speed 41mph (66km/h); water speed 4·5mph; range 300 miles (384km); vertical obstacle 3ft (0·91m); trench 8ft 4in (2·54m); gradient 60 per cent.
History: Entered US Army service in 1983.

Above: Size constraints in the troop compartment have limited the M2's deployable infantry squad to six men only.

The United States Army has had a requirement for an MICV for well over 15 years. The first American MICV was the XM701, developed in the early 1960s on the M107/M110 self-propelled gun chassis. This proved unsatisfactory during trials. The Americans then tried to modify the current M113 to meet the MICV role: a variety of different models was built and tested, but again these vehicles failed to meet the army requirement. As a result of a competition held in 1972, the FMC Corporation, which still builds the M113A2, was awarded a contract to design an MICV designated the XM723. The XM723 did not meet the requirements of the US Army and further development, based on the same chassis, resulted in the Fighting Vehicle System (FVS) which comprised two vehicles, the XM2 Infantry Fighting Vehicle and the XM3 Cavalry Fighting Vehicle. These were eventually accepted for service as the M2 and M3 Bradley Fighting Vehicles. The US Army has a requirement for some 6,882 M2/M3 vehicles, and three battalions of M2s were formed in 1983, the first at Ford Hood, Texas.

The primary task of the M2 in the eyes of the US Army is to enable infantry to fight from under armor whenever practicable, and to be able both to observe and to use their weapons from inside the vehicle. The M2 will replace some, but not all, of the current M113 APCs, as the latter are more than adequate for many roles on the battlefield. The M2 has three major advances over the existing M113 APC. First, the IFV has greater mobility and better cross-country speed, enabling it to keep up with the M1 MBT when acting as part of the tank/infantry team. Second, it has much greater firepower. Third, it has superior armor protection. The tank provides long-range firepower whilst the IFV provides firepower against softer, close-in targets. The M2's infantry also assist tanks by locating and destroying enemy anti-tank weapons.

The hull of the M2 is of all-welded aluminum construction with an applique layer of steel armor welded to the hull front, upper sides and rear for added protection. The hull sides also have a thin layer of steel armor, the space between the aluminum and steel being filled with foam to increase the buoyancy of the vehicle. The armored protection of the IFV is claimed to be effective against Soviet 14·5mm armor-piercing rounds and 155mm air-burst shell splinters.

The driver is seated at the front of the vehicle on the left, with the engine to his right. The two-man turret is in the center of the hull and the personnel compartment is at the rear. Personnel entry is effected through a large power-operated ramp in the hull rear. The two-man power operated turret is fully stabilized and is armed with a 25mm Hughes Chain Gun and a co-axial 7·62mm machine gun. The weapons can be elevated to +60° and depressed to −10°, turret traverse being 360°. Mounted on the left side of the turret is a twin launcher for the Hughes TOW ATGW. A total of 900 rounds of 25mm, 2,340 rounds of 7·62mm and seven TOW missiles are carried. The troop compartment is provided with six firing ports (two in each side and two at the rear) for the 5·56mm M231 weapon. The M231 is a specially developed version of the M16, cut-down and sealed in a ball mount. It is somewhat ironic that the outcome of a requirement for the infantry to be able to use their weapons from inside the vehicle should be an additional and specialized rifle. Three M72A2 light anti-tank weapons are also carried. The M2 is fully amphibious, although a flotation screen is required, and is propelled in the water by its tracks. An NBC system is fitted, as is a full range of night vision equipment.

Some 3,300 M3 Cavalry Fighting Vehicles are to be purchased to replace M60s and M113s in armored cavalry units and in the scout platoons of mechanized infantry and tank battalions. The M3 is outwardly identical with the M2: the major differences lie in the internal stowage and the layout of the crew compartment. The M3 carries twice the number of stowed 25mm rounds and ten stored TOW missiles. Only two cavalrymen are housed in the rear compartment and the firing ports are not used.

The chassis of the M2/M3 is also used as the basis for the Vought Multiple Launch Rocket System and the Armored, Forward-Area, Rearm Vehicle (AFARV) which has been designed to supply MBTs with ammunition when they are in the battlefield area.

Below: The turret of the M2 Bradley carries a 25mm cannon and co-axial 7·62mm machine-gun as well as two TOW missiles.

M113A2

Type: Armored personnel carrier.
Crew: 2 plus 11.
Armament: One Browning 0·5in (12·7mm) machine-gun.
Armor: 12mm-38mm (0·47-1·58in).
Dimensions: Length 15ft 11in (4·863m); width 8ft 10in (2·686m); height 8ft 2in (2·5m).
Weight: Combat 24,600lbs (11,156kg).
Ground Pressure: 7·82lb/in² (0·55kg/cm²).
Engine: General Motors Model 6V53 six-cylinder water-cooled diesel developing 215bhp at 2,800rpm.
Performance: Road speed 42mph (67·6km/h); water speed 3·6mph (5·8km/h); range 300 miles (483km); vertical obstacle 2ft (0·61m); trench 5ft 6in (1·68m); gradient 60 per cent.
History: Entered service with the United States Army in 1960. Also used by 50 other countries.

In the early 1950s the standard United States Army APC was the M75, followed in 1954 by the M59. Neither of these was satisfactory and in 1954 foundations were laid for a new series of vehicles. In 1958 prototypes of the T113 (aluminum hull) and T117 (steel hull) armored personnel carriers were built. A modified version of the T113, the T113E1, was cleared for production in mid-1959 and production commenced at the FMC plant at San Jose, California, in 1960. The vehicle is still in production today and some 70,000

have been built in the USA. It is also built in Italy by Oto Melara, which has produced a further 4,000 for the Italian Army and for export. In 1964 the M113 was replaced in production by the M113A1, identical with the earlier model but for a diesel rather than a petrol engine.

The M113A1 had a larger radius of action than the earlier vehicle. The M113 had the distinction of being the first armored fighting vehicle of aluminum construction to enter production. The driver is seated at the front of the hull on the left, with the engine to his right. The commander's hatch is in the center of the roof and the personnel compartment is at the rear of the hull. The infantry enter and leave via a large ramp in the hull rear, although there is also a roof hatch over the troop compartment. The basic vehicle is normally armed with a pintle-mounted Browning 0·5in machine-gun, which has 2,000 rounds of ammunition. The M113 is fully amphibious and is propelled in the water by its tracks. Infra-red driving lights are fitted as standard. FMC has developed a wide variety of kits for the basic vehicle including an ambulance kit, NBC kit, heater kit, dozer-blade kit, various shields for machine-guns and so on.

The current production model is the M113A2 which is essentially an M113A1 with improved engine cooling and improved suspension. Most US Army M113 and M113A1 vehicles are now being brought up to M113A2 standard.

There are more variants of the M113 family than any other fighting vehicle in service today, and there is room here to mention only some of the more important models. The M577 is the command model, with a much higher roof and no armament. There are two mortar carriers: the M125 with an 81mm mortar, and the M106 with a 107mm mortar. The flame-thrower model is known as the M132A1, and is not used outside the United States Army. The M806 is the recovery model, and this is provided with a winch in the rear of the vehicle and spades at the rear. The anti-aircraft model is known as the Vulcan Air Defense System or M163; this is armed with a six-barrelled 20mm General Electric cannon. The M548 tracked cargo carrier is based on an M113 chassis, can carry 5 tons (5,080kg) of cargo and is fully amphibious. There are many models of the M548, including the M727, which carries three HAWK surface-to-air missiles, and the M730, which carries four Chaparral short-range surface-to-air missiles. Yet another version, the M752, carries the Lance tactical missile system, whilst the M688 carries two spare missiles.

One recent model is the M901 Improved TOW Vehicle (ITV), with a retractable launcher that carries two Hughes TOW ATGWs in the ready-to-launch position. Almost 2,000 of these vehicles have been ordered by the US Army. The latest model to be ordered is the Surface-Launched Unit Fuel-Air Explosive (SLUFAE) launcher, which is an unguided rocket system based on the M548 chassis.

The M113 series and its derivatives will remain in service with the US and foreign armies for many years to come. Like the "Jeep" of World War II, it is cheap, simple to manufacture, easy to maintain, and effective in use. The US Army may well one day wish that the same applied to the M2/M3 series.

Left: In its transport role the M113 has been the Western world's most important APC for some quarter of a century.

Below left: The M901 ITV can use its elevating launcher while the vehicle and crew remain safely under cover.

Below: Key features of the M113 series are versatility, reliability and availability in considerable quantities.

LAV-25

Type: Light armored vehicle.
Crew: 3.
Armament: M242 25mm Bushmaster automatic cannon; M240 7·62mm co-axial MG.
Armor: Steel, sufficient to withstand 7·62mm AP in front, 7·62mm elsewhere.
Dimensions: Length 21ft (6·4m); width 7ft 2½in (2·2m) height 8ft 2½in (2·5m).
Weights: Empty 19,850lb (9,004kg); combat loaded 27,559lb (12,501kg).
Engine: Detroit Diesel 6V-53T, 6-cylinder turbocharged diesel; 275hp at 2,800rpm.
Performance: Maximum road speed 63mph (101km/h); road range 485 miles (781km); swimming speed 6mph (9·65km/h); gradient 70 per cent; side slope 35 per cent.

In 1981-82 the US Army's Tank-Automotive Command (TACom) carried out a series of tests for a light armored vehicle (LAV) to be procured for the US Army and US Marine Corps. Four vehicles were tested: the British Alvis Scorpion-Stormer, the Swiss-designed but Canadian-produced MOWAG "Piranha", and the Cadillac-Gage V-150 and V-300. The Scorpion-Stormer series is tracked; the remainder are wheeled. Both the Army and Marine Corps required these vehicles for employment with the Rapid Deployment Force (RDF), although the Army's original requirement was reduced from 2,315 to 680 in 1982, and is now totally in doubt. Indeed, in mid-1983 the Congress denied funds for Army procurement of the LAV because it was considered that the requirement had not been properly justified. This is not to say, however, that the Army will not get its LAV in the long run.

The US Army's basic requirement is for a Mobile Protected Gun-Near Term (MPG-N), which differs substantially from the LAV required by the USMC. The Army plans to equip its light divisions with two MPG battalions, each with 41 LAVs and 40 HMMWVs (Hummer), for reconnaissance, fire support, and anti-tank defense. These battalions appear—on paper, at least—to be too lightly equipped, even for the RDF.

The USMC contract calls for the delivery of 758 vehicles over a five-year period, the first being delivered by General Motors in October 1983.

Right: The LAV-25 has good cross-country performance and a very versatile hull able to accept a variety of turrets, the basic type sporting a 25mm cannon and co-axial machine-gun.

Far right: Among the experimental developments of the LAV series is this air-defense model with surveillance radar, four short-range SAMs and one four-barrel cannon for point defense purposes.

LVTP-7 Amphibious Assault Vehicle

LVTP-7, LVTC-7, LVTE-7, LVTH-7
Crew: 3 plus 25.
Armament: One M85 0·5in (12·7mm) machine-gun.
Armor: 7mm–30mm (0·28–1·18in).
Dimensions: Length 26ft 1in (7·943m); width, 10ft 9in (3·27m); height, 10ft 9in (3·27m).
Weight: Combat 52,150lbs (23,655kg).
Ground pressure: 8lb/in² (0·57kg/cm²).
Engine: Detroit Diesel Model 8V53T eight-cylinder turbocharged diesel developing 400bhp at 2,800rpm.
Performance: Road speed 39·5mph (63·37km/h); water speed 8·5mph (13·7km/h); range (road) 300 miles (482km); vertical obstacle 3ft (0·914m); trench 8ft (2·438m); gradient, 70 per cent.
History: Entered service with United States Marine Corps 1971. Also in service with Argentina, Italy, Spain and Thailand. No longer in production.

The standard amphibious assault carrier in service with the United States Marines in the 1950s was the LVTP-5 (Landing Vehicle Tracked Personnel-5). Although an improvement over earlier vehicles, the LVTP-5 proved very difficult to maintain in service. So, in 1964, the Marines issued a requirement for a new LVTP and the FMC Corporation was selected to build 17 prototypes. The first of these was completed in 1967 under the designation of LVTPX-12. Trials were carried out in Alaska, Panama and various other Marine installations, and in 1970 FMC was awarded a production contract for 942 vehicles. The first production LVTP-7 was completed in August 1971 and production continued until September 1974. It has now completely replaced the older LVTP-5. The role of the LVTP-7 is to transport Marines from ships off shore to the beach, and if required, to carry them inland to their objective. The hull of the LVTP-7 is of all-welded aluminium construction and varies in thickness from 20 to 45mm. The engine and transmission are at the front·of the hull and can be removed as a complete unit if required. The driver is seated at the front, on the left, with the commander to his rear. The LVTP-7 is armed with a turret-mounted M85 0·5in machine-gun. This is mounted on the right side and has an elevation of +60° and a depression of −15°; traverse is a full 360° and a total of 1,000 rounds of ammunition is carried. The personnel compartment is at the rear of the hull, where the 25 Marines are provided with bench type seats which can be quickly stowed so that the vehicle can be used as an ambulance or cargo carrier. The usual method of entry and exit is via a large ramp at the rear of the hull. Hatches are also provided over the troop compartment so that stores can be loaded when the vehicle is alongside a ship.

The LVTP-7 is propelled in the water by two water-jets, one in each side of the hull towards the rear. These are driven by propeller shafts from the transmission. Basically pumps draw water from above the track, and this is then discharged to the rear of the vehicle. Deflectors at the rear of each unit divert the water-jet stream for steering, stopping and reversing.

There are two special versions of the LVTP-7 in service. The first of these is the LVTR-7. This is used to repair disabled vehicles, for which a wide range of equipment is carried, including an hydraulic crane and winch. The second model is the LVTC-7, a special command model with additional radios and other equipment. Two other models, the LVTE-7 (Engineer) and LVTH-7 (Howitzer) were not placed in production.

All LVTP7s are now being rebuilt to the LVTP7A1 standard and fitted with new Cummins VT400 8-cylinder diesel and many other improvements including smoke generators, passive night vision equipment, improved fire suppression system, installation of PLARS, improved crew/troop compartment ventilation and improved electric weapon station. In addition, vehicles are now being produced to the LVTP7A1 standard.

Below: On land the LVTP-7 is large and clumsy, but its water performance is good and the type remains absolutely essential for the US Marine Corps' amphibious assault role, in which its 25-man or cargo load is most impressive.

Below: LVTP-7s on the move, showing the high bow that contributes to the type's seakeeping qualities. A tactical limitation is lack of organic firepower, the LVTP-7 being limited to one 0·5-inch turret-mounted machine-gun.

M109A2

Type: Self-propelled howitzer.
Crew: 6.
Armament: One 155mm howitzer; one ·5in (12·7mm) Browning anti-aircraft machine-gun.
Armor: 20mm (0·79in) maximum, estimated.
Dimensions: Length (including armament) 21ft 8in (6·612m); length (hull) 20ft 6in (6·256m); width 10ft 10in (3·295m); height (including anti-aircraft machine-gun) 10ft 10in (3·295m).
Weight: Combat 55,000lb (24,948kg).
Ground Pressure: 10·95lb/in² (0·77kg/cm²).
Engine: Detroit Diesel Model 8V71T eight-cylinder turbocharged diesel developing 405bhp at 2,300rpm.
Performance: Road speed 35mph (56km/h); range 242 miles (390km); vertical obstacle 1ft 9in (0·533m); trench 6ft (1·828m); gradient 60 per cent.
History: Entered service with the United States Army in 1963. Also used by Austria, Belgium, Canada, Denmark, Germany, Great Britain, Ethiopia, Greece, Iran, Israel, Italy, Jordan, Kampuchea, Kuwait, Libya, Morocco, the Netherlands, Norway, Oman, Pakistan, Saudi Arabia, Spain, South Korea, Switzerland, Taiwan, Tunisia and Turkey. Still in production.

The first production models of the M109 were completed in 1962, and some 3,700 examples have now been built (of which about 1,800 are in US Army service), making the M109 the most widely used self-propelled howitzer in the world. It has a hull of all-welded aluminum construction, providing the crew with protection from small arms fire. The driver is seated at the front of the hull on the left, with the engine to his right. The other five crew members are the commander, gunner and three ammunition members, all located in the turret at the rear of the hull. There is a large door in the rear of the hull for ammunition resupply purposes. Hatches are also provided in the sides and rear of the turret. There are two hatches in the roof of the turret, the commander's hatch being on the right. A 0·5in (12·7mm) Browning machine-gun is mounted on this for anti-aircraft defense. The suspension is of the torsion-bar type and consists of seven road wheels, with the drive sprockets at the front and the idler at the rear, and there are no track-return rollers.

The 155mm howitzer has an elevation of +75° and a depression of −3°, and the turret can be traversed through 360°. Elevation and traverse are powered, with manual controls for emergency use. The weapon can fire a variety of ammunition, including HE, tactical nuclear, illuminating, smoke and chemical rounds. Rate of fire is four rounds per minute for three minutes, followed by one round per minute for the next hour. A total of 28 rounds of separate-loading ammunition is carried, as well as 500 rounds of machine-gun ammunition.

The second model to enter service was the M109A1, identical with the M109 apart from a much longer barrel, provided with a fume extractor as well as a muzzle-brake. The fume extractor removes propellant gases from the barrel after a round has been fired and thus prevents fumes from entering the fighting compartment. The M109A2 has an improved shell rammer and recoil mechanism, the M178 modified gun mount, and other more minor improvements. The M109A3 is the M109A1 fitted with the M178 gun mount.

The M109 fires a round to a maximum range of 16,070 yards (14,700m); the M109A1 fires to a maximum range of 19,685 yards (18,000m). Rocket assisted projectiles (M549A1) increase the maximum range to 26,250 yards (24,000m). A new nuclear round (M785) is now under development: it is ballistically compatible with the M549A1 RAP and will utilize the same protective container as the M758 eight-inch round (*see M110A2 entry*).

The M109 can ford streams to a maximum depth of 6ft (1·828m). A

Top: The shorter barrel of the original M126 ordnance carried by the M109 requires a large balance weight just behind the muzzle brake. The M126 barrel fires HE, cargo, illuminating, smoke, agent and tactical nuclear rounds.

Above: The M109 series is the Western world's most important SP howitzer, this being an M109A1 with the longer M185 ordnance. Just visible on the left of the turret is the armored hood for the optical fire-control system.

special amphibious kit has been developed for the vehicle but this is not widely used. It consists of nine inflatable airbags, normally carried by a truck. Four of these are fitted to each side of the hull and the last to the front of the hull. The vehicle is then propelled in the water by its tracks at a maximum speed of 4mph (6·4km/h). The M109 is provided with infra-red driving lights and some vehicles also have an NBC system.

To keep the M109 supplied with ammunition in the field Bowen-McLaughlin-York have recently developed the M992 Field Artillery Ammunition Support Vehicle which is expected to enter production in the near future.

M110A2

M110, M110A1, M110A2

Type: Self-propelled howitzer.
Crew: 5 plus 8 (see text).
Armament: One 8in (203mm) howitzer.
Armor: 20mm (0.79in) maximum (estimated).
Dimensions: Length (including gun and spade in traveling position) 35ft 2½in (10.731m); length (hull) 18ft 9in (5.72m); width 10ft 4in (3.149m); height 10ft 4in (3.143m).
Weight: Combat 62,500lb (28,350kg).
Ground pressure: 10.80lb/in² (0.76kg/cm²).
Engine: Detroit Diesel Model 8V-7T eight-cylinder turbo-charged diesel developing 405bhp at 2,300rpm.
Performance: Road speed 34mph (54.7km/h); range 325 miles (523km); vertical obstacle 3ft 4in (1.016m); trench 7ft 9in (2.362m); gradient 60 per cent.
History: Original version, M110, entered service with the United States Army in 1963. Now used by Belgium, West Germany, Greece, Iran, Israel, Japan, Jordan, Saudi Arabia, South Korea, Netherlands, Pakistan, Spain, Turkey, United Kingdom and United States.

In 1956 the United States Army issued a requirement for a range of self-propelled artillery which would be air-transportable. The Pacific Car and Foundry Company of Washington were awarded the development contract and from 1958 built three different self-propelled weapons on the same chassis. These were the T235 (175mm gun), which became the M107, the T236 (203mm howitzer), which became the M110, and the

T245 (155mm gun), which was subsequently dropped from the range. These prototypes were powered by a petrol engine, but it was soon decided to replace this by a diesel engine as this could give the vehicles a much greater range of action. The M107 is no longer in service with the US Army; all have been rebuilt to M110A2 configuration. The M110A2 is also in production by Bowen-McLaughlin-York Company, and when present orders have been completed the US Army wil have a total inventory of over 1,000.

The hull is of all-welded-steel construction with the driver at the front on the left with the engine to his right. The gun is mounted towards the rear of the hull. The suspension is of the torsion-bar type and consists of five road wheels, with the fifth road wheel acting as the idler, the drive sprocket is at the front. Five crew are carried on the gun (driver, commander and three gun crew), the other eight crew members following in an M548 tracked vehicle (this is based on the M113 APC chassis), which also carries the ammunition, as only two ready rounds are carried on the M110 itself. The 203mm howitzer has an elevation of +65° and a depression of −2°, traverse being 30° left and 30° right. Elevation and traverse are both hydraulic, although there are manual controls for use in an emergency. The M110 fires an HE projectile to a maximum range of 26,575 yards (24,300m), and other types of projectile that can be fired include HE carrying 104 HE grenades, HE carrying 195 grenades, Agent GB or VX and tactical nuclear. A large hydraulically-operated spade is mounted at the rear of the hull and is lowered into position before the gun opens fire, and the suspension can also be locked when the gun is fired to provide a more stable firing platform. The gun can officially fire one round per two minutes, but a well trained crew can fire one round per minute for short periods. As the projectile is very heavy, an hydraulic hoist is provided to position the projectile on the ramming tray; the round is then pushed into the breech hydraulically before the charge is pushed home, the breechlock closed and the weapon is then fired. The M110 can ford streams to a maximum depth of 3ft 6in (1.066m) but has no amphibious capability. Infra-red driving lights are fitted as standard but the type does not have an NBC system.

All M110s in US Army service, and in an increasing number of NATO countries as well, have been brought up to M110A2 configuration. The M110A1 has a new and longer barrel, while the M110A2 is identical to the M110A1 but has a double baffle muzzle brake. The M110A1 can fire up to charge eight while the M110A2 can fire up to charge nine. The M110A1/M110A2 can fire all of the rounds of the M110 but in addition binary, high-explosive Rocket Assisted Projectile (M650), and the improved conventional munition which contains 195 M42 grenades. The latter two have a maximum range, with charge nine, of 32,800 yards (30,000m).

The M110A2 also fires the M753 rocket-assisted tactical nuclear round, which entered production in FY 1981. The M753 will be available in two versions: the first as a normal nuclear round; the second as an "Enhanced Radiation" version. These nuclear rounds are packed in very sophisticated containers to prevent unauthorized use and are subject to very stringent controls. The ER rounds will not be deployed outside the USA except in an emergency.

One major shortcoming of the M110 design has always been its lack of protection for the gun crew: it is virtually the only modern self-propelled gun to suffer such a deficiency. The US Army plans to rectify this by fitting a Crew Ballistic Shelter (CBS), a high, square gun housing that will improve survivability against small arms and shell fragments by some 33 per cent and will also provide collective NBC protection.

One of the problems with heavy artillery of this type is keeping the guns supplied with sufficient ammunition. As noted above the weapon is supported by an M548 tracked vehicle, and this in turn is kept supplied by 5- or 10-ton trucks.

Left: The M201 ordnance of the M110A2 fires the 204lb M106 HE projectile to a range of more than 23,300 yards.

Below: Like other members of the M110 family, the M110A2 lacks a turret or any other form of crew protection.

M102

Type: Light howitzer.
Caliber: 105mm.
Crew: 8.
Weight: 3,298lb (1,496kg).
Length firing: 22ft (6·718m).
Length traveling: 17ft (5·182m).
Height firing: 4·29ft (1·308m).
Height traveling: 5·22ft (1·594m).
Width: 6·44ft (1·964m).
Ground clearance: 1·08ft (0·33m).
Elevation: −5° to +75°.
Traverse: 360°.
Range: 12,576 yards (11,500m), standard ammunition; 16,513 yards (15,100m) with RAP.

The 105mm M102 was developed at Rock Island Arsenal to replace the standard 105mm M101 howitzer in both airborne and airmobile divisions. The first prototype was completed in 1962 and the weapon entered service in 1966. It was widely used in Vietnam. Improvements over the M101 include a reduction in weight, longer range, and it can be quickly traversed through 360°. Both the M101 and M102 were to have been replaced by a new 105mm howitzer called the XM204, but this was cancelled by Congress in 1977 owing to both tactical and technical problems.

The M102 is normally deployed in battalions of 18 guns (each of these having three batteries, each with 6 guns), and both the 82nd Airborne and 101st Airmobile/Air Assault Divisions each have three battalions of M102s, but these are now being replaced by the 155mm M198. It is normally towed by the M561 (6×6) Gama Goat vehicle or a 2½ ton 6×6 truck, and can be carried slung underneath a Boeing Chinook CH-47 helicopter.

When in the firing position the wheels are raised off the ground and the weapon rests on a turntable under the front of the carriage; a roller tire is mounted at the rear of the trail and this enables the weapon to be quickly traversed through 360° to be laid onto a new target. The M102 has an unusual bow shape box type trail which is of aluminum construction to reduce weight. Its breechblock is of the vertical sliding wedge type and its recoil system is of the hydropneumatic type. The barrel is not provided with a muzzle brake, although this was fitted to the prototype weapons. A wide range of ammunition can be fitted including high explosive, high explosive anti-tank, anti-personnel, illuminating, smoke, chemical, HEP-T, and leaflet. Ten rounds per minute can be fired for the first three minutes, and 3 rounds per minute in the sustained fire role.

Above: The M102 is a moderately light 105mm towed howitzer.

M114A2

Type: Howitzer.
Caliber: 155mm.
Crew: 11.
Weight: 12,700lb (5,761kg).
Length traveling: 23·9ft (7·315mm).
Width traveling: 7·99ft (2·438m).
Height traveling: 5·9ft (1·8m).
Elevation: −2° to +63°.
Traverse: 25° right and 24° left.
Range: 21,106 yards (19,300m).

In 1939, Rock Island Arsenal started the development of a new 155mm towed howitzer to replace the 155mm M1918 howitzer which at that time was the standard 155mm howitzer of the US Army (this was basically a modified French 155mm weapon built in the United States). This new 155mm weapon was designated the M1 and first production weapons were completed in 1942. Production continued until after the end of the war by which time over 6,000 weapons had been built. After the war the M1 was redesignated the M114. The 4·5 inch M1 used the same carriage as the M114 but none of these remain in service today. A self-propelled model called the M41 was also built, but again, none of these remain in service with the US Army.

When the weapon is in the firing position, it is supported on its trails and a firing jack which is mounted under the carriage. When in the traveling position, the trails are locked together and attached to the prime mover, which is generally a 6×6 truck. The M114 can also be carried slung under a Boeing CH-47 Chinook helicopter.

Its recoil system is of the hydropneumatic variable type and its breechblock is of the stepped thread/interrupted screw type. The M114 can fire a variety of ammunition of separate loading type (eg, the projectile and a charge) including an HE round weighing 95lb (43kg), tactical nuclear, illuminating and chemical. Sustained rate of fire is one round per minute. It cannot however fire the new Rocket Assisted Round which has a longer range than the standard 155mm round.

The US Marine Corps developed a new tube for the M114 which has been adopted by the US Army as the M114A2. This tube is a ballistic match for that on the M109A2 (qv), and the M114A2 can thus fire all ammunition fired by its self-propelled counterpart. The M114A2 is used by general-support artillery units of the US Army Reserve and the National Guard.

Above: The M114A1 is an elderly weapon being considerably upgraded in US service to M114A2 standard with the ordnance of the M198 for greater range and accuracy.

Below: In firing position the M114 is supported on its split trail legs and a jack to lift the carriage off the ground.

M198

Type: Towed howitzer.
Caliber: 155mm.
Crew: 10.
Weight: 15,795lb (7,165kg).
Length firing: 37ft 1in (11·302m).
Length traveling: 23ft 3in (7·086m).
Width firing: 28ft (8·534m).
Width traveling: 9ft 2in (2·79m).
Height firing (minimum): 5·91ft (1·803m).
Height traveling: 9·92ft (3·023m).
Ground clearance: 13in (0·33m).
Elevation: −4·2° to +72°.
Traverse: 22½° left and right; 360° with speed traverse.
Range: 32,808 yards (30,000m) with RAP; 24,060 yards (22,000m) with conventional round.

In the late 1960s, Rock Island Arsenal started work on a new 155mm howitzer to replace the M114, and this was given the development designation of the XM198. The first two prototypes were followed by eight further prototypes, and during extensive trials these weapons fired over 45,000 rounds of ammunition. The M198 is now in production at Rock Island; the Army has a requirement for 435 M198s while the Marine Corps requires 282. It has also been adopted by a number of other countries including Australia, India, Greece, Pakistan, Thailand and Saudi Arabia. The M198 is used by airborne, airmobile and infantry divisions. Other divisions will continue to use self-propelled artillery. The weapon will be developed in battalions of 18 guns, each battery having 6 weapons. The M198 is normally towed by a 6×6 5-ton truck or a tracked M548 cargo carrier, the latter being a member of the M113 family of tracked vehicles. It can also be carried

Above: Though heavier than the M114, the M198 (seen here in the form of a 1970 prototype) is a more modern weapon with considerably greater muzzle velocity and range. The type fires an extremely diverse assortment of tactical rounds.

M29A1

Type: Mortar.
Caliber: 81mm.
Weight of barrel: 27·99lb (12·7kg).
Weight of baseplate: 24·91lb (11·3kg).
Weight of bipod: 40lb (18·15kg).
Total weight with sight: 115lb (52·2kg).
Elevation: +40° to +85°.
Traverse: 4° left and 4° right.
Maximum range: 5,140 yards (4,700km).
Rate of fire: 30rpm for 1 minute; 4-12rpm sustained.

In service with US Army and some Allied countries, the 81mm M29 mortar is the standard medium mortar of the US Army and is in service in two basic models, infantry and self-propelled. The standard infantry model can be disassembled into three components, each of which can be carried by one man—baseplate, barrel, mount and sight. The exterior of the barrel is helically grooved both to reduce weight and to dissipate heat when a high rate of fire is being achieved.

The mortar is also mounted in the rear of a modified member of the M113 APC family called the M125A1. In this vehicle the mortar is mounted on a turntable and this enables it to be traversed quickly through 360° to be laid onto a new target. A total of 114 81mm mortar bombs are carried in the vehicle.

The mortar can fire a variety of mortar bombs including HE (the M374 bomb has a maximum range of 5,025 yards (4,595m)), white phosphorus (the M375 bomb has a maximum range of 5,180 yards (4,737m)) and illuminating (the M301 bomb has a maximum range of 3,444 yards (3,150m)). The 81mm M29 has been replaced in certain units by the new M224 60mm Lightweight Company Mortar.

Right: The M29 mortar has served the US and some other forces faithfully for a number of years, but is now obsolescent largely as a result of its weight.

M224

Type: Lightweight company mortar.
Caliber: 60mm.
Total weight: 46lb (20·9kg); (hand-held with M8 baseplate) 17lb (7·7kg).
Maximum range: 3,828 yards (3,500m).

During the Vietnam campaign, it was found that the standard 81mm M29 mortar was too heavy for the infantry to transport in rough terrain, even when disassembled into its three main components. In its place the old 60mm M19 mortar was used, but this had a short range. The M224 has been developed to replace the 81mm M29 mortar in non-mechanized infantry, airmobile and airborne units at company level, and is also issued to the US Marine Corps. The weapon comprises a lightweight finned barrel, sight, M7 baseplate and bipod, although if required it can also be used with the lightweight M8 baseplate, in which case it is hand-held. The complete mortar weighs only 46lb (20·9kg) compared to the 81mm mortar which weighs 115kg (52kg). The M224 fires an HE bomb which provides a substantial portion of the lethality of the 81mm mortar with a waterproof "horseshoe" snap-off, propellant increments, and the M734 multi-option fuze. This new fuze is set by hand and gives delayed detonation, impact, near-surface burst (0-3ft, 0-0·9m), or proximity burst (3-13ft, 0·9-3·96m).

The mortar can be used in conjunction with the AN/GVS-5 hand held laser rangefinder, this can range up to 10,936 yards (10,000m) to an accuracy of ±10·936 yards (±10m). This enables the mortar to engage a direct-fire target without firing a ranging bomb first. The M224 fires a variety of mortar bombs to a maximum range of 3,828 yards (3,500m) and is currently in production at Watervliet Arsenal. The Army has ordered 1,590 of these mortars while the Marine Corps has ordered 698.

Right: The M29 is being replaced in the company support role by the smaller M224, which is a far more versatile weapon.

under a Boeing CH-47 Chinook, but (and this is a most important drawback) its 5-ton prime mover cannot. A further problem is that the carriage is some 5in (127mm) too wide to fit into the Low-Attitude Parachute Extraction System (LAPES) rails in USAF C-130 aircraft.

When in the traveling position, the barrel is swung through 180° so that it rests over the trails. This reduces the overall length of the weapon. When in the firing position the trails are opened out and the suspension system is raised so that the weapon rests on a non-anchored firing platform. A hydraulic ram cylinder and a 24in (0·609m) diameter float mounted in the bottom carriage at the on-carriage traverse centerline provides for rapid shift of the carriage to ensure 360° traverse. This enables the weapon to be quickly laid onto a new target.

The weapon has a recoil system of the hydropneumatic type and the barrel is provided with a double baffle muzzle brake. The M198 uses separate loading ammunition (e.g. a projectile and a separate propelling charge) and can fire an HE round to a maximum range of 22,000m, or out to 30,000m with a Rocket Assisted Projectile. The latter is basically a conventional HE shell with a small rocket motor fitted at the rear to increase the range of the shell. The weapon will also be the primary user of the new Cannon Launched Guided Projectile (or Copperhead) round. Nuclear and Improved Conventional Munitions, as well as rounds at present used with the M114, can also be fired. It will also be able to fire the range of ammunition developed for the FH70. The latter is a joint development between Britain, Germany and Italy, and is now in production. Maximum rate of fire is four rounds per minute for the first three minutes, followed by two rounds per minute thereafter. A thermal warning device is provided so that the gun crew know when the barrel is becoming too hot.

Although a great improvement on its predecessors, the M198 has suffered from a number of problems. The desired range and accuracy requirements have been achieved at the expense of mobility and size. Further, unit price has increased from an original estimate of $184,000 to $421,000— although the M198 is by no means the only weapon system to suffer such problems.

Vulcan, M163/M167

Type: 20mm Vulcan air defense system.
Crew: 1 (on gun).
Weight (firing and traveling): 3,500lb (1,588kg).
Length traveling: 16ft (4·9m).
Width traveling: 6·49ft (1·98m).
Height traveling: 6·68ft (2·03m).
Elevation: −5° to +80°.
Traverse: 360°.
Effective range: 1,750 yards (1,600m).
(*Note: specification refers to the towed version.*)

The 20mm Vulcan is the standard light anti-aircraft gun of the US Army and has been in service since 1968. There are two versions of the Vulcan system in service, one towed and the other self-propelled; both are fair weather, daylight only systems. The towed version is known as the M167 and this is mounted on a two wheeled carriage and is normally towed by an M715 or M37 truck. When in the firing position the weapon rests on three outriggers to provide a more stable firing platform. The self-propelled model is known as the M163 and this is mounted on a modified M113A1 APC chassis, the chassis itself being the M741. The latter will be replaced by the twin 40mm Sergeant York DIVAD (*qv*).

The 20mm cannon used in the system is a modified version of the air-cooled six-barrel M61 Vulcan cannon developed by General Electric. It is also the standard air-to-air cannon of the US Air Force. The Vulcan cannon has two rates of fire, 1,000 or 3,000 rounds per minute, and the gunner can select either 10, 30, 60 or 100 round bursts. The M163 has 500 rounds of linked ready-use ammunition while the self-propelled model has 1,100 rounds of ready-use ammunition.

The fire control system consists of an M61 gyro lead-computing gun sight, a range-only radar mounted on the right side of the turret (developed by Lockheed Electronics), and a sight current generator. The gunner normally visually acquires and tracks the target while the radar supplies range and range rate data to the sight current generator. These inputs are converted to proper current for use in the sight. With this current the sight computes the correct lead angle and adds the required super elevation.

The turret has full power traverse and elevation, slewing rate being 60°/second, and elevation rate being 45°/second. Power is provided by an auxiliary generator.

The Vulcan air defense system is normally used in conjunction with the Chaparral SAM. Each Vulcan/Chaparral battalion has 24 Chaparral units and 24 self-propelled Vulcan systems.

Below: The M163 is a standard US Army weapon despite its limitation (especially important in European formations) to clear-weather operations through lack of sensors other than an optical lead-computing sight and range-only radar.

M16A1

Type: Rifle.
Caliber: 5·56mm.
Length overall (with flash suppressor): 38·9in (99cm).
Length of barrel: 19·9in (50·8cm).
Weight (including 30-round loaded magazine): 8·2lb (3·72kg).
Range (maximum effective): 300 yards (274m).
Rate of fire: 700-950rpm (cyclic); 150-200rpm (automatic); 45-65rpm (semi-automatic).
Muzzle velocity: 3,280ft/s (1,000m/s).

The M16 (previously the AR-15) was designed by Eugene Stoner and was a development of the earlier 7·62mm AR-10 assault rifle. It was first adopted by the US Air Force, and at a later date the US Army adopted the weapon for use in Vietnam. When first used in combat numerous faults became apparent and most of these were traced to a lack of training and poor maintenance. Since then the M16 has replaced the 7·62mm M14 as the standard rifle of the United States forces. To date over 5,000,000 have been manufactured, most by Colt Firearms and the weapon was also made under licence in Singapore, South Korea and the Philippines. Twenty-one armies use the M16. The weapon is gas-operated and the user can select either full automatic or semi-automatic. Both 20- and 30-round magazines can be fitted, as can a bipod, bayonet, telescope and night sight. The weapon can also be fitted with the M203 40mm grenade launcher, and this fires a variety of 40mm grenades to a maximum range of 382 yards (350m). The M203 has now replaced the M79 grenade launcher on a one-for-one basis. The Colt Commando is a special version of the M16 and this has a shorter barrel, flash supressor and a telescopic sight, reducing the

overall length of the weapon to 27·9in (71cm). The M231 is a special model which can be fired from within the M2 Bradley Infantry Fighting Vehicle.

There has been consistent dissatisfaction with the M16A1 in the US Army, and even more so in the other main user—the US Marine Corps. One of the major complaints is its lack of effectiveness at ranges above 340 yards (300m), which has come to a head with the increased emphasis on desert warfare with the RDF. This, combined with the high average age of current stocks, led to a major review in 1981.

As a result, a "product improved" weapon (M16A2) is now under consideration. A major feature would be a stiffer and heavier barrel, utilizing one-turn-in-seven-inches (17·8cm) rifling—as opposed to one-turn-in-twelve-inches (30·5cm)—to enable the new standard NATO 5·56mm

M60

Type: General purpose machine gun.
Caliber: 7·62mm.
Length: 43·3in (110cm).
Length of barrel: 22in (56cm).
Weight: 23lb (10·48kg) with bipod; 39·6lb (18kg) with tripod.
Maximum effective range (bipod): 984 yards (900m).
Maximum effective range (tripod): 1,968 yards (1,800m).
Rate of fire: 550rpm (cyclic); 200rpm (automatic).

The M60 is the standard GPMG of the US Army and has now replaced the older 0·30 Browning machine gun. The weapon was developed by the Bridge Tool and Die Works and the Inland Division of General Motors Corporation, under the direction of Springfield Armory. Production of the M60 commenced in 1959 by the Maremont Corporation of Saco, Maine.

The M60 is gas-operated, air-cooled and is normally used with a 100-round belt of ammunition. To avoid overheating the barrel is normally changed after 500 rounds have been fired. Its fore sight is of the fixed blade type and its rear sight is of the U-notch type and is graduated from about 656ft to 3,937ft (200 to 1200m) in about 328ft (100m) steps. The weapon is provided with a stock, carrying handle and a built in bipod. The M60 can also be used on an M122 tripod mount, M4 pedestal mount and M142 gun

Above: The M60 suffered from a number of development problems, but is now an effective though heavy GPMG.

mount for vehicles. Other versions include the M60C remote for helicopters, M60D pintle mount for vehicles and helicopters and the M60E2 internal model for AFVs.

The M60 will remain in service with the US Army for many years. It is sturdy, reliable, and highly effective.

M2 HB

Type: Heavy machine gun.
Caliber: 0·50in (12·7mm).
Length overall: 65·07in (165·3cm).
Length of barrel: 44·99in (114·3cm).
Weight (gun only): 83·33lb (37·8kg); 127·8lb (57·98kg) with tripod.
Range: 1,996 yards (1,825m) effective in ground role; 7,470 yards (6,830m) maximum; 820 yards (750m) anti-aircraft role.
Rate of fire: 450/575rpm.

The 0·50 caliber M2 machine gun was developed for the US Army in the early 1930s, as the replacement for the 0·50 M1921A1 MG. The weapon was developed by John Browning (who designed many other famous weapons including the Browning Automatic Rifle and the Browning 0·30 machine gun), and the Colt Firearms company of Hartford, Connecticut.

The M2 is air-cooled and recoil operated, and is fed from a disintegrating metallic link belt. The weapon can fire either single shot or full automatic, and various types of ammunition can be fired including ball, tracer, armor-piercing and armor-piercing incendiary. For ground targets the weapon is mounted on the M3 tripod while for the anti-aircraft role the M63 mount is used. It is also mounted on many armored fighting vehicles including the M113A1 series of APC (and variants), the M109/M108 SPH and the M578 and M88 ARV. The M55 anti-aircraft system (no longer in service with the US Army) has four M2s, and the M2 is also mounted in helicopters and in some commanders' turrets like the M85. The M2 HB MG is still being produced in the United States by Ramo Incorporated and the Maremont Corporation, and it remains in service in some 20 countries.

The M2 HB went out of production shortly after World War II, but the line was recently re-opened, mainly, but not entirely, for export sales. The letters "HB" in the designation stand for "hydraulic buffer", a modification introduced in the late 1930s.

Below: The M2 HB is one of those weapons that appears to be immortal, all its design and operational features having blended into a weapon of such devastating power and reliability that improvement seems all but impossible.

Above: The M16 helped pave the way for today's generation of 5·56mm assault rifles after a disastrous early career. This is an M16A1 with the PVS-2 Starlight night sight.

(0·218in) round to be fired. Other features under consideration are a three-round burst capability to replace the current full-automatic, an adjustable rearsight, and a modified flash eliminator. The opportunity would also be taken to introduce tougher "furniture", ie, butt-stock, pistol grip, and handguard.

A program is in hand to examine new technologies for incorporation in a possible future weapon. These include controlled-burst fire and multiple projectiles (eg, flechettes).

Above: An adjunct to the M16 is the M203 grenade-launcher, which clips under the forestock and has its own trigger.

M72A2

Type: Light anti-tank weapon (LAW).
Caliber: 66mm.
Length of rocket: 20in (50·8cm).
Weight of rocket: 2·2lb (1kg).
Muzzle velocity: 476ft/s (145m/s).
Maximum effective range: 355 yards (325m).
Length of launcher closed: 25·7in (65·5cm).
Length of launcher extended: 35in (89·3cm).
Weight complete: 4·75lb (2·15kg).

The M72 is the standard Light Anti-Tank Weapon (LAW) of the US Army and is also used by many other armies around the world. Development of weapon started in 1958 with the first production LAWs being completed by the Hesse Eastern Company of Brockton, Massachusetts, in 1962. It is also manufactured under licence in Norway by Raufoss. The LAW is a lightweight, shoulder-fired rocket launcher and its rocket has a HEAT warhead which will penetrate over 11·8in (300mm) of armor. It can also be used against bunkers, pillboxes and other battlefield fortifications.

When the M72 is required for action, the infantryman removes the safety pins, which open the end covers, and the inner tube is telescoped outwards, cocking the firing mechanism. The launcher tube is then held over the shoulder, aimed and the weapon fired. The launcher is then discarded. Improved models are known as the M72A1 and the more recent M72A2.

The successor to the M72A2 was to be the Viper, which was supposed to be so cheap and effective that it was planned to issue it to virtually every man in the front line. Weighing a little under 9lb (4·1kg), Viper has a 2·75in (70mm) diameter warhead with a performance against modern Soviet

armor that is marginal, to say the least. Following strong criticism by the General Accounting Office (GAO), the US Congress ordered a shoot-off between Viper and three European weapons: the British LAW 80, the Norwegian M72-750, and the Swedish AT4. A further complication arose when General Dynamics refused to sign a fixed-price contract for Viper. The US Army is thus faced with either buying a European LAW system off-the-shelf or soldiering on with the M72A2 until a better US-designed successor is available.

Above: Typical of the current generation of one-man high-performance anti-tank launchers is the British LAW80.

Below: The M72A2 is light and comparatively cheap, but has only marginal performance against modern MBTs.

M249

Type: Squad automatic weapon (SAW).
Caliber: 5·56mm.
Lengths: Overall 39·4in (100cm); barrel 18·5in (47cm).
Weights: Empty 15·5lb (7·03kg); with 200-round magazine 22lb (9·97kg).
Effective range: 1,421 yards (1,300m).
Rate of fire: 750rpm.
Muzzle velocity: 3,033ft/s (924m/s).

The SAW idea was conceived in 1966, but it has taken a long time to reach service. When the M16 was issued to infantry squads, all infantrymen had an automatic weapon, but with a maximum effective range of some 330 yards (300m) only. It was considered that each fire team in the squad needed a weapon of greater all-round capability than the M16, but obviously not a weapon as heavy or as sophisticated as the M60. The SAW meets this requirement, and will be issued on a scale of one per fire team, ie, two per squad. The SAW may also replace some M60s in non-infantry units.

The M249 SAW is a development of the Belgian Fabrique Nationale (FN) "Minimi". Current orders are being met from the FN factory, but it is intended to set up a production line in the USA. Current requirements are for 26,000 M249s for the Army and 9,000 for the Marine Corps in a five-year program, but further orders will doubtless follow.

The M249 is very smooth in operation and displays a reliability that is considered exceptional in light machine guns. Fully combat ready, with a magazine of 200 rounds, bipod, sling, and cleaning kit, the M249 weighs 22lb (9·97kg), which is still 1lb (0·4kg) less than an empty M60 machine gun. The M855 ball round fired from the M249 will penetrate a US steel helmet at a range of 1,421 yards (1,300m).

Overall, the M249 is superior to the Soviet PKM 7·62mm (bigger, heavier, smaller mag), and the RPK 5·45mm (bigger, lighter, smaller mag).

Above: The M249 is a light fire-support machine-gun designed for squad use as long-range partner to the M16 rifle.

Right: Designed to use its own special 200-round ammunition container, the M249 can also accommodate the M16's magazine.

M79

Type: Grenade launcher.
Caliber: 40mm.
Weight of grenade: 0·610lb (0·277kg).
Length of launcher: 29in (73·7cm).

Length of barrel: 14in (35·6cm).
Weight of launcher: (empty) 5·99lb (2·72kg); loaded, 6·5lb (2·95kg).
Muzzle velocity: 249ft/s (76m/s).
Range: 437·4 yards (400m) maximum; 383 yards (350m) effective, area targets; 164 yards (150m) effective, point targets.
Effective casualty radius: 5·46 yards (5m).
Rate of fire: 5 rounds per minute.

The 40mm M79 Grenade Launcher was developed to give the infantryman the capability to deliver accurate firepower to a greater range than could be achieved with a conventional rifle grenade. The M79 is a single shot, break-open weapon and is fired from the shoulder. It is breech loaded and fires a variety of different types of ammunition including high explosive, high explosive air burst, CS gas and smoke. Its fore sight is of the blade type and its rear sight is of the folding leaf adjustable type. The latter is graduated from 82 yards (75m) to 410 yards (375m) in about 27 yards (25m) increments. When the rear sight is in the horizontal position, the fixed sight may be used to engage targets up to 109·3 yards (100m). The M79 has been replaced in front line units by the M203 grenade launcher which is fitted to the standard M16A1 rifle.

Left: The single-shot, shoulder-fired M79 grenade launcher, in service with the Army and Marine Corps, makes up for poor effective lethal range of the grenade by having good accuracy, in the right hands.

M1911A1

Type: Pistol.
Caliber: 0·45in (11·43mm).
Length: 8·63in (21·93cm).
Length of barrel: 5·03in (12·78cm).
Weight loaded: 2·99lb (1·36kg).
Weight empty: 2·49lb (1·13kg).
Effective range: 65ft (20m).
Muzzle velocity: 826ft/s (252m/s).

The 0·45 caliber M1911 pistol was the standard American sidearm of World War I. In 1923, work on an improved model commenced at Springfield Armory, and this was standardized as the M1911A1 in 1926, and since then the weapon has been the standard sidearm of the US Army. The Army does, however, use other pistols for special missions, as the M1911A1 is rather heavy and has quite a recoil. Between 1937 and 1945, over 19 million M1911A1 pistols were manufactured by Colt, Ithaca and Remington. The weapon is semi-automatic, and all the user has to do is to pull the trigger each time he wants to fire. The magazine, which is in the grip, holds a total of seven rounds. The fore sight is of the fixed blade type and the rear sight consists of a U notch on dovetail slide. The weapon has three safety devices: the grip safety on the handle, the safety lock, and the half cock position on the hammer.

Manufacture of the M1911A1 ceased in 1945 and the cost of spare parts,

especially barrels and slides, is becoming very high. This, combined with a number of operational shortcomings (such as the heavy recoil), and the lack of commonality with the standard NATO 9mm round, has led to a long search for a replacement. This resulted in a 1982 shoot-off between four competing designs: the US Smith & Wesson 459M, the Swiss-German SIG-Sauer P226, the German Heckler & Koch P7A13, and the Italian Beretta 92SB. All four failed the test in one way or another and, as a result, in February 1982 Congress prohibited the use of any further funds in projects involving a 9mm handgun. It would, therefore, appear that the famous "45" will soldier on for many years to come.

Below: The M1911A1 pistol is a classic and well-loved weapon long out of production, and now about to be replaced.

GEMSS
Ground-Emplaced Mine-Scattering System

All NATO armies are seeking to enhance their ability to stop and defeat armored thrusts by the numerically superior Warsaw Pact forces. To this end, all forms of anti-tank weapons are being developed, and over the past decade there has been a marked revival of interest in anti-tank mines: interest both in the effect of the mines themselves and in rapid methods of laying them. The Ground-Emplaced Mine-Scattering System (GEMSS) is particularly effective, since it is mounted on a trailer that can be towed by any suitable tracked (M548 cargo carrier, M113 APC) or wheeled (5-ton truck) prime mover. GEMSS's primary purpose is quickly to lay minefields that will force attacking enemy armored vehicles into constricted areas where they will provide a rewarding target for killing weapons.

GEMSS is the M128 mine dispenser, holding up to 800 4lb (1·8kg) mines which are deployed at intervals of 32 or 64 yards (30 or 60m), the interval being determined by the rate of launch and the speed of the vehicle. The M128 dispenser is mounted on the M794 trailer.

The mines are laid on the surface and a 2,734 yard (2,500m) field can be laid in less than six hours. The anti-tank mine has a magnetic influence field; this means that it can attack the whole width of the target and does not need to be run over by the tracks. There is also an anti-personnel mine, a fragmentation weapon activated by automatically deployed trip-wire sensors. Both types of mine have anti-disturbance devices to inhibit clearance, but both also have a built-in self-destruct device which neutralizes the minefield after a pre-determined interval.

Fiftynine GEMSS units were procured by the US Army in FY 1982 and a further 52 units in FY 1983.

Below: The laying density of the GEMSS minefield is decided by launch rate and the speed of the tower, here an M113.

M992 FAASV

Type: Field artillery ammunition support vehicle (FAASV).
Crew: 9 (maximum).
Armament: One 0·5in Browning MG.
Dimensions: Length overall 22ft 3in (6·7m); width 10ft 10in (3·295m); height 10ft 7½in (3·24m).
Weights: Loaded 57,500lb (26,082kg); cargo capacity 18,920lb (8,582kg).
Engine: Detroit Diesel Model 8V71T, 8-cylinder turbocharged diesel; 405bhp at 2,350rpm.
Performance: Road speed 35mph (56km/h); road range 220 miles (354km); vertical obstacle 1ft 9in (0·53m); trench 6ft (1·83m).

Many armies are searching for an answer to the ammunition resupply problem created by the ever-increasing capability of modern artillery. This problem has a number of facets. First, most artillery is now on highly mobile self-propelled tracked chassis, and is thus able to move more often, faster, and to more inaccessible sites, Secondly, rates of fire are increasing and thus creating a greater quantitative requirement. Finally, increases in caliber have led to larger and heavier rounds which are more difficult for the "ammunition numbers" to handle.

The US Army's solution to this problem is the FAASV, which entered production in 1983, with introduction to service scheduled for 1985-86. The FAASV is based on the well-proven M109A2 chassis, but with a large armored housing in place of the turret. This housing contains removable vertical racks which are hoisted aboard by a 1,500lb (680kg) capacity, extendible-boom crane on the front of the vehicle. On arrival at the gun position, projectiles and charges are removed from these racks by an automatic stacker, assembled, fuzed, and then passed by an hydraulic conveyer directly into the supported gun.

The FAASV can carry 90 155mm projectiles and charges, or 48 8in rounds. The rate of passing rounds to the guns is 8 rounds per minute, which handsomely exceeds current rates of fire. An additional feature is that the armored rear door swings up to provide overhead protection during the transfer process.

This very promising vehicle is designed and built by Bowen-McLaughlin-York and 144 units are currently on order, although the US Army's requirement is for at least 250 units.

Below: The use of the M922 promises significant improvements in the tactical capability of M109 and M110 SP artillery.

United States Warships

Nimitz

CVN

Completed: 1975 onwards.
Names: CVN 68 *Nimitz*; CVN 69 *Dwight D. Eisenhower*;
CVN 70 *Carl Vinson*; CVN 71 *Theodore Roosevelt*,
CVN 72 *Abraham Lincoln*,
CVN 73 *George Washington* (building).
Displacement: 81,600t standard; 91,400t full load.
Dimensions: 1,092 oa x 134 wl, 251 flight deck x 37ft
(332.8 x 40.8, 76.4 x 11.3m).
Propulsion: 4-shaft nuclear; 2 A4W reactors; 260,000shp = 30kts.
Armament: *AAW:* 3 BPDMS launchers Mk 25 (3x8).
Aircraft: 24 F-14A Tomcat; 24 A-7E Corsair; 10-A6E Intruder
+ 4 KA-6D; 4 E-2C Hawkeye; 4 EA-6B Prowler;
10 S-3A Viking; 6 SH-3H Sea King.
Sensors: *Surveillance:* SPS-48, SPS-43A, SPS-10.
Fire Control: 3 Mk 115.

The Nimitz class was originally envisaged as a replacement for the three Midway-class carriers. The completion of the first nuclear-powered carrier, *Enterprise*, had been followed by the construction of two conventionally powered ships, *America* and *John F. Kennedy*. The latter had, however, only ever been thought of as "interim" designs to plug the gap between *Enterprise* and a second generation of nuclear carriers which would employ smaller numbers of more advanced reactors to provide the necessary power, and which would, it was hoped, cost less to build. The two A4W reactors which power the Nimitz class each produce approximately 130,000shp compared with only 35,000shp for each of the eight A2W reactors aboard *Enterprise*. Moreover, the uranium cores need replacing far less frequently than those originally used in *Enterprise*, giving a full 13-year period between refuellings.

The reduction in the number of reactors from eight to two allowed for major improvements in the internal arrangements below hangar-deck level. Whereas in *Enterprise* the entire centre section of the ship is occupied by the machinery rooms, with the aviation fuel compartments and munitions machinery is divided into two separate units, with the magazines between machinery is dvided into two separate units, with the magazines between them and forward of them. The improved arrangement has resulted in an increase of 20 per cent in aviation fuel capacity and a similar increase in the volume available for munitions and stores.

Flight-deck layout is almost identical to that of *John F. Kennedy*. At hangar-deck level, however, there has been a significant increase in the provision of maintenance workshops and spare parts stowage. Maintenance shops have all but taken over the large sponson which supports the flight deck, and at the after end of the hangar there is a large bay for aero-engine maintenance and testing. The increased competition for internal volume even in a ship of this size is illustrated by the need to accommodate a total complement of almost 6,300 men, compared with only 4,900 for *Enterprise*—the original *Forrestal* design on which both ships are based provided for 3,800!

Sensor provision and defensive weapons are on a par with *John F. Kennedy*. The SPS-33/34 "billboard" radars fitted to *Enterprise* and the cruiser *Long Beach* proved to be a maintenance nightmare, and *Nimitz* has been provided with conventional rotating 3-D and air search models. The position of the SPS-48 and SPS-43 antennae is reversed in comparison with *John F. Kennedy*. *Nimitz* and *Eisenhower* are scheduled to be fitted with an ASW Control Centre and specialised maintenance facilities for the S-3 Viking anti-submarine aircraft; these features were incorporated into *Carl Vinson* while building. The fourth ship of the class may receive the fixed SPY-1A planar antennae associated with Aegis.

Three Mk 25 BPDMS launchers are fitted at present, but these will shortly be replaced by the Mk 29 launcher for NATO Sea Sparrow (IPDMS). This class is also scheduled to receive three Phalanx CIWS guns.

Problems were experienced from the outset in the construction of these ships. *Nimitz* was four years late in commissioning and took seven years to build (*Enterprise* took only four). Her construction was plagued by a shortage of skilled labour and frequent strikes at the Newport News Shipyard. When she was finally completed in 1973, vital components for the A4W reactors had still not been delivered, and a further two years were to elapse before commissioning. This delayed the start of *Eisenhower* by a further four years, and produced a knock-on effect which resulted in rocketing costs. President Carter attempted, unsuccessfully, to block the authorisation of funds for the construction of a fourth carrier in favour of the smaller, less capable, but less costly CVV design. The CVV, however, was never popular with the Navy, and the Reagan administration has now committed itself to the continuation of the CVN programme.

Both *Nimitz* and *Eisenhower* serve in the Atlantic, and besides the customary deployment to the Mediterranean they have recently seen service in the Indian Ocean. *Vinson* and *Roosevelt* serve in the Pacific.

Below: The growing core of US naval power projection is found in the planned seven units of the nuclear-powered Nimitz class of CVs, here epitomized by its nameship.

Note the massive "hurricane" bow and the overhang of her massive deck, crammed with air-defense, attack, early warning, and anti-submarine warfare aircraft.

John Jordan, a contributor to many important defense journals, a consultant to the Soviet section of "Jane's Fighting Ships", and author of several technical books on modern warships.

The following technical descriptions cover the more important warships in the US Navy inventory. The warships are presented by ship type, with combat vessels arranged approximately by size.

Enterprise

CVN

Completed: 1961
Name: CVN 65 *Enterprise*
Displacement: 75,700t standard; 89,600t full load.
Dimensions: 1,123 oa x 133 wl, 248 flight deck x 36ft (342.3 x 40.5, 75.7 x 10.9m).
Propulsion: 4-shaft nuclear; 8 A2W reactors; 280,000shp = 30kts.
Armament: 3 NATO Sea Sparrow launchers Mk 29 (3x8); 3 Phalanx CIWS (3x6).
Aircraft: 24 F-14A Tomcat; 24 A-7E Corsair; 10 A-6E Intruder + 4 KA-6D; 4 E-2C Hawkeye; 4 EA-6B Prowler; 10 S-3A Viking; 6 SH-3H Sea King.
Sensors: *Surveillance:* SPS-48C, SPS-49, SPS-65.
Fire Control: 3 Mk 91.

Laid down shortly after the US Navy's first nuclear-powered surface ship, the cruiser *Long Beach, Enterprise* was completed in the remarkable short space of 3 years 9 months. The initial development work on her propulsion plant had begun as early as 1950, and the design of the reactors had benefited from the evaluation of early models installed in submarines. Even so, the problem of producing the required 280,000shp on four shafts employing first-generation reactors resulted in a solution that was costly in terms of internal volume; two A2W reactors are coupled to each shaft and the entire centre section of the ship is taken up by machinery.

Enterprise was also costly in terms of the initial purchase price—nearly double that of her conventionally-powered contemporaries of the Kitty Hawk class—but a number of strong arguments were advanced in favour of nuclear power. Reduced life-cycle costs due to infrequent refuellings made the nuclear-powered carrier a more economic proposition in the longer term, and the CVAN would be capable of undertaking lengthy transits and operations in high-threat areas at a high sustained speed. Moreover, the elimination of ship's fuel bunkers in *Enterprise* allowed a 50 per cent increase in aviation fuel capacity, and consequently in the number of consecutive days of strike operations she could sustain.

In size and general layout *Enterprise* is similar to *Kitty Hawk*. The most significant difference as completed was in the shape of the island, which comprised a "box" structure on which were mounted SPS-32/33 "billboard" radars, surmounted by a large cone for ECM and ESM antennae. The SPS-32/33 radars proved difficult to maintain, however, and when *Enterprise* was refitted in 1979-81, the entire island was removed and replaced by a more conventional structure similar to that of the *Nimitz* As refitted, she now carries conventional rotating radars of the latest types.

Like the carriers of the Kitty Hawk class *Enterprise* was to have received two Mk 10 launchers for Terrier missiles. She was completed with the large sponsons aft, but Terrier was not installed initially in a bid to keep down costs. When Terrier lost favour as a carrier weapon in the mid-1960s, it was decided instead to fit two BPDMS Sea Sparrow launchers on the after sponsons. After her recent refit *Enterprise* now carries three Mk 29 launchers for NATO Sea Sparrow, and three Phalanx CIWS guns.

Enterprise began her operational life in the Atlantic, but was transferred together with her nuclear-powered escort group to the Pacific during the Vietnam War and has remained there ever since. A second ship of the class was to have been authorised in the early 1960s but the project was deferred on grounds of cost (see *John F. Kennedy*).

Above: The USS *Enterprise* carries some 85 aircraft launched with the aid of four C13 steam catapults (two bow and two angled) and serviced with the aid of four deck-edge lifts. She was the first carrier to operate the F-14 Tomcat.

Below: Well illustrated in this high-angle shot of USS *Enterprise* are the vast flightdeck (with fore-and-aft plus angled sections), and the island superstructure set far to starboard to leave the flightdeck unobstructed.

Kitty Hawk

CV

Completed: 1961-8.
Names: CV63 *Kitty Hawk*; CV64 *Constellation*; CV 66 *America*; CV 67 *John F. Kennedy*.
Displacement: 60,100-61,000t standard; 80,800-82,000t full load.
Dimensions: 1,048-1,073 oa × 130 wl, 250-268 flight deck × 36ft. (319.3-326.9 × 39.6, 76.2-81.5 × 11m).
Propulsion: 4-shaft geared steam turbines; 280,000shp = 30kts.
Armament: 2 NATO Sea Sparrow launchers Mk29 (2x8); CV 64: 2 twin Mk 10 launchers (40 + 40) for Terrier missiles; CV 66-7: 3 BPDMS launchers Mk 25 (3x8), 3 Phalanx CIWS.
Aircraft: 24 F-14A Tomcat; 24 A-7E Corsair; 10 A-6E Intruder + 4 KA-6D; 4 E-2C Hawkeye; 4 EA-6B Prowler; 10 S-3A Viking; 6 SH-3H Sea King.
Sensors: *Surveillance:* SPS-48C, SPS-49 (SPS-37A in CV 63), SPS-10, SPS-65 (CV 67 only). *Fire Control:* 4 SPG-55A (CV 64), 2 Mk 91 (CV 63), 3 Mk 115 (CV 66-7). *Sonars:* SQS-23 (CV 66 only).

Although there are significant differences between the first pair completed and the last two vessels—*John F. Kennedy* is officially considered as a separate single-ship class—these four carriers are generally grouped together because of their common propulsion system and flight-deck layout.

Kitty Hawk and *Constellation* were ordered as improved Forrestals, incorporating a number of important modifications. The flight deck showed a slight increase in area, and the arrangement of the lifts was revised to improve aircraft-handling arrangements. The single port-side lift, which on the Forrestals was located at the forward end of the flight deck—and was therefore unusable during landing operations—was repositioned at the after end of the overhang, outside the line of the angled deck. The respective positions of the centre lift on the starboard side and the island structure were reversed, so that two lifts were available to serve the forward catapults. A further improved feature of the lifts was that they were no longer strictly rectangular, but had an additional angled section at their forward end which enabled longer aircraft to be accommodated. The new arrangement proved so successful that it was adopted by all subsequent US carriers.

Kitty Hawk and *Constellation* were designed at a time when long-range surface-to-air missiles were just entering service with the US Navy. In place of the eight 5-inch (127mm) guns of the Forrestal class these ships therefore received two Mk 10 launchers for Terrier missiles positioned on sponsons aft just below the level of the flight deck, with their 40-missile magazines behind them. The SPG-55 guidance radars were fitted close to the launchers and on the island, which became far more cluttered than that of the *Forrestal* because of the need to accommodate a much larger outfit of air search and height-finding radars. To help solve this problem a separate tall lattice mast was placed immediately aft of the island. This has carried a succession of large 3-D radars, beginning with the SPS-8B, subsequently replaced by the SPS-30, and eventually by the planar SPS-48.

America, the third ship of the class, was completed after a gap of four years and therefore incorporated a number of further modifications. She has a narrower smokestack and is fitted with an SQS-23 sonar.

In 1963 it was decided that the new carrier due to be laid down in FY 1964 would be nuclear-powered, but Congress baulked at the cost, and the ship was finally laid down as a conventionally powered carrier of a modified Kitty Hawk design. *John F. Kennedy* can be distinguished externally from her near-sisters by her canted stack—designed to keep the corrosive exhaust gases clear of the flight deck—and by the shape of the forward end of the angled deck.

Of even greater significance was the abandonment of the expensive long-range Terrier system, which took up valuable space and merely duplicated similar area defence systems on the carrier escorts, in favour of the Basic Point Defence Missile System (BPDMS), for which three octuple launchers were fitted. The SPS-48 radar, carried on a rather slimmer mast aft of the island, was fitted from the outset. Provision was made, as in *America*, for an SQS-23 sonar, but this was never installed.

John F. Kennedy marks the high point of US carrier construction, and it is significant that the later CVNs of the Nimitz class are almost identical in flight-deck layout, armament, and sensor outfit. The earlier three ships of the Kitty Hawk class are now being refitted to the same standard. In particular the Terrier launchers, together with the fire control radars, are being removed and replaced by Mk 29 launchers for NATO Sea Sparrow. It is envisaged that all four ships will eventually carry three Mk 29 launchers and three Phalanx CIWS guns. All vessels in the class are now fitted with the SPS-48 3-D radar, and the SPS-37A air search radar is being replaced by the much more compact SPS-49.

Kitty Hawk and *Constellation* have served since completion in the Pacific. *America* and *John F. Kennedy* serve in the Atlantic, with frequent deployments to the Mediterranean.

Below: The conventional powered USS *Kitty Hawk* under way as one of the Pacific Fleet's six operational CVs.

Below: Compared with her sisterships, CV63 and CV64, the carrier USS *America* has a narrow smoke stack, but has a wider flightdeck, and one of her four catapults is of the C13-1 improved type.

Below: An early shot of USS *Constellation* shows (on the port quarter) one of the two Mk10 twin Terrier launchers, slated for replacement by Mk 29 Seasparrow launchers.

Forrestal

CV

Completed: 1952-5.
Names: CV 59 *Forrestal*; CV 60 *Saratoga*; CV 61 *Ranger*;
CV 62 *Independence*.
Displacement: 60,000t standard; 78,000t full load.
Dimensions: 1,039-1,047 oa x 130wl, 238 flight deck x 37ft
(316.7-319 x 38.5, 72.5 x 11.3m).
Propulsion: 4-shaft geared steam turbines; 260-280,000shp = 33kts.
Armament: CV 59-60: 2 BPDMS launchers Mk 25 (2x8);
CV 61-62: 2 NATO Sea Sparrow launchers Mk 29 (2x8).
Aircraft: 24 F-4J Phantom; 24 A-7E Corsair; 10 A-6E Intruder
+ 4 KA-6D; 4 E-2C Hawkeye; 4 EA-6B Prowler;
10 S-3A Viking; 6 SH-3H Sea King.
Sensors: *Surveillance:* SPS-48, SPS-43A, SPS-10, SPS-58
(not in CV 61).
Fire Control: 2 Mk 115 (CV 59-60), 2 Mk 91 (CV 61-62).

Authorisation of the Forrestal class was a direct consequence of the Korean War, which re-established the value of the carrier for projecting air power against land targets. The new class was to operate the A-3 Skywarrior strategic bomber, which weighed fully 78,000lb (35,455kg) and dimensions and hangar height were increased accordingly. The original design was for a carrier similar in configuration to the ill-fated *United States*, which had a flush deck, together with a retractable bridge, and two waist catapults angled out on sponsons in addition to the standard pair of catapults forward.

The advent of the angled deck, which was tested by the US Navy in 1952 on the Essex-class carrier *Antietam*, led to the modification of *Forrestal* while building to incorporate this new development. The result was the distinctive configuration which has been adopted by all subsequent US carrier construction: a massive flight deck with considerable overhang supported by sponsons to the sides, with a small island incorporating the smokestack to starboard. The Forrestals were the first US carriers to have the flight deck as the strength deck—in previous ships it was the hangar deck—and in consequence side lifts were adopted in preference to centreline lifts and incorporated in the overhang. This resulted in a large uninterrupted hangar in which more than half the ship's aircraft could be struck down. The layout of the four side lifts proved less than satisfactory, however; in particular the port-side lift, which is at the forward end of the angled deck, cannot be used during landing operations, and the Kitty Hawk class which followed had a modified arrangement.

All four ships of the class were completed with eight 5-inch (127mm) single mountings on sponsons fore and aft. The forward sponsons created problems in heavy seas, however, and the three ships based in the Atlantic had both guns and sponsons removed in the early 1960s (*Ranger* lost her forward guns but retained the sponsons). During the 1970s all guns were replaced by BPDMS Mk 25 or IPDMS Mk 29 launchers. Eventually all four ships will have three Mk 29 launchers and three Phalanx CIWS guns.

The electronics suite has undergone considerable change and expansion since the 1950s. Large SPS-43A long-range air search aerials have been fitted on outriggers to the starboard side of the island, and the distinctive SPS-30 3-D radar was carried above the bridge from the early 1960s until replaced in the late 1970s by the SPS-48. *Saratoga* was taken in hand in October 1980 for a 3-year major modernisation (SLEP) which included replacement of the SPS-43 by the new SPS-49.

Unlike later carriers, the Forrestal class do not operate the F-14 Tomcat, but retain the F-4 Phantom. It is envisaged that the latter will eventually be replaced by the F-18 Hornet.

Below: USS *Saratoga* under way in the Red Sea, showing her two C7 and two C11-1 steam catapults.

Midway

CV

Completed: 1945-7.
Names: CV 41 *Midway*; CV 43 *Coral Sea*.
Displacement: 51-52,000t standard; 64,000t full load.
Dimensions: 979 oa x 121 wl, 259/236 flight deck x 36ft (298.4 x 36.9,
78.8/71.9 x 11m).
Propulsion: 4-shaft geared steam turbines; 212,000shp = 32kts.
Armament: 2 BPDMS launchers Mk 25 (2x8-CV 41 only);
3 Phalanx CIWS.
Aircraft: 24 F-4J Phantom; 24 A-7E Corsair; 10 A-6E Intruder
+ 4 KA-6D; 4 E-2C Hawkeye; 4 EA-6B Prowler.
Sensors: *Surveillance:* (CV 41) SPS-48A, SPS-37A, SPS-10;
(CV 43) SPS-30, SPS-43A, SPS-10.
Fire Control: 2 Mk 115.

These ships were the last war-built US carriers. Three units were completed but *Franklin D. Roosevelt* was stricken in 1977. As built, the Midway class had an axial flight deck with two centre-line lifts and a side lift amidships on the port side. They were armed with a heavy battery of 14-18 5-inch (127mm) guns and numerous smaller AA weapons. The original design was quickly overtaken by developments in jet aircraft, and the class underwent a major modernisation during the 1950s in which an 8-degree angled deck was built, incorporating the side lift at its forward end; the after lift, which would have obstructed landing operations, was removed and replaced by a second side lift to starboard aft of the island. The armament was significantly reduced and the latest 3-D and air search radars fitted. C-11 steam catapults were installed to enable the ships to operate the new generation of various types of jet aircraft.

Coral Sea, which was the last of the three to the modernised, incorporated a number of further modifications as a result of experience with her two sisters and with the Forrestal class. The position of the port-side lift was found to be unsatisfactory, and it was moved aft to clear the angled deck altogether. This enabled the angled deck itself to be extended forward with a consequent increase in deck space, and a third C-11 catapult was installed. The position of the forward centre-line lift was found to be equally unsatisfactory, as it was situated between the forward catapults and was therefore unusable during take-off operations. It was therefore removed and replaced by a third side lift forward of the island. New sponsons were built for the six remaining guns, which were now just below flight-deck level.

The conversion of *Coral Sea* was particularly successful, and she remained largely unaltered—except for the removal of the remaining guns—throughout the following two decades. Since 1978 she has been the thirteenth carrier in a 12-carrier force and has only recently been reactivated to replace *Saratoga* while the latter undergoes her SLEP.

In 1966 *Midway* was taken in hand for a major modernisation which would enable her to operate the same aircraft as the more modern US carriers. The flight deck was completely rebuilt—its total area was increased by approximately one-third—and the lifts rearranged on the pattern established by *Coral Sea*. (The new lifts are much larger, however, and have a capacity of 130,000lb (59,100kg) compared with 74,000lb (33,636kg) for those of her sister-ship). Two C-13 catapults were installed forward, enabling *Midway* to handle the latest aircraft. The armament was reduced to three 5-inch (127mm) guns (these were replaced in 1979 by two BPDMS launchers). NTDS was installed during the modernisation and the island has recently been extended to incorporate the latest sensors. Three Phalanx CIWS guns are to be fitted in the near future.

Midway, which is based in Japan, is due to remain in service until 1988, when she will replace *Coral Sea* as a training ship. Her principal limitations compared with later carriers are those inherent in the initial design; a hangar height of only 5.3m (17ft 6in)—the E-2 Hawkeye AEW aircraft needs 5.6m (18ft 4in) clearance—and a limited aviation fuel capacity—365,000 gallons compared with 750,000 gallons in the Forrestal design. In spite of their CV designation neither *Midway* nor *Coral Sea* operate fixed- or rotary-wing ASW aircraft, and both continue to operate the F-4 Phantom in place of the F-14 Tomcat.

Below: When CVN73 is delivered in the early 1990s, the World War II-vintage USS *Coral Sea* is to be used for training.

Ohio Class

SSBN

Completed:	1979 onwards.
Names:	SSBN 726 *Ohio*; SSBN 727 *Michigan*; SSBN 728 *Florida*; SSBN 729 *Georgia*; SSBN 730 *Henry M Jackson*; SSBN 731 *Alabama*; SSBN 732 *Alaska*; SSBN 733 *Nevada*; SSBN 734 onwards not yet named.
Displacement:	16,600t surfaced; 18,700t submerged.
Dimensions:	560ft oa x 42ft x 35.5ft (170.7x12.8x10.8m).
Propulsion:	Single shaft nuclear, 60,000shp=30kts dived.
Armament:	24 Trident I (C-4) SLBM; 4 21in (533mm) torpedo tubes.
Sensors:	Sonar: BQQ 5 (passive only).

While the programme of upgrading the later Polaris SLBM submarines to carry Poseidon was under way in the early 1970s, development of an entirely new missile was started. This was to have a much longer range— 4,400 miles (7,100km)—which in turn necessitated a new and much larger submarine to carry it. The missile, Trident 1, is now in service on converted Lafayette class SSBNs, while the first of the submarines purpose-built for Trident, USS *Ohio*, joined the fleet in 1982. Initially Congress baulked at the immense cost of the new system—but then the Soviet Navy introduced its own long-range SLBM, the 4,200 mile (6,760km) SS-N-8, in the Delta class. This was followed in 1976 by the firing of the first of the increased-

Right: Only the diminutive size of the man on the bridge provides any indication of the vast bulk of the Ohio class SSBN, here epitomized by the nameship of the class.

range SS-N18s (4,846 miles, 7,800km). US reaction was to speed up the Trident programme, and the first of the Ohio class submarines was laid down on 10 April 1976. Eight are now in commission with a further sixteen building or currently planned. Trident II (D-5) will be fitted from the ninth of class onwards.

The eventual number of Trident-carrying SSBNs depends on two principal factors. The first is the outcome of the new round of Strategic Arms Limitation Talks (or Strategic Arms Reduction Talks) between the Reagan administration and the USSR, which will then, of course, have to be ratified by the US Congress. Any such agreement would presumably include, as in SALT-II proposals, the maximum numbers of SLBMs and launch platforms that each super-power was prepared to permit the other to possess. The other factor is the development of new types of long-range cruise missiles, some of which can be used in a strategic role even when launched from a standard 21in (533mm) submerged torpedo tube. This, and similar progress in other fields, may restrict the need for large numbers of SLBMs in huge and very expensive SSBNs. The great advantage, however, of the current generation of very long-range SLBMs is that they can be launched from American or Soviet home waters, thus making detection of the launch platform and destruction of either the submarine or the missiles launched from it extremely difficult, if not virtually impossible.

Lafayette Class/Franklin Class

SSBN

Completed:	1962-1966.
Names:	SSBN 616 to SSBN 659.
Displacement:	7,250t surfaced; 8,250t submerged.
Dimensions:	425ft oa x 33ft x 31.5ft (129.3 x 33 x 31.5m).
Propulsion:	Single shaft nuclear; 15,000shp=30kt submerged.
Armament:	16 Poseidon C-3 SLBM (19 boats), 16 Trident D-4 SLBM 12 boats; four 21in (533mm) torpedo tubes (all).
Sensors:	Sonar BQQ-2.

The 31 Lafayette class SSBNs were the definitive US submarines of the 1960s and 1970s. The first eight were originally fitted with Polaris A-2 missiles, while the remaining 23 had the improved Polaris A-3 with a range of 2,855 miles (4,594km) and three 200KT MRV warheads. The first five boats launched their missiles with compressed air, but the remainder use a rocket motor to produce a gas-steam mixture to eject the missiles from their tubes. All Lafayettes have now been fitted to take Poseidon C-3 SLBMs, which have a range of about 3,230 miles (5,200km) with ten 50KT MIRVs.

The Lafayettes are slightly enlarged and improved versions of the Ethan Allen design, and are almost indistingsuishable from that class. The last 12 Lafayettes differ considerably from the earlier boats and are sometimes referred to as the Benjamin Franklin class. They have improved, quieter machinery and 28 more crewmen. Twelve of these are being refitted to take the larger three-stage Trident 1 C-4 SLBM, which has a range of about 4,400 miles (7,100km) and carries eight 100KT MIRVs. Although these SSBNs do not have the underwater performance of the SSNs, they have a respectable capability against surface ships or other submarines and are armed with conventional or wire-guided torpedoes and Subroc. Normally, however, they would attempt to evade detection or contact.

Daniel Webster (SSBN-626) of this class has been fitted with diving planes on a raised bow sonar instead of on the fin; although this has been successful, it has not been copied on other SSBNs.

Below: The USS *Daniel Boone* running on the surface, with a raised deck aft of the sail for 16 Trident C-4 SLBM tubes.

Los Angeles Class

SSN

Completed:	1974 onwards.
Names:	SSN 688 to SSN 777.
Displacement:	6,000t surfaced; 6,900t submerged.
Dimensions:	360ft oa x 31.75ft x 32.25ft (109.7 x 10.1 x 9.8m).
Propulsion:	Single shaft nuclear; 35,000shp=30+kt submerged.
Armament:	4 21in (533mm) torpedo tubes; Subroc, Mk 48 torpedoes, Tomahawk (15 VLS tubes to be fitted from SSN-721 onwards).
Sensors:	*Long range sonar:* BQQ-5 plus towed array. *Short range sonar:* BQS-15. *Radar:* BPS-15.

The first Los Angeles SSN entered service in 1976; thirty-six are now in commission and the eventual size of the class has yet to be decided. They are much larger than any previous SSN and have a higher submerged speed. They have the BQQ-5 sonar system and can operate Subroc, Sub-Harpoon and Tomahawk as well as conventional and wire-guided torpedoes. Thus, like all later US SSNs, although they are intended to hunt other submarines and to protect SSBNs they can also be used without modification

to sink surface ships at long range with Sub-Harpoon. Further, Tomahawk will enable them to operate against strategic targets well inland.

The Los Angeles class is very sophisticated and each boat is an extremely potent fighting machine. With a production run of at least 44, it must be considered a very successful design. However, these boats are becoming very expensive: in 1976 the cost of each one was estimated at $221.25 million; the boat bought in 1979 cost $325.6 million; the two in 1981 cost $495.8 million each. Not even the USA can continue to spend money at that rate.

Nevertheless, the Reagan Administration has ordered a speeding up of the Los Angeles building programme, calling for two in 1982 and three per year thereafter. The Tomahawk missile programme is also being accelerated: Tomahawk has been fitted from SSN-719 (the twenty-second boat to be launched, in 1983) onward.

A design for a smaller and cheaper SSN, under consideration in 1980 as a result of Congressional pressure, appears to have been shelved. There are now plants to improve the Los Angeles boats—especially their sensors, weapon systems and control equipment—and fifteen Vertical Launch System (VLS) missile tubes are being fitted in the forward main ballast tank

Right: Against a backdrop of further construction, USS *Baltimore* enters the water at Groton on December 13, 1980.

Right: An overhead view of USS *James K. Polk* emphasizes the raised rear decking and large sail-mounted hydroplanes.

area for Tomahawk missiles, thus restoring the Mark 48 torpedo load to its original figure.

Below: SSN power is well illustrated by the Los Angeles class USS *Phoenix* at speed in lumpish sea conditions.

California
CGN

Completed: 1974-5.
Names: CGN 36 *California*; CGN 37 *South Carolina*.
Displacement: 10,150t full load.
Dimensions: 596 oa x 61 x 32ft (182 x 18.6 x 9.6m).
Propulsion: 2-shaft nuclear; 2 D2G reactors; 60,000shp = 30kts.
Armament: *AAW:* 2 single Mk 13 launchers (40 + 40) Standard MR missiles, 2 5-inch (127mm) Mk 45 (2x1). 2 Phalanx 20mm CIWS.
ASW: ASROC launcher Mk 16 (1x8, reloads); 4 12.75-inch (324mm) torpedo tubes (4x1, fixed).
SSM: 8 Harpoon missiles (2x4).
Sensors: *Surveillance:* SPS-48C, SPS-40B, SPS-10.
Fire Control: 4 SPG-51D, SPG-60, SPQ-9A.
Sonars: SQS-26CX.

California and her sister *South Carolina* were built in response to the need for a new class of nuclear escorts to accompany the CVNs of the *Nimitz* class. A third ship was approved in FY 1968, but this was later cancelled.

Compared with previous CGNs, *California* is a much larger, more sophisticated vessel. The design reverted to the "double-ended" layout of *Bainbridge*, but single Mk 13 Tartar launchers were adopted in preference to the Mk 10. This was in some ways a retrograde step in that it limited the ships to the medium-range (MR) version of the Standard missile, whereas earlier CGs and CGNs could be retro-fitted with the extended-range (ER) version. It also necessitated the provision of a separate ASROC launcher, forward of which there is a magazine surmounted by a prominent deckhouse into which the missiles are hoisted before reloading.

California was the first ship to be fitted with the new lightweight 5-inch (127mm) gun, and the first to have the digital Mk 86 FC system installed. The anti-surface element of the latter—the SPQ-9 antenna—is housed within a radome on the after side of the mainmast, while the SPG-60 antenna, which besides tracking air targets can serve as a fifth illuminating channel for the missiles, is located directly above the bridge.

One ship serves in the Atlantic, the other in the Pacific. Both have recently been fitted with Harpoon and Phalanx CIWS, and will be fitted with Tomahawk.

Above: Though a twin-ended CV-escort cruiser, the USS *California* is limited by her Mk 13 single-rail launchers, which distinguish her from later CGNs.

Below: With four SPG-51D radars (two forward and two aft), USS *California* can simultaneously control four SAMs. She was the first US ship to have Mk45 guns with Mk 86 control system.

California (CGN-36).

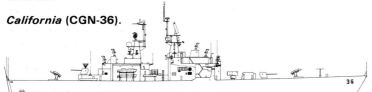

Truxtun
CGN

Completed: 1967.
Name: CGN 35 *Truxtun*.
Displacement: 8,200t standard; 9,200t full load.
Dimensions: 564 oa x 58 x 31ft (172 x 17.7 x 9.4m).
Propulsion: 2-shaft nuclear; 2 D2G reactors; 60,000shp = 30kts.
Armament: *AAW:* twin Mk 10 launcher (60) for Standard ER missiles; 1 5-inch (127mm) Mk 42.
ASW: ASROC missiles from Mk 10 launcher; 1 SH-2F helicopter; 4 12.75-inch (324mm) torpedo tubes Mk 32 (4x1, fixed).
SSM: 8 Harpoon missiles (2x4).
Sensors: *Surveillance:* SPS-48, SPS-40, SPS-10.
Fire Control: 2 SPG-55B, 1 SPG-53F.
Sonars: SQS-26.

Originally requested as one of seven Belknap-class frigates in the FY 1962 programme, *Truxtun* was given nuclear propulsion at the insistence of Congress. She emerged from the drawing board with tall, distinctive lattice masts in place of the twin macks of the oil-burning ships.

While she carried an identical weapons outfit to her near-sisters, major modifications were made to the layout. The positions of the Mk 10 launcher and the 5-inch (127mm) Mk 42 and their respective fire-control radars were reversed, and the ASROC/Terrier magazine rings were therefore located beneath the flight deck and not forward of the bridge. In place of the triple Mk 32 torpedo tubes of the Belknaps *Truxtun* has two fixed tubes located in the superstructure on either side amidships. The helicopter hangar, which is 40ft by 17ft (12.3 x 5m), is shorter and wider than that of the Belknaps.

Truxtun originally had twin 3-inch (76mm) mountings amidships, but these were replaced in the late 1970s by quadruple launchers for Harpoon. The two Mk 25 stern tubes have also been removed. Two Phalanx CIWS guns will be fitted in the near future.

Truxtun has served since completion in the Pacific Fleet, where she has combined with *Long Beach* and *Bainbridge* to form the nuclear-powered escort squadron which accompanies the carrier *Enterprise*.

Below: The USS *Truxton* is a single-ended CV-escort cruiser. The lattice masts are distinctive.

Belknap

Completed: 1964-7.
Names: CG 26 *Belknap*; CG 27 *Josephus Daniels*;
CG 28 *Wainwright*; CG 29 *Jouett*; CG 30 *Horne*;
CG 31 *Sterett*; CG 32 *William H. Standley*; CG 33 *Fox*;
CG 34 *Biddle*.
Displacement: 6,570t standard; 7,930t full load.
Dimensions: 547 oa x 55 x 29ft (166.7 x 16.7 x 8.7m).
Propulsion: 2-shaft geared steam turbines; 85,000shp = 33kts.
Armament: *AAW:* twin Mk 10 launcher (60) for Standard ER missiles;
1 5-inch (127mm) Mk 42; 2 Phalanx CIWS being fitted.
ASW: ASROC missiles from Mk 10 launcher;
1 SH-2F helicopter; 6 12.75-inch (324mm) torpedo
tubes Mk 32 (2x3).
SSM: 8 Harpoon missiles (2x4).
Sensors: *Surveillance:* SPS-48, SPS-40 (CG 29, 31-34) *or*
SPS-43 (CG 27-28, 30) *or* SPS-49 (CG 26), SPS-10F.
Fire Control: 2 SPG-55B, 1 SPG-53.
Sonars: SQS-26BX (except CG 26, SQS-53C)

The nine ships of the Belknap class, together with their nuclear-powered
half-sister *Truxtun*, constitute the final group of AAW "frigates" completed
for the US Navy during the 1960s. Outwardly they resemble their
predecessors of the Leahy class, with which they share a common hull-form
and superstructure layout. A closer look, however, reveals a shift in
emphasis in favour of significantly increased anti-submarine capabilities.

In the Belknaps the "double-ended" missile launcher arrangement was
abandoned and the 5-inch gun reinstated—a reflection, in part, of concern
about the diminishing number of vessels capable of fire support operations.
The Mk 10 Terrier launcher was given a third 20-round magazine ring
located below and between the other two. The extra capacity was used,
however, not to compensate for the reduction in Terrier rounds compared
with the *Leahy*, but in order to dispense with a separate ASROC launcher.
The upper two rings carry alternate Terrier/Standard and ASROC rounds,
while the third, which carries only SAM rounds, serves as a feed for the two
upper rings.

The additional deck space gained as a result of these modifications was
utilised to provide a helicopter platform and hangar immediately aft of the
second mack. It was envisaged that the Belknaps would operate the ill-fated
drone anti-submarine helicopter (DASH) but the programme was abandoned
before any drones were embarked. Instead, the Belknaps became the trial
class for the LAMPS helicopter programme in the early 1970s, and
introduced manned ASW helicopters to the US Navy with conspicuous
success.

**Above: USS *Horne* shows the radically different macks of the
conventionally-powered Belknap class CV-escort cruisers.**

The Belknaps carried an altogether more advanced electronics outfit to
the Leahy class. In particular the SQS-23 sonar was replaced by the much
more powerful SQS-26, while the new planar SPS-48 3-D radar replaced the
older SPS-39. Target and fire control data were coordinated by the US
Navy's first computer-based Naval Tactical Data System (NTDS). Moreover,
these systems have been constantly updated in order to keep abreast of the
aerial threat. In 1977 *Wainwright* was modified to conduct evaluation of the
SM-2 missile, following which it is now carried by all ships of the class.
Belknap, which had her entire upper works destroyed by fire following a
collision with the carrier *John F. Kennedy* in 1975, has been rebuilt with a
completely updated sensor outfit, including an SPS-49 air search radar, an
SQS-53A sonar, and SLQ-32(V)3 ECM antennae. All ships have now been
fitted with quadruple Harpoon launchers in place of the former 3-inch
(76mm) AA guns amidships, and each will receive two Phalanx CIWS guns
in the near future.

Four units of the Belknap class currently serve in the Atlantic, and five in
the Pacific. They are employed as AAW escorts for the conventionally
powered carriers.

Wainwright (CG-28).

**Below: The Belknap class has its SAM launcher and radars forward of
the bridge. This is USS *William H. Standley*.**

Bainbridge

CGN

Completed: 1962.
Names: CGN 25 *Bainbridge*.
Displacement: 7,700t standard; 8,580t full load.
Dimensions: 565 oa x 58 x 29ft (172.5 x 17.7 x 7.9m).
Propulsion: 2-shaft nuclear; 2 D2G reactors; 60,000shp = 30kts.
Armament: *AAW:* 2 twin Mk 10 launchers (40 + 40) for Standard ER missiles; 2 20mm (2x1).
ASW: ASROC launcher Mk 16 (1x8); 6 12.75-inch (324mm) torpedo tubes Mk 32 (2x3).
SSM: 8 Harpoon missiles (2x4).
Sensors: *Surveillance:* SPS-48, SPS-37, SPS-10D.
Fire Control: 4 SPG-55B.
Sonars: SQS-23.

Like the later *Truxtun*, *Bainbridge* is an offshoot of a larger class of conventionally powered AAW "frigates". She is a near-sister of the Leahy class, with which she initially shared an identical outfit of weapons and electronics. As completed, she presented a more streamlined profile than the *Leahy* because her nuclear propulsion enabled her to dispense with the tall

macks of the latter.

The layout of *Bainbridge's* weapons is identical to that of the *Leahy*, with twin Mk 10 Terrier launchers fore and aft and an ASROC box launcher forward of the bridge. From 1974 onwards the ship underwent an extensive refit aimed at upgrading her electronics. The refit included not only the installation of new surveillance radars and NTDS but also the complete remodelling of her superstructure, which now comprises two distinct blocks with much greater internal volume. The forward block is surmounted by a broad lattice mast and the after block by a heavy pole mainmast. The former 3-inch (76mm) AA guns have been replaced by quadruple Harpoon missile launchers, and two Phalanx close-in weapon systems (CIWS) guns will be fitted abreast the after SPG-55 tracker/illuminators in the near future. SPG-55 tracker/illuminators in the near future.

Bainbridge has served since completion in the Pacific, where she has combined with *Truxtun* and *Long Beach* to form the nuclear-powered escort squadron which accompanies the carrier *Enterprise*.

Below: A double-ended ship with Mk 10 twin launchers fore and aft together with pairs of SPG-55B radars and associated Mk 76 fire-control systems, the USS *Bainbridge* also possesses two Mk 141 quadruple Harpoon launchers at the after end of the superstructure, and a Mk 16 Octuple Asroc launcher just forward of the bridge.

Leahy

CG

Completed: 1962-4.
Names: CG 16 *Leahy*; CG 17 *Harry E. Yarnell*; CG 18 *Worden*; CG 19 *Dale*; CG 20 *Richmond K. Turner*; CG 21 *Gridley*; CG 22 *England*; CG 23 *Halsey*; CG 24 *Reeves*.
Displacement: 5,670t standard; 7,800t full load.
Dimensions: 553 oa x 55 x 25ft (162.5 x 16.8 x 7.6m).
Propulsion: 2-shaft geared steam turbines; 85,000shp = 32kts.
Armament: *AAW:* 2 twin Mk 10 launchers (40 + 40) for Standard ER missiles.
2 Phalanx CIWS.
ASW: ASROC launcher Mk 16 (1x8); 6 12.75-inch (324mm) torpedo tubes Mk 32 (2x3).
SSM: 8 Harpoon missiles (2x4) fitted in place 3-inch (76mm) guns.
Sensors: *Surveillance:* SPS-48, SPS-43 (SPS-49 in CG 19), SPS-10.
Fire Control: 4 SPG-55B.
Sonars: SQS-23.

The nine ships of the Leahy class, together with their nuclear-powered half-sister *Bainbridge*, constitute the second group of AAW "frigates" completed for the US Navy during the 1960s. They were designed at a time when it was thought that guns would disappear altogether from the inventory of naval weapons. They were therefore the first US Navy ships to have an all-missile main armament. They also introduced the "mack" (combined mast and stack) to US Navy construction as a means of conserving valuable centre-line deck space.

A "double-ended" layout was adopted with twin Mk 10 Terrier launchers fore and aft. There are 20-round magazine rings in line with each launcher arm, and the missiles are lifted from the top of the ring and run up at an angle of 15 degrees through a wedge-shaped deckhouse onto the launcher. Target tracking and illumination are provided by paired SPG-55B FC radars mounted atop the fore and after superstructures.

As in the earlier Coontz class, there is an 8-round ASROC launcher forward of the bridge, but no reloads are carried.

From 1967 until 1972 the Leahy class underwent an extensive modernisation programme aimed at bringing their electronics up to the same standard as the Belknaps. A large planar SPS-48 3-D radar replaced

the original SPS-39, and NTDS was installed. *Dale* has now received the new SPS-49 air search radar in place of her SPS-43, and this modification will eventually be extended to all ships of this class and the Belknap class.

All ships have had their 3-inch (76mm) AA guns removed and have received eight Harpoon in their place. They have also received two Phalanx CIWS guns.

Only three units of this class are based in the Atlantic, the remaining six

Long Beach

CGN

Completed: 1961.
Name: CGN 9 *Long Beach*.
Displacement: 14,200t standard; 17,350t full load.
Dimensions: 721 oa x 73 x 29ft (219.8 x 22.3 x 8.8m).
Propulsion: 2-shaft nuclear; 2 C1W reactors; 80,000shp = 30kts.
Armament: *AAW:* 2 twin Mk 10 launchers (40 + 80) for Standard
ER missiles; 2 5-inch (127mm) Mk 30 (2x1).
ASW: ASROC launcher Mk 16 (1x8); 6 12.75-inch
(324mm) torpedo tubes Mk 32 (2x3).
SSM: 8 Harpoon missiles (2x4).
Sensors: *Surveillance:* SPS-48C, SPS-49, SPS-65.
Fire Control: 4 SPG-55A.
Sonars: SQQ-23.

Long Beach was the US Navy's first all-missile warship, and the first surface ship with nuclear power. She was designed as an escort for the carrier *Enterprise*, and has performed this role throughout the past two decades.

As completed she had two Mk 10 Terrier launchers forward and a Mk 12 launcher aft for the long-range Talos. The depth of the hull enabled an extra pair of magazine rings to be worked in beneath the second Mk 10 launcher, giving *Long Beach* a total capacity of no less than 166 surface-to-air missiles. There was an ASROC box launcher amidships, and shortly after the ship entered service two 5-inch (127mm) guns of an older pattern were fitted to provide defence against small surface craft.

Electronics were on a par with *Enterprise* herself, with large fixed SPS-32/33 "billboard" radars mounted on a similar "turret" superstructure block. The latter proved to be a major maintenance problem, and the FY 1978 budget provided funds to fit *Long Beach* with the AEGIS system. The proposed conversion was quickly cancelled, however, as it was feared that this expenditure might result in reductions in the new CG 47 programme.

Talos was removed in 1979 and the after launcher replaced by quadruple Harpoon launchers. The following year *Long Beach* began a major refit at which the SPS-32/33 radars were removed and their functions taken over by an SPS-48 3-D radar and an SPS-49 air search radar—the latter atop lattice mainmast. Two Phalanx CIWS guns were installed on the after superstructure, and there will eventually be launchers for Tomahawk aft.

Above right: USS *Long Beach* comes alongside at San Diego. In the refit the SPS-32 and SPS-33 planar radars were removed.

Right: USS *Long Beach's* bulkily shaped superstructure was dictated by the original use of "billboard" radar antennae.

---

being allocated to the Pacific Fleet. These dispositions are almost certainly related to their much greater cruising range as compared with the preceding Coontz class, and also to their limited ASW capabilities. Two of these AAW ships would normally be allocated to each non-nuclear carrier battle group.

Below: Stern-on view of the USS *Leahy* emphasizes the centerline location of missile launchers and radars.

Below: USS *England* fires a Standard ER. Note the two after SPG-55 radars trained to port for illumination and guidance.

Iowa

Completed: 1943-44, and recommissioned 1982-88.
Names: BB 61 *Iowa*; BB 62 *New Jersey*; BB 63 *Missouri*; BB 64 *Wisconsin*.
Displacement: 58,000t full load.
Dimensions: 887.2 oa x 108.2 x 38ft (270.4 x 33 x 11.6m).
Propulsion: 2-shaft geared steam turbines; 212,000shp = 33/35kts.
Armament: SS: 9 16-inch (406mm) Mk 7 (3x3).
AAW: 12 5-inch (127mm) Mk 38 (6x2); 4 20mm Phalanx Mk 16 CIWS (4x1).
SSM: 32 Tomahawk (8 x quadruple Mk 143 ABLs); 16 Harpoon (4 x quadruple Mk 141s).
ASW: provision for four SH-60B Seahawk helicopters.
Sensors: Surveillance: SPS-49(V), SPS-67(V).
Fire Control: 4 Mk 37 GFCS with Mk 25 radar, 2 Mk 38 gun directors with Mk 13 radar, 1 Mk 40 gun director with Mk 27 radar, two Mk 51 gun directors, two Mk 63 GFCS with Mk 34 radar, 6 Mk 56 gun directors with Mk 35 radar.

Built entirely during World War II and the largest battleships ever produced apart from the two units of the Japanese Yamato class, the Iowa class was designed for unparalleled protection and speed without any sacrifice of gun armament. The result was four battleships of exemplary capability and sea-keeping. The ships were mothballed in the late 1940s, but reactivated as shore-bombardment platforms (1950-53) in the Korean War. They were then mothballed again, though *New Jersey* was again reactivated for shore-bombardment service (1968-69) in the Vietnam War, when she fired 5,688 16-inch and 14,891 5-inch rounds.

The appearance of the Soviet Kirov class battle-cruisers combined with the comparatively slow building pace of the US Navy's extremely costly nuclear-powered carriers to produce a reappraisal of the four battleships held in reserve during the late 1970s. After a great deal of intra-service and political wrangling about the exact nature of the modernization (including plans for the addition of provision for STOVL aircraft and an AEGIS air-defense system) and its cost, it was decided to reactivate and modernize these superb warships as "a valuable supplement to the carrier task force in performing presence and strike missions, while substantially increasing our ability to provide naval gunfire support for power projection and amphibious assault missions". The first three ships were recommissioned for a cost of some $330 million each (less than the capital outlay for a new Oliver Hazard Perry class frigate), re-entering active service in December 1982 (BB 62, reactivated at Long Beach NY), April 1984 (BB 61, reactivated at Ingalls Shipbuilding) and summer 1986 (BB 63, reactivated at Long Beach NY).

The reactivation and modernization programme centered on the ships' electronic and armament systems. So far as the electronic systems were concerned, the entire sensor and communications suites were modernized: SPS-49 air-search radar was added on the new lattice mast behind the control tower and above the forward funnel, provision was made for the retrofit of SPS-67 surface-search radar (since accomplished), an SLQ-32(V)3 electronic support measures system was installed, four Mk 36 RBOC chaff launchers

Ticonderoga

Completed: 1983 onwards.
Names: CG 47 *Ticonderoga*; CG 48 *Yorktown*; CG 49. . . .; CG 50. . .; CG 51. . . .; CG 52. . . .
Displacement: 9,100t full load.
Dimensions: 563 oa x 55 x 31ft (171.7 x 17 x 17.6 x 9.4m).
Propulsion: 2-shaft COGAG; 4 LM2500 gas turbines; 80,000bhp = 30kts.
Armament: AAW: 2 twin Mk 26 launchers (44 + 44) for Standard MR SM-2 missiles; 2 5-inch (127mm) Mk 45 (2x1); 2 Phalanx CIWS.
ASW: ASROC missiles from Mk 26 launcher; 2 LAMPS helicopters; 6 12.75-inch (324mm) torpedo tubes Mk 32 (2x3).
SSM: 8 Harpoon missiles (2x4).
Sensors: Surveillance: 4 SPY-1A, SPS-49, SPS-55.
Fire Control: 4 Mk 99, SPQ-9A.
Sonars: SQS-53A, SQR-19 TACTAS.

The new missile cruiser *Ticonderoga* will be the first operational vessel to be fitted with the AEGIS Combat System. It was originally envisaged that this system would be installed in nuclear-powered escorts such as the Strike Cruiser (CSGN) and the CGN 42 variant of the Virginia class, but the enormous cost of AEGIS combined with that of nuclear propulsion proved to be prohibitive under the restrictive budgets of the late 1970s. Moreover, two AEGIS escorts were required for each of the twelve carrier battle groups, and as not all of the carriers concerned were nuclear-powered, it was decided to utilise the growth potential of the fossil-fuelled Spruance design to incorporate the necessary electronics.

The AEGIS Combat System was developed to counter the saturation missile attacks which could be expected to form the basis of Soviet anti-carrier tactics during the 1980s. Conventional rotating radars are limited both in data rate and in number of target tracks they can handle, whereas saturation missile attacks require sensors which can react immediately and have a virtually unlimited tracking capacity. The solution adopted in the AEGIS system is to mount four fixed planar antennae each covering a sector of 45 degrees on the superstructures of the ship. Each SPY-1 array has more than 4000 radiating elements that shape and direct multiple beams. Targets satisfying predetermined criteria are evaluated, arranged in sequence of threat and engaged, either automatically or with manual override, by a variety of defensive systems.

At longer ranges air targets will be engaged by the SM-2 missile, fired from one of two Mk 26 launchers. The SM-2 differs from previous missiles in requiring target illumination only in the terminal phase of flight. In the initial and mid-flight phase the missile flies under auto-pilot towards a predicted interception point with initial guidance data and limited mid-course guidance supplied by the AEGIS system. This means that no less than 18 missiles can be kept in the air in addition to the four in the terminal phase, and the Mk 99 illuminators switch rapidly from one target to the next under computer control. At closer ranges back-up is provided by the two 5-inch guns, while "last-ditch" self-defence is provided by two Phalanx CIWS guns, assisted by ECM jammers and chaff dispensers.

Ticonderoga and her sisters are designed to serve as flagships, and will be equipped with an elaborate Combat Information Centre (CIC) possessing an integral flag function able to accept and coordinate data from other ships and aircraft. Eighteen units are currently projected.

Right: USS *Vincennes* (CG49), third vessel in this useful class, shows off her two Mk 26 twin launchers, two CIWS mountings and after pair of SPY-1 planar arrays.

Virginia

CGN

Completed: 1976-80.
Names: CGN 38 *Virginia*; CGN 39 *Texas*; CGN 40 *Mississippi*; CGN 41 *Arkansas*.
Displacement: 11,000t full load.
Dimensions: 585 oa x 63 x 30ft (178 x 19 x 9m).
Propulsion: 2-shaft nuclear; 2 D2G reactors; 60,000shp = 30kts.
Armament: AAW: 2 twin Mk 26 launchers (44 + 24) for Standard MR missiles; 2 5-inch (127mm) Mk 45 (2x1).
ASW: 1 LAMPS helicopter (see notes); ASROC missiles from fwd Mk 26 launcher; 6 12.75-inch (324mm) torpedo tubes Mk 32 (2x3).
SSM: 8 Harpoon missiles (2x4) being fitted.
Sensors: Surveillance: SPS-48C, SPS-40B, SPS-55.
Fire Control: 2 SPG-51D, SPG-60, SPQ-9A.
Sonars: SQS-53A.

Following closely upon the two CGNs of the California class, the *Virginia* incorporated a number of significant modifications. While the basic layout of the class is identical to that of their predecessors, the single-arm Mk 13 launchers of the *California* were superseded by the new Mk 26 twin ASROC launcher forward, and a helicopter hangar was built into the stern.

The magazine layout and missile-handling arrangements of the Mk 26 constitute a break with previous US Navy practice. In earlier missile cruisers and destroyers booster-assisted missiles such as Terrier were stowed in horizontal magazine rings, and the shorter Tartar missiles in cylindrical magazines comprising two concentric rings of vertically stowed missiles. The magazine associated with the Mk 26 launcher, however, has a continuous belt feed system with vertical stowage capable of accommodating a variety of missiles. This means that ship's length is the only limiting factor on the size of the magazine, which is capable of being "stretched" or "contracted" to suit the dimensions of the vessel in which it is to be installed. It has also eliminated the requirement for a separate launcher for ASROC. In the Virginia class ASROC rounds are carried in the forward magazine alongside Standard MR surface-to-air missiles. The elimination of the ASROC launcher and its associated reloading deckhouse has saved 5m (16.4ft) in length compared with *California*.

The installation of an internal helicopter hangar in a ship other than an aircraft carrier is unique in the postwar US Navy. The hangar itself is 42ft by 14ft (12.8 x 4.3m) and is served by a stern elevator covered by a folding hatch. Although it is envisaged that SH-2F helicopters will eventually be assigned, the ships do not at present have helicopters embarked.

The electronics outfit is on a par with *California*, with two important differences. The first is the replacement of the SQS-26 sonar by the more advanced solid-state SQS-53, and the older Mk 114 ASW FC system by the digital Mk 116. The second is the retention of only the after pair of SPG 51.

Right: In ascending order above the bridge of USS *Texas* are the antennae for the SPG-60 and SPQ-9A radars associated with the Mk 86 FCS, SPS-55 surface and SPS-48C 3D radars.

were fitted, and upgrading of the communications witnessed the addition of one OE-82 satellite communications antenna, one SRR-1 receiver, three WSC-3 transceivers and one Link 11 data receiver. In the armament sphere the main armament remained unaltered, but the secondary armament was thinned from 10 to six 5-inch twin mountings to make room for the BGM-109 Tomahawk long-range anti-ship and land-attack cruise missiles' Mk 143 Armored Box Launchers. Other additions were four quadruple launchers for Harpoon medium-range anti-ship missiles, and four Phalanx CIWS mountings to provide point-defense against sea-skimming missiles and attack aircraft. Other modifications undertaken during the pre-commissioning refit centered on improvement of habitability for a crew of 65 officers and some 1,450 enlisted men, conversion to navy distillate fuel, removal of extraneous features such as the aircraft-handling crane and development of a Combat Engagement Center for SSM and tactical control purposes.

Since her reactivation, *New Jersey* has served in the Western Pacific, off Central America and in the eastern Mediterranean. Between December 1983 and May 1984 she provided gunfire support for the US Marine Corps contingent in Lebanon, engaging targets in the Chouf mountains with 1,900lb (862kg) HC rounds out to a range of some 41,500 yards (39,950m) with fair accuracy. Of the three battleships currently in service, two serve with the Pacific Fleet and one with the Atlantic Fleet.

Left: A head-on view of USS *New Jersey* emphasizes the World War II appearance of this powerful surface combatant, the major visible modifications being the white-domed CIWS mountings and the lattice for the ship's modern sensors.

tracker/illuminators, reducing the number of available channels (including the SPG-60) from five to three. This modification looks forward to the conversion of the ships to fire the SM-2 missile, which requires target illumination only in the terminal phase. The ships are also scheduled to receive Harpoon, Tomahawk, and two Phalanx CIWS guns at future refits.

The original requirement was for eleven ships of this class, which would then combine with earlier CGNs to provide each of the CVANs projected at that time with four nuclear-powered escorts. After only four units of the class had been laid down, however, further orders were suspended while consideration was given first to the Strike Cruiser (CSGN) and then to a modified CGN 38 design with AEGIS. Both these projects were abandoned in favour of the conventionally powered CG-47 now under construction, but the CGN42 AEGIS proposal was recently revived and dropped again.

All ships of the class serve as CGN escorts; two in the Atlantic Fleet and two in the Pacific Fleet.

Below: The aft pyramid mast of USS *Arkansas* provides a home for the SPS-40B air-search radar and the TACAN beacon.

Sturgeon Class/Narwhal

SSN

Completed:	1967-75. No. in Class: 37/1.
Displacement:	3,640t surfaced; 4,650t submerged.
Dimensions:	Length 292ft (89m); Beam 32ft (9.65m); Draught 29ft 6in (8.9m).
Propulsion:	1-shaft nuclear; 1 S5W reactor; 15,000shp = 30kts.
Armament:	Harpoon SSMs; SUBROC; 4 21-inch (533mm) torpedo tubes Mk 63.

The 37 Sturgeon class SSNs are slightly enlarged and improved versions of the Permit (Thresher) class. Like them, the Sturgeons have an elongated teardrop hull with torpedo tubes set amidships, with the bow taken up by the various components of the BQQ-2 sonar system. The Sturgeon is distinguished visually from the Permit by its taller fin with the driving planes set farther down. Several problems arose between the USN and the builders of this class: *Pogy* (SSN-647) was re-allocated to another yard for completion, while *Guitarro* (SSN-665) was delayed for more than two years after sinking in 35ft (10.7m) of water while being fitted out, in an incident later described by a Congressional committee as 'wholly avoidable'.

In an attempt to reduce noise, the Sturgeon class is fitted with two contra-rotating propellers on the same shaft. Although American submarines are already significantly quieter than their Soviet counterparts, any developments which can reduce noise (and therefore the distance at which the submarine can be detected) are speedily introduced. The Sturgeons, like the Permits, will be fitted during the course of routine overhauls with the BQQ-5 sonar system introduced in the Los Angeles class.

Narwhal (SSN-671), an experimental SSN based on the Permit/Sturgeon design, was built in 1967-69 to test the S5G free-circulation reactor, which has no pumps and is therefore quieter than previous US reactors. Although *Narwhal* retains this system and is still in service, no further submarines have been built with such a system.

Below: USS *Narwhal* is similar to the boats of the Sturgeon class, but has different (and much quieter) propulsion.

Below: USS *Sea Devil* surfaces, revealing hydroplanes that can be turned to the vertical position for ice penetration.

Tullibee/ Permit (Thresher) Class

SSN

Completed:	1960-68. No. in Class: 1/13.
Displacement:	3,750t surfaced; 4,300-4,600t submerged.
Dimensions:	Length 279-297ft (84.9-89.5m); Beam 32ft (9.6m); Draught 29ft (8.8m).
Propulsion:	1-shaft nuclear; 1 S5W reactor; 15,000shp = 30kts.
Armament:	Harpoon SSMs; SUBROC; 4 21-inch (533mm) torpedo tubes Mk 63.

Tullibee is one of the smallest SSNs to be built, displacing only 2,640 tons submerged, and was an early attempt at the ideal hunter-killer submarine. The small size meant that she was very manoeuvrable and thus more likely to detect a hostile submarine before herself being detected. The torpedo tubes were fitted amidships for the first time in order to free the bows for the then new BQQ-2 conformal sonar array. She was also fitted with turbo-electric drive to eliminate the noise made by the reduction gears in earlier boats. However, small size also led to a low submerged speed, and *Tullibee* lacked space to carry the more sophisticated (and inevitably larger) equipment and electronics. No more SSNs of this size have been built for the US Navy. *Tullibee* remains in service but is no longer considered a first-line unit.

All the better features of *Tullibee* were incorporated into the Thresher class, which, after the loss of the name ship in the Atlantic in April 1963, was redesignated the Permit class. Built between 1960 and 1966, four of these boats were originally designed to take the Regulus II cruise missile: they were re-ordered as SSNs when the Regulus II was cancelled in favour of the Polaris SLBM in 1958. The last three of the class (SSN-614, -615 and -621) have a larger hull than the earlier boats; *Jack* (SSN-605) has a modified hull to accommodate contra-rotating propellers, as one of the US Navy's many attempts to find a really quiet propulsion system. The principal anti-submarine weapon is Subroc, controlled by the BQQ-2 sonar sytem; the Permits can also fire the anti-ship Harpoon missile. They will in time be fitted to take the Tomahawk SLCM and will also be retrofitted with the BQQ-5 sonar.

Below: USS *Guardfish* is typical of the Permit (originally Thresher) class of SSNs, which introduced into US Navy service genuine deep-diving capability, quiet machinery, large bow-mounted sonar and midships-mounted Mk 63 torpedo tubes.

George Washington Class/ Ethan Allen Class

SSN

Completed: 1959-63. No. in Class: 3/5.
Displacement*: 6,955t surfaced; 7,900t submerged.
Dimensions*: Length 411ft (125.1m); Beam 33ft (10.1m); Draught 30ft (9.1m).
Propulsion: 1-shaft nuclear; 1 S5W reactor; 15,000shp = 25kts.
Armament: 4 21-inch (533mm) torpedo tubes Mk 65.
*Details for Ethan Allen

The George Washington class were the US Navy's first ballistic missile submarines. In order to get Polaris to sea as quickly as possible the design was based on that of the Skipjack class SSN. In fact, *George Washington* (SSBN-598) herself was laid down as *Scorpion* (SSN-589), and was lengthened by the addition of a 130ft (40m) insert while on the stocks. The original powerplant and much of the SSN-type equipment was retained in the SSBN. The five George Washington SSBNs were in service for seven years before the first of the Soviet equivalents, the Yankee class, became operational. By the mid-1960s the relatively short range of the Polaris A-1 missiles was making the George Washingtons vulnerable to Soviet countermeasures, so during their first re-coring they were fitted with the 2,855-mile (4,595km) Polaris A-3. Their electronics were also upgraded.

Two of this class (*Theodore Roosevelt* and *Abraham Lincoln*) had their missile compartments removed in 1980 and the spent fuel disposed of. Although the bow and stern sections were then rejoined, the decommissioned hulks are now being cannibalized for spares prior to disposal. The three remaining boats are being converted to SSNs by removing all missiles and associated equipment; cement will be put into the missile tubes as ballast compensation. The cost of conversion is a mere $400,000 per boat. As SSNs, their main use will be in training and as targets on ASW exercises, thus releasing more modern SSNs for front-line duties. The three boats will only be used in this way

for two to three years, however, because of the short life remaining in their nuclear cores.

Whereas the George Washington class was built to a modified SSN design in order to get the Polaris into service as soon as possible, the five Ethan Allen SSBNs were the first to be specially designed as such. While generally similar to the George Washingtons, they are nearly 30ft (9.1m) longer and, when first commissioned, were armed with the Polaris A-2, which had a range of 1,725 miles (2,776km). They had greatly improved crew quarters, an important factor in boats which remained submerged for more than sixty days at a time. *Ethan Allen* herself became the first SSBN to fire a live SLBM, on 6 May 1962; this detonated successfully on the Christmas Island test range. These boats were fitted with Polaris A-3, but, like the George Washingtons, they will not be fitted with Poseidon or Trident. All five are now being converted to SSNs and will operate in the attack role through to the end of the 1980s at least.

Above: The Ethan Allen class was the US Navy's first custom-designed SSBN type, four of the five later becoming SSNs.

Below: Now in Pacific Fleet reserve, USS *Patrick Henry* was built as an original Polaris SSBN but converted into an SSN.

Kidd

DDG

Completed: 1981-2.
Names: DDG 993 *Kidd;* DDG 994 *Callaghan;* DDG 995 *Scott;* DDG 996 *Chandler.*
Displacement: 8,140t full load.
Dimensions: 563 oa x 55 x 30ft (171.1 x 16.8 x 8.1m).
Propulsion: 2-shaft COGAG; 4 LM2500 gas turbines; 80,000bhp = 30kts.
Armament: *AAW:* 2 twin Mk 26 launchers (24 + 44) for Standard MR missiles; 2.5-inch (127mm) Mk 45 (2x1) 2 Phalanx CIWS.
ASW: ASROC missiles from Mk 26 launcher; 2 LAMPS helicopters; 6 12.75-inch (324mm) torpedo tubes Mk 32 (2x3).
SSM: 8 Harpoon missiles (2x4).
Sensors: *Surveillance:* SPS-48, SPS-55.
Fire Control: 2 SPG-51, SPG-60, SPQ-9A.
Sonars: SQS-53.

Above: USS *Chandler* shows off the lattice masts and associated antennae of the AAW/ASW-optimized Kidd class.

Below: Ordered by Iran as an upgraded Spruance class unit, USS *Kidd* is one of the US Navy's four most capable DDGs.

The four ships of the Kidd class are AAW modifications of the Spruance-class destroyer originally ordered by Iran but acquired by the US Navy in 1979 following the fall of the Shah.

The allowances made in the Spruance design for the modular installation of a number of weapon systems then in production or under development made redesign a simple matter, as the AAW modification had been one of the variations originally envisaged. In the Kidd class twin-arm Mk 26 launchers have been fitted fore and aft in place of the ASROC and Sea Sparrow launchers of the ASW version. The forward magazine is the smaller of the two, the original intention being to fit the now-defunct 8-inch (205mm) Mk 71 gun in place of the forward 5-inch (127mm) mounting. Contrary to US Navy practice, an SPS-48 3-D radar is fitted, but there is no independent air search radar. There are also only two SPG-51 tracker/illuminators—one above the bridge and the other on a raised superstructure immediately abaft the mainmast. The electronics outfit is therefore austere by US Navy standards, but this will be remedied over the next few years by the addition of systems currently being fitted to other ships of similar capabilities. Two Phalanx CIWS guns have recently been installed.

The Kidd-class destroyers can fire ASROC missiles from their forward Mk 26 launcher, resulting in an ASW capability not far short of that of the standard Spruance.

The provision of extra air-conditioning capacity and dust separators for the gas-turbine air intakes makes these ships well suited to operations in tropical conditions.

Spruance

DD

Completed: 1975-82.
Names: DD 963 *Spruance;* DD 964 *Paul F. Foster;* DD 965 *Kinkaid;* DD 966 *Hewitt;* DD 967 *Elliott;*
DD 968 *Arthur W. Radford;* DD 969 *Peterson;*
DD 970 *Caron;* DD 971 *David W. Ray;* DD 972 *Oldendorf;*
DD 973 *John Young;* DD 974 *Comte De Grasse;*
DD 975 *O'Brien;* DD 976 *Merrill;* DD 977 *Briscoe;*
DD 978 *Stump;* DD 979 *Conolly;* DD 980 *Moosbrugger;*
DD 981 *John Hancock;* DD 982 *Nicholson;*
DD 983 *John Rodgers;* DD 984 *Leftwich;* DD 985 *Cushing;*
DD 986 *Harry W. Hill;* DD 987 *O'Bannon;* DD 988 *Thorn;*
DD 989 *Deyo;* DD 990 *Ingersoll;* DD 991 *Fife;*
DD 992 *Fletcher;* DD 997 *Hayler.*
Displacement: 7,800t full load.
Dimensions: 563 oa x 55 x 29ft (171.1 x 16.8 x 8.8m).
Propulsion: 2-shaft COGAG; 4 LM2500 gas turbines; 80,000bhp = 30 + kts.
Armament: ASW: ASROC launcher Mk 16 (1x8, 24 reloads); 2 SH-2F helicopters (only one embarked); 6 12.75-inch (324mm) torpedo tubes Mk 32 (2x3).
AAW: NATO Sea Sparrow launcher Mk 29 (1x8, 16 reloads). 2 5-inch (127mm) Mk 45 (2x1); 2 Phalanx CIWS being fitted.
SSM: 8 Harpoon missiles (2x4).
Sensors: *Surveillance:* SPS-40, SPS-55.
Fire Control: SPG-60, SPQ-9A, Mk 91.
Sonars: SQS-53.

The most controversial ships to be built for the US Navy since World War II, the Spruance class was designed to replace the war-built destroyers of the Gearing and Allen M. Sumner classes, which had undergone FRAM ASW modification programmes during the 1960s but by the early 1970s were nearing the end of their useful lives.

At 7,800t full load—more than twice the displacement of the destroyers it was to replace—the *Spruance* epitomised the US Navy's design philosophy of the 1970s. This philosophy envisaged the construction of large hulls with block superstructures which maximised internal volume, fitted out with machinery that could be easily maintained and, if necessary, replaced, and equipped with high-technology weapon systems that could be added to and

updated by modular replacement at a later stage. The object was to minimise "platform" costs, which have no military pay-off, in favour of greater expenditure on weapon systems ("payload") in order to ensure that the ships would remain first-line units throughout the 30-year life-expectancy of their hulls.

In a further attempt to minimise "platform" costs the entire class was ordered from a single shipbuilder, the Litton/Ingalls Corporation, which invested heavily in a major production facility at Pascagoula, using advanced modular construction techniques.

The only "visible" weapons aboard *Spruance* when she was completed were 5-inch (127mm) Mk 45 lightweight gun mountings fore and aft and an ASROC box launcher forward of the bridge. In view of the size and cost of the ships this caused an immediate public outcry.

The advanced ASW qualities of the Spruance class are, however, largely hidden within the hull and the bulky superstructures. The ASROC launcher, for example, has a magazine beneath it containing no less than 24 reloads. The large hangar to port of the after-funnel uptakes measures 49-54ft by 21-23ft (15-16.5m x 6.47m) and can accommodate two LAMPS helicopters. And to either side of the flight deck there are sliding doors in the hull which conceal triple Mk 32 torpedo tubes and torpedo-handling rooms.

Of even greater significance are the advanced submarine detection features of the class. The bow sonar is the new SQS-53, a solid-state improved version of the SQS-26, which can operate in a variety of active and passive modes, including direct path, bottom bounce and convergence zone. The SQS-53 has proved so successful that the SQS-35 VDS initially scheduled to be installed in these ships will not now be fitted. The adoption of an all-gas-turbine propulsion system, which employs paired LM2500 turbines *en echelon* in a unit arrangement, and which was selected partly because of the ease with which it can be maintained and because of its low manning requirements, has resulted in a significant reduction in underwater noise emission. The Spruance is therefore capable of near-silent ASW operations.

The class is also fitted with the latest computerised data systems in a well

***Arthur W Radford* (DD-968).**

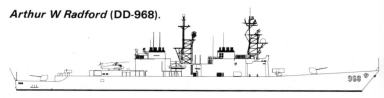

Decatur

Completed: 1956-9.
Names: DDG 31 *Decatur*; DDG 32 *John Paul Jones*; DDG 33 *Parsons*; DDG 34 *Somers*.
Displacement: 4,150t full load.
Dimensions: 418 oa x 45 x 20ft (127.5 x 13.8 x 6.1m).
Propulsion: 2-shaft geared steam turbines; 70,000shp = 32.5kts.
Armament: *AAW:* single Mk 13 launcher (40) for Standard MR missiles; 1 5-inch (127mm) Mk 42.
ASW: ASROC launcher Mk 16 (1x8); 6 12.75-inch (324mm) torpedo tubes Mk 32 (2x3).
SSM: Harpoon missiles will be fired from Mk 13 launcher.
Sensors: *Surveillance:* SPS-48, SPS-29E (SPS-40 in DDG 34), SPS-10B.
Fire Control: 1 SPG-51C, 1 SPG-53B.
Sonars: SQS-23.

These four ships were originally conventionally armed destroyers of the Forrest Sherman class. From 1965 until 1968 they underwent a major conversion to bring them up to a similar standard to the DDGs of the Charles

F. Adams class.

The three-year refit included the removal of the after 5-inch (127mm) guns and their replacement by the Tartar missile system. A Mk 13 single-arm launcher together with its cylindrical magazine replaced the after gun mounting, and immediately forward of it a large deckhouse carrying a single SPG-51 tracker/illuminator was constructed. Two massive lattice masts replaced the original tripods, giving the ships a distinctive profile. The purpose of the new mainmast was to carry the large SPS-48 3-D radar, which was just entering service. *Somers*, the last ship converted, also had her original SPS-29 air search radar replaced by an SPS-40. The initial conversion plan envisaged the operation of DASH anti-submarine drones, but when the DASH programme ran into problems, it was decided to fit an ASROC launcher instead.

It was originally intended that the entire Forrest Sherman class should undergo a similar conversion, but the cost of the programme proved to be prohibitive. Nor has the conversion proved to be particularly successful; the Decatur class suffers from excessive topweight, and although costly long-range detection and tracking facilities have been provided, the ships are limited to a single tracker/illuminator. All are now in reserve.

Below: USS *Somers* of the Decatur class, one of four such conversions currently in reserve with mechanical problems.

designed Combat Information Centre (CIC), and has the latest digital fire control systems—the Mk 86 GFCS and the Mk 116 underwater FC system.

Moreover, besides the weapon systems fitted on completion, the Spruance class was designed to accept a variety of other systems then at the development stage. All ships have now received the Sea Sparrow Improved Point Defence Missile System (IPDMS), Harpoon anti-ship missiles (aft of the first funnel), and Whiskey-3 (WSC-3) satellite communications antennae. SLQ-32(V)2 ECM antennae are now being fitted, and provision has been made for the future replacement of the ASROC and Sea Sparrow launchers by Mk 26 launchers. Eventually these will be replaced by Mark 41 Vertical Launch Systems (VLS), each of which comprises a 29- or 61-missile box able to accommodate AAW, anti-ship, and ASW missiles. The Spruance class is scheduled to receive the SQR-19 TACTAS towed array when it becomes available.

The flexibility of the Spruance design is such that it has formed the basis both for the AAW destroyers originally ordered for Iran (see Kidd class) and of the new AEGIS cruiser (see Ticonderoga class).

One additional ship of the Spruance class was ordered in 1979. DD 997 was originally to have had increased hangar and flight-deck space for helicopter and VTOL operations, but it was a modification which found greater favour with Congress than with the US Navy, which has since decided to complete the ship to the standard Spruance configuration.

Above: The blocky appearance of the Spruance class is well displayed by USS *Oldendorf* and her LAMPS I helicopter.

Below: Spruance class DDs such as USS *Kinkaid* are dedicated ASW ships with good anti-ship missiles and short-range SAMs.

Charles F. Adams

DDG

Completed: 1960-4.
Names: DDG 2 *Charles F. Adams;* DDG 3 *John King;* DDG 4 *Lawrence;* DDG 5 *Claude V. Ricketts;* DDG 6 *Barney;* DDG 7 *Henry B. Wilson;* DDG 8 *Lynde McCormick;* DDG 9 *Towers;* DDG 10 *Sampson;* DDG 11 *Sellers;* DDG 12 *Robison;* DDG 13 *Hoel;* DDG 14 *Buchanan;* DDG 15 *Berkeley;* DDG 16 *Joseph Strauss;* DDG 17 *Conyngham;* DDG 18 *Semmes;* DDG 19 *Tattnall;* DDG 20 *Goldsborough;* DDG 21 *Cochrane;* DDG 22 *Benjamin Stoddert;* DDG 23 *Richard E. Bird;* DDG 24 *Waddell.*
Displacement: 3,370t standard; 4,500t full load.
Dimensions: 437 oa x 47 x 22ft (133.2 x 14.3 x 6.7m).
Propulsion: 2-shaft geared steam turbines; 70,000shp = 31.5kts.
Armament: *AAW:* twin Mk 11 launcher (42) *or* single Mk 13 launcher (40) for Standard MR missiles; 2 5-inch (127mm) Mk 42 (2x1).
ASW: ASROC launcher Mk 16 (1x8); 6 12.75-inch (324mm) torpedo tubes MK 32 (2x3).
SSM: Harpoon misiles from Mk 13 launcher.
Sensors: *Surveillance:* SPS-39, SPS-29/37 (DDG 2-14) *or* SPS 40 (DDG-15-24), SPS-10C/D.
Fire Control: 2 SPG-51C, 1 SPG-53A/E/F.
Sonar: SQS-23.

The Charles F. Adams class is derived from the Forrest Sherman, with a Tartar launcher in place of the third 5-inch (127mm) gun mounting. It is still the standard AAW destroyer in service with the US Navy, and is employed together with the larger CGs to provide anti-air defence for the carrier battle groups.

The first 13 ships of the class were fitted with the twin-arm Mk 11 launcher but later ships have the single-arm Mk 13. The Mk 13 is a lightweight launcher with a high rate of fire—8 rounds per minute—which compensates in part for the single arm. Both launchers employ a cylindrical magazine containing two concentric rings of missiles. Overall length was increased by about 9m (29.5ft) to accommodate a Mk 16 ASROC launcher

between the funnels. The installation of Tartar and ASROC made the *Charles F. Adams* one of the most formidably armed destroyers of its period, and the design was adopted by the Federal German and the Australian Navies.

In spite of their age these ships are still highly regarded in the US Navy. They have proved to be extremely useful, well balanced ships, whose only major defect has been their temperamental high-pressure boilers. In the late 1970s it was therefore proposed that they should undergo a major modernisation programme which would extend their service life beyond the nominal 30-year mark. Funding was to have been authorised in FY 1980-3 but it was feared that expenditure of this magnitude would adversely affect

Coontz

DDG

Completed: 1959-61.
Names: DDG 37 *Farragut;* DDG 38 *Luce;* DDG 39 *Macdonough;* DDG 40 *Coontz;* DDG 41 *King;* DDG 42 *Mahan;* DDG 43 *Dahlgren;* DDG 44 *Wm. V. Pratt;* DDG 45 *Dewey;* DDG 46 *Preble.*
Displacement: 4,700t standard; 5,800t full load.
Dimensions: 513 oa x 53 x 25ft (156.2 x 15.9 x 7.6m).
Propulsion: 2-shaft geared steam turbines; 85,000shp = 33kts.
Armament: *AAW:* twin Mk 10 launcher (40) for Standard ER missiles; 1 5-inch (127mm) Mk 42.
ASW: ASROC launcher Mk 16 (1x8); 6 12.75-inch (324mm) torpedo tubes Mk 32 (2x3).
SSM: 8 Harpoon missiles (2x4).
Sensors: *Surveillance:* SPS-48 (SPS-49 in DDG 43, 46), SPS-29/37, SPS-10.
Fire Control: 2 SPG-55B, 1 SPG-53A.
Sonars: SQS-23.

The ten ships of the Coontz class constitute the first group of AAW "frigates" completed for the US Navy during the 1960s. Unlike the later ships of the Leahy and Belknap classes they have a flush-decked hull, and this feature, together with their twin lattice mast/funnel arrangement, reveals their derivation from the all-gun DLs of the early 1950s. They also have much

lower endurance than later ships, and this factor appears to have been largely responsible for their redesignation as DDGs in 1975 (the Leahy and Belknap classes became CGs). They nevertheless carry a similar armament to the later ships, have been brought up to the same standard as regards electronics, and perform an identical mission in defence of the carrier battle groups which are described and shown on pages 10-13.

The *Coontz* has a twin Mk 10 launcher aft, a single 5-inch (127mm) gun forward, an ASROC box launcher above it in "B" position, and triple anti-submarine tubes amidships. From 1968 until 1976 the class underwent a major modernisation similar to that of the *Leahy.* The SPS-39 3-D radar was replaced by an SPS-48, the Terrier guidance system was changed from command (employing SPG-49 radars) to semi-active guidance (employing the SPG-55), and a computer-based NTDS was installed—*Mahan* and *King,* which had been trials ships for the system 1961-2, had theirs updated. *Farragut* had her ASW capability enhanced by the provision of a reloading magazine for ASROC at the forward end of the superstructure, but she remained the only ship thus fitted. All ships had the original 3-inch (76mm) AA guns removed, and these were later replaced by Harpoon. In 1979 *Mahan* received the SM-2 missile, and this was subsequently fitted to the rest of the class. They have also received the SQQ-23 PAIR sonar, but will not be fitted with Phalanx.

All except *Preble* currently serve in the Atlantic, where their limited endurance is of less consequence than in the broader reaches of the Pacific.

Below: Of the 10 Coontz class DDGs nine are active with the Atlantic Fleet, including USS *Dewey* seen here.

the programme of new construction, and it was then proposed that the last ten ships would receive a less fundamental modernisation, but this was rejected by Congress.

In a revised plan just three ships (DDG-14, -20, -22) will be modernised using 'fleet maintenance funds'. The SPS-39 3-D radar will be replaced by the SPS-52B, the SPS-29/37 by an SPS-40C, and the SPS-10 by an SPS-65. The original Gun Fire Control System (GFCS) will be replaced by the digital Mk 86, with SPG-60 and SPQ-9A antennae, and the NTDS will be updated, with provision of the SYS-1 integrated automatic detection and tracking system. An SQQ-23 PAIR active/passive sonar will replace the SQS-23, and ECM capabilities will be greatly enhanced by the installation of two SLQ-32(V)2 antennae. The modernisation will require at least 18 months per ship. It is envisaged that these vessels will eventually be replaced by the DDGX now under development.

Below: USS Charles F. Adams presents a striking appearance as she steams at high speed. The SAM launcher is located aft.

Below: USS Wilson is one of 13 Charles F. Adams class DDGs with the Mk 11 twin rather than Mk 13 single SAM launcher.

Forrest Sherman

DD

Completed:	1955-9.
Names:	DD 931 Forrest Sherman; DD 942 Bigelow; DD 944 Mullinix; DD 945 Hull; DD 946 Edson (NRF). DD 951 Turner Joy. (ASW conversions). DD 937 Davis; DD 938 Jonas Ingram; DD 940 Manley; DD 941 Du Pont; DD 943 Blandy; DD 948 Morton; DD 950 Richard S. Edwards.
Displacement:	2,800t standard, 4,050t full load.
Dimensions:	418 oa x 45 x 22ft (127.5 x 13.7 x 6.7m).
Propulsion:	2-shaft geared steam turbines; 70,00shp = 32.5kts.
Armament:	(Unmodified units) ASW: 6 12.75-inch (324mm) torpedo tubes Mk 32 (2x3). AAW: 3 5-inch (127mm) Mk 42 (3x1). (ASW Conversions). ASW: ASROC launcher Mk 16 (1x8); 6 12.75-inch (324mm) torpedo tubes Mk 32 (2x3). AAW: 2 5-inch (127mm) Mk 42.
Sensors:	Surveillance: SPS-37 or SPS-40, SPS-10. Fire Control: SPG-53. Sonars: SQS-23, SQS-35 IVDS in ASW-modified ships.

The Forest Sherman class were the first postwar US destroyers. Although conventionally armed, they followed current tactical thinking in abandoning anti-ship torpedoes, which were replaced by four fixed 21-inch (533mm) "long" ASW torpedoes, and in mounting a lesser number of guns with higher performance than those of their war-built predecessors.

The conventional armament was quickly overtaken by new technological developments—in particular the advent of the nuclear submarine and the surface-to-air missile—and an extensive conversion programme was drawn up. Four ships were given the Tartar missile system (see Decatur class) but the cost of the conversion precluded its extension to the rest of the class. Eight ships were therefore given a limited ASW conversion between 1967 and 1971. The second gun mounting was replaced by an ASROC launcher and the fixed A/S tubes by triple Mk 32 trainable tubes; surveillance radars were updated and an independent variable depth sonar fitted above the stern.

Even this limited conversion programme ran into cost problems, and the remaining six ships of the class received only those modifications which entailed a minimum of structural alterations. They retained all three 5-inch (127mm) guns and were not fitted with ASROC or VDS.

From 1975 onwards Hull served as trial ship for the 8-inch (205mm) Mk 71 Major Calibre Light Weight Gun (MCLWG). The mounting replaced the forward gun until 1979, when it was removed. All are in reserve, except for DD-933, which is now a floating museum.

Below: The ASW conversion to eight Forrest Sherman class DDs saw the No. 2 5-inch gun replaced by a Mk 16 Asroc launcher.

Oliver Hazard Perry

FFG

Completed: 1977 onwards.
Names: FFG 7 *Oliver H. Perry*; FFG 8 *McInerney*;
FFG 9 *Wadsworth*; FFG 10 *Duncan*; FFG 11 *Clark*;
FFG 12 *George Philip*; FFG 13 *Samuel E. Morison*;
FFG 14 *Sides*; FFG 15 *Estocin*; FFG 16 *Clifton Sprague*;
FFG 19 *John A. Moore*; FFG 20 *Antrim*; FFG 21 *Flatley*;
FFG 22 *Fahrion*; FFG 23 *Lewis B. Puller*;
FFG 24 *Jack Williams*; FFG 25 *Copeland*; FFG 26 *Gallery*;
FFG 27 *Mahlon S. Tisdale*; FFG 28 *Boone*;
FFG 29 *Stephen W. Groves*; FFG 30 *Reid*; FFG 31 *Stark*;
FFG 32 *John L. Hall*; FFG 33 *Jarret*; FFG 34 *Aubrey Fitch*;
FFG 36 *Underwood*; FFG 37 *Crommelin*; FFG 38 *Curts*;
FFG 39 *Doyle*; FFG 40 *Halyburton*; FFG 41 *McClusky*;
FFG 42 *Klakring*; FFG 43 *Thach*; FFG 45 *De Wert*;
FFG 46 *Rentz*; FFG 47 *Nicholas*; FFG 48 *Vandegrift*;
FFG 49 *Robert G Bradley*; FFG 50 *Taylor*; FFG 51 *Gary*;
FFG 52 *Carr*; FFG 53 *Hawes*; FFG 54 *Ford*; FFG 55 *Elrod*;
FFG 56 *Simpson*; FFG 57 *Reuben James*;
FFG 58 *Samuel B Roberts*; FFHG 59 *Kauffman*;
+ 2 building.
Displacement: 3,710t full load.
Dimensions: 445 oa x 45 x 25ft (135.6 x 13.7 x 7.5m).
Propulsion: 1-shaft COGAG; 2 LM2500 gas turbines;
40,000bhp = 28kts.
Armament: *AAW:* single Mk 13 launcher (40) for Standard MR missiles;
1 76mm (3-inch) Mk 75; 1 Phalanx CIWS being fitted.
ASW: 2 LAMPS helicopters, 6 12.75-inch (324mm)
torpedo tubes Mk 32 (2x3).
SSM: Harpoon missiles from Mk 13 launcher.
Sensors: *Surveillance:* SPS-49, SPS-55.
Fire Control: STIR (modified SPG-60).
Sonars: SQS-26.

Above: The bulky superstructure of the Oliver Hazard Perry FFG is belied by the racy hull lines, and most of the class have made 30+kts on trials. This is USS *Samuel B. Roberts*.

The FFG 7 design has its origins in the Patrol Frigate first proposed in September 1970. The latter was to constitute the "low" end of the so-called "high/low" mix, providing large numbers of cheap second-rate escorts with reduced capabilities to counterbalance the sophisticated but costly specialist ASW and AAW vessels whose primary mission was to protect the carriers. Strict limitations were therefore imposed on cost, displacement and

Knox

FF

Completed: 1969-74.
Names: FF 1052 *Knox*; FF 1053 *Roark*; FF 1054 *Gray*;
FF 1055 *Hepburn*; FF 1056 *Connole*; FF 1057 *Rathburne*;
FF 1058 *Meyerkord*; FF 1059 *W.S. Sims*; FF 1060 *Lang*;
FF 1061 *Patterson*; FF 1062 *Whipple*; FF 1063 *Reasoner*;
FF 1064 *Lockwood*; FF 1065 *Stein*;
FF 1066 *Marvin Shields*; FF 1067 *Francis Hammond*;
FF 1068 *Vreeland*; FF 1069 *Bagley*; FF 1070 *Downes*;
FF 1071 *Badger*; FF 1072 *Blakely*;
FF 1073 *Robert E. Peary*; FF 1074 *Harold E. Holt*;
FF 1075 *Trippe*; FF 1076 *Fanning*; FF 1077 *Ouellet*;
FF 1078 *Joseph Hewes*; FF 1079 *Bowen*; FF 1080 *Paul*;
FF 1081 *Aylwin*; FF 1082 *Elmer Montgomery*;
FF 1083 *Cook*; FF 1084 *McCandless*;
FF 1085 *Donald B. Beary*; FF 1086 *Brewton*;
FF 1087 *Kirk*; FF 1088 *Barbey*; FF 1089 *Jesse L. Brown*;
FF 1090 *Ainsworth*; FF 1091 *Miller*;
FF 1091 *Miller*; FF 1092 *Thomas C. Hart*;
FF 1093 *Capodanno*; FF 1094 *Pharris*; FF 1095 *Truett*;
FF 1096 *Valdez*; FF 1097 *Moinester*.
Displacement: 3,011t standard; 4,100t full load.
Dimensions: 438 oa x 47 x 25ft (133.5 x 14.3 x 7.6m).
Propulsion: 1-shaft geared steam turbines; 35,000shp = 27kts.
Armament: *ASW:* ASROC launcher Mk 16 (1x8, reloadable);
1 SH-2F helicopter; 4 12.75-inch (324mm) torpedo
tubes Mk 32 (4x1).
AAW: BPDMS launcher Mk 25 (1x8) in 31 ships;
1 5-inch (127mm) Mk 42.
SSM: Harpoon missiles from ASROC Launcher.
Sensors: *Surveillance:* SPS-40, SPS-10.
Fire Control: SPG-53A/D/F, Mk 115.
Sonars: SQS-26CX, SQS-35 IVDS in some ships.

The Knox class began as a Design Work Study of the Brooke-class missile escort. Congressional opposition to the mounting costs of fitting escorts with the Tartar system resulted, however, in the abandonment of the latter class after only six units had been laid down. The *Knox* was therefore redesigned as an ASW Escort.

Although the *Knox* retained the one-shaft propulsion system of the Garcia/Brooke design, the complex pressure-fired boilers of the latter were abandoned in favour of a "safer", more conventional steam plant. This necessitated an increase in size without creating any extra space for weapons.

Originally the two 5-inch (127mm) Mk 38 guns of the *Garcia* were to have been replaced by a combination of a single 5-inch Mk 42 and the ill-fated Sea Mauler point-defence missile. The Sea Mauler was eventually replaced by the Sea Sparrow BPDMS—a system not contemplated when the *Knox* was

designed.

Other "hiccups" in the development of the *Knox* include the abandonment of a fixed "billboard" ECM antenna which influenced the design of the tall mack, of the pair of fixed torpedo tubes (for Mk 37/Mk 48 torpedoes) which were to have been fitted in the stern, and of the DASH programme.

Ultimately the abandonment of DASH worked to the ships' advantage, as it was replaced by the LAMPS I manned helicopter. As with the previous two classes of escort, the hangar received a telescopic extension, giving overall dimensions of 42-47ft by 15-18ft (12.6-14.3m x 4.4-5.6m). Taken together with the reloadable ASROC launcher and the SQS-26 sonar, this gave the *Knox* a first-class anti-submarine outfit, which rescued the design from an unpromising beginning.

Besides the Sea Sparrow BPDMS, many ships have received the SQS-35 independent variable depth sonar since completion. All will receive the SQR-18 towed array in the near future. Most ships have now had their ASROC launchers modified to fire Harpoon, and it is planned to replace Sea Sparrow with a single Phalanx CIWS mounting.

In spite of the early problems experienced the *Knox* has become one of the most useful and versatile classes of US warship. It is also the largest class of major combatants completed in the West in the postwar era, and would have been larger still but for the cancellation of ten ships authorised in FY 1968 to finance other programmes.

Below: USS *Downes* exemplifies the appearance of the Knox class with a Phalanx CIWS replacing the Mk 25 SAM launcher.

7 programme has meant a two-year gap between the completion of the first ship and the rest of the class, making it possible to iron out any problems experienced during trials with the first ship, and to incorporate any necessary modifications into the following units while building. Moreover, before even the lead ship had been completed, the individual systems with which she was to be equipped had already been tested on ships of other classes.

Like the frigates which preceded her, the *Oliver Hazard Perry* has a "second-class" propulsion plant on one screw. The layout is, however, much more compact than that of the *Knox* as a result of the adoption of gas turbines. Two LM2500s— the same model as that installed in the *Spruance*—are located side-by-side in a single engine room. Two small retractable propulsion pods fitted just aft of the sonar dome provide back-up during docking procedures, and these can drive the ship at 6 knots in an emergency.

The balance of the armament is more closely oriented to AAW than that of the *Knox*, which was a specialist ASW design. The FFG 7 has a Mk 13 launcher forward for Standard MR surface-to-air missiles and Harpoon anti-ship missiles, and an OTO-Melara 76mm (3-inch) quick-firing gun atop the bulky superstructure block. ASROC has been abandoned altogether, but there is a broad hangar aft for two LAMPS helicopters. The sonar, which is hull-mounted inside a rubber dome, is a new austere type which has neither the long range nor the multi-mode capability of the SQS-26 fitted to previous frigates. It is, however, envisaged that the FFG 7 would operate in conjunction with other frigates equipped with the SQS-26 and would receive target information from their sonars via data links.

Whereas the *Spruance* was designed to incorporate a large amount of space for future growth, the FFG 7 has been strictly tailored to accommodate only those systems envisaged in the near future. These include the SH-60 Seahawk LAMPS III (together with its RAST recovery system), the SQR-19 tactical towed array, fin stabilisers, a Link 11 data transfer system, and a single Phalanx CIWS gun. These items alone represent a lot of growth. Once these modifications have been made, however, there remains only a 50-ton margin for further growth, and if any additional items of equipment are to be fitted, others will have to be removed.

manpower requirements

Unlike its near-contemporary, the high-value *Spruance*, which had its own specialised production facility, the FFG 7 was designed to be built anywhere. Simple construction techniques were encouraged, making maximum use of flat panels and bulkheads, and passageways are generally straight. The hull structure can be prefabricated in modules of 35, 100, 200 or 400 tons, allowing the various shipyards to use the most convenient size. As a result the programme is running well to schedule with some units being delivered early, and costs have been kept remarkably close to the original estimates.

The application of the USAF-derived "fly-before-buy" concept to the FFG

Arleigh Burke

Completed: 1989-.
Names: DDG 51 *Arleigh Burke* plus another 17 planned and 11 proposed.
Displacement: 8,400t full load.
Dimensions: 466 oa x 60 x 30ft (142.1 x 18.3 x 9.1m).
Propulsion: 2-shaft COGAG; 4 LM2500 gas turbines, 80,000shp = 30+kts.
Armament: *AAW:* 2 Mk 41 Vertical Launch Systems (29x61) for Standard MR SM-2 missiles; 1 5-inch (127mm) Mk 45 (1x1); 2 20mm Phalanx Mk 16 CIWS (2x1).
ASW: ASROC missiles from Mk 41 launchers; 6 12.75-inch (324mm) torpedo tubes Mk 32 (2x3); provision for 1 SH-60B Seahawk helicopter.
SSM: 56 BGM-109 Tomahawk from Mk 41 launchers; 8 Harpoon (2x4).
Sensors: *Surveillance:* 4 SPY-1D, SPS-67(V).
Fire Control: Mk 99 MFCS with 3 SPG-62 radars, Seafire laser gun fire control, Mk 116 underwater weapons fire control.
Sonar: SQS-53C, SQR-19 TACTAS.

The proposed 29 Arleigh Burke class units are designed as guided-missile destroyer counterparts to the Ticonderoga class guided-missile cruisers in the AAW role, though useful anti-ship and anti-submarine capabilities are retained. The class is intended to replace the 1960s-vintage Adams and Coontz class DDGs from 1990, and retains good commonality with the Ticonderoga class (radar and powerplant) though at only some three-quarters of the cost through reduced radar capability, one-quarter fewer missiles, three rather than four missile illuminators, and lack of embarked helicopter and ASW command/co-ordination facilities. Recent operational experience by the US and British navies has resulted in reduced use of aluminium, and the introduction of 70 tons of Kevlar armor over vital spaces. The forward VLS has 29 cells, and that located aft has 61 cells for the careful blend of SAMs, SSMs and ASUWs. The omission of full helicopter facilities is now seen as a tactical limitation, and an Improved Arleigh Burke class is being designed to remedy this defect.

Below: Features of the Arleigh Burke class DDG are four forward-mounted planar arrays and VLS units fore and aft.

Brooke

FFG

Completed: 1966-8.
Names: FFG 1 *Brooke*; FFG 2 *Ramsey*; FFG 3 *Schofield*;
FFG 4 *Talbot*; FFG 5 *Richard L. Page*; FFG 6 *Julius A. Furer*.
Displacement: 2,640t standard; 3,245t full load.
Dimensions: 415 oa x 44 x 24ft (126.3 x 13.5 x 7.3m).
Propulsion: 1-shaft geared steam turbine; 35,000shp = 27kts.
Armament: *AAW:* single Mk 22 launcher (16) for Standard MR missiles;
1 5-inch (127mm) Mk 30.
ASW: ASROC launcher Mk 16 (reloadable in FFG 4-6);
1 SH-2F helicopter; 6 12.75-inch (324mm) torpedo
tubes Mk 32 (2x3).
Sensors: *Surveillance:* SPS-52D, SPS-10F.
Fire Control: 1 SPG-51C, Mk35.
Sonars: SQS-26AX.

The Brooke class is a Tartar modification of the Garcia class of ASW escorts.
The two classes share the same basic hull, single-shaft propulsion plant, and
general layout, but the *Brooke* has a single Mk 22 Tartar launcher in place of
the second 5-inch (127mm) Mk 30 of the *Garcia*.

The Mk 22 launcher has a single-ring magazine with a much-reduced
capacity of 16 rounds compared with the 40-round installation which is
standard to larger vessels. The above-water sensor outfit is also comparatively
austere; there is an SPS-52 3-D radar but no independent air search
antenna, and only a single SPG-51 tracker/illuminator. In spite of this

**Above: Compared with the Garcia class, the Brooke class has a Mk 22
single launcher in place of the after 5-inch gun.**

Congress baulked at the $11m increase in cost compared with the gun
armed *Garcia*, and rejected the proposal for a further 10 units in FY 1964.

Since completion, the Brooke class has undergone similar modifications

Garcia

FF

Completed: 1964-68.
Names: FF 1040 *Garcia*; FF 1041 *Bradley*;
FF 1043 *Edward McDonnell*; FF 1044 *Brumby*;
FF 1045 *Davidson*; FF 1047 *Voge*; FF 1048 *Sample*;
FF 1049 *Koelsch*; FF 1050 *Albert David*; FF 1051 *O'Callahan*.
Displacement: 2,620t standard; 3,400t full load.
Dimensions: 415 oa x 44 x 24ft (126.3 x 13.5 x 7.3m).
Propulsion: 1-shaft geared steam turbine; 35,000shp = 27kts.
Armament: *ASW:* ASROC launcher Mk 16 (1x8) reloadable in FFG
(1047-51). 1 SH-2F helicopter (except FF 1048, 1050)
6 12.75-inch (324mm) torpedo tubes Mk 32 (2x3).
AAW: 2 5-inch (127mm) Mk 30 (2x1).
Sensors: *Surveillance:* SPS-40, SPS-10.
Fire Control: Mk 35.
Sonars: SQS-26AXR (FF 1040-45) or
SQS-26BX (FF 1047-51), SQR-15 TASS
(FF 1048, 1050 only).

The Garcia-class ocean escort was evolved from the Bronstein design which,
although similar in size to contemporary European escorts, proved too small
for the US Navy. Improvements included a larger, flush-decked hull, a
heavier gun armament, and the provision of a hangar aft for DASH anti-
submarine drones. The last five units were also given a reload magazine for
ASROC at the forward end of the bridge, which has a distinctive sloping face
in these ships. The earlier units were initially fitted with two stern tubes for
Mk 25 torpedoes, but these have now been removed.

Only *Bradley* is thought to have operated DASH before the programme
was abandoned. All except *Sample* and *Albert David* (which are fitted instead
with a towed array) subsequently had their hangars enlarged and a
telescopic extension fitted to enable them to operate manned LAMPS

helicopters. This modification has brought with it a significant increase in
ASW capabilities.

A compact one-shaft steam propulsion plant employing pressure-fired
boilers was adopted to maximise the internal volume available for weapons

Bronstein

FF

Completed: 1963.
Names: FF 1037 *Bronstein*; FF 1038 *McCloy*.
Displacement: 2,360t standard; 2,650t full load.
Dimensions: 372 oa x 41 x 23ft (113.2 x 12.3 x 7m).
Propulsion: 1-shaft geared steam turbine; 20,000shp = 24kts.
Armament: *ASW:* ASROC launcher Mk 16 (1x8);
6 12.75-inch (324mm) torpedo tubes Mk 32 (2x3).
AAW: 2 3-inch (76mm) Mk 33 (1x2).
Sensors: *Surveillance:* SPS-40, SPS-10.
Fire Control: Mk 35.
Sonars: SQS-26, SQR-15 TASS.

The development of high-speed nuclear-powered submarines by the Soviet
Union in the late 1950s effectively outdated even those US Navy DEs which
were under construction at that time. The US Navy responded by designing
a new type of ocean escort radically different from its predecessors in every
respect. The result was the two ships of the Bronstein class.

Steam propulsion was adopted in place of the traditional diesels, although,
contrary to European practice, the single shaft of the DE was retained. The
most revolutionary feature of the design, however, was that the entire ship

was built around a first-class ASW outfit comprising the latest weapons and
sensors. The slim, tapered bow conceals a massive SQS-26 sonar dome,
which was originally to be matched with the ASROC anti-submarine missile
and a DASH drone, for which a flight deck was provided immediately abaft
the superstructure. When DASH was cancelled, however, the superstructure
arrangement proved too cramped to fit a hangar large enough to take a
LAMPS helicopter, and only ASROC and the triple Mk 32 tubes remain.

**Below: The two Bronstein class FFs were essentially prototypes with
bow sonar, Asroc and drone helicopters.**

Above: Though small, the Brooke class FFGs are useful AAW and ASW platforms for less intensive theaters.

to the Garcia. The two Mk 25 torpedo tubes initially incorporated in the stern have been removed and, following the abandonment of the DASH programme, the hangar has been enlarged and fitted with a telescopic extension to accommodate a LAMPS helicopter. Overall hangar dimensions are now 40-52ft by 15-17ft (12-15.8m x 4.4-5.1m).

In 1974 *Talbot* was refitted to evaluate various systems which were to be installed in the FFG 7, including the OTO Melara 76mm gun, the Mk 92 and STIR fire control systems, and the SQS-56 sonar. She has since reverted to her original configuration.

and electronics. The pressure-fired boilers proved complex to operate and maintain, however, and concern about the reliability of such a high-technology system—especially in a ship with only a single shaft—led to a reversion to conventional boilers in the succeeding Knox class.

Above left: The 10 units of the Garcia class were designed mainly for ocean escort with an ASW-optimized sensor/armament fit.

Above: USS *Davidson* (FF 1045) of the Garcia class.

The gun armament was on a par with previous DEs. A third 3-inch (76mm) gun on the low quarterdeck was removed in the mid-1970s to make room for a large towed array. The superstructure comprises a single compact block surmounted by a tall mack carrying the air search radar and ECM aerials.

Although unsatisfactory in some respects, these two ships set the pattern for all ocean escorts built for the US Navy over the next two decades.

Below: An elderly feature of the Bronstein class is the mounting for two 3-inch guns forward of the Mk 16 launcher.

Below: Despite their sleek lines, the two Bronstein class FFs lack the pace and seakeeping for ocean ASW work.

Pegasus

PHM

Completed: 1977-82.
Names: PHM 1 *Pegasus*; PHM 2 *Hercules*; PHM 3 *Taurus*;
PHM 4 *Aquila*; PHM 5 *Aries*; PHM 6 *Gemini*.
Displacement: 231t full load.
Dimensions: 132 x 28 x 6ft (40 x 8.6 x 1.9m).
Propulsion: (hullborne) 2 Mercedes-Benz diesels; 1600bhp = 12kts.
(foilborne) 1 General Electric gas-turbine;
18,000bhp = 40kts.
Armament: 8 Harpoon (2x4); 1 3-inch (76mm) Mk 75.
Sensors: *Fire Control:* 1 Mk 92 (Mk 94 in PHM 1).

The PHM was one of the four new designs in the "low" programme advocated in Zumalt's Project 60 (see Introduction). It was envisaged that squadrons of these fast patrol craft would be deployed at the various choke-points – in particular those in the Mediterranean and the NW Pacific – through which the surface units of the Soviet Navy needed to pass in order to reach open waters. High speed and a heavy armament of anti-ship missiles would enable the PHM to make rapid interceptions, and the relatively low unit cost meant that large numbers could be bought.

The Italian and Federal German Navies, with similar requirements in the Mediterranean and the Baltic respectively, participated in the development of the design. The Germans planned to build 12 units of their own in addition to the 30 originally projected for the US Navy.

Technical problems with the hydrofoil system resulted in cost increases, and opponents of the PHM programme, pointing to the limited capabilities of the design, tried to obtain cancellation of all except the lead vessel. Congress insisted, however, on the construction of the six units for which funds had already been authorised.

The propulsion system of the PHM comprises separate diesels driving two waterjets for hullborne operation and a single gas turbine for high-speed foilborne operation.

In order to fit in with the requirements of the NATO navies the OTO-Melara 76mm gun and a Dutch fire control system were adopted. The Mk 94 GFCS on *Pegasus* was bought direct from HSA but the Mk 92 systems on the other five are being manufactured under licence. The original anti-ship missile armament has been doubled, with two quadruple mounts replacing the four singles first envisaged.

Right: USS *Pegasus* shows off the hydrofoil's maneuverability and speed in benign sea conditions.

Below: USS *Aries* at speed, the two Mk 141 quadruple Harpoon launchers clearly visible over the stern.

Avenger

MCM

Completed: 1985-.
Names: MCM 1 *Avenger*; MCM 2 *Defender*; MCM 3 *Sentry*; MCM 4 *Champion*; MCM 5 *Guardian*; plus 9 planned.
Displacement: 1,040t full load.
Dimensions: 224 oa x 39 x 11.4ft (68.3 x 11.9 x 3.5m).
Propulsion: 2-shaft diesels; 4 Waukesha L-1616 or Isotta-Fraschini diesels; 2,400bhp = 14kts; plus 2 200hp electric motors for hovering.
Armament: 2 0.5-inch (12.7mm) machine-guns (2x1).
Sensors: *Surveillance:* SPS-55, SPS-56.
Sonar: SQQ-30 (SQQ-32 in later ships).

The Avenger class is planned as partial remedy for the US Navy's sadly declined mine countermeasures capability, the speciality of this class being harbor clearance in conjunction with MSH-type minehunters. Delay has resulted from continual tinkering with the design (wood hull and GRP superstructure), and the proposed 21 units have been trimmed to 14. As soon as possible the original diesels are to be replaced by low-magnetism Italian units, and the SQQ-30 variable-depth minehunting sonar superseded by the more capable SQQ-32 type, which will allow maximum use to be made of the five types of minesweeping gear (two acoustic, two magnetic and one mechanical) carried in addition to the EX 116 mine neutralization system. The ALQ-166 magnetic sweep vehicle is to be retrofitted.

Below: In definitive configuration the Avenger class has the gear for its SQQ-30 minehunting sonar forward of the bridge.

Blue Ridge

Completed: 1970-71
Names: LCC 19 *Blue Ridge;* LCC 20 *Mount Whitney.*
Displacement: 19,290t full load.
Dimensions: 620 oa x 82 wl, 108 upper deck x 27ft.
(188.5 x 25.3, 33 x 8.2m).
Propulsion: 1-shaft steam turbine; 22,000shp = 20kts.
Armament: 2 BPDMS launchers Mk 25
4 3-inch (76mm) Mk 33 (2x2).
Sensors: *Surveillance:* SPS-48, SPS-40, SPS-10.
Fire Control: 2 Mk 115, 2 Mk 35.

These two vessels were built to provide specialised command facilities for the amphibious fleets in the Pacific and Atlantic respectively. They replaced the more numerous war-built AGFs, which had inadequate speed for the new 20-knot amphibious squadrons. The basic design is that of the Iwo Jima-class LPH, with the former hangar occupied by command spaces, offices and accommodation. Prominent sponsons for LCPLs and ships' boats project from the sides, and the broad flat upper deck is lined with a

variety of surveillance, ECM/ESM and communications aerials. The LCCs are fitted with the Naval Tactical Data System (NTDS), the Amphibious Command Information System (ACIS) and the Naval Intelligence Processing System (NIPS). As completed, they had only two twin 3-inch (76mm) mountings for defence against aircraft, but two BPDMS launchers were added in 1974. Two utility helicopters are generally operated from the flight pad aft but there are no hangar or maintenance facilities.

The command facilities originally provided for a naval Commander Amphibious Task Group (CATG), a Marine Landing Force Commander (LFC), Air Control Group Commander, and their respective staffs, with accommodation for up to 200 officers and 500 enlisted men in addition to the 780-man crew.

There were plans for a third ship (AGC 21), which would have provided both fleet command and amphibious command facilities, but inadequate speed for fleet work was an important factor in her cancellation. With the demise of the Cleveland-class CGs fleet flagships in the late 1970s, however, *Blue Ridge* and *Mount Whitney* became flagships of the Seventh (W. Pacific) and the Second (Atlantic) Fleets respectively.

Below: USS *Blue Ridge* reveals her command function with sensor and communications antennae on the "flightdeck".

Tarawa

Completed: 1976-80.
Names: LHA 1 *Tarawa*; LHA 2 *Saipan*; LHA 3 *Belleau Wood*; LHA 4 *Nassau*; LHA 5 *Peleliu*.
Displacement: 39,300t full load.
Dimensions: 820 oa x 107 wl. 126 flight deck x 26ft (249 9 x 32.5, 38.4 x 7.9m)
Propulsion: 2-shaft geared steam turbines; 70,000shp = 24kts.
Armament: 2 BPDMS launchers Mk 25 (2x8); 3 5-inch (127mm) Mk 45 (3x1); 6 20mm (6x1).
Aircraft: 30 helicopters (CH-46D, CH-53D/E, AH-1T, UH-1N).
Troops: 2,000.
Landing-craft: 4 LCU, 2 LCM.
Sensors: *Surveillance:* SPS-52B, SPS-40B, SPS-10F. *Fire Control:* SPG-60, SPQ-9A, 2 Mk 115.

The last in a series of ocean-going amphibious vessels ordered during the 1960s, the Tarawa-class LHAs were to combine in a single hull capabilities which had previously required a number of separate specialist types – the LPH, the LSD, the LPD, the LCC and the LKA (see following entries). The result is a truly massive ship with more than twice the displacement of any previous amphibious unit and with dimensions approaching those of a conventional aircraft carrier. Nine ships were originally projected, to be constructed by means of advanced modular techniques at the same Litton/Ingalls yard that built the Spruance-class destroyers. In 1971, however, with the Vietnam War drawing to a close, the order was reduced to five, resulting in some financial penalties.

The increase in size of these ships is a direct consequence of the need to provide a helicopter hangar *and* a docking-well. The hangar is located directly above the docking-well; both are 268ft in length and 78ft wide (81.6 x 23.7m), and the hangar has a 20ft (6.5m) overhead to enable the latest heavy-lift helicopters to be accommodated. In order to maximise internal capacity the ship's sides are vertical for two-thirds of its length. Hangar capacity is greater than that of the Iwo Jima class, and all the helicopters can be struck down if necessary. The customary loading would include about 12 CH-46D Sea Knights, six of the larger CH-53D Sea Stallions, four AH1 SeaCobra gunships, and a couple of UH-1N utility helicopters. The Pacific-based ships have operated AV-8 Harriers and have their flight decks marked out accordingly. The flight deck is served by a side lift to port and a larger centre-line lift set into the stern. The latter can handle the new CH-53E Super Stallion heavy-lift helicopter.

The docking-well can accommodate four of the big LCUs, which can each lift three M-48 or M-60 tanks, or 150 tons of cargo. Two LCM-6 landing-craft, which can each carry 80 troops or 34 tons of cargo, are stowed immediately aft of the island and are handled by a large crane. The docking-well is divided into two by a central support structure incorporating a conveyor belt, which runs forward onto the vehicle decks. The conveyor belt is served by a group of three cargo elevators at its forward end, and by a further two elevators in the docking-well area. The elevators bring supplies for the landing force, stored in pallets each weighing approximately one ton, up from the cargo holds deep in the ship. The pallets are transferred to the landing-craft by one of 11 monorail cars which work overhead in the welldeck area. The after pair of elevators can also lift pallets directly to the hangar deck, where they are loaded onto transporters. An angled ramp leads from the hangar deck to the forward end of the island, enabling the

transfer of pallets to the flight deck for loading onto the helicopters.

Forward of the docking-well are the vehicle decks, interconnected by a series of ramps and able to accommodate some 200 vehicles. Tanks, artillery and trucks are generally stowed at the forward end, and up to 40 LVTP-7 amphibious personnel carriers, each with a capacity of 25 troops, can be accommodated. Eight LVTPs can be launched from the welldeck simultaneously with the four big LCUs.

Above the vehicle decks is the accommodation deck, with berths for some 2,000 troops in addition to the 900 crew. At the forward end there is a combined acclimatisation room/gymnasium, in which humidity and temperature can be controlled to simulate the climate in which the troops will be operating. At the after end there is a large, well equipped hospital, which can if necessary expand into accommodation spaces. Separate personnel elevators serve the hospital and the accommodation area, enabling rapid transfers to and from the flight deck.

The large block superstructure houses extensive command facilities, with accommodation for both the Commander Amphibious Task Group (CATG) and the Landing Force Commander (LFC) and their respective staffs. To enable these officers to exercise full tactical control over amphibious operations the LHAs are provided with a computer-based Integrated Tactical Amphibious Warfare Data System (ITAWDS), which keeps track of the position of troops, helicopters, vehicles, landing-craft and cargo after they leave the ship. The system also tracks the position of designated targets ashore, and aims and fires the ship's armament, which is orientated towards fire support and short-range anti-aircraft defence.

The versatility of the LHAs enables them to combine with any of the other amphibious types in the US Navy inventory. A typical PhibRon deployment would combine an LHA with an LPD and one/two LSTs. The only major limitation of the design appears to be the inability to accommodate more than one of the new air-cushion landing-craft (AALC) because of the layout of the docking-well.

Above: An LCM-6 is maneuvered off the stern well of USS *Tarawa*, which can accommodate 17 such craft.

Below: USS *Tarawa* reveals the capacious hull of her class, together with the extensive accommodation of her "island".

Iwo Jima

LPH

Completed: 1961-70.
Names: LPH 2 *Iwo Jima;* LPH 3 *Okinawa;* LPH 7 *Guadalcanal;* LPH 9 *Guam;* LPH 10 *Tripoli;* LPH 11 *New Orleans;* LPH 12 *Inchon.*
Displacement: 17,000t light; 18,300t full load.
Dimensions: 592 oa x 84 wl, 112 flight deck x 26ft (180 x 25.6, 34.1 x 7.9m).
Propulsion: 1-shaft geared steam turbine; 22,000shp = 20kts.
Armament: 2 BPDMS launchers Mk 25 (2x8); 4 3-inch (76mm) Mk 33 (2x2).
Aircraft: 25 helicopters (CH-46D, CH-53D, AH-1T, UH-1N).
Sensors: *Surveillance:* SPS-40, SPS-10. *Fire Control:* 2 Mk 115.

The US Marine Corps had initiated experiments in helicopter assault techniques as early as 1948, and in 1955 the former escort carrier *Thetis Bay* underwent a major conversion to test the "vertical envelopment" concept. Two years later the escort carrier *Block Island* was taken in hand for a similar conversion, but this was halted as an economy measure. The concept proved such a success, however, that the Navy embarked on a programme of new purpose-built helicopter carriers, which became the Iwo Jima class. As an interim measure three Essex-class carriers were modified for helicopter operations and reclassified as amphibious assault ships. These and the converted escort carriers took the "missing" LPH numbers in the series until their demise in the late 1960s.

As the ships of the Iwo Jima class were amphibious—not fleet—units, many of the refinements associated with first-line vessels were dispensed with in the interests of economy. The design was based on a mercantile hull with a one-shaft propulsion system capable of a sustained 20 knots. A large central box hangar was adopted with 20ft (6.5m) clearance, a capacity of about 20 helicopters, and with side lifts disposed *en echelon* at either end. The lifts, 50ft x 34ft (15.2 x 10.4m) and with a capacity of 44-50,000lb (20-22,725kg), can be folded upwards to close the hangar openings. Fore and aft of the hangar there is accommodation for a Marine battalion, and the ships have a well equipped hospital with 300 beds.

The flight deck is marked out with five helo spots along the port side and two to starboard. No catapults or arresting wires are fitted. Helicopter assault operations are directed from a specialised Command Centre housed in the island. The radar outfit is austere: air search and aircraft control antennae are fitted but these ships do not have the large 3-D antennae of the first-line carriers.

As completed, the *Iwo Jima* class had two twin 3-inch (76mm) mountings at the forward end of the island and two further mountings just below the after end of the flight deck. Between 1970 and 1974 the after port mounting and the first of the two forward mountings were replaced by BPDMS launchers.

From 1972 until 1974 *Guam* was test ship for the Sea Control Ship concept. In this role she operated ASW helicopters and a squadron of marine AV-8 Harrier aircraft. A new tactical command centre was installed and carrier-controlled approach (CCA) radar fitted. Although operations with the Harrier were particularly successful and have been continued on a routine basis in the larger Tarawa-class LHAs, the Sea Control Ship did not find favour with the US Navy, and *Guam* has since reverted to her assault ship role.

The Iwo Jima class generally operates in conjunction with ships of the LPD, LSD and LST types. Although *Inchon*, the last ship built, carries two LCVPs, the LPHs have no significant ability to land troops, equipment and supplies by any means other than by helicopter. The troops are therefore lightly equipped and would be employed as an advance echelon, landing behind the enemy's shore defences and relying on a follow-up frontal assault staged by more heavily equipped units brought ashore by landing-craft from the other vessels in the squadron.

Below: Derived from World War II escort carrier design, USS *Inchon* of the Iwo Jima class has two large deck-edge lifts.

LSD 41

LSD

Completed: 1984 onwards.
Name: LSD 41 *Whidbey Island*, LSD 42 *Germantown*, plus one building, 3 ordered.
Displacement: 11,140t light; 15,745t full load.
Dimensions: 609 oa x 84 x 20ft (185.6 x 25.6 x 5.9m).
Propulsion: 2-shaft diesels; 4 SEMT-Pielstick 16-cyl.; 34,000shp = 20kts
Armament: 2 Phalanx CIWS
Troops: 340.
Landing-craft: 4 LCAC.
Sensors: *Surveillance:* SPS-55.

The LSD 41 design was prepared in the mid-1970s as a replacement for the eight Thomaston-class ships. The project was subjected to delaying tactics by the Carter Administration pending a reassessment of the Navy's requirement for amphibious lift. In 1981, however, pressure from Congress compelled the Administration to order the prototype for the class, and nine follow-on ships are included in the first 5-year programme of the Reagan Administration.

Although not a particularly innovative design, the LSD 41 shows a number of improvements over its immediate predecessor, the Anchorage class. The large flight deck aft extends right to the stern, and is strong enough to accept the powerful CH-53E Super Stallion cargo-carrying helicopter now entering service with the Marines. The docking-well is identical in width to that of earlier LSDs but is 10ft (3m) longer than that of *Anchorage*. It is designed to accommodate four of the new air-cushion landing-craft (LCAC), with which it is intended to replace all conventional LCU-type landing-craft in the late

1980s. The two experimental craft at present being evaluated, the Jeff-A and Jeff-B AALCs, are 90ft (30.2m) and 87ft (26.4m) long respectively, and 47-8ft (14.3-14.6m) wide. Both have bow and stern ramps and can carry a single M-60 tank, with an alternative loading of six towed howitzers and trucks or 120,000lb (54,545kg) of cargo. This is a lower lift capacity than the conventional LCU, but the LCAC will compensate for this by carrying its load to the beach at a speed of 50 knots.

The LSD 41 is being built by modular construction techniques, and differs from previous amphibious vessels in adopting diesel propulsion in place of steam turbines. Four SEMT-Pielstick diesels manufactured under licence, are being installed in two independent paired units.

Below: The Whidbey Island class LSD has a forward-located superstructure and a massive docking well for LCACs aft.

Austin

LPD

Completed: 1965-71.
Names: LPD 4 *Austin;* LPD 5 *Ogden;* LPD 6 *Duluth;*
LPD 7 *Cleveland;* LPD 8 *Dubuque;* LPD 9 *Denver;*
LPD 10 *Juneau;* LPD 12 *Shreveport.*
LPD 13 *Nashville;* LPD 14 *Trenton;* LPD 15 *Ponce.*
Displacement: 10,000t light; 16,900t full load.
Dimensions: 570 oa x 84 x 23ft (173.3 x 25.6 x 7m).
Propulsion: 2-shaft geared steam turbines; 24,000shp = 20kts.
Armament: 4 3-inch (76mm) Mk 33 (2x2).
Aircraft: up to 6 CH-46D (see notes).
Troops: 840-930.
Landing-craft: 1 LCU, 3 LCM-6.
Sensors: *Surveillance:* SPS-40, SPS-10.

The Austin class is a development of the Raleigh class, which instituted the
LPD concept. The major modification was the insertion of a 50ft (15.2m) hull
section forward of the docking-well. This resulted in a significant increase in
vehicle space and cargo capacity (3,900 tons compared to only 2,000 tons
for the Raleigh class). The additional length available for flying operations
enabled a large telescopic hangar to be worked in immediately aft of the
superstructure, giving these ships the maintenance facilities which were
lacking in the Raleigh class. The main body of the hangar is 58-64ft (17.7-
19.5m) in length and 19-24ft (5.8-7.3m) in width; the telescopic extension
increases overall length to 80ft (24.4m).

Troop accommodation and docking-well capacity are identical to those of
Raleigh, except that LPD 7-13 are configured as amphibious squadron
(PhibRon) flagships and can accommodate only 840 troops. The latter ships
can be outwardly distinguished by their extra bridge level.

Two of the original four twin 3-inch (76mm) mountings, together with all
fire-control radars, were removed in the late 1970s. The class is scheduled
to receive two Phalanx CIWS guns as soon as these become available.

In October 1980 *Coronado* was temporarily redesignated AGF as a
replacement for the Command ship *La Salle* (see Raleigh class), which was
undergoing refit, but has since remained in that role.

**Above right: The flightdeck of USS *Shreveport* can handle a useful
number of CH-46 or CH-53 assault helicopters.**

**Right: A service life extension programme is to provide USS *Nashville*
and other Austin class LPDs with improved aviation facilities and
provision for two LCAC air-cushion vehicles.**

Anchorage

LSD

Completed: 1969-72.
Names: LSD 36 *Anchorage;* LSD 37 Portland; LSD 38 *Pensacola;*
LSD 39 *Mount Vernon;* LSD 40 *Fort Fisher.*
Displacement: 8,600t light; 13,700t full load.
Dimensions: 553 oa x 84 x 19ft (168.6 x 25.6 x 5.6m).
Propulsion: 2-shaft geared steam turbines; 24,000shp = 20kts.
Armament: 6 3-inch (76mm) Mk 33 (3x2).
Troops: 375.
Landing-craft: 3 LCU, 1 LCM-6.
Sensors: *Surveillance:* SPS-40, SPS-10.

The five dock landing ships of the Anchorage class were among the last units
to be completed in the large amphibious ship programme of the 1960s. In
spite of the advent of the LPD with its "balanced load" concept, there was
still a requirement for LSDs to carry additional landing-craft to the assault
area. The Anchorage class was therefore built to replace the ageing war-built
vessels, which had inadequate speed for the new PhibRons. It is a

development of the Thomaston class, from which its ships can be
distinguished by their tripod mast and their longer hull.

The docking-well measures 430ft by 50ft (131 x 15.2m)—an increase of
30ft (9m) in length over the Thomastons—and can accommodate three of
the big LCUs or nine LCM-8s, with an alternative loading of 50 LVTP-7s.
There is space on deck for a single LCM-6, and an LCPL and an LCVP are
carried on davits. As in the Thomaston class, there are vehicle decks above
the docking-well amidships, served by two 50-ton cranes. The Anchorage
class was designed to transport up to 30 helicopters, and there is a
removable flight deck aft for heavy-lift cargo helicopters.

The sensor outfit and armament are on a par with the contemporary LPDs
of the Austin class (which are described on pages 114-115). Four twin 3-
inch (76mm) mountings were originally fitted, but one was removed,
together with all fire control radars, in the late 1970s. The mountings
forward of the bridge are enclosed in GRP shields. Two Phalanx CIWS guns
will be fitted when the mounting becomes available.

**Below: Evident in this aerial view of USS *Pensacola* are the large
docking well of the Anchorage class LSD (with an LCU entering) and
the removable helicopter platform.**

Raleigh

Completed: 1962-63.
Names: LPD 1 *Raleigh*; LPD 2 *Vancouver*.
Displacement: 8,040t light; 13,900t full load.
Dimensions: 522 oa x 84 x 21ft (158.4 x 25.6 x 6.4m).
Propulsion: 2-shaft geared steam turbines; 24,000shp = 20kts.
Armament: 6 3-inch (76mm) Mk 33 (3x2).
Troops: 930.
Landing-craft: 1 LCU, 3 LCM-6.
Sensors: *Surveillance:* SPS-40, SPS-10.

Raleigh was the prototype of a new amphibious class employing the "balanced load" concept. Previous amphibious task forces carried troops in Attack Transports (APA), cargo in Attack Cargo Ships (AKA), and landing-craft and tanks in Dock Landing Ships (LSD). The basic principle of the "balanced force" concept is that these three capabilities are combined in a single hull. The docking-well in the Raleigh class therefore occupies only the after part of the ship, while forward of the well there are vehicle decks, cargo holds and substantial troop accommodation decks. The well itself measures 168ft x 50ft (51.2 x 15.2m) – less than half the length of the docking-well in the most modern LSDs – and is served overhead by six monorail cars, which load cargo into the awaiting landing-craft. The docking-well can accommodate one LCU and three LCM-6s, or four LCM-8s. Two further LCM-6s and four LCPLs are carried at the after end of the superstructure, and are handled by a large crane.

The docking-well is covered by a helicopter landing platform, which can receive any of the major types of helicopter in service with the Marines. The Raleigh class, unlike the later Austins, has no hangar or maintenance facilities and therefore relies on an accompanying LPH or LHA to provide helicopters for vertical assault operations. The flight deck can also be used as additional vehicle space, and there are ramps connecting the flight deck, the vehicle decks and the docking-well.

A third ship of the class, *La Salle*, serves as a Command Ship for the US Middle East Force. She was specially converted for this role and is now numbered AGF 3.

Below: USS *Raleigh* pioneered the concept of the LPD development of the LSD, but proved slightly too small.

Newport

Below: USS *Newport* and her sisters are the ultimate LSTs, but also feature a stern ramp for amphibious vehicles.

Completed: 1969-72.
Names: LST 1179 *Newport*; LST 1180 *Maniwotoc*,
LST 1181 *Sumter*; LST 1182 *Fresno*; LST 1183 *Peoria*;
LST 1184 *Frederick*; LST 1185 *Schenectady*;
LST 1186 *Cayuga*; LST 1187 *Tuscaloosa*;
LST 1188 *Saginaw*; LST 1189 *San Bernadino*;
LST 1190 *Boulder*; LST 1191 *Racine*;
LST 1192 *Spartanburg County*; LST 1193 *Fairfax County*;
LST 1194 *La Moure County*; LST 1195 *Barbour County*;
LST 1196 *Harlan County*; LST 1197 *Barnstable County*;
LST 1198 *Bristol County*.
Displacement: 8,342t full load.
Dimensions: 562 oa x 70 x 18ft (171.3 x 21.2 x 5.3m).
Propulsion: 2-shaft diesels; 6 GM (1179-81)/Alco (others);
16,500bhp = 20kts.
Armament: 4 3-inch (76mm) Mk 33 (2x2).
Sensors: *Surveillance:* SPS-10.

The twenty LSTs of the Newport class are larger and faster than the war-built vessels they replaced. In order to match the 20-knot speed of the other amphibious units built during the 1960s the traditional bow doors were suppressed in favour of a 112ft (34m) ramp which is lowered over the bows of the ship between twin fixed derrick arms. This arrangement also allowed for an increase in draught in line with the increase in displacement.

There is a large integral flight deck aft for utility helicopters. Pontoons can be slung on either side of the flight deck for use in landing operations. Each can carry an MBT and they can be mated with the stern gate. They are handled by twin derricks located immediately aft of the staggered funnel uptakes.

Below decks there is a total parking area of 19,000sq ft (5,300m²) for a cargo capacity of 500 tons of vehicles. The forecastle is connected to the vehicle deck by a ramp and to the flight deck by a passageway through the superstructure. A through-hull bow thruster is provided to maintain the ship's position while unloading offshore.

The twin 3-inch (76mm) gun mounts, located at the after end of the superstructure will be replaced by Phalanx CIWS guns when these become available.

In 1980 *Boulder* and *Racine* were assigned to the Naval Reserve Force.

Beech King Air

VC-6B

Origin: Beech Aircraft Corporation, Wichita, Kansas.
Type: VIP liaison transport.
Engines: Two 580ehp P&WC PT6A-21 turboprops.
Dimensions: Span 50ft 3in (15.32m); length 35ft 6in (10.82m); wing area 293.94sq ft (27.31m²).
Weights: Empty 5,778lb (2.621kg); loaded 9,650lb (4,377kg).
Performance: Maximum cruising speed 256mph (412km/h) at 12,000ft (3,660m); max rate of climb 1,995ft (596m)/min; service ceiling 28,100ft (8,565m); range with max fuel at max cruising speed with allowances, 1,384 miles (2,227km) at 21,000ft (6,400m) at 249mph (401km/h); typical field length, 3,500ft (1,067m).
Armament: None.
History: First flight (company prototype) 20 January 1964; VC-6A delivered to Air Force February 1966.

Development: The Model 90 King Air was essentially a Queen Air fitted with PT6 turboprop engines. With the B90 model the span was increased and gross weight raised considerably to take advantage of the power available. Large numbers of the original A90 series were bought by the Army, for many duties, but a single B90 was bought for the Air Force to serve as a VIP transport--a rare case of a single-aircraft buy of an off-the-shelf type. Originally designated VC-6A, it was later upgraded to VC-6B

Right: The Beech VC-6B is typical of twin-engined light transports that are frequently adopted by air arms for the military liaison and communications roles.

standard with small modifications. Tail number is 66-7943 and the aircraft serves with the 89th Military Airlift Group at Andrews AFB, near Washington, DC, as a unit of the 1254th Special Air Missions Squadron. Unlike previous King Air models the B90 is pressurized, and of course the VC-6B is fully equipped for flight in bad weather, by night or in severe icing conditions.

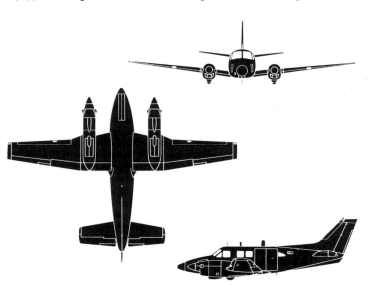

Beech Super King Air

C-12A, VC-12A

Origin: Beech Aircraft Corporation, Wichita, Kansas.
Type: Utility, VIP and mixed passenger/cargo transport.
Engines: Two 801ehp P&WC PT6A-38 turboprops.
Dimensions: Span 54ft 6in (16.61m); length 43ft 9in (13.34m); wing area 303sq ft (28.15m²).
Weights: Empty 7,800lb (3,538kg); loaded 12,500lb (5,670kg).
Performance: Maximum cruising speed, 272mph (437km/h) at 30,000ft (9,144m); service ceiling, 31,000ft (9,450m); range at maximum cruising speed, 1,824 miles (2,935km); TO/landing distances, about 2,800ft (850m).
Armament: None.
History: First flight (company prototype) 27 October 1972; first military contract, August 1974.

Development: For many years the top end of the Beechcraft range, and a Cadillac among propeller-driven executive aircraft, the T-tailed Super King

Air 200 has found wide acceptance among all the US armed forces. The Air Force purchased 30 of the initial military model, the C-12A, with engines of lower power than commercial and later military variants, resulting in reduced performance. Apart from the lower-powered engines the C-12A was basically an off-the-shelf aircraft for service in various liaison and transport roles. The cockpit is laid out for two-pilot operation, though the right seat may be occupied by a passenger. The main cabin is usually equipped for eight passengers, though other arrangements are in use, and conversion to cargo operation is quick and simple. Avionics are even more comprehensive than usual for a light twin, and provision is made in the baggage area in the rear fuselage for storing survival gear. The interior is fully pressurized and air-conditioned, and the wing and tail are deiced by pneumatic boots. Aircraft styled VC-12A are equipped for VIP duties, with the 89th Military Airlift Group at Andrews AFB, Maryland, adjacent to DC. Other C-12As are assigned to overseas HQs or embassies; for example at Ramstein AB, HQ of USAFE.

Below: The C-12 is a successful light transport in service with the US Army (C-12A, top) and US Air Force (VC-12A).

Bill Gunston, Assistant Compiler of *Jane's All the World's Aircraft*; author of many technical books and papers on military affairs.

Bell AH-IS HueyCobra

Type: Attack helicopter.

Engine: 1,800shp Lycoming T53-L-703 turboshaft.

Dimensions: Main-rotor diameter 44ft (13·4m); overall length (rotors turning) 52ft 11½in (16·14m); length of fuselage 44ft 5in (13·54m); height 13ft 5½in (4·1m).

Weights: Empty 6,598lb (2,993kg); maximum 10,000lb (4,536kg).

Performance: Maximum speed (TOW configuration) 141mph (227km/h); max rate of climb (SL, rated power) 1,620ft (494m)/min; service ceiling (rated power) 12,200ft (3,719m); hovering ceiling in ground effect, same; range (max fuel, SL, 8% reserve) 315 miles (507km).

Armament: M65 system with nose telescope sight and crew helmet sights for cueing and guiding eight TOW missiles on outboard under-wing pylons; chin turret (to 100th AH-1S) M28 with 7·62mm Minigun and 40mm M129 grenade launcher with 300 bombs, (from No 101) GE Universal turret with 20mm M197 three-barrel gun (or alternative 30mm); also wide range of cluster/fuel-air explosive and other weapons or five types of rocket fired from 7 or 19-tube launchers.

History: First flight 7 September 1965; combat service June 1967 (TOW-Cobra January 1973, AH-1S March 1977).

Development: First flown in 1965 after only six months of development, the HueyCobra is a combat development of the UH-1 Iroquois family. It combines the dynamic parts—engine, transmission, and rotor system—of the original Huey with a new streamlined fuselage providing for a gunner in the front and pilot above and behind him and for a wide range of fixed and power-aimed armament systems. The first version was the US Army AH-1G, with 1,100hp T53 engine, of which 1,124 were delivered, including eight to the Spanish Navy for anti-ship strike and 38 as trainers to the US Marine Corps. The AH-1Q is an anti-armor version often called TOWCobra because it carries eight TOW missile pods as well as the appropriate sighting system. Latest versions are the -1Q, -1R, and -1S, with more power and new equipment.

The US Army plans to upgrade many earlier models to -1S standard, which, with 324 new production aircraft, will give a total fleet of 982. Several hundred are already in service. Thus, the HueyCobra, developed in just six months in 1965, will remain in front-line service with the US Army well into the 1990s and probably beyond the year 2000.

Below: Revealed as an AH-1S by its flat-plate canopy, this HueyCobra shows off the family's remarkably slim fuselage and stub wings fitted with four weapon hardpoints.

Above: The US Marine Corps' AH-1W SuperCobra is the most capable current version, with two powerful engines for excellent performance carrying a versatile weapons load.

Bell UH-1H Iroquois (Huey)

XH-40, UH-1 Iroquois series (Models 204, 205 and 212)

Type: Utility helicopter.

Engine: Originally, one Lycoming T53 free-turbine turboshaft rated at 600-640shp, later rising in stages to 825,930, 1,100 and 1,400shp; (212) 1,800shp P&WC PT6T-3 (T400) coupled turboshafts, flat-rated at 1,250shp and with 900shp immediately available from either following failure of the other.

Dimensions: Diameter of twin-blade main rotor (204, UH-1B, C) 44ft 0in (13·41m), (205,212) 48ft 0in (14·63m) (tracking tips, 48ft 2¼in, 14·69m); (214) 50ft 0in (15·24m); overall length (rotors turning) (early) 53ft 0in (16·15m), (virtually all modern versions) 57ft 3¼in (17·46m); height overall (modern, typical) 14ft 4¾in (4·39m).

Weights: Empty (XH-40) about 4,000lb (1,814kg), (typical 205) 4,667lb (2,110kg), (typical 212) 5,549lb (2,517kg); maximum loaded (XH-40) 5,800lb (2,631kg), (typical 205) 9,500lb (4,309kg), (212/UH-1N) 10,500lb (4,762kg).

Performance: Maximum speed (all) typically 127mph (204km/h); econ cruise speed, usually same; max range with useful payload, typically 248 miles (400km).

Armament: See text.

History: First flight (XH-40) 22 October 1956, (production UH-1) 1958, (205) August 1961, (212) 1969.

Development: Used by more air forces, and built in greater numbers, than any other military aircraft since World War II, the "Huey" family of helicopters grew from a single prototype, the XH-40, for the US Army. Over 20 years the gross weight has been almost multiplied by three, though the size has changed only slightly. Early versions seat eight to ten, carried the occasional machine-gun, and included the TH-1L Seawolf trainer for the US Navy. Prior to 1962 the Army/Navy designation was basically HU-1, which gave rise to the name Huey, though the (rarely used) official name is Iroquois. Since 1962 the basic designation has been UH-1 (utility helicopter type 1).

In August 1961 Bell flew the first Model 205 with many changes of which the greatest was a longer fuselage giving room for up to 14 passengers or troops, or six litters (stretchers) and an attendant, or up to 3,880lb (1,759kg) of cargo. All versions have blind-flying instruments, night lighting, FM/VHF/UHF radios, IFF transponder, DF/VOR, powered controls, and searchlight. Options include a hook for a slung load, rescue hoist, and various fits of simple weapons or armor. Newest and most important of the Model 205 helicopters in US military service is the UH-1H, which remained in production until 1980. Ten have been converted as EH-1H Quick Fix EW (electronic-warfare) machines, but this role has been taken over by the more powerful EH-60A. Two were given augmented avionics and special equipment as UH-1V medevac transports.

Some 3,900 UH-1s are currently in US Army service; about 3,500 are the UH-1H model, which was introduced in 1967. Some 2,700 of the -1Hs are scheduled to remain in service beyond the year 2000 for a wide range of

duties, and apart from fitting glassfiber composite blades they will be completely upgraded with over 220 new items or improvements including a radar-warning receiver, chaff/flare dispenser, IR jammer, exhaust IR suppressor, radar altimeter, DME, and secure communications even in NOE (nap of the Earth) flying.

Above: The UH-1H was the most widely produced variant of the basic Huey, and has proved a highly adaptable tactical type.

Below: The 20th Special Operations Squadron is based in Florida with low-visibility UH-1N utility helicopters.

Bell OH-58C Kiowa

OH-58A to D and TH-57

Type: Light observation helicopter/Army Helicopter Improvement Program (AHIP).

Engine: (OH-58A, TH-57A) one 317shp Allison T63-700 turboshaft, (OH-58C) 420shp T63-720.

Dimensions: Diameter of two-blade main rotor 35ft 4in (10·77m); length overall (rotors turning) 40ft 11¾in (12·49m); height 9ft 6½in (2·91m).

Weights: Empty (C) 1,585lb (719kg), (D) 2,825lb (1,281kg); maximum (C) 3,200lb (1,451kg).

Performance: Maximum speed 139mph (224km/h); service ceiling (C) 19,000ft (5,791m); range (SL, no weapons, 10% reserve) 299 miles (481km).

Armament: Usually none (see text).

History: First flight (OH-4A) 8 December 1962, (206A) 10 January 1966, (production OH-58C) 1978, (AHIP) 1983.

Development: The loser in the US Army Light Observation Helicopter contest of 1962, the 206 was marketed as the civil JetRanger, this family growing to encompass the more powerful 206B and more capacious 206L LongRanger. In 1968 the US Army re-opened the LOH competition, naming Bell now winner and buying 2,200 OH-58A Kiowas similar to the 206A but with larger main rotor. Since 1976 Bell has been rebuilding 585 OH-58A Kiowas to OH-58C standard with uprated engine, flat-plate canopy to reduce glint, new instrument panel, improved avionics, and many minor improvements. Standard armament kit, not always fitted, is the M27 with a 7·62mm Minigun firing ahead.

In 1981 Bell was named winner of the AHIP (Army Helicopter Improvement Program) for a "near-term scout". The first of five prototype Model 406 AHIP machines flew in 1983. Features include a new rotor with four

composite blades driven by a much more powerful T63-type (Model 250) engine, very comprehensive protection systems, and a mast-mounted ball with TV and FLIR (forward-looking infra-red), laser ranger/designator, inertial navigation, and one or two pairs of MLMS missiles.

The AHIP will serve in air cavalry, attack helicopter, and field artillery units. One of its main tasks will be target acquisition and laser designation for Hellfire missiles, Copperhead, and other US Army/USAF laser-guided munitions. The number of OH-58As and -58Cs to be converted to AHIP standard has yet to be decided, but the first 16 were delivered in FY85. Yet another version, the Model 406CS (Combat Scout) is now flying.

Below: Rebuilt to AHIP standard with a four-blade rotor and over-rotor sensor mounting, the OH-58A becomes the OH-58D.

Boeing B-52 Stratofortress

B-52D, G and H

Origin: Boeing Airplane Company (from May 1961 The Boeing Company), Seattle, Washington.

Type: Heavy bomber and missile platform.

Engines: (D) eight 12,100lb (5,489kg) thrust P&WA J57-19W or 29W turbojets, (G) eight 13,750lb (6,237kg) thrust P&WA J57-43W or -43WB turbojets, (H) eight 17,000lb (7,711kg) thrust P&WA TF33-1 or -3 turbofans.

Dimensions: Span 185ft 0in (56.39m); length (D, and G/H as built) 157ft 7in (48.0m); (G/H modified) 160ft 11in (49.05m); height (D) 48ft 4½in (14.7m), (G/H) 40ft 8in (12.4m); wing area 4,000sq ft (371.6m²).

Weights: Empty (D) about 175,000lb (79,380kg), (G/H) about 195,000lb (88,450kg); loaded (D) about 470,000lb (213,200kg), (G) 505,000lb (229,000kg), (H) 505,000 at takeoff, inflight refuel to 566,000lb (256,738kg).

Performance: Maximum speed (true airspeed, clean), (D) 575mph (925km/h), (G/H) 595mph (957km/h); penetration speed at low altitude (all) about 405mph (652km/h, Mach 0.53); service ceiling (D) 45,000ft (13.7km), (G) 46,000ft (14.0km), (H) 47,000ft (14.3km); range (max fuel, no external bombs/missiles, optimum hi-alt cruise) (D) 7,370 miles (11,861km), (G) 8,406 miles (13,528km), (H) 10,130 iles (16,303km); takeoff run, (D) 11,100ft (3,383m), (G) 10,000ft (3,050m), (H) 9,500ft (2895m).

Armament: (D) four 0.5in (12.7mm) guns in occupied tail turret, MD-9 system, plus 84 bombs of nominal 500lb (227kg) in bomb bay plus 24 of nominal 750lb (340kg) on wing pylons, total 60,000lb (27,215kg); (G) four 0.5in (12.7mm) guns in remote-control tail turret, ASG-15 system, plus 8 nuclear bombs or up to 20 SRAM, ALCM or mix (eight on internal dispenser plus 12 on wing plyons); (H) single 20mm six-barrel gun in remote-control tail turret, ASG-21 system, plus bombload as G.

History: First flight 15 April 1952; later, see text.

Development: Destined to be the longest-lived aircraft in all aviation history, the B-52 was designed to the very limits of the state of the art in 1948-49 to meet the demands of SAC for a long-range bomber and yet achieve the high performance possible with jet propulsion. The two prototypes had tandem pilot positions and were notable for their great size and fuel capacity, four double engine pods and four twin-wheel landing trucks which could be slewed to crab the aircraft on to the runway in a crosswind landing. The B-52A changed to a side-by-side pilot cockpit in the nose and entered service in August 1954, becoming operational in June 1955. Subsequently 744 aircraft were built in eight major types, all of which have been withdrawn except the B-52D, G and H.

The B-52D fleet numbered 170 (55-068/-117, 56-580/-630 built at Seattle and 55-049/-067, 55-673/-680 and 56-657/-698 built at Wichita) delivered at 20 per month alongside the same rate for KC-135 tankers in support. The B-52G was the most numerous variant, 193 being delivered from early 1959 (57-6468/-6520, 58-158/-258 and 59-2564/-2602, all from Wichita), introducing a wet (integral-tank) wing which increased internal fuel from 35,550 to 46,575 US gal and also featured shaft-driven generators, roll control by spoilers only, powered tail controls, injection water in the leading edge, a short vertical tail, rear gunner moved to the main pressurized crew compartment and an inner wing stressed for a large pylon on each side. The final model, the B-52H, numbered 102 (60-001/-062 and 61-001/-040), and was essentially a G with the new TF33 fan engine and a new tail gun.

During the Vietnam war the B-52D was structurally rebuilt for HDB (high-density bombing) with conventional bombs, never considered in the original design. The wings were given inboard pylons of great length for four tandem triplets of bombs on each side, and as noted in the data 108 bombs could be carried in all with a true weight not the 'book value' given but closer to 89,100lb (40,400kg). Another far-reaching and costly series of structural modifications was needed on all models to permit sustained operations at low level, to keep as far as possible under hostile radars, again not previously considered. The newest models, the G and H were given a stability

Above: Even the B-52H model is becoming old, a condition signalled by practice for other roles such as minelaying.

Below: Six folded ALCMs on the starboard underwing pylon of a B-52G of 416th Bomb Wing at Griffiss AFB, New York.

augmentation system from 1969 to improve comfort and airframe life in turbulent dense air. From 1972 these aircraft were outfitted to carry the SRAM (Short-Range Attack Missile), some 1,300 of which are still with the SAC Bomb Wings. Next came the EVS (Electro-optical Viewing System) which added twin chin bulges. The Phase VI ECM (electronic counter-measures) cost $362.5 million from 1973. Quick Start added cartridge engine starters to the G and H for a quick getaway to escape missile attack. Next came a new threat-warning system, a satellite link and 'smart noise' jammers to thwart enemy radars. From 1980 the venerable D-force was updated by a $126.3 million digital nav/bombing system. Further major changes to the G and H include the OAS (offensive avionics system) which is now in progress costing $1,662 million. The equally big CMI (cruise-missile interface) will eventually fit the G-force for 12 AGM-86B missiles on the pylons, the first wing becoming operational in December 1982. In the late 1980s it is proposed to carry out further modifications to fit a Common Strategic Rotary Launcher (CSRL), which can carry SRAMs, ALCMs, advanced cruise missiles or free-fall nuclear bombs.

The last B-52D was retired in late 1983, leaving some 265 B-52Gs and Hs in SAC's active inventory, equipping 15 Bomb Wings, all with home bases in the continental USA. Large number are also in storage.

Below: Features of all B-52s, including this B-52H, are tandem landing gear, slim fuselage and twin-engine pods.

Boeing C-135 family

Origin: Boeing Airplane Company (from May 1961 The Boeing Company), Seattle, Washington.
Type: Tankers, transports, EW, Elint, command-post and rsearch aircraft.
Engines: (A and derivatives) four 13,750lb (6,273kg) thrust P&WA J57-59W or -43WB turbojets, (B and derivatives) four 18,000lb (8165kg) thrust P&WA TF33-3 turbofans, (RE) four 22,000lb (9,979kg) thrust CFM56-1B11 turbofans.
Dimensions: Span (basic) 130ft 10in (39.88m); length (basic) 134ft 6in (40.99m); height (basic) 38ft 4in (11.68m), (tall fin) 41ft 8in (12.69m; wing area 2,433sq ft (226m²).
Weights: empty (KC-135A basic) 98,466lb (44,664kg), (KC, operating weight) 106,306lb (48,220kg), (C-135B) 102,300lb (46,403kg); loaded (KC, original) 297,000lb (134,719kg), (KC, later max) 316,000lb (143,338kg), (C-135B) 275,000lb (124,740kg) (typical of special variants).
Performance: Maximum speed (all) about 580mph (933km/h); typical high-speed cruise, 532mph (856km/h) at 35,000ft (10.7km); initial climb (J57, typical) 1,290ft (393m)/min, (TF33) 4,900ft (1,494m)/min; service ceiling (KC, full load) 36,000ft (10.9km), (C-135B) 44,000ft (13.4km); mission radius (KC) 3,450 miles (5,552km) to offload 24,000lb (10,886kg) transfer fuel, 1,150 miles (1,950km) to offload 120,000lb (54,432kg); field length (KC, ISA+17°C) 13,700ft (4,176m).
Armament: None.
History: First flight 31 August 1956, variants see text.

Development: Boeing risked more than the company's net worth to build a prototype jetliner, first flown in July 1954. An important factor behind the gamble was the belief the USAF would buy a jet tanker/transport to replace the Boeing KC-97 family, and this belief was justified by the announcement of an initial order for 29 only three weeks after the company prototype flew, and long before it had done any inflight refuelling tests. The KC-135A Stratotanker differed only in minor respects from the original prototype,

Below: The KC-135 plays a key role in USAF operations, and many older aircraft are being upgraded to KC-135R standard.

whereas the civil 707 developed in a parellel programme was a totally fresh design with a wider fuselage, airframe of 2024 alloy designed on fail-safe principles and totally revised systems. The KC-135A was thus a rapid programme and deliveries began on 30 April 1957, building up to a frantic 20 per month and eventually reaching 732 aircraft.

The basic KC-135A has a windowless main fuselage with 80 tip-up troop or ground-crew seats and a cargo floor with tiedown fittings. Fuel is carried in 12 wing tanks and nine in the fuselage, only one of the latter being above the main floor (at the extreme tail). All but 1,000 US gal (3,785 lit) may be used as transfer fuel, pumped out via a Boeing high-speed extensible boom steered by a boom operator lying prone in the bottom of the rear fuselage. Only one receiver aircraft can be refuelled at a time, keeping station by watching rows of lights along the underside of the forward fuselage. The original short fin was later superseded by a tall fin and powered rudder, and many tankers were given an ARR (air refuelling receiver) boom receptacle. The KC force numbers 615 active aircraft in 35 squadrons, including 80 aircraft in Reserve units. The 100th ARW (Air Refuelling Wing) at Beale AFB exclusively uses the KC-135Q with special avionics and JP-7 fuel for the SR-71 aircraft.

MATS, now MAC, bought 15 C-135A and 30 C-135B Stratolifter transports, the Bs with fan engines with reversers and much sprightlier performance with less noise and smoke. These remained windowless but had the refuelling boom removed (though retaining the operator's blister) and were equipped for 126 troops or 89,000lb (40,370kg) cargo loaded through a large door forward on the left side. In MATS these aircraft were soon replaced by the C-141. The final new-build versions were the four RC-135A survey/mapping aircraft for MATS and ten RC-135B for strategic reconnaissance. Thus, total C-135 production for the USAF numbered 808, completed in February 1965.

Since then the family has swelled by modification to become perhaps the most diverse in aviation history, the following all being USAF variants: EC-135A, radio link (SAC post-attack command control system); EC-135B, AF Systems Command, ex-RIA (Range Instrumented Aircraft) mainly twice-rebuilt; EC-135C, SAC command posts; EC-135G, ICBM launch and radio link (with boom); EC-135H, airborne command posts; EC-135J, airborne command posts (Pacaf); EC-135K, airborne command posts (TAC); EC-135L, special SAC relay platforms; EC-135N, now C-135N, Apollo range, four with A-LOTS pod tracker; EC-135P, communications/command posts; KC-135A, original designation retained for SAC relay links; KC-135R, also RC-135R, special recon/EW rebuilds; NC-135A, USAF, NASA and AEC above-ground nuclear-test and other radiation studies; NKC-135A, Systems Command fleet for ECM/ECCM, laser, ionosphere, missile vulnerability, icing, comsat, weightless, boom and other research; RC-135B and C, recon aircraft with SLAR cheeks and other sensors; RC-135D, different SLARs and thimble noses; RC-135E, glassfibre forward fuselage and inboard wing pods; RC-135M, numerous electronic installations, fan engines; RC-135S, most M installations plus many others; RC-135T, single special SAC aircraft; RC-135U, special sensors and aerials cover almost entire airframe, including SLAR cheeks, extended tailcone and various chin, dorsal, ventral and fin aerials; RC-135V, rebuild of seven Cs and one U with nose thimble, wire aerials and ventral blades; RC-135W, latest recon model mostly rebuilt from M with SLAR sheeks added; WC-135B, standard MAC weather platforms.

Boeing E-4 AABNCP

E-4B

Origin: Boeing Aerospace Company, Kent, Washington.
Type: Advanced airborne command post.
Engines: Four 52,500lb (23,814kg) thrust General Electric F103-100 turbofans.
Dimensions: Span 195ft 8in (59.64m); length 231ft 10in (70.66m); wing area 5,500 sq ft (511m²).
Weights: Empty, not disclosed but about 410,000lb (186 tonnes); loaded 820,000lb (371,945kg).
Performance: Maximum speed, 700,000lb (317,515kg) at 30,000ft (9,144m), 602mph (969km/h); typical cruising speed, 583mph (939km/h) at 35,000ft (10,670m); maximum range with full tanks, 7,100 miles (11,426km); takeoff field length, ISA, 10,400ft (317m); cruise ceiling, 45,000ft (13,715m).
Armament: None.
History: First flight (747 prototype) 9 February 1969, (E-4A) 13 June 1973.

Development: This unique variant of the commercial 747 transport is being procured in small numbers to replace the various EC-135 airborne command posts of the US National Military Command System and SAC. Under the 481B AABNCP (Advanced Airborne National Command Post) programme the Air Force Electronic Systems Division awarded Boeing a contract in February 1973 for the first two unequipped aircraft, designated E-4A and powered by JT9D engines, to which a third aircraft was added in July 1973. E-Systems won the contract to instal interim equipment in these three E-4A aircraft, the first of which was delivered to Andrews AFB in December 1974. The next two were delivered in 1975.

The third E-4A differed in being powered by the GE F103 engine, and this

Boeing E-3 Sentry

E-3A

Origin: Boeing Aerospace Company, Kent, Washington.
Type: Airborne Warning and Control System (AWACS) platform.
Engines: Four 21,000lb (952kg) thrust P&WA TF33-100/100A turbofans.
Dimensions: Span 145ft 9in (44,42m); length 152ft 11in (46.61m); height 41ft 4in (12.6m) (over fin); wing area 3,050sq ft (283.4m²).
Weights: Empty, not disclosed but about 162,000lb (73,480kg), loaded 325,00lb (147,400kg).
Performance: Maximum speed 530mph (853km/h); normal operating speed, about 350mph (563km/h); service ceiling, over 29,000ft (8.85km); endurance on station 1,000 miles (1,609km) from base, 6h.
Armament: None.
History: First flight (EC-137D) 5 February 1972, (E-3A) 31 October 1975; service delivery (E-3A) 24 March 1977.

Development: The USAF had been one of the pioneers of overland surveillance platforms, mainly using EC-121 Warning Stars (based on the Super Constellation, and continuing in unpublicized service until almost 1980). During the 1960s radar technology had reached the point at which, with greater power and rapid digital processing, an OTH (over the horizon) capability could be achieved, plus clear vision looking almost straight down to detect and follow high-speed aircraft flying only just above the Earth's surface. One vital ingredient was the pulse-doppler kind of radar, in which the 'doppler shift' in received frequency caused by relative motion between the target and the radar can be used to separate out all reflections except those from genuine moving targets. Very clever signal processing is needed to eliminate returns from such false 'moving targets' as leaves violently distributed by wind, and the most difficult of all is the motion of the sea surface and blown spray in an ocean gale. For this reason even more clever radars are needed for the overwater mission, and the USAF did not attempt to accomplish it until quite recently.

While Hughes and Westinghouse fought to develop the new ODR (overland downlock radar), Boeing was awarded a prime contract on 8 July 1970 for the AWACS (Airborne Warning And Control System). Their proposal was based on the commercial 707-320; to give enhanced on-station endurance it was to be powered by eight TF34 engines, but to cut costs this was abandoned and the original engines retained thought driving high-power electric generators. The aerial for the main radar, back-to-back with an IFF (identification friend or foe) aerial and communications aerials, is mounted on a pylon above the rear fuselage and streamlined by adding two D-shaped radomes of glassfibre sandwich which turn the girdler-like aerial array into a deep circular rotordome of 30ft (9.14m) diameter. This turns very slowly to keep the bearings lubricated; when on-station it rotates at 6rpm (once every ten seconds) and the searchlight-like beam is electronically scanned under computer control to sweep from the ground up to the sky and space, picking out every kind of moving target and processing the resulting signals at the rate of 710,000 complete 'words' per second. The rival radars were flown in two EC-137D aircraft rebuilt from existing 707s, and the winning Westinghouse APY-1 radar was built into the first E-3A in 1975. The first E-3A force was built up in TAC, to support quick-reaction deployment and tactical operation by all TAC units. The 552nd AWAC Wing received its first E-3A at Tinker AFB, Oklahoma, on 24 March 1977, and went on operational duty a year later. Subsequently the 552nd have operated in many parts of the world. It was augmented from 1979 by NORAD (North American Air Defense) personnel whose mission is the surveillance of all North American airspace and the control of NORAD forces over the Continental USA.

From the 22nd aircraft in 1981 an overwater capability has been incorporated, and from No 24 the systems are to an upgraded standard linked into the JTIDS (Joint TActical Information Distribution System) shared by all US services as well as NATO forces which use 18 similar aircraft. The USAF total fleet is 34 aircraft: the first 24 E-3As are now being upraded to E-3B and the last 10 to E-3C standards.

Below: 71-1408 was the second of two EC-137D prototypes for the E-3 Sentry series, and was later designated an E-3A.

was made standard and subsequently retrofitted to the first two aircraft in December 1973 a fourth aircraft was contracted for, and this was fitted with more advanced equipment resulting in the designation E-4B. All AABNCP aircraft have been brought up to the same standard and are designated E-4B. The first E-4B (75-0125), the fourth in the E-4 series, was delivered on 21 December 1979. The E-4B has accommodation for a larger battle staff on its 4,620 sq ft (429.2m²) main deck, which is divided into six operating areas: the National Command Authorities area, conference room briefing room, battle staff, communications control centre and rest area. The flight deck includes a special navigation station (not in 747s) and crew rest area, essential for air-refuelled missions lasting up to 72 hours. Lobe areas under the main deck house technical controls and stores for on-board maintenance.

One of the world's most costly military aircraft types, the E-4B is designed for unique capabilities. its extraordinary avionics, mainly communications but including many other types of system, were created by a team including Electrospace Systems, Collins, Rockwell, RCA and Burroughes, co-ordinated by E-Systems and Boeing. Each engine drives two 150kVA alternators, and a large air-conditioning system (separate from that for the main cabin) is provided to cool the avionics compartments. Nuclear thermal shielding is extensive, and among the communications are an LF/VLF using a wire aerial trailed several miles behind the aircraft, and an SHF (super high frequency) system whose aerials are housed in the dorsal blister that was absent from the E-4A. Since November 1975 the sole operational management for the AABNCP force has been vested in SAC, and the main base is Offutt AFB, Nebraska, which is also home to the 55th Strategic Recon Wing, user of the EC-135 command posts. All four aircraft of the E-4B fleet are now in service and their Electro-Magentic Pulse (EMP)-protected electronic system represent a vital and unique C³ capability for the USA.

Left: 73-1676 was the first of three E-4A command post aircraft (seen here after upgrading to E-4B) to carry the president and other officials clear of nuclear devastation for the control of the USA's surviving military assets.

Boeing T-43

T-43A

Origin: The Boeing Company, Seattle, Washington.
Type: Navigator trainer.
Engines: Two 14,500lb (6,577kg) thrust P&WA JT8D-9 turbofans.
Dimensions: Span 93ft 0in (28.35m); length 100ft 0in (30.48m); wing area 980 sq ft (91.05m²).
Weights: Empty 64,090lb (29,071kg); loaded 115,500lb (52,391kg).
Performance: Maximum cruising speed 562mph (904km/h); normal cruising speed, about 464mph (747km/h) at 35,000ft (10.67km); range with MIL-C-5011A reserves, 2,995 miles (4,820km).
Armament: None.
History: First flight (737-100) 9 April 1967, (T-43A) 10 April 1973.

Development: Vietnam experience revealed a serious deficiency of facilities for training modern navigators, the only aircraft for this purpose being 77 T-29 piston-engined machines based on the immediate post-war Convair-Liner. In May 1971 the Air Force announced an $87.1 million order for 19 off-the-shelf Boeing 737-200s, with an option (not taken up) for a further ten. The 19 aircraft were delivered in the 12 months from June 1973, and all have since operated with the 323rd Flying Training Wing at Mather AFB, California. Numerous change orders were issued to the basic 737-200, though engines and equipment items are treated as commercial (there is no military designation for the JT8D). There is only a single door and nine windows along each side of the cabin, the floor is strengthened to carry heavy avionics consoles and operating desks, there are additional avionics aerials, and an 800 US-gal (3027 lit) auxiliary fuel tank is installed in the aft cargo compartment. In addition to the two pilots and supernumerary there are stations for 12 pupil navigators, four advanced trainees and three instructors. Training is given under all weather conditions and at all heights, with equipment which is often modified to reflect the conditions experienced in operational types.

Below: The T-43A is an extremely cost-effective way of training 16 high-quality navigators at the same time.

Boeing VC-137

VC-137B, C

Origin: The Boeing Company, Seattle, Washington.
Type: Special missions transport.
Engines: Four 18,000lb (8,165kg) thrust P&WA JT3D-3 turbofans.
Dimensions: Span (B) 130ft 10in (39.87m), (C) 145ft 9in (44.42m); length (B) 144ft 6in (44.04m), (C) 152ft 11in (46.61m); wing area (B) 2,433sq ft (226m²), (C) 3,010sq ft (279.64m²).
Weights: Empty (B) about 124,000lb (56,250kg), (C) about 140,500lb (63,730kg); loaded (B) 258,000lb (117,025kg), (C) 322,000lb (146,059kg).
Performance: Maximum speed (B) 623mph (1002km/h), (C) 627mph (1010km/h); maximum cruise, (B) 618mph (995km/h) (C) 600mph (966km/h); initial climb (B) 5,050ft (1539m)/min, (C) 3,550ft (1,082m)/min; service ceiling (B) 42,000ft (12.8km), (C) 38,500ft (11.73km); range, maximum payload, (B) 4,235 miles (6,820km), (C), 6,160 miles (9915km).
Armament: None.
History: First flight (civil -120B) 22 June 1960, (-320B) 31 January 1962.

Development: These aircraft bear no direct relationship to the prolific C135 family but were commercial airliners (hence the civil engine designation) bought off-the-shelf but specially furnished for the MAC 89th Military Airlift Group, based at Andrews AFB, Maryland, to fly the President and other senior executive officials. All have rear cabins with regular airline seating but a special midships HQ/conference section and a forward communications centre with special avionics in contact with stations on land, sea, in the air and in space. There are special security provisions. The two VC-137Bs were bought as early 707-153s with JT3C-6 engines and were redesignated on fitting turbofan engines. The first VC-137CC (62-6000), a much larger aircraft equivalent to a 707-320B, was the original Presidential Air Force One. It is now back-up to today's Air Force One, 72-7000.

Below: When fitted with TF33 turbofans the first VC-137A (and its two companions) were redesignated VC-137B.

Boeing Vertol H-46 family

CH-46 and UH-46 Sea Knight

Origin: Boeing Vertol, Morten, Pennsylvania.
Type: Transport, search/rescue, and minesweeping helicopter.
Powerplant: Two 1,250-1,870shp General Electric T58 turboshafts.
Dimensions: Diameter of each three-blade main rotor 50ft (15.24m); fuselage length 44ft 10in (13.66m); height 16ft 8½in (5.09m); total area of rotor discs 4,086sq ft (379.6m²).
Weights: Empty (CH-46D) 10,732lb (4,868kg), (CH-46E) 11,585lb (5,240kg); max loaded (D) 23,000lb (10,432kg), (E) 21,400lb (9,706kg).
Performance: Typical cruise 120mph (193km/h); range with 30min reserve (6,600lb, 3,000kg payload) 109 miles (175km), (2,400lb, 1,088kg payload) 633 miles (1,020km).
Armament: Normally none.
History: First flight (107) April 1958, (prototype CH-46A) 27 August 1959.

Development: In the mid-1950s Vertol (later Boeing Vertol) developed the twin-turbine Model 107. From this the H-46 series, named Sea Knight in US service, was developed as a Marine Corps assault transport carrying 25 equipped troops or cargo payloads up to 7,000lb (3,175kg), with water landing and takeoff capability.

Of all-metal construction, the H-46 has the engines installed on each side of the large fin-like rear rotor pylon, a large unobstructed rectangular cabin, integrated cargo loading systems, full all-weather navaids, fixed twin-wheel tricycle landing gears and power-folding blades on the tandem rotors. Total deliveries amounted to 624, completed in 1970.

The basic CH-46 fleet is being updated with approximately 3,000 glassfiber rotor blades, uprated T58-16 engines of 1,870shp,

Above: Older CH-46 helicopters are being upgraded to CH-46E by the US Navy using Boeing-supplied kits.

crash-attenuating crew seats, combat-resistant fuel system and improved rescue gear. The new helicopter is designated CH-46E. Conversions are being done "in house" by Naval Air Systems Command with the aid of 345 update kits being supplied during 1985-88. A dedicated SAR (search and rescue) model is HH-46, while the US Navy uses the UH-46 for ship replenishment. Small numbers were delivered of the RH-46A for MCM (mine countermeasures).

Boeing Vertol CH-47D Chinook

CH-47A, B, C and D Chinook (data for D)

Type: Medium transport helicopter.
Engines: Two 3,750shp Lycoming T55-L-11A free-turbine turboshafts.
Dimensions: Diameter of main rotors 60ft (18·29m); length, rotors turning, 99ft (30·2m); length of fuselage 51ft (15.54m); height 18ft 7in (5·67m).
Weights: Empty 20,616lb (9,351kg); loaded (condition 1) 33,000lb (14,969kg); (overload condition II) 46,000lb (20,865kg).
Performance: Maximum speed (condition I) 189mph (304km/h); (II) 142mph (229km/h); initial climb (I) 2,880ft (878m)/min; (II) 1,320ft (402m)/min; service ceiling (I) 15,000ft (4,570m); (II) 8,000ft (2,440m); mission radius, cruising speed and payload (I) 115 miles (185km) at 158mph (254km/h) with 7,262lb (3,294kg); (II) 23 miles (37km) at 131mph (211km/h) with 23,212lb (10,528kg).
Armament: Normally none.
History: First flight (YCH-47A) 21 September 1961, (CH-47C) 14 October 1967, (D) 11 May 1979.

Development: Development of the Vertol 114 began in 1956 to meet the need of the US Army for a turbine-engined all-weather cargo helicopter able to operate effectively in the most adverse conditions of altitude and temperature. Retaining the tandem-rotor configuration, the first YCH-47A flew on the power of two 2,200shp Lycoming T55 turboshaft engines and led directly to the production CH-47A. With an unobstructed cabin 7½ft (2·29m) wide, 6½ft (1·98m) high and over 30ft (9·2m) long, the Chinook proved a valuable vehicle, soon standardized as US Army medium helicopter

and deployed all over the world. By 1972 more than 550 had served in Vietnam, mainly in the battlefield airlift of troops and weapons but also rescuing civilians (on one occasion 147 refugees and their belongings were carried to safety in one Chinook) and lifting back for salvage or repair 11,500 disabled aircraft valued at more than $3,000 million. The A model gave way to the CH-47B, with 2,850hp engines and numerous improvements. Since 1967 the standard basic version has been the CH-47C, with much greater power and increased internal fuel capacity. Most exports by BV are of this model, which in 1973 began to receive a crashworthy fuel system and integral spar inspection system.

In the late 1970s there was a resurgence of orders, and by 1981 they were nearing 1,000, with many new customers. Argentina's Type 308 is an Antarctic logistic/rescue machine with radar, duplex inertial navigation and range of 1,265 miles (2,036km). Canada's CH-147s have many advanced features, but the 33 Chinook HC.1 transports of the RAF are to an even later standard with 44 seats or 24 stretcher casualties, triple cargo hooks (front and rear, 20,000lb, 9,072kg; center at 28,000lb, 12,700kg), Decca TacNav, doppler and area navigation, new cockpit lighting, L-11E engines driving folding glass/carbon-fiber blades and amphibious capability in Sea State 3.

Development work on the RAF Chinook has led to the CH-47D for the US Army. The first 436 D models will be converted from older machines, but these will be followed by 91 new-builds, for a total inventory of 527. These feature 3,750shp L-712 long-life engines, 7,500shp transmission, redundant and uprated electrics, glassfiber blades, modular hydraulics, triple cargo hook, advanced light control system, new avionics, single-point fueling, survivability gear, and T62 APU.

Below: The CH-47D is the US Army's most capable and versatile medium-lift helicopter, the twin-rotor design allowing the carriage of a considerable slung load (including artillery) or 44 fully equipped troops embarked in the cabin.

British Aerospace AV-8 Harrier I

AV-8A, TAV-8A and AV-8C

Origin: British Aerospace, UK.
Type: Single-seat attack and close-support, (TAV) dual combat-capable trainer.
Powerplant: One 21,500lb (9,752kg) Rolls-Royce Pegasus 103 vectored-thrust turbofan.
Dimensions: Span 25ft 3in (7.7m); length 45ft 7in (13.89m); height 11ft 4in (3.45m); wing area 201.1sq ft (18.68m²).
Weights: Empty (AV) 12,020lb (5,452kg); maximum (not VTOL) 25,000lb (11,340kg).
Performance: Maximum speed (SL, clean) over 737mph (1,186km/h); dive Mach limit, 1.3; time from vertical lift-off to 40,000ft (12.2km) 2min 23s; range with one inflight refuelling, over 3,455 miles (5,560km).
Armament: Two 30mm Aden gun each with 130 rounds; external weapon load of up to total of 5,000lb (2,270kg) including bombs, Paveway smart bombs, Mavericks, cluster dispenser, rocket launcher and Sidewinder AAMs.
History: First flight (AV-8A) August 1970, (AV-8C) May 1979.

Development: Adopted in 1969 by the US Marine Corps as a close-support multirole aircraft of use in amphibious assaults, the AV-8A is a slightly Americanized and simplified version of the RAF Harrier GR.3, lacking the latter's inertial navigation and laser nose but with certain US equipment specified by the customer. A total of 102 were supplied, together with eight TAV-8A dual trainers, deliveries beginning in January 1971. Units equipped have always been the training squadron, VMA(T)-203 at MCAS Cherry Point and three combat squadrons, VMA-231, 513 and 542. Attrition has at times been severed, mainly through reasons other than failures of the aircraft, and prolonged and generally very successful operations have been mounted from every kind of ship and shore airfield. In 1979-84 a total of 47 AV-8As have been upgraded to AV-8C standard with life-improving strakes and retractable flap under the fuselage, a liquid-oxygen system, secure voice radio and improved UHF, passive radar receivers facing to front and rear and a flare/chaff dispenser. The C-model was the standard USMC Harrier until the arrival of the Harrier II.

Below: The AV-8 is essentially an Americanized version of the Harrier GR.3 'bomb truck' with greater air-combat power.

Cessna O-2 Skymaster

Model 337, O-2A

Origin: Cessna Aircraft Company, Wichita, Kansas.
Type: Forward air control and reconnaissance.
Engines: Tandem 210hp Continental IO-360C six-cylinder.
Dimensions: Span 38ft 2in (11.63m); length 29ft 9in (9.07m); wing area 202.5sq ft (18.8m²).
Weights: Empty 2,848lb (11,292kg); loaded (max) 5,400lb (2,448kg).
Performance: Maximum speed 200mph (322km/h); cruising speed 144mph (232km/h); initial climb 1,180ft (360m)/min; service ceiling 18,000ft (5,490m); takeoff or landing over 50ft (15m), 1,675ft (510m); range with max fuel, 1,325 miles (2,132km).
Armament: Can carry underwing 7.62mm Minigun pod, light rockets or other light ordnance.
History: First flight (337 prototype) 28 February 1961, (O-2A) early 1967.

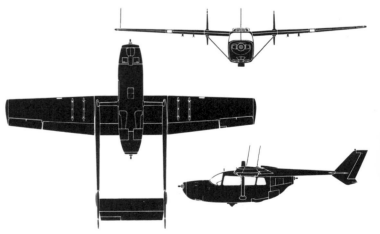

Above: Three-view of the standard Cessna O-2A.

Below: O-2A of the 22nd Tactical Aircraft Support Squadron.

Development: The USAF placed a contract with Cessna for a military version of the Model 337 Skymaster 'push/pull' twin to supplement and then replace the single-engined O-1. Features included side-by-side dual controls for pilot and observer (the latter having extra windows low on the right side), four underwing pylons for flares or many other loads, and extensive navaids and communications systems. By 1971 a total of over 350 had been delivered, plus some 160 O-2B spy-war aircraft. Today large numbers of O-2A serve in utility and FAC rfoles with TAC's 24th CW at Howard AFB, Canal Zone, 507th TACW at Shaw AFB, SC, and 602nd TACW at Bergstrom, Texas; USAFE's 601st TCW at Sembach; Alaska's 25th TASS at Eielson AFB; and in the following ANG units: 105th TASW, White Plains, NY; 110th TASG, Battle Creek, Mich; 111th TASG, Willow Grove, Pa; 115th TASW, Traux Field, Wis; 163rd TASG, Ontario, Calif; and 182nd TASG, Peoria, Ill.

Cessna T-37

Model 318, T-37B, A-37B Dragonfly

Origin: Cessna Aircraft Company, Wichita, Kansas.
Type: T-37, primary trainer; A-37, light attack.
Engines: (T) two 1,025lb (465kg) thrust Teledyne CAE J69-25 turbojets, (A) two 2,850lb (1293kg) thrust General Electric J85-17A turbojets.
Dimensions: Span (T) 33ft 9.3in (10.3m), (A, over tanks) 35ft 10.5in (10.93m); length (T) 29ft 3in (8.92m), (A, excl refuelling probe) 28ft 3.25in (8.62m); wing area 183.9 sq ft (17.09m²).
Weights: Empty (T) 3,870lb (1,755kg), (A) 6,211lb (2,817kg); loaded (T) 6,600lb (2,993kg) (A) 14,000lb (6,350kg).
Performance: Maximum speed (T) 426mph (685km/h), (A) 507mph (816km/h); normal cruising speed (T) 380mph (612km/h), (A, clean) 489mph (787km/h); initial climb (T) 3,020ft (920m)/min, (A) 6,990ft (2130m)/min; service ceiling (T) 35,100ft (10,700m), (A) 41,765ft (12,730m); range (T, 5% reserves, 25,000ft/7,620m cruise) 604 miles (972km), (A, max fuel, four drop tanks) 1,012 miles (1628km), (A, max payload including 4,100lb/1860kg ordnance) 460 miles (740km).
Armament: (T) None, (A) GAU-2B/A7.62mm Minigun in fuselage, eight underwing pylons (four inners 870lb/394kg each, next 600lb/272kg and outers 500lb/227kg) for large number of weapons, pods, dispensers, clusters, launchers or recon/EW equipment.
History: First flight (T) 12 October 1954, (A) 22 October 1963.

Development: After prolonged study the Air Force decided in 1952 to adopt a jet primary pilot trainer, and after a design competition the Cessna Model 318 was selected. Features included all-metal stressed-skin construction, side-by-side seating in a cockpit with ejection seats and a single broad clamshell canopy, two small engines in the wing roots with nozzles at the trailing edge, fixed tailplane half-way up the fin, manual controls with electric trim, hydraulic slotted flaps and hydraulic tricycle landing gear of exceptional track but short length, placing the parked aircraft low on the ground. The introduction was delayed by numerous trivial modifications and even when service use began in 1957 pupils were first trained on the T-34. Altogether 534 T-37As were built, but all were brought up to the standard of the T-37B, of 1959, which had more powerful J69 engines, improved radio, navaids and revised instrument panel. After 41 had been converted to A-37As further T-37As were bought in 1957 to bring the total of this model to 447. They serve in roughly equal numbers with the advanced T-38A at all the USAF's pilot schools: 12th Flying Training Wing at Randolph; 14th at Columbus (Miss); 47th at Laughlin; 64th at Reese; 71st at Vance; 80th at Sheppard and 82nd at Williams.

The A-37 was derived to meet a need in the early 1960s for a light attack aircraft to fly Co-In (counter-insurgent) missions. Cessna had previously produced two T-37C armed trainers (many of this model were later supplied to Foreign Aid recipients, including South Vietnam in the 1960s), and later these aircraft were then rebuilt as AT-37 prototypes (designation YAT-37D) with much more powerful engines and airframes restressed for increased weights which, in stages, were raised to 14,000lb (6,350kg). No fewer than eight underwing pylons plus wingtip tanks were added, giving a great weapon-carrying capability whilst offering performance significantly higher than that of the trainer. Redesignated A-37A, a squadron converted from T-37Bs on the production line was evaluated in Vietnam in 1967. Altogether 39 A-37As were built by converting T-37Bs on the line, followed by 511 of the regular USAF production model with full-rated J85 engines, 6g structure, flight-refuelling probe, greater internal tankage and other changes. The A-37 Dragonfly proved valuable in south-east Asia, where many were left in South Vietnamese hands after the US withdrawal. After the end of the US involvement the A-37B was withdrawn from regular USAF service but it continues to equip a Reserve wing and two Air National Guard groups. The AFR's 434th TFW flies the A-37B at Grissom AFB, Bunker Hill, Indiana, and the ANG units are the 174th TFG (Syracuse, NY) and the 175th (Baltimore, Md).

Below: Though still a useful light attack aircraft, the armed A-37B is now used mainly for the second-line FAC role.

Bottom: The problems of the Northrop T-46 have further extended the use and life of the side-by-side T-37B trainer in widespread service with Air Training Command.

Cessna T-41

Model 172, T-41A Mescalero, T-41C.

Origin: Cessna Aircraft Company, Wichita, Kansas.
Type: Primary pilot trainer.
Engine: (A) one 150hp Lycoming O-320-E2D, (C) 210hp Continental IO-360-D.
Weights: Empty (A) 1,363lb (618kg); loaded (A) 2,300lb (1,043kg).
Performance: Maximum speed (A) 144mph (232km/h), (C) 153mph (246km/h); maximu mcruising speed (A) 138mph (22km/h), (C) 145mph (233km/h); initial climb (A) 645ft (196m)/min, (C) 880ft (268m)/min; service ceiling (A) 13,100ft (3,995m), (C) 17,000ft (5,180m).

Armament: None
History: First flight (civil 172) 1955, (T-41A) August 1964.

Development: The high cost of pupil wastage (failure) in all-jet training prompted the Air Force to reconsider its policy, and in July 1964, after two years of study, the decision was taken to introduce a light piston-engined machine for initial training, to weed out pupils with an initial 30h at relatively low cost. The Model 172 was picked off-the-shelf, and 170 were ordered as the T-41A Mescalero, total orders to date being 237 (the last in 1973). Joint civil/military serials are carried, without national insignia, and the USAF aircraft are operated by eight civilian contract schools located near USAF undergraduate pilot schools. In addition 52 more powerful T-41Cs were purchased for cadet training at the Air Force Academy at Colorado Springs. These resemble the civil 172E but have fixed-pitch propellers.

Right: This T-41C carries dual civil and military serials, and is operated by the 557th Flying Training Squadron, the air component of the Air Force Academy at Colorado Springs.

Below: Three-view of the Cessna T-41A Mescalero.

de Havilland Canada C-7

DHC-4 C-7A, C-7B

Origin: The de Havilland Aircraft of Canada, Toronto.
Type: STOL tactical transport.
Engines: Two 1,450hp Pratt & Whitney R-2000-7M2 Twin Wasp 14-cylinder.
Weights: Empty (A) 16,795lb (7,618kg), (B) 18,260lb (8,283kg); loaded (A) 26,000lb (11,794kg), (B) 31,300lb (14,198kg).
Performance: Maximum speed 216mph 9348km/h); typical cruising speed, 182mph (293km/h); initial climb 1,355ft (413m)/min; service ceiling, (A) 27,700ft (8,443m), (B) 24,800ft (7,559m); range (B) from 242 miles (389km) with max payload of 8,40lb (3,964kg) to 1,307 miles (2,103km) with maximum fuel; takeoff or landing over 50ft (15m), about 1,200ft (366m).
Armament: None.
History: First flight 30 July 1958; service delivery (US Army inventory) January 1961.

Development: A specialized STOL (short takeoff and landing) transport aimed mainly at the military market, the piston-engined Caribou has a fairly small interior roughly with the capacity and load capability of a C-47 (DC-3) but with a full-section rear loading ramp which can also be used for air dropping. Features include high-lift flaps, manual controls from a dual

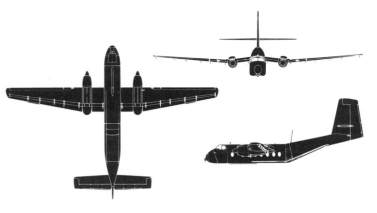

Above: Three-view of the DHC C-7A (withour radar).

cockpit, nose radar and pneumatic boot deicers on all leading edges. The US Army purchased 159 of which the final 103 were to a later standard with increased weight. Normal loads included 32 troops or two Jeeps or similar small vehicles. In 1967, at the height of their involvement in Vietnam, a political decision transferred these aircraft to the Air Force. The last C-7 unit was the ANG's 135th TAG, but a few are still flying.

Below: C-7A of the 94th TAW at Dobbins AFB, Georgia.

Fairchild A-10 Thunderbolt II

A-10A, A-10/T, A-10/NAW

Origin: Fairchild Republic Company, Farmingdale, NY.
Type: Close-support attack aircraft.
Engines: Two 9,065lb (4,112kg) thrust General Electric TF34-100 turbofans.
Dimensions: Span 57ft 6in (17.53m); length 53ft 4in (16.26m); height (regular) 14ft 8in (4.47m), (NAW) 15ft 4in (4.67m); wing area 506sq ft (47m²).
Weights: Empty 21,519lb (9761kg); forward airstrip weight (no fuel but four Mk 82 bombs and 750 rounds) 32,730lb (14,846kg); maximum 50,000lb (22,680kg). Operating weight empty, 24,918lb (11,302kg), (NAW) 28,630lb (12,986kg).
Performance: Maximum speed, (max weight, A-10A) 423mph (681km/h), (NAW) 420mph (676km/h); cruising speed at sea level (both) 345mph (555km/h); stabilized speed below 8,000ft (2,440m) in 45° dive at weight 35,125lb (15,932kg), 299mph (481km/h); maximum climb at basic design weight of 31,790lb (14,420kg), 6,000ft (1,828m)/min; service ceiling, not stated; takeoff run to 50ft (15m) at maximum weight, 4,000ft (1,220m); operating radius in CAS mission with 1.8 hour loiter and reserves, 288 miles (463km); radius for single deep strike penetration, 620 miles (1,000km); ferry range with allowances, 2,542 miles (4091km).
Armament: One GAU-8/A Avenger 30mm seven-barrel gun with 1,174 rounds, total external ordnance load of 16,000lb (7,257kg) hung on 11 pylons, three side-by-side on body and four under each wing; several hundred combinations of stores up to individual weight of 5,000lb (2,268kg) with maximum total weight 14,638lb (6,640kg) with full internal fuel.
History: First flight (YA-10A) 10 May 1972; (production A-10A) 21 October 1975, (NAW) 4 May 1979.

Development: After prolonged study of lightweight Co-In and light armed reconnaissance aircraft the Air Force in 1967 initiated the A-X programme for a new-generation CAS (close air support) aircraft. It had never had such

an aircraft, this mission being previously flown by fighters, bombers, attack and even FAC platforms, including such diverse types as the F-105 and A-1. Emphasis in A-X was not on speed but on lethality against surface targets (especially armour), survivability against ground fire (not including SAMs), heavy ordnance load and long mission endurance. Low priority was paid to advanced nav/attack avionics, the fit being officially described as 'austere'.

Below: The A-10A can carry a magnificent weapons load (here just a quartet of AGM-65 Mavericks) and loiter for extended periods over the battlefield, but is considered too slow.

Fairchild C-123 Provider

C-123K

Origin: Fairchild Engine and Airplane Corporation, Hagerstown, Md (now Fairchild Republic Company, Farmingdale, NY).
Type: Tactical airlift transport.
Engines: Two 2,500hp Pratt & Whitney R-2800-99W Double Wasp 18-cylinder plus two 2,850lb (1,293kg) thrust GE J85-17 auxiliary turbojets.
Dimensions: Span 110ft 0in (33.53m); length 76ft 3in (23.92m); wing area 1,223sq ft (113.6m²).
Weights: Empty 35,366lb (16,042kg); loaded 60,000lb (27,216kg).
Performance: Maximum speed (with jets) 228mph (367km/h); maximum cruising speed, 173mph (278km/h); initial climb (no jets) 1,150ft (351m)/min; service ceiling 29,000ft (8,839m); range with maximum payload of 15,000lb (6,804kg), 1,035 miles (1,666km).
Armament: None.
History: First flight (XC-123) 14 October 1949, (K) 27 May 1966.

Development: The history of this tactical transport goes back to Chase Aircraft, of Trenton, NJ. Here the largest of a series of advanced stressed-skin transports and gliders (including a four-jet transport) was designed by M. Stoukoff in 1949, won an Air Force order for 300 but fell down when Kaiser-Frazer failed to build them. Fairchild stepped in, bought Chase and delivered the 300 on schedule. So good were these machines that they were updated in many ways, the final C-123K model having underwing-jet pods.

Typical loads include trucks, artillery, 61 troops or 50 litter (stretcher) patients with six sitting wounded and six attendants. The last units to be equipped with the C-123K were two AFRES units, 302nd TAW (Rickenbaker AFB, Ohio), and 439th (Westover AFB, Mass); only a few remain in service.

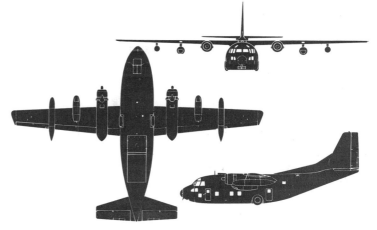

Above: Three-view of the Fairchild C-123K Provider.

Below: C-123K of the 310th Air Commando Squadron in Vietnam.

After a major competition the Northrop A-9A and Fairchild A-10A were pitted against each other in a flyoff contest throughout 1972, after which the A-10A was announced the Air Force's choice on 18 January 1973. Including six DT&E (development, test and evaluation) aircraft the planned force was to number 733, to be deployed in TAC wings in the USA and Europe, and also to a growing number of AFR and ANG squadrons.

The original A-10A was a basically simple single-seater, larger than most tactical attack aircraft and carefully designed as a compromise between capability, survivability and low cost. As an example of the latter many of the major parts, including flaps, main landing gears and movable tail surfaces, are interchangeable left/right, and systems and engineering features were designed with duplication and redundancy to survive parts being shot away. The unusual engine location minimizes infra-red signature and makes it almost simple to fly with one engine inoperative or even shot off. Weapon pylons were added from tip to tip, but the chief tank-killing ordnance is the gun, the most powerful (in terms of muzzle horsepower) ever mounted in an aircraft, firing milk-bottle-size rounds at rates hydraulically controlled at 2,100 or 4,200 shots/min. The gun is mounted 2° nose-down and offset to the left so that the firing barrel is always on the centrelilne (the nose landing gear being offset to the right).

The basic aircraft has a HUD (head-up display), good communications fit increase in the overall programme to 825 to sustain the desired force to the mid-1990s. Significantly, half the 60 aircraft in the FY81 budget were two-seaters, which though priced $600,000 higher are expected to effect savings by reducing the demand for chase aircraft.

In 1979 Fairchild flew a company-funded NAW (night/adverse weather) demonstrator with augmented avionics and a rear cockpit for a WSO seated at a higher level and with good forward view. Both the regular and NAW aircraft can carry a Pave Penny laser seeker pod under the nose, vital for laser-guilded munitions, and the NAW also has a Ferranti laser ranger, FLIR (forward-looking infra-red), GE low-light TV and many other items including a Westinghouse multimode radar with WSO display. It is probable that during the rest of the decade A-10As will be brought at least close to the NAW standard, while the two-seat NAW might be procured alongside or in place of future buys of the basic A-10A.

Below: The A-10A's disposable load depends on 11 laterally-dispersed hardpoints for 16,000lb (7,257kg) of stores.

General Dynamics F-16 Fighting Falcon

F-16A, B

Origin: General Dynamics Corporation, Fort Worth, Texas.
Type: Multi-role righter (B) operational fighter/trainer.
Engine: One 23,840lb (10,814kg) thrust Pratt & Whitney F100-200 afterburning turbofan.
Dimensions: Span 31ft 0in (9.449m) 32ft 10in/1.01m over missile fins); length (both versions, excl probe) 47ft 7.7in (14.52m); wing area 300.0 sq ft (27.87m²).
Weights: Empty (A) 15,137lb (6,866kg), (B) 15,778lb (7,157kg); loaded (AAMs only) (A) 23,357lb (10,594kg), (B) 22,814lb (10,348kg), (max external load) (both) 35,400lb (16,057kg). (Block 25 on) 37,500lb (17,010kg).
Performance: Maximum speed (both, AAMs only) 1,350mph (2,173km/h, Mach 2.05) at 40,000ft (12.19km); maximum at SL, 915mph (1,472km/h, Mach 1.2); initial climb (AAMs only) 50,000ft (15.24km)/min; service ceiling, over 50,000ft (15.24km); tactical radius (A, six Mk 82, internal fuel, HI-LO-HI) 340 miles (547km); ferry range, 2,415 miles (3,890km).
Armament: One M61A-1 20mm gun with 500/515 rounds, centreline pylon for 300 US gal (m1,136lit) drop tank or 2,200lb (998kg) bonb, inboard wing plyons for 3,500lb (1,587kg) each, middle wing pylons for 2,500lb (1,134kg) each (being uprated under MSIP-1 to 3,500lb), outer wing pylons for 250lb (113.4kg), all ratings being at 9 g.
History: First flight (YF) 20 January 1974, (production F-16A) 7 August 1978; service delivery (A) 17 August 1978.

Development: The Fighting Falcon originated through a belief by the Air Force that there might be a more cost/effective fighter than the outstanding but necessarily expensive F-15. In a Lightweight Fighter (LWF) programme of 1972 it sought bids from many design teams, picked GD's Model 401 and Northrop's simplified P.530 and evaluated two prototypes of each as the YF-16 and YF-17. GD's engineering team created a totally new aircraft with such advanced features as relaxed static stability (a basic distribution of shapes and masses to attain greater combat agility, overcoming a marginal longitudinal stability by the digital flight-control system), large wing/body flare to enhance lift at high angles of attack and house a gun and extra fuel, a straight wing with hinged leading and trailing flaps used to incrase manoeuvrability in combat (the trailing surfaces being rapid-action flaperons), fly-by-wire electrically signalled flight controls, a futuristic cockpit with reclining zero/zero seat for best resistance to g, with a sidestick controller instead of a control column and one-piece canopy/windscreen of blown polycarbonate, and a miniature multi-mode pulse-doppler radar. On 13 January 1975 the Air Force announced full development of the F-16 not just as a simple day air-combat fighter but also to meet a greatly expanded requirement calling for comprehensive all-weather navigation and weapon delivery in the air/surface role.

This vitally important programme growth was triggered largely by the recognition that there existed a near-term European market, and in June 1975 orders were announced by four European NATO countries (Belgium, Denmark, Netherlands and Norway). These organized with GD and P&WA a large multinational manufacturing programme which in the longer term has greatly expanded the production base. In July 1975 the Air Force ordered

Below: Even when carrying the ALQ-119 ECM pod, the F-16A retains considerable weapons-carriage capability and its almost legendary aerial agility. These are 8th TFW aircraft.

General Dynamics F-106 Delta Dart

F-106A, B

Origin: General Dynamics Convair Division, San Diego, California.
Type: All-weather interceptor, (B) operational trainer.
Engine: One 24,500lb (11,130kg) thrust Pratt & Whitney J75-17 afterburning turbojet.
Dimensions: Span 38ft 3in (11.67m); length (both) 70ft 8¾in (21.55m); wing area 661.5 sq ft (61.52m²).
Weights: Empty (A) about 24,420lb (11,077kg); loaded (normal) 34,510lb (15,668kg).
Performance: Maximum speed (both) 1,525mph (2,455km/h) or Mach 2.3 at 36,000ft (11km); initial climb, about 29,000ft (8,839m)/min; service ceiling 57,000ft (17,374m); range with drop tanks 1,800 miles (2,897km).
Armament: One 20mm M61A-1 gun, two AIM-4F plus two AIM-4G Falcons, plus one AIR-2A or -2G Genie nuclear rocket.
History: First flight (aerodynamic prototype) 26 December 1956, (B) 9 April 1958; squadron delivery June 1959.

Development: Derived from the earlier F-102 Delta Dagger, the F-106 had a maximum speed approximately twice as high and completely met the requirements of Aerospace Defense Command (Adcom) for a manned interceptor to defend the continental United States. Linked via its complex and bulky MA-1 electronic fire-control system through a digital data link into the nationwide SAGE (semi-automatic ground environment), the 106 served much longer than intended and in fact never did see a successor,

despite the continued threat of the manned bomber, though there were numerous engineering improvements and some substantial updates including the addition of the gun (in a neat installation in the missile bay, causing a slight ventral bulge) as well as improved avionics, an infra-red sensor of great sensitivity facing ahead for detecting heat from hostile aircraft and assisting the lock-on of AAMs, and a flight-refuelling boom receptacle. Convair completed many other studies including improved electric power system, solid-state computer, the AIMS (aircraft identification monitoring system) and an enhanced-capability variant for Awacs control. The last of 277 F-106As and 63 tandem-seat F-106B armed trainers were delivered in 1961. Adcom was disbanded in 1980 and F-106s now fly only with fighter units in the ANG. One also flies with NASA on storm hazard research.

Below: The F-106A is disappearing from first-line service.

six pre-production F-16As and two F-16Bs with tandem dual controls and internal fuel reduced from 1,072.5 US gal (4,060lit) to 889.8 (3,368). Both introduced a flight-refuelling boom receptacle (into which a probe can be inserted) and provision for a 300 US gal (1,136lit) centreline drop tank and two 370gal (1,400lit) wing tanks. All eight aircraft were delivered by June 1978, by which time the Air Force had announced a programme for 1,184 F-16As and 204 F-16Bs, with the name Fighting Falcon.

Few aircraft have been as excitedly received as the F-16, which by sheer engineering excellence and painstaking development is as close to the optimum combat aircraft as it is possible to get in its timescale. Even so, it was naturally prey to occasional troubles, notably the prolonged stall-stagnation engine difficulty that had earlier hit the F-15 with an almost identical engine. Following intensive test programmes at Edwards, Nellis and by an MOT&E (multi-national operational test and evaluation) team the 388th TFW at Hill AFB, Utah, began to convert on 6 January 1979 and has subsequently not only achieved a string of 'firsts' with the F-16 but has set impressive records in the process. Next came the 56th TFW at MacDill, Florida, followed by the 474th at Nellis, Nevada, the 8th TFW at Kunsan, S Korea, the 50th TFW at Hahn, W. Germany (in USAFE) and the 363rd at Shaw, S. Carolina. Thanks to the large production base and wide international deployment (extending to Israel, S Korea, Egypt, Pakistan and other countries beyond those previously listed) global deployment of Air Force F-16 units is proving exceptionally simple, the aircraft having swiftly attained an exceptional level of reliabilty which is enhanced by outstanding maintenance and self-test features.

Enthusiasm by pilots and ground crew has been exceptional, but an event which dramatically highlighted how far the F-16 had come since 1974 was its first participation in a numerically scored inter-service competition. In the searching USAF/RAF contest held at RAF Lossiemouth on 16-19 June

Above: This F-16A of the 388th TFW at Hill AFB carries a centerline ALQ-119 pod, two drop tanks and four Sidewinder AAMs (two AIM-9Js inboard and two AIM-9Ls at the tips).

1981 teams of F-16s (388th TFW), F-111s, Jaguars and Buccaneers were required under realistic wartime scenarios to penetrate defended airspace, engage hostile fighters and bomb airfields and road convoys. The F-16s were the only aircraft to hit all assigned surface targets, while in air combat their score was 86 kills against no losses; rival teams suffered 42 losses and collectively scored but a single kill. The F-16 also scored very much better against Rapier SAM threats, while in the ground-crew part of the contest the 388th achieved an average turnround time between sorties of 10½ minutes, including refuelling, loading six Mk 82 bombs and 515 rounds of ammunition. Since its introduction to TAC the F-16 has had the highest Mission Capable Rate in the command, and has been the only multirole aircraft to achieve the command goal of 70%.

In 1982 production had passed 600 aircraft, with plenty of spare capacity at Fort Worth for up to 45 per month if necessary. Though this excellent output was attained by sticking to an agreed standard of build, improvements have been continual, and many more are in prospect. During production the inlet was strengthened to carry EO/FLIR and laser pods, a graphite/epoxy tailplane of larger size was introduced to match increased gross weight (see data), and the central computer and avionics were changed for a much 'expanded package'. Later the 30mm GEpod gun, Maverick missile, Lantirn and AMRAAM advanced missile will be introduced, the new AAM being linked with the programmable APG-66 radar for stand-off interception capability. Later still the striking bat-like SCAMP (supersonic-cruise aircraft modification program) may result in still higher performance with double bombloads.

General Dynamics F-111

F-111A, D, E and F, FB-111A and EF-111A

Origin: (except EF) General Dynamics Corporation, Fort Worth, Texas; (EF) Grumman Aerospace Corporation, Bethpage, NY.
Type: A,D,E,F, all-weather attack; FB, strategic attack; EF, tactical ECM jammer.
Powerplant: Two Pratt & Whitney TF30 afterburning turbofans, as follow, (A, C, EF) 18,500lb (8,390kg) TF30-3, (D,E) 19,600lb (8,891kg) TF30-9, (FB) 20,350lb (9,231kg) TF30-7, (F) 25,100lb (11,385kg) TF30-100.
Dimensions: Span (fully spread) (A,D,E,F,EF) 63ft 0in (19.2m), (FB) 70ft 0in (21.34m), (fully swept) (A,D,E,F,E,F) 31ft 11½in (9.74m), (FB) 33ft 11in (10.34m); length (except EF) 73ft 6in (22.4m), (EF) 77ft 1.6in (23.51m); wing area (A,D,E,F,EF, gross, 16°) 525 sq ft (48.77m²)
Weights: Empty (A) 46,172lb (20,943kg), (D) 49,090lb (22,267kg), (E) about 47,000lb (21,319kg), (EF) 53,418lb) (24,230kg), (F) 47,481lb (21,537kg), (FB) close to 50,000lb (22,680kg); loaded (A) 91,500lb (41,500kg), (D,E) 92,500lb (41,954kg), (F) 100,000lb (45,360kg), (FB) 114,300lb (51,846kg), (EF) 87,478lb (39,680kg).
Performance: Maximum speed at 36,000ft (11km), clean and with max afterburner, (A,D,E) Mach 2.2, 1,450mph (2,335km/h), (FB) Mach 2, 1,320mph (2,124km/h), (F) Mach 2.5, 1,653mph (2,660km/h), (EF) Mach 1.75, 1,160mph (1,865km/h); cruising speed, penetration, 571mph (919km/h); initial climb (EF) 3,592ft (1,95m)/min; service ceiling at combat weight, max afterburner, (A) 51,000ft (15,500m), (F) 60,000ft (18,290m), (EF) 54,700ft (16,670m); range with max internal fuel (A,D) 3,165 miles (5,093km), (F) 2,925 miles (4,707km), (EF) 2,484 miles (3,998km); takeoff run (A) 4,000ft (1,219m), (F) under 3,000ft (914m), (FB) 4,700ft

(1,433m), (EF) 3,250ft (991m).
Armament: Internal weapon bay for two B43 bombs or (D,F) one B43 and one M61 gun; three pylons under each wing (four inboard swivelling with wing, outers being fixed and usable only at 16°, otherwise being jettisoned) for max external load 31,500lb (14,288kg); (FB only) provision for up to six SRAM, two internal; (EF) no armament.
History: First flight 21 December 1964, service delivery (A) June 1967 ▶ (EF) July 1981.

Below: The F-111F used by the 48th TFW is the most capable strike version of the 'Aardvark' in USAF tactical service.

181

Above: Key to F-111F capability is the 'Pave Tack' retractable laser pod with weapons such as these GBU-15s.

Development: In 1960 the Department of Defense masterminded the TFX (tactical fighter experimental) as a gigantic programme to meet all the fighter and attack needs of the Air Force, Navy and Marine Corps, despite the disparate requirements of these services, and expected the resultant aircraft to be bought throughout the non-Communist world. In fact, so severe were the demands for weapon load and, in particular, mission range that on the low power available the aircraft had inadequate air-combat capability and in fact it was destined never to serve in this role, though it is still loosely described as a 'tactical fighter'. After prolonged technical problems involving escalation in weight, severe aerodynamic drag, engine/inlet mismatch and, extending into the early 1970s, structural failures, the F-111 eventually matured as the world's best long-range interdiction attack aircraft which in the hands of dedicated and courageous Air Force crews pioneered the new art of 'skiing'--riding the ski-toe locus of a TFR (terrain-following radar) over hills, mountains and steep-sided valleys in blind conditions, in blizzards or by night, holding a steady 200ft (91m) distance from the ground at high-subsonic speed, finally to plant a bomb automatically within a few metres of a previously computed target.

Basic features of the F-111 include a variable-sweep 'swing wing' (the first in production in the world) with limits of 16° and 72.5°, with exceptional high-lift devices, side-by-side seating for the pilot and right-seat navigator (usually also a pilot) or (EF) electronic-warfare officer, large main gears with low-pressure tyres for no-flare landings on soft strips (these prevent the carriage of ordnance on fuselage pylons), a small internal weapon bay, very great internal fuel capacity (typically 5,022 US gal, 19,010 litres), and emergency escape by jettisoning the entire crew compartment, which has its own parachutes and can serve as a survival shelter or boat.

General Dynamics cleared the original aircraft for service in 2½ years, and built 141 of this F-111A version, which equips 366TFW at Mountain Home AFB, Idaho (others have been reserved for conversion into the EF-111A). It is planned to update the A by fitting a digital computer to the original analog-type AJQ-20A nav/bomb system, together with the Air Force standard INS and a new control/display set. The F-111E was similar but had larger inlet ducts and engines of slightly greater power; 94 were delivered and survivors equip the 20th TFW at Upper Heyford, England. These are to receive the same updates as the A. Next came the F-111D, which at great cost was fitted with an almost completely different avionic system of a basically digital nature including the APQ-130 attack radar, APN-189 doppler and HUDs for both crew-members. This aircraft had great potential but caused severe technical and manpower problems in service and never fully realized its capabilities, though it remains a major advance on the A and E. The 96 built have always equipped the 27th TFW at Cannon AFB, New Mexico. The F-111F is by far the best of all tactical F-111 versions, almost entirely because Pratt & Whitney at last produced a really powerful TF30 which incorporated many other advanced features giving enhanced life with fewer problems. With much greater performance than any other model the F could if necessary double in an air-combat role though it has no weapons for this role except the gun and if necessary AIM-9. The 106 of this model served at Mountain Home until transfer to the 48th TFW in England, at Lakenheath. The most important of all F-111 post-delivery modifications has been the conversion of the F force to use the Pave Tack pod, normally stowed in the weapon bay but rotated out on a cradle for use. This complex package provides a day/night all-weather capability to acquire, track, designate and hit surface targets using EO, IR or laser guided weapons. The first squadron

Grumman A-6 Intruder and EA-6 Prowler

A-6A, B, C, E, EA-6A and B, and KA-6D

Origin: Grumman Aerospace Corporation, Bethpage, NY.
Type: (A-6A, B, C, E, F) two-seat carrier-based all-weather attack; (EA-6A) two-seat ECM/attack; (EA-6B) four-seat ECM; (KA-6D) two-seat air-refueling tanker.
Powerplant: (A-6A to E) two 9,300lb (4,218kg) thrust Pratt & Whitney J52-8A turbojets; (EA-6B) two 11,200lb (5,080kg) J52-408; (A-6F) two 10,800lb (4,900kg) General Electric F404-400D turbofans.
Dimensions: Span 53ft (16.5m); length (except EA-6B) 54ft 7in (16.64m); (EA-6B) 59ft 5in (18.11m); height (A-6A, A-6C, KA-6D) 15ft 7in (4.75m); (A-6E and F, EA-6A and B) 16ft 3in (4.95m); wing area 528.9sq ft (49.1m²).
Weights: Empty (A-6A) 25,684lb (11,650kg); (EA-6A) 27,769lb (12,596kg); (EA-6B) 27,769lb (12,596kg); (EA-6B) 34,581lb (15,686kg); (A-6E) 25,630lb (11,625kg); max loaded (A-6A and E) 60,400lb (27,397kg); (EA-6B) 58,500lb (26,535kg).
Performance: Max speed (clean A-6A) 684mph (1,102km/h) at sea level or 625mph (1,006km/h, Mach 0.94) at height, (EA-6A) over 630mph (10,131km/h), (EA-6B) 599mph (964km/h) at sea level, (A-6E) 648mph (1,043km/h) at sea level; initial climb (A-6E, clean) 8,600ft (2,621m)/min; service ceiling (A-6A 41,660ft (12,700m), (A-6E) 44,600ft (13,595m), (EA-6B) 39,000ft (11,582m), range with full combat load (A-6E) 1,077 miles (1,733km); ferry range with external fuel (all) about 3,100 miles (4,890km).
Armament: All attack versions, including EA-6A, five stores locations each rated at 3,600lb (1,633kg) with max total load of 15,000lb (6,804kg); typical load thirty 500lb (227kg) bombs; (EA-6B, KA-6D) none.
History: First flight (YA2F-1) 19 April 1960; service acceptance of A-6A 1 February 1963; first flight (EA-6A) 1963, (KA-6D) 23 May 1966, (EA-6B) 25 May 1968, (A-6E) 27 February 1970; final delivery (A-6E) after 1987, (F) 1996.

Development: Despite its seemingly outdated concept, the A-6 Intruder will remain in low-rate production throughout the foreseeable future as the standard equipment of all the heavy attack squadrons of the US Navy and Marine Corps. The design was formulated during the later part of the Korean War, in 1953, when the need for a truly all-weather attack aircraft was first recognized. After much refinement of the requirement an industry competition was held in 1957.

Above: Test launch of a Tomahawk from an A-6 Intruder.

Grumman's G-128 design being chosen late in that year. The YA2F-1 prototype was notable for its downward tilting engine jet-pipes, intended to give STOL performance, but these were not featured in the production machine.

Basic characteristics of all aircraft of the family include a conventional long-span wing with almost full-span flaps on both the leading and trailing edges. Ahead of the trailing-edge flaps are "flaperons" used as lift spoilers and ailerons, while the tips contain split airbrakes which are fully opened on each carrier landing. Plain turbo-jets were used, and these remained in all successive production versions but are now being replaced (see later text). The nose is occupied by a giant radar array, with a fixed inflight-refueling probe above the center-line in front of the side-by-side cockpit with Martin-Baker seats (slightly inclined and staggered) which can be tilted back to reduce fatigue.

Grumman delivered 482 of the original A-6A model, ending in December 1969, and 62 of these were converted into KA-6D air-refueling tankers which can transfer over 21,000lb (9,526kg) of fuel through the hosereel. This remains the standard tanker of the 14 carrier air wings, with limited attack capability and equipment for use as an air/sea rescue control platform. The A-6A, B and C are no longer in use, the standard attack model being the A-6E. This has been equipped with totally new radar, the Norden APQ-148 replacing two radars in earlier versions, as well as an IBM/Fairchild computer-based attack and weapon-delivery system.

to convert was the 48th TFW's 494th TFS, in September 1981. Their operations officer, Maj Bob Rudiger, has said: 'Important targets that once required several aircraft can now be disabled with a single Pave Tack aircraft, the radar tells the pod where to look, and the laser allows us to put the weapon precisely on target.'

The long-span FB-111A was bought to replace the B-58 and early models of B-52 in SAC, though the raising price resulted in a cut in procurement from 210 to 76, lentering service in October 1969. It has so-called Mk IIB avionics, derived from those of the D but configured for SAC missions using nuclear bombs or SRAMs. With strengthened structure and landing gear the FB has a capability of carrying 41,250lb (18,711kg) of bombs, made up of 50 bombs of 825lb (nominal 750lb size) each. This is not normally used, and the outer pylons associated with this load are not normally installed. The FB equips SAC's 380th BW at Plattsburgh AFB, NY, and the 509th at Pease, New Hampshire. No go-ahead has been received for numerous extremely capable stretched FB versions.

Last of the F-111 variants, the EF-111A is the USAF's dedicated EW

platform, managed by Grumman (partner on the original Navy F-111B version) and produced by rebuilding F-111As. The USA acknowledges the Soviet Union to have a lead in both ground and air EW, and thousands of radars and other defence emitters in Eastern Europe would make penetration by NATO aircraft extremely dangerous. The vast masking power of the EF-110A, which equals that of the Navy EA-6B and in fact uses almost the same ALQ-99E tac-jam system (but with a crew of only two instead of four), is expected to be able to suppress these 'eyes' and enable NATO aircraft to survive. An aerodynamic prototype flew in March 1977, the ALQ-99 was flying in an F-111 in May 1977, and production deliveries began in mid-1981 to the 366th TFW. The Air Force plans to have 42 aircraft rebuilt as EFs, for service with all USAFE penetrating attack units and others in TAC and possibly other commands.

Below: Vital support for F-111 interdiction aircraft is provided by the EF-111 electronic escort aircraft carrying the ALQ-99E automated ECM system.

In 1974 an A-6E was fitted with the TRAM (target recognition and attack multisensor) package, comprising a stabilized chin turret containing a FLIR and a laser interlinked with the radar for detection, identification and weapon-guidance at greater ranges in adverse conditions. Other updates with TRAM include the Litton ASN-92 CAINS (carrier aircraft inertial navigation system), a new CNI suite and automatic carrier landing. It was planned to deploy 318 A-6Es, but production has been continued with new airframes being produced at six a year until 1987. In that year it is planned to switch to the A-6F.

Meanwhile a major update program has fitted TRAM to all the 250 A-6Es in frontline carrier air wings, and to the similar aircraft equipping the five all-weather VMA (AW) attack squadrons of the Marines. Since 1981 all new and updated A-6Es have also been equipped to launch the Harpoon stand-off attack and anti-ship missile. Boeing has developed new long-life replacement wing structures.

Under a 1984 contract Grumman is developing the totally upgraded A-6F, for first flight in late 1989 and production from 1990. Apart from the more fuel-efficient engines the main improvements will be a new Norden radar, new cockpit with electronic displays, processors and HUD (all displays and computer common with the F-14D), and two extra pylons for self-defence AAMs (Sidewinder or AIM-132 ASRAAM).

The EA-6B Prowler is the standard electronic warfare platform of the Navy carrier air wings and Marine Corps. Though it is based on the

airframe of the A-6E, with local reinforcement to cater for the increased weights, fatigue life and 5.5g load factor, it is gutted of attack avionics and instead houses the AIL ALQ-99 tactical jamming system, which covers all anticipated hostile emitter frequency bands. Surveillance receivers are grouped in the fairing on the fin, and the active jammers are mounted in up to five external pods, each energized by a nose windmill generator and containing two (fore/aft) transmitters covering one of seven selected frequency bands. To manage the equipment a crew of four is carried, comprising pilot (left front), and ECM officer in the right front seat to manage navigation, communications, defensive ECM and chaff/flare dispensing, and two more ECMOs in the rear seats who can each detect, assign, adjust and monitor the jammers.

All VAQ (fixed-wing EW) squadrons of the Navy fly the EA-6B, as do the three Marine EW squadrons. Production at six per year is continuing to 1990. All in service have been updated with new avionics in two stages of ICAP (increased capability), and Norden is supplying about 100 advanced APS-130 navigation radars for retrofit to existing Prowlers. During the rest of the decade Grumman has to define a further update stage for the EA-6B, with many of the A-6F features.

Below: Portly and somewhat low of outright performance, the A-6E is still an unrivalled carrierborne attack and strike platform because of its phenomenal nav/attack system.

Grumman E-2C Hawkeye

E-2A, B and C Hawkeye, TE-2C and C-2A Greyhound

Origin: Grumman Aerospace Corporation, Bethpage, NY.
Type: Carrier- and land-based airborne early warning and control (AWACS) platform.
Powerplant: Two 4,910ehp Allison T56-A-425 turboprops (from 1986 two 5,250ehp T56-A-427).
Dimensions: Span 80ft 7in (24.56m); length 57ft 6.75in (17.54m); height 18ft 3.8in (5.58m) wing area 700sq ft (65.03m²).
Weights: Empty 37,945lb (17,211kg); max take-off 51,817lb (23,503kg).
Performance: Max speed 374mph (602km/h); cruising speed 310mph (500km/h); service ceiling 30,800ft (9,390m); endurance (max fuel) 6.1h.
Armament: None.
History: First flight (E-2) 21 October 1960, (E-2C) 20 January 1971; first delivery (E-2A) 19 January 1964.
Development: Unique in offering a valuable and comprehensive AEW package in an aircraft of compact dimensions and moderate operating cost, the Hawkeye has managed to make the transition from being a highly specialized aircraft for US Navy carrier air wings to become a major contender for sales in the world market for operation from land airfields.

Together with some EC-121 variants, the original E-2A of 1961 was the first aircraft to have the new style of rotodome in which the antenna itself was given a streamlined fairing instead of being housed inside a radome. The size of airframe needed to house the APS-96 radar was such that considerable ingenuity was needed; for example, four fins and rudders are used, all mounted at 90° to the dihedral tailplane and all well below the wake of the rotodome. The rotodome itself is set at a positive incidence to lift at least its own weight, while on a carrier it is retracted a short distance to enable it to clear the roof of the hangar. The dome rotates once every 10 seconds when in operation, and the

Above: Launch of an E-2C Hawkeye from USS *Saratoga* in 1986.

radar gives surveillance from a height of 30,000ft (9,144m) within a radius of 300 miles (480km). Ten years into the program, the APS-96 was replaced by the APS-125 with an Advanced Radar Processing System (ARPS) which gives a much improved discrimination and detection capability over both land and water. With this new radar the aircraft designation changed to E-2C; it entered service as such in 1973 and remains the standard 'eyes' of the US Navy at sea, with numerous updates in the subsequent years.

The two pilots occupy a wide flight deck. Behind them, amidst a mass of radar racking and the high-capacity vapor-cycle cooling system (the radiator for which is housed in a large duct above the fuselage), is the pressurized Airborne Tactical Data System (ATDS) compartment. This is the nerve-center of the aircraft, manned by the combat information officer, air control officer and radar operator. They are presented with displays and outputs not only from the main radar but also from some 30 other electronic devices, including passive detectors and communications systems. These combine to give a picture of targets,

Grumman F-14 Tomcat

F-14A, C and D

Origin: Grumman Aerospace Corporation, Bethpage. NY.
Type: Two-seat carrier-based multi-role fighter.
Power plant: (F-14A) two 20,900lb (9,480kg) thrust Pratt & Whitney TF30-412A two-shaft afterburning turbofans, being replaced by TF30-414A, same rating, (A+, D) 29,000lb (13,154kg) General-Electric F110-400 augmented turbofans.
Dimensions: Span (68° sweep) 38ft 2in (11.63m), (20° sweep) 64ft 1½in (19.54m); length 62ft 8in (19.1m); height 16ft (4.88m); wing area 565sq ft (52.49m²).
Weights: Empty 40,104lb (18,191kg); loaded (normal) 58,539lb (26,553kg), (max) 74,348lb (33,724kg).
Performance: Maximum speed 1,544mph (2,485km/h, Mach 2.34) at height, 910mph (1,470km/h, Mach 1.2) at sea level; initial climb at normal gross weight, over 30,000ft (9,144m)/min; service ceiling over 56,000ft (17,070m); range (fighter with external fuel) about 2,000 miles (3,200km) (F-14D, over 3,000 miles, 4,828km).
Armament: One 20mm M61-A1 multi-barrel cannon in fuselage; four AIM-7 Sparrow and four or eight AIM-9 Sidewinder air-to-air missiles, or up to six AIM-54 Phoenix and two AIM-9; maximum external weapon load in surface attack role 14,500lb (6,577kg).
History: First flight 21 December 1970; initial deployment with Navy carriers October 1972; first flight (F-14B) 12 September 1973, (F-14D) 1987.

Development: When Congress finally halted development of the compromised F-111B version of the TFX in mid-1968, Grumman was already well advanced with the project design of a replacement. After a competition for the VFX requirement Grumman was awarded a contract for the F-14 in January 1969. The company had to produce a

Below: This long-range interception F-14A reveals the separation of the engines permitting the carriage of four AIM-54s under the fuselage as well as two under the wings.

tracks and trajectories, and signal emissions, all duly processed and, where appropriate, with IFF interrogation replies. Passive Detection System (PDS) receivers are located on the nose and tail, and on the tips of the tailplane (horizontal stabilizer) for the lateral coverage. An E-2C mission can last six hours, and at a radius of 200 miles (322km) the time on station at 30,000ft (9,144m) can be almost 4 hours. This is appreciably shorter than the 10 hours at this radius of the E-3A and Nimrod, but Grumman claims a 2:1 price differential in acquisition and operating costs (the E-2C costs $58 million).

The E-2C can detect airborne targets anywhere in a 3,000,000 cubic mile surveillance envelope, and it is claimed that a target as small as a cruise missile can be detected at ranges over 115 miles (185km), fighters at ranges up to 230 miles (370km), and larger aircraft at 289 miles (465km). All friendly and enemy maritime movements can also be monitored. The AN-ALR-59 PDS can detect the presence of electronic emitters at ranges up to twice that of the radar system. High speed data

processing enables the E-2C automatically to track more than 250 targets at the same time, and to control more than 30 airborne intercepts. A new Total Radiation Aperture Control antenna (TRAC-A) is now under development, and this will enable the range to be increased, reduce the sidelobes and enhance the ECCM capability.

Production of the E-2C is slow but steady, with the 95th airframe due to be delivered in 1987. Grumman has for many years had a team working on improved Hawkeyes, some with turbofan propulsion, and even on a completely new replacement (E-7). In mid-1986 the most likely new-generation aircraft appeared to be a similar airframe with 8,000hp Allison 501-M78 propfan engines. The increase in power of some 60 per cent would greatly improve operating height and endurance.

Below: The over-fuselage rotodome holds the antenna for the E-2C's capable but constantly updated surveillance radar.

detailed mock-up by May and build 12 development aircraft. Despite sudden loss of the first aircraft on its second flight, due to total hydraulic failure, the program has been a complete technical success and produced one of the world's outstanding combat aircraft.

Basic features include use of an automatically scheduled variable-sweep wing, to match the aircraft to the conflicting needs of carrier compatibility, dog-fighting and attack on surface targets at low level; pilot and naval flight officer (observer) in tandem; an extremely advanced airframe, with tailplane skins of boron-epoxy composite and similar novel construction methods, and one canted vertical tail above each engine; and the extremely powerful Hughes AWG-9 radar which, used in conjunction with the Phoenix missile (carried by no other combat aircraft), can pick out and destroy a chosen aircraft from a formation over 100 miles (160km) away. For close-in fighting the gun is used in conjunction with snap-shoot missiles, with the tremendous advantage that, as a launch platform, the Tomcat is unsurpassed. Grumman claim it to be unrivalled, and to be able—by automatic variation of wing sweep—to out-maneuver all previous combat aircraft. Introduction to the US Navy was smooth and enthusiastic, with VF-1 and -2 serving aboard *Enterprise* in 1974. But costs escalated beyond prediction, Grumman refusing at one time to continue the program and claiming its existing contracts would result in a loss of $105 million. For the same reason the re-engined F-14B, with the later-technology and much more powerful F401 engine, was held to a single prototype. In 1975 ongoing production agreements were concluded and by mid-1985 total deliveries amounted to a useful 505 aircraft, excluding 80 supplied to Iran.

The basic aircraft has remained virtually unchanged, though prolonged trouble with the engines has led to the P-414A version of the TF30 which it was hoped would improve safety and reliability. This engine arrived in late 1983 together with a new radar, programmable signal processor, a new target identification system, embodying Northrop's TCS (TV camera set) which has been slowly retrofitted to existing Tomcats since 1981, a laser-gyro inertial system, completely new cockpit displays and completely new threat-warning and internal self-protection jammer system. In 1980-81, as a replacement for the RA-5C and RF-8G, 49 F-14As were fitted with Tarps (tac air recon pod system), containing optical cameras and an infra-red sensor.

Because of severe cost-escalation of the 'cheap' F/A-18A the latter is now roughly the same price as the Tomcat, which is accordingly expected to be expanded from a 497-aircraft program. From 1987 the standard engine will be the General Electric F110, previously flown as the F101DFE engine in the ex-F-14B 'SuperTomcat' in 1981. This engine should revitalize this basically tremendous aircraft and keep it one the top line through the 1990s. The new engine powers the otherwise unchanged F-14A+, and from 1990 will also power the F-14D. This will also have further updated avionics and weapons, and to a large degree can be regarded as a new airplane.

Above: This F-14A totes four AIM-54s, two AIM-7s and two AIM-9s for interception at varying ranges from itself.

Below: The decisive moment as the long-burn motor of an AIM-54 cuts in, rapidly boosting the missile to Mach 3·8.

185

Grumman OV-1 Mohawk

OV-1A to -1D, EV-1, JOV, RV

Type: (OV) multi-sensor tactical observation and reconnaissance; (EV) electronic warfare; (JOV) armed reconnaissance; (RV) electronic reconnaissance.

Engines: Two 1,005shp Lycoming T53-7 or -15 free-turbine turboprops; (OV-1D) two, 1,160shp T53-701.

Dimensions: Span (-1A, -C) 42ft (12.8m); (-1, -D) 48ft (14.63m); length 41ft (12.5m); (-1D with SLAR, 44ft 11in); height 12ft 8in (3.86m).

Weights: Empty (-1A) 9,937lb (4,507kg); (-1B) 11,067lb (5,020kg); (-1C) 10,400lb (4,717kg); (-1D) 12,054lb (5,467kg); maximum loaded (-1A) 15,031lb (6,818kg); (11B, C) 19,230lb (8,722kg); (-1D) 18,109lb (8,214kg).

Performance: Maximum speed (all) 297-310mph (480-500km/h); initial climb (-1A) 2,950ft (900m)/min; (-1B) 2,250ft (716m)/min; (-1C), 2,670ft (814m)/min; (-1D) 3,618ft (1,103m)/min; service ceiling (all) 28,800-31,000ft (8,534-9,449m); range with external fuel (-1A) 1,410 miles (2,270km); (-1B) 1,230 miles (1,980km); (-1C) 1,330 miles (2,140km); (-1D), 1,011 miles (1,627km).

Armament: Not normally fitted, but can include a wide variety of air-to-ground weapons including grenade launchers, Minigun pods and small guided missiles.

History: First flight (YOV-1A) 14 April, 1959; service delivery, February 1961; final delivery (new aircraft) December 1970.

Development: Representing a unique class of military aircraft, the OV-1

Above: The APS-94 SLAR carried by the Mohawk provides clear radar imagery of terrain and features to the side of the aircraft flight path, automatic exposure and development of film providing a near-realtime permanent record.

Mohawk is a specially designed battlefield surveillance machine with characteristics roughly midway between lightplanes and jet fighters. One of its requirements was to operate from rough forward airstrips and it has

---

Kaman SH-2 Seasprite

UH-2, HH-2 and SH-2 in many versions (data for SH-2D)

Origin: Kaman Aerospace Corporation, Bloomfield, Connecticut.

Type: Ship-based multirole helicopter (ASW, anti-missile defense, observation, search/rescue and utility).

Powerplant: Original versions, one 1,050 or 1,250hp General Electric T58 turboshaft; all current versions, two 1,350hp T58-8F.

Dimensions: Main-rotor diameter 44ft (13.41m); overall length (blades turning) 52ft 7in (16m); fuselage length 40ft 6in (12.3m); height 13ft 7in (4.14m); main-rotor disc area 1,520sq ft (141.2m²).

Weight: Empty 6,953lb (3,153kg); max 13,300lb (6,033kg), (1985 on) 13,500lb (6,124kg).

Performance: Max speed 168mph (270km/h); max rate of climb (not vertical) 2,440ft (744m)/min; service ceiling 22,500ft (6,858m); range 422 miles (679km).

Armament: See below.

History: First flight (XHU2K-1) 2 July 1959; service delivery (HU2K-1, later called UH-2A) 18 December 1962; final delivery (new) 1972, (conversion) 1975, (rebuild) 1982.

Development: Originally designated HU2K-1 and named Seasprite, this exceptionally neat helicopter was at first powered by a single T58 turbine engine mounted close under the rotor hub and was able to carry a wide range of loads, including nine passengers, in its unobstructed central cabin, with two crew in the nose. The main units of the

tailwheel-type landing gear retract fully. About 190 were delivered and all were later converted to have two T58 engines in nacelles on each side.

For well over 20 years the Seasprite has been standard equipment aboard US Navy frigates, in various versions including the HH-2C rescue/utility with armor and various armament including chin Minigun turret and waist-mounted machine guns or cannon; others are unarmed HH-2D. One has been used in missile firing (Sparrow III and Sidewinder) trials in the missile-defense role. All Seasprites have since 1970 been drastically converted to serve in the LAMPS (light airborne multi-purpose system) for anti-submarine and anti-missile defense.

The SH-2D has more than two tons of special equipment including powerful chin radar, sonobuoys, MAD gear, ECM, new navigation and communications systems and Mk 44 and/or Mk 46 torpedoes. All have been brought up to SH-2F standard with improved rotor, higher gross weight and improved sensors and weapons.

Though only the interim LAMPS platform, the SH-2 is a substantial program. The first of 88 new SH-2F Seasprites became operational in 1973, and by 1982 Kaman had delivered 88, plus 16 rebuilt SH-2Ds. Moreover, despite the existence of the much bigger and more costly SH-60B LAMPS III, 18 new-production SH-2Fs were ordered in 1981 and these were being delivered during 1984-85. The final nine have increased maximum weight (this may be cleared later on the whole fleet after small changes). A second batch of 18 new Seasprites was funded in FY83, and six each in FY84, 85 and 86 for service into the next century.

Right: Carrying extensive electronics, the SH-2F Seasprite LAMPS I helicopter is carried by smaller warships.

Lockheed C-5A Galaxy

C-5A, C-5B

Origin: Lockheed-Georgia Company, Marietta, Ga.

Type: Heavy strategic airlift transport.

Powerplant: Four 41,000lb (18,597kg) thrust General Electric TF39-1 turbofans.

Dimensions: Span 222ft 8½in (67.88m); length 247ft 10in (75.54m); height 65ft 1½in (19.85m); wing area 6,200sq ft (576.0m²).

Weights: Empty (basic operating) 337,937lb (153,285kg), loaded (2,25g) 769,000lb (348,810kg).

Performance: Maximum speed (max weight, 25,000ft/7,620m) 571mph (760km/h); normal long-range cruising speed, 518mph (834km/h); initial climb at max wt., rated thrust, 1,800ft (549m)/min; service ceiling, (615,000lb/278,950kg) 34,000ft (10.36km); range with design payload of 220, 967lb (100,228kg), 3,749 miles (6,033km); range with 112,600lb (51,074kg) payload, 6,529 miles 7,991 miles (12,860km); takeoff distance at max wt. over 50ft (15m), 8,400ft (2,560m); landing from 50ft (15m), 3,600ft (1,097m).

Armament: None.

History: First flight 30 June 1968; service delivery, 17 December 1969; final delivery from new, May 1973.

Development: Growing appreciation of the need for an extremely large

logistics transport to permit deployment of the heaviest hardware items on a global basis led in 1963 to the CX-HLS (Heavy Logistics System) specification calling for a payload of 250,000lb (113,400kg) over a coast-to-coast range and half this load over the extremely challenging unrefuelled range of 8,000 miles (12,875km); it also demanded the abililty to fly such loads into a 4,000ft (1,220m) rough forward airstrip. Such performance was theoretically possible using a new species of turbofan, of high bypass ratio, much more powerful than existing engines. In August 1965 GE won the engine contract, and two months later Lockheed won the C-5A aircraft. Design was undertaken under extreme pressure, the wing being assigned to CDI, a group of British engineers from the cancelled HS.115 and TSR.2 programmes. About half the value of each airframe was subcontracted to suppliers in the US and Canada, and construction of the first aircraft (66-8303) began as early as August 1966.

Meeting the requirements proved impossible, and cost-inflation reduced the total buy from 115 (six squadrons) to 81 (four squadrons), of which 30 were delivered by the end of 1970. As a cargo airlifter the C-5A proved in a class of its own, with main-deck width of 19ft (5.79m) and full-section access at front and rear. The upper deck houses the flight crew of five, a rest area for a further 15 and a rear (aft of the wing) area with 75 seats. Features include high-lift slats and flaps, an air-refuelling receptacle, advanced forward-looking radars and a unique landing gear with 28 wheels offering the required 'high flotation' for unpaved surfaces, as weel as free castoring to facilitate ground manoeuvring, an offset (20° to left or right) swivelling capability for use in crosswinds, fully modulating anti-skid brakes and the ability to kneel to bring the main deck close to the ground. Despite highly exceptional STOL (short takeoff and landing) qualities and good low-speed control with full-span slats and triple fans and rudders. Pilot and observer sit in side-by-side Martin Baker J5 seats and all versions have extremely good all-round view and very comprehensive navigation and communications equipment. All versions carry cameras and upward-firing flares for night photography. Most variants carry UAS-4 infra-red surveillance equipment and the -1B carries APS-94 SLAR (side-looking airborne radar) in a long pod under the right side of the fuselage, with automatic film processing giving, within seconds of exposure, a permanent film record of radar image on either side of the flight path. The -1D combined the functions of the two previous versions in being quickly convertible to either IR or SLAR missions. Underwing pylons can carry 150 US gal drop tanks, ECM (electronic countermeasures) pods, flare/chaff dispensers, or, in the JOV-1A such weapons as FFAR pods, 0.50in gun pods or 500lb (227kg) bombs—though a 1965 Department of Defense rule forbids the US Army to arm its fixed-wing aircraft! The EV-1 is the OV-1B converted to electronic surveillance with an ALQ-133 target locator system in centerline and tip pods. The RV-1C and -1D are conversions of the OV-1C and -1D for permanent use in the electronic reconnaissance role. Total production of all versions was 371, and since the mid-1970s the USA has maintained a continuing modernization programme involving (by 1983) 91 earlier models to OV-1D standard, and four to RV-1D, to maintain a force of 110 OV-1Ds and 36 RV-1Ds into the 1990s.

Right: An overhead view of the OV-1 Mohawk shows the type's wide fuselage with side-by-side seating, turboprop engines, two drop tanks and carriage of the APS-94 SLAR pod under the starboard side of the fuselage.

publicized faults, most of which were quickly rectified, the C-5A was soon giving invaluable service; but a deep-rooted difficulty was that the wing accrued fatigue damage much more rapidly than had been predicted. Several costly modification programmes proved incomplete solutions, and in 1978 Lockheed's proposal for the introduction of a new wing was accepted. This wing uses a totally different detailed design in different materials, and though the moving surfaces are largely unchanged even these are to be manufactured again, the slats, ailerons and flap tracks for the second time being assigned to Canadair. Between 1982-87 all 77 surviving

aircraft are to be re-winged. This is being done with minimal reduction in airlift capability by MAC's 60th MAW at Travis, 436th at Dover, Delaware, and 443rd at Altus AFB, Oklahoma.

In 1982 the US Congress authorized a programme to procure an additional 50 aircraft to a new C-5B standard, with a long crack-free airframe life, improved avionics and four General Electric TF39-GE-1C turbofan engines. The first flew on 10 September 1985.

Below: The C-5A is the USAF's primary strategic transport.

Lockheed C-130 Hercules

C-130A to P, DC-130, EC-130, HC-130, JHC-130, JC-130, MC-130, RC-130, WC-130.

Origin: Lockheed-Georgia Company, Marietta, Ga.
Type: Originally, multirole airlift transport; special variants, see text.
Powerplant: Four Allison T56 turboprops, (B and E families) 4,050ehp T56-7, (H family) 4,910ehp T56-15 flat-rated at 4,508ehp.
Dimensions: Span 132ft 7in (40.41m); length (basic) 97ft 9in (29.79m), (HC-130H, arms spread) 106ft 4in (32.41m); wing area 1,745sq ft (162.12m²).
Weights: Empty (basic E, H) 72,892lb (33 063kg); operating weight (H) 75,832lb (34,397kg); loaded (E,H) 155,000lb (70,310kg), max overload 175,000lb (79,380kg).
Performance: Maximum speed at 175,000lb (E, H), also max cruising speed, 386mph (621km/h); economical cruise, 345mph (556km/h); initial SL climb (E) 1,830ft (558m)/min, (H) 1,900ft (579m)/min; service ceiling at 155,000lb, (E) 23,000ft (7,010m), (H) 26,500ft (8,075m); range (H with max payload of 2,487 miles (4,002km; ferry range with reserves (H), 4,606 miles (7,412km); takeoff to 50ft (15m) (H at 175,000lb), 5,160ft (1,573m); landing from 50ft (15m) (H at 100,000lb/45,360kg), 2,700ft (823m).
Armament: Normally none.
History: First flight (YC-130A) 23 August 1954, (production C-130A) 7 April 1955; service delivery December 1956.

Development: When the Berlin Airlift and Korean war highlighted the need for more capable military transport aircraft, several obvious features were waiting to be combined in one design. Among these were a high wing and unobstructed cargo compartment, a flat level floor at truck-bed height above the ground, pressurization and air-conditioning, full-section rear door and vehicle ramp, turboprop propulsion for high performance, a modern flight deck with all-round vision, and retractable landing gear with 'high flotation' tyres for use from unprepared airstrips. All were incorporated in the Lockheed Model 82 which in June 1951 won an Air Force requirement for a new and versatile transport for TAC. By sheer good fortune the Allison single-shaft T56 turboprop matured at precisely the right time, along with a new species of advanced Aeroproducts or HamStan propeller and several other new-technology items including high-strength 2024 aluminium alloy, machined skin planks for the wings and cargo floor, metal/metal bonding and titanium alloys for the nacelles and flap skins. Another new feature was a miniature APU (auxiliary power unit) in one of the landing-gear blisters to provide ground power for air-conditioning and main-engine pneumatic starting.

Two YC-130 prototypes were built at Burbank, with 3,250hp T56-1 engines, but long before these were completed the programme was moved to the vast Government Plant 6 in Georgia which had been built to produce the B-29 under Bell management and restored to active use by Lockheed in January 1951. The new transport was ordered as the C-130A in September 1952 and the work phased in well with the tapering off of the B-47. When the 130, soon dubbed the Herky-bird, joined the 463rd Troop Carrier Wing at Ardmore in 1956 it caused a stir of a kind never before associated with a mere cargo transport. Pilots began to fly their big airlifters like fighters, and to explore the limits of what appeared to be an aircraft so willing it would do impossible demands. This was despite increases in permitted gross weight from 102,000lb to 116,000 and then to 124,200lb (56,335kg). At an early stage the nose grew a characteristic pimple from switching to the APN-59 radar, and provision was made for eight 1,000lb (454kg) Aerojet assisted takeoff rockets to be clipped to the sides of the fuselage, to augment the thrust of full-rated 3,750hp engines.

In December 1958 Lockheed flew the first extended-range C-130B with more powerful engines driving four-blade propellers. The Air Force bought

Above: Operated by MAC in the operational and tactical transport roles, the Hercules provides the USAF with unparalleled capability to support the US Army in the field, especially with the most capable C-130H model.

132 to supplement the 204 A-models, the latter progressively being rebuilt as AC-130 gunships, DC-130 drone (RPV) controllers, JC-130 spacecraft tracking and retrieval aircraft and C-130D wheel/ski aircraft with Arctic/Antarctic equipment. The next basic model, and bought in largest numbers (389), was the E, first flown on 25 August 1961. With this a minor structural rework enabled wing pylons to carry large drop tanks of 1,360 US gal (5,145lit), meeting the strategic range requirements of MATS (now MAC) and thus opening up a new market for the 130 beyond the tactical sphere. MATS (MAC) received 130 of the E model, and TAC re-equipped with 245 and transferred the A and B models to the ANG and Reserve, giving these reserve forces undreamed-of airlift capability. Some B-models were converted for other roles, new duties including weather reconnaissance (WC-130) and a single STOL aircraft with extra pod-mounted T56 engines supplying a boundary-layer control system, designated NC-130. Among currently serving rebuilds of the E are the EC-130E tactical command and control platform, with several unique avionic systems, and the MC-130E used with special avionics and low-level flight techniques for clandestine exfiltration and airdrop missions.

Latest basic type is the C-130H, first delivered in April 1975, with more powerful engines flat-rated at the previous level to give improved takeoff from hot/high airstrips. Variations include the HC-130H extended-range model for the Aerospace Rescue and Recovery Service with a fold-out nose installation for the snatching of people or payloads from the ground. The JHC-130H model has further gear for aerial recovery of space capsules. A more advanced model, with special direction-finding receivers but without long-range tanks, is the HC-130N. The HC-130P model combines the mid-air retrieval capability with a tanking and air-refuelling function for helicopters.

This evergreen aircraft is by far the most important Air Force tactical airlifter and fulfils a host of secondary functions. Though civil and RAF versions have been stretched to match capacity to payload, this has not been done by the USAF. Production continues, and six H models were ordered for the AFRes and ANG in July 1981. New roles being studied by the Air Force include the C-130H-MP maritime patroller with offshore surveillance equipment, and the CAML (cargo aircraft minelayer) system using hydraulically powered pallets for rapid-sequence deployment of large sea mines. Should CAML be adopted, Air Force C-130s could fly minelaying missions for the Navy.

Below: The AC-130H is a dedicated Hercules gunship, in this instance flown by the 7th Special Operations Squadron.

Lockheed C-141 StarLifter

C-141A and B

Origin: Lockheed-Georgia Company, Marietta, Ga.
Type: Strategic airlift and aeromedical transport.
Powerplant: Four 21,000lb (9,525kg) thrust Pratt & Whitney TF33-7 turbofans.
Dimensions: Span 159ft 11in (48.74m); length (A) 145ft. 0in (44.2m), (B) 168ft 3½in (51.29m); wing area 3,228sq. ft (299.9m²).
Weights: Empty (A) 133,733lb (60,678kg), (B) 148,120lb (67,186kg); loaded (A) 316,600lb (143,600kg), (B) 343,000lb (155,585kg).
Performance: Maximum speed (A) 571mph (919km/h), (B, also max cruising speed) 566mph (910km/h); long-range cruising speed (both) 495mph (796km/h), initial climb (A) 3,100ft (945m)/min, (B) 2,920ft (890m)/min; service ceiling, 41,600ft (12,68km); range with maximum payload of (A, 70,847lb/32,136kg) 4,080 miles (6,565km), (B, 90,880lb/41,222kg) 2,935 miles (4,725km); takeoff to 50ft (15m) (B) 5,800ft (1,768m).
Armament: None.
History: First flight 17 December 1953; service delivery 19 October 1964; first flight of C-141B, 24 March 1977.

Development: In the late 1950s MATS (now MAC) anticipated a severe future shortage of long-range airlift capacity, the C-133 being an interim propeller aircraft and the much larger C-132 being cancelled. As interim solutions orders were placed for the C-135 jet and for a long-range version of the C-130, but on 4 May 1960 a requirement was issued for a purpose-designed transport which was won by Lockheed's Model 300 submission in March 1961. Ordered at once as the C-141, it followed the lines of the C-130, and even had the same 10ft x 9ft (3.1 x 2.77m) body cross-section (a choice which perhaps proved erroneous, as from the start the internal cube volume was totally inadequate for the available weightlifting ability). The C-141 was, in other respects, much larger, with a wing of almost twice the area, swept at only 23° (¼-chord) for good field length but resulting in lower speeds than equivalent civil transports. Features included a full-section ramp/door, side paratroop doors, upper-surface roll/airbrake spoilers, four reversers, tape instruments, an all-weather landing system and advanced loading and positioning systems for pallets and other loads.

The first five C-141As were ordered in August 1961, at which time the requirement was for 132 aircraft, but following extremely rapid development and service introduction further orders were placed for a total of 285. Several of the first block were structurally modified to improve the ability of the floor to support the skids of a containerized Minuteman ICBM, a weight of 86,207lb (30,103kg). One of these aircraft set a world record in parachuting a single mass of 70,195lb (31,840kg). Standard loads included 10 regular 463L cargo pallets, 154 troops, 123 paratroops or 80 litter

Above: Development of the C-141B conversion variant has finally made the StarLifter weight- rather than volume-limited, providing far greater operational capacity as inflight-refuelling capability was added at the same time.

(stretcher) patients plus 16 medical attendants. Usable volume was 5,290 cu ft (150m³), not including the ramp. Service experience proved exemplary and in the Vietnam war C-141s, many of them specially equipped for medical missions and flown with extraordinary skill to ensure a smooth ride even through severe weather, maintained essentially a daily schedule on a 10,000-mile (16,000km) trip with full loads both ways.

It was this full-load experience which finally drove home the lesson that the C-141 could use more cubic capacity. Lockheed devised a cost/effective stretch which adds 'plugs' ahead of and behind the wing which extend the usable length by 23ft 4in (7.11m), increasing the usable volume (including the ramp) to 11,399cu ft (322.71m³). The extended aircraft, designated C-141B, carriers 13 pallets or much larger numbers of personnel. It also incorporates an improved wing/body fairing which reduces drag and fuel burn per unit distance flown, while among other modifications the most prominent is a dorsal bulge aft of the flight deck housing a universal (boom or drogue) flight-refuelling receptacle. The first conversion, the YC-141B, was so successful that the Air Force decided to have Lockheed rework all the surviving aircraft (277), to give in effect the airlift ability of 90 additional aircraft with no extra fuel consumption.

Two hundred and seventy C-141As were converted to B standard in the early 1980s and equip 14 squadrons assigned to the following MAWs: 60th at Travis, California; 63rd at Norton, California; 437th at Charleston, S Carolina; 438th at McGuire, NJ; 443rd at Altus, Oklahoma; and to part of the 314th TAW at Little Rock, Arkansas.

Lockheed P-3 Orion

P-3A, B and C with derivatives

Origin: Lockheed-California Company, Burbank, California.
Type: Maritime patrol and ASW aircraft, (EP) EW platform; data are for P-3C Update.
Powerplant: Four 4,910ehp (4,510shp) Allison T56-14 turboprops.
Dimensions: Span 99ft 8in (30.37m); length 116ft 10in (35.61m); height overall 33ft 8½in (10.27m); wing area 1,300sq ft (120.77m²).
Weights: Empty 61,491lb (27,890kg); normal loaded 135,000lb (61,235kg); max 142,000lb (64,410kg).
Performance: Max speed (15,000ft/4,570m at 105,000lb/47,625kg) 473mph (761km/h); patrol speed 237mph (381km/h); takeoff over 50ft (15m) 5,490ft (1,673m); mission radius (3h on station at low level) 1,550 miles (2,494km), (no time on station) 2,383 miles (3,853km).
Armament: Internal bay can accommodate eight AS torpedoes, or two Mk 101 nuclear depth bombs plus four torpedoes or a variety of mines and other stores; ten underwing pylons carry mines, depth bombs, torpedoes, Harpoon anti-ship missiles or other stores. Total expendable load 20,000lb (9,072kg).
History: First flight (aerodynamic prototype YP3V, converted Electra) 19 August 1958; (YP-3A) November 1959, (P-3A) 15 April 1961, (P-3C) 18 September 1968; service delivery (A) August 1962, (C Update) April 1974, (Update II) August 1977, (Update III) August 1983.

Development: Derived from the L-188 Electra passenger airliner, the P-3 Orion was specifically ordered as an off-the-shelf type, for operation in the ocean patrol and ASW role from shore bases. Nobody expected it to have a production run of over 30 years; moreover, it has become virtually the standard aircraft in its class and in the Netherlands has now even replaced the Atlantic which was a 'clean sheet of paper' design. The P-3 inherited from the L-188 good short-field performance, outstanding handling even with three of the broad-bladed propellers

feathered, thermal de-icing (bleed air on the wings, electric on the tail) and a pressurized fuselage with a circular section giving a maximum cabin width of 10ft 10in (3.3m). Instead of adding a giant weapon bay, as was done with the Nimrod, Lockheed merely put in a shallow bay under the floor and made up the required payload with external pylons. Typically the P-3 is flown by a flight crew of five, with the centre fuselage occupied by the tactical crew, also numbering five. There is the usual dinette and two folding bunks at the extreme rear.

Early P-3A and B versions are still serving with some export customers, though all have had some updating and a few in the USA have been converted for other roles. US Navy squadrons VQ-1 and -2 replaced their EC-121 Warning Stars with the EP-3E, gross rebuilds of early P-3s to serve in the Elint role. Distinguished by their giant 'doghouse' radomes and other antennas above and below the fuselage, the EP-3Es are equipped for detecting, fixing and recording emissions from unfriendly ships, their main sensors being passive receivers, direction finders and signal analysers.

▶

Below: The P-3B variant of the Orion ocean patrol and ASW aircraft is now used only by Naval Air Reserve squadrons.

The US Navy and Lear Siegler developed a modification kit to update early P-3s, especially the P-3B, with new navaids and sensors; the RNZAF aircraft have been thus modified. The only current P-3A operator is Spain, whose aircraft are ex-USN and replaced leased examples. Even the improved P-3B in the US Navy serves only with Reserve squadrons.

Standard model today is the P-3C Update III. This has APS-115 radar, ASA-64 MAD in the tail boom, a battery of sonobuoys and other sonics installations in the rear fuselage, and launchers for A- and B-size buoys immediately aft of the wing. In many Orions, including P-3Cs of early

vintage, the chin position is occupied by a glass-paned gondola housing a KA-74A gimbal-mounted surveillance camera; today, this is replaced by a retractable FLIR. Another variable feature is the choice of pods on the two inboard pylons under the wing roots. It is common to find the ALQ-78 ESM (passive receiver, with what look like anhedralled delta wings) on the left pylon and the AXR-13 LLLTV on the right. Today the latter is usually replaced by the nose FLIR, and the ESM will eventually be replaced by a completely new AIL system in wingtip pods which will also provide targeting data for the Harpoon missiles, provision for which was incorporated at the Update II stage. The three Update stages

Lockheed S-3 Viking

S-3A Viking, US-3A and S-3B
Origin: Lockheed-California Company, Burbank, California.
Type: Four-seat carrier-based anti-submarine aircraft.
Powerplant: Two 9,275lb (4,207kg) General Electric TF34-2 or TF34-400 two-shaft turbofans.
Dimensions: Span 68ft 8in (20.93m); length 53ft 4in (16.26m); height 22ft 9in (6.93m); wing area 598sq ft (55.56m²).
Weights: Empty 26,600lb (12,065kg); normal loaded for carrier operation 42,500lb (19,277kg); maximum loaded 47,000lb (21,319kg).
Performance: Maximum speed 506mph (814km/h); initial climb, over 4,200ft (1,280m)/min; service ceiling, above 35,000ft (10,670m); combat range, more than 2,303 miles (3,705km); ferry range, more than 3,454 miles (5,558km).
Armament: Split internal weapon bays can house four Mk 46 torpedoes, four Mk 82 bombs, four various depth bombs or four mines; two wing pylons can carry single or triple ejectors for bombs, rocket pods, missiles, tanks or other stores, the S-3B carrying two AGM-84A Harpoon missiles.
History: First flight 21 January 1972; service delivery October 1973; operational use (VS-41) 20 February 1974; final delivery 1980.

Development: Designed to replace the evergreen Grumman S-2, the S-3 is perhaps the most remarkable exercise in packaging in the history of aviation. It is also an example of an aircraft in which the operational equipment costs considerably more than the aircraft itself. Lockheed-California won the Navy competition in partnership with LTV (Vought) which makes the wing, engine pods, tail and F-8-type landing gear. The long-span wings have high-lift flaps and spoilers, ESM receiver pods on the tips, and form integral tanks inboard of the fold hinges. The latter are skewed so that the folded wings can overlap each other. The vertical tail also folds to lie flat.

Lockheed built eight development prototypes plus 179 inventory aircraft. In 1984 conversion began to S-3B standard, with updated equipment and avionics and provision to launch Harpoon anti-ship cruise missiles. Developed versions, including a COD transport, tanker, ECM and AEW versions are also possible, for both carrier and land operation. The US-3A transport carries most of its payload in large underwing pods, but the Navy has decided to stick with the C-2A Greyhound (though four US-3As are in service in the Philippines). The KS-3A air-refueling tanker proved satisfactory on test, but none has been procured to augment the small fleet of EKA-3B and KA-6D tankers, mainly because of the high cost of reopening the production line.

Right: An armed S-3A prepares for launch from USS Saratoga.

Lockheed SR-71

SR-71 A, B and C
Origin: Lockheed-California Company, Burbank, California.
Type: A, strategic reconnaissance; B, C, trainer.
Powerplant: Two 32,500lb (14,742kg) thrust Pratt & Whitney J58-1 (JT11D-20B) continuous-bleed afterburning turbojets.
Dimensions: Span 55ft 7in (16.94m); length 107ft 5in (32.74m); wing area 1,800sq ft (167.2m²).
Weights: Empty, not disclosed, but about 65,000lb (29.5t); loaded 170,000lb (77,112kg).
Performance: Maximum speed (also maximum cruising speed), about 2,100mph (3,380km/h) at over 60,000ft (18,29m); world record speed over 15/25km course, 2,193mph (3,530km/h), Mach 3.31); maximum sustained height (also world record), 85,069ft (25,929m); range at 78,740ft (24km) at 1,983mph (3191km/h, Mach 3) on internal fuel, 2,982 miles (4,800km); corresponding endurance, 1h 30min; endurance at loiter speed, up to 7h.
Armament: None.
History: First flight (A-11) 26 April 1962; (SR-71A) 22 December 1964; service delivery, January 1966.

Development: Unbelievably, Lockheed and the Air Force succeeded in designing, building and completing the flight-test programme of these extremely large and noisy aircraft in total secrecy. President Johnson disclosed the existence of the basic A-11 design in February 1964. It was created by Lockheed's Advanced Development Projects team—the so-called Skunk Works—under vice-president C.L. 'Kelly' Johnson in 1959-61 The requirement was for a platform able to succeed the U-2 for clandestine reconnaissance, and as height was no longer sufficient protection, speed had to be added (which in turn translated into still greater height). The engineering problems with the titanium-alloy airframe, the unprecedented propulsion system (which at cruising speed glows orange-white at the rear yeat gets most of its thrust from the inlet) and even the hydraulic system which had to use totally new materials and techniques. Basic features included a modified delta wing with pronounced camber on the outer leading edges, extremely large lifting strakes extended forwards along the body and nacelles, twin inwards-canted pivoted fins above the nacelles, outboard ailerons, inboard elevators and main gears with three wheels side-by-side. The original A-11 shape also featured fixed ventral fins under the rear of the nacelles and a larger hinged central ventral fin.

The first three aircraft (60-6934/6) were built as YF-12A research interceptors, with a pressurized cockpit for a pilot and air interception officer, Hughes ASG-18 pulse-doppler radar, side chines cut back to avoid the radome and provide lateral locations for two IR seekers, and tandem missile bays for (usually) eight AIM-47 AAMs. In 1969-72 two participated in a joint programme with NASA to investigate many aspects of flight at

around Mach 3. These aircraft investigated surface finishes other than the normal bluish-black which resulted in the popular name of 'Blackbird' for all aircraft of this family.

It is believed that about 15 aircraft were delivered to the Air Force with a generally similar standard of build, though configured for the reconnaissance/strike role. Designated A-11, they could carry a centreline pod which could be a 1-megaton bomb but was usually a GTD-21 reconnaissance drone looking like a scaled-down single-engined A-11 and with cameras, IR and (variously, according to mission) other sensors in a bay behind the multi-shock centrebody nose inlet. Some dozens of these RPVs were delivered, painted the same heat-reflective black and with similar flight performance (engine has not been disclosed) but with rather shorter endurance. Those not consumed in missions (about 17) were stored at Davis-Monthan.

have dramatically multiplied processor speed and memory, added navaids such as VLF/Omega to the original INS and mix of doppler and Loran, and completely new subsystems for managing and processing the sonics, including a new receiver and the IBM Proteus acoustic processor. Lockheed is also flying a demonstrator of an AEW&C (airborne early warning and control) P-3 aimed at export customers.

Right: The P-3C Update I is structurally and aerodynamically akin to the P-3B, but carries radically improved electronics and, from Update II models, four Harpoon anti-ship missiles.

The A-11/GTD-21 held the fort until, in 1964, the definitive long-range recon/strike RS-71A came into service. (It was announced by President Johnson as the SR-71A and as he was never corrected the 'SR' designation became accepted.) This also can carry a 1-MT bomb pod or GTD-21 or derived RPV, but details of missions and payloads have not been disclosed. With an airframe and increased-capacity fuel system first flown on the fourth A-11 (designated YF-12C) it is longer, has no rear ventrals, optimized forward chines extending to the tip of the nose, and no missile bay but extremely comprehensive and in some cases unique reconnaissance systems for the surveillance of from 60,000 to 80,000 square miles

Below: Despite the age of the basic design, the SR-71A remains unrivalled in terms of sheer performance.

(155,000 to 207,000km²) per hour. The backseater, with a separate clamshell canopy with inserted panes of heat-resistant glass, is the RSO, reconnaissance systems officer. Both crew wear Astronaut suits and follow pre-flight procedures based on those of space missions. The first SR-71A was assigned to a new unit, the 4,200th SRW, at Beale AFB, California, in 1966, which worked up the optimum operating procedures and techniques for best coverage, optimum fuel consumption, minimal signatures and precision navigation, burning special JP-7 fuel topped up in flight by KC-135Q tankers also based at Beale. To facilitate the demanding process of crew conversion to this extremely costly aircraft an operational trainer, the SR-71B, was purchased, at least two being slotted into the main batch of 29 (or more) which began at 61-7950. This has a raised instructor cockpit and dual pilot controls, and also includes the reconnaissance systems for RSO training.

After the first crews had qualified as fully operational, in 1971, the parent wing was restyled the 9th SRW, with two squadrons. This has ever since operated in a clandestine manner, rarely more than two aircraft being despatched to any overseas theatre and missions normally being flown by single aircraft. It is not known to what extent subsonic cruise is used; in the normal high-speed regime the skin temperature rises from -49°C to 550/595°C, and the fuel serves as the heat sink and rises to a temperature of about 320°C before reaching the engines; at least one SR-71C was produced as an SR-71A rebuild, following loss of an SR-71B. It has been estimated that the SR-71As seldom fly more than 200 hours per year, mainly on training exercises. No recent estimate has been published of their vulnerability.

Below: The lines of the SR-71A are indicative of the type's superb performance, while the chines also provide useful volume for highly classified reconnaissance systems.

Lockheed TR-1

U-2A, B, C, CT, D, R, WU-2 family and TR-1A & B.

Origin: Lockheed California Company, Burbank, California.
Powerplant: One Pratt & Whitney unaugmented turbojet, (A and some derivatives) 11,200lb (5,080kg) thurst J57-13A or -37A, (most other U-2) versions) one 17,000lb (7,711kg) thrust J75-13, (TR-1) 17,000lb (7,711kg) J75-13B.
Dimensions: Span (A,B,C,D,CT) 80ft 0in (24,38m), R, WU-2C, TR-1) 103ft 0in (31.39m); length (typical of early versions) 49ft 7in (15.1m), (R, TR) 63ft 0in (19.2m); wing area (early) 565sq ft (52.49m²), (R, TR) 1,000sq ft (92.9m²).
Weights: Empty (A) 9,920lb (4,500kg), (B,C,CT,D) typically 11,700lb (5,305kg), (R) 14,990lb (6,800kg), (TR) about 16,000lb (7,258kg); loaded (A) 14,800lb (6,713kg), (B,C,CT,D, clean) typically 16,000lb (7,258kg), (with 89 US gal wing tanks) 17,270lb (7,833kg), (R) 29,000lb (13,154kg), (TR) 40,000lb (18,144kg).
Performance: Maximum speed (A) 494mph (795km/h), (B,C,CT,D) 528mph (850km/h), (R) about 510mph (821 1km/h), (TR) probably about 495mph (797km/h); maximum cruising speed (most) 460mph (740m/h), (TR) 430mph (692km/h); operational ceiling (A) 70,000ft (21.34km), (B,C, CT, D) 85,000ft (25.9km), (R,TR) about 90,000ft (27.43km); maximum range (A) 2,200 miles (3,540km), (B,C,CT,D) 3,000 miles (4,830km), (R) about 3,500 miles (5,833km), (TR) about 4,000 miles (6,437km); endurance on internal fuel (A) 5½ h, (B,C,CT,D) 6½ h, (R) 7½ h, (TR) 12 h.
Armament: None.
History: First flight (A) 1 August 1955; service delivery February 1956; operational service, June 1957.

Development: First of the two families of clandestine surveillance aircraft produced by Lockheed's 'Skunk Works' under the brilliant engineering leadership of C.L. 'Kelly' Johnson, the U-2 was conceived in spring 1954 to meet an unannounced joint USAF/CIA requirement for a reconnaissance and research aircraft to cruise at the highest attainable altitudes. The entire programme was cloaked in secrecy, test flying (under Tony LeVier) took place at remote Watertown Strip, Nevada, and no announcement was made of delivery to the Air Force of 56-675 and -676, the two prototypes. The original order comprised 48 single-seaters and five tandem-seat aircraft, initially the back-seater being an observer or systems operator. The operating unit was styled Weather Reconnaissance Squadron, Provisional

Above: The TR-1A is designed for long endurance at high altitude, and carries a mass of sensors in its wing pods.

(1st) and soon moved to Atsugi AB, Japan, while the WRS,P (2nd) moved to Wiesbaden, Germany, with basing also at Lakenheath, England. The WRS,P(3rd) remained at Edwards to develop techniques and handle research.

Intense interest in the aircraft, grey and without markings, prompted an announcement that they were NASA research aircraft, with Utility designation U-2, but after numerous unmolested missions over the Soviet Union, China and other territories, one of the CIA aircraft was shot down near Sverdlovsk on 1 May 1960. Future missions were flown by USAF pilots in uniform, with USAF markings on the aircraft. Several more J75-powered aircraft were shot down over China and Cuba, and attrition was also fairly high from accidents, because the U-2 is possibly the most difficult of all modern aircraft to fly. Features include an all-metal airframe of sailplane-like qualities, with a lightly loaded and extremely flexible wing, tandem bicycle landing gears, outrigger twin-wheel units jettisoned on takeoff (the landing tipping on to a downturned wingtip), an unpressurized cockpit with UV-protected sliding canopy of F-104 type, special low-volatility fuel, and large flaps, airbrakes and braking parachute.

McDonnell Douglas A-4 Skyhawk

A-4A to S and TA-4 series

Origin: Douglas Aircraft Company, El Segundo, California, later moved to McDonnell Douglas, Long Beach, California.
Type: Single-seat attack bomber; TA, dual-control trainer.
Powerplant: (B, C) one 7,700lb (3,493kg) thrust Wright J65-16A single-shaft turbojet (US Sapphire); (E, J) 8,500lb (3,856kg) Pratt & Whitney J52-6 two-shaft turbojet; (F) 9,300lb (4,218kg) J52-8A; (M, N) 11,200lb (5,080kg) J52-408A.
Dimensions: Span 27ft 6in (8.38m); length (A) 39ft 1in (11.91m), (B) 39ft 6in (12.04m) (42ft 10¾in, 13.07m over FR probe), (E,F) 40ft 1½in (12.22m), (M, N) 40ft 3¼in (12.27m), (TA series, excluding probe) 42ft 7¼in (12.98m); height 15ft (4.57m), (early single-seaters 15ft 2in, TA series 15ft 3in); wing area 260sq ft (24.15m²).
Weights: Empty (A) 7,700lb (3,493kg), (E) 9,284lb (4,211kg), (typical modern single-seat, eg M) 10,465lb (4,747kg), (TA-4F) 10,602lb (4,809kg); maximum loaded (A) 17,000lb (7,711kg), (B) 22,000lb (9,979kg), (all others, shipboard) 24,500lb (11,113kg), (land-based) 27,420lb (12,437kg).
Performance: Maximum speed (clean) (B) 676mph (1,088km/h), (E) 685mph (1,102km/h), (M) 670mph (1,078km/h), (TA-4F) 675mph (1,086km/h); maximum speed (4,000lb-1,814kg bombload) (F) 593mph (954km/h), (M) 645mph (1,038km/h); initial climb (F) 5,620ft (1,713m)/min, (M) 8,440ft (2,572m)/min; service ceiling (all, clean) about 49,000ft (14,935m); range (clean, or with 4,000/1,814kg weapons and maximum fuel, all late versions) about 920 miles (1,480km); maximum range (M) 2,055 miles (3,307km).
Armament: Standard on most versions, two 20mm Mk 12 cannon, each with 200 rounds; pylons under fuselage and wings for total ordnance load of (A, B, C) 5,000lb (2,268kg), (E, F) 8,200lb (3,720kg), (M, N) 9,155lb (4,153kg).
History: First flight (XA4D-1) 22 June 1954, (A-4A) 14 August 1954, squadron delivery October 1956, (A-4C) August 1959, (A-4E) July 1961, (A-4F) August 1966; (A-4M) April 1970, (A-4N) June 1972, first of TA series (TA-4E) June 1965.

Development: Most expert opinion in the US Navy refused to believe

the claim of Ed Heinemann, chief engineer of what was then Douglas El Segundo, that he could build a jet attack bomber weighing half the 30,000lb (13,600kg) specified by the Navy. The first Skyhawk, nicknamed 'Heinemann's Hot Rod', not only flew but gained a world record by flying a 311 miles (500km) circuit at over 695mph (1,118km/h). Today over 30 years later, greatly developed versions are still in use. These late versions do weigh close to 30,000lb, but only because the basic design has been improved with more powerful engines, increased fuel capacity and much heavier weapon load. The wing was made in a single unit, forming an integral fuel tank and so small it did not need to fold. The tall main gears fold forwards, the legs lying under the main wing box and the wheels ahead of it. The rudder has a single skin down the centre, with ribs on each side.

Hundreds of Skyhawks have served aboard carriers, but in the US involvement in SE Asia 'The Scooter' (as it was affectionately known) flew many kinds of mission from land bases. In early versions the emphasis was on improving range and load and the addition of all-weather avionics. The F model introduced the dorsal hump containing additional avionics, and the M, the so-called Skyhawk II, marked a major increase in mission effectiveness. Most of the TA-4 trainers closely resembled the corresponding single-seater, but the TA-4J and certain other models have simplified avionics and are used not only for advanced pilot training but also by the 'Top Gun' and similar fighter-pilot training units for dissimilar aircraft combat training.

In the Vietnam War hundreds of A-4s saw intensive action from the summer of 1964. The types involved were the A-4C, D, E, F, M and TA-4F, operated by many squadrons of the Navy and Marine Corps. In August 1965, during the 37-month Rolling Thunder bombing campaign against North Vietnam, two A-4Es became the first Navy aircraft, and almost the first in history to be brought down by SAMs. Vast amounts of ordnance were delivered, usually with great accuracy.

Though production was completed in 1979 after 26 unbroken years, with deliveries amounting to 2,405 attack models and 555 two-seaters, updating programs continue to improve survivors in Navy and Marine Corps service. There is also a major rebuild program which since 1980 has given the Marines 23 two-seat TA-4F trainers rebuilt as OA-4M FAC (Forward Air Control) platforms with avionics basically as in the A-4M and rear canopy sections faired into the 'camel hump'. Many versions, both new and ex-US service, have been exported.

Right: The A-4 series is obsolescent by the latest front-line attack standards, but still serves usefully in other roles. These are TA-4Js operated for aggressor training.

into a bulged upper platform carrying the tailplane. All known U-2R aircraft have been matt black, serving with various overseas commands.

The latest variant, the TR-1, is basically a further updated U-2R with ASARS (advanced Synthetic-Aperture Radar System), in the form of the UPD-X side-looking airborne radar, and with dramatically increased integral-tank fuel capacity, which results in very much higher gross weight. A single-seater, like the R, the TR-1A carries extensive new avionics in its pods, as well as much more comprehensive ECM. Mission equipment is also carried in the nose, in the Q-bay behind the cockpit and between the inlet ducts. Because of the long endurance the Astronaut-suited pilot has special facilities for his personal comfort and for taking warm food. The first batch comprised two TR-1As (80-1061 and 1062) and a third aircraft (1063) which was actually first to be delivered, on 10 June 1981, via the Air Force to NASA with designation ER-2 for earth-rescource missions. Next followed three more TR-1As and a two-seat TR-1B, the eventual fleet expected to number 33 As and two Bs. The main base is at Alconbury, England and the mission is to look 35 miles (55km) into Communist territory.

Right: The TR-1 is more "flyable" than the U-2, but the TR-1B two-seat conversion trainer is still vitally important.

From 1959 the J75 engine was installed, and with the U-2C the inlets were splayed out at the front, the U-2D being the original two-seat version and the U-2CT (conversion trainer) being one of at least six rebuilds, in this example as a dual-control pilot trainer with the instructor seated at an upper level. Most CTs have been stationed at the Air Force Flight Test Center and Test Pilot School, both at Edwards. The AFFTC also uses several other versions, including D variants with special instrumentation, dorsal or ventral inlets for sampling, and various external payloads, with a variety of black, white and other paint schemes. Both C and D models have large dorsal 'doghouse' fairings for sampling, sensing or avionic equipment.

Because of high attrition the line was reopened in 1968 with 12 considerably larger aircraft styled U-2R (68-10329 to 10340). While most earlier models could carry 80 US gal (336lit) tanks on the leading edge, the R was supplied with large wing pods permanently installed and accommodating various payloads as well as 105 US gal (398lit) fuel. Wet wings increased internal capacity, and the R also introduced a stretched airframe able to accommodate all necessary fuel and equipment internally. Front and rear main gears were moved closer together and the rear fuselage was formed

McDonnell Douglas AH-64 Apache

Model 77, AH-64

Type: Armed helicopter.

Engines: Two 1,536shp General Electric T700-700 free-turbine turbo-shafts.

Dimensions: Diameter of four-blade main rotor 48ft 0in (14·63m); length overall (rotors turning) 57ft ½in (17·39m); length of fuselage 49ft 1½in (14·97m); height to top of hub 13ft 10in (4·22m).

Weights: Empty 10,268lb (4,657kg); maximum loaded 17,650lb (8,006kg)

Performance: Maximum speed (13,925lb/6,316kg) 192mph (309km/h); maximum cruising speed 182mph (293km/h); max vertical climb 2,880ft (878m)/min; max range on internal fuel 380 miles (611km); ferry range 1,121 miles (1,804km).

Armament: Four wing hardpoints can carry 16 Hellfire missiles or 76 rockets (or mix of these weapons); turret under fuselage (designed to collapse harmlessly upwards in crash landing) houses 30mm Chain Gun with 1,200 rounds of varied types of ammunition.

History: First flight (YAH-64) 30 September 1975; entry into service scheduled 1984.

Development: A generation later than the cancelled Lockheed AH-56A Cheyenne (the world's first dedicated armed escort and attack helicopter), the AH-64 was selected as the US Army's standard future attack helicopter in December 1976. This followed competitive evaluation with the rival Bell YAH-63, which had tricycle landing gear and the pilot seated in front of the co-pilot/gunner. The basic development contract also included the Chain Gun, a lightweight gun (in 30mm calibre in this application) with a rotating lockless bolt. In 1977 development began of the advanced avionics, electro-optics and weapon-control systems, progressively fitted to three more prototypes, followed by a further three—designated Total Systems Aircraft—flown by early 1980. The 56-month development ended in mid-1981 and limited production began at the end of that year. Total US Army requirement is for 572 machines, but actual procurement may be rather less, because of rapid cost escalation.

McDonnell Douglas (formerly Hughes) is responsible for dynamic components, while Teledyne Ryan produces the bulk of the rest of the airframe (fuselage, wings, engine nacelles, avionic bays, canopy and tail unit). The entire structure is designed to withstand hits with any type of ammunition up to 23mm calibre. The main blades, for example, each have five stainless-steel spars, with structural glassfiber tube linings, a laminated stainless steel skin and composite rear section, all bonded together. The main sensors are PNVS (pilot's night vision system) and TADS (target acquisition and designation sight) jointly developed by Martin Marietta and Northrop.

Both crew members are equipped with the Honeywell IHADSS (integrated helmet and display sight system) and each can in emergency fly the helicopter and control its weapons. The helicopter's nose sight incorporates day/night FLIR (forward-looking infra-red) laser ranger/designator and laser tracker. The AH-64 carries an ordnance load of some 2,650lb (1,202kg), which can include up to 16 Hellfire anti-tank missiles, 76 2·75in (6·98cm) rockets, up to 1,200 rounds for its 30mm cannon, or lesser combinations of these.

Above: The AH-64A is heavy but agile, and possesses excellent armament matched to an advanced targeting system.

Below: The Apache's most important weapon is the laser-homing Hellfire, a "fire-and-forget" anti-tank missile.

McDonnell Douglas C-9

C-9A, VC-9A

Origin: Douglas Aircraft Company, Long Beach, California.
Type: Aeromedical airlift transport.
Powerplant: Two 14,500lb (6,577kg) thrust Pratt & Whitney JT8D-9 turbofans.
Dimensions: Span 93ft 5in (28.47m), length 119ft 3½in (36,37m), wing area 1,000.7sq ft (92.97m²).
Weights: Empty about 60,500lb (27,443kg); loaded 108,000 or 121,000lb (48,989 or 54,884kg).
Performance: Maximum speed 583mph (938km/h); maximum cruising speed 564mph (907km/h); initial climb 2,900ft (885m)/min; takeoff field length, 5,530ft (1,685m); range with maximum payload of 22,000lb (9,979kg), about 1,990 miles (3,203km).
Armament: None.
History: First flight (DC-9) 25 February 1955; service delivery 10 August 1968.

Development: While the Navy requested a completely re engineered DC-9 (as the C-9B Skytrain II) the Air Force bought the DC-9-30 off the shelf, with few modifications as its standard aeromedical transport over tactical ranges. It has three entrances, two with special hydraulic stairways and the third a large door forward on the left side with a hydraulic elevator for loading litters (stretcher patients). Normal loads can be up to 40 litter patients and/or 40 seated, plus two nurses and three aeromedical technicians. There are galleys

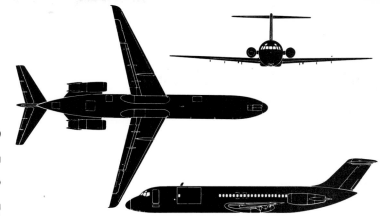

Above: Three-view of the McDonnell Douglas C-9A.

and toilets front and rear, as well as a special care compartment with its own environmental controls. A total of 21 C-9As was delivered in 1968-73, equipping the 375th AAW at MAC's headquarters at Scott AFB, Illinois, and the 435th TAW at Rhein Main airport, Germany. The VIP VC-9A (originally VC-9C) force comprises three aircraft assigned to the 89th MAG SAMW at Andrews, near Washington DC.

Below: The C-9A is a dedicated aeromedical transport fitted out as a flying hospital, as such boosting the morale of fighting men in remoter areas by offering the real advantages of rapid movement to well-equipped hospitals.

McDonnell Douglas C-17

C-17A

Origin: Douglas Aircraft Company, Long Beach, California.
Type: Long-range heavy airlift transport.
Powerplant: Four 37,600lb (17,055kg) thrust Pratt & Whitney PW2037 turbofans.
Dimensions: Span 165ft 0in (50.29m); length 170ft 8in (52.02m); height 53ft 6in (16.31m); wing area 3,800sq ft (353m²).
Weights: Empty 259,000lb (117,480kg); loaded 572,000lb (259,455kg).
Performance: Normal cruising speed about 495mph (797km/h); takeoff field length with maximum payload, 7,600ft (2,320m); landing field length with max payload, 3,000ft (914m); range with maximum payload, 2,765 miles (4,445km); ferry range 5,755 miles (9,265km).
Armament: None.
History: First flight, possibly 1986; delivery about 1989; full operational capability, 'early 1990s'.

Development: After years of study, which originally centred on tactical aircraft to replace the C-130 (YC-14 and YC-15) but moved to global ranges with the announcement of the Rapid Deployment Force, the USAF was able to issue an RFP for the new C-X long-range heavy airlift transport in October 1980. Douglas's selection was announced in August 1981, but it took until 1985 before the USAF firmly committed itself to the programme.
In early 1982 the Reagan administration stated that it did not plan further development of the C-17, but in mid-year let a "modestly paced" R&D programme to McDonnell Douglas for further work on the project. The Fiscal Year 1985 programme, however, announced full-scale engineering development; the first prototype will fly in 1989 and IOC is expected for late 1991, in a programme which may eventually rival that of the C-130.
The C-17 will be an extremely modern aircraft in all respects, with a 25° supercritical wing carrying four of the newest engines, each with a reverser,

blowing back close under the wing to give powered lift when the titanium flaps are lowered. Ground mobility will be exceptional, with four main gears each with a row of three low-pressure tyres, allowing the fully loaded aircraft to turn in an 80ft (24.5m) strip and reverse back up a 2.5% (1 in 40) gradient. The cargo floor will be 87ft (26.5m) long, 216in (5.49m) wide and have headroom of 142in (3.6m) under the wing and 162in (4.1m) elsewhere. Maximum payload will be 17,200lb (78.1t), and apart from an M1 tank (plus other loads) the C-17 could carry wheeled vehicles two-abreast and Jeeps three-abreast. Three electronic displays on the flight deck enable the flight crew to be reduced to two pilots and a loadmaster. The C-17 will combine ground mobility at least as good as a C-130 with cargo capability of a C-5A.

Below: The C-17A is designed to carry Hercules-type loads over global ranges into Hercules-type tactical airstrips.

195

McDonnell Douglas F-4 Phantom II

F-4C, D, E, G and RF-4C

Origin: McDonnell Aircraft Company, St Louis, Missouri.
Type: (C,D,E) all-weather interceptor and attack, (G) EW platform, (RF) reconnaissance.
Powerplant: (C,D,RF) to 17,000lb (7,711kg) thrust General Electric J79-15 afterburning turbojets, (E,G) two 17,900lb (8,120kg) J79-17.
Dimensions: Span 38ft 5in (11.7m); length (C,D) 58ft 3in (17.76m), (E,RF) 63ft 0in (19.2m); wing area 530sq ft (49.2m²).
Weights: Empty (C) about 28,000lb (12.7t), (D) 28,190lb (12,787kg), (E) 30,328lb (13,757kg), (G) about 31,000lb (14.06t), (RF) 29,300lb (13.29t); maximum loaded (C,D,RF) 58,000lb (26.3t), (E,G) 60,360lb (27.5t).
Performance: Maximum speed (C,D,E, Sparrow AAMs only external load) 910mph (1,464km/h, Mach 1.19) at low level, 1,500mph (241km/h, Mach 2.27) over 35,000ft (10.67km); initial climb, low level (AAMs only external load) 28,000ft (8,534m)/min; service ceiling 60,000ft (18.29km) without external stores; range on internal fuel (no external weapons) typically 1,750 miles (2,817km), ferry range (clean except three tanks), (C,D,RF) 2,300 miles (3,700km), (E,G) 2,660 miles (4,281km); takeoff run (clean) 5,000ft (1,525m); landing run 3,000ft (914m).
Armament: (C,D) Up to 16,000lb (7,257kg) assorted stores on external pylons including four AIM-7 Sparrow AAMs recessed into underside of fuselage/wing junction and two more AIM-7, or four AIM-9 Sidewinder, on inboard pylons; (E) same plus 20mm M61A-1 gun under nose; (G) typically three AIM-7 Sparrow recessed, three Mavericks or one Standard ARM plus two AIM-9 on each inboard pylon, and one Shrike on each outboard pylon, plus any other ordnance carried by other versions; (RF) none.
History: First flight (Navy F4H-1) 27 May 1958, (Air Force F-4C) 27 May 1963.

Development: Though it was the result of the manufacturer's initiative rather than an order by a customer, the F4H-11 Phantom II was by a wide margin the most potent fighter of the late 1950s, with outstanding all-round flight performance (resulting in 21 world records), the best radar performance of any Western fighter, the greatest load-carrying capability, and exceptional range and slow-flying qualities to fit it for oceanic operations from carriers. By the early 1960s the Air Force had recognised that it beat even the specialist land-based types at their own missions, and after prolonged study decided to buy the basic F-4B version with minimal changes. The original Air Force designation of F-110 Spectre was changed to F-4C Phantom II under the unified 1962 system, the F-4C being a minumum-change version of the Navy B and preceded (from 24 January 1962) by the loan to TAC of 30 B models ex-Navy.

After buying 583 F-4Cs with dual controls, a boom receptacle, Dash-15 engines with cartridge starters, larger tyres and increased-capacity brakes, inertial navigation and improved weapon aiming, the Air Force procured 793 of the F-4D model which was tailored to its own land-based missions, with APQ-109 radar, ASG-22 servoed sight, ASQ-91 weapon-release computer for nuclear LABS manoeuvres, improved inertial system and 30-kVA alternators. Visually, many Ds could be distinguished by removal of the AAA-4 IR detector in a pod under the radar, always present on the C. Next came the extremely sophisticated RF-4C multi-sensor reconnaissance aircraft, a major rebuild in a programme which preceded the D by two years and was the first Air Force variant to be authorised. Designed to supplement and then replace the RF-101 family the RF-4C was unarmed but was modified to carry a battery of forward-looking and oblique cameras, IR linescan, SLAR (side-looking airborne radar) and a small forward oblique mapping radar, as well as more than 20 auxiliary fits including photo flash/flare cartridges in the top of the rear fuselage, special ECM and HF shunt aerials built into the fin behind the leading edge on each side. TAC purchased 505 of this model in 1964-73.

All these variants were very heavily engaged in the war in SE Asia in 1966-73, where political rules combined with other problems to reduce their air-combat performance. Prolonged call for an internal gun resulted in the F-4E, which had the most powerful J79 engine to permit the flight performance to be maintained despite adding weight at both ends. In the nose was the new solid-state APQ-120 radar and the M61 gun, slanting down on the ventral centreline with the 6 o'clock firing barrel near-horizontal, and at the rear was a new (No 7) fuel cell giving enhanced range. The first E was delivered to TAC on 3 October 1967, about three months after first flight, and a total of 949 in all were supplied to maintain the F-4 as leading TAC aircraft with an average of 16 wings equipped throughout the period 1967/77. From 1972 all Es were rebuilt with a slatted leading edge, replacing the previous blown droop which permitted much tighter accelerative manoeuvres to be made, especially at high weights, without stall/spin accidents of the kind which had caused many losses in Vietnam.

Below: The F-4E is still in widespread USAF service, but requires ECM pods for survivability over the modern battlefield.

Above: An F-4E of the 3rd TFW in afterburner shows off the Phantom's still fearsomely aggressive appearance.

The final Air Force variant is the F-4G, the standard Advanced Wild Weasel platform replacing the F-105F and G which pioneered Wild Weasel missions in the late 1960s. The name covers all dedicated EW and anti-SAM missions in which specially equipped electronic aircraft hunt down hostile SAM installations (using radar for lock-on, tracking or missile guidance) and destroy them before or during an attack by other friendly aircraft on nearby targets. The F-4G (the same designation was used previously for modified F-4Bs of the Navy) is a rebuild of late-model F-4E (F-4E-42 through -45) fighters, and has almost the same airframe. It is the successor to the EF-4C, two squadrons of which were fielded by TAC from 1968 and which demonstrated excellent performance with a simpler system. In the F-4G the main EW system is the AN/APR-38, which provides very comprehensive radar homing and warning and uses no fewer than 52 special aerials, of which the most obvious are pods facing forward under the nose (replacing the gun) and facing to the rear at the top of the vertical tail. The system is governed by a Texas Instruments reprogrammable software routine which thus keeps up the date on all known hostile emitters. Offensive weapons normally comprise triple AGM-65 EO-guided Mavericks on each inboard pylon plus a Shrike on each outer pylon; alternatively weapons can include the big Standard ARM (Anti-Radiation Missile), AGM-88 HARM (High-speed ARM) or various other precision air/ground weapons. A Westinghouse ALQ-119 jammer pod is fitted in the left front missile recess, the other three recesses carrying Sparrow AAMs for self-protection. Another change is to fit the F-15 type centreline tank which can take 5g when full with 600 US gal (2,27 1lit). The G total is 116 aircraft.

Today the F-4 is still the most numerous combat aircraft in the Air Force. User units include: TAC, 4th TFW (E) at Seymour-Johnson, N Carolina; 31st TFW (E), Homestead, Florida; 33rd TFW (E), Eglin, Florida; 35th TFW (C,E,G), George, California; 56th TFW (D,E), MacDill, Florida; 57th FIS (E), Keflavik, Iceland; 57th TTW (E), Nellis, Nevada; 58th TTW (C), Luke, Arizona; 67th TRW (RF), Bergstrom, Texas; 347th TFW (E), Moody, Georgia; 363rd TRW (RF), Shaw, S Carolina; and 474th TFW (D), Nellis. USAFE, 10th TRW (RF), Alconbury, England; 26th TRW (RF), Zweibrücken, Germany; 50th TFW (E), Hahn, Germany; 52nd TFW (E,G), Spangdahlem, Germany; 86th TFW (E), Ramstein, Germany; 401st TFW (C), Torrejon, Spain; and 406th TFT (various), Zaragoza, Spain. Pacaf, 3rd TFW (D), Clark, Philippines; 8th TFW (E), Kunsan, Korea; 18th TFW (C, RF), Kadena, Okinawa; and 51st CW (E), Osan, Korea. Alaska, 21st CW (E), Elmendorf. Afres, 915th TFG (C), Homestead. ANG, 117th TRW (RF), Birmingham, Alabama; 119th FIG (C), Fargo, N Dakota; 122nd TFW (C), Ft Wayne, Indiana; 123rd TRW (RF), Louisville, Kentucky; 124th TRG (RF), Boise, Idaho; 131st TFW (C), St Louis, Mo; 148th TRG (RF), Duluth, Minnesota; 149th TFG (C), Kelly, Texas; 152nd TRG (RF), Reno, Nevada; 154th CG (C), Hickam, Hawaii; 155th TRG (RF), Meridian, Mississippi; 159th TFG (C), New Orleans, Louisiana; 183rd TFG (C), Springfield, Illinois; 186th TRG (RF), Meridian; 187th TRG (RF), Montgomery, Alabama; and the 191st FIG (D), Selfridge, Michigan.

McDonnell Douglas F-15 Eagle

F-15A,B,C,D and E

Origin: McDonnell Aircraft Company, St Louis, Missouri.
Type: Air-superiority fighter with secondary attack role.
Powerplant: Two 23,930lb (10,855kg) thrust Pratt & Whitney F100-100 afterburning turbofans.
Dimensions: Span 42ft 9¾in (13.05m); length (all) 63ft 9in (19.43m); wing area 608sq ft (56.5m²).
Weights: Empty (basic equipped) 28,000lb (12.7t); loaded (interception mission, max internal fuel plus four AIM-7, F-15A) 41,500lb (18,824kg), (C) 44,500lb (20,185kg); maximum with max external load (A) 56,500lb (25,628kg), (C) 68,000lb (30,845kg).
Performance: Maximum speed (over 36,000ft/10 973m with no external load except four AIM-7), 1,653mph (2,660km/h, Mach 2.5); with max external load or at low level, not published; initial climb (clean) over 50,000ft (15.24km)/min, (max wt) 29,000ft (8.8km)/min; service ceiling 65,000ft (19.8km); takeoff run (clean) 900ft (274m); landing run (clean, without brake chute) 2,500ft (762m); ferry range with three external tanks, over 2,878 miles (4,631km), (with Fast packs also) over 3,450 miles (5,560km).
Armament: One 20mm M61A-1 gun with 940 rounds, four AIM-7F (later AMRAAM) fitting against fuselage, four AIM-9L (later Asraam) on flanks of wing pylons, total additional ordnance load 16,000lb (7,257kg) on five stations (two each wing, one centreline).
History: First flight (A) 27 July 1972, (B) 7 July 1973; service delivery (Cat II test) March 1974, (inventory) November 1974.

Above: The F-15A has very useful fuel capacity, but still benefits from the attentions of a KC-135A on long missions.

Above: The F-15E demonstrator shows off its pace with four AIM-9 Sidewinder AAMs. Note the two hardpoints on the starboard engine trunk for AIM-7F Sparrow AAMs.

Below: The F-15A's APG-63 radar has displayed impressive reliability as well as the ability to find and track aerial targets at great range. Data are shown on the HUD and HDD.

Development: Recognizing its urgent need for a superior long-range air-combat fighter the Air Force requested development funds in 1965 and issued an RFP in September 1968 for the FX, the McDonnell proposal being selected in late 1969, with the F100 engine and Hughes APG-63 radar following in 1970. Inevitably the demand for long range resulted in a large aircraft, the wing having to be so large to meet the manoeuvre requirement that it has a fixed leading edge and plain unblown trailing-edge flaps. Two of the extremely powerful engines were needed to achieve the desired ratio of thrust/weight, which near sea level in the clean condition exceeds unity. The inlet ducts form the walls of the broad fuselage, with plain vertical rectangular inlets giving external compression from the forward-raked upper lip and with the entire inlet pivoted at the top and positioned at the optimum angle for each flight regime. The upper wall of the inlet forms a variable ramp, and the lower edge of the fuselage is tailored to snug fitting of the four medium-range AAMs. The gun is in the bulged strake at the root of the right wing, drawing ammunition from a tank inboard of the duct. There is no fuel between the engines but abundant room in the integral-tank inner wing and between the ducts for 11,600lb (5,260kg, 1,739 US gal, 6,592lit), and three 600 US gal (2,270lit) drop tanks can be carried each stressed to 5g manoeuvres when full. Roll is by ailerons, only at low speeds, the dogtoothed slab tailplanes taking over entirely at over Mach 1, together with the twin rudders, which are vertical.

Avionics and flight/weapon control systems are typical of the 1970 period, with a flat-plate scanner pulse-doppler radar, vertical situation display presenting ADI (attitude/director indicator), radar and EO information on one picture, a HUD, INS and central digital computer. In its integral ECM/IFF subsystems the F-15 was far better than most Western fighters, with Loral radar warning (with front/rear aerials on the left fin tip), Northrop ALQ-135 internal counter-measures system, Magnavox EW warning set and Hazeltine APX-76 IFF with Litton reply-evaluator. High-power jammers, however, must still be hung externally, any of various Westinghouse pods normally occupying an outer wing pylon. While the APG-63 offered a fantastic improvement (over any previous Air Force radar) in its ability to track low-level targets, fairly straightforward location of cockpit switches giving a Hotas (Hands on throttle and stick) capability which dramatically improved dogfight performance. Though it was, and remains, concerned at the price, the Air Force got in the F-15A everything it was looking for, and in 1973 announced a force of 729 aircraft including a proportion of tandem dual-control F-15B operational trainers.

Production at St Louis has been running at 90 to 144 aircraft per year, with some 1,000 F-15s delivered by late 1986. Recipient units began with TAC's 57th TTW at Nellis, 58th TTW at Luke, 1st TFW at Langley, 36th TFW at Bitburg (Germany), 49th TFW at Holloman, 33rd TFW at Eglin, 32nd TFS at Camp New Amsterdam (Netherlands) and 18th TFW at Kadena (Okinawa). Some of these units have received the current production variants, the F-15C and two-seat F-15D. These have a vital electronic modification in a reprogrammable signal processor, giving instant ability to switch from one locked-on target to another, to keep looking whilst already locked to one target, to switch between air and ground targets and, by virtue of an increase in memory from 24K to 96K (96,000 'words'), to go into a high-resolution mode giving the ability to pick one target from a tight formation even at near the limit of radar range. To some extent the latter capability will remain not fully realized until a later medium-range AAM is used (the Air Force has studied the Navy AIM-54 Phoenix but not adopted it). The British Sky Flash would give a major improvement now, especially in severe jamming, but again has not been adopted. The C and D also have 2,000lb (907kg) of additional internal fuel and can carry the Fast (Fuel and sensor, tactical) packs cunningly devised by McDonnell to fit flush along the

Above: An F-15C of the 32nd TFS shows off its potent interception fit of four Sparrows and four Sidewinders.

sides of the fuselage. These actually reduce subsonic drag and offer far less supersonic drag than the drop tanks whilst adding a further 9,750lb (4,422kg) fuel, or an assortment of sensors (cameras, FLIR, EO, LLTV or laser designator) or a mix of fuel and sensors.

In the second half of 1981 the F-15C re-equipped the 48th FIS at Langley, previously an F-106A unit in now-defunct Adcom, and the Air Force is now procuring aircraft to an eventual level of 1,266, partly in order to replace the aged F-106 in CONUS defence. For the future, while one variant of F-1 has been subjected to prolonged study as the USAF's Asat (Anti-satellite) aircraft, firing a large air/space missile based on a SRAM motor followed by an Altair II carrying a nuclear warhead, prolonged testing and demonstration of a company-funded Strike Eagle has now led to the F-15E of which 392 are to be procured, with IOC in 1988. This will serve as the Enhanced Tactical Fighter to replace the F-111 (the alternative being the Panavia Tornado) and also as the Advanced Wild Weasel (with far greater capability than the F-4G). The key is the SAR (synthetic-aperture radar) built into the APG-63, which very greatly improves resolution of fine detail against even distant ground targets. With a Pave Tack (FLIR/laser) pod the backseater in the two-seat F-15E can handle what are considered to be the best tactical navigation/target/weapon avionics in the world (apart from the strictly comparable Tornado). External weapon carriage is increased to 24,000lb (10,885kg), including laser-guided and anti-radiation weapons, Harpoon anti-ship missiles, dispensers and other stores. Whether the large existing F-15 force can eventually be brought up to this impressive standard has not been disclosed.

Below: Visible in the starboard wing of this 18th TFW F-15C is the muzzle port of the close-range M61A1 20-mm cannon.

McDonnell Douglas F/A-18 Hornet

F/A-18A, TF-18A and RF-18

Origin: McDonnell Aircraft Company, St Louis, Missouri, with Northrop associate contractor.

Type: Carrier-based and land-based dual-role fighter and attack, with reconnaissance capability (RF-18).

Powerplant: Two General Electric F404-400 afterburning turbofans, each "in 16,000lb (7,258kg) thrust class".

Dimensions: Span (with missiles) 40ft 4¾in (12.31m), (without missiles) 37ft 6in (11.42m); length 56ft (17.07m); height 15ft 3½in (4.66m); wing area 400sq ft (36.16m²).

Weights: Empty 23,050lb (10,455kg); loaded (fighter) 36,710lb (16,651kg), (attack) 49,224lb (22,328kg); max loaded (catapult limit) 50,064lb (22,710kg).

Performance: Max speed (clean, at altitude) 1,190mph (1,915km/h, Mach 1.8), (max weight, sea level) subsonic; sustained combat maneuver ceiling, over 49,000ft (14,935m); combat radius (air-to-air mission, high, no external fuel) 461 miles (741km); ferry range, more than 2,300 miles (3,700km).

Armament: One 20mm M61 gun with 570 rounds in upper part of forward fuselage; nine external weapon stations for max load (Catapult launch) of 13,400lb (6,080kg), including bombs, sensor pods, missiles (including Sparrow) and other stores, with tip-mounted Sidewinders.

History: First flight (YF-17) 9 June 1974; (first of 11 test F-18) 18 November 1978 (production F/A-18) 1980; service entry 1982.

Development: It is remarkable that this twin-engined machine designed for carrier operations should have won three major export sales almost entirely because of its ability to kill hostile aircraft at stand-off distance using radar-guided AAMs (which with a few trivial changes could be done by its losing rival, the F-16). From the outset in 1974 the Hornet was designed to be equally good at both fighter and attack roles, replacing the F-4 in the first and the A-7 in the second. It was also hoped that the Hornet—strictly the F-18 but usually designated F/A-18 by the Navy to emphasize its dual role—would prove a "cheaper alternative" to the F-14, but predictably the long and not wholly successful development process has resulted in an aircraft priced at well over $20 million; indeed the initial Spanish contract for 72 aircraft plus spares and training is priced at $3,000 million, or $41.7 million each.

Where the Hornet is unquestionably superior is in the engineering of the aircraft itself, which is probably the best yet achieved in any production combat type, and in particular in the detail design for easy routine maintenance and sustained reliability. Though not a large aircraft, with dimensions between those of the compact European Tornado and the F-4, and significantly smaller than the F-15, the F-18 combines the Tornado's advantage of small afterburning engines and large internal fuel capacity and avionics and weapons configured from the start for both F and A missions. Of course, in the low-level attack role it cannot equal Tornado because it has a large wide-span fixed wing, giving severe gust response, and suffers from relatively low maximum speed and lack of terrain-following radar; but in the typical Navy/Marines scenario with a mission mainly over the sea and a dive on target these shortcomings are less important. Originally it had been planned to buy an F-18 for the Navy and an A-18 for the Marines, still a single seater but with small changes. It proved possible to build a

Below: The F/A-18A is agile and able to carry a powerful warload, and also offers its pilot superb fields of vision. It is gradually replacing F-4 Phantoms and A-7 Corsair IIs.

common airplane for both services.

In weapon carriage the Hornet is first class with plenty of pylons and payload capability, and clearance for a wide spectrum of stores. In the fighter mission it is excellent, now that the wing has been redesigned to meet the specified rates of roll, and unlike its most immediate rival, the F-16, it has from the start carried a high-power liquid-cooled radar, the Hughes APG-65, matched with radar-guided AAMs. It would be easy to criticize the armament as the only old part of a new aircraft, but in fact the M61 gun is still hard to beat, and the AIM-7 Sparrow and -9 Sidewinder AAMs have been so updated over the years that both remain competitive. The fundamental shortcoming of the Sparrow in requiring continuous illumination of the target—which means the fighter must keep flying towards the enemy long after it has fired its missile—is a drawback to all Western fighters, and will remain so until AIM-120 (AMRAAM) is in service in 1987. In most air-combat situations the Hornet can hold its own, and compared with previous offensive (attack) aircraft is in a different class; it is in the long-range interdiction role that Hornet has significant shortcomings. These center chiefly on radius with a given weapon load, though it has been pointed out this can be rectified to some extent by using larger external tanks and by air refueling, the airplane being equipped with a British-style retractable probe permanently installed in the upper right side of the nose. Forward vision is good, though unlike the F-16 there is a transverse frame. The cockpit will always be a major "plus" for this aircraft, with Hotas controls (the stick being conventional instead of a sidestick), up-front CNI controls and three excellent MFDs (multi-function displays) which replace virtually all the traditional instruments. This cockpit goes further than anything previously achieved in enabling one man to handle the whole of a defensive or an offensive mission. But this is not to deny that a second crewmember would not ease the workload, especially in hostile airspace, and there have been studies of a two-seat version since the start of the program, though escalating costs have made its go-ahead increasingly unlikely.

There is, of course, a two-seat dual-pilot version for conversion training; this retains weapons capability and the APG-65 radar, but has about 6 per cent less internal fuel. There is also a prototype of a dedicated reconnaissance RF-18, testing of which began in 1984. This has a new nose, with the gun and ammunition replaced by a recon package which would normally include optical cameras and/or AAD-5 IR linescan. It is stated that this model could be converted "overnight" into the fighter/attack configuration.

The first Navy/Marines training squadron, VFA-125, commissioned at NAS Lemoore in November 1980. Three Marine Corps squadrons, VMFA-314, -323 and -531, were equipped by mid-1984, with three others following, while Navy squadrons are now also converting at lower priority. Until 1984 the Hornet was cleared operationally only for the fighter mission, because the Marines needed to replace the F-4 in this role more urgently. The attack mission depends to some degree on adding the laser spot tracker and FLIR on the Sparrow AAM fuselage pylons.

In the summer of 1984 inspection of aircraft based at the Naval Air Test Center at Patuxent River showed evidence of a structural problem—cracking of the tips of the fins and the fin/fuselage attachment. Investigation showed that this was due to the effect of side forces on the fins in conjunction with vortices. As an interim measure, angle of attack was limited to 25° below 30,000ft when the aircraft was flying between 300-400kts. Modification kits were quicky devised and installed in the field, while modified fins entered production later that year. All Hornets now in service are without airframe restrictions.

The planned Navy/Marines buy is 1,366 plus ten prototypes. Thanks to major foreign sales, small components are made in Canada, Australia and Spain under offset agreements.

Above: As shown by the Hornet's moderately large wing of little sweep, high performance is subordinated to features such as agility, tactical flexibility and weapon carriage.

Below: The movable leading- and trailing-edge flaps give the Hornet a wing of fully variable camber, contributing to excellent handling in all flight regimes.

McDonnell Douglas F-101

F-101B

Origin: McDonnell Aircraft Company, St Louis, Missouri.
Type: All-weather interceptor.
Powerplant: Two 14,990lb (6,800kg) thrust Pratt & Whitney J57-55 afterburning turbojets.
Dimensions: Span 39ft 8in (12.09m); length 67ft 4¾in (20.55m); wing area 368sq ft (34.22m²).
Weights: Empty (equipped) 28,000lb (12.7t); loaded (intercept) 39,900lb (19.1t), maximum 46,673lb (21,171kg).

Performance: Maximum speed (40,000ft/18.1km, clean), 1,220mph (1963km/h, Mach 1.85); initial climb, 17,000ft (5,180m)/min; service ceiling, 52,000ft (15.85km); range on internal fuel, 1,550 miles (2,495km).
Armament: Three AIM-4D or AIM-26 Falcon AAMs in internal bay and/or two AIR-2A Genie nuclear rockets externally.
History: First flight (F-101A) 29 September 1954, (B) 27 March 1957; service delivery (B) 18 March 1959.

Development: The original F-101A was intended as a 'penetration fighter' for SAC, but actually went to TAC as an attack aircraft. The F-101B

Below: F-101B tandem-seat all-weather fighters of the Oregon Air National Guard's 123rd Fighter Interceptor Squadron.

McDonnell Douglas
KC-10A Extender

KC-10A

Origin: Douglas Aircraft Company, Long Beach, California.
Type: Air-refueling tanker and heavy cargo transport.
Powerplant: Three 52,500lb (23,814kg) thrust General Electric F103 (CF6-50C2) turbofans.
Dimensions: Span 165ft 4½in (50.41m); length 181ft 7in (55.35m); height 58ft 1in (17.7m); wing area 3,958sq ft (367.7m²).
Weights: Empty (tanker role) 240,026lb (108,874kg); maximum loaded 590,000lb (267,620kg).
Performance: Max speed (max weight, at 25,000ft/7,620m) about 600mph (966km/h); max cruising speed (30,000ft/9,144m) 555mph (893km/h); takeoff field length 10,400ft (3,170m); max range (with max cargo load) 4,370 miles (7,032km).
Armament: None.
History: First flight (DC10) 29 August 1970, (KC-10A) 12 July 1980.

Development: Selected in December 1977 as the USAF's future ATCA (Advanced Tanker/Cargo Aircraft), the KC-10 (the A is often omitted from the designation) is in production under a single multi-year contract which is to deliver 60 by the end of 1987. The first entered service with the 32nd Air Refueling Sqd at Barksdale AFB in March 1981, followed by deliveries to the 9th ARS at March and the 911th ARS at Seymour Johnson in 1984. Associate AF Reserve squadrons share the new aircraft at each base.

Basically the KC-10 is a commercial DC-10-30CF convertible passenger/freighter, with military avionics and equipment, and with a major revision to the fuselage. Above the floor the area is equipped mainly for cargo, with a main cargo door and five passenger doors, but no windows other than four to add natural light. Under the floor are seven Goodyear flexible fuel cells with capacity of 117,829lb (53,446kg, 18,125gal, 68,610lit) of fuel. At the rear is a boom operator station with an extra-large high-speed refueling boom with FBW control, able to transfer fuel at 1,500gal (5,678lit)/min. The KC-10 is also equipped with a British-type hose drum unit and drogue. This enables it to refuel airplanes of the Navy, Marines and friendly air forces which are probe-equipped. The entire on-board fuel capacity, comprising the underfloor cells plus the basic tankage of 238,236lb (108,062kg), can be used as transfer fuel. It is possible to transfer

200,000lb (90,718kg) of fuel to receiver aircraft at a distance of 2,200 miles (3,540km) from the KC-10s base and return. The KC-10 also has an air-refueling receptacle. The above-floor area is equipped with portable winches and power rollers, and can accommodate 27 USAF Type 463L pallets, or 25 with access along both sides. Max cargo payload is 169,370lb (76,825kg). At the forward end of the cabin is seating for essential support personnel (typically 14), and six crew, as well as four rest bunks.

In service KC-10s act as "lead ship" on overseas fighter deployments.

interceptor, one of a series of later variants, differed from all others in having engines with large high-augmentation afterburners, and a second crew-member, accommodated at the expense of reduced fuselage fuel, to manage the MG-13 radar fire-control system tied in with the missile armament. By 1961 the Air Force had received 480 of this version together with the closely related TF-101B dual trainer which retained full armament. At one time 16 Adcom squadrons flew this reliable and well-liked aircraft, and it was also in wide-scale service with the CAF. Its final days of front-line service were seen with various units of the Air National Guard, before being replaced by the F-4 and F-15 in US service and by the CF-18 in the CAF. A number of examples are still flying, however, particularly on EW tasks.

Below: Three-view of RF-101C with side (bottom) of RF-101G.

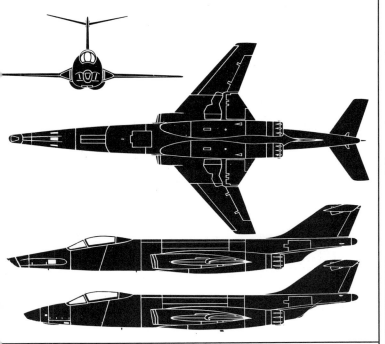

They are supported by the manufacturer under a separate contract, and the operational reliability rate is stated to have exceeded 99 per cent overall, with several months at 100 per cent. Deliveries by early 1986 totaled 44. A fleet of 17 KC-10s can fully support the transatlantic deployment of an F-4 wing, instead of the 40 KC-135s formerly needed. Their longer range reduces the need for foreign landing rights.

Below: The KC-10A offers an unrivalled combination of transport and inflight-refueling capabilities.

McDonnell Douglas OH-6A Cayuse

Type: Light observation helicopter.
Engine: One Allison turboshaft T63-5A flat-rated at 252·5shp.
Dimensions: Diameter of four-blade main rotor 26ft 4in (8·03m); length overall (rotors turning) 30ft 3¼in (9·24m); height overall 8ft 1½in (2·48m).
Weights: Empty 1,229lb (557kg), maximum loaded 2,700lb (1,225kg).
Performance: Max cruise at S/L 150mph (241km/h); typical range on normal fuel 380 miles (611km).
Armament: See text.
History: First flight (OH-6A) 27 February 1963.

Development: Original winner of the controversial LOH (Light Observation Helicopter) competition of the US Army in 1961, the OH-6A Cayuse is one of the most compact flying machines in history, relative to its capability. The standard machine carries two crew and four equipped troops, or up to 1,000lb (454kg) of electronics and weapons including the XM-27 gun or XM-75 grenade launcher plus a wide range of other infantry weapons. The US Army bought 1,413 and several hundred other military or para-military examples have been built by Hughes or licencees. In 1986 the Model 500 was in production with, or offering, nine military helicopters all significantly uprated compared with the Cayuse, and bristling with advanced avionics, sensors, weapons and protective features, but the only sale to the US military has been USA funding of a single research Notar (NO TAil Rotor) helicopter modified from an OH-6A.

Virtually all OH-6As in the US Army inventory are now with National Guard or Army Reserve units.

Below: The Defender series was developed as a private venture, and offers excellent armed capability, especially with mast-mounted sight and TOW anti-tank missiles.

Below: Modified to use low-pressure exhaust gases rather than a tail rotor, this OH-6A is flown experimentally.

McDonnell Douglas/BAe T-45 Goshawk

T-45A and B

Origin: McDonnell Douglas, Long Beach, USA; British Aerospace is principal subcontractor.

Type: Advanced pilot trainer.

Powerplant: One 5,340lb (2,422kg) Rolls-Royce/Turboméca Adour 851 turbofan.

Dimensions: Span 30ft 9¾in (9.39m); length 36ft 7¾in (11.17m); height 13ft 3in (4.04m); wing area 179.6sq ft (16.69m²).

Weights: Empty (A) approx 8,756lb (3,972kg); loaded (clean) 12,440lb (5,642kg).

Performance: Maximum speed 645mph (1,038km/h); dive Mach limit 1.2; max rate of climb (gross wt) 9,300ft (2,835m)/min; service ceiling 50,000ft (15.24km); sortie endurance 4h.

Armament: Has full Hawk capability but no requirement for weapons at present.

History: First flight (Hawk) 21 August 1974, (T-45B) 1987, (A) 1988.

Development: Having had perhaps the quickest and more troublefree complete development of any modern military aircraft, the basic Hawk T.1 for the RAF entered service as a replacement for the Hunter and Gnat in 1976 and has subsequently set the world's best-ever record for any jet combat aircraft for low maintenance burden and low attrition (in the first 130,000 hours one aircraft was lost, through collision with a ship). In November 1981 a proposal by McDonnel Douglas, British Aerospace and Sperry Flight Systems was outright winner of the US Navy VT/XTS contest for a future undergraduate pilot trainer to replace the T-2C Buckeye and TA-4J Skyhawk. The three companies proposed a total system, of which aircraft and direct support represented some 85 per cent by value. Despite Congressional opposition the win was so clear-cut that it has been allowed to go ahead, and the first FSD (full-scale development) contact was signed in September 1982. The first stage involves delivery of 54 T-45B Hawk trainers from 1987 for land-based training. These are basically similar to the Hawk T.1 but have a strengthened landing gear with long-stroke main legs and twin-wheel nose gear, a modified rear fuselage with twin lateral airbrakes and revised cockpit instrumentation and avionics. From 1988 these would be supplemented by the T-45A, of which 253 are to be delivered, which in addition will have a nose-tow catapult facility and arrester hook. Though the fuel savings over today's aircraft are calculated at 35 to 55 per cent, the T-45A is not scheduled to enter service until 1991.

Right: The superbly efficient British Aerospace Hawk Mk 50 is paving the way for the T-45 Goshawk advanced pilot trainer for the US Navy's training program.

McDonnell Douglas/BAe AV-8B Harrier II

AV-8B

Origin: Joint prime contractors McDonnell Aircraft Company, St Louis, Missouri, and British Aerospace, UK.

Type: Multirole close-support attack fighter.

Powerplant: One 21,700lb (9,843kg) thrust Rolls-Royce F402-406 Pegasus vectored-thrust turbofan.

Dimensions: Span 30ft 4in (9.25m); length 46ft 4in (14.12m); height 11ft 8in (3.56m); wing area 230sq ft (21.37m²).

Weights: Empty 13,086lb (5,936kb); max (VTO) 19,185lb (8,702kg), (STO) 31,000lb (14,061kg).

Performance: Max speed (clean, SL) 668mph (1,075km/h); dive Mach limit 0.93; combat radius (STO, seven Mk 82 bombs plus tanks, lo profile, no loiter) 748 miles (1,204km); ferry range 2,441 miles (3,929km).

Armament: Seven external pylons, centerline rates at 1,000lb (454kg) inboard wing 2,000lb (907kg), centre wing 1,000lb (454kg) and outboard 630lb (286kg), for total external load of 7,000lb (3,175kg) for VTO or 17,000lb (7,711kg) for STO, (GR.5) two additional AAM wing pylons; in addition ventral gun pods for one 25mm GAU-12/U gun and 300 rounds.

History: First flight (YAV-8B rebuild) 9 November 1978, (AV-8B) November 1981; entry into service 1983.

Above: Comparison of the AV-8A (background) and AV-8B shows the great development the latter's LIDs, nose and wings.

Development: Through developed directly from the original British Aerospace Harrier, the Harrier II is a totally new aircraft showing quite remarkable improvement and refinement in almost every part. This is especially the case in radius of action with any given weapon load, but it also extends to the scope and variety of possible loads, and to the general comfort and pleasure of flying. The original Harrier required a lot of attention, especially during accelerating or decelerating transitions, and suffered from poor all-round view and a distinctly traditional cockpit, whereas the Harrier II offers a completely new experience which makes full use of technology stemming from the F-15 and F18. At the same time, apart from the wing, which is a wholly new long-span structure made almost entirely from graphite composites, the new aircraft is a joint effort with inputs from both partners.

The wing is the most obvious visible difference, compared with earlier Harriers. Apart from giving vastly greater lift, at the expense of extra drag, it houses much more fuel, so that total internal fuel capacity is 50 per cent greater. With eight sinewave spars and composite construction it is virtually unbreakable, with essentially limitless fatigue life, and the curved Lerx (leading-edge root extensions) greatly enhance combat maneuverability and bring turn radius closer to what the customers require. Under the wing are six stores pylons, four of them plumbed for tanks which in the Marine Corps AV-8B are normally of 300gal (1,136lit) size. The extra pylons on the GR.5 are in line with the outrigger landing gears and will normally carry AIM-9L Sidewinders.

Left: With LIDs fitted under the fuselage the AV-8B has seven hardpoints, each seen here with one Snakeye retarded bomb of the type carried for the basic support mission.

The under-fuselage gun pods are specially configured to serve as LIDs (lift-improvement devices) which, joined across the front by a rectractable dam, provide a cushion of high-pressure air under the aircraft which counters the suck-down effect of rising air columns around the fuselage. In the AV-8B a 25mm gun is housed in the left pod with its ammunition fed from the right pod.

In the matter of avionics and EW the Harrier II is dramatically updated, the basic kit including INS (Litton ASN-130A or, in the GR.5, a Ferranti set), digital air-data and weapons, computers, large field of view HUD, fiber-optic data highways and comprehensive RWR and ECM systems. The primary weapon-delivery system is the Hughes ARBS (angle/rate bombing system), with dual-wavelength TV/laser target acquisition and tracking. A multimode radar is being studied. The RWR system's forward-looking receivers are in the wingtips, rather than in a fin-tip fairing as in early Harriers. The ALQ-164 jammer pod can be attached on the centerline pylon. A bolt-on inflight-refueling probe pack can be added above the left inlet duct, the probe being extended hydraulically when required. The cockpit is largely redesigned, with a large-angle HUD, UFC as on the F/A-18, MFD and ACES II seat. Every Marine converting from the AV-8C finds the Harrier II like a step into the next century.

The Marines expect to receive a total of 300 AV-8Bs, not including four FSD (full-scale development) machines or two-seaters. Deliveries are now taking place and the first squadron achieved IOC in late 1985, by which time there were 33 AV-8Bs at Cherry Point. Harrier IIs are being delivered to VMAT-203 training squadron, to the three previous AV-8C squadrons and to five A-4 squadrons. Marines will also buy a planned 28 two-seat TAV-8Bs.

Below: The AV-8B has far superior pilot visibility plus greater power and a larger wing for weightier warloads.

Northrop F-5

F-5A Freedom Fighter, F-5B, F-5E Tiger II, F-5F

Origin: Northrop Corporation, Hawthorne, California.
Type: Light tactical fighter.
Powerplant: Two General Electric J85 afterburning turbojets, (A/B) 4,080lb (1,850kg) thrust J85-13 or -13A, (E/F) 5,000lb (2,270kg) thrust -21A.
Dimensions: Span (A/B) 25ft 3in (7.7m) (A/B over tip tanks) 25ft 10in (7.87m), (E/F) 26ft 8in (8.13m), (E/F over AAMs) 27ft 11⁷in (8.53m) length (A) 47ft 2in (14.38m), (B) 46ft 4in (14.12m), (E) 48ft 2in (14.68m), (F) 51ft 7in (15.72m); wing area (A/B) 170sq ft (15.79m²), (E/F) 186sq ft (17.3m²).
Weights: Empty (A) 8,085lb (3,667kg), (B) 8,361lb (73,792kg), (E) 9,683lb (4,392kg), (F) 10,567lb (4,793kg); max loaded (A) 20,576lb (9,333kg), (B) 20,116lb (9,124kg), (E) 24,676lb) (11,193kg), (F) 25,225lb (11,442kg).
Performance: Maximum speed at 36,000ft (11km), (A) 925mph (1,489km/h, Mach 1.4), (B) 886mph (1,425km/h, Mach 1.34), (E) 1,077mph (1,734km/h, Mach 1.63), (F) 1,011mph (1,628km/h, Mach 1.53); typical cruising speed 562mph (904km/h, Mach 0.85); initial climb (A/B) 28,700ft (8,750m)/min, (E) 34,500ft (100,516m)/min, (F) 32,890ft (1,025m)/min; service ceiling (all) about 51,000ft (15.54km); combat radius with max weapon load and allowances, (A, hi-lo-hi) 215 miles (346km), (E, lo-lo-lo) 138 miles (222km); range with max fuel (all hi, tanks dropped, with reserves) (A) 1,565 miles (2,518km), (E) 1,779 miles (2,863km).
Armament: (A/B) total military load 6,200lb (2,812kg) including two 20mm M-39 guns and wide variety of underwing stores, plus AIM-9 AAMs for air combat; (E/F) Very wide range of ordnance to total of 7,000lb (3,175kg) not inculding two (F-5F, one) M-39A2 guns each with 280 rounds and two AIM-9 missiles on tip rails.
History: First flight (N-1,56C) 30 July 1959, (production F-5A) October 1963, (F-5E) 11 August 1972.

Development: The Air Force showed almost no interest in Northrop's N-156C Freedom Fighter, which was built with company funds and rolled out in 1959 without US markings. Eventually Northrop secured orders for over 1,000 F-5A and B fighters for foreign customers, and 12 of the MAP (Mutual Assistance Program) F-5As were evaluated by the Air Force in Vietnam in a project called Skoshi Tiger, which demonstrated the rather limited capability of this light tactical machine, as well as its economy and strong pilot appeal. When the USAF withdrew from SE Asia it left behind many F-5As and Bs, most having been formally transferred to South Vietnam, and few of these remain in the inventory. In contrast the slightly more powerful and generally updated F-5E Tiger II succeeded in winning Air Force support from the start, and the training of foreign recipients was handled mainly by TAC, with ATC assistance. The first service delivery of this version was to TAC's 425th TFS in April 1973. This unit at Williams AFB, Arizona (a detached part of the 58th TTW at Luke), proved the training and combat procedures and also later introduced the longer F which retains both the fire-control system and most fuselage fuel despite the second seat. Ultimately the Air Force bought 112 F-5Es, both as tactical fighters and (over half the total) as Aggressor aircraft simulating potential enemy aircraft in DACT (Dissimilar Air Combat Training). About 60 F-5Es and a small number of Fs continue in Air Force service in the development of air-combat techniques, in Aggressor roles, in the monitoring of fighter weapons meets and various hack duties. The F-5Es are painted in at least eight different

Northrop T-38 Talon

T-38A

Origin: Northrop Corporation, Hawthorne, California.
Type: Advanced trainer.
Powerplant: Two 3,850lb (1,746kg) thrust General Electric J85-5A afterburning turbojets.
Dimensions: Span 25ft 3in (7.7m); length 46ft 4½in (14.1m); wing area 170sq ft (15.79m²).
Weights: Empty 7,200lb (3,266kg); loaded 11,820lb (5,361kg).
Performance: Maximum speed, 858mph (1,381km/h, Mach 1.3) at 36,000ft (11km); maximum cruising speed, 627mph (1,009km/h) at same height; initial climb 33,600ft (10.24km)/min; service ceiling 53,600ft (16.34km); range (max fuel, 20min loiter at 10,000ft/3km) 1,140 miles (1,835km).
Armament: None.
History: First flight (YT-38) 10 April 1959, (T-38A) May 1960; service delivery 17 March 1961.

Development: Throughout the second half of the 1950s Northrop's project team under Welko Gasich studied advanced lightweight fighters of novel design for land and carrier operation, but the first genuine service interest was in the N-156T trainer, a contract for Air Force prototypes being signed in December 1956. Unique in the world, except for the Japanese FST-2, in being designed from the outset as a jet basic trainer with supersonic speed on the level, the T-38 was an attractive lightweight version of contemporary fighters, with twin afterburning engines, extremely small sharp-edged wings, area ruling for reduced transonic drag, inboard powered ailerons and slab tailplanes with slight anhedral. The instructor is seated behind and 10in (0.25m) higher than his pupil, both having rocket-assisted seats. To assist the pilot, yaw and pitch flight-control channels incorporate stability augmenters, and great care was taken in 1959-61 to produce an aircraft that pupils could handle. Strictly classed as a basic pilot trainer, the T-38A nevertheless is an advanced machine to which undergraduate pilots come only after completing their weed-out on the T-41A and their complete piloting course on the T-37A jet. The Air Force procured about 1,114 Talons, of which some 800 remain in inventory service with ATC. Their accident rate of some 0.9/11,2 per 100,000 flight hours is half that for the USAF as a whole. An Advanced Squadron of T-38As is based at each ATC school (see Cessna T-37 for list). Many Talons are used as hacks by senior officers, for command liaison and for research, while others are assigned to TAC's 479th TTW at Holloman.

Right: The T-38A serves with Air Training Command in the advanced role, and has proved a remarkably successful type with an excellent record of reliability and safety.

Republic F-105 Thunderchief

F105B, D, F and G

Origin: Republic Aviation Corporation (now Fairchild Republic Co), Farmingdale, NY.
Type: (B,D) single-seat fighter/bomber, (F) two-seat operational trainer, (G) EW/ECM platform.
Engine: One Pratt & Whitney J75 two-shaft afterburning turbojet; (B) 23,500lb (10,660kg) J75-5; (D, F, G) 24,500lb (11,113kg) J75-19W.
Dimensions: Span 34ft 11¼in (10.65m); length (B, D) 64ft 3in (19.58m); (F, G) 69ft 7½in (21.21m); height (B, D) 19ft 8in (5.99m), (F, G) 20ft 2in (6.15m).
Weights: Empty (D) 27,500lb (12,474kg); (F, G) 28,393lb (12,879kg); maximum loaded (B) 40,000lb (18,144kg); (D) 52,546lb (23,834kg); (F, G) 54,000lb (24,495kg).
Performance: Maximum speed (B) 1,254mph; (D, F, G) 1,480mph (2,382km/h, Mach 2.25); initial climb (B, D, typical) 34,500ft (10,500m)/min; (F, G) 32,000ft (9,750m)/min; service ceiling (typical) 52,000ft (15,850m); tactical radius with 16 750lb bombs (D) 230 miles (370km); ferry range with maximum fuel (typical) 2,390 miles (3,846km).
Armament: One 20mm M-61 gun with 1,029 rounds in left side of fuse-lage; internal bay for ordnace load of up to 8,000lb (3,629kg), and five external pylons for additional load of 6,000lb (2,722kg).
History: First flight (YF-105A) 22 October 1955; (production B) 26 May 1956; (D) 9 June 1959; (F) 11 June 1963; final delivery 1965.

Development: The AP-63 project was a private venture by Republic Aviation to follow the F-84. Its primary mission was delivery of nuclear or conventional weapons in all-weathers, with very high speed and long range. Though it had only the stop-gap J57 engine the first Thunderchief exceeded the speed of sound on its first flight, and the B model was soon in production for Tactical Air Command of the USAF. Apart from being the biggest single-seat, single-engine combat aircraft in history, the 105 was notable for its large bomb bay and unique swept-forward engine inlets in the wing roots. Only 75 B were delivered by 600 of the advanced D were built, with Nasarr

Below: The F-105G was developed for the "Wild Weasel" role but was soon supplanted for defense suppression by the F-4.

colour schemes, three of which reproduce Warsaw Pact comouflage schemes while others are low-visibility schemes. The F-5Fs at Williams are silver, with broad yellow bands and vertical tails. User units include the 58th TTW (425th TFS, as described), 57th TTW at Nellis (a major tactical and air combat centre for the entire Air Force), 3rd TFW, Clark AFB, Philippines

Above: These F-5E Tiger IIs serve with the 527th TFS in the dissimilar air combat training (aggressor) role for USAFE.

(Pacaf), 527th Aggressor TFS, attached to the 10th TRW at RAF Alconbury, England; and various research establishments in Systems Command.

monopulse radar and doppler navigation. Production was completed with 143 tandem-seat F with full operational equipment and dual controls. The greatest of single-engined combat jets bore a huge burden throughout the Vietnam war. About 350 D were rebuilt during that conflict with the Thunderstrick (T-stick) all-weather blind attack system--a few also being updated to T-stick II--with a large saddleback fairing from cockpit to fin. About 30 F were converted to ECM (electronic countermeasures) attackers, with pilot and observer and Wild Weasel and other radar homing, warning

and jamming systems. Westinghouse jammers and Goodyear chaff pods were carried externally. Prolonged harsh use over 20-odd years had by 1982 degraded flight performance of these tough and well-liked aircraft, whose nicknames of Thud, Ultra Hog (the F-84 having been the original Hog and the F-84F the Super Hog) and Lead Sled in no way reflected pilot dissatisfaction with what had been in its day the nearest thing to a one-type air force. By 1982 all had gone from the regular units and survivors were grouped in three Afres squadrons for a short period; 457th and 465th TFSs converted to F-4s in 1982-83 and the last F-105 unit, 466th TFS, carried out the final operational flight on February 25 1984. A few aircraft remain operational, the last of the remarkable Republic fighters.

Below: A formation of F-105Ds seen on the occasion of their transfer from the 35th TFW to AFRES and ANG units in 1980.

Rockwell B-1

B-1A, B

Origin: Rockwell International, North American Aerospace Operations, El Segundo, California.

Type: Strategic bomber and missile platform.

Powerplant: Four General F101-GE-102 augmented turbofans each rated at 29,900lb (13 563kg) with full afterburner.

Dimensions: (B-1A) Span (fully spread) 136ft 8½in (41.67m), (fully swept, to 67° 30ft) 78ft. 2½in (23.84m); length (including probe) 150ft 2½in (45.78m); wing area (spread, gross) 1,950sq ft (181.2m²).

Weights: Empty (B-1A) about 145,000lb (65,772kg), (B) over 160,000lb (72,576kg); maximum loaded (A) 395,000lb (179,172kg), (B) 477,000lb (216,367kg).

Performance: Maximum speed (B, over 36,000ft/11km) about 1,000mph (1,600km/h, Mach 1.5), (B, 500ft/152m) 750mph (1,205km/h, Mach 0.99); typical high-altitude cruising speed, 620mph (1,000km/h); range with maximum internal fuel, over 7,000 miles (11,265km); field length, less than 4,500ft (1,372m).

Armament: Eight ALCM internal plus 14 external; 24 SRAM internal plus 14 external; 12 B28 or B43 internal plus 8/14 external; 24 B61 or B83 internal plus 14 external; 84 Mk 82 internal plus 44 external (80,000lb, 36,288kg).

History: Original (AMSA) study 1962; contracts for engine and airframe 5 June 1970; first flight 23 December 1974; decision against production June 1977; termination of flight-test programme 30 April 1981; announcement of intention to produce for inventory, September 1981; planned IOC, 1 July 1987.

Development: Subject of a programme whose length in years far outstrips the genesis of any other aircraft, the B-1 was the final outcome of more than ten years of study to find a successor to the cancelled B-70 and RS-70 and subsonic in-service B-52. Originally planned as an extremely capable swing-wing aircraft with dash performance over Mach 2, the four prototypes were built with maximum wing sweep of 67° 30ft and were planned to have variable engine inlets and ejectable crew capsules of extremely advanced design. The latter feature was abandoned to save costs, and though the second aircraft reached Mach 2.22 in October 1978 this end of the speed spectrum steadily became of small importance. By 1978 the emphasis was totally on low-level penetration at subsonic speeds with protection deriving entirely from defensive electronics and so-called 'stealth' characteristics. Not very much could be done to reduce radar cross-section, but actual radar signature could be substantially modified, and the effort applied to research and development of bomber defensive electronic systems did not diminish.

The original B-1A featured a blended wing/body shape with the four engines in paired nacelles under the fixed inboard wing immediately outboard of the bogie main gears. Though designed more than ten years ago, the aerodynamics and structure of the B-1 remain highly competitive, and the extremely large and comprehensive defensive electronics systems (managed by AIL Division of Cutler-Hammer under the overall avionics integration of Boeing Aerospace) far surpassed those designed into any other known aircraft, and could not reasonably have been added as post-flight modifications. During prototype construction it was decided to save further costs by dropping the variable engine inlets, which were redesigned to be optimized at the high-subsonic cruise regime. Another problem, as with the B-52, was the increased length of the chosen ALCM, which meant that the original SRAM-size rotary launcher was no longer compatible. The original B-1 was designed with three tandem weapon bays, each able to house many free-fall bombs or one eight-round launcher. Provision was also

Above: Advanced avionics and variable geometry could make the B-1B a superb low-level penetration bomber for the USA.

originally made for external loads. A particular feature was the LARC (Low-Altitude Ride Control), an active-control modification which by sensing vertical accelerations due to atmospheric gusts at low level and countering these by deflecting small foreplanes and the bottom rudder section greatly reduced fatigue of crew and airframe during low-level penetration. All four prototypes flew initially from Palmdale and exceeded planned qualities. The third was fitted with the ECM system and DBS (doppler beam-sharpening) of the main radar, while the fourth had complete offensive and defensive electronics and was almost a production B-1A. The Carter administration decided not to build the B-1 for the inventory, and the four aircraft were stored in flyable condition after completing 1,985.2h in 247 missions.

After further prolonged evaluation against stretched FB-111 proposals the Reagan administration decided in favour of a derived B-1B, and announced in September 1981 the intention to put 100 into the SAC inventory from 1986, with IOC the following year. The B-1B dispenses with further high-altitude dash features, the wing sweep being reduced to about 59° 30ft. As well as refined engines the B-1B can carry much more fuel; a detailed weight-reduction programme reduces empty weight, while gross weight is raised by over 37 tonnes. Main gears are stronger, wing gloves and engine inlets totally redesigned, many parts (ride-control fins, flaps and bomb doors, for example) made of composite material, pneumatic starters with cross-bleed fitted, offensive avionics completely updated (main radar is Westinghouse's APG-66), the ALQ-161 defensive avionics subsystem fitted, RAM (radar-absorbent material) fitted at some 85 locations throughout the airframe, and the whole aircraft nuclear-hardened and given Multiplex wiring. Radar cross-section will be less than one-hundredth that of a B52. Deploying this LRCA (Long-Range Combat Aircraft) is intended to bridge the gap until the next generation 'stealth' aircraft is fielded in a programme so shrouded in secrecy that no IOC date has yet been announced.

Below: Careful contouring of the airframe and engine nacelles helps to minimize the B-1B's radar signature.

Rockwell OV-10 Bronco

OV-10A

Origin: Rockwell International, designed and built at Columbus, Ohio, Division of North American Aircraft Operations (now Columbus plant of NAA Division).
Type: Forward air control.
Powerplant: Two 715ehp Garrett T76-416/417 turboprops.
Dimensions: Span 40ft 0in (12.19m); length 41ft 7in (12.67m); wing area 291sq ft (27.03m²).
Weights: Empty 6,893lb (3,127kg); loaded 9,908lb (4,494kg), overload 14,444lb (6,552kg).
Performance: Maximum speed (sea level, clean) 281mph (452km/h); initial climb (normal weight), 2,600ft (790m)/min; service ceiling, 24,000ft (7,315m); takeoff run (normal weight), 740ft (226m); landing run, same; combat radius (max weapon load, low level, no loiter), 228 miles (367km); ferry range, 1,382 miles (2,224km).
Armament: Carried on five external attachments, one on centreline rated at 1,200lb (544kg) and four rated at 600lb (272kg) on short body sponsons which also house four 7.62mm M60 machine guns with 500 rounds each.

History: First flight 16 July 1965, (production oV-10A) 6 August 1967; USAF combat duty, June 1968.

Development: This unique warplane was the chief tangible outcome of prolonged DoD studies in 1959-65 of Co-In (Counter-Insurgency) aircraft tailored to the unanticipated needs of so-called brushfire wars using limited weapons in rough terrain. The Marines issued a LARA (Light Armed Recon Aircraft) specification, which was won by NAA's NA-300 in August 1964. Features included superb all-round view for the pilot and observer seated in tandem ejection seats, STOL rough-strip performance and a rear cargo compartment usable by five paratroops or two casualties plus attendant. Of the initial batch of 271 the Air Force took 157 for use in the FAC role, deploying them immediately in Vietnam. Their ability to respond immediately with light fire against surface targets proved very valuable, and the OV-10 was always popular and a delight to fly. In 1970 LTV Electrosystems modified 11 for night-FAC duty with sensors for detecting surface targets and directing accompanying attack aircraft, but most OV-10s now in use are of the original model. Units include TAC's 1st SOW at Hurlburt Field, Florida; the 602nd TACW, Bergstrom AFB, Texas; the 601st TCW, Sembach AB, Germany; Pacaf's 51st CW, Osan, Korea; and certain specialized schools.

Below: An OV-10A of the 19th TASS in South Korea.

Rockwell T-39 Sabreliner

T-39A, B and F

Origin: North American Aviation (later Rockwell International Sabreliner Division), El Segundo, California.
Type: (A) pilot proficiency/support, (B) radar trainer, (F) EW trainer.
Powerplant: Two 3,000lb (1,361kg) thrust Pratt & Whitney J60-3 turbojets.
Dimensions: Span 44ft 5in (13.53m); length (original A) 43ft 9in (13.33m); wing area 342.05sq ft (31.79m²).
Weights: Empty (A) 9,300lb (4,218kg); loaded 17,760lb (8,056kg).
Performance: Maximum speed (A) 595mph (958km/h) at 36,000ft (11km); typical cruising speed, 460mph (740km/h, Mach 0.7) at 40,000ft (12.2km); maximum range (A), 1,950 miles (3,138km).
Armament: None.
History: First flight (NA-246 prototype) 16 September 1958, (T-39A) 30 June 1960; service delivery, October 1960.

Development: The Air Force's UTX requirement issued in August 1956 was the first in the world for an executive-jet type aircraft, though at that time the main mission was expected to be training and utility transport. The winning design from NAA, which had only the faintest kinship to the Sabre, was planned with wing-root engines but these were moved to the novel rear-fuselage position before construction began. The wing was swept and slatted, and stressed to fighter-type g loads. Rather cramped, the main cabin had two rounded-triangle windows each side and a door forward on the left immediately behind the comfortable flight deck. The prototype was put through Phase II at Edwards only six weeks after first flight, and so captivated Air Force pilots that seven T-39s were ordered in January 1959.

Ultimately the Air Force bought 149, the majority serving as pilot-proficiency trainers, utility transports and, in a few cases, as VIP aircraft. Some spent their lives on research and special trials, the 6th to 9th were delivered with Nasarr radar to train F-105D pilots (designation T-39B), and at least three As were substantially modified as T-39F electronic-warfare trainers, originally for crews of the F-105G Wild Weasel aircraft. Though usually absent from published lists, almost all the T-39 force remain at work, many being assigned to combat wings (eg, the 86th TFW at Ramstein, Germany).

Below: The T-39A serves on administrative support with three MAC squadrons, each divided into four regional detachments.

Shorts 330

UTT and Sherpa

Origin: Short Brothers, UK.
Type: Utility STOL transport.
Engines: Two 1,198shp P&WC PT6A-45R turboprops.
Dimensions: Span 74ft 8in (22.76m); length 58ft 0.5in (17.69m); height overall 16ft 3in (4.95m); wing area 453.0sq ft (42.1m²).
Weights: Empty 14,000lb (6,350kg); max (UTT) 24,600lb (11,158kg), (Sherpa) 22,900lb (10,387kg).
Performance: Max cruising speed (UTT) 231mph (372km/h), (Sherpa) 218mph (352km/h); STOL takeoff to 50ft (15m) 2,110ft (644m); STOL landing ground run 770ft (235m); range (max fuel, UTT in passenger role) 1,053 miles (1,695km), (Sherpa, 5,000lb/2,268kg cargo, full diversions and 45min hold) 770 miles (1,239km).
Armament: None.
History: First flight (330) 22 August 1974, (Sherpa) 23 December 1982.
Users: (Military) (UTT) two unidentified Far East air forces, (Sherpa) USA(AF).

Development: Shorts twin turboprop transports have enjoyed a sales boom that since 1982 has accelerated dramatically. These two new versions are certain to become global best-sellers, and could well trigger off sales for such other roles as offshore patrol, SAR and photo-survey, if not armed tactical and maritime missions as well.

The basic aircraft have a long-span wing for good STOL performance, an unpressurized fuselage with rectangular cross-section (76in/1.93m wide and high in the UTT and 78in/1.98m wide and high in the Sherpa) and rough-field landing gear with the main units retracting into small sponsons.

The 330/UTT (utility tactical transport) is little changed from the 330-200 civil airliner, the main differences being clearance to an operational necessity weight raised to 24,000lb (see data), to allow payload to rise to 8,000lb (3,360kg), military avionics, and an interior configured for 33 troops, 30 para-troops (for whom the two rear doors are changed to open inwards) plus jumpmaster, or 15 stretchers plus four seated personnel. Range with 30 troops and their full equipment exceeds 691 miles (1,120km). In 1984 two Asian air forces placed major orders.

The Sherpa is a dedicated cargo aircraft, with a full-section rear ramp door operated from within or outside the aircraft and set to any desired height. The full cabin section is unobstructed over a length of almost 30ft (9.1m), and loads weighing up to 7,500lb (3,402kg) can include light vehicles, four LD3 or seven

Sikorsky S-61 family

SH-3A and -3D Sea King, HH-3A, RH-3A and many other variants

Origin: Sikorsky Aircraft, Division of United Technologies Corporation, Stratford, Connecticut.
Type: See below.
Powerplant: Two General Electric T58, free-turbine turboshaft; (SH-3A and derivatives) 1,250shp T58-8B; (SH-3D and derivatives) 1,400shp T58-10, (S-61R versions) 1,500hp T58-5).
Dimensions: Diameter of main rotor 62ft (18.9m); length overall 72ft 8in (22.15m), 61R) 73ft (22.25m); height overall 16ft 10in (5.13m); main-rotor disc area 3,019sq ft (280.5m²).
Weights: Empty (simple transport versions, typical) 9,763lb (4,428kg), (ASW, typical) 11,865lb (5,382kg), (armed CH-3E) 13,255lb (6,010kg); maximum loaded (ASW) about 18,626lb (8,449kg), (transport) usually 21,500lb (9,750kg), (CH-3E) 22,050lb (10,000kg).
Performance: Maximum speed (typical, maximum weight) 166mph (267km/h); initial climb (not vertical but maximum) varies from 2,200 to 1,310ft (670-400m)/min, depending on weight; service ceiling typically 14,700ft (4,480m); range with maximum fuel typically 625 miles (1,005km).
Armament: See below.
History: First flight (HSS-2) 11 March 1959, (CH-3) 17 June 1963.

Development: One of the most famous families of helicopters in the world, the S-61 stemmed from a Navy requirement of 1957 for a more powerful machine than the HSS-1 Seabat. Though the latter was a fine helicopter it was incapable of flying the hunter/killer ASW mission. Modern turbine engines promised a quantum jump in capability. Britain's Royal Navy merely put turbine engines in the HSS-1, but the US Navy got Sikorsky to create an entirely new helicopter, the S-61. This was procured as the HSS-2, inevitably called "Hiss 2". It virtually made all previous helicopters obsolete. As had been done in 1955 by Mil in the USSR, it had its two turbine engines mounted close beneath the rotor, above the fuselage, driving direct into the main gearbox. This got the engines and transmission completely away from the cockpit and cabin, and left the interior completely unobstructed. For the first time the fuselage was made in the form of a flying boat hull, with a watertight planing bottom. Struts as the sides carried stabilizing floats accommodating the retracted twin-wheel main landing gears, the tailwheel being at the stern. Streamlining was excellent, there being no trace of any pod/boom configuration, and the complete tail and five-blade main rotor could be folded to stow the big helicopter in small warship hangars. Twin T58 engines offered not only unprecedented power from a small weight and bulk, whilst eliminating cooling problems, but also freed the Navy from the need to have stocks of high-octane gasoline and for the first time almost removed the threat of engine failure. The boat hull was an extra; operations from the sea were not normally intended.

The HSS-2, called SH-3 from 1962, was the first fully equipped ASW helicopter. It had a full spectrum of sensors including radar, dunking sonar, dispensed sonobuoys and MAD (magnetic-anomaly detection) "bird" towed on a cable. These all feed information to the tactical

Sikorsky S-64

S-64, CH-54A and B Tarhe

Origin: Sikorsky Aircraft Division of United Technologies, Stratford, USA.
Type: Crane helicopter.
Engines: (CH-54A) two 4,500shp Pratt & Whitney T73-1 turboshafts, (CH-54B) two 4,800shp T73-700.
Dimensions: Diameter of six-blade main rotor 72ft 0in (21·95m); length overall (rotors turning) 88ft 6in (26·97m); height overall 18ft 7in (5·67m).
Weights: Empty (A) 19,234lb (8724kg); maximum loaded (A) 42,000lb (19,050kg), (B) 47,000lb (21,318kg).
Performance: Maximum cruise 105mph (169km/h); hovering ceiling out of ground effect 6,900ft (2100m); range with max fuel and 10 per cent reserve (typical) 230 miles (370km).
Armament: Normally none.
History: First flight (S-64) 9 May 1962; service delivery (CH-54A) late 1964, (B) late 1969.
User: USA (Army).

Development: Developed from the first large US Army helicopter, the S-56, via the piston-engined S-60, the S-64 is an efficient weight-lifter which in Vietnam carried loads weighing up to 20,000lb (9072kg). The CH-54A Tarhes used in that campaign retrieved more than 380 shot-down aircraft, saving an estimated $210 million, and carried special vans housing up to 87 combat-equipped troops. The improved CH-54B, distinguished externally by twin main wheels, has lifted loads up to 40,780lb (18,497kg) and reached a height of 36,122ft (11,010m). There is no fuselage, just a structural beam joining the tail rotor to the cockpit in which seats are provided for three pilots, one facing to the rear for manoeuvring with loads. The dynamic components (rotor, gearboxes, shafting) were used as the

Right: Betrayed by its layout as a flying crane helicopter, the CH-54 series serves only with National Guard units.

basis for those of the S-65. With cancellation of the HLH (Heavy-Lift Helicopter) the S-64 remains the only large crane helicopter in the West. A total of just over 100 were built, all the last batches being very small numbers for a late emerging civil market. By 1981 the CH-54 could be outperformed by the latest Chinook and Super Stallion, but its withdrawal from the USA is not scheduled until late in the decade.

CO8 containers or the largest afterburning fighter engines.

In March 1984 the Sherpa was selected by the USAF as its EDSA (European distribution system aircraft), requiring an initial 18 aircraft with options on a further 48, worth with supporting services some $660 million. They will run a shuttle service radiating from Zweibrücken AB and linking an initial 20 USAF bases in Europe, with major spokes leading to warehouses at RAF Kemble, England, and Torrejón AB, near Madrid.

The USAF Sherpas are well equipped with avionics and equipment, including single UHF and HF radios, dual VHF-AM/FM, two flight directors, dual VOR/ILS, a Litton LTN-96 ring laser gyro inertial navigation system, Tacan, dual ADF, flight data recorder, cockpit voice recorder, IFF transponder, GPWS, radar altimeter, and a Collins RNS-300 colour weather radar with terrain mapping.

The Sherpa, which serves with the 10th Military Airlift Squadron of Military Airlift Command, has cabin floor flat throughout its length, with a locally reinforced center cabin area. It can be expected to carry specialist role equipment, including that for onboard sorting of letters and small packages. Roller conveyor systems are standard.

Right: The C-23 serves in Europe for the rapid delivery of tactically urgent supplies such as repaired engines.

---

compartment amidships manned by two sensor operators. Along the sides could be carried up to 840lb (381kg) of weapons including a homing torpedo or depth bombs. Deliveries continued with SH-3Ds with greater power, SH-3G and 3H with later equipment, RH-3As for MCM (mine countermeasures) and VH-3As for the DC-based Executive Flight Detachment to carry the President and other VIPs. The HH-3A was a special combat rescue model operated mainly by HC-7 in Vietnam. It had high-speed refueling and fuel dumping, armor, uprated engines and twin TAT-102 turrets each with a 7.62mm Minigun.

In 1962 the AF borrowed three Sea Kings and decided to get a special version to meet its own long-range transport requirements. The result was the CH-3C (S-61R), a major redesign with an ordinary land fuselage and a full-width rear ramp door. The landing gear was changed to tricycle type with all units retractable, the twin-wheel nose gear being raised into an open nose compartment and the twin-wheel main gears folding into large rear sponsons. The fuselage was made watertight for emergency sea descents. Provision was made for firing 0.50in guns from the cabin windows, and in the special HH-3E Jolly Green Giant version for Vietnam new equipment included two or four Miniguns, extra armor, an inflight refueling probe and jettisonable external tanks. These did a tremendous job rescuing downed aviators and even bringing back crashed aircraft in Vietnam, while others stood by during space launchings.

Right: The HH-3E was developed for combat search-and-rescue in the Vietnam War with features such as additional fuel tankage (and an inflight-refueling probe), armor protection and armament for the suppression of ground fire.

Sikorsky S-65/S-80, H-53 family

CH-53, HH-53 and RH-53 Sea Stallion, HH-53 Super Jolly (Green), CH-53E Super Stallion and export models

Origin: Sikorsky Aircraft, Division of United Technologies, Stratford, Connecticut.
Type: (C) assault transport helicopter, (M) mine countermeasures.
Powerplant: (Early versions) two 2,850shp General Electric T64-6 turboshafts; (CH-53D and G) 3,925shp T64-413; (RH-53D) 4,380shp T64-415; (CH-53E) three 4,380shp T64-415.
Dimensions: Diameter of main rotor (most, six blades) 72ft 3in (22.02m), (CH-53E, seven blades) 79ft (24.08m); length overall (rotors turning) 88ft 2in (26.9m); (CH-53E) 99ft 1in (30.2m); length of fuselage 67ft 2in (20.47m), (E) 73ft 4in (22.35m); height overall 24ft 11in (7.6m), (E), 28ft 5in (8.66m); main-rotor disc area (small) 4,070sq ft (378.1m²), (large) 4,902sq ft (455.37m²).
Weights: Empty (CH-53D) 23,485lb (10,653kg), (E) 33,226lb (15,071kg); max loaded (most) 42,000lb (19,050kg), (RH-53D) 50,000lb (22,680kg), (E) 73,500lb (33,339kg).
Performance: Max speed 196mph (315km/h); typical cruising speed 173mph (278km/h); initial climb (most) 2,180ft (664m)/min, (E) 2,750ft (838m)/min; range (with payload, optimum cruise) (most) 540 miles (869km), (E) 1,290 miles (2,075km).
Armament: (HH-53B) three 7.62mm Miniguns, plus optional 20mm cannon and grenade launchers.
History: First flight 14 October 1964, (E) 1 March 1974; service delivery (CH-53A) May 1966, (E) March 1981, (MH) 1 September 1983.

Development: Designed as a heavy assault transport helicopter for the US Marine Corps, the initial Sea Stallion CH-53A version of the S-65 was basically a considerably enlarged version of the S-61, but with a conventional fuselage instead of a boat hull. The dynamic parts — gearboxes, transmission and rotors—were based on those of the CH-54 (S-64) but with the main rotor having a titanium hub and folding blades. Other features include an unobstructed cabin 7ft 6in (2.29m) wide and 6ft 6in (1.98m) high, with full-width rear ramp doors for loading vehicles or air dropping; tricycle landing gear with twin-wheel units, the main gears retracting forwards into large sponsons which contain the four fuel tanks; and in some verisons fixed streamlined external tanks which carry the navigation lights.

The Marine requirement was to carry 38 equipped troops; other loads can include 8,000lb (3,629kg) of cargo, or 25 litters and four attendants. The initial buy was for 139, named Sea Stallion, and they quickly established a high reputation for good performance; despite ▶

Below: A seven-blade main rotor and three engines help make the CH-53E a decisive assault transport helicopter.

their size, one was put through a test program involving prolonged looping and rolling. A group of 15 CH-53As were modified for Navy use as RH-53A minesweepers (MCM, mine countermeasures).

Sikorsky then secured orders from the USAF, initially for the HH-53B, for the Aerospace Rescue & Recovery Service, with engines uprated to 3,080shp; six-man crew; retractable inflight-refueling probes, jettisonable external tanks and with armament and armor for operations in Vietnam. The HH-53C Super Jolly, built in greater numbers, had 3,435shp engines, and various changes including the ability to hoist the Apollo capsules from the ocean, with the external hoist rated at 20,000lb (9,072kg). The CH-53C Super Jolly was a simple transport version of the HH-53C, while the Marines returned in 1969 with a big order for 126 CH-53Ds, with engines at first of 3,695shp and finally 3,925shp, automatic blade folding and the ability to carry 55 troops (though in an unchanged fuselage). Eight HH-53Cs plus the prototype were converted into HH-53H (Pave Low) night and all-weather search and rescue Super Jollies with IR sensors, B-52 type inertial navigation and terrain-following radar. This sub-family ended with 20 RH-53D Sea Stallions for the Navy, for MCM duties; they have refueling probes and external tanks. Several were lost in the abortive Iran rescue operation of 24 April 1980.

After long delays Sikorsky got a go-ahead in 1978 for the CH-53E, which is so greatly uprated it has a different maker's designation of S-80E, and is named Super Stallion. Seldom has a helicopter been so improved in capability as the Stallion, because from an original total of 5,700hp the CH-53E has no less than 13,140hp, from three of the most powerful T64 engines, the extra unit being at the rear of the others just to the left of the centerline. The power is absorbed by a new rotor with seven lengthened and redesigned blades, the entire mechanical drive train being redesigned to handle the increased power. The fuselage is longer and better streamlined, the tail is completely redesigned (eventually maturing with a large fin inclined to the left and carrying a kinked gull tailplane on the right, opposite the enlarged tail rotor), and largely redesigned structure and systems bring them into

Sikorsky S-70

S-70, UH-60A Black Hawk, EH-60 (SOTAS) SH-6 OB Seahawk and UH-60D Night Hawk

Origin: Sikorsky Aircraft, Division of United Technologies Corporation, Stratford, Connecticut.
Type: (UH) combat assault transport, (EH) electronic warfare and target acquisition, (HH) combat rescue, (SH) ASW and anti-ship helicopter.
Powerplant: (UH, EH) two 1,560shp General Electric T700-700 turboshafts, (SH, HH) two 1,690shp T700-401.
Dimensions: Diameter of four-blade rotor 53ft 8in (16.36m); length overall (rotors turning) 64ft 10in (19.76m); length (rotors/tail folded) (UH) 41ft 4in (12.6m), (SH) 41ft ½in (12.5m); height overall (UH) 16ft 10in (5.13m), (SH) 17ft 2in (5.23m); main-rotor disc area 2,261sq ft (210.05m²).
Weights: Empty (UH) 10,624lb (4,819kg), (SH) 13,648lb (6,191kg); max loaded (UH) 20,205lb (9,185kg) (normal mission weight 16,260lb, 7,375kg), (HH) 22,000lb (9,979kg), (SH) 21,884lb (9.925kg).
Performance: Max speed (UH) 184mpg (296km/h); cruising speed (UH) 167mph (269km/h) (SH) 155mph (249km/h); range at max weight, 30min reserves, (UH) 373 miles (600km), (SH) about 500 miles (805km).
Armament: (UH) See below, (EH) electronic only, (SH) two Mk-46 torpedoes and alternative dropped stores, plus offensive avionics.
History: First flight (YUH) 17 October 1974, (productin UH) October 1978, (SH) 12 December 1979; service delivery (UH) June 1979.

Development: This helicopter family owes little to any previous Sikorsky type, and when the first version (the UH-60A Black Hawk) was designed in the late 1970s it was packed with new technology. The original requirement came from the US Army, which needed a UTTAS (utility tactical-transport aircraft system) for general battlefield supply duties. The basic role called for a crew of three and a cabin for 11 troops with full equipment, but the UH-60A can readily be fitted with 14 troop seats, or alternatively with six litters. The cargo hook can take a load of 8,000lb (3,629kg), and a typical frontline load can be a 105mm gun, 50 rounds of packaged ammunition and the gun crew of five. The UH-60A can also be used for command and control or for reconnaissance missions. The design was made especially compact so that it would fit into a C-130; a C-5 can carry six.

The UH-60A proved to be a particularly successful machine, with surprising agility and good all-weather avionics. As with all later versions most of its critical parts are designed to withstand 23mm gunfire, and in a gruelling kind of combat life it has proved one of the most 'survivable' of all helicopters. Originally there was no call for armament, apart from provision for the troops to fire a 7.62mm M60 LMG from a pintle mount on each side of the cabin (and standard kit includes chaff/flare dispensers for self defense). In the 1980s, however the Army began re-equipping its Black Hawk fleet with the ESSS (external stores support system) which adds large 'wings' with four pylons on which can be hung anything from motorcycles to 16 Hellfire precision missiles. Gun pods are another alternative, as is the M56 mine-dispensing system. For self-ferry duties four external tanks can be attached, giving a range of 1,323 miles (1,230km).

As expected the UH-60A is a big program, with deliveries about 770 at the time of writing, with a predicted eventual total for the Army of 1,715. Another 11 have gone to the USAF, nine being used for recovery and rescue missions at Elgin AFB. The EH-60A Black Hawk is a specialized ECM version packed with 1,800lb (816kg) of equipment designed to detect, monitor and jam enemy battlefield communications. This installation is called Quick Fix II, the main item being the ALQ-151 ECM kit. The Army plans to buy 132 of this version as its SEMA (special electronics mission aircraft. It also hopes to fund 78 of another version, the EH-60B, fitted with the SOTAS (stand-off target acquisition system),

main element of which is a large target-indicating radar whose signals are relayed to a ground station. This program has run into cost and schedule problems, and was halted in late 1981.

The main USAF model is the HH-60A Night Hawk, which uses almost the same airframe but has uprated engines and transmission more akin to that of the SH-60B Sea Hawk. The Night Hawk is planned as the next-generation all-weather combat rescue and special missions vehicle. Features include external tanks and additional internal fuel to achieve a full-load combat radius of 288 miles (463km), flight-refueling probe, various new weapons provisions in the fuselage, added protection systems, and a mass of avionics including all-weather terrain following with a FLIR and the LANTIRN, as well as special communications and a pilot's helmet display like that of the AH-64A Apache. The USAF hopes to afford 90, the first of which is flying in Europe 1 camouflage, as well as 66 HH-60Es which will save money by having no FLIR, radarmap display or helmet display. The Marines HMS-1 Executive Flight Detachment flies nine VH-60A (VIP) transports.

Yet another quite different version is the US Navy's SH-60B Seahawk. This, the Sikorsky S-70L, was built to meet the need for a LAMPS III (light airborne multi-purpose system), packaged into a shipboard helicopter. In fact the SH-60B is much larger and more costly than most shipboard machines, because of the strenuous demands for equipment and weapons to handle ASW and ASST (anti-ship surveillance and targeting) in all weather. Apart from all the obvious changes needed for operation from destroyers and frigates, the Seahawk has uprated engines and transmission and a totally new fuselage with APS-124 search radar under the cockpit and forward part of the cabin, side chin-mounted ESM pods, a MAD station on the right, a battery of 25 sonobuoy launchers on the left with four more reloads inside the fuselage (125 buoys in all), and an impressive array of sensors, navaids, communications, processing systems and self-defense measures. Normal ASW armament comprises two torpedoes. There is no FR probe, but the Seahawk can be coupled to a refueling hose from a ship and refuel at the hover or while maintaining station at sea.

The Navy achieved operational capability in 1984, and expects to receive 203 of these big machines for use from 106 surface warships. They can also fly Vertrep (vertical replenishment), medevac, fleet support, SAR and communications relay missions. The Navy expects to buy a further 175 of the SH-60F type, for its CV-helo missions. These will operate from carriers in the direct protection of the battle fleet, using AQS-13 dipping sonar instead of buoys, and also flying planeguard SAR missions.

Below: UH-60A in assault guise with a vehicle as slung load.

line with the latest state of the art. Only 55 seats are fitted still, but the external cargo load can be 32,000lb (14,515kg). Sikorsky is delivering two a month, and by mid-1986 had supplied the Marines with 100 of the 200+ total scheduled for the 1990s.

The newest version is the MH-53E AMCM (airborne MCM) Sea Dragon, for the US Navy. The major change in this model is the 1,000gal (3,785lit) increase in internal fuel, housed in giant sponsons, but the hydraulics and electrical systems are also improved, and new avionics are fitted to facilitate the difficult task of clearing minefields. The very capable MH-53E supplements the RH-53D. Late in 1984, the MH-53E underwent shipboard compatibility tests at the Naval Air Station, Norfolk, Va. The successful outcome of these trials is being followed by orders expected to total 35.

Right: A US Navy MH-53E Sea Dragon, the dedicated mine countermeasures version of the CH-53E Super Stallion. Each giant sponson tank holds 1,017 US gal (3,850l) of fuel.

Vought A-7 Corsair II

A-7D, K

Origin: Vought Corporation, Dallas, Texas.
Type: (D) attack, (K) combat trainer.
Powerplant: One 14,250lb (6,465kg) thrust Allison TF41-1 turbofan.
Dimensions: Span 38ft 9in (11.8m); length (D) 46ft 1½in (14.06m), (K) 48ft 11½in (14.92m); wing area 375sq ft (34.83m).
Weights: Empty (D) 19,781lb (8,972kg); loaded (D) 42,000lb (19,050kg).
Performance: Maximum speed (D, clean, SL), 690mph (1,110km/h), (5,000ft/1,525m, with 12 Mk 82 bombs) 646mph (1,040km/h); tactical radius (with unspecified weapon load at unspecified height), 715 miles (1,151km); ferry range (internal fuel) 2,281 miles (3,671km), (max with external tanks) 2,861 miles (4,604km).
Armament: One 20mm M61A-1 gun with 1,000 rounds, and up to 15,000lb (6,804kg) of all tactical weapons on eight hardpoints (two on fuselage each rated 500lb/227kg, two inboard wing pylons each 2,500lb/1,134kg, four outboard wing pylons each 3,500lb/1,587kg).
History: First flight (Navy A-7A) 27 September 1965, (D) 26 September 1968, (K) January 1981.

Development: The Corsair II was originally derived from the supersonic F-8 Crusader fighter to meet a Navy need for a subsonic tactical attack aircraft with a much heavier bomb load and greater fuel capacity than the A-4. So effective did the A-7 prove that in 1966 it was selected to equip a substantial proportion of TAC wings, and ultimately 457 were acquired. Compared with the Navy aircraft the A-7D introduced a more powerful engine (derived from the Rolls-Royce Spey) with gas-turbine self-starting, a multi-barrel gun, and above all a totally revised avionic system for continuous solution of navigation problems and precision placement of free-fall weapons in all weather. The folding wings and arrester hook were retained, and other features included a strike camera, boom receptacle instead of a probe, boron carbide armour over cockpit and engine, and a McDonnell Douglas Escapac seat. Avionics have been further improved over the years, but the APQ-126 radar had been retained, programmable to ten operating models, together with British HUD, inertial system, doppler radar, direct-view storage tube for radar or Walleye guidance, and central ASN-91 digital computer. For laser-guided weapons the Pave Penny installation is hung externally in a pod, but the ALR-46(V) digital radar warning system is internal. There is no internal jamming capability, however, and the usual ECM payload is an ALQ-101 or -119 hung in place of part of the bombload.

Production of the A-7D has long been completed, but Vought has recently also completed delivery of 31 dual-control A-7K Corsair IIs which retain a full weapons capability. 16 of these have been assigned to the ANG's 162nd TFTG at Tucson and a pair to each of the 11 ANG's 13 operational units equipped with the A-7D. These units are the 112th TFG, Pittsburgh, Pennsylvania; 114th TFG, Sioux Falls, Iowa; 121st TFW, Rickenbacker AFB, Ohio; 127th TFW, Selfridge AFB, Michigan; 132nd TFW, Des Moines, Iowa; 138th TFG, Tulsa, Oklahoma; 140th TFW, Buckley, Colorado; 150th TFG, Kirtland AFB, New Mexico; 156th TFG, San Juan, Puerto Rico; 162nd TFG (TFTG), Tucson; 169th TFG, McEntire Field, S Carolina; 178th TFG, Springfield, Ohio; and the 185th TFG, Sioux City, Iowa. In the 1981 Gunsmoke tactical gunnery meet at Nellis the 140th, from Colorado, shot their way to the top team title with an exceptional 8,800 out of 10,000 points (the team chief, Lt-Col Wayne Schultz, winning the Top Gun individual award). The meet involves not only gunnery but bombing and maintenance/loading contests. The chief of the judges said: 'Some of the scores are phenomenal—pilots are so accurate they don't need high explosive to destroy a target, they are hitting within 1½ to 2 metres, with ordinary free-fall bombs.' Few tactical aircraft are as good at attack on surface targets.

Below: The A-7 is a weapon of the Air National Guard, this A-7D serving with the 188th TFS of the New Mexico ANG. It is possible that the A-7 may be radically upgraded.

US Rockets and Missiles

ALCM, AGM-86B

Origin: Boeing Aerospace Co., USA.
Type: Air-launched cruise missile.
Dimensions: With wings/tailplane extended, length 20·7ft (6·32m); body diameter 25·4in (64·5cm); span 12ft (3·66m).
Launch weight: 2,825lb (1,282kg).
Propulsion: One Williams F107-101 turbofan with sea-level rating of 600lb (272kg) static thrust.
Range: Max without belly tank, 760 miles (1,200km).
Flight speed: Cruise, about Mach 0·65; terminal phase, possibly Mach 0·8.
Warhead: W-80 thermonuclear as originally developed for SRAM-B.

One of the most important weapons in the West's inventory, ALCM (Air-Launched Cruise Missile) was presented by President Carter as a new idea when he terminated B-1 as a bomber; he even said B-1 had been developed "in absence of the cruise missile factor", whose presence in 1976 made the bomber unnecessary. This is simply not true. The cruise missile never ceased to be studied from 1943, and — apart from such USAF examples as Mace and Snark — it was cruise-missile studies in 1963-6 that led to AGM-86 SCAD (Subsonic Cruise Armed Decoy) approved by DoD in July 1970. This was to be a miniature aircraft powered by a Williams WR19 turbofan, launched by a B-52 when some hundreds of miles short of major targets.

Like Quail, SCAD was to confuse and dilute hostile defences; but the fact that some or all would carry nuclear warheads — by 1963 small enough to fit such vehicles — meant that SCAD could do far better than Quail. No longer could the enemy ignore decoys and wait and see which were the bombers. Every SCAD had to be engaged, thus revealing the locations and operating frequencies of the defence sites, which could be hit by surviving SCADs, SRAMs or ARMs. SCAD was to be installationally interchangeable with SRAM, with a maximum range of around 750 miles (1,207km).

SCAD ran into tough Congressional opposition, but the USAF knew what it was about and in 1972 recast the project as ALCM, retaining the designation AGM-86A. SCAD had had only a secondary attack function, but ALCM is totally a nuclear delivery vehicle, and like SRAM has the ability to multiply each bomber's targets and increase defence problems by approaching from any direction along any kind of profile. Compared with SRAM it is much easier to intercept, being larger and much slower, but it has considerably greater range and allows the bomber to stand off at distances of at least 1,000 miles (1,609km).

The original AGM-86A ALCM was interchangeable with SRAM, so that a B-52G or H could carry eight on the internal rotary launcher plus 12 externally, and an FB-111A four externally plus two internally (though the latter aircraft has never been named as an ALCM carrier). This influenced the shape, though not to the missile's detriment, and necessitated folding or retracting wings, tail and engine air-inlet duct. Boeing, who won SCAD and carried across to ALCM without further competition, based ALCM very closely on SCAD but increased the fuel capacity and the sophistication of the guidance, with a Litton inertial platform (finally chosen as the P-1000) and computer (4516C), updated progressively when over hostile territory by McDonnell Douglas Tercom.

In 1976 the decision was taken to aim at maximum commonality with AGM-109 Tomahawk, but the guidance packages are not identical. The engine in both missiles is the Williams F107 of approximately 600lb (272kg) thrust, but in totally different versions; the ALCM engine is the F107-101, with accessories underneath and different starting system from the Dash-400 of AGM-109. The warhead is W-80, from SRAM-B.

AGM-86A first flew at WSMR on 5 March 1976. Many of the early flights failed — one undershot its target by a mile because its tankage had been underfilled! — but by the sixth shot most objectives had been attained and 1977 was spent chiefly in improving commonality with Navy AGM-109, in preparation for something unforeseen until that year: a fly-off against AGM-109 Tomahawk in 1979 to decide which to buy for the B-52 force. It was commonly said Boeing was told to make AGM-86A short on range to avoid competing with the B-1. In fact no more fuel could be accommodated and still retain compatibility with SRAM launchers, and in 1976 Boeing proposed an underbelly auxiliary fuel tank for missiles carried externally.

A better answer was to throw away dimensional compatibility with SRAM and develop a considerably stretched missile, called AGM-86B. This has a fuselage more than 30 per cent longer, housing fuel for double the range with a given warhead. Other changes include wing sweep reduced to 25°, thermal batteries for on-board electrical power, all-welded sealed tankage, improved avionics cooling and 10 year shelf life. President Carter's decision to cancel the B-1 in June 1977 opened the way for Boeing to promote this longer missile, which could still be carried externally under the wings of a B-52 but would not have fitted into the weapon bays of a B-1.

From July 1979 Boeing's AGM-86B was engaged in a fly-off against GD's AGM-109. Results were hardly impressive, each missile losing four out of ten in crashes, quite apart from other mission-related failures, but after a long delay the USAF announced choice of Boeing on 25 March 1980. A month later it was announced that the USAF/Navy joint management was dissolved and that the USAF Systems Command would solely manage 19 follow-on test flights in 1980 and subsequent production of 3,418 missiles by 1987. The first two rounds assigned to SAC joined the 416th BW at Griffiss AFB in January 1981. Since then about half the 169 operational B-52G bombers have been converted to carry up to 12 rounds each, in two tandem triplets, and in 1982 President Reagan increased the buy to 3,780 missiles by 1990 to permit 96 B-52H bombers to be equipped also. From 1986 the internal bomb bays are being rebuilt by Boeing-Wichita to permit each aircraft to carry a further eight rounds on an internal rotary launcher. Each B-52, after conversion, has a permanently attached wing-root "strakelet", visible in satellite pictures, as demanded by SALT II provisions. The pre-loaded wing pylons will be carried only in time of emergency.

The production B-1B carries the same eight-barrel rotary launcher as the rebuilt B-52, and except for the first few aircraft also carries a further 14 on eight external racks.

Below: The AGM-86B is the main weapon of SAC's B-52 fleet, and possesses good range plus a useful warhead delivered with great accuracy. But the ALCM is undoubtedly too slow.

Bill Gunston, Assistant Compiler of Jane's *All the World's Aircraft;* author of many technical books and papers on military affairs.

This catalogue includes the major rockets and missiles in service with the US armed forces and important projects under development. They are arranged in alphabetical order.

ALMV (ASAT)

Origin: Boeing Aerospace Co/LTV, USA.
Type: Air-launched Miniature Vehicle (Anti-Satellite).
Dimensions: Length 17·71ft (5·4m); body diameter 15·7 to 19·7in (40 to 50cm) both approximate.
Launch weight: Missile 2,645lb (1,200kg); homing vehicle 35·3lb (16kg).
Propulsion: First-stage, Thiokol; second-stage Vought Altair III (Thiokol).
Range: 100 to 256 miles (60 to 160km) depending on flight profile.
Flight speed: Mach 3 + .
Warhead: Vought.

For many years the US Department of Defense, and particularly the USAF and the US Army, have been studying Anti-Satellite (ASAT) weapons systems. The Air Force studies·led in 1979 to a program for operational hardware, with a USAF contract for $78·2m being awarded to the Vought Corporation for an ASAT system to be deployed by about 1985. This was to comprise an advanced interceptor vehicle with guidance so accurate it would destroy targets by physical impact, no explosive warhead being necessary.

This weapon, designated the Air-Launched Miniature Vehicle, is now in the testing stage; it is launched by an F-15 fighter and then boosted into orbital height by two rocket stages. The first stage is based on the Short Range Attack Missile (SRAM), a Boeing Aerospace product, and Boeing has developed this stage, as well as providing integration services and managing development of the mission control centre. The second stage is the Altair III, the Thiokol motor which for many years has been the fourth stage of Vought's Scout vehicle. McDonnell Douglas has modified the F-15 to serve as the launch platform. An $82.3m contract was voted in 1980 and a further $268m in 1981 to continue development through to the flight testing, which had been planned to begin in 1984.

In February 1985 US Secretary of State for Defense Caspar Weinberger stated that ASAT was in the test and evaluation stage, and it was later announced that this had been a complete success, with live hits on space targets. ASAT is believed now to be in service.

Above: Third test launch of the ASAT weapon from a climbing F-15 fighter. The satellite target was destroyed.

AMRAAM

Origin: Hughes Aircraft, Missile Systems Group, USA.
Type: Advanced medium-range AAM.
Dimensions: Length 145·7in (3·7m); body diameter 7·0in (178mm).
Launch weight: 326lb (148kg).
Propulsion: Advanced internal rocket motor.
Performance: Speed probably about Mach 4; maximum range in excess of 30 miles (48km).
Warhead: Expected to be lighter than 50lb (22kg).

Also called BVR (Beyond Visual Range) missile, the Advanced Medium-Range AAM is the highest priority AAM programme in the United States, because AIM-7F is becoming long in the tooth and is judged urgently in need of replacement in the 1980s by a completely new missile. AMRAAM is a joint USAF/USN programme aimed at producing a missile having higher performance and lethality than any conceivable advanced version of Sparrow, within a package that is smaller, lighter, more reliable and cheaper.

AMRAAM will obviously be matched with later versions of F-14, -15, -16 and -18 equipped with programmable signal processors for doppler beam-sharpening and with advanced IR sensors able to acquire individual targets at extreme range. The missile will then be launched automatically on inertial mid-course guidance, without the need for the fighter to illuminate the target, the final terminal homing being by a small active seeker.

The task clearly needs a very broad programme to investigate not only traditional sensing and guidance methods but also new ones such as target aerodynamic noise, engine harmonics and laser scanning to verify the external shape and thus confirm aircraft type. Multiple-target and TWS (track-while-scan) are needed, and AMRAAM has a high-impulse motor giving rapid acceleration to a Mach number higher than 4, with subsequent manoeuvre by TVC and/or tail controls combined with body lift, wings not being needed. Mid-course guidance is Nortronics inertial, and the small Hughes active terminal radar now uses a TWT (travelling-wave tube) transmitter.

The original list of five competing groups was narrowed to two in February 1979, and at the end of 1981 Hughes was picked over Raytheon to build 94 test missiles, with options on 924 for inventory plus follow-on production (which,

because the US buy alone is expected to exceed 13,000 for the USAF and 7,000 for the Navy/Marines, is expected to be split between two contractors, Raytheon probably becoming second-source).

In 1980 West Germany and the UK signed a memorandum of understanding assigning AMRAAM to the USA and ASRAAM to the two European nations. Since then work has gone ahead on integrating the US missile into the RAF Tornado F.2, replacing Sky Flash, and the Luftwaffe F-4F (the latter possibly being refitted with APG-65 or improved APG-66 radar under the Peace Rhine programme). The Tornado Foxhunter radar may need a small L-band transmitter to provide mid-course updating.

Testing of full-scale development rounds started in 1984, and the production run began with 174 in 1985 and 1,042 in 1986.

Below: Smaller and lighter than the AIM-7 it is designed to replace, the AIM-120 offers a "fire-and-forget" capability. This is one of 94 test missiles, seen under an F-14A's wing.

Asroc, RUR-5A

Origin: Honeywell Aerospace and Defense Group, USA.
Type: Anti-submarine rocket.
Dimensions: Length 181in (4·6m); body diameter 12·8in (32·5cm); span 33·25in (84·5cm).
Launch weight: 960lb (435kg).
Propulsion: Naval Propellant Plant solid tandem boost motor, basic missile is torpedo.
Guidance: Ballistic in flight.
Range: 1·25 to 6·2 miles (2 to 9·97km).
Flight speed: Transonic.
Warhead: Standard Mk 44/46 torpedo, HE or nuclear warhead.

Operational since 1961, this elementary all-weather ASW weapon used sonar and fire-control computer to slew and elevate the launcher (Mk 46 or Mk 10 Terrier/Standard/Asroc launcher). The Asroc flies a ballistic trajectory to the vicinity of the target. The rocket is jettisoned after burnout, and a parachute decelerates the Mk 46 torpedo for a safe water entry, thereafter homing on the target in the usual way. As an alternative, the payload can be a 1kT nuclear depth charge likewise lowered by parachute. Though obsolescent, Asroc is still operational aboard 27 cruisers, 87 destroyers and 65 frigates of the US Navy, and is being installed aboard each new DD-963 destroyer. It is also in service on some 59 ships of 11 other navies.

Below: The Asroc is now elderly in its short-range RUR-5A version, and the development of a vertical-launch longer-range model ignores the ASW limitations of the Mk 46 torpedo.

CWW GBU-15

Origin: Rockwell International, USA.
Type: Modular glide (smart) bomb.
Dimensions: Length 154in (3·91m); body diameter 18in (457mm); span 59in (1,499mm).
Launch weight: 2,450lb (1,111kg).
Propulsion: None.
Performance: Speed, subsonic: range, typically 5 miles (8km) but highly variable with launch height and speed.
Warhead: Mk 84 bomb, 2,000lb (907kg).

The CWW (cruciform-wing weapon) is the modern successor to the Vietnam-era Pave Strike Hobos (homing-bomb system), of which GBU-8 (guided bomb unit) was the chief production example. Like GBU-8, GBU-15 is a modular system comprising standard GP (general purpose) bombs to which a target-detecting device and trajectory-control fins are added. The full designation of the basic production missile is GBU-15(V)/B, and it is also called a modular guided glide bomb (MGGB) or modular guided weapon system.

Though the payload and structural basis may be the CBU-75 cluster munition the normal basis is the Mk 84 2,000lb (907kg) bomb. To the front are added an FMU-124 fuze, a tubular adapter and either of two target-detecting devices, TV or IIR (imaging infra-red). At the rear are added an autopilot, displacement gyro, primary battery, control module and data-link module, and the weapon is completed by attaching four canard fins and four large rear wings with powered control surfaces on the trailing edges. (An alternative PWW, planar-wing weapon, by Hughes, is no longer active).

GBU-15 is launched at medium to extremely low altitudes. In the former case it is guided over a direct line of sight to the target. In the latter it is launched in the direction of the target, while the carrier aircraft gets away at very low level. It is steered by a data-link by the operator in the aircraft who has a display showing the scene in the seeker in the nose of the missile (TV is the usual method). The missile climbs until it can acquire the target, and then pushes over into a dive. The operator has the choice of steering the missile all the way to the target or locking-on the homing head. Extensive trials from F-4, F-111 and B-52 aircraft are complete and substantial deliveries have been made to USAF.

Below: The medium- low-altitude CWW GBU-15 "smart" bomb under the wing of an F-4. Tiseo EO sensor is above the pylon.

Chaparral, MIM-72C

Origin: Ford Aeronutronic Division, USA.
Type: Mobile surface-to-air guided missile system.
Dimensions: Length 114·5in (2·91m); body diameter 5in (12·7cm); span 25in (64cm).
Launch weight: 185lb (84kg).
Propulsion: Rocketdyne Mk 36 Mod 5 single-stage solid motor.
Guidance: Initial optical aiming, IR homing to target heat emitter.
Range: About 2·5 miles (4km).
Flight speed: About Mach 2·5.
Warhead: (MIM-72A) 11lb (5kg) HE-frag with pre-formed splinters; (MIM-72C) M-250 (Picatinny Arsenal) blast-frag.

When the purpose-designed Mauler missile was abandoned this weapon was substituted as a makeshift stop-gap, the missile being the original Sidewinder 1C modified for ground launch. A fire unit has four missiles on a manually tracked launcher, carried on an M730 (modified M548) tracked vehicle, with a futher eight rounds on board ready to be loaded by hand. Owing to the severe cutbacks in the Americanized Roland, Chaparral has continued to fill the gap, and is now widely used by the Army and Marine Corps, usually with an equal number of Vulcan air-defense gun systems. The missile now in production is MIM-72C, which not only carries the better warhead noted above, but also has improved DAW-1 all-aspect guidance and the Harry Diamond Labs M-817 proximity fuze. Though totally inadequate, Chaparral is having to remain the USA's forward-area low-altitude SAM system for at least the next decade instead of being replaced by Roland, a problem exacerbated by the failure of the gun-

based DIVAD system. Urgent efforts are being made to improve it with a blind-fire radar, smokeless motor and Stinger IFF, and it is anticipated that Chaparral will now remain in service until the late 1990s.

Below: The Chaparral system was introduced as a stop-gap, and suffers from a number of important tactical limitations.

Dragon M47 FGM-77A

Origin: McDonnell Douglas Astronautics (second course production by Raytheon and Kollsman), USA.
Type: Infantry anti-tank/assault missile.
Dimensions: Length 29·3in (74cm); body diameter 4·5in (11·4cm); fin span 13in (33cm).
Launch weight: 24·4lb (11·1kg).
Propulsion: Recoilless gas-generator thruster in launch tube; sustain propulsion by 60 small side thrusters fired in pairs upon tracker demand.
Guidance: See text.
Range: 3,300ft (60-1,000m).
Flight speed: About 230mph (370km/h).
Warhead: Linear shaped charge, 5·4lb (2·45kg).

Dragon was designed as a medium-range complement to TOW (*qv*). In service since 1971, Dragon comes sealed in a glass-fibre launch tube with a fat rear end containing the launch charge. The operator attaches this to his tracker, comprising telesopic sight, IR sensor and electronics box. When the missile is fired, its 3 curved fins flick open and start the missile spinning. The operator holds the sight on the target and the tracker automatically commands the missile to the line of sight by firing appropriate pairs of side thrusters. The launch tube is thrown away and a fresh one attached to the tracker. The Army and Marine Corps use the basic Dragon, while developments involve night sights and laser guidance.

The Dragon system is not without its problems. Perhaps the most important is that the missile body diameter of 4·5in (11·4cm) sets the limit on the size of the warhead. The effectiveness of a shaped charge warhead is a function of its diameter, and at least 6in (15cm) is likely to be needed to counter the new armours coming into service on the latest Soviet tanks. In addition, the missile is slow; this aggravates the difficulties of the operator, who must hold his breath throughout the flight of the missile. The operator is also adjured to grasp the launch-tube tightly, for if he does not his shoulder may rise at the moment of launch, thus sending the missile into the ground. Finally, the rocket thrusters have been found to deteriorate in storage, and many need replacement.

Initial plans for a Dragon replacement centred on a progamme designated IMAAWS, but this was halted in 1980.

Above: The Dragon is a bulky piece of kit, and the missile's low speed leaves the operator exposed for too long a period. A replacement is now being sought as a matter of urgency.

HARM, AGM-88A

Origin: Texas Instruments Inc., USA.
Type: Anti-radiation missile.
Dimensions: Length 13ft 8½in (4·17m); body diameter 10in (254mm); span 44in (1,118mm).
Launch weight: 796lb (361kg).
Propulsion: Thiokol single-grain (280lb, 127kg, filling of non-aluminized HTPB) reduced-smoke boost/sustain motor.
Performance: Speed over Mach 2; range/height variable with aircraft to about 11·5 miles (18·5km).
Warhead: Fragmentation with proximity fuze system.

Neither Shrike nor Standard ARM is an ideal air-launched ARM and in 1972 the Naval Weapons Center began R&D and also funded industry studies for a High-speed Anti-Radiation Missile (HARM). Among the objectives were much higher flight speed, to lock-on and hit targets before they could be switched off or take other action, and to combine the low cost and versatility of Shrike, the sensitivity and large launch envelope of Standard ARM, and completely new passive homing using the latest microelectronic digital techniques and interfacing with new aircraft systems. In 1974 TI was selected as system integration contractor, assisted by Hughes, Dalmo-Victor, Itek and SRI (Stanford Research Institute).

The slim AGM-88A missile has double-delta moving wings and a small fixed tail. The TI seeker has a simple fixed aerial (antenna) yet gives broadband coverage, a low-cost autopilot is fitted, and Motorola supply an optical target detector forming part of the fuzing for the large advanced-design warhead. Carrier aircraft include the Navy/Marines A-6E, A-7E and F/A-18, and the Air Force APR-38 Wild Weasal F-4G and EF-111A, with Itek's ALR-45 radar warning receiver and Dalmo-Victor's DSA-20N signal analyser both interfaced. Proposed carriers include the B-52, F-16 and Tornado. HARM can be used in three modes. The basic use is Self-protect, the ALR-45 detecting threats, the launch computer sorting the data to give priorities and pass to the missile a complete set of digital instructions in milliseconds, whereupon the missile can be fired. In the Target of Opportunity mode the very sensitive seeker locks-on to "certain parameters of operation and also transmissions associated with other parts of a radar installation" which could not be detected by Shrike or Standard ARM. In the pre-briefed mode HARM is fired 'blind' in the general direction of known enemy radiation emitters; if the latter are 'silent' the missile self-destructs, but if one of them radiates, HARM at once homes on to it.

Test flights began in 1976; redesign followed and following prolonged further tests delivery to user units began in early 1983.

Below: The combination of F-4G "Wild Weasel" aircraft and AGM-88A missiles provides the US Air Force with excellent capability against hostile radars. The memory of the missile means that the launch aircraft need pop up out of cover merely to acquire the target (with APR-38 radar-homing and ALR-45 radar-warning receiver systems) and launch the missile, which then homes automatically even if the emitter shuts down.

Harpoon, AGM-84A

Origin: McDonnell Douglas Astronautics, USA.
Type: Anti-ship missile.
Dimensions: Length 12ft 7in (3·84m); body diameter 13·5in (343mm); span 30in (762mm).
Launch weight: 1,160lb (526kg).
Propulsion: One Teledyne CAE J402-400 turbojet, sea-level thrust 661lb (300kg).
Performance: Speed Mach 0·75; range over 57 miles (92km).
Warhead: NWC 500lb (227kg) penetration/blast with impact/delay and proximity fuzing.

This extremely important weapon system began as an ASM in 1968, but three years later was combined with a proposal for a ship- and submarine-launched missile system. McDonnell Douglas Astronautics (MDAC) was selected as prime contractor in June 1971. The main development contract followed in July 1973, and of 40 prototype weapon systems 34 were launched in 1974-5, 15 being the RGM-84A fired from ships (including the PHM *High Point* whilst foilborne) and three from submarines, the other 16 being air-launched. At first almost wholly trouble-free, testing suffered random failures from late 1975, and the clearance for full-scale production was delayed temporarily. Production of all versions amounted to 315 in 1976, and about 2,900 by early 1984.

Target data, which can be OTH if supplied from a suitable platform, are fed before launch to the Lear-Siegler or Northrop strapdown inertial platform which can steer the missile even if launched at up to 90° off the desired heading. Flight control is by cruciform rear fins. A radar altimeter holds the desired sea-skimming height, and no link with the aircraft is required. Nearing the target the Texas Instruments PR-53/DSQ-58 active radar seeker searches, locks-on and finally commands a sudden pull-up and swoop on the target from above.

The Naval Weapons Center and MDAC are also studying possible versions with supersonic speed, torpedo-carrying payload, imaging IR homing, passive radiation homing, nuclear warhead, vertical launch, midcourse guidance up-dating and other features.

MDAC expects to make at least 5,000 systems by 1988 despite the delayed start. Of these well over 2,000 will be for the US Navy, for surface ships, sub-marines, and P-3C, A-6E, S-3B, A-7E and F/A-18A aircraft. The S-3 carries two missiles and the other types four. Production is at the rate of 40 missiles per month. Among the aircraft systems is a missile firing simulator.

Sixteen Western navies use Harpoon, including nine in NATO. All users classify Harpoon as the principal anti-surface weapon.

Above: The Harpoon is one of the most important weapons in the US inventory, the AGM-84A version providing aircraft such as the P-3C Orion with powerful anti-ship capability.

Below: An RGM-84A surface-launched Harpoon leaves the port rail of the Mk 11 twin SAM/anti-ship launcher of the Charles F. Adams class destroyer USS *Lawrence*.

Hawk, MIM-23B

Origin: Raytheon Company, Missile Systems Division, USA.
Type: Transportable surface-to-air missile system.
Dimensions: Length 16ft 6in (5·03m); body diameter 14in (360mm); span 48·85in (1,190mm).
Launch weight: 1,383lb (627·3kg).
Propulsion: Aerojet M112 boost/sustain solid rocket motor.
Guidance: CW radar SARH.
Range: 25 miles (40km).
Flight speed: Mach 2·5.
Warhead: HE blast/frag, 120lb (54kg).

Hawk (Homing All-the-Way Killer) was the world's first missile with CW guidance. When developed in the 1950s it looked a good system, but by modern standards it is cumbersome, each battery having a pulse acquisition radar, a CW illuminating radar, a range-only radar, two illuminator radars, battery control center, six three-missile launchers and a tracked loader, the whole weighing many tons. AN SP version has ground support items on wheels and towed by tracked launchers or loaders. Hawk became operational in August 1960 and is deployed widely throughout the Army and Marine Corps and 17 other nations. Improved Hawk (MIM-23B) has a better guidance system, larger warhead, im-proved motor and semi-automatic ground systems ("certified rounds" are load-ed on launchers without the need for further attention). Further development is

attempting to improve CW radar reliability and improve pulse-acquisition speed by allowing automated threat-ordering of all targets that could be of impor-tance. Since the early 1970s it has been planned to replace certain Hawk units by Patriot, but Hawk and its improved versions will remain in service for many years.

Below: Its associated fire-control system is bulky, but the Hawk itself remains a capable and widely deployed SAM.

Hellfire

Origin: Rockwell International, USA.
Type: Laser-guided "fire and forget" missile.
Dimensions: Length 64in (1,626mm); body diameter 7in (178mm).
Launch weight: 98·86lb (44·84kg).
Propulsion: Thiokol TX657 reduced-smoke "all-boost" motor.
Range: Up to "several kilometers", "far in excess of present anti-armor systems".
Flight speed: Transonic, quickly builds to Mach 1·17.
Warhead: Firestone 20lb (9kg) 7in-diameter hollow charge.

A direct descendent of Rockwell's Hornet, this missile has applications against hard point targets of all kinds, though it was officially described as "the USA's next-generation anti-armor weapon system". Numerous development firings took place from 1971 before full engineering go-ahead was received in October 1976. It has semi-active laser homing with a very advanced seeker from Martin Marietta. The seeker has a Cassegrain telescope under the hemispherical glass nose sending signals to the electronics section with microprocessor logic. Steering is by four canard controls, and Hellfire can pull 13g at Mach 1·17. The US Under-Secretary of Defense, The Hon. William J. Perry, said "This missile most often goes right through the center of the bull's eye". The primary carrier is the AH-64A Apache helicopter (16 rounds) but Hellfire is also carried by the USMC AH-1T Cobra. Numerous Hellfires have been launched without prior lock-on, some of them in raid-fire homing on different multiple targets using ground designators with individual coding. The missile notices the laser radiation in flight, locks-on and homes at once. IOC was attained in 1985. This missile will probably also be developed with "launch-and-leave" IIR guidance. Some 60,000 missiles will be procured over the life of the programme.

Above: The Hellfire was designed primarily for the AH-64A, but its comparative lightness and "fire-and-forget" laser homing prompted its adoption for types such as this UH-60A.

Lance, MGM-52C

Origin: Vought Corporation, USA.
Type: Battlefield missile.
Dimensions: Length 20·24ft (6·17m); body diameter 22in (56cm).
Launch weight: 2,833 to 3,376lb (1,285-1,527kg) depending on warhead.
Propulsion: Rocketdyne P8E-9 storable-liquid 2-part motor with infinitely throttleable sustainer portion.
Guidance: Simplified inertial.
Range: 45 to 75 miles (70-120km) depending on warhead.
Flight speed: Mach 3.
Warhead: M234 nuclear 468lb (212kg, 10kT), W-70-4 ER/RB (neutron) or Honeywell M251, 1,000lb (454kg) HE cluster.

In service since 1972, this neat rocket replaced the earlier Honest John rocket and Sergeant ballistic missile, with very great gains in reduced system weight, cost and bulk, and increases in accuracy and mobility. Usual vehicle is the M752 (M113 family) amphibious tracked launcher, with the M688 carrying two extra missiles and a loading hoist. For air-dropped operations a lightweight towed launcher can be used. In-flight guidance accuracy, with the precisely controlled sustainer and spin-stabilization, is already highly satisfactory, but a future missile could have DME (Distance Measuring Equipment) command guidance. The US Army has 8 battalions, 6 of which are deployed in Europe with 6 launchers each; the 2 remaining battalions are at Fort Sill, Okla. Lance production lasted from 1971 to 1980, during which time 2,133 missiles were built. Lance is in service with the armies of Belgium, FRG, Italy, Israel, Netherlands and the UK.

Lance is the most powerful long-range missile currently under the direct control of the tactical ground commander. Its importance lies in its potential for breaking up Warsaw Pact second and third echelon forces before they can be committed.

A successor in this vital mission is under development as the Corps Support Weapon System (CSWS). This is intended to carry an even wider variety of payloads over ranges up to 124 miles (200km), using simpler support equipment and requiring fewer men.

Above: The black plumes from the Lance midsection are the exhausts of the spin-stablization rocket motors.

Below: Lance in the field on the lightweight towed launcher developed for air-drop capability.

Maverick, AGM-65

Origin: Hughes Aircraft, USA.
Type: Air-to-surface missile.
Dimensions: Length 98in (2,490mm); body diameter 12in (305mm); span 28·3in (720mm).
Launch weight: (AGM-65A, shaped-charge) 436lb (210kg), (65A, blast/frag) 635lb (288kg).
Propulsion: Thiokol boost/sustain solid motor, from 1972 TX-481 and from 1981 TX-633 with reduced smoke.
Performance: Speed classified but supersonic; range 0·6-10 miles (1-16km) at sea level, up to 25 miles (40km) after Mach 1·2 release at altitude.
Warhead: Choice of Chamberlain shaped charge (83lb, 37·6kg, charge) or Avco steel-case penetrator blast/frag.

Smallest of the fully guided or self-homing ASMs for US use, AGM-65 Maverick was approved in 1965 and, following competition with Rockwell, Hughes won the programme in June 1968. An initial 17,000-missile package was fulfilled in 1975, and production has continued at reduced rate on later versions. The basic missile, usually carried in triple clusters under the wings of the F-4, F-15, F-16, A-7, A-10 and Swedish AJ37A Viggen, and singly by the F-5 and the BGM-34 RPV, has four delta wings of very low aspect ratio, four tail controls immediately behind the wings, and a dual-thrust solid motor.

In mid-1978 Hughes completed production of 26,000 AGM-65A Mavericks and for three years had no production line. Unguided flights began in September 1969, and the missile has been launched at all heights down to treetop level.

The pilot selects a missile, causing its gyro to run up to speed and light a cockpit indicator. The pilot then visually acquires the target, depresses his uncage switch to remove the protective cover from the missile nose, and activates the video circuitry. The TV picture at once appears on a bright display in the cockpit, and the pilot then either slews the video seeker in the missile or else lines up the target in his own gunsight. He depresses the track switch, waits until the cross-hairs on the TV display are aligned on the target, releases the switch and fires the round. Homing is automatic, and the launch aircraft at once escapes from the area.

In the 1973 Yom Kippur war AGM-65A was used operationally, in favorable conditions. It requires good visibility, and the occasional $48,000 A-model breaks its TV lock and misses its target — for example, because of overwater glint.

AGM-65B, Scene-Magnification Maverick, has new optics, a stronger gimbal mount and revised electronics. The pilot need not see the target, but instead can search with the seeker and cockpit display which presents an enlarged and clearer picture. Thus he can identify the target, lock-on and fire much quicker and from a greater slant range. AGM-65B was in production (at up to 200 per

Below: The versatile Maverick air-to-surface missile has been developed in many forms, this being an AGM-65E with semi-active laser homing matched to many NATO designators.

Midgetman

Origin: USAF and commercial contractors, USA.
Type: Road-mobile, inter-continental ballistic missile.
Dimensions: Length 45·27ft (13·8m); body diameter 45·2in (115cm).
Launch weight: 30,000lb (13,600kg); payload weight 1,003lb (455kg).
Propulsion: Solid-fuel, three-stage.
Range: 6,000nm.
Warhead: Mk 21 with 500kT warhead.

The debate on the future national requirements for ICBMs and what shape such ICBMs should take has raged in the USA for a number of years. In an effort to resolve the argument on the MX (Peacekeeper) President Reagan set up a Commission on Strategic Forces, known by the name of its chairman as the Scowcroft Commission. This body recommended the prompt deployment of 100 Peacekeepers and the longer term development of a road-mobile 'small ICBM', now popularly designated 'Midgetman'.

Midgetman was designed initially with the specifications shown above, which were agreed in the FY84 Budget. The intention was that it should have a single re-entry vehicle (Mark 21 with 500kT warhead), thus reversing the recent trend for MIRVS. It would also be moved around the country on a purpose-built Hard Mobile Launcher (HML). Development contracts have been let for the various sub-systems and testing is now under way in some areas; for example, the Martin Marietta and Boeing submissions for the HML are now running in prototype form.

As happens so often in weapons systems development, however (and especially with US strategic missile programmes), the military requirement is changing and there are strong pressures to increase the weight, and thus the size of the missile. There are proposals to add warheads, thus returning to the MIRV concept, which would actually reduce the cost of the programme, as well as to add penetration aids to overcome Soviet ABM systems. The latter would add some 4·92ft (1·5m) to the first stage (for a total missile length of 50·2ft/15.3m) and 8,813lb (4,000kg) to the all-up weight, and generate sufficient space for a second warhead of a new, lighter design.

The HML has to be capable of using existing roads and bridges. This means that total weight must be below about 200,000lb (91,000kg), and the vehicle must be no more than about 13·8ft (4.2m) wide, so that it uses less than half the normal road width. Two consortia have produced prototypes: Boeing, Goodyear Aerospace and PACCAR, and Martin Marietta and Caterpillar. Both are articulated vehicles, with low overall height, rounded triangular shapes, and with a degree of 'hardening'. The Martin Marietta HML runs on rubber tracks on rubber wheels, while the Boeing design has wheels. The choice between the two is due to be made in 1986/87.

Arguments between the Pentagon, the Senate and the House of Representatives continue. In late 1986 it is difficult to determine what the final shape, size and cost of the Midgetman system might take, but it seems safe to say that the programme may well become as controversial as MX.

Above: Details of the "Midgetman" small ICBM are sparse, though it seems likely that if the type goes ahead it will use land-mobile basing and carry a single warhead with considerable accuracy over a range of some 6,000 miles (9,655km).

month) from May 1980 to May 1983.

AGM-65C Laser Maverick was for close-air support against laser-designated targets, the lasers being the infantry ILS-NT200 or the airborne Pave Knife, Pave Penny, Pave Spike, Pave Tack or non-US systems. Flight testing began in January 1977, using the Rockwell tri-Service seeker. Troop training has established the method of frequency and pulse coding to tie each missile to only one air or ground designator, so that many Mavericks can simultaneously be homed on many different sources of laser radiation.

AGM-65C was replaced by AGM-65E with "tri-Service" laser tracker and

Below: The Maverick family's several guidance types suit the missile to most tactical aircraft (including this F-16B two-seater), and three warhead types have also been developed.

digital processing which in 1982 entered production for the US Marine Corps with heavy blast/frag warhead. Westinghouse tested Pave Spike with the Minneapolis-Honeywell helmet sight for single-seat aircraft.

In May 1977 engineering development began on AGM-65D IR-Maverick, with Hughes IIR tri-Service seeker. Considerably more expensive than other versions, the IIR seeker — especially when slaved to an aircraft-mounted sensor such as FLIR, a laser pod or the APR-38 radar warning system — enables the Maverick to lock-on at least twice the range otherwise possible in northwest Europe in mist, rain or at night. Of course, it also distinguishes between "live targets" and "hulks". Using the centroid seeker in place of the original edgelock optics, AGM-65D was tested from an F-4 in Germany in poor weather in January-March 1978.

While Hughes continues to produce the common center and aft missile sections, delay with the laser-seeker E-version meant that AGM-65D got into pilot production first.

All AGM-65A Mavericks have the same 130lb (59kg) conical shaped-charge warhead, but different warheads are in prospect. The Mk 19 250lb (113kg) blast/fragmentation head is preferred by the Navy and Marines, giving capability against small ships as well as hard land targets, and may be fitted to C and D versions with new fuzing/arming and a 4in (102mm) increase in length. Another warhead weighs 300lb (136kg), while in December 1976 the Air Force expressed a need for a nuclear warhead.

Hughes' Tucson, Arizona, plant is likely to be hard-pressed to handle TOW, Phoenix and residual Roland work on top of enormously expanded Maverick production. By far the largest numbers are expected to be of the IIR Maverick, AGM-65D, of which well over 30,000 rounds are predicted at a rate of 500 per month.

Prolonged tests have confirmed the long range, which at last matches the flight limitations of the missile itself, and AGM-65D is the standard missile for use with the Lantirn night and bad-weather sensor system now being fitted to F-16s and A-10s.

The Navy is expected to procure AGM-65F, which is almost the same missile but fitted with the heavy penetrator warhead of AGM-65E, and with modified guidance software exactly matched to give optimum hits on surface warships. With this missile family Hughes has achieved a unique capability with various guidance systems and warheads, resulting in impressively large production and interchangeability.

Minuteman, LGM-30

Origin: Boeing Aerospace Co., USA.
Type: ICBM.
Dimensions: Length 59·7ft (18·2m); body diameter (first stage) 6ft (183cm).
Launch weight: 76,015lb (34,475kg).
Propulsion: First stage, Thiokol TU-120 (M55E) solid rocket, 200,000lb (91,000kg) thrust for 60 sec; second stage, Aerojet SR19 solid rocket, with liquid-injection thrust-vector control, 60,000lb (27,200kg) thrust; third stage Aerojet/Thiokol solid rocket, 34,876lb (16,000kg) thrust, plus post-boost control system.
Guidance: Inertial.
Range: Over 8,000 miles (12,875km).
Warhead: Three (sometimes two) General Electric Mk 12 MIRVs.

Minuteman was designed in 1958-60 as a smaller and simpler second-generation ICBM using solid propellant. Originally envisaged as a mobile weapon launched from trains, it was actually deployed (probably mistakenly) in fixed hardened silos. Minuteman I (LGM-30B) became operational in 1963 but is no longer in use. Minuteman II (LGM-30F) became operational from December 1966, and today 450 are still in use, and replacement of expired component-lifetimes has recently started. By 1978 all the re-entry vehicles were of the Mk 11C type hardened against EMP; consideration has been given to prolonging missile life, and improving accuracy, by retrofitting the NS-20 guidance used on Minuteman III (LGM-30G). The latter, operational since 1970, has a new third stage and completely new re-entry vehicles forming a fourth stage with its own propulsion, guidance package and pitch-roll motors; as well as several warheads, individually targetable, it houses chaff, decoys and possibly other penaids.

Production of LGM-30G Minuteman III ended in late 1977, but the force is continually being updated, with improved silos, better guidance software, and the Command Data Buffer System, which, with other add-ons, reduces retargeting time per missile from around 24 hours to about half an hour, and allows it to be done remotely from the Wing's Launch Control Center or from an ALCS (Airborne Launch Control System) aircraft or an NEACP (National Emergency Airborne Command Post). The latter comprise the E-4B while the ALCS authority is vested in nine EC-135C aircraft which can monitor 200 Minuteman missiles and, via improved satellite communications links, retarget and launch any of these missiles even if their ground LCC (Launch Control Center) is destroyed. Installation of the Mk 12A RV began in 1979. This has various advantages and carries the 330kT W-78 warhead, but it is about 16kg heavier and this slightly reduces range and MIRV footprint.

One hundred Minuteman silos are due to be converted to take the Peacekeeper ICBM, and an unspecified number of Minuteman IIs are allocated to the Emergency Rocket Communications System. The elderly Titan II ICBM, of which 52 were in service in 1980, is being phased out, the process being due for completion in 1987.

Above: The use of MIRVs, such as the three Mk 12s carried by the LGM-30F, allow separated targets to be engaged, as shown by the tracks of these six MIRVs from two Minuteman IIIs.

Below: Though expensive, test launches such as that of this Minuteman III validate the ongoing program of updates which keep these strategic vehicles right "up to the mark".

MLRS

Origin: Vought Corporation (prime contractor), USA.
Type: Multiple rocket system.
Dimensions: Rocket length 13ft (3·96m); diameter 8·94in (227mm).
Launch weight: Rocket 600lb (272kg).
Propulsion: Atlantic Research solid rocket motor.
Range: Over 18·6 miles (30km).
Flight speed: Just supersonic.
Warhead: Dispenses payload of sub-munitions, initially 644 standard M42 bomblets.

Known from 1972 until 1979 as the GSRS (General Support Rocket System), the MLRS (Multiple Launch Rocket System) entered service with 1st Infantry Division (Mechanized) at Fort Riley, Kansas, in 1983. It has the same battlefield mobility as armored formations, being carried on a tracked vehicle with a trainable and elevating launcher; this can be rapidly loaded with two six-round containers without the crew of three leaving their cab. Each box houses six preloaded tubes, with a 10-year shelf life. The crew can ripple-fire from two to 12 rounds in less than one minute, the fire control re-aiming after each shot. The rocket is highly accurate and is intended to carry any of three types of sub-munition, M42 shaped-charge grenade-size,scatterable anti-armor mine, or guided sub-missiles. In the future a binary chemical warhead may also be developed. Each launcher load of 12 missiles is said to "place almost 8,000 sub-munitions in an area the size of four (US) football fields". The first production system was delivered to the Army in early 1982, by which time $317 million had been voted for the first 112 vehicles and 6,210 rockets. Production is intended to rise to 5,000 rounds per month in a programme costing an estimated $4·2 billion.

The carrying vehicle is designated a Self-propelled Launcher Loader (SPLL) and is based on the M2 IFV (qv). The SPLL weighs some 50,000lb (22,680kg) fully loaded and is air-portable in a C-141 StarLifter. It can travel at 40mph (64km/h) and can ford a depth of 40in (1·01m), but is not amphibious.

One of the major problems with high rate-of-fire rocket systems is that of resupply, and MLRS is no exception. Each battery of nine launchers will have its own ammunition platoon of 18 resupply vehicles and trailers, and there will be many more farther back in the logistic system.

In mechanized and armoured divisions there will be one MLRS battery in the general support battalion (with two batteries of M110A2), while light divisions will have an independent battery. There will be an MLRS battalion of three batteries with each corps.

The MLRS is also the subject of a major NATO programme involving France, Italy, the Federal Republic of Germany, and the United Kingdom.

Below: An MLRS launcher looses off one of its 12 rockets.

Patriot, MIM-104

Origin: Raytheon Missile Systems Division and Martin Orlando Divison, USA.
Type: Self-propelled air defence missile system.
Dimensions: Length 209in (5·31m); body diameter 16in (40·6cm); span 36in (92cm).
Launch weight: 2,200lb (998kg).
Propulsion: Thiokol TX-486 single-thrust solid motor.
Guidance: Phased-array radar command and semi-active homing.
Range: About 37 nautical miles (68·6km).
Flight speed: About Mach 3.
Warhead: Choice of nuclear or conventional blast/frag.

Originally known as SAM-D, this planned successor to both Nike Hercules and Hawk has had an extremely lengthy gestation. Key element in the Patriot system is a phased-array radar, which performs all the functions of surveillance, acquisition, track/engage and missile guidance. The launcher carries 4 missiles each in its shipping container, from which it blasts upon launch. Launchers, spare missiles boxes, radars, computers, power supplies and other items can be towed or self-propelled. Patriot is claimed to be effective against all aircraft or attack missiles even in the presence of clutter or intense jamming or other ECM.

Fundamental reasons for the serious delay and cost-escalation have been the complexity of the system, the 1974 slowdown to demonstrate TVM (track via missile) radar guidance, and inflation. Unquestionably the system is impressive, but often its complication and cost impress in the wrong way and the number of systems to be procured has been repeatedly revised downwards.

The authorized development programme was officially completed in 1980, when low-rate production was authorized. In 1983 production was cautiously stepped up and the first operational units were formed in mid-1984. The US Army plans to have 81 Patriot batteries, for which its hardware requirements are 103 fire units and 6,200 missiles. The system is also being purchased by Japan and a number of NATO nations.

Below: The production-standard Patriot fire unit has four box launchers. This is an impressive test firing.

Paveway LGBs

Origin: Texas Instruments, USA.
Type: Laser-guided unpowered bombs.
Launch weight: As for original bombs plus about 30lb (13·6kg).
Propulsion: As for original bombs plus from 6 to 20in (152-500mm) length and with folding tailfins.
Performance: Speed, free-fall; range, free-fall so varies with release height, speed.
Warhead: As in original bombs.

This code-name identifies the most diverse programmes in history aimed at increasing the accuracy of tactical air-to-surface weapons. This USAF effort linked more than 30 separately named systems for airborne navigation, target identification and marking, all-weather/night vision, weapon guidance and many other functions, originally for the war in SE Asia. In the course of this work the "smart bombs" with laser guidance managed by the Armament Development and Test Center at Elgin AFB, from 1965, were developed in partnership with TI, using the latter's laser guidance kit, to form an integrated family of simple precision weapons. The first TI-guided LGB was dropped in April 1965.

All these bombs are extremely simple to carry, requiring no aircraft modification or electrical connection; they are treated as a round of ordnance and loaded like a free-fall bomb. Carrier aircraft have included the A-1, A-4, A-6, A-7, A-10, A-37, F-4, F-5, F-15, F-16, F/A-18, F-100, F-105, F-111, AV-8A, B-52 and B-57.

Targets can be marked by an airborne laser, in the launch aircraft or another aircraft, or by forward troops. Like almost all Western military lasers the matched wavelength is 1·064 microns, the usual lasers (in Pave Knife, Pave Tack or various other airborne pods) being of the Nd/YAG type. More recently target illumination has been provided by the Atlis II, LTDS, TRAM, GLLD, MULE, LTM, Lantirn and TI's own FLIR/laser designator.

In all cases the guidance unit is the same, the differences being confined to attachments and the various enlarged tail fins. The silicon detector array is divided into four quadrants and is mounted on the nose of a free universal-jointed housing with an annular ring tail. As the bomb falls this aligns itself with the airstream, in other words the direction of the bomb's motion. The guidance computer receives signals from the quadrants and drives four control fins to equalize the four outputs. Thus, the sensor unit is kept pointing at the source of laser light, so that the bomb will impact at the same point. Electric power is provided by a thermal battery, energised at the moment of release, and power to drive the fins comes from a hot-gas generator.

Users include the RAF for use on Mk13/18 1,000lb (454kg) bombs carried by Buccaneers, Tornados and Jaguars. Total production of Paveway guidance units has been very large; in the early 1970s output was at roughly 20,000 per year, at a unit price of some $2,500.

Since 1980 the Paveway II weapons have been in production including a simpler and cheaper seeker section, and a folding-wing aerofoil group. Portsmouth Aviation has integrated the system with RAF bombs used from Harriers over the Falklands. Paveway III has flick-out lifting wings and a microprocessor and can be dropped at treetop height.

Peacekeeper

Origin: Martin Marietta Denver Aerospace, USA.
Type: ICBM.
Dimensions: Length 70·8ft (21·6m); diameter 7·6ft (2·34m).
Launch weight: 195,015lb (8,845kg).
Propulsion: Stages 1, 2 and 3 use HTBP propellant, upper stages having extendable-skirt exit cones; stage 4 has hypergolic liquid propellants feeding a vectoring main chamber and eight small altitude-control engines.
Guidance: High-precision inertial.
Range: Over 6,900 miles (11,100km).
Warhead: Ten Mk 12A MIRVs each of 330kT yield.

Like the B-1 bomber the Peacekeeper (formerly MX) weapon system consumed money at a prodigious rate for many years without making the slightest contribution to Western defence or deterrence. Though the need has been self-evident for many years, and there are no problems in producing the missile, arguments raged for many years on how to base it. In 1974 a packaged Minuteman was pulled by parachute from a C-5A, and prolonged research has established the feasibility of an air basing concept.

Early in MX development (pre-1978) all interest centred on mobile deployment using road (curiously, not railway) cars or various forms of transporter/launcher driven around underground rail networks, in most variations with the missile erected so that it would break through the surface in virgin terrain. The Carter administration favoured the MPS (multiple protective shelter) scheme, but the Reagan administration found this faulty and announced in December 1981: ''. . . initial deployment will be in existing Minuteman silos. At least 40 MXs will be deployed, with the first unit of ten missiles operational in late 1986. The Specific location . . . will be determined in spring 1982 . . . In addition, the Air Force has initiated R&D to find the best long-term option . . . The options include the following: ballistic-missile defence of silo-based or deceptively based missiles; DBS, deep-basing system, in underground citadels; and air-mobile basing . . . Congress approved $1,900m for Fiscal 1982 and some

$2,500m has been spent to date. The cost to produce 226 missiles and deploy 40 in Minuteman silos is estimated at 1,800-1,900m in 1982 dollars.''

Next, the Senate Armed Services Committee rejected Minuteman-silo-basing and asked for a permanent basing plan by 1 December 1982. This resulted in other suggestions, notably DUB (deep underground basing) about 3,280ft (1,000m) down in rock, with a self-contained tunnelling machine for each launch capsule and crew, and CSB (closely spaced basing). The latter, called ''dense pack'', relies on the so-called fratricide effect in that debris from each nuclear warhead is supposed to disable those following behind (it apparently being assumed that hostile warheads would be spaced only a second or two apart). President Reagan approved CSB in May 1982, for 100 missiles spaced at 1,640ft (500m) intervals over a region almost 4 miles (6km +) across, but the validity of CSB was later doubted by several authorities. The first cold-launch pop-up test took place in January 1982, and the first MX flight test in January 1983.

The definitive plan is that 100 Peacekeeper ICBMs will be deployed, (starting in 1986 and completing in 1990) in former Minuteman silos near the FE Warren AFB in Wyoming. Better C³ systems will be installed and more sophisticated shock isolation devices fitted, but the silos will not be further hardened.

Below: Canister test for the Peacekeeper missile, 25 February 1982. Such tests are essential to success of the ''cold launch'' system.

Below: An MX test launch in May 1982, with the sabots beginning to fall away as the missile clears the tube.

Right: Released from an F-15, this GBU-16B/B laser-guided bomb shows the layout of the weapon before the fins deploy.

Below: Underwing fit of two GBU-12D/Bs on an Alkan carrier.

Pershing, MGM-31

Origin: Martin Orlando Division, USA.
Type: Battlefield missile.
Dimensions: Length 34·5ft (10·51m); body diameter 40in (1·01m); fin span about 80in (2·02m).
Launch weight: About 10,150lb (4,600kg).
Propulsion: Two Thiokol solid motors in tandem, first stage XM105, second stage XM106.
Guidance: Army-developed inertial made by Eclipse-Pioneer (Bendix).
Range: 100 to 460 miles (160-740km).
Flight speed: Mach 8 at burnout.
Warhead: Nuclear, usually W-50 of approximately 400kT.

Originally deployed in 1962 on XM474 tracked vehicles as Pershing 1, the standard US Army long-range missile system has now been modified to 1a standard, carried on 4 vehicles based on the M656 5-ton truck. All are transportable in a C-130. In 1976 the 3 battalions with the US 7th Army in Europe were updated with the ARS (Azimuth Reference System), allowing them quickly to use unsurveyed launch sites, and the SLA (Sequential Launch Adapter) allowing one launch control centre easily to fire three missiles. To replenish inventory losses caused by practice firings, 66 additional Pershing 1a missiles were manufactured in 1978-80.

Deployment of Pershing 1a in mid-1983 totalled 108 launchers with US Army Europe and 72 with West German forces (these latter being operated by the Luftwaffe, not the Army). The US has started to replace its Pershing 1as with Pershing IIs on a one-for-one basis, but the intentions of the West German government are not yet known.

Pershing II has been studied since 1969 and has been in full development since 1974. It mates the existing vehicle with Goodyear Radag (Radar area-correlation guidance) in the new nose of the missile. As the forebody plunges down towards its target the small active radar scans the ground at 120rpm and correlates the returns with stored target imagery. The terminal guidance corrects the trajectory by means of new delta control surfaces, giving c.e.p. expected to be within 120ft (36m). As a result a lighter and less-destructive warhead (reported to be based on the B61 bomb of some 15kT) can be used, which extends maximum range. The Pershing II is fitted with an "earth-penetrator" device which enables the nuclear warhead to "burrow" deep underground before exploding. This is clearly intended for use against buried facilities such as HQs and communications centres.

Development of Pershing II was envisaged as being relatively simple and cheap, but it has, in the event, proved both complicated and expensive. One problem has been with the rocket motors, which are entirely new to obtain the greatly increased range. A further complication was the sudden elevation of the Pershing II programme into a major international issue, with the fielding of the missiles becoming a test of US determination. The problems were further compounded by repeated failures in the test programme, but the final test was a success and full production has gone ahead. First fielding took place in December 1984 and all 108 are due to be deployed by December 1988.

The reason for the furore over Pershing II stems from its quite exceptional accuracy. The "hard-target kill potential" of a nuclear warhead is derived from the formula: $(Raw Yield)^{2/3} \div (c.e.p.)^2$. This means that the effect can be increased by two methods. In the first, the raw yield is increased, but this not only leads to a larger warhead, and thus a larger missile, but also the rate of increase in effect decreases as the raw yield is increased, ie, there is a law of diminishing returns. The other method of achieving a greater effect is to increase the ac-curacy (ie, decrease the c.e.p.), and as the effect increases by the square of the c.e.p., this is far more efficacious. Hence, the c.e.p. of 120ft (36m) has led to a warhead of much less raw yield but very much greater effect than that fitted to the Pershing 1a. This seems to place a number of hard tagets in the western USSR in danger.

Below: The Pershing II uses the same two-stage powerplant as the Pershing I, but has a smaller and more accurate warhead.

Poseidon C-3

Origin: Lockheed Missiles and Space Co., USA.
Type: SLBM.
Dimensions: Length 34ft (10·36m); diameter 74in (188cm).
Launch weight: Approx 65,000lb (29,500kg).
Propulsion: First stage, Thiokol solid-fuel motor with gas-pressurized gimballed nozzle; second stage, Hercules motor with similar type nozzle.
Guidance: Inertial.
Range: See *Warhead*.
Warhead: MIRV system carrying maximum of 14 MIRVs for 2,485 miles (4,000km), or 10 MIRVs for the maximum range of 3,230 miles (5,198km). Each warhead of 50kT yield.

The result of lengthy studies into the benefits of later technology, Poseidon C-3 SLBMs were first installed in Franklin and Lafayette class SSBNs, starting with USS *James Madison* (SSBN-627). This boat carried out the first Poseidon deployment on 31 March 1971. Compared with the Polaris A-3 (now only serving on the four British SSBNs), Poseidon has at least equal range, carries double they payload, and has twice the accuracy (ie, half the circular area probable/CEP) as well as much improved MIRV and penetration aid (penaid) capability. A modification programme, started in 1973 to rectify deficiencies which showed up after the 1970 IOC, was completed in 1978. More than 40 missiles, which were withdrawn from submarines after operational patrols, have been fired with excellent results.

Poseidon C-3 was installed on 31 Franklin and Lafayette SSBNs, and 12 of the latter have since been retrofitted with Trident missiles. The remaining 19 Poseidon boats will remain in service well into the 1990s, and there are no plans to convert any more to take Trident, nor are there likely to be any more than routine updates to the missiles themselves.

At maximum range ten Mark 3 MIRVs (each of 50kT yield) can be flown, together with numerous penaids. At such ranges CEP is of the order of ½nm (0·8km). At shorter ranges more MIRVs are carried.

Compared with over 1,000 Soviet SLBMs, the US fields 640 including 496 Poseidon C-3/C-4.

Below: A Poseidon C-3 erupts from the water, its first-stage motor igniting for the boost phase of the SLBM's flight.

Phoenix, AIM-54

Origin: Hughes Aircraft, USA.
Type: Long-range AAM.
Dimensions: Length 157·8in (4·01m); body diameter 15in (380mm); span 36·4in (925mm).
Launch weight: 985lb (447kg).
Propulsion: Aerojet (ATSC) Mk 60 or Rocketdyne Flexadyne Mk 47 long-burn solid motors.
Performance: Speed Mach 5-plus; range over 124 miles (200km).
Warhead: Continuous-rod (132lb, 60kg) with proximity and impact fuzes.

By far the most sophisticated and costly AAM in the world this missile provides air defence over an area exceeding 12,000 square miles (31,000km²) from near sea level to the limits of altitude attained by aircraft or tactical missiles. But it can be fired only from the F-14 Tomcat and costs nearly half a million dollars.

Following the classic aerodynamics of the Falcon family, Phoenix was originally AAM-N-11 and Hughes aircraft began development in 1960 to replace the AIM-47A and Eagle as partner to the AWG-9 for the F-111B. This advanced fire-control system was the most capable ever attempted, and includes a very advanced radar (derived from the ASG-18 carried in the YF-12A) of high-power PD type with the largest circular aerial (of planar type) ever carried by a fighter. It has look-down capability out to ranges exceeding 150 miles (241km), and is backed up by an IR tracker to assist positive target identification and discrimination.

AWG-9 has TWS capability, and, had it been fitted, an F-111B with the maximum load of six Phoenix missiles would have been able to engage and attack six aircraft at maximum range simultaneously, weather and conditions and target aspect being of little consequence; indeed the basic interception mode assumed is head-on, which is one of the most difficult at extreme range.

Propulsion is by a long-burning Rocketdyne (Flexadyne) Mk 47 or Aerojet Mk60 motor, giving a speed to burnout of Mach 3·8. Combined with low induced drag and the power of the large hydraulically driven tail controls this gives sustained manoeuvrability over a range not even approached by any other AAM, despite the large load of electrical battery, electrical conversion unit, autopilot, electronics unit, transmitter/receiver and planar-array seeker head (all part of the DSQ-26 on-board guidance) as well as the 132lb (60kg) annular blast fragmentation warhead with Downey Mk 334 proximity fuze, Bendix IR fuze and DA fuze.

Hughes began flight test at PMIC in 1965, using a DA-3B Skywarrior, achieving an interception in September 1966. In March 1969 an F-111B successfully engaged two drones, and subsequently Phoenix broke virtually all AAM records including four kills in one pass (out of a six-on-six test, there being one no-test and one miss), a kill on a BQM-34A simulating a cruise missile at 50ft (15m), and a kill on a BQM-34E flying at Mach 1·5 tracked from 153 miles (246km), the Phoenix launched at 127 miles (204km) and impacting 83·5 miles (134km) from the launch point. The first AWG-9 system for the F-14A Tomcat, which replaced the F-111B, was delivered in February 1970. Production of Phoenix AIM-54A at Tucson began in 1973, since when output averaged about 40 per month. By the third quarter of 1978 output had passed 2,500; it then slowed sharply and production ended in 1980.

Since late 1977 production missiles were of the AIM-54B type with sheet-metal wings and fins instead of honeycomb structure, non-liquid hydraulic and thermal-conditioning systems, and simplified engineering. In 1977 Hughes began a major effort to produce an updated Phoenix to meet the needs of the 1990s. This missile, AIM-54C, has totally new all-digital electronics, more reliable and flexible in use than the analog unit, with a solid-state radar replacing the previous klystron tube model. Accuracy is improved by a new strapdown inertial reference unit from Nortronics, and ECCM capability is greatly enhanced. Another improvement is the new proximity fuze developed by the Naval Weapons Center. Following the test and delivery of 30 pilot-production rounds in the second half of 1981, full production started in 1982 and annual deliveries were: 1983-108, 1984-265. 1985-265. A total of 635 are scheduled to be delivered in 1987-88.

Below: The Phoenix is in its element as the high-altitude long-range interception missile carried by the F-14A Tomcat.

Below: The most powerful air-defense combination in the world is represented by the F-14 swing-wing fighter, its AWG-9 radar system and six AIM-54A Phoenix AAMs.

Rapier and Tracked Rapier

Origin: British Aerospace Dynamics, UK.
Type: Self-propelled air defence missile system.
Dimensions: Length 7·35ft (2·24m); diameter 5·23in (0·133m); wingspan 15in (0·381m).
Launch weight: 93·9lb (42·6kg).
Propulsion: 2-stage solid-propellant rocket motor.
Guidance: Command to line-of-sight.
Range: Slant range 4 miles (6·5km); altitude limits 164 to 9,849ft (50 to 3,000m).
Flight speed: Mach 2 + .
Warhead: Semi-armor-piercing with crush fuze and HE.

The original Rapier model consisted of a wheeled fire-unit towed behind a 1-tonne vehicle, and mounting four missiles. The fire unit included a surveillance radar, an IFF coder/decoder and a microwave command transmitter. Intended for use against fast, low-flying targets, Rapier is designed actually to impact the target, and has repeatedly shown its ability to do so, both in peacetime tests and in combat. The requirement to operate in bad weather and at night led to the development of the DV181 (Blind-fire) radar.

The next and inevitable development was the Tracked Rapier, originally developed by BAe with the former Shah's Iran in mind. It uses the M548 cargo-carrying derivative of the US Army's MII3 APC. The crew of three travel in an aluminium-armored cab, and behind this is an air-conditioner and a power unit protected from missile efflux by a blast shield. The firing-unit is mounted on a turntable on the rear of the vehicle, with eight missiles at instant readiness.

Well over 14,000 missiles have been produced so far in what promises to be a very long production run. Towed Rapier is already in service with, or on order for, the services of 12 nations, including the USAF. Tracked Rapier has so far only been ordered by the British Army.

The latest development is Rapier Laserfire, a palletized installation which can fit on any flat-platform 3- or 4-tonne vehicle, and has an automatic laser tracker.

Below: The Rapier system offers exceptional single-shot kill probability with a direct hit. All-weather capability is provided by Blind-fire radar, each directing four launchers.

Redeye, FIM-43A

Origin: General Dynamics, USA.
Type: Shoulder-fired infantry surface-to-air missile.
Dimensions: Length 48in (122cm); body diameter 2·75in (7cm); span 5·5in (14cm).
Launch weight: 18lb (8·2kg); whole package weighs 29lb (13kg).
Propulsion: Atlantic Research dual-thrust solid.
Guidance: Initial optical aiming, IR homing.
Range: Up to about 2 miles (3·3km).
Flight speed: Low supersonic.
Warhead: Smooth-case frag.

The first infantry SAM in the world, Redeye entered US Army service in 1964 and probably 100,000 had been delivered to the Army and Marine Corps by 1970. It has severe limitations. It has to wait until aircraft have attacked and then fire at their departing tailplanes; there is no IFF. Flight speed is only just enough to catch modern attack aircraft and the guidance is vulnerable to IRCM. Engagement depends on correct identification by the operator of the nature of the target aircraft. He has to wait until the aircraft has passed, aim on a pursuit course, listen for the IR lock-on buzzer, fire the missile and then select a fresh tube. The seeker cell needs a cooling unit, three of which are packed with each missile tube.

Below: Among the Redeye's failings is its restriction to stern chase of a target aircraft that has already attacked.

Below: Morale rather than AA capability was boosted by the Redeye man-portable SAM system with all its limitations.

Roland

Origin: International (Americanized and manufactured by Hughes Aircraft Co., with participation by Boeing Aerospace and others).
Type: Self-propelled air defence missile system.
Crew: 3.
Dimensions: Length 7·87ft (2·4m); diameter 6·3in (0·16m); wingspan 1·64in (0·5m).
Launch weight: 146·6lb (66·5kg).
Propulsion: Two-stage solid-propellant rocket motor.
Guidance: Optical or radar.
Range: Slant range 3·9 miles (6·3km); altitude limits 66 to 16,400ft (20 to 5,000m).
Flight speed: Mach 1·6.
Warhead: HE with impact and proximity fuzes.

In the mid-1960s France and Germany started development of an air defence system, with two modes: clear-weather (Roland 1) and all-weather (Roland 2). The system entered service in 1980.

The US Army selected Roland in 1975 to be mounted on the M109 chassis, with large orders promised, but progressive cutbacks have ended with 27 firing units.

The missile can be used in both clear and all-weather conditions, and has always been intended for use in a gun/missile mix. The Argentine Army deployed a Roland unit to port Stanley in the South Atlantic War, and it fired 8 out of its 10 missiles, but only one possible success (a Sea Harrier) resulted.

Below: The US Roland system is based on a chassis containing eight reload rounds, plus a turret with acquisition and tracking radars, an optical sight and two ready-use SAMs.

Below: A US Roland leaves one of the two launch tubes on the M109 launch vehicle, discarding its sabots in the process.

Seasparrow RIM-7H

Origin: Raytheon Co., USA.
Dimensions: Length 12ft (3·6m); diameter 7·8in (200mm); span 3·4in (1·02m).
Launch weight: 441lb (200kg).
Propulsion: Solid.
Range: 15 miles (25km).
Warhead: HE.

NATO Seasparrow (RIM-7H) is a development of the US Navy's Seasparrow (RIM-7E) which is based on the air-launched Sparrow. RIM-7E still forms the basis of the USN's Basic Point Defense System (BPDMS), serving aboard many DDGs, FFGs and CGNs, though it is being superseded by the RIM-7H version. This is an improved PDMS in CVs, Spruance and other class DDs, some LCCs, LPHs and LHAs, and large replenishment vessels. It is also the subject of a massive international co-production programme involving several NATO nations, and serves aboard frigates of Belgium, Canada, Denmark, Italy, Netherlands, Norway, Spain and West Germany. Some NATO nations, including Turkey, have land-based Seasparrow sites; and Japan has also purchased the system.

NATO Seasparrow entered full-scale production in 1973 and there are now over 100 systems installed. The RIM-7H version was also used in Italy's Albatross system.

Basically, RIM-7H is a high-performance version of the Sparrow AAM with folding fins. It is fired from a lightweight 8-round box launcher, is reloaded manually, has automatic tracking, uses continuous wave (CW) semi-active homing guidance and the Mk91 fire control radar system.

RIM-7M entered USN and other NATO service in 1983. This is a vertical launch system, whose missile has a Jet Vane Control unit added, which controls the initial tip-over, orientation and course control, after which the normal guidance control takes over.

Below: Mk 29 launch of a RIM-7 from the Mk 29 launcher on the starboard quarter of the carrier US *Kitty Hawk*.

Below: Launch of a RIM-7 Seasparrow from one of the USS *John F. Kennedy's* three point-defense Mk 29 octuple launchers.

Shillelagh, MGM-51A

Origin: Ford Aeronutronic Division, USA.
Type: Gun-launched guided missile.
Dimensions: Length 45in (114cm); body diameter 5·95in (15·2cm); fin span 11·4in (29cm).
Launch weight: 60lb (27kg).
Propulsion: Amoco single-stage solid with hot-jet jetavators.
Guidance: Optical tracking and IR command link.
Range: Up to about three miles (4,500m).
Flight speed: High subsonic.
Warhead: Octol shaped charge 15lb (6·8kg).

Very large numbers of these advanced anti-tank missiles were supplied to the US Army in 1966-70, for firing from the 152mm dual purpose gun fitted to the General Sheridan AFV and M60A2 main battle tank. The gunner, who can fire a missile or a conventional round depending on the target, has only to keep the target centred in optical cross-hairs for the IR guidance to keep the missile centred on the line of sight. Firings were carried out from UH-1 helicopters, but an air-launched version is not in use. In 1976-78 trials were in hand of a proposed new guidance system using laser designators (either at the launch point or elsewhere) with a view to modifying the existing missiles, but no production followed.

Below: A Shillelagh missile leaves the gun of an M551. The system suffers considerable tactical and technical problems.

Below: One of the Shillelagh's main tactical limitations is a minimum effective range of some 1,300 yards (1,188m).

Shrike, AGM-45

Origin: Naval Weapons Center (NWC), with production by TI, USA.
Type: Passive homing anti-radiation missile.
Dimensions: Length 120in (3·05m); body diameter 8in (203mm); span 36in (914mm).
Launch weight: (Approximately, depending on sub-type) 390lb (177kg).
Propulsion: Rockwell (Rocketdyne) Mk 39 or Aerojet (ATSC) Mk 53 (polybutadiene) or improved Mk 78 (polyurethane, dual-thrust) solid motor.
Range: 18 to 25 miles (29 to 40km).
Flight speed: Mach 2.
Warhead: Blast/frag, 145lb (66kg), proximity fuze.

Based in part on the Sparrow AAM, this was the first anti-radar missile (ARM) in the US since World War II. Originally called ARM and designated ASM-N-10, it was begun as a project at NOTS (later NWC) in 1961, and in 1962 became AGM-45A. Production by a consortium headed by Texas Instruments (TI) and Sperry Rand/Univac began in 1963 and Shrike was in use in SE Asia three years later with Wild Weasel F-105Gs and EA-6As. Early experience was disappointing and there have since been numerous models, identified by suffix numbers, to rectify faults or tailor the passive homing head to a new frequency band identified in the potential hostile inventory. Carried by the US Navy/Marines A-4, A-6, A-7 and F-4, the Air Force F-4, F-105 and EF-111 and the Israeli F-4 and Kfir, Shrike is switched on while flying towards the target and fired as soon as the TI radiation seeker has locked-on. After motor cutoff Shrike flies a ballistic path until control-system activation. The seeker has a monopulse crystal video receiver and continually updates the guidance by determining the direction of arrival of the hostile radiation, homing the missile into the enemy radar with its cruciform centre-body wings driven in "bang/bang" fashion by a hot-gas system. There were at least 18 sub-types in the AGM-45-1 to -10 families, with over 13 different tailored seeker heads, of which the USAF bought 12,863 by 1978 and the Navy a further 6,200. In the Yom Kippur war Israel used Shrike tuned to 2965/2900 MHz and 3025/3050 MHz to defeat SA-2 and SA-3 but was helpless against SA-6. In 1978-81 additional procurement centred on the -9 and -10 for the USAF to be carried by F-4G and EF-111A platforms, together with modification kits to equip existing rounds to home on to later SAM and other radars.

Below and bottom: The principal limitations of the Shrike are individual seekers tuned to specific emitters, and a ballistic flight path in the event of emitter shutdown.

Sidewinder, AIM-9

Origin: Original design by US Naval Weapons Center; commercial production by Philco (now Ford Aerospace) and later GE, today shared by Ford Aerospace and Raytheon, USA.
Type: Close-/medium-range AAM.
Dimensions: Types vary between 111·4in and 120·9in (2,830 and 3,070mm long).
Launch weight: Between 155 and 195lb (70·4 and 88·5kg) for various types.
Propulsion: Solid motor (various, by Rockwell, Aerojet or Thiokol, with Aerojet Mk 17 qualified on 9B/E/J/N/P and Thiokol Mk 36 or reduced-smoke TX-683 qualified on 9L/M).
Performance: Range between 2 and 11 miles (3·2 and 17·7km); mission time, between 20 and 60 seconds.
Warhead: (B/E/J/N/P) 10lb (4·5kg) blast/fragmentation with passive IR proximity fuze (from 1982 being refitted with Hughes DSU-21/B active laser fuze), (D/G/H) 22·4lb (10·2kg) continuous rod with IR or HF proximity fuze, (L/M) 25lb (11·4kg) advanced annular blast/fragmentation with active laser IR proximity fuze.

One of the most influential missiles in history, this slim AAM was almost un-American in development for it was created out of nothing by a very small team at NOTS China Lake, operating on the proverbial shoe-string budget. Led by Doctor McLean, this team was the first in the world to attack the problem of passive IR homing guidance, in 1949, and the often intractable difficulties were compounded by the choice of an airframe of only 5in (127mm) diameter, which in the days of vacuum-tube electronics was a major challenge. In 1951 Philco was awarded a contract for a homing head based on the NOTS research and today the guidance team at Newport Beach, now called Ford Aerospace and Communications, is still in production with homing heads for later Sidewinders. The first XAAM-N-7 guided round was successfully fired on 11 September 1953. The first production missiles, called N-7 by the Navy, GAR-8 by the USAF and SW-1 by the development team, reached IOC in May 1956.

These early Sidewinders were made of sections of aluminium tube, with the seeker head and control fins at the front and four fixed tail fins containing patented rollerons at the back. The rolleron is similar to an air-driven gyro wheel, and one is mounted in the tip of each fin so that it is spun at high speed by the slipstream. The original solid motor was made by Hunter-Douglas, Hercules and Norris-Thermador, to Naval Propellant Plant design, and it accelerated the missile to Mach 2·5 in 2·2 sec.

Sidewinder Guidance Sections

	AIM-9B: 80,900 produced by Philco and GE and c15,000 by European consortium; 10,000+ updated by Ford.
	AIM-9C/D: 9C SARH model by Motorola (1,000+), 9D with better IR/speed/manoeuvre, 950+ by Ford for US Navy.
	AIM-9E: 9B rebuilt with new cooled wide-angle seeker, about 5,000 for USAF by Ford (Aeronutronic).
	AIM-9G/H: 9G improved 9D with off-boresight lock-on (2,120 Raytheon, USN); 9H solid-state (3,000 Ford AF).
	AIM-9L/M: 9L 3rd generation all-aspect (Ford and Raytheon, also Europe); 9M improved ECCM/motor (Raytheon).
	AIM-9J/N: J rebuilt B/E with new front end (Ford c14,000 for AF); N (formerly J1) further improved (c,7,000).
	AIM-9P improved B/E/J or new production, new motor/fuze and better reliability, c13,000 by Ford for USAF.

The Sidewinder Family

Model	Guidance	Length	Control fin span	Launch wt	Mission time	Range	Production
AIM-9B	Uncooled PbS.25° look. 70 Hz reticle. 11°/sec tracking	111.4in (2830mm)	22.0in (559mm)	155lb (70.4kg)	20 sec	2 miles (3.2 km)	80,900
9B FGW.2	CO_2 cooling, solar dead zone reduced to 5°	114.5in (2908mm)	22.0in (559mm)	167lb (75.8kg)	20 sec	2.3 miles (3.7 km)	15,000
AIM-9C	Motorola SARH	113.0in (2870mm)	24.8in (630mm)	185lb (84.0kg)	60 sec	11 miles (17.7 km)	1,000
AIM-9D	N_2 cooled PbS, 40° look, 125 Hz reticle, 12°/sec tracking	113.0in (2870mm)	24.8in (630mm)	195lb (88.5kg)	60 sec	11 miles (17.7 km)	1,000
AIM-9E	Peltier-cooled PbS, 40° look, 100 Hz reticle, 16.5°/sec tracking	118.1in (3000mm)	22.0in (559mm)	164lb (74.5kg)	20 sec	2.6 miles (4.2 km)	5,000 (ex-9B)
AIM-9G	As -9D plus SEAM	113.0in (2870mm)	24.8in (630mm)	191lb (86.6kg)	60 sec	11 miles (17.7 km)	2,120
AIM-9H	As -9G plus solid-state, 20°/sec tracking	113.0in (2870mm)	24.8in (630mm)	186lb (84.5kg)	60 sec	11 miles (17.7 km)	7,720
AIM-9J	As -9E plus part-solid-state	120.9in (3070mm)	22.0in (559mm)	172lb (78.0kg)	40 sec	9 miles (14.5 km)	10,000 (ex-9B)
AIM-9L	Argon-cooled InSb. fixed reticle, tilted mirror system	112.2in (2850mm)	24.8in (630mm)	188lb (85.3kg)	60 sec	11 miles (17.7 km)	11,700+
AIM-9M	As -9L, better motor and ECCM	112.2in (2850mm)	24.8in (630mm)	190lb (86.0kg)	60 sec	11 miles (17.7 km)	3,500+
AIM-9N	As -9E plus part-solid-state	120.9in (3070mm)	22.0in (559mm)	172lb (78.0kg)	40 sec	9 miles (14.5 km)	7,000
AIM-9P	As -9N plus reliability improvements	120.9in (3070mm)	22.0in (559mm)	172lb (78.0kg)	60 sec	11 miles (17.7 km)	13,000

The beauty of this missile was its simplicity, which meant low cost, easy compatibility with many aircraft and, in theory, high reliability in harsh environments. It was said to have "less than 24 moving parts" and "fewer electronic components than the average radio". At the same time, though the guidance method meant that Sidewinder could be carried by any fighter, with or without radar, it was erratic in use and restricted to close stern engagements at high altitude in good visibility. The uncooled PbS seeker gave an SSKP of about 70 per cent in ideal conditions, but extremely poor results in bad visibility, cloud or rain, or at low levels, and showed a tendency to lock-on to the Sun, or bright sky, or reflections from lakes or rivers.

The pilot energised his missile homing head and listened for its signals in his headset. It would give a growl when it acquired a target, and if it was nicely positioned astern of a hot jetpipe the growl would become a fierce strident singing that would rise in intensity until the pilot let the missile go. There were plenty of QF-80, Firebee and other targets that had early Sidewinders up their jetpipe in the 1950s, but unfortunately real-life engagements tended to have the wrong target, or the wrong aspect, or the wrong IR-emitting background. In October 1958, however, large numbers of Sidewinders were fired by Nationalist Chinese F-86s against Chinese MiG-17s and 14 of the latter were claimed in one day. This was the first wartime use of AAMs.

The staggering total of nearly 81,000 of the original missile were built in three almost identical versions which in the new 1962 scheme were designated AIM-9, 9A and 9B. Nearly all were of the 9B form, roughly half by Raytheon. A further 15,000 were delivered by a European consortium headed by BGT, which

Below: Superb air-to-air shot of an F-16A Fighting Falcon sporting a pair of 370 US gal drop tanks and two AIM-120 Amraam medium-range air-to-air missiles under the wings, and a pair of Sidewinder short-range air-to-air missiles on the wingtip rails. These last are of the AIM-9J/N or AIM-9P series, based on the AIM-9B and AIM-9E but with much enhanced seekers and control systems for greater capacity.

Below: Weighing in at 190lb (86kg) AIM-9L/M is still a fair overhead load for three men during the arming of an F-15.

in the late 1960s gave each European missile a new seeker head of BGT design known as FGW Mod 2. This has a nose dome of silicon instead of glass, a cooled seeker and semi-conductor electronics, and transformed the missile's reliability and ability to lock-on in adverse conditions.

By 1962 SW-1C was in use in two versions, AIM-9C by Motorola and -9D by Ford. This series introduced the Rocketdyne Mk 36 solid motor giving much greater range, a new airframe with tapered nose, long-chord controls and more swept leading edges on the tail fins, and completely new guidance. Motorola produced the 9C for the F-8 Crusader, giving it SARH guidance matched to the Magnavox APQ-94 radar, but for various reasons this odd man out was unreliable in performance and was withdrawn. In contrast, 9D was so successful it formed the basis of many subsequent versions, as well as MIM-72C Chaparral. The new guidance section introduced a dome of magnesium fluoride, a nitrogen-cooled seeker, smaller field of view, and increased reticle speed and tracking speed. The control section introduced larger fins, which were detachable, and high-power actuators fed by a longer-burning gas generator. The old 10lb (4·54kg) warhead with passive-IR fuze was replaced by a 22·4lb (10·2kg) annular blast fragmentation head of the continuous-rod type, fired by either an IR or HF proximity fuze.

AIM-9E was fitted with a greatly improved Ford seeker head with Peltier (thermoelectric) cooling, further-increased tracking speed and new electronics and wiring harnesses, giving increased engagement boundaries especially at low level. AIM-9G has so-called SEAM. (Sidewinder Expanded Acquisition Mode), an improved 9D seeker head, but was overtaken by 9H. The latter introduced solid-state electronics, even faster tracking speed, and double-delta controls with increased actuator power, giving greater manoeuvrability than any previous Sidewinder as well as limited all-weather capability. AIM-9J is a rebuilt 9B or 9E with part-solid-state electronics, detachable double-delta controls with greater power, and long-burning gas generator. Range is sacrificed for high acceleration to catch fast targets.

There are J-1 and J-3 improved or "all-new" variants. A major advance came with Sidewinder 9L, with which NWC (as NOTS now is) at last responded to the prolonged demands of customers and the proven accomplishments of BGT. The latter's outstanding seeker head developed for Viper was first fitted to AIM-9L to give Alasca (All-Aspect Capability), a great missile that was merely used by Germany as a possible fall-back in case 9L failed to mature. AIM-9L itself, in full production from 1977, has long-span pointed delta fins, a totally new guidance system and an annular blast fragmentation of preformed rods, triggered by a new proximity fuze in which a ring of eight GaAs laser diodes emit and a ring of silicon photodiodes receive.

About 16,000 of the 9L series were made by 1983, and at least a further 9,000 are likely to be made by a new BGT-led European consortium which this time includes BAe Dynamics and companies in Norway and Italy. Pilot production deliveries began in 1981, and BAe received its first production contract (for £40 million) in February 1982. No European missiles had reached British squadrons in April 1982 and 100 AIM-9L were supplied for use by Harriers and Sea Harriers in the South Atlantic from US stocks. The lethal combination of aircraft and AIM-9s gained 25 known victories.

AIM-9M is a revised L. 9N is the new designation of J-1 (all are 9B or 9E rebuilds). 9P are rebuilds of 9B/E/J. and additional 9P missiles are being made from new.

Sparrow, AIM-7

Origin: Raytheon Co., and General Dynamics, USA, as second source production.
Type: Medium-/long-range AAM.
Dimensions: Length (E, F) 144in (3660mm), (M) 145in (3680mm); body diameter 8in (203mm); span 40in (1020mm).
Launch weight: (E) 452lb (205kg), (F, M) 503lb (228kg).
Propulsion: (7E) Aerojet or Rockwell Mk 52 Mod 2 PB/AP solid motor, (7F, M) Hercules or Aerojet Mk 58 high-impulse solid motor.
Performance: Speed (both) about Mach 4; range (E) 28 miles (44km). (F, M) 62 miles (100km).
Warhead: (E) 66lb (30kg) continuous-rod warhead, (F, M) 88lb (40kg) Mk 71 advanced continuous-rod warhead, in each case with proximity and DA fuzes.

Considerably larger than other contemporary American AAMs, this missile not only progressed through three fundamentally different families, each with a different prime contractor, but late in life mushroomed into totally new versions for quite new missions as an ASM (Shrike) and a SAM (two types of Sea Sparrow).

Sperry Gyroscope began the programme as Project Hot Shot in 1946, under the US Navy BuAer contract. By 1951 Sperry had a contract for full engineering development of XAAM-N-2 Sparrow I, and the suffix I was added because by that time there was already a Sparrow II. The first representative guided flight tests took place in 1953. This missile was a beam rider, with flush dipole aerials around the body which picked up the signals from the fighter radar beam (assumed to be locked-on to the target) and drove the cruciform delta wings to keep the missile aligned in the centre of the beam. At the tail were four fixed fins, indexed in line with the wings. Propulsion was by an Aerojet solid motor, and missile assembly took place at the Sperry-Farragut Division which operated a Naval Industrial Reserve plant at Bristol, Tennessee.

IOC was reached in July 1956, and Sparrow I was soon serving in the Atlantic and Pacific Fleets, and with the Marine Corps.

In 1955 Douglas obtained limited funding for Sparrow II, as main armament for the proposed F5D-1 Skylancer. Amazingly, however, the company did not switch to SARH guidance but to fully active radar, and this was tough in a missile of 8in (203mm) diameter, a figure common to all Sparrows. In mid-1956 the Navy decided to terminate Sparrow II, but it was snapped up by the Royal Canadian Air Force as armament for the Arrow supersonic interceptor. After severe difficulties Premier Diefenbaker cancelled Sparrow II on 23 September 1958, and the Arrow itself the following February.

Three years previously Raytheon had begun to work on Sparrow III, taking over the Bristol plant in 1956. Sparrow III uses almost the same airframe as Sparrow II but with SARH guidance. By the mid-1950s Raytheon had become one of the most capable missile companies, possibly because its background was electronics rather than airframes. It built up a missile engineering centre at Bedford, Massachusetts, with a test base at Oxnard (not far from Point Mugu), California; production of Sparrows was finally shared between Bristol and a plant at South Lowell, near Bedford.

Most of the airframe is precision-cast light alloy. Early Sparrow III missiles had an Aerojet solid motor, not cast integral with the case, and introduced CW guidance. AIM-7C, as it became, reached IOC in 1958 with Demons of the Atlantic and Pacific fleets. AIM-7D introduced the Thiokol (previously Reaction Motors) prepacked liquid motor, and was also adopted by the Air Force in 1960 as AIM-101 to arm the F-110 (later F-4C) Phantom. All fighter Phantoms can

carry four Sparrows recessed into the underside of the fuselage, with target illumination by the APQ-72, APQ-100, APQ-109, APQ-120, or APG-59 (part of AWG-10 or -11) radar. In the Italian F-104S Starfighter the radar is the Rockwell R-21G/H, and in the F-14 Tomcat the powerful Hughes AWG-9. The AIM-7D was also the basis for PDMS Sea Sparrow.

AIM-7E, the next version (also used in the NATO Sea Sparrow system), uses the Rocketdyne free-standing solid motor with Flexadyne propellant (Mk 38), which gives a slightly increased burnout speed of Mach 3·7. The warhead is of the continuous-rod type, the explosive charge being wrapped in a tight drum made from a continuous rod of stainless steel which shatters into about 2,600 lethal fragments. DA and proximity fuzes are fitted. Many thousands of 7E missiles were used in Vietnam by F-4s, but, owing to the political constraints imposed on the American fighters, were seldom able to be fired. Accordingly AIM-7E2 was developed with shorter minimum range, increased power of maneuvre and plug-in aerodynamic surfaces requiring no tools. The AIM-7C, D and E accounted for over 34,000 missiles.

Introduced in 1977, AIM-7F has all-solid-state guidance, making room for a more powerful motor, the Hercules Mk 58, giving further-enhanced flight speed and range, as well as a larger (88lb, 40kg) warhead. Claimed to lock-on reasonably well against clutter up to 10 db, -7F is compatible with CW PD radars (and thus with the F-15 and F-18), and has a conical-scan seeker head. In 1977 GD Pomona was brought in as second source supplier and with Raytheon was expected to deliver about 19,000 missiles by 1985, split roughly between the Navy and Air Force, plus hoped-for exports.

In 1982 both contractors switched to AIM-7M, developed by Raytheon. This has an inverse-processed digital monopulse seeker generally similar to Sky Flash in giving greatly improved results in adverse conditions. GD's first contract was for 690, following 3,000 of the 7F type.

Below: Launch of an AIM-7 with APG-65 radar guidance from FSD Hornet during early armament trials.

The Sparrow Faimly

1950 designation	1962	Guidance	Length	Span	Launch wt	Range	Production
AAM-N-2 Sparrow I	AIM-7A	Radar beam riding	140in (3.56m)	39in (0.99m)	310lb (141kg)	5 miles (8 km)	c2,000
AAM-N-3 Sparrow II	AIM-7B	Active radar homing	144in (3.66m)	39in (0.99m)	420lb (191kg)	?	c100
AAM-N-6 Sparrow III	AIM-7C	SARH CW	144in (3.66m)	40in (1.02m)	380lb (172kg)	25 miles (40 km)	2,000
AAM-N-6A/AIM-101	AIM-7D	SARH CW	144in (3.66m)	40in (1.02m)	440lb (200kg)	25 miles (40 km)	7,500
AAM-N-6B	AIM-7E	SARH CW	144in (3.66m)	40in (1.02m)	452lb (205kg)	28 miles (44 km)	25,000
—	AIM-7F	SARH CW solid-state	144in (3.66m)	40in (1.02m)	503lb (228kg)	62 miles (100 km)	3,000
—	AIM-7M	SARH CW solid state	145in (3.68m)	40in (1.02m)	503lb (228kg)	62 miles (100 km)	1,800+

SRAM, AGM-69

Origin: Boeing Aerospace, USA.
Type: Fully maneuvrable self-guided wingless rocket.
Dimensions: Length (with tail fairing for external carriage) 190in (4·83m), (without fairing) 168in (4·27m); body diameter 17·5in (444·5mm); span (three fins at 120°) each tip is 15in (381mm) from axis of missile.
Launch weight: 2,230lb (1,012kg).
Propulsion: Originally Lockheed Propulsion Co two-pulse solid motor; Thiokol is in low-rate production with a long-life motor with numerous improvements.
Range: Very variable depending on launch height and selected profile — 35 to 105 miles (56 to 169km).
Flight speed: Mach 2·8 to 3·2.
Warhead: Nuclear W-69, 200kT, air burst and DA fuzes.

Throughout the 1950s nuclear warheads became even smaller, and by 1960 studies showed that a missile that could be carried by a fighter could deliver a large nuclear warhead from a range exceeding 100 miles (161km). In the event

the SRAM (Short-Range Attack Missile) has not been used by fighters, but by aircraft of SAC, primarily to neutralise potential hostile defenses such as radars, SAMs and other AA systems. The adjective "short-range" has taken on a new meaning, while the compact lightweight design of this high-performance weapon multiplies in dramatic fashion the number of targets that one bomber can engage. Boeing, the final prime contractor, began SRAM studies in December 1963, ahead of the drafting of SOR-212 in 1964 which resulted in the establishment of WS-104A. A keen competition followed in 1965, with selection in November 1965 of Boeing and Martin and final choice of Boeing (now Boeing Aerospace Co) on 31 October 1966. A dummy SRAM was dropped from a B-52 in December 1967, live flights began in 1969, and IOC was reached in early 1972. Production of 1,500 AGM-69A missiles was completed in July 1975, the missile then equipping 18 SAC bases operating the B-52G and H and FB-111A.

Originally there were to be different guidance systems, Sylvania supplying a radar-homing version and an IR-homer also being required. These were not procured, and AGM-69A has only inertial guidance by Singer-Kearfott, with a Delco on-board computer to command very varied flight profiles. Four basic trajetories are: semi-ballistic; terrain-following; pull-up from "under the radar" followed by inertial dive; and combined inertial and terrain-following. The small, almost perfectly streamlined missile is said to have a radar cross-section "about

Standard ARM (RGM/AGM-78)

Origin: General Dynamics, USA.
Type: Anti-radar missile (AGM, air-launched; RGM, ship-launched).
Dimensions: Length 15ft (4·57m); body diameter 13·5in (34·3cm); fin span 42·9in (109cm).
Launch weight: Basic 1,356lb (615kg), Mod 1 1,800lb (816kg).
Propulsion: Aerojet Mk 27 Mod 4 dual-thrust solid motor.
Guidance: Passive radar seeker by Maxson and GD/Pomona.
Range: 15 miles (25km).
Flight speed: Over Mach 2.
Warhead: Conventional, impact/prox fuze.

Announced in 1966, Standard ARM is a development of the Standard ship-to-air SAM. The first model used the TI seeker head of the Shrike ARM but improved guidance is now fitted. This missile has augmented, and is now replacing, Shrike in US Navy A-6 squadrons and USAF units flying the F-105, F-4 and possibly other aircraft such as the A-10; it has also been reported as carried by the Navy EA-6B Prowler EW aircraft and the E-2C Hawkeye AEW platform. Carrier aircraft can be fitted with TIAS (Target identification and Acquisition System) to help the missile strike home despite the enemy radar being intermittently or permanently switched off; in the USAF Standard ARM is linked with the Wild Weasel system and would probably be carried by the EF-4E (F-4G) and EF-111A. (See HARM.) RGM-66D is an interim US Navy ship-to-ship missile which can hit radar-emitting targets beyond the horizon. It is fitted to two patrol gunboats (in stern box launcher); RGM-66E is tailored to the Asroc launcher and is interim ARM on six DDGs and six FFGs.

Below: An AGM-78 Standard ARM under the wing of a "Wild Weasel" F-105G, an aircraft type now out of service.

Below: F-4G "Wild Weasel" fully equipped with radar-sensing avionics and AGM-45, AGM-65, AGM-78 and AGM-88 missiles.

Standard, RIM-66/67

Origin: General Dynamics, USA.
Type: Ship-to-air missile; also surface-to-surface, see text.
Dimensions: Length (MR) 15ft (4·57m), (ER) 27ft (8·23m); body diameter 13·8in (35cm); fin span (MR) 42in (107cm), (ER) 62in (157cm).
Launch weight: (MR) about 1,300lb (590kg), (ER) about 2,350lb (1,060kg).
Propulsion: (MR) dual-thrust solid, Aerojet/Hercules Mk 56 Mod O; (ER) boost, Atlantic Research Mk 30 Mod 2, sustainer, Naval propellant Plant Mk 12 Mod 1.
Guidance: Semi-active radar homing, varies with ship installation.
Range: (SM-1, MR) about 15 miles (24km), (SM-2, MR) about 30 miles (48·5km), (SM-1 ER) 35 miles (56km), (SM-2, ER) 60 miles (96km).
Flight speed: (MR) about Mach 2.5 (ER) over Mach 2·5.
Warhead: (SM-1) Usually Mk 90 (about 6,000 fragments, plus blast and incendiary) with Mk 45 proximity fuze.

RIM-66A (SM-1 MR) and RIM-67A (SM-2 ER) are Standard Missile 1 Medium Range and Extended Range, and were respectively developed to replace Tartar and Terrier as standard US Navy ship-to-air weapons, RGM-66D is a horizon-limited surface-to-surface version. Both are in US Navy use, and the same weapon was the basis of AGM-78 and RGM-66D Standard ARM described separately. RIM-66C, SM-2 (Standard Missile 2), is also being developed in MR and ER forms, the latter having a tandem boost motor as in the ER version of SM-1. SM-2 is a similar airframe but has totally different guidance and augmented propulsion, and forms part of the complex Aegis ship-defence system having capability against missiles and multiple threats. Guidance includes a new two-way link for mid-course command and terminal homing with higher ECM resistance. The Aegis system incorporates giant SPY-1A phased-array radars facing all round each ship, the first CG-47 *Ticonderoga* which, despite delays and massive cost-escalation, joined the fleet in 1983.

Below: The RIM-67B Standard-2 ER has an inertial reference unit to optimize the flight profile and so extend range.

as large as a bullet''. The B-52 can carry eight on a rotary launcher reminiscent of a revolver cylinder in the aft bomb bay (exceptionally, and at the expense of other loads, it can carry three such launchers internally), plus two tandem triplets on each former Hound Dog pylon, modified for SRAM compatibility, a total of 20 missiles. The FB-111A can carry up to six, four on swivelling wing pylons and two internally. The bombardier selects each missile in turn, checks the updating of the KT-76 inertial guidance and lets it drop. The motor accelerates it to about Mach 3, fast enough to fly and steer with body lift and three tail fins (there are no wings). Nearing the target the second propulsion stage is ignited.

About 1,300 missiles remain available to SAC's dwindling forces. AGM-69B, an improved missile with nuclear hardening throughout, the W-80 warhead, a completely new Thiokol HTPB-propellant motor and greatly increased computer memory, was almost ready for production for the B-1, which can carry 32; AGM-69B was cancelled in 1977 following discontinuance of the production programme for B-1. The remaining A-series missiles must, however, be fitted with the new Thiokol motor, because of ageing problems, and computer memory and nuclear-hardening improvements are also projected. There is no money for production of new missiles, despite attractions of large carrier aircraft such as the 747-200F which could carry 72 internally.

Below: A B-52H shows off its underwing carriage of 12 SRAMs on pylons originally schemed for the AGM-28 Hound Dog.

Stinger, FIM-92A

Origin: General Dynamics, USA.
Type: Portable air-defence missile system.
Dimensions: (Missile) length 60in (152cm); body diameter 2·75in (7cm); span 5·5in (14cm).
Launch weight: 24lb (10·9kg); whole package 35lb (15·8kg).
Propulsion: Atlantic Research dual-thrust solid.
Guidance: Passive IR homing (see text).
Range: In excess of 3·1 miles (5km).
Flight speed: About Mach 2.
Warhead: Smooth-case frag.

Designed in the mid-1960s as a much-needed replacement for Redeye, Stinger has had a long and troubled development but is at last in service. An improved IR seeker gives all-aspect guidance, the wavelength of less than 4·4 microns being matched to an exhaust plume rather than hot metal, and IFF is incorporated (so that the operator does not have to rely on correct visual identification of oncoming supersonic aircraft).

In FY 1981 the first 1,144 missiles for the inventory were delivered at $70·1m, and totals for 1982 and 1983 were respectively 2,544 at $193·4m and 2,256 at $214·6m. Total requirements for the US Army and Marine Corps are currently some 17,000 fire units and 31,484 missiles.

An improvement programme called Stinger-POST (Passive Optical Seeker Technique) is now in hand. This operates both the ultra-violet and infra-red spectra, the combination of the two frequency bands giving improved discrimination, longer detection range, and greater ECCM options. The Soviet counterparts are SA-7 and its replacement, SA-14.

Left: Though slow in development and early production, the Stinger offers US ground forces a more potent and versatile man-portable SAM system than the ineffective Redeye.

Below: Launch of the 24lb (11kg) FIM-92A Stinger missile, whose guidance is optimized for all-aspect engagement.

Subroc, UUM-44A

Origin: Goodyear Aerospace, USA.
Type: Submarine-to-Submarine rocket.
Dimensions: Length 20ft 5in (6·25m); body diameter (boost motor) 21in (53·3cm).
Launch weight: 4,086lb (1,853kg).
Propulsion: Thiokol TE-260G solid tandem boost motor with four jetavator nozzles.
Guidance: Kearfott SD-510 inertial system.
Range: Up to 35 miles (56km).
Flight speed: Supersonic.
Warhead: W-55 nuclear (estimated 1kT, radius about 4 miles (6·4km).

Standard ASW weapon of the US Navy attack submarines, Subroc is launched from a 21in torpedo tube in the conventional way. The missile arches up through the water and at a safe distance the rocket ignites, guiding the weapon towards its target both before and after breaking the ocean surface. Steering is accomplished by the jetavators during powered flight. At motor cutoff the warhead vehicle is separated and continues to its target guided by aerodynamic fins. Entry to the water is cushioned, after which the warhead sinks to the correct depth before detonating. Subroc has been operational since 1965. Attack submarines usually carry four to six missiles each. In 1979 Congress decided not to introduce a revised rocket motor and new digital guidance system, and instead Subroc will be replaced in the early 1990s by the new Anti-Submarine Warfare-Stand-Off weapon (ASW-SOW).

Below left: A startled seagull clears the area as a Subroc pierces the surface with its booster rocket already ignited.

Below: A technician prepares to pressure-test a UUM-44A in a water chamber as part of the weapon's certification process.

Titan II, LGM-25C

Origin: Martin Marietta Corporation, USA.
Type: ICBM deployed in hardened silo.
Dimensions: Length 102ft 8½in (31·30m); body diameter 120in (305cm).
Launch weight: 330,000lb (149,690kg).
Propulsion: First stage, Aerojet LR87 twin-chamber engine burning nitrogen tetroxide and Aerozine; second stage Aerojet LR91, similar but one smaller chamber (all chambers gimballed).
Guidance: Inertial, IBM/AC Spark Plug.
Range: 9,300 miles (15,000km).
Flight speed: 15,000mph (24,000km/h) at burnout.
Warhead: General Electric Mk 6 RV containing thermonuclear warhead (W-53, estimated 9MT) and penaids.

By far the biggest and oldest of America's surviving strategic missiles. Titan was begun in the mid-1950s as a later alternative to Atlas with the bold feature of a second stage that had to ignite in space. Titan II, operational since 1963, combined silo emplacement with hypergolic (self-igniting) propellants which reduced reaction time from hours to one minute. A total force of only 54 missiles was deployed, in three wings centred at Davis-Monthan, McConnell and Little Rock AFBs, but hypergolic-fuel explosions in 1978 and 1980 reduced this total to 52 missiles. In March 1978 work began on replacing the original guidance by the USGS (Universal Space Guidance System) used on the Titan III space launcher, chiefly to reduce maintenance cost from about $173 million to $101 million per year, and this was completed in 1981. Since 1980 there has been much rethinking on when to start dismantling this force, which is the only one in the West to offer anything like the range and throw-weight of the far more numerous Soviet ICBMs. Following an accident and increasing criticism of this ageing force it has been gradually phased out, with the last missiles being deactivated in FY87.

Below: The Titan II offers warhead power and range unmatched by later weapons, but is now obsolete and being phased out.

Below: Test launch of a Titan II from a silo at Vandenberg AFB. The single Mk 6 re-entry vehicle has a CEP of some 1,425 yards (1,303m), and has a yield estimated at 9 megatons.

Tomahawk, AGM-109

Origin: General Dynamics, USA.
Type: Air-to-surface missile.
Dimensions: Length (H,K) 234in (5·94m), (I) 192in (4·88m); body diameter 21in (533mm); span (wings extended) 103in (2·616m).
Launch weight: (H) 2,900lb (1,315kg), (I) 2,225lb (1,009kg), (K) 2,630lb (1,193kg).
Propulsion: Modified Teledyne CAE J402-400 turbojet (660lb, 300kg, sea-level thrust).
Performance: Speed 550mph (885km/h); range (sea level, Mach 0·6) (H) 293 miles (472km), (I)350 miles (564km), (K) 316 miles (509km).
Warhead: (H) 58 TAAM bomblet/mine payloads, 1,060lb (481kg); (I) WDU-7B or -18B unitary warhead, 650lb (295kg); (K)WDU-25A/B unitary warhead, 937lb (425kg).

The General Dynamics AGM-109 was one of the chief versions of the Tomahawk strategic nuclear cruise missile, first tested in air drops from P-3 Orions and A-6 Intruders in 1974. It differed from the ship/submarine/GLCM versions in having no rocket boost motor or launch capsule/box. Main propulsion, at first a J402, switched like other versions to a Williams F107 turbofan in competition with the Boeing AGM-86B as the ALCM for SAC. When the Boeing missile was chosen, Tomahawk was recast in different roles, and eventually in 1981 the naval versions were all terminated, chiefly on cost grounds. GLCM continued as a tactical weapon of the Air Force, and a completely new version,

MRASM (Medium-Range ASM) was launched in 1981 as a non-nuclear cruise missile for wide use by the Air Force arming many types of aircraft beginning with the B-52 and F-16.

MRASM has been taken to a high pitch of development — interestingly enough with the original pure-jet engine, but in a much modified form able to fly 8-hour missions burning the new JP-10 fuel and with a positive oil storage, retapered turbine, oxygen start system and zirconium-coated combustor. The basic missile has been developed in three forms, differing in payload and guidance. AGM-109H is the baseline airfield attack missile, with DSMAC II (digital scene-matching area-correlation) guidance and carrying a heavy payload of 58 TAAM (tactical airfield attack missile) bomblets or mines, discharged from upward-facing tubes along the fuselage.

This version is in competition with short-range or free-fall anti-airfield weapons, and justifies its high cost by the fact it is a launch-and-leave missile which eliminates the need for the carrier aircraft to come within 300 miles (483km) of the target.

AGM-109I is a dual-role weapon proposed to the Navy for use by A-6E squadrons. It has a large unitary warhead and both DSMAC II and IIR (imaging IR) guidance for either anti-ship or land attack missions. AGM-109K is a pure sea-control missile with only IIR guidance; the scene-matching and large fuel-cell power plant are replaced by an enlarged warhead.

Below: The AGM-109H resembles other members of the Tomahawk family on the outside, but is somewhat different on the inside, with turbojet rather than turbofan propulsion, and a payload of 58 upward-ejected minelets for airfield attack.

Tomahawk (Sea), BGM-109A, B, C and E

Origin: General Dynamics, USA.
Type: SLCM.
Dimensions: Length, loosely given as 21ft (6·4m) with boost motor, but varies type to type; length in flight, typically 18·25ft (5.56m); body diameter 21in (533mm); span 8·3ft (2·54m) or 8·6ft (2·61m).
Launch weight: All naval versions, typically 4,190lb (1,900kg).
Propulsion: One Williams F107-WR-400 turbojet rated at 600lb (272kg); launch by 7,000lb (3,175kg) Atlantic Research solid rocket motor.
Guidance: (A) INS(Tercom), (B/E) strapdown AHRS/active radar, (C) INS(Tercom + Dsmac).
Range: (A, C) 1,553 miles (2,500km), (B/E) 280 miles (450km).
Flight speed: 550mph (885km/h).
Warhead: (A) W-80 thermonuclear, (B/E, C) conventional, Bullpup type.

Since it was first developed in December 1972 the Tomahawk family has diversified, so that, despite losing the big USAF buy of an air-launched strategic version to Boeing's AGM-86B, four variants remain active programmes: three for the US Navy described here, and one for the USAF for land mobile deployment described next. The three Navy versions are all basically similar and differ in fuel capacity, guidance and warhead. All have conventional light-alloy aircraft-type airframes, with a tubular body, pivoted wings which unfold to zero sweep after launch, four powered tail fins for trajectory control and a ventral inlet. In naval versions of the missile the tail fins and inlet also deploy after launch.

The BGM-109A version is the TLAM-N (Tactical Land Attack Missile, Nuclear). It has inertial mid-course guidance updated by Tercom (terrain-contour-matching) guidance in the terminal phase, giving outstanding accuracy despite the fact that it has an extremely powerful warhead (thus, it can be used against hardened targets). It is deployed aboard submarines and surface warships. In the submarine mode it is delivered encapsulated in a stainless-steel container which provides environmental protection even at great ocean depths as well as control, communication and launch facilities, including gas-drive cold launch. In the SSN-688 class attack submarines 12 vertical launch tubes are

Above: The revitalized battleships of the New Jersey class each carry 32 BGM-109A/C TLAM land-attack and BGM-109B/E TASM anti-ship versions of the Tomahawk SLCM for launch from four quadruple Mk 143 ABLs (Armored Box Launchers). Such a launch from the USS *New Jersey* is illustrated. (The white-topped system beneath the missile, on the right, is a Phalanx Mk 16 close-in weapon system, CIWS), now fitted to many US warships.

built into the bow section outside the pressure hull (the original plan was to fire from existing torpedo tubes). Retired Polaris-type SSBNs are being studied as CMC (cruise-missile carrier) boats with up to 80 rounds.

BGM-109B/E is the TASM (Tactical Anti-Ship Missile), with conventional Bullpup-type warhead, much less fuel and active radar homing based on that of Harpoon. It follows a pre-programmed flight profile and can be fired from submarine capsules or surface ships, vertical launch tubes being planned for CG-47, DD-963 and DDG-X class ships. Funding continues to support development of

Tomahawk (Land), BGM-109G

Origin: General Dynamics, USA.
Type: GLCM.
Dimensions: Length, 19·6ft (6.0m) body diameter 20·5in (520mm); span 8·2ft (2·5m).
Launch weight: 3,200lb (1,451kg).
Propulsion: One Williams F107-WR-400 turbofan rated at 600lb (272kg); launch by 7,000lb (3,175kg) Atlantic Research solid rocket motor.
Guidance: INS/Tercom, + Dsmac.
Range: 1,550 miles (2,500km).
Flight speed: 550mph (885km/h).
Warhead: W-84 nuclear or thermonuclear (classified).

In most essentials BGM-109G is identical to the long-range naval versions of Tomahawk, but it has Dsmac (digital scene-matching area-correlation) guidance and the new W-84 warhead. Its mission designation is GLCM (Ground-Launched Cruise Missile), and it is assigned to the Air Force for deployment relatively close to potential trouble-spots, notably Europe. Under the desperately needed NATO TNF (theater nuclear force) modernization programme a total of 464 GLCMs are being stationed in NATO European nations under the management of TAC on behalf of SAC.

Each missile is packaged with aerodynamic surfaces and engine inlet retracted inside an aluminium drum. Tanks are filled and guidance pre-targeted. The BGM-109G may then be left for many months without attention. For use the canister is loaded aboard the TEL (transporter/erector/launcher) vehicle, a GD product weighing 33 tons which carries four missile tubes in a single box which can be elevated to the desired launch angle. Each Combat Flight Group comprises four TELs (16 rounds) and two LCCs (launch control centres), the latter also being built into a vehicle, in this case weighing 36 tons largely because of the CBR protection for the crew. Thus the total force will comprise 29 Flights totalling 116 TEL vehicles. These are divided between sites in Britain, West Germany, Belgium, Italy and (possibly) the Netherlands.

Deployment of what the so-called peace movement calls "cruise" was subject to a huge campaign of opposition by European protesters who appeared not to understand that, in any time of political crisis, the GLCMs would be driven many miles from their peacetime base to hidden locations in other parts of the host country. Thus, unlike the nuclear bombers which have been parked on NATO airbases for years, these missiles cannot invite retaliation because an enemy could not know their future locations. The scale of the Communist propaganda reaction is a fair measure of this missile's deterrent power.

During the October 1986 talks in Iceland, Soviet and American negotiations failed to reach agreement on withdrawal of theater nuclear missiles from Europe.

Above: Test launch of a BGM-109G ground-launched cruise missile from its four-round TEL vehicle, specially designed to permit GLCM operations away from fixed (and therefore vulnerable) base locations.

Above: After submarine launch and a 400 mile (640km) approach flight, a BGM-109C is seen just before impacting a concrete target during a live warhead test on 25 July, 1984.

Right: The devastating effect of the 1,000lb (453kg) warhead (derived from that of the AGM-12C Bullpup ASM) is evident as the target bunker is totally destroyed by the BGM-109C.

this variant, the ship installations and the required OTH (over the horizon) command/control systems.

BGM-109C is TLAM-C, the conventional counterpart to BGM-109A and like other versions planned for both sea and land warfare, and its guidance will have the super-accurate Dsmac (Digital scene-matching area correlation), in which scenes ahead of the missiles are scanned and analysed into digital information which is compared with information on the target approach terrain stored in the guidance system.

TOW 2, BGM-71

Origin: Hughes Aircraft, USA.
Type: Heavy anti-tank missile.
Dimensions: Length 55·1in (140cm); body diameter 6in (15·2cm); span (wings extended) 13·5in (34·3cm).
Launch weight: (BGM-71A) 47·4lb (21·5kg).
Propulsion: Hercules K41 boost (0·05s) and sustain (1s) motors.
Range: 213 to 4,000yd (65 to 3,750m).
Flight speed: 625mph (1,003km/h).
Warhead: (BGM-71A) Picatinny Arsenal 8·6lb (3·9kg) shaped-charge with 5·3lb (2·4kg) explosive.

The TOW (Tube-launched, Optically-tracked, Wire-guided) missile is likely to set an all-time record in the field of guided-missile production. Prime contractor Hughes Aircraft began work in 1965 to replace the 106mm recoilless rifle. The missile's basic infantry form is supplied in a sealed tube which is clipped to the launcher. The missile tube is attached to the rear of the launch tube, the target sighted and the round fired. The boost charge pops the missile from the tube, firing through lateral nozzles amidships. The 4 wings indexed at 45° spring open forwards, and the 4 tail controls flip open rearwards. Guidance commands are generated by the optical sensor in the sight, which continuously measures the position of a light source in the missile relative to the LOS and sends steering commands along twin wires. These drive the helium-pressure actuators working the four tail controls in pairs for pitch and yaw. In 1976 production switched to ER (Extended-Range) TOW with the guidance wires lengthened from 9,842ft (3,000m) to the figure given. Sight field of view reduces from 6° for gathering to 1·5° for smoothing and 0·25° for tracking.

TOW reached IOC in 1970, was used in Vietnam and the 1973 Middle East war, and has since been produced at a higher rate than any other known missile. The M65 airborne TOW system equips the standard American attack helicopter, the AH-1S TowCobra and the Marines' twin-engine AH-1J and -1T Improved SeaCobra, each with a TSU (Telescopic Sight Unit) and two quad launchers. Other countries use TOW systems on the BO 105, Lynx, A109, A129, 500MD and other attack helicopters.

In late 1981 production began of the Improved TOW, with a new warhead triggered by a long probe, extended after launch to give 15in (381mm) stand-off distance for greater armor penetration. The shaped-chargehead, with LX-14 filling and a dual-angle deformable liner, is also being retrofitted to many existing rounds.

Hughes is now producing TOW 2, which has several I-TOW improvements, plus a new warhead with the same diameter as the rest of the missile with a mass of 13lb (5·9kg) and an even longer (21·25in, 540mm) extensible probe, calculated to defeat all tanks of the 1990s. Flight performance is maintained by a new double-base motor giving about 30 per cent greater total impulse, and the command guidance link has been hardened.

Below: A McDonnell Douglas 500MG light attack helicopter fires a TOW missile, targeting and flight-control information being provided by the mast-mounted sight.

Left: A retouched photo sequence shows the launch of a TOW 2 up to the ignition of the flight motor (left).

Trident C-4

Origin: Navy, and Lockheed Missiles and Space Co., USA.
Type: Submarine-launched ballistic missile.
Dimensions: Length 34ft (10·36mm); diameter 6·1ft (188cm).
Launch weight: 70,000lb (32,000kg).
Propulsion: Three tandem stages; advanced solid motors with thrust vectoring.
Guidance: Inertial.
Range: 4,400 miles (7,100km).
Warhead: Eight Mark 4 100kT MIRV. Mark 500 Evader MaRV may be installed later.

Some 24 extremely large submarines of the Ohio class, each boat mounting 24 launch tubes, carry this large, long-range SLBM system. Flight testing of the Trident I (C-4) missile improved after a somewhat shaky start and the system is now operational. Trident I (C-4) has been installed in 12 units of the Franklin/Lafayette class and the first such conversion, USS *Francis Scott Key* (SSBN-657), joined the fleet as the first operational Trident-armed submarine on 20 October 1979. Trident II (D-5), a longer missile which has much improved throw-weight and/or range, is currently under development. It will fit the C-4 launch tubes for diameter, but, being somewhat longer, will not only need new tubes but also a new submarine launch platform and will be fitted in the ninth and subsequent Ohio class SSBNs.

The British Government has announced plans to purchase Trident missiles, which will be installed in a new class of British-built SSBNs. As with Polaris, an entirely British front-end will be fitted, thus ensuring ultimate national control over deployment and targetting. After initially deciding to order the C-4, the British Government changed its mind and ordered the D-5, but stated that the total number of warheads per missile would never exceed that planned for the C-4.

According to US Secretary of Defense Caspar Weinberger Trident II (D-5) will be "the first US SLBM capable of retaliating effectively against hardened Soviet targets". It is only a small step from this to a first-strike counter-force capability.

Above: An overhead view of the Ohio class submarine USS *Michigan* shows the raised decking and hatches behind the sail for the boat's complement of 24 Trident C-4 SLBMs.

Walleye, AGM-62

Origin: Martin Marietta, USA.
Type: Guided unpowered bomb.
Dimensions: Length (I) 135in (3·44m), (II) 159in (4·04m); body diameter (I) 12·5in (317mm); (II) 18in (457mm); span (I) 45·5in (1·16m), (II) 51in (1·3m).
Launch weight: (I) 1,100lb (499kg), (II) 2,400lb (1,089kg).
Propulsion: None.
Performance: Speed subsonic; range (I) 16 miles (26km), (II) 35 miles (56km).
Warhead: (I) 825lb (374kg), (II) based on Mk 84 bomb.

An unpowered glide bomb with TV guidance, AGM-62 Walleye was intended to overcome the aircraft-vulnerability hazard of visual radio-command ASMs. Walleye quickly proved successful, and in January 1966 Martin was awarded the first production contract. This was later multiplied and in November 1967 the need for Walleye in SE Asia resulted in Hughes Aircraft being brought in as second-source. In 1969 the Navy described this missile as "The most accurate and effective air-to-surface conventional weapon ever developed anywhere".

Walleye I has a cruciform of long-chord delta wings with elevons, a gyro stabilized TV vidicon camera in the nose, and ram-air windmill at the tail to drive the alternator and hydraulic pump. The pilot or operating crew-member identifies the target, if necessary using aircraft radar, aims the missile camera at it, focusses it and locks it to the target using a monitor screen in the cockpit. The aircraft can then release the missile and turn away from the target, though it must keep the radio link with the missile. In theory the missile should glide straight to the target, but the launch operator has the ability to break into the control loop and, watching his monitor screen, guide it manually into the target.

In 1968 the Navy funded several developments — Update Walleye, Walleye II, Fat Albert and Large-Scale Walleye among them — which led to the enlarged Walleye II (Mk 5 Mod 4) for use against larger targets. In production by 1974, Walleye II was deleted from the budget the following year and replaced by the first procurement of ER/DL (Extended Range/Data-Link) Walleye II (Mk 13 Mod 0). The ER/DL system was originally planned in 1969 to allow a launch-and-leave technique at greater distance from the target, the missile having larger wings to improve the glide ratio, and the radio data-link allowing the operator to release the missile towards the target and then, when the missile was much closer, acquire the target on his monitor screen, focus the camera and lock it on.

Operations in SE Asia showed that it would be preferable to use two aircraft, the first to release the Walleye (if possible already locked on the approximate target position) and then escape and the second, possibly miles to one side, to update the lock-on point and monitor the approach to the target.

Below: The Walleye is an extremely accurate guided bomb for use by tactical aircraft such as this A-4F Skyhawk.

Left: A Walleye I under test in 1969, when it soon became apparent that the type's capabilities could be enhanced by larger wings, giving greater stand-off range.

Above: Test launch of a Trident C-4 SLBM at the Eastern Space and Missile Center based at Patrick AFB in Florida. The C-4 has demonstrated a CEP of 500 yards (457m) or less.

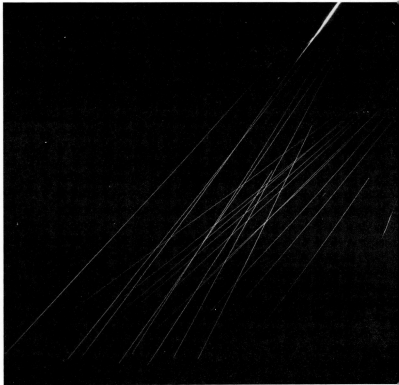

Above: Multiple ballistic exposure photograph of Trident I C4 re-entry body, seen from P-3C Orion at 20,000ft (6,096m) 15nm from impact point during 1980 test.

INDEX

Page numbers in bold type refer to subjects of captions or charts, etc.

A

Acheson, Dean, 19
Advanced Self-Protection Jammer (ASPJ), 105
Advanced Tactical Fighter (AFT), 105-6
Aerospace Rescue and Recovery Service (ARRS), 110
Afghanistan: Soviet invasion, 20, 26
Air Force, US
 Academy, 10
 Communications Command (AFCC), 111
 Logistics Command (AFLC), 111
 organization, 100-11
 Reserve (AFRES), 109-10
 Systems Command (AFSC), 111
 Technical Applications Center, 101
Air National Guard (ANG), 15, 106, 109-11
Air Tactical Data System, 79
Air Training Command, 110
Air University (AU), 111
Airborne Division, 82nd, **73**
Aircraft Carriers
 aircraft complement, 83
 deployment, 77
 see also Warships, US
Aist (Soviet hovercraft), 122
Alamo siege, **11**
Alaskan Air Command (AAC), 108
Alternate National Military Command Center (ANMCC), 35
American Civil War, 13-14
American Revolution, 13
Andropov, Yuri, 20
ANZUS alliance, 25
Aquino, Corazon, 25
Armacost, Michael, 48
Army Reserve Strength, 70
Assured Destruction (AD), 54-6
Atlantic Conveyor (supply ship), 83
Australia: relations with US, 25
Automatic Digital Network (AUTODIN), 36
Automatic Secure Voice Network (AUTOSEVOCOM), 36
Automatic Voice Network (AUTOVON), 36

B

Ballistic Missile Early Warning System (BMEWS), 59-60
Battalion Landing Teams (BLT), 92
Battalion strength
 mechanized infantry, 68-9
 tank, 68
Bay of Pigs raid, 28
Beech Aircraft Corporation
 Beech King Air, 168
 Beech Super King Air, 108, 110, **168**
Begin, Lee, 103
Begin, Menachem, 26
Bell Corporation
 AH-1S HueyCobra, **65**, 91
 OH-58C Kiowa, 69-70, **170**
 UH-1H Iroquois (Huey), **170**
Berlin confrontation, 18
Boeing Aerospace Company
 ALCM, AGM-86B, **53**, 102-3, **214**

ALMV (ASAT), **215**
 Minuteman, LGM-30, 20, 52-3, **54**, **56**, 100, 104, **221**
 SRAM, AGM-69, 102, 107, **230**, **231**
Boeing Company 105, 109
 B-52 Stratofortress, 52, **53**, **57**, 100, **101**, 102-3, **171**
 C-18, 107
 C-135 family, 104, 107, 110, 111, **172**
 E-3 Sentry, 79, 101, **104**, 105-8, **110**, **173**
 E-4 AABNCP, 104, 172, **173**
 T-43, 110, **174**
 VC-137, **174**
Boeing-Vertol CH-47D Chinook, 135, **175**
Boeing-Vertol H-46 family, 91, 99, **175**
Boyce, John, 51
Bradley, Omar, 17
Brezhnev, Leonid, 20
Bridge Tool and Die Works: M60 machine gun, **93**, 99, 136
British Aerospace
 AV-8 Harrier I, 85, 91, 94, **176**
 AV-8B Harrier II, 204, **205**
British Aerospace Dynamics: Rapier, **225**
British Secret Service, 45
Brown, Harold, 39-40, 57, 60
Browning, John 136
Brzezinski, Zbigniew, 39
Budget Committees of Congress, 35
Bureau of Intelligence and Research of the US State Department, 48-9
Burham, David, 51
Bush, George, 24
Byrnes, Secretary, 19

C

Canada
 US failure to conquer, 13
 US relations with, 28-9
Carter, Jimmy, 18-28 passim, 57
Casey, William, 50-1
Castro, Fidel, 27-8, **29**
Central Intelligence Agency
 operations, 44-7
 organization, **44**
Cessna Aircraft Company
 O-2 Skymaster, 108, **176**
 T-37, 110, **177**
 T-41, 110, **177**
Chernenko, Konstantin, 20, 112
Chief of Naval Operations (CNO), 81
China, People's Republic of, 19, 24-5
Chippewa (battle), **10**
Chrysler: M60 tank, **68**, **94**, 124, **125**
Chun Doo Hwan, 22
Church, Frank, 18
Churchill, Winston, 17, 44
Civil Reserve Air Fleet (CRAF), 109
Clark, William, 38
Close-in Battle doctrine, 63
Coast Guard, US, 82-3
Colt Firearms
 M2HB machine gun, **136**
 M16A1 rifle, 93, 136, **137**
 M1911A1 pistol, **138**
Combat aircraft, US
 air control: Rockwell OV-10 Bronco, 108, **209**
 ASW
  Lockheed P-3 Orion, 47, 79, 81, **189**, 190
  Lockheed S-3 Viking, 190, **191**
 attack

British Aerospace AV-8 Harrier I, 85, 91, 94, **176**
 Cessna A-37B, **110**
 Fairchild A-10 Thunderbolt II, 100, 105, 107, **108**, 110-11, **178**, 179
 General Dynamics F-111, 52, 100, **101**, 103, 105, **181**, **182**, **183**
 Grumman A-6 Intruder & EA-6 Prowler, 83, 91, **182**, **183**
 Vought A-7 Corsair II, 100, 111, **213**
AWACS
 Boeing E-3 Sentry, 79, 101, **104**, 105-8, **110**, **173**
 Grumman E-2C Hawkeye, **184**, 185
bomber
 Boeing B-52 Stratofortress, 52, **53**, **57**, 58, 86, 100, **101**, 102-3, **171**
 McDonnell Douglas A-4 Skyhawk, 91, 192, **193**
 Rockwell B-1, 52, 57, **58**, **208**
command post: Boeing E-4 AABNCP, 104, 172, **173**
fighter
 General Dynamics F-16 Fighting Falcon, 15, 101, **105**, 106-10 passim, **111**
 Grumman F-14 Tomcat, 76, 79, 83, 85, 105, **184**, 185
 McDonnell Douglas F-15 Eagle, 46, **105**, 106, **107**, 108, 111, **198**, **199**
 McDonnell Douglas F/A18 Hornet, 83, 85, 90, **91**, 94, 105, **200**, **201**
 McDonnell Douglas/BAe AV-8B Harrier II, 204, **205**
 Northrop F-5, 109, 206, **207**
 Republic F-105 Thunderchief, **206**, **207**
helicopter
 Bell AH-1S HueyCobra, **65**, **88**, 91, **169**
 Bell OH-58C Kiowa, 69-70, **170**
 Bell UH-1H Iroquois (Huey), 110, **170**
 Boeing-Vertol CH-47D Chinook, 135, **175**
 Boeing-Vertol H-46 family, 91, 99, **175**
 Kaman SH-2 Seasprite, **186**, **187**
 McDonnell Douglas AH-64 Apache, 69, **194**
 McDonnell Douglas OH-6A Cayuse, **203**
 Sikorsky CH-53 Super Stallion, 91, 94, **95**
 Sikorsky HH-60A Nighthawk, **110**
 Sikorsky S-61 family, 110, 210, **211**
 Sikorsky S-64, 210
 Sikorsky S-65/S-80, H-53 family, 110, **211**, 212
 Sikorsky S-70, **212**, **213**
interceptor
 General Dynamics F-106 Delta Dart, 106, 111, **180**
 McDonnell Douglas F-4 Phantom II, 79, 85, 90, 100, **107**, 108, **109**, 110, 111, **196**, **197**
 McDonnell Douglas F-101, **202**, **203**
light transport
 Beech King Air VC-6B, 168

Beech Super King Air C-12A, VC-12A, 108, 110, **168**
reconnaissance
 Cessna O-2 Skymaster, 108, 176
 Grumman OV-1 Mohawk, 102, **186**, **187**
 Lockheed SR-71, 46, 107, 190, **191**
surveillance
 Lockheed TR-1, 46, **107**, **192**, **193**
tilt wing
 552-MV22 Osprey, **99**
trainer
 Boeing T-43, 110, **174**
 Cessna T-37, 110, 177
 Cessna T-41, 110, **177**
 McDonnell Douglas/BAe T-45 Hawk, 204, **205**
 Northrop T-38 Talon, 206, **207**
 Rockwell T-39 Sabreliner, **209**
transport
 Boeing C-135 family, 104, 107, 110, 111, **172**
 Boeing VC-137, **174**
 de Haviland Canada C-7, 178
 Fairchild C-123 Provider, **179**
 Lockheed C-5A, C-5B Galaxy, 100, **109**, 110, 186, **187**
 Lockheed C-130 Hercules, **47**, **95**, 101, 109-11, **188**
 Lockheed C-141 Starlifter, 101, 109, 110, **189**
 McDonnell Douglas C-9, 109, **195**
 McDonnell Douglas C-17, 109, **195**
 McDonnell Douglas KC-10A Extender, 104, 109, 110, **202**, **203**
 Shorts 330, 110, 210, **211**
Combat Aviation Brigade strength, 69-70
Commandant Marine Corps (CMC), 88
corps strength, 67
Critical Communications Net (CRITCOM), 48
Cuban confrontation, 18, 27-8

D

de Haviland Aircraft of Canada: C-7, **178**
Deep Battle doctrine, 63-7
Defense
 Advanced Research Projects Agency (DARPA), 33
 Communications Agency (DCA), 33
 Communications System (DCS), 36
 Contract Audit Agency (DCAA), 34
 Intelligence Agency (DIA), 33, 45, 47
 Investigative Service (DIS), 34
 Legal Services Agency, 34
 Logistics Agency, 33-4
 Mapping Agency (DMA), 34
 Meteorological Satellite Program, 104
 Nuclear Agency (DNA), 33
 Resources Board, 35
 Security Assistance Agency (DSAA), 34
Department of Defense
 budgets 35
 change 37-40
 field commands 34-5
 organization 30-7

Direct Reporting Units (DRU), 101
Division
 artillery strength, 70
 strength, 67-8
 support command strength, 70
Douglas Aircraft Company
 A-4 Skyhawk, 91, 192, **193**
 AH-64 Apache, 69, **194**
 C-9, 109, **195**
 C-17, 109, **195**
 KC-10A Extender, 104, 109, 110, **202**, **203**
Douhet, Giulio, 38
Drug Enforcement Administration (DEA), 49

E

Egypt, 20
Eilath (Israeli destroyer), 76, 83
Eisenhower, Dwight, 17, 27, 39
Eisenhower, USS, 78
El Salvador, 28
Electronic Security Command (ESC), 101, 111
Enterprise, USS, 78
Estonia, 19

F

Fabrique Nationale: M249 squad automatic weapon, **93**, **138**
Fairchild Republic Company
 A-19 Thunderbolt II, 100, 105, 107, **108**, 110-11, **178**, 179
 C-123 Provider, **179**
Falkland Islands conflict, 27
Federal Bureau of Investigation (FBI), 49
Field commands of Department of Defense, 34-5
Finland, 19
Feet, US
 composition, **84**
 Marine Force Atlantic (FMLANT), 91
 Marine Force Pacific (FMFPAC), 91
 operating areas, **81**
 organization, **81**
Flexible Response, 54
FMC Corporation: LVTP-7 amphibious assault vehicle, 95, **130**
Force Service Support Groups (FSSG), 90
Ford, Gerald, 20, 22, 28
Ford Aeronautic Division
 Chaparral, MIM-72C, 70, **216**
 Shillelagh, MGM-51A, **227**
 Sidewinder, AIM-9, 79, 85, 94, 105, **228**, **229**
Forward Area Air Defense (FAAD), 95
Frunze (Soviet warship) 122

G

Gemayel, Mr., 26
General Dynamics, 103, 105
 aircraft
  F-16 Fighting Falcon, 15, 101, **105**, 106-10 passim, **111**, **180**, **181**
  F-106 Delta Dart, 106, 111, **180**
  F-111, 52, 100, **101**, 103, 105, **181**, **182**, **183**
 missiles
  Redeye, FIM-43A, **226**
  Sparrow, AIM-7, 79, 85, 94, 105, **230**

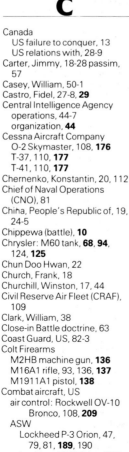

Standard, RIM-66/67, **231**
Standard ARM (RGM/AGM-78), 107, **231**
Stinger, FIM-92A, 95, 109, **232**
Tomahawk, AGM-109, **234**
Tomahawk (Land), BGM-109G, **235**
Tomahawk (Sea), BGM-109A, B, C & E, 79, 84-6, **234**, **235**
General Electric Corporation M60 machine gun, **93**, 99, **136**
M163/M167 Vulcan, 129, **135**
General Motors: M55 tank, 126, **127**
George Washington, USS, 53
Global Positioning System (GBS), 104
Goldwater, Barry, 39
Goodyear Aerospace: Subroc, UUM-44A, **232**
Gorbachev, Mikhail, 18
Grant, Ulysses S., 13, 14
Grenada invasion, 10, 13, **17**, 18, **28**, 71-2
Gromyko, Andrei, 21
Ground forces' weapons, US
air defense system: Vulcan, M163/M167, 129, **135**
ammunition support vehicle: M992FAASV, **139**
amphibious assault vehicles LVTP-5, 130
LVTP-7, 95, **88**, **130**
anti-tank weapon: M72A2, 95, **137**
armored personnel carrier M25, 129
M59, 129
M75, 129
M106, 129
M113, 128, **129**, **139**
M577, 129
armored vehicle: LAV-25, 94, **95**, **130**
cargo carrier: M548, 129
combat engineer vehicle: M727, 129
flame thrower vehicle: M132 A1, 129
grenade launcher M79, 138
M203, **137**, 138
ground emplaced mine-scattering system, **139**
howitzer M102, **133**
M109A2, **131**
M110A2, **132**
M114A2, **133**
M198, 94, 134
infantry fighting vehicle M2/M3, **68**, **128**
M901, **129**
machine gun M2HB, **136**
M60, **93**, 99, **136**
missile carrier M688, 129
M729, 129
M730, 129
M901, **129**
mortar M29A1, 134
M224, 134
pistol: M1911A1, **138**
recovery vehicle: M806, 129
remote controlled vehicle: Mastiff, **99**
rifle: M16, 93, 136, **137**
squad automatic weapon: M249, **93**, **138**
tank M1 Abrams, 16, 68, **69**, 94, **126**, **127**

M48, 124, **125**
M60, **68**, **94**, 124, **125**
M67, 125
M68, 68, **125**
M551 Sheridan, 126, **127**
MBT-70, 126
Grumman Aerospace Corporation, 105
A-6 Intruder & EA-6 Prowler, 83, 91, **182**, **183**
E-2C Hawkeye, **184**, **185**
F-14 Tomcat, 76, 79, 83, 85, **105**, **184**, **185**
OV-1 Mohawk, 102, **186**, **187**
Gus (Soviet hovercraft), 122

H

Habib, Philip, 26
Haig, Alexander, 24, 27
Halsey, Admiral William, 11
Harlan County, USS, **88**
Helsinki Accords, 20
High Mobility Multi-Purpose Wheeled Vehicle (HMMWV), 95
Honduras, exercises in, 27
Honeywell Aerospace and Defense: Asroc, RUR-5A, **216**
Horton, John, 50-1
Hughes Aircraft AMRAAM, 105, 215
Maverick, AGM-65, 107, **220**, **221**
Phoenix, AIM-54, 79, **225**
Roland, **226**
TOW-2, BGM-71, 95, **236**
Hughes/Navy laser beam director, **60**

I

Inchon, USS, **96**
Indian wars, 13-14
Infantry, US, **62**
Intelligence, military, 42-51
US agencies, **45**
Iranian embassy siege, 10, **18**, 26
Iraqi-Iranian war, 26
Israel: relations with US, 25-6
Ithaca: M1911A1 pistol, **138**

J

Japan: relations with US, 23-4
Johnson, Lyndon, 27-8
Joint Tactical Information Distribution System (JTIDS), 105
Joint TACtical Missile System (JTACMS), 107
Jones, Gen. David, 30, 37-9

K

Kaman Aerospace Corporation: SH-2 Seasprite, 186, **187**
Kampiler, William, 51
Kennedy, John F., 27-8, 39
KGB, 51
King, Ernest J., 17
Kirov (Soviet warship), 122
Kissinger, Henry, 19, 21
Komer, Robert, 39
Korea, 12, 19
downing of airliner, 20, 47, 51
relations with US, 22-3
war generating distrust, 15
Kurile Islands, 19

L

Latin America: US concerns with, 27-8
Latvia, 19
LAW 80, British, **137**
Lebanon: peacekeeping force, 12, **25**, 26, **98**
Lebed (Soviet warship), 122
Lee, Andrew Daulton, 51
Lee, Robert E., 14
Lehman, John F., 35, 39
Leyte Gulf battle, 11-12
Liberty, USS, 45
Libya raid, 13
briefing map, **27**
Light Airborne Multipurpose System (LAMPS), 85
Light Anti-armor Weapon (LAW), 99
Light Armored Vehicle Battalion (LAVB), 90, 94
Light Infantry Division (LID), 72-3
Lithuania, 19
Lockheed: F-19 Stealth Fighter, 105-6
Lockheed-California Company P-3 Orion, 47, 79, 81, **189**, 190
S-3 Viking, 190, **191**
SR-71, 46, 107, 190, **191**
TR-1, 46, **107**, **192**, 193
Lockheed-Georgia Company C-5A Galaxy, 100, **109**, 110, 186, **187**
C-130 Hercules, **47**, 95, 101, 109-11, **188**
C-141 Starfighter, 101, 109, 110, **189**
Lockheed Missiles and Space Poseidon C-3, 52, 56, **224**
Trident C-4, 57, 85, **236**, **237**
Low Intensity Conflict (LIC), 62, 72
Lundy's Lane battle, 10

M

MacArthur, General of the Army Douglas, 10, 17
McCormack-Curtis amendment, 32
McDonnell Douglas AV-8B Harrier II, 204, **205**
F-4 Phantom II, 79, 85, 90, 100, 106, **107**, 108, **109**, 110, 111, **196**, **197**
F-15 Eagle, 46, **105**, 106, **107**, 108, 111, **198**, **199**
F-101, **202**, **203**
F/A 18 Hornet, 105, **200**, **201**
OH-6A Cayuse, **203**
T-45 Hawk, 204, **205**
McDonnell Douglas Astronautics Dragon, M47 FGM-77A, 68, **217**
Harpoon, AGM-84A, 79, 84-6, **218**
McNamara, Secretary, 54-5
Mahan, Rear Admiral Alfred Thayer, 14
Marcos, Ferdinand, 25
Maremont Corporation: M60 machine gun, **93**, 99, **136**
Marine Air Control Group (MACG), 95
Air Ground Task Force (MAGTF), 90, 92
Aircraft Wing (MAW), 95
Amphibious Brigade, **93**
Amphibious Force (MAF), 92, **93**
Amphibious Unit (MAU), 92, **93**
Marine Corps

in Beirut, **98**
integration with Navy, **81**
organization, 90-2
strength, 90
Marine Division: structure, **90**
Marine Integrated Fire and Air Support System (MIFASS), 99
Maritime Prepositioned Ships (MPS), 85
Marshall, Gen. George C., 17
Marshall Plan, 19
Martin Marietta Corporation Titan II, LGM-25C, 52, **53**, **54**, **58**, 104, **233**
Walleye, AGM-62, **237**
Martin Marietta Denver Aerospace: Peacekeeper, 21, **52**, 58-9, 104, **223**
Martin Marietta Low-Altitude Navigation and Targeting in Night (LANTIRN), 105
Martin Orlando Division: Pershing, MGM 13, **13**, 14, 20, 21, 104, 108, 115, **224**
Massive Retaliation, 54
Meuse-Argonne Offensive, 11, 17
Mexico: US relations with, 29
Middle East: US security concerns, 25-7
Military Airlift Command (MAC), 109-10
Miller, Richard, 51
MILSTAR Satellite Communication System, 60, 104
Minimally Attended Radar (MAR), 108
Minimum Essential Emergency Communications Network (MEECN), 36-7
Mondale, Walter, 22
Mubarak, Mr., 26
Muldoon, Robert, **24**
Mutual Assured Destruction (MAD), 54-6

N

Nakasone, Yasuhiro, 23-4
Narrangansett, **20**
National Command Authorities (NCA), 35-6
Emergency Airborne Command Post (NEAPC), 35
Guard, 15, 37-8
strength, 70
Intelligence Estimate (NIE): production cycle, **51**
Military Command Center (NMCC), 35
Military Command System (NMCS) 35-6
Security Act (1947), 30-1, 44, 88, 90
Security Agency (NSA), 33, 46
Security Council, 30
Naval Academy, 10
bases, 78
Reserve strength, 82
Navy, US composition, **80**
& Marine Corps integration, **81**
organization, 80-3
Tactical Data System (NTDS), 79
New Jersey, USS, **16**, **151**
New Zealand: relations with US, 25
Nicaragua, 28
Nimitz, Chester, 17
Nimitz, USS, 78
Nixon, Richard, 19, 22, 27-8

North American Aerospace Defense Command (NORAD), 104
North Atlantic Treaty Organization (NATO), 18-21 passim
air force, 120-1
Northrop Corporation, 103, 105
F-5, 109, 206, **207**
T-38 Talon, 110, 206, **207**

O

Office of Strategic Services (OAS), 50
Ogorodnikova, Svetlana, 51
Organization of American States (OAS), 28

P

Pacific Air Forces (PACAF), 108-9
Pacific Car and Foundry Company: M110 howitzer, 132
Park, President, 22
Pave Paws radar program, 59-60
Pearl Harbor intelligence failure, 42-4
Penkovsky, Col. Oleg, 45
Persian Gulf, US concerns with, 26-7
Pershing, Gen. John J., 11
Pettit, Lieut. Col. James, 11
PFC Dewayne T. Williams, USS, **97**
Philippines, the: relations with US, 19, 25
Pincher, Chapman, 45
Point Salines Airport, 13, 71
Poland, 19, 21
Polk, James K., 13
Ponce, USS, **88**
Position Location Reporting System (PLRS), 99
Pratt & Whitney, 109

Q

Quarles, Secretary, 53-4

R

Rabin, Yitzhak, **25**
Rapid Deployment Force (RDF), 71, 98
Rawdon, F., 25
Raytheon Company Hawk, MIM-23B, 95, **218**
Patriot, MIM-104, **222**
Seasparrow, RIM-7H, 85, **227**
Sidewinder, AIM-9, 79, 85, 94, 105, **228**, **229**
Sparrow, AIM-7, 79, 85, 94, 105, **230**
Reagan, Ronald, **18**, 20
& arms control, 61
& Israel, 26
& Korea, 22
& Latin America, 28
& Mexico, 29
& missile deployment, 21
& Navy, 38
& SDI, 60
& Triad improvement, 58
Rear Battle doctrine, 67
Remington: M1911A1 pistol, **138**
Republic Aviation Company: F-105 Thunderchief, **206**, 207
Richardson, Elliot, 39
Ripley, Eleazar Wheelock, 10

Rock Island Arsenal
 M102 howitzer, **133**
 M114A2 howitzer, **133**
 M198 howitzer, 94, 134
Rockets and missiles, US
 air defense
  Patriot, MIM-104, **222**
  Phoenix, AIM-54, 79, **225**
  Rapier, **225**
  Roland, **226**
  Sidewinder, AIM-9, 79, 85,
   94, 105, **228, 229**
  Sparrow, AIM-7, 79, 85,
   94, 105, **230**
  Stinger, FIM-92A, 95, 109,
   232
 air-to-surface
  Maverick, AGM-65, 107,
   220, 221
  Tomahawk, AGM-109,
   234
 anti-radar: Standard ARM
  (RGM/AGM-78), 107,
  231
 anti-radiation
  HARM, AGM-88A, 107,
   217
  Shrike, AGM-45, 107, **228**
 anti-satellite: ALMV (ASAT),
  215
 anti-ship: Harpoon, AGM-
  84A, 79, 84-6, **218**
 anti-submarine: Asroc, RUR-
  5A, **216**
 anti-tank
  Dragon M47 FGM-77A,
   68, **217**
  TOW-2, BGM-71, 95, **236**
 battlefield
  Lance, MGM-52C, 107,
   219
  Pershing, MGM-13, **13**,
   14, 20, 21, 104, 108,
   115, **224**
 cruise
  ALCM, AGM-86B, **53**,
   102-3, **214**
  Tomahawk (Land),
   BGM-109G, **235**
  Tomahawk (Sea), BGM-
   109A, B, C, & E, 79,
   84-86, **234, 235**
 glide: CWW GBU-15, **216**
 guided bomb: Walleye,
  AGM-62, **237**
 gun-launched: Shillelagh,
  MGM-51A, **227**
 inter-continental
  Midgetman, 59, **220**
  Minuteman, LGM-30, 20,
   52, 53, **54, 56,** 57, 100,
   104, **221**
  Peacekeeper, 21, **52,** 58-9,
   104, **223**
  Titan II, LGM-25C, 52, **53,**
   54, 58, 104, **233**
 laser-guided
  Hellfire, 69, **219**
  Paveway LGBs, **222, 223**
 medium range: AMRAAM,
  105, 215
 Multiple rocket; MLRS, **69,**
  222
 naval defense: Seasparrow
  RIM-7H, 85, 227
 self-guided rocket: SRAM,
  AGM-69, 102, 107, **230,**
  231
 ship-to-air: Standard, RIM-
  66/67, **231**
 submarine launched
  Polaris, 52, 54, **55**
  Poseidon C-3, 52, 56, **224**
  Trident C-4, 57, 85, **236,**
   237
 submarine-to-submarine:
  Subroc, UUM-44A, **232**
 surface-to-air
  Chaparral, MIM-72C, 70,
   216

Hawk, MIM-23B, 95, **218**
Redeye, FIM-43A, **236**
Rockeye cluster munition, 107
Rockwell International, 105
 aircraft
  B-1, 52, 57, **58, 208**
  OV-10 Bronco, 108, **209**
  T-39 Sabreliner, **209**
 missiles
  CWW GBU-15, **216**
  Hellfire, 69, **219**
Rogers, Gen. Bernard W., 34
Rumania, 19

S

Sadar, Anwar, 25
St. Mihiel offensive, 17
Sakhalin, 19
Satellite Early Warning System,
 104
Satellite Surveillance, 46-7
Satellites, US
 Big Bird, 46, **47**
 KH-1, 46, **47**
 Landsat, **47**
Saudi Arabia, 26
Schlesinger, James R., 22, 56-7
Schmidt, Helmut, 107
Scott, Winfield, 10
Scowcroft, Lieut. Gen. Brent,
 58-9
Separate Operating Agencies
 (SOA), 101
Sheffield, HMS, 83
Shenandoah, the, 13
Sheridan, Maj. Gen. Philip, 13
Sherman, Maj. Gen. William
 Tecumseh, 13
Shevchenko, Arkady, 45
Shipbuilding & Conversion, **85**
Short Brothers 330, 110, 210,
 211
Shoulder-Launched
 Multipurpose Assault
 Weapon (SMAW), 95
Shultz, George, 24
Sidra, Gulf of, 13
Signal Intelligence satellite
 (SIGINT), 46-7
Sikorsky Aircraft
 S-61 family, 110, 210, **211**
 S64, 210
 S-65/S-80, H-53 family, 110,
  211, 212
 S-70, **212, 213**
Slava (Soviet warship), 122
Snepp, Frank, 48
Souvremenny (Soviet warship),
 122
Soviet air forces, 118-20
Soviet aircraft
 aircraft
  An-12 Cub, 119
  An-22 Cock, 119
  Il-76 Candid, 114, 119
  Ilyushin Mainstay, 103,
   122
  MiG-15, 100
  MiG-21 Fishbed, 119, 120
  MiG-23/-27 Flogger, 107,
   119, 120
  MiG-25 Foxbat, 120
  MiG-29 Fulcrum, 119, 122
  MiG-31 Foxhound, 103,
   119, 122
  Mya-4 Bison, 106, 114
  Su-7 Fitter-A, 120
  Su-15 Flagon, 119
  Su-17/20/22 Fitter series,
   119-20
  Su-24 Fencer, 107, 114,
   120
  Su-25 Frogfoot, 120
  Su-27 Flanker, 103, 119,
   122
  Tu-22 Backfire, 83, 106,
   108, 112, 114
  Tu-95 Bear, 106, 112, 114

Tupolev Blackjack, 106,
  112
 Yak-28 Brewers, 120
 Yak-38 Forger, 122
 helicopters
  Helix, 122
  Hind, 116
  Hip, 116
  Hokum, 117
  Mi-26 Halo, 117
  Mi-28 Havoc, 117
Soviet amphibious forces, 122
Soviet army weapons
 infantry vehicles
  BMP, 117-8
  BTR-60, 117
  BTR-80, 117
 tank T-72, 95
Soviet chemical warfare, 118
Soviet ground forces
 organization, 115-18
Soviet laser weapons, 122-3
Soviet missiles
 AS-4, 114
 AS-15, 106, 112, 114
 Frog rockets, 115
 SA-4, 118
 SA-9-13, 118
 SA-11, 118
 SA-N-4, 122
 SA-N-6, 122
 SA-X-12, 118, 122
 Scaleboard, 115
 SS-1C Scud, 115
 SS-11, 113
 SS-12, 115
 SS-13, 113
 SS-17, 113
 SS-18, 20, 113
 SS-19, 113
 SS-20, 21, 108, 114
 SS-21, 115
 SS-23, 115
 SS-25, 112, 113
 SS-N-5, 114
 SS-N-12, 121, 122
 SS-N-18, 114
 SS-N-20, 114
 SS-NX-21, 114
 SS-NX-23, 112, 114
 SS-NX-24, 114
 SS-X-24, 113
 SSC-X-4, 114
 ZSU-23-4, 118
Soviet naval forces, 121-2
Soviet space program, 123
Soviet warships
 Akula, 114
 Delta IV SSBN, 112, 114
 Golf, 114
 Kilo, 121
 Kiev, 121
 Mike, 114
 Sierra, 114
 Typhoon, 112
 Victor, 114
 Yankee, 114
Spaatz, Carl A., 17
Space Command
 (SPACECOM), 100
Spain, war with, 14
Special Operations Forces
 (SOF), 73
Spetsnaz, 118
Sputnik, 52
Stalin, Josef, 44, 112
Stoner, Eugene, 136
Strategic Air Command, 101-5
Strategic Arms Limitation Talks
 (SALT), 18, 20, 56-8, 61, 114
Strategic Arms Reduction Talks
 (START), 18-21, 61
Strategic Defense Initiative
 (SDI), 13, 18, 21, 60
 concepts, **61**
 Organization (SDIO), 33
Strategic Integrated
 Operations Plan (SIOP), 37
Strategic Intelligence Machine,
 42

Sun Tzu, 99
Suzuki, Zenko, 23
Syria, 12, 20

T

Tactical Air Command, 105-7
Tactical Air Operations Module
 (TAOM), 99
Taft, Senator, 19
Taiwan, 19, 24
Taylor, Maxwell D., 40
Texas, Republic of, 13
Texas Instruments
 HARM, AGM-88A, 107, **217**
 Paveway LGBs, **222, 223**
 Shrike, AGM-45, 107, **228**
Thatcher, Margaret, **20**
Ticonderoga, USS, 85
Tower, John, 38
Treaty of Paris, 13
Triad, the US strategic, 52-60
Truman, Harry S., 19
Truman Doctrine, 18, 19
Tsaplya (Soviet warship), 122

U

Udaloy (Soviet warship), 122
United States Air Force
 Academy, 101
United States Air Forces in
 Europe (USAFE), 107-8
US Joint Chiefs of Staff (JCS),
 31-2
US Joint Command Structure:
 intelligence flow, **49**
USAF Historical Research
 Center, 101
USAF/US Army Joint
 Surveillance and Target
 Attack Radar System
 (JSTARS), 107
Ustinov, Mr., 21
Utenok (Soviet warhsip), 122

V

Valley Forge battle, 10
Vandenberg, Senator, 19
Vietnam war, **11,** 12, 79-84
 generating distrust, 15
Vinson, USS, 78
von Clausewitz, Maj. Gen. Carl,
 42
von Steuben, Baron, 10
Vought Corporation
 aircraft: A-7 Corsair II, 100,
  111, **213**
 missiles
  Lance, MGM-52C, 107,
   219
  MLRS, 69, **222**

W

Walker, John, 51
War of 1812-1815, 13
War with Mexico 1846-1848,
 13
Warsaw Pact air forces, 120-1
Warships, US
 aircraft carrier classes
  Enterprise CVN, **141**
  Forrestal CV, **143**
  Kitty Hawk CV, **142**
  Midway CV, **143**
  Nimitz CVN, **140**
 amphibious vessel classes
  Anchorage LSD, **166**
  Austin LPD, **166**
  Landing Craft Air Cushion
   LCAC, 95-6, **99**
  LSD 41, 96, **165**
  Newport LST, **167**
  Raleigh LPD, **167**

Tarawa LHA, 85, **164**
Wasp, **96**
ASW escort classes
 Brooke FFG, **160, 161**
 Knox FF, **158**
command ships class: Blue
 Ridge LCC, **163**
destroyer classes
 Arleigh Burke, **159**
 Charles F. Adams DDG,
  156, **157**
 Decatur DDG, **155**
 Forrest Sherman DD, **157**
 Kidd DDG, **154**
 Spruance DD, 85, 154, **155**
fast patrol craft: Pegasus
 PHM, **162-3**
frigate classes:
 Bainbridge CGN, **148**
 Belknap CG, **146**
 Coontz DDG, **156**
 Leahy CG, 146, **147**
 Oliver Hazard Perry FFS,
  85, **158-9**
 Truxton CGN, **146**
helicopter carrier class: Iwo
 Jima LPH, **96, 165**
missile cruiser class:
 Ticonderoga CG, 85, **150**
nuclear escort classes
 California CGN, **146**
 Long Beach CGN, **149**
 Virginia CGN, 150, **151**
ocean escort classes
 Bronstein FF, **160-1**
 Garcia FF, **160-1**
submarine classes
 Ethan Allen SSBN, **153**
 George Washington, **153**
 Lafayette/Franklin SSBN,
  144
 Los Angeles SSN, 85, **144**
 Ohio SSN, 85, **144**
 Sturgeon Class/Narwhal,
  152
 Tullibee/Permit (Thresher)
  SSN, **152**
Washington, George, 10
Weinberger, Caspar W., **19, 25,**
 35, 60
West Point, 10
Wilson, Woodrow, 14
Wisconsin, USS, 79
World War I: US participation,
 14
World War II
 origin of intelligence, 42-4
 US participation, 14-15
Worldwide Military Command
 and Control System
 (WWMCCS), 36-7

Y

Yun Po-Sun, 22

Z

Zhang Aiping, **24**

PRINTED IN BELGIUM BY

proost
INTERNATIONAL BOOK PRODUCTION